The Official ABAP® Reference

 PRESS

SAP PRESS and SAP Technical Support Guides are issued by
Bernhard Hochlehnert, SAP AG

SAP PRESS is a joint initiative of SAP and Galileo Press. The know-how
offered by SAP specialists combined with the expertise of the publishing
house Galileo Press offers the reader expert books in the field. SAP PRESS
features first-hand information and expert advice, and provides useful skills
for decision-making.

SAP PRESS offers a variety of books on technical and business related topics
for the SAP user. For further information, please also visit our Web site:
www.sap-press.com.

W. Heuvelmans, A. Krouwels, B. Meijs, R. Sommen
Enhancing the Quality of ABAP Development
2004, 504 pp., ISBN 1-59229-030-2

A. Schneider-Neureither (Ed.)
The ABAP Developer's Guide to Java
Leverage your ABAP skills to climb up the Java learning curve
2005, 500 pp., ISBN 1-59229-027-2

K. Kessler, P. Tillert, P. Dobrikov
Java Programming with the SAP Web Application Server
2005, approx. 520 pp., ISBN 1-59229-020-5

F. Heinemann, C. Rau
Web Programming in ABAP with the SAP Web Application Server
2005, 2nd ed., approx. 580 pp. ISBN 1-59229-060-4

J. Meiners, W. Nüßer
SAP Interface Programming
A comprehensive reference for RFC, BAPI, and JCo programming
2004, 380 pp., ISBN 1-59229-034-5

Horst Keller

The Official
ABAP® Reference

Volume II

 PRESS

Contents at a Glance

Contents

Part 9 User Dialogs

28 Messages   727

Part 10 Processing External Data

29 Open SQL   743

32 The ABAP File Interface   843

33 Data Consistency 881

Part 11 Program Parameters

34 Parameters in the SAP Memory 895

35 Language Environment 901

36 Date and Time Information 913

Part 12 Program Processing

37 Testing and Checking Programs 927

38 Dynamic Program Development 937

Part 13 External Programming Interfaces

Part 14 Obsolete Statements

42   Obsolete Statements   1017

Part 15 Appendix

A   Conversion Rules for Assignments   1091

B Language-like Classes and Interfaces   1115

C Language-like Function Modules   1123

D Predefined Treatable Exceptions   1129

Part 9
User Dialogs

25 Dynpros

25.1 Overview

Dynpro is the short form for "dynamic program." Along with the new features of the SAP Web Application Server, Dynpros form the basis of user dialogs in an SAP system.

A dynpro is the object of the repository and always exists as a component of an ABAP program. It consists of a screen layout with its screen elements and the dynpro flow logic. Dynpro fields are assigned to the screen elements.

The flow logic contains processing blocks for events that are triggered before a screen layout is sent and after user action occurs on the displayed screen layout. Dynpros are edited using the Screen Painter tool.

25.1.1 User Interface

To execute user dialogs, input and output services must be accessible through a User Interface (UI). A user interface is used for the interaction between a user and a program. If parts of the user interface are displayed in the window on the screen, this is a Graphical User Interface (GUI). The SAP-specific implementation for executing dialog-based applications with dynpros is the SAP GUI, which is installed as a software component of the SAP System on the presentation server. It contains all the control elements required for the execution of dialogs between the user and the program. The control elements of the SAP GUI are shown in Figure 25.1.

On the screen, the SAP GUI presents the screen of a dynpro in a window. The screen can contain screen elements for displaying contents or for receiving user actions. The screen and its screen elements are processed using the Layout Editor belonging to the Screen Painter tool. Each screen element has properties that are statically predefined in the Screen Painter and that, in part, can be modified dynamically in the ABAP program.

As a further part of the graphical user interface, each standard window contains a menu bar, a standard toolbar, and an application toolbar. Windows that are displayed as modal dialog windows contain only application toolbars. The bars are independent components of the ABAP program and are grouped together in a GUI status. Also, they are assigned to a dynpro by setting the GUI status. In addition to the graphical elements, the function keys are a part of the user interface. They are defined as an independent component of the ABAP program and therefore a part of a

GUI status. The components of the GUI status and the GUI status itself are processed using the Menu Painter tool. For the most part, the control elements presented by the user interface are linked with the function codes, which can be evaluated in the ABAP program. The description of the current GUI status can be found in the system field sy-pfkey.

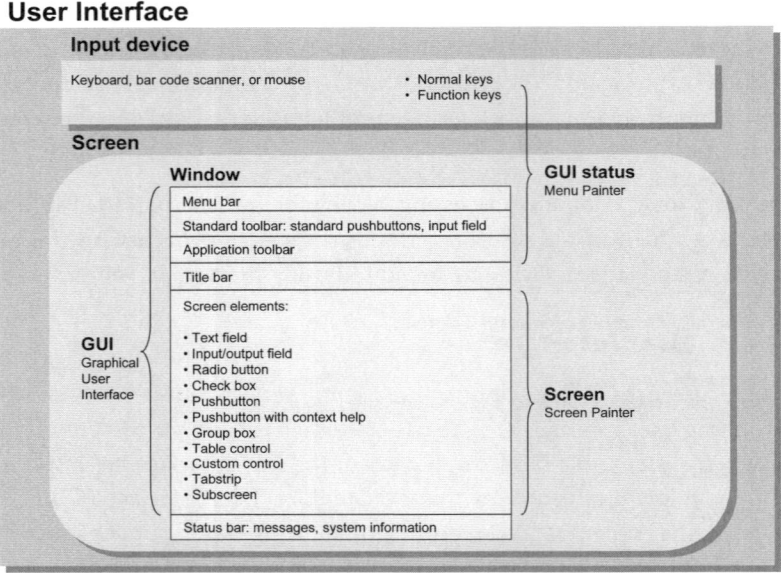

Figure 25.1 Components of a User Interface

A SAP GUIs window is fully complete when it has the title bar and the status bar. The title bar, which is also edited using the Menu Painter, contains the heading of the window. The status bar displays information that can be transmitted, among others, during the execution of an ABAP program by a MESSAGE statement. In addition, it contains system information that can be displayed or hidden through an icon on the right-hand side of the bar.

25.1.2 Screen Layout

The screen layout of a dynpro is created in the Layout Editor of the Screen Painters. The window in Figure 25.2 shows a screen layout that contains all possible screen elements. Above the screen, the menu bar, the standard toolbar, the title bar, and the application toolbar are to be seen; below it, the status bar is to be seen.

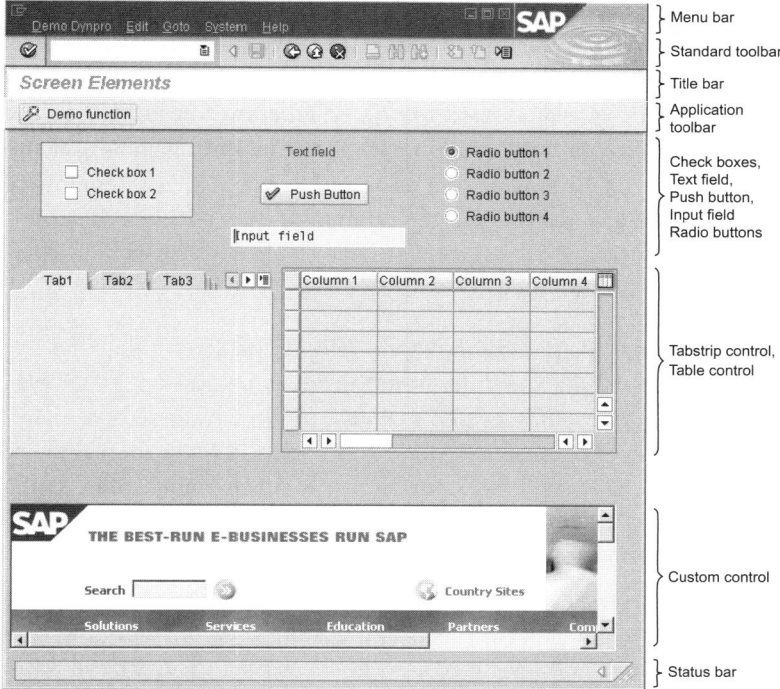

Figure 25.2 Screen Elements

25.1.3 Dynpro Fields

The dynpro flow logic does not contain any data declarations. With the exception of the OK field already created when the screen itself is created, all other data objects of a dynpro (dynpro fields) created when the screen elements are defined in the Layout Editor are assigned to the latter. The data types of dynpro fields are defined either through reference to the flat data types of the ABAP Dictionary or through reference to global fields of the ABAP program. After process-before-output (PBO) processing (see Section 25.2.1) and before the screen layout is sent, there is a data transport of global data objects for the respective ABAP program to dynpro fields of the same name. After a user action on the screen layout, and before or during process-after-input (PAI) editing (see Section 25.2.1), the data transport takes place in the reverse order.

Transport of all dynpro fields occurs at the end of PBO processing, with the exception of those fields that are defined in table controls or in step loops. The latter are processed in loops in the flow logic and transported from the ABAP program to the dynpro after each loop execution. During

PAI, first the content of all dynpro fields that do not belong to any table control or step loop and are not listed in any `FIELD` statement are transported into the fields with the same name in the ABAP program. The contents of the fields of a table control or step loop are transported to the ABAP program row by row or group by group at the beginning of the respective loop run. The fields that are listed in the `FIELD` statements of the dynpro flow logic are transported upon execution of the corresponding `FIELD` statement.

Note

▶ On the screen, the content of dynpro fields is character-type. Thus the value described there can differ from the initial description. This is particularly valid for the description of initial values. On the screen, all initial fields except for those of type STRING and SSTRING are filled with blanks, while internally they contain a type-fitting initial value. Initial fields of type STRING or SSTRING are empty also on the screen, which means that the cursor cannot be moved in the output length.

▶ If dynpro fields with reference to flat structures are defined in the ABAP Dictionary, the global data objects of the ABAP program with the same names must have been declared as interface work areas using the statement `TABLES` (see Section 6.9.1). Otherwise, no data transport will take place.

25.1.4 Dynpro Flow and Dynpro Sequences

Dynpros are called either through transaction codes (see Section 10.3.1) or using the statement `CALL SCREEN` (see Section 25.3.1). During the call, the PBO event is triggered and its event block is processed in the dynpro flow logic. Afterwards, the screen layout of the dynpro is displayed in the current or in a new pop-up level (in the case of modal dialog boxes). After a user action in the user interface of this window, the event PAI (or POH or POV) is triggered and its event block is processed in the dynpro flow logic. In the event blocks of the dynpro flow logic, dialog modules of the appropriate ABAP program are called. When PAI processing is closed, the next dynpro of the current dynpro is called automatically.

Each dynpro has a next dynpro. In particular, a dynpro can also be its own next dynpro. The next dynpro is either statically predefined or it is set in the ABAP program using the statements `SET SCREEN` or `LEAVE TO SCREEN`. In this way, a dynpro is automatically part of a dynpro sequence. Each next dynpro always belongs to a single pop-up level and is executed in a single window. The number of the current dynpro can be taken from the system field `sy-dynnr`.

The flow of a dynpro sequence is determined by the respective next dynpro in the dynpro concerned. During processing, a dynpro always has a next dynpro. At the beginning of processing, this is statically predefined, but it can be overwritten in the program. The first dynpro of a dynpro sequence is the initial dynpro. A dynpro sequence is ended by calling the next dynpro with the dynpro number 0.

If one dynpro sequence is embedded in another, the calling dynpro sequence is continued after the completion of the embedded dynpro sequence. If the dynpro sequence is not embedded, the current program is ended.

25.2 Statements in the Dynpro Flow Logic

The dynpro flow logic is the procedural part of a dynpro. It is created using an ABAP-like programming language on the **Flow logic** tab page in the Screen Painter. The syntax rules of the dynpro flow logic are largely similar to the rules for ABAP (see Chapter 2). In particular, statements are ended using a period, chained statements can be formed, and the same rules apply for comments.

The dynpro flow logic, like an ABAP program, is structured from processing blocks. Possible processing blocks are the four event blocks for the dynpro events PBO, PAI, POH, and POV, which all start with the key word `PROCESS`. These event blocks contain a small set of statements that are described in the following sections and which offer the following functions:

▶ Call dialog modules of the ABAP program

▶ Control data transports to the ABAP program

▶ Treat error messages

▶ Execute loops using table controls

▶ Call subscreens

Statement	Section
PROCESS	25.2.1
MODULE	25.2.2
FIELD	25.2.3

Statement	Section
CHAIN, ENDCHAIN	25.2.4
LOOP, ENDLOOP	25.2.5
CALL SUBSCREEN	25.2.6

The statements in the event blocks of the dynpro flow logic are normally processed sequentially. Branches result from error handling following input checks in dialog modules (see Section 25.2.3.3). Screen elements in table form are processed in loops (see Section 25.2.5).

25.2.1 Dynpro Flow Logic Event Blocks

PROCESS

Introduction of dynpro flow logic event blocks.

Syntax

```
PROCESS { {BEFORE OUTPUT}
         | {AFTER INPUT}
         | {ON HELP-REQUEST}
         | {ON VALUE-REQUEST} }.
```

The keyword PROCESS defines the processing blocks of the dynpro flow logic. The corresponding events are triggered in the following manner by the ABAP runtime environment while processing a dynpro:

▶ The event PROCESS BEFORE OUTPUT (PBO) is triggered by the runtime environment before the screen of a dynpro is sent to the presentation server. After processing the relevant event block, the contents of global fields of the ABAP program are transported to dynpro fields of the same names and is then displayed as a screen layout in the window.

▶ The event PROCESS AFTER INPUT (PAI) is triggered by a user action on the user interface, which is associated with a function code. At the PAI event or during the processing of the relevant event block (see Section 25.2.3.1), the contents of the dynpro fields are transported to the data objects with the same names in the corresponding ABAP program. Before execution of the relevant event block, automatic input checks are executed (see *ABAP—Introduction to Programming SAP Applications* by Horst Keller and Sascha Krüger, SAP PRESS 2001); these are defined either in the system or in the ABAP Dictionary. While the event block and the PBO event block of the next dynpro are processed, the screen of the current dynpro remains in the display, but the user interface is inactive. After the PAI processing is finished, the event PBO of the next dynpro is triggered or, if the current dynpro is the last one in its dynpro sequence, the execution returns to the position from which the dynpro sequence was called.

► The events PROCESS ON HELP-REQUEST (POH) and PROCESS ON VALUE-REQUEST (POV) are triggered by the request for the field help (**F1**) or the input help (**F4**) for a screen element of the screen layout. In the relevant event block, the MODULE statement is executed, which is associated with the FIELD statement for the dynpro field of the selected screen element. If several FIELD statements exist for the same dynpro field, only the first is executed. The content of the field specified under FIELD is not automatically passed to the called module in the event block at POH or POV. After POH or POV processing is finished, the system returns to processing the screen layout displayed on the presentation server, without triggering the PBO event.

There must be at least one PROCESS BEFORE OUTPUT statement in the dynpro flow logic. In addition, PROCESS BEFORE OUTPUT must always be placed before PROCESS AFTER INPUT. PROCESS ON HELP-REQUEST or PROCESS ON VALUE-REQUEST can only be specified if PROCESS AFTER INPUT is specified first. Other processing blocks except the four that start with PROCESS are not allowed in the dynpro flow logic.

Notes

► Processing of the event blocks at PAI of the current and at PBO of the next dynpro form one dialog step.

► Specifying the event blocks at POH and POV overrules field and input helps defined by the system or in the ABAP Dictionary. You must specify those only if the predefined helps are not sufficient.

25.2.2 Calling Dialog Modules

```
MODULE
```

The statement MODULE of the dynpro flow logic calls the dialog module mod of the ABAP program. You can use MODULE either as a keyword or as an addition of the statement FIELD. When using it as an addition, the call of the dialog module depends on the conditions for the dynpro fields (see Section 25.2.3).

Syntax

```
MODULE mod [ AT {EXIT-COMMAND|CURSOR-SELECTION} ]
           [ ON {CHAIN-INPUT|CHAIN-REQUEST} ].
```

As a keyword, the statement calls the dialog module mod of the respective ABAP program. At the event PAI, you can use the additions AT and ON to specify conditions for the call of the dialog module.

At the event PBO, you can call any dialog module defined in the ABAP program with the addition OUTPUT. At the events PAI, POH and POV, you can call any dialog module defined with the addition INPUT or without any addition (see Section 4.3). If the dialog module mod does not exist in the ABAP program, an untreatable exception is triggered. After processing a dialog module in the ABAP program, processing of the dynpro flow logic is resumed after the position of the call as long as the dynpro processing is not completed within the dialog module.

You can use MODULE as a keyword only at the events PBO and PAI. At the events POH and POV, you can use MODULE only as an addition to the FIELD statement (see Section 25.2.3).

Note

Do not mix up the MODULE statement of the dynpro flow logic with the identically called statement MODULE for defining dialog modules in the ABAP program (see Section 4.3).

25.2.2.1 Calling a dialog module for function type "E"

Syntax

```
... AT EXIT-COMMAND ...
```

The addition AT EXIT-COMMAND at the event PAI causes the module mod to be called if:

▶ The function used to trigger the event PAI has the function type "E"

▶ Into the input field of the standard toolbar, the user entered a character string starting with "/E" and confirmed it using **Enter**

The dialog module is called before the automatic input checks defined in the system or in the ABAP Dictionary and independent of its position in the event block. The only dynpro field transported to the ABAP program is the OK field. If the function that triggered the PAI event does not fulfill any of the above prerequisites, the MODULE statement is not executed.

If several `MODULE` statements have the `AT EXIT COMMAND` addition, only the first one is executed. If no `MODULE` statement has the addition `AT EXIT COMMAND`, normal PAI processing is executed: The predefined input checks are executed and then the PAI event block is processed sequentially. Provided the screen processing is not terminated in the dialog module `mod`, after the return from the dialog module, the complete PAI processing is executed. You must not use the addition `AT EXIT COMMAND` in connection with the statement `FIELD` (see Section 25.2.3.2).

Note

The function type of a function is determined in the Screen Painter or Menu Painter. Usually those functions of the user interface are defined with function type "E" that are assigned to the icons **Back**, **Exit** and **Cancel** in the standard toolbar of the GUI status. Therefore, the called dialog module should terminate the dynpro processing and enable security checks if required.

25.2.2.2 Calling a dialog module during field selection

Syntax

```
... AT CURSOR-SELECTION ...
```

The `AT CURSOR-SELECTION` addition at the event PAI causes the module `mod` to be called only if:

▶ The function used to trigger the event PAI has the function code "CS" and the function type "S"

▶ The cursor is placed on a single input or output field of the screen layout at the moment of the user action

The call occurs within the usual PAI processing, meaning that the automatic input checks defined in the system or in the ABAP Dictionary are executed and the `MODULE` statement is called according to its position in the event block. You can use the addition in connection with the `FIELD` statement (see Section 25.2.3.2).

If the PAI event is triggered under the above circumstances, the function code is not passed to `sy-ucomm` and the OK field. They keep their previous values.

Note

The function type and function code of a function are determined in the Screen Painter or in the Menu Painter. We recommend that you assign the function code "CS" in the Menu Painter to function key **F2** in order to simultaneously assign the double-click function of the mouse to it. This allows you to assign dialog modules to the selection of input or output fields.

25.2.2.3 Conditional call within a processing chain

Syntax

```
... ON {CHAIN-INPUT|CHAIN-REQUEST} ...
```

These conditions make sense only within chains using the CHAIN and END-CHAIN statements (see Section 25.2.4). They check the individual conditions ON INPUT or ON REQUEST (see Section 25.2.3.4) for all dynpro fields that are specified so far within the current chain after FIELD. The dialog module is called if at least one of the dynpro fields fulfills the respective condition.

Example

Typical structure of a simple dynpro flow logic. At PBO, a dialog module status_0100 is called to set the GUI status, at PAI, a dialog module leave_100 is called to handle functions with the function type "E" and a dialog module user_command_0100 to handle the other user actions.

```
PROCESS BEFORE OUTPUT.
  MODULE status_0100.

PROCESS AFTER INPUT.
  MODULE leave_100 AT EXIT-COMMAND.
  MODULE user_command_0100.
```

The relevant ABAP program must implement the dialog modules and may have a structure like the one below. Because dialog modules have no local data, we recommend handling the actual processing within procedures that you call depending on the function code.

```
DATA: ok_code TYPE sy-ucomm,
      ...

MODULE status_0100 OUTPUT.
  SET PF-STATUS 'STATUS_0100'.
ENDMODULE.

MODULE leave_100 INPUT.
  CASE ok_code.
    WHEN 'BACK'.
```

```
      ...
    WHEN 'CANCEL'.
      ...
    WHEN 'EXIT'.
      LEAVE PROGRAM.
    ...
  ENDCASE.
ENDMODULE.

MODULE user_command_0100 INPUT.
  CASE ok_code.
    WHEN ...
      CALL ...
      ...
  ENDCASE.
ENDMODULE.
```

25.2.3 Controlling Data Transfer and Flow Logic

```
FIELD
```

The FIELD statement controls the data transport from the dynpro to the ABAP program during the event PAI. It can be combined with the MODULE statement to conditionally call dialog modules and to allow you to check the input.

Syntax

```
FIELD dynp_field [MODULE mod [cond]] [WITH hlp].
```

The FIELD statement can be used in the event blocks at PBO, PAI, POH and POV, but it has no effect in the event block at PBO. For dynp_field, you must specify a dynpro field of the current dynpro. The statement has the following effect.

▶ In the event block at PAI, FIELD controls the time when the data transport from the dynpro field dynp_field to the global data object with the same name of the ABAP program takes place (see Section 25.2.3.1).

▶ In the event block at PAI, FIELD can be combined with a MODULE statement to call a module mod according to the conditions cond for the dynpro field dynp_field (see Section 25.2.3.2) and to allow input checks with error handling (see Section 25.2.3.3).

▶ In the event blocks at POH and POV, `FIELD` can either be combined with a `MODULE` statement (without the *cond* condition) to call a module `mod` with self-programmed field or input help, or with the addition `WITH` of POH, a data element additional documentation can be called (see Section 25.2.3.4).

25.2.3.1 Data transport at point of time PAI

If the statement `FIELD` is used in the event block at point of time PAI, then the statement controls the data transport for the specified dynpro field. By default, all dynpro fields are transported to the ABAP program at the event PAI and before the processing of the corresponding event block. If you use one or multiple `FIELD` statements, only such dynpro fields as are not listed after a `FIELD` statement are transported directly at the PAI event.

The transport of the content of a dynpro field `dynp_field` specified after `FIELD` to the homonymous global ABAP data object takes place at the execution of the corresponding `FIELD` statement. If a dynpro field is listed in more than one `FIELD` statement, its value is transferred when the first corresponding `FIELD` statement is executed. There are the following exceptions:

▶ The statement `FIELD` has no effect for the OK field. The OK field is always transported directly at the event PAI.

▶ A field whose content is initial to PBO, and which is not changed by the user, is not transported by the `FIELD` statement. If this field in a PAI module is filled with a value before the execution of the `FIELD` statement, then the value is not overwritten with the initial value by the `FIELD` statement.

Notes

▶ The effect of the statement `FIELD` upon the data transport to the event PAI is independent from the link to a `MODULE` statement.

▶ A dynpro field should not be used in a PAI-module before it is transported by the dynpro. Otherwise, the ABAP field contains the same value as at the end of the previous dialog step.

▶ When dynpro fields are defined with reference to flat structures in the ABAP Dictionary, the homonymous global data objects of the ABAP program must be declared with the statement `TABLES` as interface work area (see Section 6.9.1). Otherwise, with or without `FIELD`, no data transport takes place.

▶ If a dynpro field is defined with reference to a data element in the ABAP-Dictionary to which is assigned an obsolete field-exit on a customer system, then the function module of the field-exit can be executed during the transport. In general, this changes the value of the dynpro field.

25.2.3.2 Link with the MODULE statement to the PAI event

Syntax

```
FIELD dynp_field MODULE mod [cond].
```

After the `FIELD` statement of the dynpro flow logic, at the event PAI you can call the dialog module `mod` using the `MODULE` statement. If no condition `cond` is specified, the module is called immediately after the data transport specified in `FIELD`.

Besides two conditions of the normal module call (see Section 25.2.2), after `FIELD` you can specify special conditions `cond` for the call of the dialog module, which concern the screen field `dynp_field`.

Syntax of *cond*

```
...  { ON INPUT }
   | { ON REQUEST }
   | { ON *-INPUT }
   | { ON {CHAIN-INPUT|CHAIN-REQUEST} }
   | { AT CURSOR-SELECTION } ...
```

The conditions check the dynpro field for the initial value and for the user input. The conditions ON CHAIN-INPUT, ON CHAIN-REQUEST and AT CURSOR-SELECTION have the same meaning as if used after a stand-alone MODULE statement (see Section 25.2.2).

Note
Two obsolete conditions *cond* are described in Section 42.14.1.

Check initial value

Syntax

```
... ON INPUT ...
```

With this condition, the module `mod` is called only if the screen field `dynp_field` has a non-initial content. All dynpro fields except for those of type STRING or SSTRING are empty if they contain only blanks in the screen presentation. Dynpro fields of the type STRING or SSTRING are empty if they do not contain any characters.

If the input field has the special attribute ***-Input** and the user has entered an asterisk as first character in the input field of dynpro field `dynp_field`, the condition `ON INPUT` is not met. Instead, the condition `ON *-INPUT` is fulfilled (see below).

Note

On the screen, an empty field of type STRING or SSTRING is recognizable if the cursor can only be set on the start of the field.

Check input

Syntax

```
... ON REQUEST ...
```

With this condition, the module `mod` is called only if the value of the dynpro field `dynp_field` has been changed by input after the event PBO. It is considered as input if the existing input is overwritten with the same value or if the initial value of the field is entered explicitly. Besides user input, the following value input results in a call of `mod`:

▶ Transfer of a default value set via **System · User Profile · Hold Data**. However, this requires the dynpro property **Hold Data** to be active (see Section 25.3.13).

▶ Transfer of a default value from the SAP Memory. This requires that in the **PARAMETER-ID** property of a screen element an SPA/GPA parameter is specified (see Chapter 34).

▶ Transfer of data that is passed in the call of a dialog transaction using the addition `USING` of the `CALL TRANSACTION` statement (see Section 10.3.1).

▶ Transfer of a default value predefined in the system or in the ABAP Dictionary for input/output fields of certain types.

Check *-input

Syntax

```
... ON *-INPUT ...
```

With this condition, the module `mod` is called only if the user entered an asterisk (*) as a first character in the input field of the dynpro field `dynp_field` and if the input field has the special attribute ***-Input**. The content of `dynp_field` is passed to the ABAP program without the leading asterisk.

25.2.3.3 Handling of messages at event PAI

If the statement `FIELD` in the event block on PAI is linked with a `MODULE` statement, then the statement controls the handling of warnings and error messages sent in the called module using the statement `MESSAGE` (see Chapter 28).

Handling outside a processing chain

If `FIELD` is listed outside a processing chain that is introduced with `CHAIN` (see Section 25.2.4), and if a warning or an error message is sent in the dialog module specified after `MODULE`, then the PAI processing is interrupted and the screen layout is displayed again without triggering the event PBO. The input field belonging to `dynp_field` is the only field ready for input on the current screen layout and can be overwritten by the user. If the value in the input field is changed by the user, the PAI processing is continued after a user action with the first `FIELD` or `CHAIN` statement that is linked with the dynpro field `dynp_field`. If the value in the input field is not changed by the user, then the PAI processing is continued again with the current `FIELD` statement. Previous statements of the PAI event block are not processed again.

Handling within a processing chain

If `FIELD` is listed within a processing chain introduced by `CHAIN`, and if a warning or an error message was sent within a module that was called within the processing chain, then the PAI processing is interrupted and the screen displayed again without triggering the event PBO. All input fields of the dynpro fields listed within the processing chain after `FIELD` statements are ready for input. If the value of at least one of these input fields is changed by the user, then the PAI processing continues after a user action at the first `FIELD` or `CHAIN` statement that is linked with one of the changed dynpro fields. If none of the input fields is changed by the user, the PAI processing continues again directly at the `CHAIN` statement of the current processing chain. Previous statements of the PAI event block are not processed again.

Notes

▶ If an error message occurs at the user input as described in Chapter 28, then the user must correct the input values until no error message is sent, whereas after a warning, the input values can be confirmed unchanged. The warning is not sent again at the second execution of the `MESSAGE` statement.

▶ If warnings or error messages are sent in modules without reference to `FIELD` or `CHAIN`, then the PAI processing is interrupted and the screen layout is displayed again without triggering the PBO event and without a field on the screen layout being ready for input. In the event of an error message, the user must terminate the processing. In order to do this, an according option must be created on the user interface (see for example Section 25.2.2.1), otherwise the program can only be terminated from the outside.

25.2.3.4 Field- and input help

In the event blocks on POH and POV, only `FIELD` statements are possible. The statement `MODULE` can only be used as an addition of the statement `FIELD`. At these events, no automatic data transport takes place from the dynpro to the ABAP program and the statement `FIELD` has no effect. The statement `FIELD` can either be linked with the statement `MODULE` or be specified with the addition `WITH` on POH.

If the statement `FIELD` is listed more than once for the same dynpro field, only the first statement is executed. If the event blocks on POH and POV are not implemented, then field or input help fields are displayed which are defined in the system or the ABAP Dictionary. If no help is defined, a message to this effect appears in the task bar.

Calling a dialog module

Syntax

```
FIELD dynp_field MODULE mod.
```

If the statement `FIELD` is linked to a statement `MODULE` in the event block on POH or POV, then—if you select the function keys **F1** or **F4** on the assigned screen element—the specified dialog module `mod` is called. After processing of the dialog module, the system returns to the display of the current screen without triggering the event PBO and without automatically transporting data from the ABAP program to the dynpro. After calling the dialog module, you are not allowed to specify a condition `cond`.

Note

A field or input help should be programmed in the called dialog module. If data are to be transported between dynpro and ABAP program, this must be programmed there as well. For both tasks, you can use function modules like, for example, DYNP_VALUES_READ or DYNP_VALUES_UP-DATE.

Calling of the additional data element documentation

Syntax

```
FIELD dynp_field [MODULE mod] WITH hlp.
```

If you use the addition WITH in the event block on POH, then the additional data element documentation specified in hlp is displayed when you select the function key **F1** on the corresponding screen element. The preconditions are that the dynpro-field dynp_field was defined with reference to a data element of the ABAP Dictionary and that additional data-element documentation was created there for the current dynpro and the current program.

For hlp, you have to specify a global, numeric data object of the ABAP-program containing the number of the additional data-element documentation. With MODULE, you can call a dialog module mod to fill the data object hlp.

Note

The additional data element documentation replaces the data element documentation which is displayed by default for dynpro fields that are defined with reference to a data element. The additional data element documentation has to be specifically designed for the current dynpro and the current program. Links between the additional data element documentation and dynpros of programs are stored in the database table THLPF. Such a link is created if the additional data element documentation for a dynpro field was created via forward navigation in the Screen Painter. The link is not created if the additional data element documentation was created directly in the ABAP Dictionary.

25.2.4 Processing Chains

```
CHAIN
```

Linking processing steps of the dynpro flow logic.

Syntax

```
CHAIN.
  . . .
ENDCHAIN.
```

The statements CHAIN and ENDCHAIN of the dynpro flow logic define processing chains. Between CHAIN and ENDCHAIN, the statements FIELD and MODULE can be specified. The statements between CHAIN and ENDCHAIN form a processing chain. Processing chains cannot be nested. The CHAIN statement can be specified in the event blocks at PAI and PBO, but has no effect in the event block at PBO.

A processing chain allows the joint processing of all the dynpro fields stated between CHAIN and ENDCHAIN after FIELD statements:

▶ The contents of all dynpro fields combined to a processing chain by the FIELD statements can be checked in the shared conditions ON CHAIN-INPUT and ON CHAIN-REQUEST of the MODULE statement (see Section 25.2.2.3).

▶ A warning or error message in a module called within a processing chain resets all input fields whose dynpro fields have been combined in this processing chain using FIELD statements to ready-for-input. After a user input, the PAI processing resumes at the latest at the CHAIN statement (see Section 25.2.3.3).

Example
Call dialog modules to check input values. The dynpro fields input1 and input2 are checked in individual dialog modules check_1 and check_2. The dynpro fields input3 to input5 are checked in a processing chain in a shared dialog module check_chain. Warning or error messages in the dialog modules either make only one input field input1 or input2 ready for input again or all three input fields input3 to input5.

```
PROCESS AFTER INPUT.
  MODULE leave_dynpro AT EXIT-COMMAND.
  FIELD input1 MODULE check_1 ON REQUEST.
  FIELD input2 MODULE check_2 ON REQUEST.
  CHAIN.
    FIELD input3.
    FIELD input4.
    FIELD input5.

    MODULE check_chain ON CHAIN-REQUEST.
  ENDCHAIN.
  MODULE handle_user_command.
```

25.2.5 Processing Table Controls

25.2.5.1 Table Controls

Table Controls are labeled screen elements for displaying and processing table-like data on dynpros. In a table control, a maximum of 255 screen elements is summarized in a table control row, which can be repeated multiple times within the table control on the screen. The fields of a row need to be created only once as dynpro fields in the dynpro and as global data objects in the ABAP program.

To edit the displayed table control lines, table controls offer an area on the screen which offers column headers, marking of rows and columns, horizontal and vertical scrolling via scroll bars, the definition of lead columns, and saving of the current settings (see Figure 25.2). Parts of the user actions in table controls are processed from the presentation server. Vertical scrolling, the saving of settings and changes of screen size (if the **Resizing** properties have been set accordingly when defining the table controls) trigger the event PAI.

A column of the table controls can be defined as a marking column in which the screen element is displayed like a push-button and treated like a checkbox (see the first column of the table control in Figure 25.2). A checked selection key sets the content of the assigned dynpro field to "X", an unchecked key sets the content to " ". The state of the selection key is transported at the event PAI to a data object of the same name in the ABAP program, and at PBO you can set the marker via the content of the data object.

Table Controls encapsulate step loops (see Section 42.14.2) and make their independent use obsolete. The processing of table controls in the dynpro flow logic accordingly bases on the step-loop technique using the statement LOOP. Contrary to the processing of independent step loops, the loops of the dynpro flow logic are linked with the addition WITH CONTROL with the table controls of the dynpros during the processing of table controls.

In the ABAP-program, table controls must be declared with the statement CONTROLS; a special structure for the handling of the table control is created (see Section 25.3.10.1).

25.2.5.2 Table Controls in Flow Logic

```
LOOP
```

Processing table controls.

Syntax

```
LOOP [AT itab [INTO wa] [steploop_options]]
    WITH CONTROL contrl.
  ...
ENDLOOP.
```

Definition of a loop in the dynpro flow logic which is linked to a table control contrl. The loop sequentially processes the presented rows of the table control contrl by executing one loop pass per table control row. For contrl, you must directly specify the name of a table control of the dynpro. If the table control does not exist, the loop is ignored. The statement block between LOOP and ENDLOOP can contain the keywords FIELD, MODULE, CHAIN and ENDCHAIN of the flow logic (as well as the obsolete ones SELECT and VALUE, see Section 42.14.1). You cannot nest loops. You can execute loops either with or without reference to an internal table.

If table controls are defined in a dynpro, you must define one loop for each table control both in the PBO processing block and in the PAI processing block.

System Fields
Within the loop pass, the system field sy-stepl contains the number of the current table control row, counted from the top visible row. The system field sy-loopc contains the total number of table control rows displayed on the screen.

Note
To link the loop with a table control, use the addition WITH CONTROL. The statement LOOP without this addition processes stand-alone step loops and is obsolete (see Section 42.14.2).

A loop without reference to an internal table

Syntax

```
LOOP WITH CONTROL contrl.
  ...
ENDLOOP.
```

If the addition AT itab is not specified, during a loop pass the contents of the screen fields of the current row of table control contrl are transported from (at event PBO) or to (at event PAI) the data objects with the same names of the ABAP program. During PBO processing, the transport is done at the end of, during PAI processing at the beginning of the loop pass. The addition `WITH CONTROL` must be specified both at PBO and PAI.

Notes

▶ For dynpro fields of the table control that are defined with a reference to the flat structures in the ABAP Dictionary, the data objects with the same names of the ABAP program must be declared exactly like normal dynpro fields with `TABLES`, otherwise there will be no data transport.

▶ In the loop, you can call dialog modules to process the relevant data objects of the ABAP program. For example, you can read data from an internal table at PBO and write it back to this internal table at PAI after processing it on the screen.

A loop with reference to an internal table

Syntax

```
LOOP AT itab [INTO wa] [steploop_options]
          WITH CONTROL contrl.

  ...
ENDLOOP.
```

If you specify the addition `AT itab`, during the loop-processing of the table control the internal table `itab` of the corresponding ABAP program is processed sequentially in parallel. For each row of the table control, one row of the internal table is processed. The internal table `itab` must be an index table. You can specify the additions `INTO`, `CURSOR`, `FROM`, `TO` and `WITH CONTROL` only at PBO, but not at PAI. At PAI, the internal table is used for reference to the table control.

Use the addition `INTO` to specify a work area `wa` to which, at PBO, at the end of each loop pass the current row of the internal table is assigned. If you do not specify the addition `wa`, an internal table with a header row must be used, which will then be used implicitly instead of `wa`. The content of `wa` or of the header row is transported after the assignment to the fields with the same names in the current row of the table control. The work area `wa` must be a global data object of the ABAP program matching the row type of the internal table. At the event PAI, only the work area `wa` or the header row of the internal table is filled with the content of the table control rows at the beginning of each loop pass. The content of the internal table is not automatically changed.

Syntax of *steploop_options*

```
... [CURSOR top_line] [FROM n1] [TO n2] ...
```

The syntax of the additions CURSOR, FROM and TO is identical to the processing of step loops (see Section 42.14.2.2). When looping over table controls, you are allowed to use these additions, but they are not really necessary because the table controls are designed to be controlled by the structure of type CXTAB_CONTROL created via CONTROLS in the ABAP program (see Section 25.3.10.1). Here, top_line of the component TOP_LINE corresponds to this structure while the number of rows to be displayed can be controlled using the component LINES instead of n1 and n2. If n1 is still specified for table controls, the content of the component CURRENT_LINE is calculated as follows, differing from Table 25.2: $sy\text{-}stepl + (TOP\_LINE - 1) + (n1 - 1)$.

Notes

▶ For dynpro fields of the table control defined with a reference to flat structures in the ABAP Dictionary, the data objects with the same names of the ABAP program must be declared identically to normal screen fields using TABLES. Otherwise there will be no data transport.

▶ Between LOOP and ENDLOOP, at PBO no dialog module has to be called to read the data from the internal table. At PAI, however, this is necessary if you want to evaluate the transported data. For example, you can modify the internal table according to the user entries.

Example

If on the screen of a dynpro a table control FLIGHT_TAB is defined, the relevant dynpro flow logic may look as described below. The loop is executed with reference to the internal table spfli_tab. At PBO, the loop calls a dialog module prepare_tab to fill the internal table. In the loop, at PBO no dialog module is called because the table control in this case is filled automatically. At PAI, in the loop a dialog module modify_tab is called to store the changes the user entered in the table control in the internal table. You can find the relevant programming section of the ABAP program in the example in Section 25.3.10.1.

```
PROCESS BEFORE OUTPUT.
  MODULE prepare_tab.
  LOOP AT spfli_tab INTO spfli WITH CONTROL flight_tab.
  ENDLOOP.
```

```
PROCESS AFTER INPUT.
  LOOP AT spfli_tab.
    MODULE modify_tab.
  ENDLOOP.
```

25.2.6 Calling Subscreens

25.2.6.1 Subscreens

You can incorporate other screen layouts into the screen layout of a dynpro in the form of subscreens using the statement CALL SUBSCREEN. To do
this, you have to define subscreen areas on the screen layout of the current dynpro. Each subscreen area has a unique name and can be adjusted
to support screen-size changes. If this is set, every change of the screen
size of the current window triggers the event PAI.

Subscreens are the screen layouts of special subscreen dynpros. When
you incorporate subscreens, you also incorporate the flow logic of the
subscreen dynpros. Subscreens can incorporate other subscreens by
themselves. A subscreen does not possess its own OK field. Instead, the
function codes are put into the OK field of the incorporating dynpro at
every user action on subscreens. In the PAI event block of a subscreen
dynpro, a statement MODULE with the addition AT EXIT-COMMAND is never
executed.

Note
Subscreen dynpros are defined as normal dynpros in the Screen Painter
and are indicated there as such. Selection screens can also be defined as
subscreen-dynpros (see Section 26.2.1.3).

25.2.6.2 Subscreens in Tabstrip Controls

A tabstrip control is a screen element that consists of multiple tabstrip
pages. Every tabstrip page contains a single-line tab title which is linked
to a function code which makes it possible to access the tabstrip page
with a single click. Below the tab title, a tabstrip page consists of a subscreen area. A subscreen area must be assigned to every tab title. To do
this, you have two options:

▶ Scrolling in the SAP GUI
  A tab title is assigned to each subscreen area and the function codes of
  the individual tab titles are defined with the function type "P". If the
  user selects a tab title, the event PAI is not raised. The corresponding
  subscreens are incorporated once into every individual subscreen area

using the statement CALL SUBSCREEN of the flow logic. If the user selects a tab title, then the SAP GUI scrolls to the corresponding tabstrip page and displays its content.

▶ **Scrolling in the ABAP program**
To each tab title, the same subscreen area is assigned and the function codes of the individual tab titles are defined without typing. If the user selects a tab title, then the event PAI is triggered. The corresponding subscreen is dynamically incorporated into the subscreen area CALL SUBSCREEN when scrolling using the statement CALL SUBSCREEN of the flow logic. In the ABAP program, you must activate the corresponding tabstrip page and the correct subscreen dynpro must be scheduled for the subscreen area (see Section 25.3.10.2).

Note
When you scroll in the SAP GUI and select a tab title, then no input checks are carried out and no data is transported to the ABAP program. Not until a user action triggers the event PAI are all entries checked and the data of all subscreens transported. When scrolling in the ABAP program, the entries are checked at every selection of a tab title and the data of the current tabstrip page is transported to the ABAP program of the subscreen dynpro.

25.2.6.3 Calling a Subscreen in the Dynpro Flow Logic

```
CALL SUBSCREEN
```

For including a subscreen, there is one variant for the event PBO and one variant for the event PAI. You cannot use the CALL SUBSCREEN statement between the LOOP and ENDLOOP or the CHAIN and ENDCHAIN statements.

PBO

Syntax

```
CALL SUBSCREEN sub_area INCLUDING prog dynnr.
```

This statement includes the subscreen dynpro of the program specified in prog and of the dynpro number specified in dynnr in the subscreen area sub_area of the current dynpro and processes its PBO flow logic at this point. After processing the PBO of the subscreen dynpro, the flow logic of the current dynpro continues after the CALL statement.

You must specify the area `sub_area` directly. For `prog`, either a character-type data object of the current ABAP program or a text field literal is expected. For `dynnr` a data object of type `n` and length 4 of the current ABAP program or a text field literal is expected. If the specified subscreen dynpro cannot be found, an untreatable exception is triggered.

If the program is specified as a literal containing "SAPLX...", it must have been delivered as a customer exit and the subscreen must have been activated using the transaction CMOD. Otherwise the statement is ignored. If no subscreen dynpro is included in a subscreen area at PBO, the area remains empty.

If the specified subscreen dynpro is not defined in the current ABAP program, the specified program is loaded into the internal mode and LOAD-OF-PROGRAM is triggered. The flow logic of the subscreen dynpro calls the dialog modules of its own ABAP program, and the global fields of its own program are transported to the subscreen dynpro. During the processing of a subscreen, the system field `sy-dynnr` contains the dynpro number of the processed subscreen.

In the dialog modules of the subscreen, the GUI status and the current next dynpro may not be changed; the statements SET { TITLEBAR | PF-STATUS } and { LEAVE | SET } SCREEN would trigger an untreatable exception there.

PAI

Syntax

```
CALL SUBSCREEN sub_area.
```

This statement calls the PAI flow logic of the subscreen dynpro included in the subscreen area `sub_area`. The subscreen dynpro must have been included at PBO into the subscreen area (see above). For the dialog modules called by the PAI flow logic, the same applies as for those called at PBO. Data transport between the subscreen dynpro and its ABAP program happens at the moment of calling or is delayed during the execution of the FIELD statements in the PAI flow logic of the subscreen dynpro.

Notes

▶ If, due to using subscreens, the names of the screen elements displayed on a screen layout are not unique, several screen fields can be assigned to one global data object of the ABAP program, and several data transports can take place for it at PBO and PAI.

▶ As the function codes of subscreen dynpros are placed into the OK field of the including dynpro, we recommend that you choose unique function code names.

▶ Because the screen fields of subscreen dynpros are transported into those global data objects of the program in which the subscreen dynpros are defined, for external calls you must make sure that this data is transported to the calling program. If you want to define subscreen dynpros to be reusable, you should encapsulate them in function groups and use function modules for setting the global data and for transporting them to the caller.

Example

If, on a dynpro, a tabstrip control with untyped tab titles and a subscreen area named SUB are defined, the respective dynpro flow logic may look as shown below. The CALL SUBSCREEN statement includes the subscreen dynpro of the same ABAP program whose number is contained in the ABAP data object dynnr in the subscreen area SUB. You can find the corresponding ABAP program code in the example in Section 25.3.10.2.

```
PROCESS BEFORE OUTPUT.
  MODULE prepare_tabstrip.
  CALL SUBSCREEN sub INCLUDING sy-repid dynnr.

PROCESS AFTER INPUT.
  CALL SUBSCREEN sub.
  MODULE handle_user_command.
```

25.3   ABAP Statements for Dynpros

You can use the following statements for calling and processing dynpros in an ABAP program:

Statement	Section
CALL SCREEN	25.3.1
SET PF-STATUS	25.3.2
GET PF-STATUS	25.3.3
SET TITLEBAR	25.3.4
SUPPRESS DIALOG	25.3.5
LOOP AT SCREEN	25.3.6
MODIFY SCREEN	25.3.7

Statement	Section
SET CURSOR	25.3.8
GET CURSOR	25.3.9
CONTROLS	25.3.10
REFRESH CONTROL	25.3.11
EXIT FROM STEP-LOOP	25.3.12
SET HOLD DATA	25.3.13
SET SCREEN	25.3.14
LEAVE [TO] SCREEN	25.3.15

25.3.1 Calling a Dynpro Sequence

CALL SCREEN

Calling a dynpro sequence directly.

Syntax

```
CALL SCREEN dynnr [STARTING AT col1 lin1
                  [ENDING   AT col2 lin2]].
```

This statement calls the dynpro with the dynpro number specified in dynnr. For dynnr, a data object of type n and length 4 is expected. The call starts a new dynpro sequence which is embedded into the current dynpro sequence. The dynpro with dynpro number dynnr is the initial dynpro of the dynpro sequence. In a dynpro sequence started by a transaction code, you can nest up to 50 other dynpro sequences.

The called dynpro sequence is terminated as soon as one of the involved dynpros branches to a next dynpro with number 0. The program continues after CALL SCREEN.

The statement CALL SCREEN accesses the dynpros of the relevant main program of the current program group and these use the global data and dialog modules of the main program. Except when calling a dynpro in an externally called subprogram, the main program usually is the current program. If the specified dynpro does not exist in the main program of the program group, an untreatable exception occurs.

By default, the screen layouts of all the dynpros of the called dynpro sequence are displayed in the current window. With the addition START-ING AT you can open a modal dialog window.

Modal Dialog Window

Use the addition STARTING AT to open a new popup level and to display all screen layouts of the called dynpro sequence in a modal dialog window. The upper left corner of the dialog window is determined by the values col1 and lin1 for column and line. The values refer to the window with popup level 0. The lower right corner is set automatically, or you can use col2 and lin2 to specify it after ENDING AT. For col1, lin1, col2 and lin2, data objects of type i are expected. The values of col1, lin1 should be smaller than those of col2, lin2, because otherwise the behavior is undefined. The maximum popup level is 9.

Notes

▶ The called dynpro should not be a selection screen. To call a selection screen, use the statement CALL SELECTION-SCREEN.

▶ When nesting dynpro sequences and creating popup levels, remember that during the program execution, you usually are already within a (nested) dynpro sequence and that the system itself can also create other dynpro sequences or popup levels (for example field or input help or messages in dialog windows). For this reason, you should never use the maximum values of 50 dynpro sequences or 9 popup levels within a program.

▶ If, during the processing of a modal dialog window, a new dynpro sequence is called, it must be started in another popup level. You cannot use the statement CALL SCREEN without the addition STARTING AT in this case.

▶ When calling a dynpro in a dialog window, you should specify the window as a modal dialog window in its properties and set an appropriate GUI status beforehand. We recommend limiting a dynpro sequence in a modal dialog window to one dynpro only.

25.3.2   Setting the GUI Status

    SET PF-STATUS

Setting the GUI status. This section describes the setting of the GUI status for windows in which the screen picture of a dynpro is specified. For the use of these statements, see Section 27.5.1. For the GUI status of selection screens, see Section 26.1.3.

Syntax

```
SET PF-STATUS status [OF PROGRAM prog] [EXCLUDING fcode].
```

During dynpro processing, this statement defines the GUI status defined in `status` for the subsequent screen layouts. The components of the set status become active in the user interface the next time a screen layout is sent onwards, and they remain active until the end of the program or until the next `SET PF-STATUS` statement. The name of the current GUI status can be read from the system field `sy-pfkey`.

For `status`, a character-type data object must be specified that contains either the name of the GUI status of the main program of the current program group, or the name of the program specified in upper case in `prog`, or which only contains blank characters. If the status is not available, an empty status is displayed, in which no control elements are active except for the predefined system functions. Of these functions, only the Enter key, to which an empty function code is assigned in this case, triggers the event PAI. If the data object `status` contains only blank characters, the standard list status is set and the additions have no effect (see Section 27.5.1).

By default, a GUI status defined in the current main program is used. The addition `OF PROGRAM` can be used to set the GUI status of the program specified in `prog`. A character-type data object that contains the name of the ABAP program in upper case is expected for `prog`.

The addition `EXCLUDING` can be used to deactivate functions of the set GUI status. An inactive function cannot be selected in the user interface. For `fcode`, either a character-type data object or an internal table with a flat character-type data type can be specified. In the GUI status, functions with function codes contained in the field or in the rows of the internal table are deactivated. Only one function code can be specified for each row of the table. The codes are not case-sensitive. Function codes specified in `fcode` for which there is no function in the GUI status are ignored.

Notes

▶ At the latest, the GUI status of a dynpro must be set during the event PBO. If no GUI status is set for a dynpro, the empty status described above is used.

▶ If the set GUI status contains dynamic function texts, the function texts are read from the assigned global data objects of the program in which the GUI status is defined. If these do not exist, question marks (?) are displayed. For dynamic function texts, an explicitly specified program `prog` is loaded into the current program group if it does not already exist in the internal mode. This makes it possible to access its global data objects.

Example

Setting the GUI status STATUS_0100 of the main program in a PBO module, whereby the functions with the function codes "CHANGE" and "SAVE" are deactivated.

```
DATA fcode TYPE TABLE OF sy-ucomm.

...

MODULE status_0100 OUTPUT.
  APPEND 'CHANGE'  TO fcode.
  APPEND 'SAVE'    TO fcode.
  SET PF-STATUS 'STATUS_0100' EXCLUDING fcode.
ENDMODULE.
```

25.3.3 Determining the GUI Status

```
GET PF-STATUS
```

Reading the GUI status of a window.

Syntax

```
GET PF-STATUS status [PROGRAM prog] [EXCLUDING fcode].
```

This statement assigns to the data object `status` the currently set GUI status whose value is also available in the `sy-pfkey` system field. For `status`, you must specify a character-like variable. If no status is set, `status` is initialized (in the window, the empty status is displayed, see Section 25.3.2). If the standard list status is set, `status` is set to the value "STLI".

Use the addition PROGRAM to assign the name of the program in which the current GUI status is defined to the variable `prog`. For `prog`, a character-like data object is expected.

Use the addition EXCLUDING to insert the function codes that are inactive in the current GUI status row by row into the internal table `fcode`. For `fcode`, you can specify an internal table with a flat character-like data type. Only those function codes are determined that have been deactivated with the addition of the same name of the SET PF-STATUS statement, and not the statically deactivated function codes in the GUI status.

Example

Determining the current status in a PAI module.

```
DATA: status TYPE string,
      prog   TYPE string,
      fcode  TYPE SORTED TABLE OF sy-ucomm
             WITH NON-UNIQUE KEY table_line.

...

MODULE user_command_100 INPUT.
  ...
  GET PF-STATUS status PROGRAM prog EXCLUDING fcode.
  ...
ENDMODULE.
```

25.3.4   Setting the GUI Title

`SET TITLEBAR`

Setting the title bar of a window. This section describes the setting of a title for windows in which the screen sequence of a dynpro is specified. For the use of these statements, see Section 27.5.2. For the title of selection screens, see Section 26.1.3.

Syntax

```
SET TITLEBAR title [OF PROGRAM prog]
                   [WITH text1 ... text9].
```

During the dynpro processing, this statement specifies the GUI title specified in `title` for the subsequent screen layouts. The title is displayed in the title bar from the next sending of one screen until the end of the program or until the next SET TITLEBAR statement. The name of the current GUI title is displayed in the system field `sy-title`.

A character-type data object that contains the name of a GUI title of the main program of the current program group or of the program specified in `prog` in upper case is expected for `title`. If the title does not exist, `sy-subrc` is set to 4 and the word "SAP" is displayed in the title bar.

By default, a GUI title defined in the current main program is used. When using the addition OF PROGRAM, a GUI title of the progam specified in `prog` can be set. A character-type data object is expected for `prog` that contains the name of an ABAP program in upper case.

When using the addition `WITH`, you can replace the placeholders of the GUI title with the contents of the data objects `text1` to `text9`. The data objects `text1` to `text9` must be of a character-type flat data type. The placeholders of the GUI title can be defined in the form "&" or "&i", where `i` can be a number between 1 and 9. The characters are replaced as follows:

▶ The numbered placeholders "&i" are replaced with the contents of the data objects `text1` to `text9`, whose names contain the same number `i` for the second digit.

▶ The non-numbered placeholders "&" are replaced with the contents of the remaining data objects `text1` to `text9` according to their order.

If no data object is specified for a placeholder, it is represented by a blank character. Two successive characters "&&" in the title bar are not replaced with the contents of `text1` to `text9`, but with the character "&".

Notes

▶ The GUI title of the screen must be set before the PBO event. If no GUI title is set for a dynpro, the word "SAP" is displayed in the title bar.

▶ The title bar can contain a maximum of 70 characters of a title. A title that exceeds this limit after the replacement of placeholders is truncated to the right.

Return values

sy-subrc	Meaning
0	GUI title is set.
4	GUI title cannot be found.

Example

Setting the GUI title TITLE_0100 of the program specified in `prog` in a PBO module. The placeholders "&1" and "&2" of the title are replaced with the contents of `p1` and `p2`.

```
DATA: title  TYPE string,
      prog   TYPE string,
      p1(10) TYPE c,
      p2(10) TYPE c.

...
```

```
MODULE status_0100 OUTPUT.
  ...
  title = 'TITLE_0100'.
  prog  = ...
  p1 = ...
  p2 = ...
  SET TITLEBAR title OF PROGRAM prog WITH p1 p2.
  ...
ENDMODULE.
```

25.3.5 Suppressing the Display

SUPPRESS DIALOG

Hiding the screen layout of a dynpro.

Syntax

SUPPRESS DIALOG.

If this statement is specified during PBO processing, then the current dynpro is processed without displaying the screen layout, while the screen layout of the previous dynpro remains visible. After PBO processing, the system triggers the event PAI in such as way as if a user had pressed the Enter key. The function code assigned to this key in the current GUI status is then transported to sy-ucomm and to the OK field. Outside of PBO processing, this statement has no effect.

If a termination message, an error message, an information message, or a warning is sent during PAI processing with the statement MESSAGE, then the screen layout of the current dynpro is displayed together with the message.

Example

You can use the SUPPRESS DIALOG statement to display lists while dynpros are processed without displaying the screen layout of that dynpro during whose processing the list is created (compare also the example in Section 27.6).

```
MODULE call_list OUTPUT.
  SUPPRESS DIALOG.
  SET PF-STATUS space.
  WRITE 'Basic List'.
  LEAVE TO LIST-PROCESSING AND RETURN TO SCREEN 0.
ENDMODULE.
```

25.3.6 Determining Attributes of Screen Elements

LOOP AT SCREEN

Reading the screen element attributes of a dynpro.

Syntax

```
LOOP AT SCREEN [INTO wa].
  ...
ENDLOOP.
```

The statements LOOP AT SCREEN ... ENDLOOP define a loop around a statement block. For every screen element of the current dynpro to which a dynpro field is assigned, one loop pass is executed. After the LOOP statement either the predefined work-area screen (see Section 5.3.4) or the work area wa (when using INTO) contains the properties of the respective screen element. wa must have the same data type as screen.

While processing a table control or a step loop (that is, within a LOOP loop of the dynpro flow logic), the current properties for its screen elements are determined in the current row or group. Outside of the processing of a table control or step loop, for its screen elements the statically pre-defined properties of all rows or groups are determined.

Table 25.1 shows the components of screen and their assignment to the field properties in the dynpro.

Component	Length	Type	Attribute	Description
name	132	c	Name	Name
group1	3	c	Group1	Modification group
group2	3	c	Group2	Modification group
group3	3	c	Group3	Modification group
group4	3	c	Group4	Modification group
required	1	c	Required-entry field	Mandatory field
input	1	c	Input	Input-enabled field
output	1	c	Output	Display field
intensified	1	c	Intensified	Intensified field

Table 25.1 The screen Structure

Component	Length	Type	Attribute	Description
invisible	1	c	Invisible	Invisible element
length	1	x	visLength	Field length
active	1	c	Input/Output/Invisible	Active field
display_3d	1	c	Two-dimensional	Box
value_help	1	c	Input help	Input help key
request	1	c	–	Input exists
values_in_combo	1	c	Dropdown listbox	Value help exists

Table 25.1 The screen Structure (cont.)

The component `name` in the loop contains the name of the current dynpro field. The components `group1` to `group4` can contain three-character IDs which were assigned to the current screen element at the time of its definition. These IDs allow you to combine the screen elements in up to four different modification groups. In the statement block after `LOOP AT SCREEN`, these can be queried in logical expressions in order to process several screen elements in the same way.

The other components of the table `screen` represent the display properties of the current screen element. With the exception of `length`, they can contain 0 or 1, where 1 is "active" and 0 is "inactive".

Except `active`, all components of the structure `screen` directly correspond to one attribute of the current screen element. The component `active` has no match in the attributes. If you change its content with `MODIFY SCREEN` (see Section 25.3.7), this affects the attributes **Input**, **Output** and **Invisible** and thus the components `input`, `output` and `invisible` of the structure `screen`.

As of Release 6.20, the structure `screen` is described by the data type SCREEN in the ABAP Dictionary. With Release 6.10, it was determined by the type `syscr_screen` of the type group SYSCR. Before Release 6.10, it was created system-internally with a bound data type.

Note
The statement `LOOP AT SCREEN` behaves similar to the statement `LOOP` in a loop on an internal table with header line (see Section 22.2.2), where instead of an internal table a system table is used.

25.3.7 Modifying Attributes of Screen Elements

```
MODIFY SCREEN
```

Changing the attributes of the current dynpro's screen elements.

Syntax

```
MODIFY SCREEN [FROM wa].
```

This statement can be used in the statement block after `LOOP AT SCREEN` only (see Section 25.3.6) and makes sense only during PBO processing. If `FROM` is not specified, `MODIFY SCREEN` modifies the attributes of the current screen element with the values from the predefined `screen` work area (see Table 25.1). If a `wa` work area is specified, its contents are used for the modification.

The `wa` work area must have the same data type as `screen`. The `name` component must contain the name of the current screen element; otherwise the statement is not executed. Up to the `group1` to `group4` and `length` components, all remaining components of `screen` and `wa` must contain either the value 0 or 1. The value 0 deactivates the corresponding field attribute, and 1 activates it.

If `MODIFY SCREEN` is executed during PBO processing, the modified attributes for the display of the screen layout affect the current dynpro after PBO processing. The attributes of the screen element of the dynpro are reset to their static attributes at the start of each PBO processing, so that the execution of `MODIFY SCREEN` during PAI processing does not affect the display of the following screen picture.

The ACTIVE component

The `active` component is used to set the `input`, `output` and `invisible` components at once. At the start of PBO processing, the `active` component has always the value 1. If `active` is set to 0 with `MODIFY SCREEN`, `input` and `output` are automatically set to 0 and `invisible` is set to 1. Other values in `input`, `output` and `invisible` are ignored. Conversely, setting `input` and `output` to 0 and `invisible` to 1 automatically sets `active` to 0, and a different value in `active` is ignored.

Modifications in Table Controls and Step Loops

During the processing of a table control or a step loop, the changes affect the current line of the table control or the current step loop group. Before the processing of a table control, the change to the attributes of a screen element that is part of a line in the table control does not affect the table control since the values are transferred from the structure created using CONTROLS (see Section 25.3.10.1). Before a step loop is processed, the change to the attributes of a screen element that is part of a step-loop group affects all groups in the step loop.

Modifications in Tabstrip Controls

If the active component for a tab title of a tabstrip control is set to 0, the whole tabstrip page is hidden.

Example

In the following PBO module, an input field called val is made mandatory and converted to a light display.

```
MODULE modify_0100 OUTPUT.
  LOOP AT SCREEN.
    IF screen-name = 'VAL'.
      screen-required   = '1'.
      screen-intensified = '1'.
      MODIFY SCREEN.
    ENDIF.
  ENDLOOP.
ENDMODULE.
```

25.3.8 Setting the Cursor

SET CURSOR

Setting the screen cursor. This section describes the setting of the cursor in screen layouts of dynpros. For the use of these statements for lists, see 27.5.3.

Syntax

```
SET CURSOR { {FIELD field [LINE line] [[DISPLAY] OFFSET off]}
           | {col lin} }.
```

During PBO processing, this statement sets the cursor in the screen layout of the current dynpro. The cursor can be positioned by entering a screen element after FIELD or by entering an absolute position using col and lin. Outside of PBO processing, the cursor is positioned in the next list displayed on the screen (see Section 27.5.3).

If the SET CURSOR statement is not specified, depending on the definition of the screen the cursor is set according to the following hierarchy:

1. On the **Cursor position** determined statically in the dynpro properties.

2. On the first input field of the dynpro.

3. On the first screen element of the dynpro.

4. On the input field in the system toolbar.

25.3.8.1 Positioning in Screen Elements

Syntax

```
... FIELD field [LINE line] [[DISPLAY] OFFSET off] ...
```

The cursor is positioned on the screen element whose name is contained in upper case in `field`. The data object `field` must be character-type and flat. The screen layout or a table control is scrolled in the display so that the screen element on which the cursor is positioned is visible. If the specified screen element is not found, the statement is ignored.

If the specified screen element is part of a table control or a step loop, the line of the table control or group of the step loop in which the cursor is positioned on the specified screen element must be specified using the addition `LINE`. For the data object `line`, the type `i` is expected. If there is no line or group for the value of `line`, or the addition `LINE` is not specified, the statement is ignored. The statement is also ignored if the addition `LINE` is specified and the screen element is not part of a table control or step loop.

If the addition `OFFSET` is not specified, the cursor is set to the first position of the screen element. Using the addition `OFFSET`, the cursor can be set to the position in a screen element entered in `off`. In this case, the counting begins at 0. The position of the cursor is only visible in input/output fields. In other screen elements, the whole element is selected. For the data object `off`, the type `i` is expected. If the value of `off` is greater than the length of the screen element, the addition is ignored. If the value of `off` is negative, the cursor is positioned at the end of the screen element. As of Release 6.20, the addition `DISPLAY` is standard and can be omitted.

25.3.8.2 Absolute Specification of a Position

Syntax

```
... col lin ...
```

The cursor is positioned in the column specified in `col` and in the line specified in `lin` in the screen layout if a screen element is available in this position that is not part of a table control or tabstrip control. For `col` and `lin`, data objects of type `i` are expected. The counting of the columns starts at 2. If the screen element is not an input/output field, the whole element is marked. The statement is ignored if no screen element is available at the specified positions, if the cursor is positioned in a table control or tabstrip control, or if negative values are entered in `col` or `lin`.

25.3.9   Evaluating the Cursor Position

```
GET CURSOR
```

Evaluating the position of the screen cursor. This section describes the specification of the cursor position in screen layout of dynpros. For the use of the statements for lists, see Section 27.4.

Syntax

```
GET CURSOR { {FIELD field [field_properties]}
           | {LINE line} }.
```

If this statement is specified during PAI processing, it transfers—depending on the specification for `FIELD` or `LINE`—either the name of the screen element, or the number of the row of a table control or of the group of a step loop (on which the screen cursor is positioned after a user action) into the data objects `field` or `line`. For `field`, a character-type (before Release 6.10 flat) variable is expected. For `line`, a variable of the type `i` is expected. In `field_properties`, further information on the cursor position can be read.

If the cursor is in the input field of the standard toolbar or on a push-button in the screen layout, the statement is ignored and the specified variables remain unchanged. If the cursor in the first variant is not in a screen element of the current dynpro but on a bar in the GUI status, the contents of `field` and the variables specified in `field_properties` are initialized. If the cursor in the second variant is not on a screen element that is part of a table control or a step loop, the variable `line` is initialized.

Note
In the second variant, the same additions `VALUE`, `LENGTH`, and `OFFSET` can be specified after `LINE` as specified for the use of the statement for lists

(see Section 27.4). However, the variables specified during PAI processing are always initialized.

Return values

sy-subrc	Meaning
0	If FIELD is specified, the cursor is on a screen element of the current dynpro or on the input field of the standard toolbar. If LINE is specified, the cursor is on a screen element within a table control or a step loop.
4	If FIELD is specified, the cursor is on a toolbar in the GUI status or, if LINE is specified, the cursor is outside a table control or a step loop.

Syntax of *field_properties*

```
... [VALUE val] [LENGTH len] [OFFSET off]
    [LINE lin] [AREA area] ...
```

The VALUE addition assigns the formatted content of the screen element on which the cursor is positioned to the data object val as a character string. For val, a character-type (prior to Release 6.10 flat) variable is expected.

The addition LENGTH assigns the length of the screen element on which the cursor is positioned to the data object len. For len, a variable of the type i is expected.

The addition OFFSET assigns the position of the cursor within the screen element on which the cursor is positioned to the data object off. For off, a variable of the type i is expected.

If the screen element on which the cursor is positioned is within a table control or a step loop, the addition LINE assigns the number of the row of the table control or the group of the step loop to the data object lin. Otherwise, lin is set to 0. For lin, a variable of the type i is expected.

If the screen element on which the cursor is positioned is within a table control, the addition AREA assigns the name of the table control to the data object area. Otherwise, area is initialized. For area, a character-type (prior to Release 6.10 flat) variable is expected.

25.3.10 Declaring a Control

CONTROLS

Declaration of a control.

Syntax

```
CONTROLS contrl TYPE { {TABLEVIEW USING SCREEN dynnr}
                     | {TABSTRIP} }.
```

With the CONTROLS statement, for each dynpro used in the program, all table controls and tabstrip controls defined there have to be declared in the declaration section. Otherwise an untreatable exception occurs when the corresponding dynpro is called. For contrl, the name of the control that is defined in the dynpro has to be specified directly. After TYPE, TABLEVIEW or TABSTRIP must be used to specify whether it is a table control or a tabstrip control.

For each control, the CONTROLS statement creates a structure with the name of the control in the ABAP program. The structure components enable the respective control to be processed in the ABAP program.

In the case of table controls, you must specify in dynnr the number of a dynpro on which a table control with the name contrl is defined. The start values of certain components of the structure contrl are obtained from the definition of this table control (see Table 25.2). For dynnr, you can specify a literal or constant of the type n and the length 4.

Note

For table controls, corresponding loops have to be programmed in the dynpro flow logic (see Section 25.2.5). For tabstrip controls, suitable subscreens have to be called (see Section 25.2.6).

25.3.10.1 Processing Table Controls in the ABAP Program

If you specify the type TABLEVIEW, a deep structure is created with the name of the control and of the type cxtab_control of the type group CXTAB. During dynpro processing, the components of the structure contain the attributes of the table control. Using this structure you can read and change the attributes of the relevant table control.

At the top level, the deep structure cxtab_control contains components for the general attributes of the table control (see Table 25.2). The component COLS is an internal table of the structure cxtab_column and contains the attributes of individual columns (see Table 25.3). The structure cxtab_column contains a structured component screen, which has the same structure as the predefined structure screen and contains the attributes of the screen element of each column. With the exception of the component `current_line`, all components of the structure `cxtab_control` can be set in the ABAP program.

When a dynpro in which a table control called `contrl` is defined is called for the first time, the start values of certain components of the structure are obtained from the definition of the table control whose screen is specified after the `USING` addition (see Table 25.2).

Component	Description
`fixed_cols`	Number of lead columns. Start value is taken from the definition of the table control in dynpro `dynnr`.
`lines`	Controls the vertical scroll bar of the table control. If the `LOOP` loop is executed in the dynpro flow logic without reference to an internal table (see Section 25.2.5.2), that start value of `LINES` is 0 and must be set in the program so that the scroll bar can be used. With reference to an internal table, `LINES` is set to the current number of lines in the internal table if the table control is being processed for the first time. However, since the time of occurrence is not defined for this, you should set the value of `LINES` explicitly to the number of lines of the internal table before the PBO processing.
`top_line`	Topmost displayed row for next PBO. Set at PAI by the position of the vertical slider box.
`current_line`	Current row during a `LOOP` loop in the dynpro flow logic. If the `FROM` addition to the `LOOP` statement is not specified (see Section 25.2.5.2, the value of `current_line` corresponds to the result of `sy-step1 + (top_line - 1)`.
`left_col`	Number of the first horizontally scrollable column displayed after the lead columns. Is set at PAI by the position of the horizontal slider box.
`line_sel_mode`	Row selection mode: "0" if no rows can be selected , "1" if one line , "2" if several lines . Start value is taken from the definition of the table control in dynpro `dynnr`.
`col_sel_mode`	Column selection mode: "0" if no columns can be marked, "1" if one column, "2" if several columns. Start value is taken from the definition of the table control in dynpro `dynnr`.
`line_selector`	Flag ("X" or " ") that specifies whether there is a marking column. Start value is taken from the definition of the table control in dynpro `dynnr`.
`h_grid`	Flag ("X" or " ") that specifies whether there are horizontal separators. Start value is taken from the definition of the table control in dynpro `dynnr`.

Table 25.2 The cxtab_control Structure

Component	Description
v_grid	Flag ("X" or " ") that specifies whether there are vertical separators. Start value is taken from the definition of the table control in dynpro dynnr.
cols	Control table for individual columns (see Table 25.3).
invisible	Flag ("X" or " ") that specifies whether or not the table control is visible in the window or not.

Table 25.2 The cxtab_control Structure (cont.)

Component	Description
screen	Structure for the attributes of the screen element of the current column (see Table 25.1). The components can be set for the values described in Section 25.3.6 either directly or using MODIFY SCREEN. The latter overwrites a direct value assignment.
index	Current position of the column in the table control. Start value is taken from the definition of the table control in the dynpro dynnr. It is set to the current value at PAI.
selected	Flag ("X" or " ") that specifies whether or not column is selected. It is set to current value at PAI.
vislength	Visible length of column. Start value is taken from the definition of the table control in dynpro dynnr.
invisible	Flag ("X" or " ") that specifies whether or not the column is visible in the table control.

Table 25.3 The cxtab_column Structure

Notes

▶ In a table control, you can scroll vertically using a scroll bar if the component lines of the structure cxtab_control was set to the correct row number before the PBO processing of the table control (see Table 25.2). Every time you scroll with the scroll bar, the event PAI is triggered with an empty function code, and the component top_line of the structure cxtab_control is automatically set to the new topmost row before the time of PBO.

▶ For program-controlled scrolling, it is sufficient to assign a value to the component top_line of the structure cxtab_control during PBO processing. For page-by-page scrolling, the number of pages to be scrolled can be obtained from the system field sy-loopc during the loop processing (see Section 25.2.5.2). sy-loopc contains the number of currently displayed rows, while the component LINES of the structure cxtab_control contains the number of rows in the entire table control.

Example

If a table control is defined on the dynpro with the number 100, whose rows are defined with reference to the database table SPFLI in the ABAP Dictionary, the corresponding programming of the ABAP program can appear as shown below. In a PBO module `prepare_tab`, an internal table `spfli_tab` is filled with data from the database table. The number of rows of `spfli_tab` is assigned to the component lines of the structure `flight_tab` created using CONTROLS; this is done to activate the scroll bar of the table control. In a PAI module `modify_tab`, the row of the internal table is modified whose table key matches that of the interface work area `spfli` defined using TABLES. The PAI module `modify_tab` is called for every displayed row of the table control. The corresponding dynpro flow logic can be seen in the example in Section 25.2.5.2.

```
CONTROLS flight_tab TYPE TABLEVIEW USING SCREEN '0100'.

TABLES spfli.

DATA spfli_tab TYPE SORTED TABLE OF spfli
               WITH UNIQUE KEY carrid connid.

...

MODULE prepare_tab OUTPUT.
  IF spfli_tab IS INITIAL.
    SELECT *
           FROM spfli
           INTO TABLE spfli_tab.
    flight_tab-lines = lines( spfli_tab ).
  ENDIF.
ENDMODULE.

MODULE modify_tab INPUT.
  MODIFY TABLE spfli_tab FROM spfli.
ENDMODULE.
```

25.3.10.2 Processing Tabstrips in the ABAP Program

If you specify the type TABSTRIP, a deep structure is created with the name of the control and of the type `cxtab_tabstrip` of the type group CXTAB. From this structure, only the component `activetab` is required in the program.

During the PBO processing, the active tabstrip page is specified by assigning the function code of a tab title to the component `activetab`. The first tabstrip page is active by default. When scrolling in the SAP GUI (see Sec-

tion 25.2.6.2), the tabstrip control can thus be initialized. For any scrolling in an ABAP program (see Section 25.2.6.2), the tabstrip page selected
by the user must be activated by this assignment. You must also ensure
that the desired subscreen is included in the dynpro flow logic using the
CALL SUBSCREEN statement (see Section 25.2.6.3).

During PAI processing, the component ACTIVETAB contains the function
code of the active tab title. When scrolling in the SAP GUI, you can thus
ascertain which tabstrip page is currently displayed.

Note

The same as for normal subscreens (see Section 25.2.6.3) applies to the
inclusion of the subscreens of tabstrips using CALL SUBSCREEN as for normal subscreens.

Example

If, on a dynpro, a tabstrip control is defined with three untyped tab titles
with the function codes "TAB1", "TAB2", and "TAB3" and a subscreen area
SUB, the scrolling can be programmed in ABAP as follows. In a PBO module prepare_tabstrip the component activetab of the structure tab_
strip created using CCNTROLS is assigned the function code of the first tab
title. After a tab title has been selected, this component is set to the relevant function code in the PAI module handle_user_command. The number of the desired subscreen dynpro is assigned to the data object dynnr
that is used for including the subscreen in the dynpro flow logic. The corresponding programming of the dynpro flow logic can be seen in the example in Section 25.2.6.

```
CONTROLS tab_strip TYPE TABSTRIP.

DATA: ok_code TYPE sy-ucomm,
      dynnr   TYPE sy-dynnr.

...

MODULE prepare_tabstrip OUTPUT.
  IF tab_strip-activetab IS INITIAL OR
     dynnr IS INITIAL.
    tab_strip-activetab = 'TAB1'.
    dynnr = '0110'.
  ENDIF.
ENDMODULE.

MODULE handle_user_command INPUT.
  CASE ok_code.
    WHEN 'TAB1'.
```

```
      dynnr = '0110'.
    WHEN 'TAB2'.
      dynnr = '0120'.
    WHEN 'TAB3'.
      dynnr = '0130'.
    ...
  ENDCASE.
  IF ok_code(3) = 'TAB'.
    tab_strip-activetab = ok_code.
  ENDIF.
ENDMODULE.
```

25.3.11 Initializing Table Control

`REFRESH CONTROL`

Initializing a table control.

Syntax

`REFRESH CONTROL contrl FROM SCREEN dynnr.`

This statement assigns values to certain components of the structure con-trl. For contrl, a structure must be specified that was created using the statement CONTROLS for a table control. The values are taken from the definition of the table control with the same name. Its screen is specified in dynnr. The values of the components are set. These values are the components for which the start values are taken from the definition of a table control (see Table 25.2). For dynnr, a data object of the type n of length 4 is expected. It must contain the number of a dynpro on which a table control name contrl is defined.

25.3.12 Exiting Step-Loop Processing

`EXIT FROM STEP-LOOP`

Leaving a step loop.

Syntax

`EXIT FROM STEP-LOOP.`

During the processing of table controls or step loops with the statement LOOP in the dynpro flow logic, this statement effects the immediate termination of the loop. The current ABAP processing block is instantly left and the dynpro flow logic continues after the statement ENDLOOP. During the PBO-processing, the statement effects that the current and the following table control lines or step-loop groups are not displayed on the screen. If the statement is not processed during the execution of a LOOP loop in the dynpro flow logic, then the program terminates with a termination message.

25.3.13 Holding Input Data

```
SET HOLD DATA
```

Activating or deactivating functions of input data.

Syntax

```
SET HOLD DATA {ON|OFF}.
```

During PBO processing, this statement turns the following standard menu entries in the GUI status of the dynpro either on with the ON addition or off with the OFF addition:

▶ System · User specifications · Hold data
  This function saves the entries made by the user in the input fields of the dynpros for the duration of the current user session. For every new display of the screen layout, these values are placed in the corresponding input fields as default values; in this way, the values transported from the ABAP program are overwritten.

▶ System · User specifications · Set data
  This function works like the **Hold data** function, except that here the corresponding input fields are no longer ready for input for all subsequent calls of the dynpro.

▶ System · User specifications · Delete data
  This function deletes all saved data and makes the input fields that were locked with **Set data** ready for input again for all subsequent calls of the dynpro.

At the beginning of every PBO processing, the setting made in the static characteristics of the screen under **Hold data** is set so that the execution of SET HOLD DATA during PAI processing does not have an effect on the display of the subsequent screen layout.

Note

The above menu entries can be selected in every GUI status but are only effectual when they are activated in the static characteristics of the dynpro with **Hold data** or with the statement SET HOLD DATA.

25.3.14 Setting the Next Dynpro

```
SET SCREEN
```

Setting the next dynpro within a dynpro sequence.

Syntax

```
SET SCREEN dynnr.
```

This statement sets the dynpro with the screen number specified in dynnr as the next dynpro for the processing of the current dynpro. For dynnr, a data object of type n and length 4 is expected. It must contain either the dynpro number of a screen in the main program of the current program group or the value 0, otherwise a non-catchable exception will be triggered. The specified next dynpro overwrites the previously-set next dynpro.

The next dynpro is automatically called when the system finishes the PAI processing of the current dynpro. If the dynpro number of the next dynpro is 0, the current next dynpro is ended.

Note

One next dynpro is always set during the processing of a dynpro. After you have called a screen, the next dynpro whose characteristics are defined statically applies. This next dynpro can be overwritten with the SET SCREEN statement for the duration of the current next dynpro processing.

25.3.15 Leaving a Dynpro

```
LEAVE SCREEN
```

Leaving the current dynpro.

Syntax

```
LEAVE { SCREEN | {TO SCREEN dynnr} }.
```

This statement ends the processing of the current dynpro. The current processing block of the ABAP program and the current processing block of the dynpro are left immediately.

The variant LEAVE SCREEN calls the current next dynpro. This is either statically specified in the properties of the current dynpro or has been set before using the statement SET SCREEN.

The variant LEAVE TO SCREEN calls the dynpro with the number dynnr as the next dynpro. A data object of the type n of the length 4 is expected for dynnr. It must contain either the dynpro number of a dynpro in the main program of the current program group or the value 0. Otherwise, an exception that cannot be handled is raised. This statement is a short form of the statements SET SCREEN dynnr and LEAVE SCREEN.

Note
This statement does not terminate the entire dynpro sequence; it branches to an additional dynpro in the same sequence. Only if the number 0 is used to branch to the next dynpro, LEAVE SCREEN also terminates the dynpro sequence.

26 Selection Screens

26.1 Overview

26.1.1 Selection Screens as Dynpros

Selection screens are special dynpros that can be defined in executable programs, function groups and module pools. Selection screens are defined in the global declaration section of relevant ABAP programs with the statements `SELECT-OPTIONS`, `SELECTION-SCREEN` and `PARAMETERS`, without using the Screen Painter. The screen layouts of selection screens can contain subsets of the screen elements of general dynpros.

Selection screens lie in the same namespace as the dynpros of the program. Additionally, dynpro number 1000 is reserved for a standard selection screen. Apart from the standard selection screen, you can define independent selection screens. Independent selection screens can only be defined in function groups and module pools.

When an ABAP program is activated, the components of the program selection screen, i.e., screens with screen elements and dynpro flow logic, are automatically generated.

26.1.2 Selection Screen Tasks

Selection screens have two major tasks:

▶ They enable users to input parameters (single values) and selection criteria (interval selections in tabular form);

▶ They represent the executable interface programs whose input fields can be supplied by the calling program with `SUBMIT` (see Section 10.2.2.3).

26.1.3 GUI Status of Selection Screens

The GUI status of a selection screen is generated automatically during the generation of a program. A statement `SET PF-STATUS` at the time of the selection screen PBO does not affect this GUI status. To define a separate GUI status for a selection screen or to deactivate the functions of the screen generated, you can use one of the function modules RS_SET_SELSCREEN_STATUS or RS_EXTERNAL_SELSCREEN_STATUS in exceptional cases. The title in the title bar of the standard selection screens cannot be changed and is always the title of the executable program as defined in the program properties.

26.1.4 Selection Screen Events

No dialog modules for selection screens can be defined in the ABAP program. Instead, the runtime environment triggers specific events during PBO and PAI processing of the dynpros, which can be handled in corresponding event blocks during the selection-screen processing (see Section 26.5.5).

26.1.5 Selection Screens and Logical Databases

In a logical database, you can also define a standard selection screen. If an executable program is linked to a logical database, its standard selection screen is composed of the logical database and its own database.

26.1.6 Statements for Selection Screens

The statements for defining and calling selection screens are as follows:

Statement	Section
SELECTION-SCREEN	26.2
PARAMETERS	26.3
SELECT-OPTIONS	26.4
CALL SELECTION-SCREEN	26.5.4

26.2 Creating and Laying Out Selection Screens

SELECTION-SCREEN

The key word SELECTION-SCREEN introduces statements for creating and changing the layout of selection screens. All screen elements and attributes of selection screens that are not determined using PARAMETERS and SELECT-OPTIONS are defined using SELECTION-SCREEN. These statements can be divided into the following areas and are covered in the corresponding sections.

1. Creating selection screens (Section 26.2.1)

2. Layout of selection screens (Section 26.2.2)

3. Using elements from other selection screens (Section 26.2.3)

4. Variants for the selection screens of logical databases (Section 26.2.4)

26.2.1 Creating Selection Screens

Variants of the statement SELECTION-SCREEN create selection screens. Selection screens can be created as normal dynpros or as subscreen dynpros. The standard selection screen for executable programs is created automatically.

26.2.1.1 The Standard Selection Screen

Each executable program already contains a standard selection screen with the dynpro number 1,000. The screen elements on the standard selection screen are defined by all PARAMETERS, SELECT-OPTIONS and SELECTION-SCREEN statements that are not within the definition of a stand-alone selection screen, in other words, that are not defined between the following statements:

```
SELECTION-SCREEN BEGIN OF SCREEN ...
...
SELECTION-SCREEN END OF SCREEN ...
```

If a standard selection screen contains the screen for the executable program and the screen for a logical database, the screen elements for the executable program are listed below those for the logical database.

Function groups and module pools do not have a standard selection screen. Here, you must place the three statements PARAMETERS, SELECT-OPTIONS and SELECTION-SCREEN within the definition of the stand-alone selection screen.

Note
We advise grouping all the statements that define the standard selection screen and listing them in the global declaration section, together with the definitions of stand-alone selection screens.

26.2.1.2 Creating Independent Selection Screens as Normal Dynpros

Syntax

```
SELECTION-SCREEN BEGIN OF SCREEN dynnr [TITLE title]
                                      [AS WINDOW].
...
SELECTION-SCREEN END OF SCREEN dynnr.
```

These statements can be executed in the global declaration section of executable programs, function groups and module pools. You create a stand-alone selection screen with the dynpro number `dynnr`. You must specify the dynpro number directly, and it must have no more than four digits.

All the `PARAMETERS`, `SELECT-OPTIONS`, and `SELECTION-SCREEN` statements that are executed within these statements define the screen elements for the stand-alone selection screen. You cannot define a further selection screen within the definition of a selection screen.

You can use the `TITLE` addition to define a title for the title bar of your stand-alone selection screen. For the title `title`, you can specify either a name of your choice with a maximum of eight characters or the name of a text symbol from the program in the form `text-###`, where *###* is the three-character ID of the text symbol. If you specify a name of your choice, the runtime environment generates a type `c` global variant of the same name that is 70 characters in length. When the selection screen is displayed, the content of the text symbol or global variable are displayed in the title bar. If the specified text symbol is not found, the name of the text symbol is displayed as the title in the form "TEXT-###". If the `TITLE` addition is not specified, the system uses the title of the program defined in the program attributes.

You can use the `AS WINDOW` addition to define a stand-alone selection screen for display in a modal dialog window. The actual shape of the window is not defined until it is accessed by `CALL SELECTION-SCREEN`. The `AS WINDOW` addition also displays warnings and error messages that occur during the processing of a selection screen event as a modal dialog window.

Note

The specified dynpro number `dynnr` must not already be assigned to existing dynpros or selection screens. You should also note that the number 1,000 for the standard selection screen cannot be used for a stand-alone selection screen in an executable program.

Example

Definition and access of a selection screen as a modal dialog window.

```
SELECTION-SCREEN BEGIN OF SCREEN 500 TITLE title
                                     AS WINDOW.
PARAMETERS name TYPE sy-uname.
SELECTION-SCREEN END OF SCREEN 500.
```

```
title = 'Input name'.

CALL SELECTION-SCREEN '0500' STARTING AT 10 10.
```

26.2.1.3 Creating Independent Selection Screens as Subscreen Dynpros

Syntax

```
SELECTION-SCREEN BEGIN OF SCREEN dynnr AS SUBSCREEN
                                       [NO INTERVALS]
                                       [NESTING LEVEL n].
...
SELECTION-SCREEN END OF SCREEN dynnr.
```

These statements serve the same function as the statements for creating selection screens as normal dynpros, but here the selection screen is defined as a subscreen dynpro.

Like all subscreen dynpros, selection screens defined as subscreen dynpros can be included in other dynpros or selection screens, or in subscreen areas and tabstrip pages. However, they cannot be accessed with a CALL SELECTION-SCREEN statement.

If you specify NO INTERVALS, the addition of the same name NO INTERVALS is used implicitly in the SELECT-OPTIONS statement when defining all the selection criteria for this selection screen, and the subscreen is narrowed accordingly.

The NESTING LEVEL addition allows you to adjust the width of the subscreen if it is to be included in a tabstrip in one or more frames. You must specify n directly as a number between 0 and 4. To ensure that the width is adjusted correctly, the number n must be the same as the number of frames that surround the tabstrip. If the tabstrip is not in a frame, you can specify the addition with a 0 or simply omit it.

Note
If selection screens defined as subscreens are included in dynpros, you should note that—as is the case with normal subscreen dynpros—the CALL SUBSCREEN statement in the dynpro flow logic must be executed at PBO and PAI so that the data is transported between the selection screen and the ABAP program User actions on selection screens defined as subscreens trigger standard selection-screen processing (see Section 26.5.5), even if they are included in dynpros.

Example

Define the selection screens 100 and 200 as subscreen dynpros and include them in a tabstrip control on the standard selection screen in an executable program.

```
REPORT ...

SELECTION-SCREEN BEGIN OF SCREEN 100 AS SUBSCREEN.
PARAMETERS: p1(10) TYPE c,
            p2(10) TYPE c,
            p3(10) TYPE c.
SELECTION-SCREEN END OF SCREEN 100.

SELECTION-SCREEN BEGIN OF SCREEN 200 AS SUBSCREEN.
PARAMETERS: q1(10) TYPE c,
            q2(10) TYPE c,
            q3(10) TYPE c.
SELECTION-SCREEN END OF SCREEN 200.

SELECTION-SCREEN: BEGIN OF TABBED BLOCK mytab
                                FOR 10 LINES,
                  TAB (20) button1 USER-COMMAND push1
                                    DEFAULT SCREEN 100,
                  TAB (20) button2 USER-COMMAND push2
                                    DEFAULT SCREEN 200,
                  END OF BLOCK mytab.

INITIALIZATION.
  button1 = 'Selection Screen 1'.
  button2 = 'Selection Screen 2'.
```

26.2.2 Laying Out Selection Screens

You create the selection screen input fields using the commands PARAMETERS and SELECT-OPTIONS. By default, each of these commands creates its own row on the selection screen. The following variants of the command SELECTION-SCREEN allow you to create selection screens in different ways. With them, you can define other screen elements and influence the order of elements on the selection screen.

The following commands can be executed within the definition of a selection screen in the global declaration part of executable programs, function groups and module pools.

▶ Blank lines: SELECTION-SCREEN SKIP

▶ Horizontal lines: SELECTION-SCREEN ULINE

- Output fields: `SELECTION-SCREEN COMMENT`
- Pushbuttons: `SELECTION-SCREEN PUSHBUTTON`
- Lines with several elements: `SELECTION-SCREEN BEGIN OF LINE`
- Blocks: `SELECTION-SCREEN BEGIN OF BLOCK`
- Tabstrip controls: `SELECTION-SCREEN BEGIN OF TABBED BLOCK`

The `SELECTION-SCREEN FUNCTION KEY` statement enables pushbuttons to be activated in the application toolbar.

Some screen elements of a selection screen can be assigned to modification groups using the addition `MODIF ID`. Modification groups are linked to the column `group1` in the system table `screen` (see Table 25.1). The modification groups that are assigned to the columns `group2` and `group3` of the system table `screen` are set by the system when a selection screen is generated. The content of `group4` is intended for internal use only.

- `group2` contains the value "DBS" for screen elements that are defined in a logical database.
- `group3` can contain the values from Table 26.1.

Abbreviation	Meaning of screen element
BLK	Frame or title of a block
COF	Output field that is linked with a parameter or selection criterion with the addition `FOR FIELD`
COM	Output field that is not linked to a parameter or selection criterion
HGH	Input field for the upper interval limit of a selection criterion
ISX	Input field of a parameter that is linked to a search help by means of the addition `AS SEARCH PATTERN`
LOW	Input field for the lower interval limit of a selection criterion
OPU	Icon for the selection option of a selection criterion
PAR	Input field of a parameter
PBU	Pushbutton
TAB	Tab title
TOT	Output field for text in front of the input field of the upper interval limit of a selection criterion
TST	Tabstrip

Table 26.1 Modification Groups of Selection Screens

Abbreviation	Meaning of screen element
TXT	Output field for text in front of the input field of a parameter or the lower interval limit of a selection criterion
ULI	Horizontal line
VPU	Pushbutton for multiple selection of a selection criterion

Table 26.1 Modification Groups of Selection Screens (cont.)

Notes

▶ The maximum width of a selection screen is 83. If you exceed this width, either the screen will be cut off or the selection screen will not be generated. In the case of blocks with a frame, the maximum width is reduced by the width of the frame.

▶ All screen elements that can be created using the command SELECTION-SCREEN are located in a namespace. This is the case even if the elements were created in different selection screens. In the case of selection-screen elements for which a global data object is generated when they are created, the namespace of the program data object also has to be taken into account. If you want to use an element or a data object in multiple selection screens, you can use the addition INCLUDE of the command SELECTION-SCREEN (see Section 26.2.3).

▶ Sharing of a namespace particularly applies to a standard selection screen composed of the selection screens of a logical database and the program itself. The elements defined in the program cannot be allowed to conflict with the elements in the logical database.

26.2.2.1 Creating Blank Lines

Syntax

```
SELECTION-SCREEN SKIP [n] [ldb_additions].
```

This statement creates n blank lines on the current selection screen among the lines already filled. You must specify the value n directly as a single-digit positive number. If you do not specify n, the system creates one blank line.

The additions *ldb_additions* can only be used in a selection-include for a logical database (see Section 26.2.4.4).

26.2.2.2 Creating Horizontal Lines

Syntax

```
SELECTION-SCREEN ULINE [[/] [pos](len)] [MODIF ID modid]
                       [ldb_additions].
```

This statement creates a horizontal line on the current selection screen. If you do not make a formatting specification [/] [pos] (len), the system creates a new line across the width of the selection screen beneath the lines already filled. The maximum length of this line is 83.

The formatting specification [/] [pos] (len) is used to position the line on the selection screen. len specifies the length of the line and pos the column from which it is drawn. Only if several elements are displayed in one line (see Section 26.2.2.5), can you omit this specification, and the line will be drawn starting from the current item. If an oblique symbol (/) is entered, you must specify a length and the system draws the line on a new row; otherwise it is drawn on the current row. If several elements are displayed in a line, you can omit the oblique (/). If there are conflicts with existing screen elements, the system will be unable to generate the selection screen.

You must specify the length len directly as a positive number with a maximum of two digits. If a line is too long, it will be cut off outside of blocks with frames (see Section 26.2.2.6) at position 83 and at the right edge of the block inside a block with a frame. You can either specify a number between 1 and 83 for pos or one of the expressions pos_low or pos_high. The expression pos_low specifies the position in which the input field for a parameter or the first input field for a selection criterion is to be displayed. The expression pos_high specifies the position in which the second input field for a selection criterion is to be displayed. If the statement is part of a block with a frame (see Section 26.2.2.6), the system interprets a number specified in pos to determine the field's position relative to the frame.

The addition MODIF ID assigns the line to the modification group modid which is assigned to the column group1 in the system table screen. This means it can be modified using a MODIFY SCREEN statement before the selection screen is displayed.

The additions ldb_additions can only be used in a selection-include for a logical database (see Section 26.2.4.4).

26.2.2.3 Creating Output Fields

Syntax

```
SELECTION-SCREEN COMMENT [/] [pos] (len)
                         { text |{ [text] FOR FIELD sel} }
                         [VISIBLE LENGTH vlen]
                         [MODIF ID modid]
                         [ldb_additions].
```

This statement creates an output field on the current selection screen and enters the content of `text` in this field. For `text`, specify either the name of the text symbol of the program in the form `text-###` (where `###` is the three-digit ID for the text symbol) or any name with a maximum of eight characters. If another name than a text symbol is entered, the runtime environment generates a global variable of the same name of type `c` and length 83. If the specified text symbol is not found, no text is entered in the output field.

The position of the output field must be specified using `[/] [pos] (len)`. The syntax and the meaning of `[/] [pos] (len)` are the same as in the generation of horizontal lines. In this case, `len` defines the length of the output field in the dynpro of the selection screen. If an output field extends beyond position 83 or sticks out of a block with a frame, the visible length is shortened accordingly and the content is displayed as movable in the visible length.

If the addition `FOR FIELD` is used, the output field is linked to a parameter or a selection criterion `sel` of the same program defined by `PARAMETERS` or `SELECT-OPTIONS`. Its name `sel` must be specified directly. When this link is made, the field help or input help for `sel` is displayed when the user selects the output field using the function keys **F1** and **F4**. The link also means that the output field is assigned to the same modification group. Furthermore, the output field is hidden if `sel` is made invisible using a variant. If `FOR FIELD` is specified, `text` does not have to be specified. The output field is then filled either with the specified name `sel`, or, if it exists in the current text pool, with the corresponding selection text.

The addition `VISIBLE LENGTH` defines the visible length `vlen` of the output field. `vlen` must be specified directly as a positive number. If `vlen` is greater than `len`, the visible length is set to `len`. If `vlen` is smaller than `len`, the output field is displayed in the length of `vlen` with movable content and a quick info of the whole content.

The addition MODIF ID assigns the output field to the modification group modid, which is assigned to the column group1 of the system table screen. It can thus be modified using the statement MODIFY SCREEN before the selection screen is displayed.

The additions *ldb_additions* can only be used in the selection-include of a logical database (see Section 26.2.4.4).

Note

The addition FOR FIELD causes the output field to behave in exactly the same way as the output fields generated automatically by PARAMETERS or SELECT-OPTIONS in response to parameters or selection criteria. Automatically generated fields are not displayed in a line if multiple elements are output and can thus be replaced by user-defined linked output fields.

Example

Output fields, horizontal lines and empty lines on the standard selection screen of an executable program. The first output field is highlighted in the display.

```
SELECTION-SCREEN COMMENT /1(50) comm1 MODIF ID mg1.
SELECTION-SCREEN ULINE.
SELECTION-SCREEN SKIP.

SELECTION-SCREEN COMMENT /1(30) comm2.
SELECTION-SCREEN ULINE /1(50).
PARAMETERS: r1 RADIOBUTTON GROUP rad1,
            r2 RADIOBUTTON GROUP rad1,
            r3 RADIOBUTTON GROUP rad1.
SELECTION-SCREEN ULINE /1(50).

AT SELECTION-SCREEN OUTPUT.
  comm1 ='Selection Screen'.
  comm2 ='Select one'.
  LOOP AT SCREEN.
    IF screen-group1 = 'MG1'.
      screen-intensified = '1'.
     MODIFY SCREEN.
   ENDIF.
 ENDLOOP.
```

26.2.2.4 Creating Pushbuttons

Syntax

```
SELECTION-SCREEN PUSHBUTTON [/] [pos] (len) button_text
                            USER-COMMAND fcode
                            [VISIBLE LENGTH vlen]
                            [MODIF ID modid]
                            [ldb_additions].
```

This statement creates a pushbutton on the current selection screen. The text on the pushbutton is determined by the content of button_text. The rules that apply to text also apply to button_text when creating an output field.

You must specify the position of the output field using [/] [pos] (len). The syntax and meaning of [/] [pos] (len) are the same as when creating horizontal lines, although in this case len defines the length of the push-button in the dynpro of the selection screen. If a pushbutton extends beyond position 83 or beyond the edge of a block with a frame, it is cut off at the right hand side.

If you specify the USER-COMMAND addition, the pushbutton must be assigned a function code fcode. The function code fcode must be speci-fied directly and can only contain a maximum of 20 characters.

Before you can work with the pushbutton, you must specify a TABLES statement to declare an interface work area for the structure SSCRFIELDS from the ABAP Dictionary.

If the user selects the pushbutton on the selection screen, the runtime environment triggers the event AT SELECTION-SCREEN and the function code fcode is transferred to the ucomm component in the interface work area sscrfields.

The VISIBLE LENGTH addition defines the visible length vlen of the push-button and its text. The syntax and meaning of this addition are the same as when creating output fields, although a pushbutton is never displayed as shorter than the text defined for it.

The MODIF ID addition assigns the pushbutton to the modification group modid that is assigned to the column group1 on the system table screen. This means it can be modified using a MODIFY SCREEN statement before the selection screen is displayed.

The additions *ldb_additions* can only be used in the selection-include of a logical database (see Section 26.2.4.4).

Notes

▶ You can use the function module ICON_CREATE to assign an icon, a quick info text and a corresponding text to a pushbutton. When you do this, you must specify an adequate length `len` for the pushbutton so that the icon can be displayed internally and adjust the visible length with `VISIBLE LENGTH`.

▶ Once the event block in AT SELECTION-SCREEN has been processed, the system returns to displaying the selection screen. To exit selection-screen processing and continue the execution of the program, you can only choose **Execute** or **Cancel**. This means that pushbuttons on selection screens are intended primarily for dynamic modifications to the selection screen rather than for a control of the program.

Example

Define and access a stand-alone selection screen 500 with two pushbuttons in an executable program. An icon and a quick info text are created for the second pushbutton.

```
TABLES sscrfields.

TYPE-POOLS icon.

SELECTION-SCREEN:
  BEGIN OF SCREEN 500 AS WINDOW TITLE title,
    PUSHBUTTON 2(10)  but1 USER-COMMAND cli1,
    PUSHBUTTON 12(30) but2 USER-COMMAND cli2
                           VISIBLE LENGTH 10,
  END OF SCREEN 500.

AT SELECTION-SCREEN.
  CASE sscrfields.
    WHEN 'CLI1'.
      ...
    WHEN 'CLI2'.
      ...
  ENDCASE.

START-OF-SELECTION.
  title = 'Push button'.
  but1  = 'Button 1'.

  CALL FUNCTION 'ICON_CREATE'
    EXPORTING
```

```
          name  = icon_information
          text  = 'Button 2'
          info  = 'My Quickinfo'
       IMPORTING
          RESULT = but2
       EXCEPTIONS
          OTHERS = 0.

    CALL SELECTION-SCREEN '0500' STARTING AT 10 10.
```

26.2.2.5 Creating Lines with Several Elements

Syntax

```
SELECTION-SCREEN BEGIN OF LINE.
...
[SELECTION-SCREEN POSITION pos [ldb_additions]].
...
SELECTION-SCREEN END OF LINE.
```

The first and last statements define a new line below the existing elements on the selection screen. All the screen elements within these statements that are defined with PARAMETERS and SELECTION-SCREEN statements are placed in this line one after the other without spaces.

The SELECTION-SCREEN POSITION statement can be used to define the output position for the following screen element. The position pos can either be specified directly as a number between 1 and 83 or using pos_low or pos_high expressions. The expression pos_low specifies the position in which the input field for a parameter or the first input field for a selection criterion is displayed as standard. The expression pos_high specifies the position in which the second input field for a selection criterion is to be displayed as standard. If you make a different specification of the position in the statement defining the following element, this is taken into account. The statement SELECTION-SCREEN POSITION is only possible within the definition of a line. If there are conflicts with existing screen elements, the selection screen cannot be generated. The additions ldb_additions can only be used in a selection-include for a logical database (see Section 26.2.4.4).

The following applies within the definition of a line:

▶ You cannot specify selection criteria defined with SELECT-OPTIONS. Otherwise, the display is not defined.

- ► You cannot define other lines with SELECTION-SCREEN BEGIN OF LINE.
- ► You cannot define blocks or tabstrips with SELECTION-SCREEN BEGIN OF [TABBED] BLOCK.
- ► The oblique symbol (/) is not allowed in formatting specifications.
- ► You can omit the position specification pos in formatting specifications.
- ► Output fields are not created for selection texts for the parameters displayed in these kinds of lines. Instead, these can be created by specifying a SELECTION-SCREEN COMMENT.

Note

If a screen element is assigned a position greater than 83 or is positioned outside a block with a frame, the selection screen is not generated. When input and output fields that were positioned beforehand extend beyond the end of the line, the visible length is shortened and the content is displayed in the visible length and can be scrolled. In this case, pushbuttons and horizontal lines are cut off at position 83 or where the frame of the block ends.

Example

A pushbutton, an input field, and an output field in a line of the standard selection screen of an executable program.

```
SELECTION-SCREEN: BEGIN OF LINE,
                  PUSHBUTTON 2(10) push
                  USER-COMMAND fcode,
                  POSITION 16.
PARAMETERS para(20) TYPE c.
SELECTION-SCREEN: COMMENT 40(40) text,
                  END OF LINE.

INITIALIZATION.
  push = 'Push'.
  text = '<--- Fill field, then push button!'.
```

26.2.2.6 Creating Blocks

Syntax

```
SELECTION-SCREEN BEGIN OF BLOCK block
                          [WITH FRAME [TITLE title]]
                          [NO INTERVALS].

...
SELECTION-SCREEN END OF BLOCK block.
```

These statements define a block with the name `block` on the current selection screen. You must specify the name `block` directly, and it must contain a maximum of 20 characters.

All screen elements on the selection screen defined with `PARAMETERS`, `SELECT-OPTIONS` and `SELECTION-SCREEN` statements within these statements are part of the block `block`. You can create additional blocks within the definition of a block.

The addition `WITH FRAME` draws a frame around a block that is not empty. A maximum of five blocks can be nested. You can specify the addition `TITLE` to define a title for a block with a frame. For the title `title`, you can specify either the name of a text symbol in the program in the form `text-###` (where ### stands for the three-character ID of the text symbol) or a name of your choice containing a maximum of eight characters. If you specify a name of your choice, the runtime environment generates a global variable of the same name, belonging to type `c` and with a length of 70. When the selection screen is displayed, the content of the text symbol or the global variable is positioned at the top left hand corner of the frame. If the specified text symbol is not found, the system does not create a title.

If you specify `NO INTERVALS`, the addition of the same name `NO INTERVALS` is used implicitly and the width of the block is reduced accordingly when defining all the selection criteria for this block in a `SELECT-OPTIONS` statement. If the block has a frame, the blocks nested therein transfer also the `NO INTERVALS` addition.

Note
Each block is assigned a selection screen event `AT SELECTION-SCREEN ON BLOCK` in which the user entries within the block can be processed together (see Section 4.4.3).

Example
Grouping radio buttons in a block with a frame and title on the standard selection screen of an executable program.

```
SELECTION-SCREEN BEGIN OF BLOCK rad1
                          WITH FRAME TITLE title.
PARAMETERS: r1 RADIOBUTTON GROUP gr1,
            r2 RADIOBUTTON GROUP gr1,
            r3 RADIOBUTTON GROUP gr1.
SELECTION-SCREEN END OF BLOCK rad1.
```

```
INITIALIZATION.
  title = 'Selection'.
```

26.2.2.7 Creating Tabstrip Controls

Syntax

```
SELECTION-SCREEN BEGIN OF TABBED BLOCK tblock FOR n LINES.
...
SELECTION-SCREEN TAB (len) tab USER-COMMAND fcode
               [DEFAULT [PROGRAM prog] SCREEN dynnr].
...
SELECTION-SCREEN END OF BLOCK tblock.
```

The first and the last statements define a tabstrip area with the name tblock on the current selection screen. The name tblock must be specified directly and can contain a maximum of 16 characters. The number of lines in the tabstrip area is determined by a number n which must be specified directly and can contain a maximum of three characters but must not exceed 197.

Within the statements defining a tabstrip area, there can only be SELECTION-SCREEN statements with a TAB addition, and these can only be used in this location. These statements define tab titles with the name tab and a length of len. The names tab must be specified directly and can contain a maximum of eight characters. The lengths len must be specified directly as positive numbers, with a maximum of two characters and a value no more than 79. If the width of all the tab titles is greater than the width of the area, the system automatically sets up a scroll bar so that you can access all the tab pages.

The system automatically creates a type c global variable of the same name and with a length of 83 for each tab title. The content of the variables is displayed as the label for the tab title on the selection screen.

Each tab title must be assigned a function code fcode with the USER-COMMAND addition. The function codes fcode must be specified directly and can contain a maximum of 20 characters. When the user chooses a tab, the corresponding function code can be determined from the system field sy-ucomm after the event AT SELECTION-SCREEN.

Each tab title must be assigned a subscreen dynpro whose screen layout is displayed as a tab page when the tab title is selected.

Static assignment

If the addition DEFAULT is specified, the tab title is assigned the subscreen dynpro for the number dynnr of the program prog. You must specify the dynpro number and program directly. If the addition PROGRAM is not specified, the system searches for the subscreen dynpro in the current program. If the addition DEFAULT is not specified, the selection screen must be dynamically assigned a subscreen dynpro before it is displayed. A subscreen dynpro that is assigned statically with DEFAULT can also be overwritten dynamically.

If the DEFAULT addition is specified, you can specify that the screen element for a tab title is displayed when the selection screen is sent by assigning the name of the tab title to the component activetab. The other components are filled with the values specified for DEFAULT when the selection screen is sent. The first page is displayed as standard.

Dynamic assignment

A global structure of the same name is created for each tabstrip area in the current program. This structure contains the three components prog of type c with a length of 40, dynnr of type c with a length of 4, and activetab of type c with a length of 132. Before the selection screen is called, these components can be assigned the name of the ABAP program in which the desired subscreen dynpro is defined, the number of the subscreen dynpro, and the function code for the tab title. An assignment to the component activetab at the time AT SELECTION-SCREEN has no effect and is automatically overwritten with the function code for the selected tab title before the event AT SELECTION-SCREEN OUTPUT is reached for the current selection screen.

Note

If an assigned subscreen dynpro is not a selection screen, the dialog modules that are accessed during its flow logic must be defined in the current program. If an assigned subscreen dynpro is a selection screen, user actions on the subscreen lead to the event AT SELECTION-SCREEN. These actions include selecting a tab title. The event AT SELECTION-SCREEN is executed first for the subscreen that is part of the selection screen and then for the selection screen itself.

Example

Definition of a tabstrip control mytab on the standard selection screen and inclusion of the selection screens 100 und 200, which are defined as subscreen dynpros, in an executable program. The assignment of the subscreen dynpros to the tab titles takes place dynamically. For an example of a static assignment with the addition DEFAULT, see the description of the definition of selection screens as subscreen dynpros in Section 26.2.1.

```
SELECTION-SCREEN BEGIN OF SCREEN 100 AS SUBSCREEN.
PARAMETERS: p1(10) TYPE c,
            p2(10) TYPE c,
            p3(10) TYPE c.
SELECTION-SCREEN END OF SCREEN 100.

SELECTION-SCREEN BEGIN OF SCREEN 200 AS SUBSCREEN.
PARAMETERS: q1(10) TYPE c,
            q2(10) TYPE c,
            q3(10) TYPE c.
SELECTION-SCREEN END OF SCREEN 200.

SELECTION-SCREEN: BEGIN OF TABBED BLOCK mytab
                                FOR 10 LINES,
                  TAB (20) button1 USER-COMMAND push1,
                  TAB (20) button2 USER-COMMAND push2,
                  END OF BLOCK mytab.

INITIALIZATION.
  button1 = 'Selection Screen 1'.
  button2 = 'Selection Screen 2'.
  mytab-prog = sy-repid.
  mytab-dynnr = 100.
  mytab-activetab = 'PUSH1'.

AT SELECTION-SCREEN.
  CASE sy-dynnr.
    WHEN 1000.
      CASE sy-ucomm.
        WHEN 'PUSH1'.
          mytab-dynnr = 100.
        WHEN 'PUSH2'.
          mytab-dynnr = 200.
        WHEN OTHERS.
        ...
      ENDCASE.
    ...
  ENDCASE.
```

26.2.2.8 Activating Pushbuttons in the GUI Status

Syntax

```
SELECTION-SCREEN FUNCTION KEY n [ldb_additions].
```

In the GUI status of the selection screen set by the system, the application toolbar contains five inactive pushbuttons to which the function codes "FC01" to "FC05" are assigned. This statement activates the pushbutton of the function code "FC0n," whereby a value between 1 and 5 must be entered for n.

To enable the use of the pushbuttons, the statement TABLES must be used to declare an interface work area of the structure SSCRFIELDS from the ABAP Dictionary.

If a text is assigned to the component functxt_0n of the interface area sscrfields before the selection screen is called, this text is displayed on the relevant pushbutton. Otherwise, the pushbutton does not contain any text.

When the user chooses a pushbutton in the application toolbar, the runtime environment triggers the event AT SELECTION-SCREEN and the corresponding function code is transferred to the component comm of the interface work area sscrfields.

The additions ldb_additions can only be used in the selection-include of a logical database (see Section 26.2.4.4).

Notes

▶ To assign icons, Quickinfo and an appropriate text to the pushbuttons, a data object can be defined of the structured type SMP_DYNTXT from the ABAP dictionary. You must assign the ID of the icon, a quickinfo, and the corresponding text to the components of this data object. The content of the whole structure must then be assigned to the component functxt_0n of the interface work area sscrfields.

▶ After the event block behind AT SELECTION-SCREEN is processed, the system returns to the display of the selection screen. To exit selection-screen processing or to continue by executing the program, the user can only choose **Execute** or **Cancel**. Pushbuttons on selection screens can therefore normally be used for dynamic modifications to the selection screen rather than for program control.

Example

Activation of two pushbuttons with icons and quick info in the application toolbar of the standard selection screen of an executable program. Selecting one of these buttons pre-assigns different values to the input fields.

```
REPORT demo_sel_screen_function_key.

TYPE-POOLS icon.
DATA functxt TYPE smp_dyntxt.
TABLES sscrfields.

PARAMETERS: p_carrid TYPE s_carr_id,
            p_cityfr TYPE s_from_cit.
SELECTION-SCREEN: FUNCTION KEY 1,
                  FUNCTION KEY 2.

INITIALIZATION.
  functxt-icon_id       = icon_ws_plane.
  functxt-quickinfo     = 'Preselected Carrier'.
  functxt-icon_text     = 'LH'.
  sscrfields-functxt_01 = functxt.
  functxt-icon_text     = 'UA'.
  sscrfields-functxt_02 = functxt.

AT SELECTION-SCREEN.
  CASE sscrfields-ucomm.
    WHEN 'FC01'.
      p_carrid = 'LH'.
      p_cityfr = 'Frankfurt'.
    WHEN 'FC02'.
      p_carrid = 'UA'.
      p_cityfr = 'Chicago'.
    WHEN OTHERS.
      ...
  ENDCASE.

START-OF-SELECTION.
  ...
```

26.2.3 Adopting Elements of Other Selection Screens

The following variant of the statement SELECTION-SCREEN enables elements that were already created in other selection screens of the same program to be adopted by a selection screen.

Syntax

```
SELECTION-SCREEN INCLUDE
    { parameter | selcrit | output | pushbutton | block }.
```

You can transfer parameters, selection criteria, output fields, pushbuttons, or whole blocks. Elements can be included in all and from all selection screens of the program. No elements can be included within the same selection screen. An element cannot be used more than once in the same selection screen. The definition of the selection screen from which the elements are transferred must be arranged before the current selection screen.

26.2.3.1 Adopting a Parameter

Syntax of *parameter*

```
... PARAMETERS para
              [OBLIGATORY [OFF]]
              [MODIF ID modid]
              [ID id] ...
```

The PARAMETERS addition creates the screen elements for the parameter para on the current selection screen. You must specify a parameter for para that has already been declared with a PARAMETERS statement on a previous selection screen. All the properties of the parameter are copied from the original selection screen.

The additions OBLIGATORY and MODIF ID have the same meaning as in the PARAMETERS statement, and these additions overwrite the corresponding properties copied from the original selection screen. If the parameter on the original selection screen is declared with an OBLIGATORY addition, this property can be deactivated on the current selection screen by specifying OFF.

The ID addition can only be used in a selection-include of a logical database (see Section 26.2.4.4).

Note
The INCLUDE addition in this variant ensures that the global variant para can be filled with values by several selection screens at the same time.

26.2.3.2 Adopting a Selection Criterion

Syntax of *selcrit*

```
... SELECT-OPTIONS selcrit
                   [OBLIGATORY [OFF]]
                   [NO INTERVALS [OFF]]
                   [NO-EXTENSIONS [OFF]]
                   [MODIF ID modid]
                   [ID id] ...
```

The SELECT-OPTIONS addition creates the screen elements for the selection criterion selcrit on the current selection screen. You must specify a selection criterion for selcrit that has already been declared with a SELECT-OPTIONS statement on a previous selection screen. All the properties of the selection criterion are copied from the original selection screen.

The OBLIGATORY, NO INTERVALS, NO-EXTENSIONS, and MODIF ID additions have the same meaning as in the SELECT-OPTIONS statement, and these additions overwrite the corresponding properties copied from the original selection screen. If the selection criterion was declared with OBLIGATORY, NO INTERVALS or NO-EXTENSIONS additions on the original selection screen, you can deactivate these properties on the current selection screen by specifying OFF.

The ID addition can only be used in a selection-include for a logical database (see Section 26.2.4.4).

Note
The INCLUDE addition in this variant ensures that the selection table selcrit can be filled with values from several selection screens at the same time.

26.2.3.3 Adopting Text for Output Fields

Syntax of *output*

```
... COMMENT [/] [pos] (len) text
            [FOR FIELD sel]
            [MODIF ID modid]
            [ID id] ...
```

The COMMENT addition creates an output field on the current selection screen. You must specify a name for text that has already been used in a previous selection screen to create an output field with a SELECTION-SCREEN COMMENT statement. You cannot specify the name of a text symbol. The new output field represents the content of the global variables text already generated for the original selection screen.

The additions have the same meaning as in the SELECTION-SCREEN COMMENT statement. If FOR FIELD is not specified, the assignment of the original selection screen is copied.

The ID addition can only be used in a selection-include of a logical database (see Section 26.2.4.4).

Note
The INCLUDE addition in this variant ensures that the global variable text can be used by several selection screens at the same time.

26.2.3.4 Adopting Text for Pushbuttons

Syntax of *pushbutton*

```
... PUSHBUTTON [/][pos](len) button_text
              [USER-COMMAND fcode]
              [MODIF ID modid]
              [ID id] ...
```

The PUSHBUTTON addition creates a pushbutton on the current selection screen. You must specify a name for button_text that has already been used to create a pushbutton with a SELECTION-SCREEN PUSHBUTTON statement on a previous selection screen. You cannot specify the name of a text symbol. The content of the global variable button_text that was generated for the original selection screen is used as the text for the new pushbutton.

The additions have the same meaning as in the SELECTION-SCREEN PUSHBUTTON statement. If USER-COMMAND is not specified, the function code from the original selection screen is copied.

The ID addition can only be used in a selection-include of a logical database (see Section 26.2.4.4).

Note
The INCLUDE addition in this variable ensures that the global variable button_text can be used by several selection screens at the same time.

26.2.3.5 Adopting a Block Definition

Syntax of *block*

```
... BLOCKS block [ID id] ...
```

The `BLOCKS` addition creates a block `block` on the current selection screen. The block specified for `block` must have been created already on a previous selection screen with a `SELECTION-SCREEN BEGIN OF [TABBED] BLOCK` statement.

The new block has exactly the same structure and contains the same screen elements as the original block. The properties of all the parameters, selection criteria, output fields, and pushbuttons in the new block are copied from the corresponding elements in the original block, just as though they were copied individually with a `SELECTION-SCREEN INCLUDE` statement.

If a block is copied within a block with a frame, the width of the original block is adjusted to fit the area within the frame. The original block cannot contain any elements outside this area.

The `ID` addition can only be used in a selection-include of a logical database (see Section 26.2.4.4).

Note
The `INCLUDE` addition in this variant ensures that, once a block structure has been defined, the structure and the corresponding global variables can be used by several selection screens at the same time.

Example
Reusing the standard selection screen of an executable program in a stand-alone selection screen that has the number 500.

```
SELECTION-SCREEN: BEGIN OF BLOCK block,
                  COMMENT /1(40) text,
                  ULINE.
PARAMETERS: p1(10) TYPE c,
            p2(10) TYPE c,
            p3(10) TYPE c.
SELECTION-SCREEN END OF BLOCK block.

SELECTION-SCREEN: BEGIN OF SCREEN 500 AS WINDOW,
                  INCLUDE BLOCKS block,
                  END OF SCREEN 500.
```

```
INITIALIZATION.
  text = 'Standard Selection'.

START-OF-SELECTION.
  ...
  CALL SELECTION-SCREEN '0500' STARTING AT 10 10.
```

26.2.4 Variants and Additions for Selection Screens of Logical Databases

A standard selection screen can be defined in a logical database. The standard selection screen of the logical database is grouped together with the standard selection screen of an executable program that is linked to the logical database, to form a shared standard selection screen.

You define the standard selection screen of a logical database in the selection-include program of the logical database. The name of this include program is DBldbSEL, where "ldb" is the name of the logical database. The elements of the standard selection screen of a logical database are defined using the usual statements PARAMETERS, SELECT-OPTIONS and SELECTION-SCREEN. The statement SELECTION-SCREEN has some variants and additions that are intended specially for use in the logical database and can only be used in the selection-include.

26.2.4.1 Creating Versions of the Standard Selection Screen

Syntax

```
SELECTION-SCREEN BEGIN OF VERSION vers text.
...
SELECTION-SCREEN EXCLUDE { {PARAMETERS para}
                         | {SELECT-OPTIONS selcrit}
                         | {RADIOBUTTON GROUPS radi}
                         | {BLOCKS block}
                         | {IDS id}                    }.
...
SELECTION-SCREEN END OF VERSION vers.
```

These statements define a version vers of the standard selection screen of the logical database. For vers you must specify a positive figure with a maximum of three characters in length. For text you must specify a text symbol from the database program in the form text-###, where ### represents the three-character ID of the text symbol. Between the statements SELECTION-SCREEN BEGIN OF VERSION and SELECTION-SCREEN END

OF VERSION—and only there—you can only make SELECTION-SCREEN statements that have EXCLUDE additions.

The definition of a version must be specified after the definition of the standard selection screen. Each version is based on the standard selection screen. The internal SELECTION-SCREEN EXCLUDE statements remove the specified para parameters, the selcrit selection criteria, the radi radio button groups and the block blocks from the version. The IDS addition removes all the elements of the standard selection screen for which the ID id was created when they were defined with the addition ID.

When an executable program is linked with a logical database in the program attributes, you can enter the number vers in the **Selection Screen Version** field, so that this version is used instead of the full standard selection screen from the logical database. Use the content of the text symbol specified in text to describe the version in the input help (**F4**) of the entry field.

Note
You can also enter a selection screen version as a standard value in the program attributes of the database program. You then must enter the number 1000 in the attributes of an executable program that is to use the full standard selection screen. You can determine which version has been used in the database program using the function module RS_SELSCREEN_VERSION.

26.2.4.2 Designating a Node for Field Selection

Syntax

```
SELECTION-SCREEN FIELD SELECTION
                 FOR {NODE|TABLE} node [ID id].
```

This statement defines a node node in the structure of the logical database for field selection. If a node is of type T, you can use the TABLE addition instead of NODE. The statement cannot be used for type C nodes. For a description of the node types, see the NODES statement in Section 6.9.2.

If a node is defined for field selection, you can use an executable program linked to the logical database in the GET statement to control which fields in the node are to be read by the logical database. If you use the function module LDB_PROCESS, the FIELD_SELECTION parameter must be specified accordingly (see Section C.3).

For more information on the ID addition, see Section 26.2.4.4.

Note

While the database program is running, the names of the fields to be read are available in the internal table SELECT_FIELDS in the structure RSFS_ TAB_FIELDS from type group RSFS.

26.2.4.3 Designating a Node for Free Selections

Syntax

```
SELECTION-SCREEN DYNAMIC SELECTIONS
             FOR {NODE|TABLE} node [ID id].
```

This statement defines a node node in the structure for the logical database for free selections. If a node is of type T, you can use the TABLE addition instead of NODE. The statement cannot be used for type C nodes. For a description of the node types, see the NODES statement in Section 6.9.2.

If a node is defined for free selections, the user can determine—while the selection screen is defined—the components of the node for which he wants to enter further selections, even when entry fields are not defined on the selection screen.

For more information on the ID addition, see Section 26.2.4.4.

Note

While the database program is running, the selections entered by the user are available in various forms in the internal table DYN_SEL in structure RSDS_TYPE of the type group RSDS, such as generated WHERE conditions for Open SQL.

26.2.4.4 Additions in Logical Databases

This section describes the additions *ldb_additions*, to be specified for some of the preceding variants of the statement AT SELECTION-SCREEN if they are listed in the selection-include of a logical database.

Syntax of *ldb_additions*

```
... FOR {TABLE|NODE} node [ID id] ...
```

These additions assign either a node in the logical database or an ID to screen elements.

Assignment to a node

```
... FOR {TABLE|NODE} node ...
```

This addition means that all the screen elements created with SELECTION-SCREEN in the selection-included for a logical database must be assigned to a node node in the structure for the logical database. If a node is of type T, you can use the TABLE addition instead of NODE. For a description of the node types, see the NODES statement (see Section 6.9.2).

When the system generates the standard selection screen for an executable program that is linked to the logical database, it only displays screen elements for which an interface work area is declared with NODES or TABLES for the assigned node node or a node below it in the hierarchy. If you use the function module LDB_PROCESS, the assigned node node must be requested so that the screen element is created (see Section C.3).

The FOR TABLE|NODE addition must be specified for the variants of the SELECTION-SCREEN statement with POSITION, PUSHBUTTON, SKIP, or ULINE. You must either assign a node or specify the FOR FIELD addition for the variant with COMMENT.

The FOR TABLE|NODE addition must not be used in statements to define blocks or lines with the additions BEGIN|END OF [TABBED] LINE or when copying elements with INCLUDE.

Note
If none of the elements in a block or a line are created on the selection screen, the entire block or line is not created.

Defining an identifier

Syntax

```
... ID id ...
```

This addition defines an ID id containing a maximum of three characters for a screen element defined in the selection-include for a logical database with a SELECTION-SCREEN statement. The ID must be specified directly.

The ID can be used to exclude screen elements from a selection screen version with a SELECTION-SCREEN EXCLUDE statement.

An ID definition can be combined with the variants of the statement SELECTION-SCREEN with COMMENT, DYNAMIC SELECTIONS, FIELD SELECTION, FUNCTION KEY, INCLUDE, PUSHBUTTON, SKIP and ULINE.

Note
You cannot define an ID for blocks defined with BEGIN OF [TABBED] BLOCK
since these are already identified by the name of the block.

26.3 Defining Parameters

Parameters are components of a selection screen to which a global elementary data object is assigned in the ABAP program and to which an
input field is assigned on the selection screen.

PARAMETERS

Declaration of parameters.

Syntax

```
PARAMETERS { {para[(len)]} | {para [LENGTH len]} }
           [type_options]
           [screen_options]
           [value_options]
           [ldb_options] .
```

Declaration of a para parameter of length len. The name of the para
parameter may contain a maximum of eight characters. This statement is
permitted in the global declaration part of executable programs, function
groups and module pools. In function groups and module pools it is only
permitted within the definition of an independent selection screen (statement SELECTION-SCREEN BEGIN OF SCREEN). In executable programs, it is
otherwise automatically assigned to the standard selection screen.

The length len can only be specified if the data type specified in *type_
options* (see Section 26.3.1) is generic in terms of the length (c, n, p and
x). The length len must be specified as a numeric literal or as a numeric
constant. If len is not specified, the length is set to 1 for a generic data
type, or else it is set to the length of the data type. As of Release 6.10, it
is possible to specify the length using the LENGTH addition.

In detail, the PARAMETERS statement has the following effect:

▶ The statement declares a global variable para of the specified length in
  the program. The type of the data object is specified in *type_options*.

▶ On the current field, an input field with the same name and a suitable
  external data type is created in a new line at position 35. The length of
  the input field is aligned with the length of the parameter. The maxi-

mum length of the input field is 132. The maximum visible length of the input field is between 39 and 45, depending on the nesting depth in blocks with frames. If the `len` length is greater than the maximum visible length, the content is displayed as movable.

In front of the input field, in the first possible position, an automatically generated output field is displayed as a description whose length is between 23 and 30 characters, depending on the nesting depth in blocks with frames. The output field contains either the name of the `para` parameter or the selection text to which the parameter is assigned in the text elements of the program. If the user requests field or input help on the output field using the **F1** or **F4** function keys, the same output is displayed as when the input field itself is selected.

The attributes of the elements on the selection screen can be influenced in *screen_cptions* (see Section 26.3.2) and with the SELEC-TION-SCREEN statement.

▶ Before the selection screen is sent, the content of the `para` data object is transported to the input field on the selection screen. If the length of the parameter is greater than 132, the content is truncated from the right. After a user action on the selection screen, the content of the input field is transported to the data object, where various events are triggered (see Section 4.4.3). The content of character-type fields is converted into uppercase by default. Settings with regard to the content of the input field can be made in *value_options* (see Section 26.3.3).

▶ If parameters are defined in the selection-include of a logical database, further *ldb_options* additions are necessary or possible (see Section 26.3.4).

Note

If a parameter with a length greater than 132 is supplied with SUBMIT when an executable program is called, the value is similarly truncated from the right at position 132. It is not truncated only if the parameter is declared with the NO-DISPLAY addition.

26.3.1 Data Type of the Parameter

Syntax of *type_options*

```
... {TYPE type [DECIMALS dec]}
  | {LIKE dobj}
  | {LIKE (type_name)} ...
```

These additions define the data type of the parameter. If none of the additions is specified, the parameter is of type c. The data type can be defined through static reference to an existing data type type, either through static reference to a data object dobj, or through dynamic reference to a data type from the ABAP Dictionary in type_name.

If the addition NO-DISPLAY is not specified, the data type of a parameter must be elementary and flat, and the numeric type f is not allowed. If the addition NO-DISPLAY is specified, any arbitrary data types, except reference types, are possible (see Section 26.3.2.2).

Note
If there is a reference to data types from the ABAP Dictionary, the parameter adopts all the properties defined there as screen-relevant. During the transport of data from and to the input field, conversion routines defined in the domain are executed. The text defined in the ABAP Dictionary can be adopted as a selection text. However, you have to make sure that the input field on the selection screen is linked to a data object of the program and has no relation to the dictionary, as is the case for dynpro fields are created in the screen painter in relation to the dictionary. This has an effect particularly on the automatic support for the input help (**F4**) and for the value check. The functionality of the input help is restricted in such a way that the dependencies between the fields and of input already entered cannot be taken into account. A value check does not take place automatically but can be activated with the addition VALUE CHECK.

26.3.1.1 Static Reference to a Data Type

Syntax

```
... TYPE type [DECIMALS dec] ...
```

With this addition, the parameter receives the data type type. For type, you can specify:

▶ The built-in ABAP types c, d, i, n, p, t, and x

▶ A generic data type from the ABAP Dictionary or a non-generic data type from the same program, already defined using TYPES and which is elementary and flat and not of the type f (for exceptions, see Section 26.3.2.2).

With the specification of the built-in ABAP type p, you can use DECIMALS to define the number of decimal places dec within the interval limits specified in Section 5.2. Without the specification of DECIMALS, the number of decimal places is 0.

If `type` is a type from the ABAP Dictionary that has the type CHAR, length 1 and—in the domain—the fixed values "X" and " ", the input field on the selection screen is automatically displayed as if the addition AS CHECKBOX were specified (see Section 26.3.2).

Example
Declaration of a parameter with reference to the component CARRID of the database table SPFLI. On the selection screen, a three-digit input field with a field and input help that can be called is created.

```
PARAMETERS p_carrid TYPE spfli-carrid.
```

26.3.1.2 Static Reference to a Data Object

Syntax

```
... LIKE dobj ...
```

With this addition, the parameter adopts all the properties of a data object `dobj` already declared, in particular also a possible reference to the ABAP Dictionary. For `dobj`, a data object must be specified that is elementary and flat, and not of the type `f` (for exceptions, see Section 26.3.2.2).

For compatibility reasons, you can use the addition LIKE to refer to—with the exception of the properties of data objects—the components of flat structures, database tables or views in the ABAP Dictionary.

26.3.1.3 Dynamic Reference to a Data Type

```
... LIKE (type_name) ...
```

Using this addition, you create the data object `para` of the data type `c` of the length 132. The nput field that actually appears on the selection screen is displayed in a length and with a field and input help that matches the data type as specified in `type_name`.

For `type_name`, a flat, character-type data object is used that—when the selection screen is called—contains the name of a component of a flat structure or a database table of the ABAP Dictionary in uppercase letters. If no selection text for the parameter is created in the currently loaded text pool, the respective field descriptor from the ABAP Dictionary appears in the output field. When the data is transported from the input field to the data object `para`, the content is converted just as though it had been assigned by the respective ABAP data type (no formatting characters, decimal separation character as a period symbol, data format of YYYYMMDD, and so on).

If the content of `type_name` is not a structure component of the ABAP Dictionary, the input field is displayed according to the actual type of the parameter. If no selection text is created for the parameter in the currently loaded text pool, the output field contains the text "Dynamic Parameter".

Note

The field `type_name` of the program in which the selection screen is defined is used. If the selection screen is defined in a logical database, the field `type_name` of the database program is used, even if the selection screen from the assigned executable program is displayed.

Example

Dynamic formatting of the input field of the parameter `p_dyn`. On the selection screen, a three-digit input field with the input help for the column CARRID in the database table SPFLI is displayed. If the parameter does not have a selection text, the text "Airline Carrier" is displayed in the output field.

```
DATA comp(60) TYPE c.

PARAMETERS p_dyn LIKE (comp).

INITIALIZATION.
  comp = 'SPFLI-CARRID'.
```

26.3.2 Attributes of Screen Elements

Syntax of *screen_options*

```
... { {[OBLIGATORY|NO-DISPLAY] [VISIBLE LENGTH vlen]}
    | {AS CHECKBOX [USER-COMMAND fcode]}
    | {RADIOBUTTON GROUP group [USER-COMMAND fcode]}
    | {AS LISTBOX VISIBLE LENGTH vlen [USER-COMMAND fcode]
                                     [OBLIGATORY]    } }
  [MODIF ID modid] ...
```

These additions can be used to declare the input field as a required field, hide the input field on the selection screen, and determine the visible length of the field. The input field can be displayed as a checkbox, radio button or drop-down-list box. All screen elements of the parameter can be assigned to a modification group.

Note
The additions cannot be combined in just any combinations. The syntax diagram shows the permitted combinations.

26.3.2.1 Declaring an Input Field as a Required Field

Syntax

```
... OBLIGATORY ...
```

This addition defines the input field of the parameter on the selection screen as a required field. If no entry is made in this field, the user cannot use the **Execute** function (**F8**) to leave the selection screen, they can only use the functions **Back**, **Exit** or **Cancel**.

26.3.2.2 Suppressing the Generation of the Input Field

Syntax

```
... NO-DISPLAY ...
```

This addition means that no screen elements are generated for the parameter on the selection screen. In an executable program, a parameter of this type serves exclusively as a part of the interface defined by the selection screen. It can be supplied with a value by the calling program when called with SUBMIT.

If the addition NO-DISPLAY is specified, a parameter can have any data types except for reference types. These parameters can only be supplied using the WITH addition to the SUBMIT statement (see Section 10.2.2.3). In this case, in contrast to the general conversion rule for deep types, the same rules apply as when importing data from a data cluster (see Section 31.3.1).

Note
The length of a value transferred to a parameter for which there is no input field, is not subject to the 132-character restriction that applies for parameters with input fields.

26.3.2.3 Defining the Visible Length of the Input Field

Syntax

```
... VISIBLE LENGTH vlen ...
```

This addition defines the visible length of the input field as `vlen`, whereby `vlen` is entered directly as a positive number. If `vlen` is smaller than the length of the parameter and smaller than the maximum visible length, the input field is displayed in the length defined in `vlen` with a movable content. Otherwise, the addition is ignored.

26.3.2.4 Creating a Checkbox

Syntax

```
... AS CHECKBOX [USER-COMMAND fcode] ...
```

This addition specifies that the input field in the first position of the selection screen is displayed as a checkbox, with the corresponding description next to it on the right. The checkbox is marked if the value of `para` is "X" or "x". Otherwise, it is not marked.

The parameter must be created with the type `c` and length 1. An explicit length `len` is not permitted. If the addition `TYPE` is used, this can only be followed by the generic type `c` or a non-generic data type of type `c` and length 1.

The addition `USER-COMMAND` can be used to assign a function code `fcode` to the parameter. The function code `fcode` must be directly specified and may have a maximum length of 20 characters. To evaluate the function code, an interface work area of the structure SSCRFIELDS from the ABAP Dictionary must be declared using the statement `TABLES`. When the user selects the checkbox on the selection screen, the runtime environment triggers the event `AT SELECTION-SCREEN` and transfers the function code `fcode` to the component `ucomm` of the interface work area `sscrfields`.

Notes

▶ If the `TYPE` addition is used to make a reference to a data type in the ABAP Dictionary of type CHAR and length 1, and for which the valid values in the domain are defined as "X" and " ", the parameter is automatically displayed as a checkbox on the selection screen.

▶ If the addition `USER-COMMAND` is specified without the addition `AS CHECKBOX`, and the parameter is of type `c` of length 1, it is also displayed as a checkbox.

▶ The addition `USER-COMMAND` can, for example, be used for screen modifications with the addition `MODIF ID` (see the example in Section 26.3.2.7).

26.3.2.5 Creating Radio Button Groups

Syntax

```
... RADIOBUTTON GROUP grp [USER-COMMAND fcode] ...
```

This addition has the effect that the input field is displayed as a radio button on the selection screen. The radio button is marked if the value of `para` is "X" or "x". Otherwise, it is not marked.

As of Release 6.40, the radio button is displayed in the first position on the selection screen, and the output field is displayed next to it on the right. In versions prior to Release 6.40, the output field is displayed in the first position of the selection screen, and the radio button is displayed in position 34.

`grp` is used to define the radio button group for the parameter. The name `grp` is entered directly as a character string with a maximum of four characters. Within a selection screen, there must be a minimum of two parameters in the same radio button group. There cannot be more than one radio button group with the same name in one program, even if they are defined in different selection screens.

The parameter must be specified with the type `c` and length 1. An explicit length specification `len` is not permitted. If the addition `TYPE` is used, it can only be followed by the generic type `c` or a non-generic data type of type `c` and length 1.

In a radio button group, only one parameter can be defined with the addition `DEFAULT`, and the specified value must be "X". By default, the first parameter in a radio button group is set to the value "X", and the rest are set to " ".

The addition `USER-COMMAND` can be used to assign a function code `fcode` to the first parameter in a radio button group. The function code `fcode` must be specified directly and have a maximum length of 20 characters. To evaluate the function code, an interface work area of the structure SSCRFIELDS from the ABAP Dictionary must be declared using the statement `TABLES`. When the user selects any radio button of the radio button group on the selection screen, the runtime environment triggers the event `AT SELECTION-SCREEN` and transfers the function code `fcode` to the component `ucomm` of the interface work area `sscrfields`.

Note

It is recommended to define the radio buttons of a radio button group directly underneath each other. If the selection screen also contains other elements, it is recommended to define each radio button group within a block surrounded by a frame.

26.3.2.6 Generating a Drop-Down List Box

Syntax

```
... AS LISTBOX VISIBLE LENGTH vlen [USER-COMMAND fcode] ...
```

This addition generates a drop-down list box for an input field on the selection screen. If the parameter is created with a data type from the ABAP Dictionary and the data type is linked to the input help in the Dictionary, the first column of the input help is displayed in the list box. Otherwise, a single-line list box is displayed containing the current value of the parameter.

The addition `VISIBLE LENGTH` must be used to specify the visible length of the input field (see Section 26.3.2.3).

The addition `USER-COMMAND` can be used to assign a function code `fcode` to the drop-down list box. The function code `fcode` must be specified directly and can have a maximum length of 20 characters. To evaluate the function code, an interface work area of the structure SSCRFIELDS from the ABAP Dictionary must be declared using the statement `TABLES`. When the user selects a line of the list box on the selection screen, the runtime environment triggers the event `AT SELECTION-SCREEN` and transfers the function code `fcode` to the component `ucomm` of the interface work area `sscrfields`.

Notes

▶ The visible length needs to be explicitly specified, because in general, the length of the list box entries differs from the actual length of the parameter.

▶ Without the addition `USER-COMMAND`, selecting a line in the drop-down list box does not lead to the event `AT SELECTION-SCREEN`.

Example

The parameter `p_carrid` is displayed with length 20 and with the name "Lufthansa" already entered. The user can select a different airline carrier, in which case a three-character abbreviation is assigned to the parameter.

```
PARAMETERS p_carrid TYPE spfli-carrid
                AS LISTBOX VISIBLE LENGTH 20
                DEFAULT 'LH'.
```

26.3.2.7 Assigning the Input Field to a Modification Group

Syntax

```
... MODIF ID modid ...
```

The addition `MODIF ID` assigns all the screen elements of the parameter to the modification group `modid`, which is assigned to the column `group1` of the system table `screen`. This enables them to be modified using the statement `MODIFY SCREEN` before the selection screen is displayed. The name of the modification group `modid` must be directly specified and can have a maximum length of three characters.

Note

The modification groups that are assigned to the columns `group2` and `group3` of the system table `screen` are set when the system generates a selection screen and are described in Table 26.1.

Example

The elements of block `b2` are assigned to the modification group `b12`. A checkbox `show_all` allows the user to select whether or not these elements are displayed. The display is changed immediately, because selecting the checkbox triggers the event `AT SELECTION-SCREEN`. The function code is not required. Instead, the content of `show_all` is evaluated to PBO.

```
PARAMETERS show_all AS CHECKBOX USER-COMMAND flag.

SELECTION-SCREEN BEGIN OF BLOCK b1 WITH FRAME.
PARAMETERS: p1(10) TYPE c,
            p2(10) TYPE c,
            p3(10) TYPE c.
SELECTION-SCREEN END OF BLOCK b1.

SELECTION-SCREEN BEGIN OF BLOCK b2 WITH FRAME.
```

```
PARAMETERS: p4(10) TYPE c MODIF ID b12,
            p5(10) TYPE c MODIF ID b12,
            p6(10) TYPE c MODIF ID b12.
SELECTION-SCREEN END OF BLOCK b2.

AT SELECTION-SCREEN OUTPUT.
  LOOP AT SCREEN.
    IF show_all <> 'X' AND
       screen-group1 = 'BL2'.
       screen-active = '0'.
    ENDIF.
    MODIFY SCREEN.
  ENDLOOP.
```

26.3.3   Attributes of the Value and the Passing of Values

Syntax of *value_options*

```
...  [DEFAULT val]
     [LOWER CASE]
     [MATCHCODE OBJECT search_help]
     [MEMORY ID pid]
     [VALUE CHECK] ...
```

Using these additions, you can define a start value that allows lowercase lettering, a search help, a SPA/GPA parameter, or the execution of a check against a value list.

26.3.3.1   Defining the Start Value

Syntax

```
...  DEFAULT val ...
```

This addition creates a start value for the content of the parameter para. The start value val can either be specified as a literal or as a data object already defined.

If the data type of the specified start value does not match the data type of the declaration, it is converted according to the rules in Section A.2. Without the addition DEFAULT, the initial value that suits the data type is used as a start value (see Table 5.2).

There are two occasions when a start value can be passed to the parameter:

▶ When an executable program is started using SUBMIT, all the values val specified using DEFAULT are passed at the program start between the events LOAD-OF-PROGRAM and INITIALIZATION to the respective parameter para.

▶ If a program is not loaded into the internal mode using a call with SUBMIT, but using a dialog or a OO-transaction or through an external procedure call, all the values val specified using DEFAULT are passed to the respective parameters para when an arbitrary selection screen is called for the first time using CALL SELECTION-SCREEN before the event AT SELECTION-SCREEN OUTPUT.

In both cases, all the parameters are supplied with their start values, irrespective of the selection screen on which they are defined. If a parameter is not initial at the time of the data transfer, the start value will not be passed.

Note

The respective input field on the selection screen is only filled with the start value if the value for para is no longer changed before the selection screen is transmitted. The system displays exactly the value that the parameter has at the end of the processing of the event AT SELECTION-SCREEN OUTPUT.

26.3.3.2 Enabling Lowercase Letters

Syntax

```
... LOWER CASE ...
```

This addition prevents the content of character-type fields from being converted to uppercase letters when the input field on the selection screen is transported to the data object para in the program and vice versa.

The addition LOWER CASE cannot be used together with the additions AS CHECKBOX or RADIOBUTTON.

26.3.3.3 Linking a Search Help

```
... MATCHCODE OBJECT search_help ...
```

This addition links the input field of the parameter to a search help search_help from the ABAP Dictionary. The name of the search help must be entered directly. For the input field of the parameter on the selection screen, the input help key is displayed. When the input help (**F4**) is requested, the user is shown the hit list from the search help. When an entry is selected, the respective value is placed into the input field. If no search help for the specified name exists in the ABAP Dictionary, a message is displayed in the status line when the input help is requested.

The addition MATCHCODE OBJECT cannot be used together with the additions AS CHECKBOX or RADIOBUTTON.

Note
The predecessors of search helps in the ABAP Dictionary were so called matchcode objects. This is why you have the name MATCHCODE OBJECT for this addition. Matchcode objects that have not yet been replaced by search helps continue to be supported by this addition.

Example
Linking the parameter p_carrid with a suitable search help. When you choose the input help on the selection screen, a list with the names of the airline carriers is displayed. If a name is selected, the corresponding abbreviation is placed in the input field.

```
PARAMETERS p_carrid TYPE s_carr_id
          MATCHCODE OBJECT demo_f4_de.
```

26.3.3.4 Linking a SPA/GPA Parameter

Syntax

```
... MEMORY ID pid ...
```

This addition links the input field of the parameter with a SPA/GPA parameter in the SAP Memory (see Section 34.1.3). The name of the SPA/GPA parameter must be specified directly and with a maximum of 20 characters.

When the selection screen is called, the input field is filled with the current value of the SPA/GPA parameter in the SAP memory, provided the data object para is initial after the processing of the event AT SELECTION-SCREEN OUTPUT. Otherwise, the value of para is displayed. If there is a user action on the selection screen, the content of the input field is assigned to the SPA/GPA parameter in the SAP memory. If no SPA/GPA parameter exists for the specified name, it will be created.

Note

The addition DEFAULT overrides the addition MEMORY ID.

Example

The parameter p_prog is linked with the SPA/GPA parameter RID, which, in turn, is linked with the input field for the program name in the dynpros of the ABAP Workbench. Accordingly, the input field of the parameter is filled with the name of the program last processed.

```
PARAMETERS p_prog TYPE sy-repid MEMORY ID rid.
```

26.3.3.5 Checking a Value List

Syntax

```
... VALUE CHECK ...
```

This addition can only be specified if the type of parameter is defined through a reference to a data type from the ABAP Dictionary.

If you have a user action on the selection screen, the current content of the input field is checked against the fixed values that may be defined in the domain of the data type. If the data type is a component of a foreign key table, a check against the check table is executed. If the check is not successful, an error message is displayed in the status line of the selection screen. If the program was called through SUBMIT without a display of the selection screen, it is displayed in the case of an error.

The addition VALUE CHECK cannot be used together with the additions AS CHECKBOX, RADIOBUTTON or NO-DISPLAY.

Note

The check against a check table is executed even if the input field is empty. Therefore, we recommend the use of the addition OBLIGATORY at the same time.

26.3.4 Additions for Selection Screens of Logical Databases

Syntax of *ldb_options*

```
... FOR {TABLE|NODE} node
    [HELP-REQUEST]
    [VALUE-REQUEST]
    [AS SEARCH PATTERN] ...
```

These additions are only possible in the selection-include program of a logical database (see also Section 26.2.4). They must be used to assign a node in the logical database to the parameter. Subroutines for self-defined help can be called, and a special parameter can be defined for evaluating the search help linked with the logical database.

26.3.4.1 Assignment to a Node

Syntax

```
... FOR {TABLE|NODE} node ...
```

With this addition, the parameter has to be assigned to a node `node` of the structure of the logical database. If a node is of type T, then, instead of `NODE`, the `table` addition of equal status can be used. You can find a description of the node types with the `NODES` statement in Section 6.9.2.

For the generation of the selection screen of an executable program which is linked to the logical database, input fields are created only for those parameters for which an interface work area for the assigned node `node`, or a node beneath it in the hierarchy, is declared with `NODES` or `TABLES` in the executable program. When using the LDB_PROCESS function module, the assigned `node` node must be requested so that the parameter appears on the selection screen (see Section C.3).

26.3.4.2 Enabling User-Defined Field Help

Syntax

```
... HELP-REQUEST ...
```

With this addition, the `para_HLP` subroutine (`para` is the name of the parameter) of the database program of the logical database is called, providing the user selects the **F1** field help for a screen element of the parameter on the selection screen. The addition is ignored if the subroutine is not available.

If the parameter is defined in the ABAP Dictionary with a reference to a data type, the field help that is defined there is not displayed.

Note
In the subroutine that is called, the field help display can be programmed or called using suitable function modules such as HELP_OBJECT_SHOW. If the input help is selected, no other selection screen events can be triggered and there is no automatic pass by value between the selection screen and the program.

26.3.4.3 Enabling User-Defined Input Help

Syntax

```
... VALUE-REQUEST ...
```

This addition results in calling of the para_VAL subroutine (para is the name of the parameter) of the database program of the logical database, providing that the user selects the **F4** input help on a screen element of the parameter on the selection screen. The input help key is displayed for the input field of the parameter on the selection screen. If the subroutine is not available, the addition is ignored.

If the parameter is defined in the ABAP Dictionary with a reference to a data type, the input help that is defined there is not displayed.

Note
In the subroutine that is called, the input help display can be programmed or called using suitable function modules such as F4IF_INT_TABLE_VALUE_REQUEST. If the input help is selected, no other selection screen events are called and there is no automatic pass by value between the selection screen and the program. As for general dynpros (see Section 25.2.3), you have to use suitable function modules for this. The parameter that is changed in the subroutine is transported to the selection screen.

26.3.4.4 Generating Complex Parameters for Search Help

Syntax

```
... AS SEARCH PATTERN ...
```

This addition enables the evaluation of a search help in the database program. For this, the logical database has to be assigned to a search help in the transaction SE36. Except for the mandatory addition FOR TABLE|NODE, the AS SEARCH PATTERN addition can only be combined with the MODIF ID addition. In particular, you cannot define a type with the TYPE addition.

The data type of the parameter is the syldb_sp internal table from the SYLDB type group. This table has three columns: hotkey (search help ID), string (search string) and trange (deep data type for complex search help). The selection screen displays a framed block with the title "Selection using search help," which contains input fields for the search help ID and the search string as well as a pushbutton for complex search help.

After the selection-screen processing, the list of values provided by the search help is available in the `ldb_SP` internal table in the database program. Instead of the `PUT_root` subroutine, the `PUT_ldb_SP` subroutine is called. Here, "ldb" is the name of the logical database and "root" is the name of the root node. This subroutine can read the actual data using the list of values in `ldb_SP` and can then call the `PUT_root` subroutine, where the `GET root` event is triggered with the `PUT root` statement.

26.4   Defining Selection Criteria

Selection criteria are components of a selection screen, to which a selection table is assigned in the ABAP program. On the selection screen, two input fields and a pushbutton for multiple selections are created for a selection criterion.

SELECT-OPTIONS

Declaration of selection criteria.

Syntax

```
SELECT-OPTIONS selcrit FOR {dobj|(type_name)}
               [screen_options]
               [value_options]
               [ldb_options].
```

This declares a selection criterion `selcrit` for a data object `dobj` or a type specified in `type_name` (see Section 26.4.1). The name of the selection criterion `selcrit` is limited to a maximum of eight characters. This statement is allowed in the global declaration part of executable programs, function groups and module-pools. In function groups and module-pools it is only allowed within the definition of an independent selection screen (statement `SELECTION-SCREEN BEGIN OF SCREEN`). In executable programs, it is otherwise automatically assigned to the standard selection screen.

The statement `SELECT-OPTIONS` has the following effect:

▶ The statement declares a selection table in the program with the name `selcrit`. A selection table is an internal standard table with a header line and a standard key. In selection tables, you can save multiple logical conditions. The content of selection screens can be analyzed in a logical expression (see Section 13.5) and in the expression of a WHERE-condition in Open SQL (see Section 29.2.4). Selection tables have the following four columns:

- ▶ `sign` of type `c` of length 1. The content of `sign` determines for every row whether the result of the condition formulated in the column is included or excluded in the entire resulting set of all rows. Evaluable values are "I" for include and "E" for exclude.

- ▶ `option` of type `c` of length 2. `option` contains the selection option for the condition of the row in the form of logical operators. Analyzable operators are "EQ", "NE", "GE", "GT", "LE", "LT", "CP" and "NP" if column `high` is initial, and "BT" and "NB" if the column `high` is not initial. With the options "CP" and "NP", the data type of the columns `low` and `high` must be of the data type `c`, and `low` must contain at least one wildcard character "+" or "*" in which "+" masks a single character and "*" an arbitrary, character chain that also can be empty.

- ▶ `low` of the data type defined after `FOR` (see Section 26.4.1). This column is designated for the comparison value in individual comparisons or for the lower interval limits in interval limitations.

- ▶ `high` of the data type defined after `FOR` (see Section 26.4.1). This column is designated for the upper interval limits in interval limitations.

▶ Two input fields with the name `selscrit-low` and `selscrit-high` are created on the current selection screen using a matching external data type in a new line at the positions 35 and 60. The length of the input fields bases upon the length of the data type which is defined after `FOR` (see Section 26.4.1). The maximum length of the input fields is 45. The maximum visible length of the input fields, depending on the nesting depth, is in blocks with frames of between 10 and 18. If the length is larger than the maximum visible length, then the content is scrollable.

Before the first input field, an automatically generated output field is displayed as an identifier in the first possible position whose length is, depending on the nesting depth, in blocks with frames between 20 and 30. The output field either contains the name of the selection criterion `selcrit`, or the selection text which is assigned to the selection criterion in the text elements of the program. If the user requests a field- or input-help on the output field using the function key **F1** resp. **F4**, the same output is displayed as if one of the input fields is chosen.

A pushbutton **Multiple selection** is created after the second input field. If you select this pushbutton, a dialog screen with four tabstrip control pages appears, in which the input fields are again displayed in tabular form in Table Controls. The tabstrip pages are separated based on individual value comparisons, interval limitations and settings for the column `sign`.

As a user, you can select an input field with a double-click on the selection screen or with the dialog window for multiple selection. On the selection screen, you also can choose the value for the column `sign`. On the dialog screen for multiple selection, you can do this by selecting the respective tabstrip page. If the selection option is not equal to "EQ" or "BT", then it is displayed as an icon directly in front of the first input field. The color of the icon is green if the content of the column `sign` is "I", and red if it is "E".

The selection options "CP" and "NP" can be selected only if the first input field contains one of the wildcard characters "*" or "+". If one of these characters is specified, the selection option is automatically set to "CP" when there is a user action.

The attributes of the elements on the selection screen can be influenced with the statement `screen_options` (see Section 26.4.2) or the statement `SELECTION-SCREEN`.

▶ The first row of the selection table `selcrit` is linked with the input fields on the selection screen. All rows are displayed in the dialog box for multiple selection. Before sending the selection screen, the content of the selection table is transported to the selection screen and displayed in the corresponding location. If the lengths of the columns `low` and `high` in the first row of the selection table are larger than 45, then the excessive content is cut off to the right. In the remaining rows, excessive content is only cut off if the dialog window for multiple selection is displayed. After a user action on the selection screen or in the dialog window for multiple selections, the content of the input fields and the selected settings are transported into the internal table, whereby several events are raised (see Section 26.2.4). In doing so, the content of character type fields is converted to uppercase by default. All settings regarding the content of the input field can be done in `value_options` (see Section 26.4.3).

▶ If selection criteria are defined in the selection-include of a logical database, further additions `ldb_options` are necessary or possible (see Section 26.2.4).

▶ If in an executable program, a selection criterion is defined for a component of a node of the linked logical database declared by `TABLES` or

NODES, and the noce in question is intended for free selection on the logical database (see Section 26.2.4), then the selection table is transferred to the logical database after selection-screen processing and is treated there as a free selection. Furthermore, in this case, the input fields for the corresponding free selection are displayed directly on the selection screen, without the necessity for the user having to select them via the function **Free selection**.

Note

If a selection criterion for data types is supplied with a length greater than 45 when calling an executable program with SUBMIT, the values of the columns low and high in the first row of the selection table are then truncated to the right of position 45. The remaining rows are not truncated. The first row is also not truncated only if the selection criterion is declared with the NO-DISPLAY addition.

26.4.1 Data Type of the LOW and HIGH Selection Table Columns

Syntax

```
... FOR {dobj|(type_name)} ...
```

This addition determines the data type of the columns low and high in the selection table. The data type can be defined by means of a static reference to an existing data object dobj or by a dynamic reference to a data type from the ABAP Dictionary in type_name.

If the addition NO-DISPLAY is not specified, the data type of columns low and high in the selection table must be elementary and flat and the numeric type f is not allowed. If the addition NO-DISPLAY is specified, any flat data types are possible (see Section 26.4.2.2).

Note

When referring to data types from the ABAP Dictionary, the selection criterion takes over all the screen-relevant attributes defined there. Any conversion routines defined in the domain are executed during data transport from and to the input field. The text defined in the ABAP Dictionary can be copied as a selection text. However, you have to make sure that the input fields on the selection screen are linked to a global data object of the program and do not have a real connection with the dictionary, as is the case with dynpro fields that are created in the screen painter with a reference to the dictionary. This has an effect particularly on the automatic support for the input help (**F4**) and on the value check. Compared to general dynpros, the functionality of the input help is restricted in such a way that dependencies between fields and of input already made is not taken into account. An automatic value check does not take place.

26.4.1.1 Static Reference to a Data Object

Syntax

```
... FOR dobj ...
```

If you specify this addition, the columns `low` and `high` in the selection table take over all the attributes of a data object `dobj` that already has been declared The most important of such attributes would be a reference to the ABAP Dictionary. For `dobj`, you must specify a data object that is elementary and flat and not of the type `f` (for exceptions, see Section 26.4.2.2).

Example
Typical declaration and use of a selection criterion.

```
DATA spfli_wa TYPE spfli.

SELECT-OPTIONS s_carrid FOR spfli_wa-carrid.

SELECT *
      FROM spfli
      INTO spfli_wa
      WHERE carrid IN s_carrid.
   ...
ENDSELECT.
```

26.4.1.2 Dynamic Reference to a Data Type

Syntax

```
... FOR (type_name) ...
```

If you specify this addition, the columns `low` and `high` in the selection table are created with the data type `c` of the length 45. The input fields are displayed on the selection screen, yet in a length and with a field and input help that matches the data type specified in `type_name`.

For `type_name`, you must specify a flat character-like data object that contains the name of a component in a flat structure from the ABAP Dictionary in block capitals when the selection screen is accessed. If the text pool currently loaded does not contain a selection text for the parameter, the output field displays the corresponding field label from the ABAP Dictionary. When data is transported from the input field to the selection table, the content is converted as if it were assigned by the corresponding ABAP data type (no formatting characters, period as a decimal separator, date format YYYYMMDD and so on).

If the content of type_name is not a structure component in the ABAP Dictionary, the input fields are displayed according to the actual type of the columns low and high. If a selection text for the parameter is not created in the text pool currently loaded, the output field contains the text "Generic Select-Option".

A dynamic reference to a data type is not possible in the selection-include for a logical database.

Example
Dynamic design of the selection criterion selcrit on the selection screen 500 based on the entries in the standard selection screen for an executable program.

```
PARAMETERS: dbtab(30)  TYPE c,
            column(30) TYPE c.

DATA type_name(80) TYPE c.

SELECTION-SCREEN BEGIN OF SCREEN 500 AS WINDOW.
SELECT-OPTIONS selcrit FOR (type_name).
SELECTION-SCREEN END OF SCREEN 500.

CONCATENATE dbtab '-' column INTO type_name.

CALL SELECTION-SCREEN 500 STARTING AT 10 10.
```

26.4.2 Attributes of Screen Elements

Syntax of *screen_options*

```
... [OBLIGATORY|NO-DISPLAY]
    [VISIBLE LENGTH vlen]
    [NO-EXTENSION]
    [NO INTERVALS]
    [MODIF ID modid] ...
```

You can use these additions to declare the first input field as a required field, to suppress the display on the selection screen, and to define the visible length. You can suppress the display of the second input field and the pushbutton for multiple selections. All screen elements of the selection criterion can be assigned to a modification group.

Note

In addition to the additions available, you can use the function module SELECT_OPTIONS_RESTRICT to restrict the number of selection options available and to prohibit the value "E" for the column sign in the selection table before the selection screen is sent.

26.4.2.1 Declaring the First Input Field as a Required Field

Syntax

```
... OBLIGATORY ...
```

This addition defines the first input field of the selection criterion on the selection screen as a required field. If this field is blank, the user cannot leave the display of the selection screen using the **Execute** function (**F8**), but only using the functions **Back**, **Exit** or **Cancel**.

26.4.2.2 Suppressing the Generation of Input Fields

Syntax

```
... NO-DISPLAY ...
```

If you specify this addition, no screen elements are created on the selection screen for the selection criterion. In an executable program, a selection criterion of this type is used exclusively as part of the interface defined by the selection screen. It can be supplied with a value by the calling program when it is called with SUBMIT.

If the addition NO-DISPLAY is specified, the low and high columns in the selection table can have any flat data types. These selection tables can only be supplied with data with a WITH addition to the SUBMIT statement (see Section 10.2.2.3).

Note

The length of the values transferred to the columns low and high in the selection table for which there is no input field is not restricted to 45 characters, as is the case for selection criteria with input fields.

26.4.2.3 Defining the Visible Length of the Input Field

Syntax

```
... VISIBLE LENGTH vlen ...
```

This addition defines a visible length of `vlen` for the input fields, where `vlen` must be specified directly as a positive number. If `vlen` is shorter than the length of the columns `low` and `high` in the selection table and shorter than the maximum visible length, the input field is displayed at a length of `vlen` and the entry can be moved. Otherwise, the addition is ignored.

26.4.2.4 Preventing Multiple Selection

Syntax

```
... NO-EXTENSION ...
```

If you specify this addition, the pushbutton for multiple selections is not created on the selection screen.

Note
The user cannot access the dialog window for multiple selections on the selection screen, which means they cannot edit selection tables containing several lines.

26.4.2.5 Preventing the Second Input Field

Syntax

```
... NO INTERVALS ...
```

If you specify this addition, the second input screen is not created on the selection screen.

Note
The user can only specify a single comparison in the first line of the selection table on the selection screen. The dialog window for multiple selections still allows interval selections.

Example
Declaration of a selection criterion for which only a single comparison is possible on the selection screen but no multiple selections.

```
DATA spfli_wa TYPE spfli.

SELECT-OPTIONS s_carrid FOR spfli_wa-carrid
                         NO-EXTENSION
                         NO INTERVALS.
```

26.4.2.6 Assigning Input Fields to a Modification Group

Syntax

```
... MODIF ID modid ...
```

The addition MODIF ID assigns all the screen elements for the selection criterion to the modification group modid that is assigned to the column
group1 in the system table screen. This means they can be modified with
a MODIFY SCREEN statement before the selection screen is displayed. You
must specify the name of the modification group modid directly, and it
can contain a maximum of three characters.

Note
The modification groups that are assigned to the columns group2 and
group3 in the system table screen are set by the system when a selection
screen is generated and are described in Table 26.1.

26.4.3 Attributes of the Value and Passing of Values

Syntax of *value_options*

```
... [DEFAULT val1 [TO val2] [OPTION opt] [SIGN sgn]]
    [LOWER CASE]
    [MATCHCODE OBJECT search_help]
    [MEMORY ID pid] ...
```

These additions allow you to specify a start value, to use lower case, and
to integrate a search help or a SPA/GPA parameter.

26.4.3.1 Defining the Default Value

Syntax

```
... DEFAULT val1 [TO val2] [OPTION opt] [SIGN sgn] ...
```

This addition defines start values for the columns in the first line of the
selection table. Without the addition DEFAULT, initial values of the corresponding type are used as start values.

val1 and val2 are used to define start values for the columns low and high. These start values can either be specified as literals or as previously defined data objects. If the data type of the specified start values does not match the data type of the columns, these are converted according to the rules in Section A.2.

The addition OPTION is used to define the start value for the option column. If the addition TO is not specified, you must specify one of the expressions eq, ne, ge, gt, le, lt, cp or np directly for opt. If the addition TO is specified, you must either specify bt or nb. If the addition OPTION is not used, the content of the option column is set to "EQ" or "BT". If you specify cp or np, the start value in val1 must contain at least one of the wildcard characters "*" oder "+" at the time of the data transfer to the selection table, otherwise the program terminates.

The addition SIGN is used to define the start value for the sgn column. You must either specify i or e directly for sgn. If the addition SIGN is not used, the content of column sign is set to "I".

For the points in time when the start values are transferred to the first position in the selection table, the same applies as for the addition DEFAULT to the PARAMETERS statement (see Section 26.3.3.1). If the selection table is not initial when the transfer takes place, the start values are not transferred to the first position. Only the header line in the selection table is filled with these values, which does not influence the selection criterion.

Note
The corresponding input fields on the selection screen are only filled with the start values if the first line in the selection table is not changed before the selection screen is sent. The system displays exactly the value contained in the selection table when the event AT SELECTION-SCREEN OUT-PUT has been processed. Start values for multiple selections can only be defined by inserting lines in the selection table.

26.4.3.2 Enabling Lowercase Letters

Syntax

```
... LOWER CASE ...
```

This addition prevents the content of character-like fields from being converted to block capitals when the data is transported from the input fields on the selection screen to the selection table.

26.4.3.3 Linking a Search Help

Syntax

```
... MATCHCODE OBJECT search_help ...
```

This addition links the input fields for the selection criterion to a search help search_help from the ABAP Dictionary. You must specify the name of the search help directly. The addition has the same effect on the input fields as when it is used with a PARAMETERS statement for an input field for a parameter (see Section 26.3.3.3).

26.4.3.4 Linking a SPA/GPA Parameter

Syntax

```
... MEMORY ID pid ...
```

This addition links the first input field to a SPA/GPA parameter in the SAP Memory (see Section 34.1.3). You must specify the name of the SPA/GPA parameter directly, and it can contain a maximum of 20 characters. The addition has the same effect on the first input field as when it is used with a PARAMETERS statement for an input field of a parameter (see Section 26.3.3.4).

26.4.4 Additions for Selection Screens of Logical Databases

Syntax of *ldb_options*

```
... [ HELP-REQUEST   [ FOR {LOW|HIGH} ] ]
    [ VALUE-REQUEST  [ FOR {LOW|HIGH} ] ]
    [ NO DATABASE SELECTION ] ...
```

The first two additions are only possible in a selection-include for a logical database (see Section 26.2.4). They can be used to access subroutines for user-defined help. The addition NO DATABASE SELECTION is only possible in an executable program that is connected to a logical database and controls the transfer of the selection table to the logical database.

26.4.4.1 Enabling User-Defined Field Help

Syntax

```
... HELP-REQUEST [ FOR {LOW|HIGH} ] ...
```

If you specify this addition, the program accesses the subroutine `selcrit_HLP` when the user chooses the field help **F1** on an input field in the selection criterion. The subroutine `selcrit_HLP` must be defined in the database program on the logical database, where `selcrit` stands for the name of the selection criterion.

You can specify `FOR LOW` or `FOR HIGH` to access either the subroutine `selcrit-LOW_HLP` or the subroutine `selcrit-HIGH_HLP`, depending on whether the field help is selected for the first or second input field. The addition does not affect the other field.

If one of the subroutines does not exist, choosing **F1** on the input field has no effect. If the selection criterion is defined with reference to a data type in the ABAP Dictionary, the field help defined there for the corresponding field is not displayed.

Note
The subroutines can be used in the same way as in a `PARAMETERS` statement to program a field help.

26.4.4.2 Enabling User-Defined Input Help

Syntax

```
... VALUE-REQUEST [ FOR {LOW|HIGH} ] ...
```

If you specify this addition, either the subroutine `selcrit-LOW_VAL` or `selcrit-HIGH_VAL` is called, depending on whether the user chooses the input help **F4** on the first or second input field of the selection criterion. The subroutines `selcrit-LOW_VAL` and `selcrit-HIGH_VAL` must be defined in the database program of the logical database, where `selcrit` stands for the name of the selection criterion. If you specify `FOR LOW`, the addition only affects the first input field, and if you specify `FOR HIGH`, it only affects the second.

If one of the subroutines does not exist, choosing **F4** for the input field has no effect. If the selection criterion is defined with reference to a data type in the ABAP Dictionary, the input help defined there for the respective field is not displayed.

Note
The subroutines can be used in the same way as for a `PARAMETERS` statement to program an input help. When the user chooses the input help, this does not trigger any other selection screen events, and there is no automatic value transfer between the selection screen and the program.

26.4.4.3 Preventing the Transfer of the Selection Table to the Logical Database

Syntax

```
... NO DATABASE SELECTION ...
```

If you specify this addition, the selection table is not transferred to the logical database as a free selection after selection-screen processing.

This addition affects processing if the following is the case:

▶ It is used in an executable program that is connected to a logical database.

▶ A component of a node in the connected logical database is specified for dobj after the addition FOR and is declared in the program with a TABLES or NODES statement.

▶ The node on the logical database is designed for free selections.

26.5 Calling Selection Screens

Selection screens can be called as follows:

▶ With the statement SUBMIT (see Section 26.5.1)

▶ As a selection screen of a report transaction (see Section 26.5.2)

▶ As an initial dynpro of a dialog transaction (see Section 26.5.3)

▶ Via the statement CALL SELECTION-SCREEN (see Section 26.5.4)

Every call starts the selection-screen processing (see Section 26.5.5).

26.5.1 Call via SUBMIT

At the execution of an executable program via the statement SUBMIT, the standard selection screen or the selection screen specified in the statement between the events INITIALIZATION and START-OF-SELECTION is called if it contains at least one input field or one pushbutton (see Section 10.2.1).

26.5.2 Call via Report Transaction

At the execution of a report transaction, the assigned executable program is started with SUBMIT, and the selection screen determined for the transaction between the events INITIALIZATION and START-OF-SELECTION is called.

26.5.3   Call via Dialog Transaction

If, at a dialog transaction, the selection screen of the corresponding program is defined as an initial dynpro, then the selection screen is called first
at the execution of the program via the transaction code. However, this
selection screen is not treated as the first dynpro of a dynpro sequence
(see Section 26.5.5).

26.5.4   Calling in the Program

```
CALL SELECTION-SCREEN
```

Calling a selection screen.

Syntax

```
CALL SELECTION-SCREEN dynnr
                 [STARTING AT col1 lin1
                 [ENDING    AT col2 lin2]]
                 [USING SELECTION-SET variant].
```

This statement calls the selection screen with the dynpro number specified in dynnr and starts selection-screen processing. For dynnr a data
object of the type n and the length 4 is expected.

The statement CALL SELECTION-SCREEN accesses the selection screens of
the respective main program of the current program group, and these
work with the parameters and selection screens of the main program and
trigger the selection-screen processing in the main program (see Section
26.5.5). The main program is generally the current program, except for
the case when calling a selection screen in an externally called subroutine.
An uncatchable exception occurs if the specified selection screen is not
contained in the main program of the program group.

You can call any selection screen of the main program, particularly the
standard selection screen. By default, the selection screen is set in the
window of the preceding dynpro. With the addition STARTING AT, you
create a modal dialog window and the selection screen is displayed in it.
The upper left corner of the dialog window is determined by the values in
col1 and lin1 for column and row. These values refer to the window
with the pop-up level 0. The lower right corner is either set automatically
or can be specified in col2 and lin2 after ENDING AT. For col1, lin1, col2
and lin2, data objects of the type i are expected. The values of col1,

lin1 should be smaller than col2, lin2; otherwise the behavior will be undefined.

With the addition USING SELECTION-SET, the parameters and selection criteria of the selection screen are supplied with a variant specified in variant. The transfer of the values to the respective data objects of the program takes place immediately before the event AT SELECTION-SCREEN OUTPUT. For variant, you have to specify a character-type data object which, at the execution of the statement contains the name in capital letters of a variant of the main program that was stored for the selection screen. If you specify a non-existing variant or a variant of another selection screen of the main program, then the addition is ignored.

Return values

sy-subrc	Meaning
0	The user selected the function **Execute** or **Execute + Print** on the selection screen.
4	The user selected **Exit, Cancel** or **Terminate** on the selection screen.

Notes

▶ The statement CALL SCREEN must not to be used to call selection screens, as otherwise the proper execution of the selection-screen processing cannot be guaranteed.

▶ If the called selection screen is displayed in a dialog window, we recommend that you use the addition AS WINDOW when specifying the selection screen.

Example
Refer to the example in Section 26.2.1.

26.5.5 Selection-Screen Processing

Selection-screen processing encapsulates the dynpro flow logic and the sending of the selection screen . No dialog modules of the program are called. Instead, various selection screen events are triggered for which event blocks can be programmed. In PBO-processing, the event AT SELECTION-SCREEN OUTPUT is triggered. During PAI-processing, a variety of different events AT SELECTION-SCREEN are triggered, depending on the user action. The corresponding event key words are described in Section 4.4.3. Selection-screen processing of a displayed selection screen is ended exclusively via the following functions:

► **Execute** or **Execute + Print**

The selection screen events of PAI processing are triggered. After that, the event `START-OF-SELECTION` is triggered at standard selection screens called via `SUBMIT`, and the program run is as described in Section 10.2.1. The program is ended in selection screens called via dialog transactions. A call in the program resumes the program after the statement `CALL SELECTION-SCREEN`.

► **Return**, **End**, or **Cancel**

Only the event `AT SELECTION-SCREEN ON EXIT-COMMAND` is triggered. After that the program is ended at standard selection screens called via `SUBMIT` and dialog transactions. Otherwise, `sy-subrc` is set to 4 and the program resumes after the statement `CALL SELECTION-SCREEN`.

For all other user actions, the selection screen is called again automatically after ending the selection-screen processing.

Note

To avoid ending the program following the processing of a selection screen called via a dialog transaction, you must during the selection-screen processing call either a next dynpro with `LEAVE TO SCREEN` or a new dynpro sequence with `CALL SCREEN`. The `SET SCREEN` statement is not sufficient.

27 Lists

27.1 Overview

27.1.1 Lists as Screens

Lists are screens that do not contain screen elements in their display areas but rather text output defined with ABAP statements. Lists are displayed as part of a special list dynpro, which is a component of the list-processor system program.

27.1.2 Lists in ABAP Programs

An ABAP program can process several lists, which are stored in one or several list buffers. In every call of a dynpro sequence, a new list buffer is opened and assigned to this screen sequence. One list buffer can contain up to 21 lists: one basic list and 20 details lists. To each list is assigned a list index, which organizes the lists in the list buffer in hierarchical levels. The first list of a list buffer is the basic list with the list index 0. All other lists, whose list indexes are increased continuously starting at 1, are details lists.

The output statements of an ABAP program write to the current list, whose list index is determined by the `sy-lsind` system field. The current list after the call of a screen sequence is the basic list. As long as the basic list is not finished, no other list levels can be created.

27.1.3 Basic List

The basic list is displayed either implicitly during the processing of an executable program (see the statement `SUBMIT` in Section 10.2) or explicitly using the `LEAVE TO LIST-PROCESSING` statement (see Section 27.6.1). In both cases, the list processor is called, and it then sends the list to the list screen. Displaying a list concludes this list in the list buffer. It can no longer be written to, but it can be read or modified.

27.1.4 Details Lists

Every user action on a displayed list, in triggering a list event for which an event block is defined in the ABAP program (see Section 4.4.4), creates a new details list. The list index of this details list is always one more than the list index of the list on which the event was triggered. The latter index is contained in the `sy-listi` system field. The output statements of the event block write to the current details list. If the event block is finished normally, the details list is displayed automatically in the list screen.

Due to user actions on displayed lists, in the list buffer a stack of up to 20 details lists can be built up. The list with the highest list index (sy-lsind) is always the current list of the ABAP program, while the list with the list index one below the highest (sy-listi) is displayed on the screen. With certain list processing statements, you can use the list index to access all lists within the stack for reading or changing.

The details list stack in a list buffer can be reduced in two ways:

1. A user action on a displayed details list is linked to the function code "BACK". This function code causes the system to return to the display of the previous list and decreases the value of sy-lsind by 1. On the basic list, "BACK" has the effect that you leave the screen sequence.

2. To the system field sy-lsind, a value is assigned within an event block for a list event. If the value of sy-lsind after finishing the event block is smaller than the list index of the current list and greater or equal to 0, then the current list replaces the list of this list level, and all lists whose list index is greater than the value of sy-lsind are deleted from the list buffer. Other values of sy-lsind are reset to the index of the current list after the event block is finished.

27.1.5   Structure of a List

A list is made up of list rows with a fixed width of up to 1,023 characters. The row width of the current list is stored in the sy-linsz system field. The number of rows of a list is limited only by the storage capacity of the system.

A list is divided into pages. Every list starts on page 1. The current page of the current list is stored in the sy-pagno system field. The output position on the current page in the list buffer is determined by the list cursor, which is provided in the system fields sy-colno (column) and sy-linno (row). A page can contain up to 60,000 rows. The number of rows per page is stored for the current list in the sy-linct system field. The value 0 represents the maximum number of rows per page.

On every page of a list, you can use rows for a page header and a page footer. The rows of the page header of the basic list are filled by default with a standard page header from the text elements of the ABAP program. The standard page header consists of a standard title and can contain column headings. The standard title is fixed so that it does not disappear when you scroll the page vertically on the screen.

At the list event TOP-OF-PAGE, you can fill the page header with additional rows. You can fill the page footer only at the list event END-OF-PAGE (see Section 4.4.4). The entire page header of the list displayed on top is fixed so that it does not move when you scroll the page vertically. The column headings of the standard page header, and the rows filled at TOP-OF-PAGE are moved when you scroll horizontally.

27.1.6   Print Lists

The lists in the list buffer are screen lists. Their content is displayed in the list screen, either after an implicit call of the list processor in an executable program (see Section 10.2.1) or after an explicit call using LEAVE TO LIST-PROCESSING (see Section 27.6.1).

When creating lists, it is also possible to exclude individual or all pages of one or more lists from the screen display and to send them to the SAP spool system instead. To do this, you use the addition PRINT ON of the statement NEW-PAGE. All these pages together then form the print list.

27.1.7   Lists and ABAP Objects

The list processing statements covered in this section are based on global data and events of the runtime environment and are no longer completely supported in ABAP Objects and when using ABAP Objects.

27.1.8   Lists and Unicode

During list display or printing, the contents stored in the list buffer are copied onto the list, with the following differences between non-Unicode and Unicode systems:

▶ In non-Unicode systems, every character requires as much space in the list buffer as columns on the list. In single-byte systems, one character occupies one byte in the list buffer and one column on the list. A character, which in a multi-byte system occupies several bytes in the list buffer, also occupies the same number of columns on the list. Therefore, in non-Unicode systems, all characters stored in the list buffer are displayed on the list.

▶ In Unicode systems, every character usually occupies one place in the list buffer. This place is displayed by a fixed number of bytes. On the list, however, a character can occupy more than one column, especially

Eastern Asiatic characters. Since on the list only as many columns are available as there are places in the list buffer, in this case fewer characters can be displayed on the list than are stored in the list buffer. The list output is shortened accordingly (the page is displayed according to the alignment) and receives an indicator (">" or "<"). On a displayed list, you can choose **System · List · Unicode-Display** to display the entire list content (as of Release 6.20, Support Package 29).

For these reasons, the horizontal position of the list cursor is equal to the output column of a displayed or printed list only in non-Unicode systems. In Unicode systems, this can be guaranteed only for the upper and lower output boundaries of the individual output.

27.1.9 Statements for List Processing

Statement	Section
BACK	27.2.5
DETAIL	42.15.1
DESCRIBE LIST	27.3.4
END-OF-PAGE	4.4.4
FORMAT	27.2.3
GET CURSOR	27.4
HIDE	27.2.10
LEAVE LIST-PROCESSING	27.6.2
LEAVE TO LIST-PROCESSING	27.6.1
MODIFY LINE	27.3.2
NEW-LINE	27.2.5
NEW-PAGE	27.2.8
POSITION	27.2.6
PRINT-CONTROL	27.2.12
READ LINE	27.3.1
RESERVE	27.2.9
SCROLL	27.3.3
SET BLANK LINES	27.2.4
SET COUNTRY	35.5

Statement	Section
SET CURSOR	27.5.3
SET LEFT SCROLL-BOUNDARY	27.2.7
SET MARGIN	27.2.11
SET PF-STATUS	27.5.1
SET TITLEBAR	27.5.2
SET USER COMMAND	11.4.2
SKIP	27.2.5
SUMMARY	42.15.1
TOP-OF-PAGE	4.4.4
ULINE	27.2.2
WINDOW	27.5.4
WRITE	27.2.1

In addition to these, there are list-control additions with introductory statements in Section 3.2.1 and with the statement SUBMIT in Section 10.2.3, as well as the event keywords for list events in Section 4.4.4.

27.2 Creating Lists

27.2.1 Writing Data in Lists

WRITE

Data output into a list.

Syntax

```
WRITE {[AT] [/][pos][(len|*|**)]} dobj
      [int_format_cptions]
      [ext_format_cptions]
      [list_elements]
      [QUICKINFO info].
```

This statement writes the content of the data object dobj onto the current page of the current list in the list buffer. All flat data types and the data type string are allowed for dobj; flat structures are treated as a data object of type c and must be character-type in Unicode systems. The data object `dobj` can be specified by a field symbol or a dereferenced data reference (for Release 6.10 and later). The format of the output is predefined but can be modified with the additions `AT` and `int_format_options`. The output that has been formatted in this way can be formatted further with `ext_format_options`, and `list_elements` allows specific list elements to be displayed.

The output position is either determined by the list cursor or specified with `pos` after `AT`. At the start of every output, the output position in the list buffer is the same as that in the list representation. In Unicode systems, the positions of individual characters within an output field can differ between the list representation and the list buffer. In both cases, though, the output length is the same.

The output length is either determined through the data type of `dobj` (see Table 27.1) or can be specified with `len|*|**` after `AT` (see Section 27.2.1.3). `len` specifies an absolute length, whereas since Release 6.20 (Support Package 29) `*` or `**` ensure that characters in Unicode systems are not truncated by mistake. If the last line of the current page is reached and a subsequent line is output, a new page is generated. The maximum number of lines is determined by the addition `LINE-COUNT` of the introductory statement or the statement `NEW-PAGE`. For basics lists, the `END-OF-PAGE` event is triggered when the area reserved for the page footer is reached, and a new page is subsequently generated.

If, after the positioning of the list cursor with a previous output statement, the output length is larger than the area available in the current line of the list buffer, the output goes to the next line. If this line is also not sufficient for a complete output, the output length is correspondingly shortened and the output is displayed in this line.

If the list cursor is positioned using the `pos` specification or a statement `BACK`, `NEW-LINE`, `NEW-PAGE`, `POSITION` or `SKIP` and not with a previous output statement, then the output is always displayed in the current line, and the output length is shortened if necessary.

After the output is displayed, the list cursor is positioned by default in the second position after the output; the `sy-colno` and `sy-linno` system fields are set accordingly.

If the data object `dobj` is declared with reference to a data type from the ABAP Dictionary, the field and input help defined there are available in the list displayed on the screen.

Note

In the default setting, the system does not place a new line in a list that contains only blank characters. Such a line is displayed only if the list cursor is directly positioned in an existing line, i.e. not via a line break. You can change this setting with the statement SET BLANK LINES ON.

27.2.1.1 Pre-Defined Output Formats

The pre-defined output format depends upon the data type and user related pre-settings:

Output length and alignment

The default settings for the output length and alignment of the pre-defined ABAP types are listed in Table 27.1.

Data type	Output length	Alignment
c	Length of dobj, max. 255	left-aligned
d	8	left-aligned
f	24	right-aligned
i	11	right-aligned
n	Length of dobj, max. 255	left-aligned
p	2 x length of dobj (+ 1 if there is a decimal separator)	right-aligned
string	In non-Unicode programs and before Release 6.20, this is the number of characters in dobj. In Unicode programs since Release 6.20 (Support Package 29) it is the number of columns required in the list. If this number is greater than the number of characters in dobj, superfluous characters are filled with blanks when they are written into the list buffer. If the output is left-aligned, they are filled on the right; if it is right-aligned they are filled on the left, and if the output is centered, they are filled on the right and left in alternation.	left-aligned
t	6	left-aligned
x	2 x length of dobj, max. 255	left-aligned
xstring	2 x number of bytes contained	left-aligned

Table 27.1 Pre-defined Output Lengths and Alignments

In Unicode programs since Release 6.20 (Support Package 29), the output length of text field literals is specified in the same way as the output

length of data objects of the type `string`. The actual data type (`c`) is only taken into account in non-Unicode programs.

Note

When the implicit output length is used, fewer characters may be displayed in the list than are stored in the list buffer. As of Release 6.20 (Support Package 29), this can happen to all data objects except those of the type `string`. In the case of data objects of the type `string` and text field literals, it is assumed that all the characters are to be displayed. For this reason, the implicit output length is calculated according to the characters in the data object so that it corresponds to the number of columns required in the list. Any blanks possibly appended in the list buffer during this process are cut off again when the data is written to the actual list.

Formats from the ABAP Dictionary

You can define a different output length and a different conversion routine for the domain for data objects whose data types are defined with reference to the ABAP Dictionary. The output length specified there is used instead of the implicit output length from Table 27.1. It is not possible to define an output length in the ABAP Dictionary for the data types RAWSTRING, SSTRING, and STRING, so that the length specified in Table 27.1 always applies to these data types.

Decimal Separators, Date and Time Format

The format in which decimals are displayed (selection of decimal and thousand separators) is predefined in the **Fixed values** in the user master record of the current user. You can change these settings using a SET COUNTRY statement (see Section 35.4).

Data objects of the type `d` are also displayed according to the mask defined in the user master record or with SET COUNTRY. The separators are displayed if the available output length is sufficient. The predefined output length displayed in Table 27.1 is not sufficient.

In type `t` data objects, colons are displayed as separators between hours, minutes and seconds, if the available output length is sufficient. The output length displayed in Table 27.1 is not sufficient.

Formats for Character-Like, Byte-Like, and Numeric Data Objects

Character-like data objects are displayed according to the code page. Unicode systems can contain characters that occupy more columns in the list than storage positions in the list buffer.

Byte-like data objects are displayed in the hexadecimal form in which one byte is displayed by two characters.

In the numeric data types i and p, the field on the far right is reserved for the plus/minus sign. The field displays a minus sign "-" for negative values and a blank for positive values. The thousand separators defined in the user master record are displayed if the available output length is sufficient.

A type f data object is displayed in the scientific notation preceded by a plus/minus sign (blank for positive numbers), a position before the decimal separator, a maximum of 16 fractional portions, the character "E" and a three-character exponent with a plus or minus sign.

Formats for Lines

The characters "-" and "|" are replaced by corresponding line elements if they are given out immediately one after the other, either horizontally or vertically. Line elements are horizontal and vertical lines, corners, crosses, and t-bars. The characters are replaced with solid lines. A single "|" is always replaced with a vertical line. As of Release 6.20 (Support Package 29), the replacement with line elements takes place relative to the display in the list and not relative to the definition in the list buffer. This means that the characters "-" and "|" can be linked to form lines in Unicode systems even if they are not specified one after the other in the list buffer.

27.2.1.2 The Influence of Output Length

When data is written with a WRITE statement, the output is stored in the list buffer and displayed from there when the list is called.

Each time a data object is given out with a WRITE statement, an output length is defined either implicitly (see Table 27.1) or explicitly (if len is specified after the addition AT, see 27.2.1.3). The output length defines the following:

▶ The number of positions (or memory spaces) available for characters in the list buffer

▶ The number of columns (or cells) available in the actual list

Output Length in the List Buffer

If the output length is shorter than the length of the format specified for the data object or defined with int_format_options, the output is shortened as follows when it is written to the list buffer.

▶ In data objects of the numeric data types i and p, the thousand separators are removed from left to right and the object is then cut off on the left. These objects are marked with an asterisk ("*") in the first position.

▶ In data objects of the type f, the number of decimal places is reduced and the number is rounded accordingly. If the output length is too short for scientific notation, asterisks ("*") are displayed instead of the numbers.

▶ All other data types are cut off on the right and not marked; the separators are removed first in the data types d and t.

If the output length is greater than the length of a predefined or self-defined format, this output length is filled in the list buffer and output is arranged there according to the predefined or self-defined alignment. Space that is not required is filled with blanks.

Output Length in the List

When displaying or printing a list, the content stored in the list buffer is transferred to the list as follows:

▶ In non-Unicode systems, each character requires the same amount of space in the list buffer as columns in the list. In single-byte systems, a character occupies one byte in the list buffer and one column in the list, while a character that occupies several bytes in the list buffer in multi-byte systems also occupies the same number of columns in the list. For this reason, all the characters stored in the list buffer are displayed in the list in non-Unicode systems.

▶ In Unicode systems, each character usually occupies one position in the list buffer. However, a character can occupy more than one column in the list (this is particularly the case with East Asian characters). However, because the list only contains the same number of columns as there are positions in the list buffer, the list can only display fewer characters than are stored in the list buffer. The list output is shortened accordingly, and the page formatted according to the alignment specified and assigned an indicator (">" or "<"). To display the entire content of a list, choose **System · List · Unicode-Display** (as of Release 6.20, Support Package 29).

Class for Calculating Output Lengths

The methods of the system class CL_ABAP_LIST_UTILITIES (see Appendix B.1.9) can be used to calculate output lengths in the list buffer and in the list display (as of Support Package 29). The return values of these methods can be used to program a correct column alignment for ABAP lists, even if they contain characters that require more than one column.

27.2.1.3 Defining the Output Position and Length

The output position and length for the current statement WRITE can be defined after AT. The output position of already existing outputs in the list buffer is overwritten with the output length of the new output. After overwriting an already existing output, the list cursor is placed at the next position, not two positions over.

The components of the position and length specification /, pos and len resp. * and ** must be listed with no spaces and in the specified sequence. If pos and len are not specified at all or are declared as numeric literals, the addition AT can be omitted.

* and ** can be used since Release 6.20, Support Package 29.

▶ With / the output is displayed in the next line after the current line. If no position pos is specified, the output is written from the first column onward. The specification of / has no effect immediately after positioning the list cursor in a list line that is not the result of a previous output statement. This is the case during the initial writing to a list page and after the explicit positioning with the statements SKIP, NEW-LINE, NEW-PAGE and BACK.

▶ The output position in the list buffer is determined by pos. For pos a data object of the type i is expected, which contains a value within the current list width. No output is displayed if the value in pos is less than 1 or greater than the current list width.

▶ The output length is determined by specifying len, * or ** in brackets. Using len, an absolute value can be specified. For len a data object of type i is expected, which contains a value within the current list width. No output is displayed if the content of len is less from or equal to 0. In Unicode systems, the number of characters displayed in the list can be different than the number of characters stored in the list buffer by specifying len. By specifying * or **, the output length depends on the data type of the data object dobj, as shown in Table 27.2.

Data type	*	**
c	Number of columns needed in the list to display the entire content; no final blank characters are taken into account. In Unicode systems, this length can be greater than the implicit length from Table 27.1.	Doubled data object length.
string	Implicit length from Table 27.1	Doubled number of characters contained therein.
n, x, xstring	Implicit length from Table 27.1	Implicit length
d	10	10
t	8	8
i, f, p	Necessary length to give out the current value, including thousands separator; value determined after evaluating possible additions CURRENCY, DECIMALS, NO-SIGN, ROUND or UNIT.	Necessary length to give out the maximum possible value, including thousands separator; value determined after evaluating possible additions CURRENCY, DECIMALS, NO-SIGN, ROUND or UNIT.

Table 27.2 Dependence of Output Lengths * and ** on Data Type

A conversion routine executed with reference to a data type in the ABAP Dictionary, when len is specified, is carried out for the lengths specified therein. When * or ** are specified, the routine is carried out for the output lengths specified in the ABAP Dictionary. When specifying * or **, the output length is then determined according to the aforementioned rules from the result of the conversion routine. The specification of * or ** when using formatting templates (USING EDIT MASK, DD/MM/YYYY etc.) is described in the respective sections (see Section 27.2.1.4).

Notes

▶ The specification of the output length len after AT should always be preferred over the use of a length specification for the data object dobj (partial field access, see Section 2.2.5). In contrast to partial field access, the specification of the output length is not restricted to byte- and character-type data objects. Furthermore, the assignment of the list output to the data object is lost during a partial field access, in that it can no longer be addressed in the list.

▶ Since Release 6.20 (Support Package 29), the specification of * or ** for the output length ensures that, independent of the data type, all characters from dobj are presented in Unicode systems, even when more columns are needed in the list than there are positions in the list buffer. With *, the minimum possible length is used, and with **, the maximum possible length is used.

▶ When an output position is specified within an already existing output, you should ensure that the position always refers to the characters stored in the list buffer. If characters that require more than one column in the list are displayed in a Unicode system, the displayed output position can differ from the specified output position. In addition, the displayed content of a partially overwritten output can be shifted, depending on the characters that overwrote the output.

Example

This example gives out a text field `text` at different positions and with different output lengths.

```
DATA: text TYPE string VALUE '0123456789ABCDEF',
      col  TYPE i       VALUE 25,
      len  TYPE i       VALUE 5.

WRITE text.
WRITE /5(10) text.
WRITE AT col(len) text.
```

27.2.1.4 Formatting Options

The formatting options *int_format_options* format the content of `dobj`.

Syntax of *int_format_options*

```
... [LEFT-JUSTIFIED|CENTERED|RIGHT-JUSTIFIED]
    [NO-GAP]
    [UNDER other_dobj]
    { { [EXPONENT exp]
        [NO-GROUPING]
        [NO-SIGN]
        [NO-ZERO]
        [CURRENCY cur]
        { { [DECIMALS dec]
            [ROUND scale] }
          | [UNIT unit] } }
      | [TIME ZONE tz] }
    [USING {{NO EDIT MASK}|{EDIT MASK mask}}]
    [date_mask] ...
```

These format options override the predefined settings. Without the specification of these additions, the output format depends implicitly on the data type (see Section 27.2.1.1). The result of formatting is adjusted to match the output length. If, during the output, a conversion routine is executed, all the formatting options—except for NO-GAP and UNDER—are ignored.

The additions can be used together with the following limitations:

▶ The addition UNIT cannot be used together with the additions DECIMALS and ROUND.

▶ The addition TIME ZONE cannot be used together with the additions CURRENCY, DECIMALS, EXPONENT, NO-GROUPING, NO-SIGN, NO-ZERO, ROUND, or UNIT.

The individual additions are described below.

Alignment

Syntax

```
... LEFT-JUSTIFIED | CENTERED | RIGHT-JUSTIFIED ...
```

This addition defines whether the output formatted according to the other options is aligned left-justified, centered, or right-justified inside the current output length in the list buffer. Closing blanks are ignored in the case of fields of the type c, and they are treated like the other characters in the case of fields of type string.

During alignment, the superfluous positions in the list buffer are filled up, either right-justified, left-justified, or alternating right- and left-justified. If the output length is not sufficient, the characters are cut off to the right for the left-justified and centered, and to the left for the right-justified alignment.

If the output length in the list display is not sufficient in Unicode systems, characters are cut off during the transfer of data from the list buffer into the list. They are cut off to the right for left-justified, and to the left for right- justified output. In the case of centered output, blanks are first removed in alternating fashion on both sides—whereby the cut-off starts on the side with more blanks—and then the other characters on the right side. If characters are cut off during data transfer from the list buffer into the list, since Release 6.10 this is made visible on the left side with the character "<" and on the right side with the character ">".

Example

Output of three literals left, in the middle, and to the right of an output area 60 characters in length.

```
WRITE:  /(60) 'Left'    LEFT-JUSTIFIED,
        /(60) 'Center' CENTERED,
        /(60) 'Right'  RIGHT-JUSTIFIED.
```

List cursor and positioning

Syntax

```
... NO-GAP ...
```

The list cursor is positioned directly after the output and not in the position in the list buffer after the next one.

Example

The output for the two following WRITE statements is " NoGap".

```
WRITE:  'No' NO-GAP. 'Gap'.
```

Syntax

```
... UNDER other_dobj ...
```

The output takes place in the current line at the position where, in a previous WRITE statement, the data object other_dobj was given out. The data object other_dobj must be written in the same way as in the respective WRITE statement, that is, including possible offset/length specifiations and so on. If the data object other_dobj was not given out beforehand, the addition is ignored.

The addition UNDER cannot be used together with a position specification pos after AT.

Note

You must manually set vertical positioning. If the list cursor is in the same position as the output of other_dobj, this will be overwritten.

Example

Table-type output of flight connections.

```
DATA:  carrid TYPE spfli-carrid,
       connid TYPE spfli-connid.

WRITE:  10 'Carrier', 40 'Connection'.
ULINE.
```

```
SELECT carrid connid
      FROM spfli
      INTO (carrid,connid).
  WRITE: / carrid UNDER 'Carrier',
          connid UNDER 'Connection'.
ENDSELECT.
```

Formatting numerical outputs

The following additions cannot be used together with the addition TIME
ZONE.

Syntax

```
... EXPONENT exp ...
```

This addition defines the exponent for the output of data objects of the
data type f. For all other data types, the addition is ignored. For exp, a
data object of the type i contains the required exponent. The mantissa is
adjusted by moving the decimal point and inserting zeros to the exponent. If exp contains the value 0, no exponent is given out. If the value of
exp is larger than the exponent in dobj plus 16, only zeros are displayed
in the mantissa. If the value of exp is less than the exponent in dobj, and
the output length is not sufficient for the required positions before the
decimal separator, the addition is ignored. If the value in exp is positive
and more than three digits, only the first three positions of the exponent
are displayed.

Example

The output of the WRITE statement is "1.414". The standard output for an
output length of 6 would be "1E+00".

```
DATA float TYPE f.
```

```
float = sqrt( 2 ).
```

```
WRITE (6) float EXPONENT 0.
```

Syntax

```
... NO-GROUPING ...
```

This addition suppresses the thousands separator in the output of data
objects of data types i or p. In all other data types, the addition is
ignored.

Syntax

```
... NO-SIGN ...
```

This addition suppresses the plus/minus sign in the output of data objects of data types i, p, or f. In all the other data types, the addition is ignored.

If the addition NO-SIGN is used with the length specification * or ** after AT, it is used first and the output length is determined from the result.

Example

Output with red background color instead of a plus/minus sign.

```
IF number < 0.
  WRITE number NO-SIGN COLOR = 6.
ENDIF.
```

Syntax

```
... NO-ZERO ...
```

If dobj has a numeric data type and contains the value 0, blanks are given out for the length of the output. If dobj has the data type c, n, or string, leading zeros are displayed by blanks.

Example

Output of 22 blanks with red background color instead of the standard output "0.0000000000000000E+00".

```
DATA float TYPE f.

SET BLANK LINES ON.
IF float = 0.
  WRITE float NO-ZERO COLOR = 6.
ENDIF.
```

Places after the decimal point for numerical outputs

The following additions cannot be used together with the addition TIME ZONE.

Syntax

```
... CURRENCY cur ...
```

This addition defines currency-dependent decimal places for the output of data objects of data types i or p. For all other data types, except for f, the addition is ignored. For cur, a three-digit, character-type field is expected that contains a currency key from the column CURRKEY of the database table TCURX in uppercase letters. The system determines the number of decimal places from the column CURRDEC of the respective row in the database table TCURX. If the content of cur is not found in TCURX, two decimal places are used. The following applies for numeric data types:

▶ In the case of data types of type i, a decimal separator is inserted at the position determined by cur and the thousands separators are moved accordingly.

▶ In the case of data objects of type p, the decimal places defined in the definition of the data type are ignored completely. Irrespective of the actual value and without rounding actions, the decimal separators and the thousand separators are inserted at the positions in the numbers determined by cur.

▶ In the case of data objects of type f, the addition CURRENCY has the same effect as the addition DECIMALS (see below). Here, the number of decimal places is determined by cur.

If the addition CURRENCY with length specification * or ** is used after AT, it is used first and the output length is determined from the result.

Note

The addition CURRENCY is appropriate for displaying data objects of type i or p without decimal places, whose contents are currency amounts in the smallest unit of the currency.

Example

The output of the WRITE statement is "123456.78".

```
DATA int TYPE i VALUE 12345678.
WRITE int NO-GROUPING CURRENCY 'EUR'.
```

Syntax

```
... DECIMALS dec ...
```

This addition defines the number of displayed decimal places for the output of data objects of data types i, p, or f. For all other data types, the addition is ignored. For dec, a data object of type i is expected that contains the number of required decimal places. If the content of dec is less than 0, it is treated as 0, and the content of data objects of data types i or p is previously multiplied by 10 to the power of dec. For the individual numeric data types, the following applies:

▶ In the case of data objects of type i, a decimal separator and as many zeros as are specified in dec are added on. The content of dec can be maximum 14. Otherwise, an exception that cannot be handled will be triggered. If the content of dec is 0, the output is unchanged.

▶ In the case of data objects of type p, as many decimal places as are specified in dec are displayed, irrespective of the number of decimal places defined in the data type. The content of dec can be maximum 14. Otherwise, an exception that cannot be handled will be triggered. If dcbj has more decimal places, it is rounded to the decimal places in dec. If dobj has fewer decimal places, a corresponding number of zeros are inserted.

▶ In the case of data objects of type f, the content of dec determines the number of decimal places in scientific notation. If the content of dec is greater than 16, it will be treated like 16. If the content of dec is greater than the number of decimal places in dobj, a corresponding number of zeros will be inserted. If the content of dec is less than the number of decimal places in dobj, it will be rounded to the decimal places defined in dec.

If the addition DECIMALS is used with the length specification * or ** after AT, it is used first and then the output length is determined from the result.

If the addition CURRENCY is specified as well, it is executed first in the case of data types i and p, and then the addition DECIMALS is applied. In the case of data type f, the addition CURRENCY is ignored if it is specified together with DECIMALS.

Example
The output for the WRITE statement is "1234.57".

```
DATA pack TYPE p DECIMALS 4 VALUE '1234.5678'.
WRITE pack NO-GROUPING DECIMALS 2.
```

Syntax

```
... ROUND scale ...
```

If dobj has the data type p, this addition multiplies the value of the data object, before the output, by 10^{-scale}. In all other data types, the addition is ignored. For scale, a data object of type i is expected that contains the value of the required scale.

If the value of `scale` is greater than 0 and the addition `DECIMALS` is not specified, the interim result is rounded to the number of decimal places defined in the data type. If the addition `DECIMALS` is specified, it is rounded to the number of decimal places specified in `dec`, and these are then given out.

If the addition `ROUND` is used with the length specification `*` or `**` after `AT`, it is used first and the output length is determined from the result.

If the addition `CURRENCY` is specified, this is used for the content of `dobj` before multiplication. If the addition `DECIMALS` is not specified, the number of decimal places specified through `cur` is used for both the rounding off and the output. If the addition `DECIMALS` is specified, the value in `dec` is used.

Example
The output of the `WRITE` statement is "123456.7800".

```
DATA pack TYPE p VALUE '12345678'.
WRITE pack NO-GROUPING ROUND 2 DECIMALS 4.
```

Syntax

```
... UNIT unit ...
```

During the output of data objects of data type `p`, this addition cuts off decimal places that have the value 0 and lack the exactness of a unit of measure. For all other data types, except `f`, this addition is ignored. For `unit`, a three-digit, character-type field is expected that contains a unit key from the column MSEHI of the database table T006 in uppercase letters. The system determines the number of decimal places from the column DECAN of the corresponding row in the database table T006. If the content of `unit` is not found in T006, the addition is ignored.

▶ If the data type of `dobj` is `p` and has at least as many decimal places as specified by `unit`, and if no positions are thus cut off that are not equal to 0, then `dobj` is given out with this number of decimal places.

▶ In the case of data objects of type `f`, the addition `UNIT` will be treated like the addition `DECIMALS` (see above). Here, the number of decimal places is determined by `unit`.

If the addition `UNIT` is used with the length specification `*` or `**` after `AT`, it is used first and the output length is determined from the result.

If the addition CURRENCY is used at the same time, this is used first for data type p and then the addition UNIT is used. In the case of data type f, the addition UNIT is ignored.

Example

If no decimal places are specified for the number "PC" in T006, the output of the WRITE statement is "1234".

```
DATA pack TYPE p DECIMALS 4 VALUE '1234.0000'.
WRITE pack NO-GROUPING UNIT 'PC'.
```

Time stamp format

Syntax

```
... TIME ZONE tz ...
```

This addition edits a time stamp in relation to a time zone. The data object dobj must be of type p of length 0 without decimal places, or of type p of length 11 with seven decimal places. The content of dobj is interpreted as though it contained the long or the short form of a time stamp in UTC reference time (see Section 36.1.2).

For tz, a data object of type TIMEZONE from the ABAP Dictionary must be specified. It must contain a time zone from the column TZONE of the database table TTZZ in uppercase letters. If tz is initial, the UTC reference time is given out.

The time stamp in dobj is converted to the time zone given in tz and is edited from the left as follows.

▶ First, the date is given out. The format depends on the settings in the user master record or on any data mask date_mask specified concurrently. After the date, a blank is given out.

▶ Second, the time is given out in the format predefined for type t. Colons (:) are inserted here as separators between hours, minutes, and seconds.

▶ If the time stamp is in the long form, a comma (,) is given out directly after the time, and after that the milliseconds.

▶ If the value of tz is not contained in the database table TTZZ or if dobj does not contain any valid time stamp, the content of dobj is given out without conversion. Before the date, an asterisk (*) is entered, and the last position of the time is cut off.

The editing takes place in an interim result of length 19 if the time stamp is in its short form, or of length 27 if the time stamp is in the long form. If the output length is shorter than 19 in the short form or 27 in the long form, first all the separators in date and time are removed in the interim result, then the blanks between date and time are removed, and only then the characters are cut off at the right. If, at the same time, a date mask *date_mask* is specified, the separators in the date are not removed.

Note

The data objects `dobj` and `tz` can be declared in relation to the data types TIMESTAMP, TIMESTAMPL, and TIMEZONE in the ABAP Dictionary.

Example

Output of a UTC time stamp in Tasmanian time. In summer, the output is "28.06.2002 04:00:00".

```
DATA: time_stamp TYPE timestamp,
      tzone      TYPE timezone.

time_stamp = 20020627180000.

tzone = 'AUSTAS'.
WRITE / time_stamp TIME ZONE tzone.
```

Conversion routines and formatting templates

Syntax

```
... USING { {NO EDIT MASK} | {EDIT MASK mask} } ...
```

This addition overrides a conversion routine defined by reference to the ABAP Dictionary. The addition NO EDIT MASK only switches off the execution of an assigned conversion routine. The addition EDIT MASK calls either another conversion routine or defines an edit mask. For `mask`, a byte-type data object is expected.

In order to call an arbitrary conversion routine CONV, `mask` must contain two equals signs, followed directly by the name of the conversion routine: "==CONV". During output, the content of `dobj` is passed to the function module CONVERSION_EXIT_CONV_OUTPUT, converted there, and then the result is displayed. If the function module is not found, an exception that can be handled is triggered (as of Release 6.10). The statement DESCRIBE FIELD contains an addition in order to fill `mask` accordingly.

If the output length is specified explicitly with `len`, the conversion routine is executed for the specified length; otherwise it is executed for the implicit output length from Table 27.1. If * or ** is specified for the output length after `AT` (as of Release 6.20, Support Package 29), the appropriate rules are used for the converted result.

If the first two characters in `mask` are not equals signs, the content is interpreted as an edit mask in which some characters have a particular meaning. Then the `WRITE` statement does not then output the content of `dobj` directly, but the character string in `mask` as follows.

▶ If the first two characters in `mask` are "LL" or "RR", these are not given out, They control whether the edit mask is left-justified or right-justified. If the first two characters are other characters, the edit mask is left-justified.

▶ All "_" characters are replaced from the left (in the case of "LL") or from the right (in the case of "RR") with characters for character-type types or numbers for the types p or i from `dobj`. In the case of fields of type c, closing blanks are ignored. Data objects of type f or x are converted into type c before editing. Superfluous characters "_" in `mask` are replaced by blanks. Characters from `dobj` for which there are no characters "_" in `mask` are not displayed.

▶ If `dobj` is of type i or p, the first character from the left "V" in `mask` is replaced with "-" in the case of a negative number and by a blank in the case of a positive number.

▶ All the other characters of the edit mask are displayed unchanged.

If no output length is specified after `AT`, the implicit output length of `dobj` (from Table 27.1) is used. If `len` is specified for the output length, the value of `len` is used. If * is specified for the output length (as of Release 6.20, Support Package 29), the length set is exactly that required for the list display. If, in Unicode systems, characters of the edit mask are replaced by characters that take up more than one column on the list, the output length is increased accordingly and the output is filled with blanks in the list buffer. If ** is specified for the output length (as of Release 6.20, Support Package 29), double the length of the edit mask `mask` is used.

If other formatting options are specified concurrently for an edit mask, these are used first, and then the special characters in the edit mask are replaced by the interim result. The date masks *date_mask* are an exception to this. If these are specified, the edit mask is ignored.

Notes

▶ In Unicode systems, you must remember that a character "_" in the edit mask does not necessarily correspond to a column in the list display since the space required in the display depends on the character to be replaced.

▶ The minus sign for a negative number is not displayed if no edit character "V" is specified. The decimal separator of a packed number with decimal places must be specified at the required position in the edit mask.

Example

Edited output of time duration. In the first output, the function module CONVERSION_EXIT_DURA_OUTPUT is executed. This converts the duration specified in seconds into minutes. In the second output, the edit mask is given out according to the rules above. However, the underscore characters "_" are replaced by the characters from time.

```
DATA: dura TYPE i,
      time TYPE t VALUE '080000'.

dura = sy-uzeit - time.
time = dura.

WRITE /(30) dura USING EDIT MASK '==SDURA'.
WRITE /(30) time USING EDIT MASK
                    'RRThe duration is __:__:__'.
```

Date format

Syntax of *date mask*

```
... DD/MM/YY   | MM/DD/YY
  | DD/MM/YYYY | MM/DD/YYYY
  | DDMMYY     | MMDDYY      | YYMMDD ...
```

These additions have the same effect as edit masks for the output of data objects of data type d. For all other data types, this addition is ignored.

The content of a data object of type d is interpreted according to the specified masks. Here, YYYY stands for the year, MM for the month, and DD for the day. The individual additions assign the content of dobj accordingly. Here, the two last year numbers are used for YY, and all the year numbers are used for YYYY. For the character /, the separator that is defined in the user master record for date output is inserted.

If the output length is defined implicitly or specified using `len`, this is used. If it is too short, the edited output is cut off to the right. If the output length is specified using * or **, it is set to the length of the specified edit mask (6, 8, or 10).

Note

The behavior for abbreviation differs from the way data output is handled according to the user master record, where the separators are removed first and then cut off.

Example

The output of the WRITE statement is, for example, "230402".

```
WRITE sy-datum DDMMYY.
```

27.2.1.5 Formatting Options

The *ext_format_options* formatting options format the outputs WRITE formatted by `int_options` over the entire output length. The following additions of the statement FORMAT can be specified as *ext_format_options* after WRITE .

Syntax of *ext_format_options*

```
...  [COLOR         {{{color [ON]}|OFF}|{= col}}]
     [INTENSIFIED   [{ON|OFF}|{= flag}]]
     [INVERSE       [{ON|OFF}|{= flag}]]
     [HOTSPOT       [{ON|OFF}|{= flag}]]
     [INPUT         [{ON|OFF}|{= flag}]]
     [FRAMES        [{ON|OFF}|{= flag}]]
     [RESET]  ...  .
```

The meaning of the additions is the same as for the statement FORMAT (see Section 27.2.3), except that they only affect the output of the current WRITE statement. If the additions are not specified, the standard settings described in FORMAT or the settings set by the previous FORMAT statements are used.

Note

The use of such an addition in the WRITE statement overrides the standard settings or the formats set by the previous FORMAT statements for exactly one output and for exactly the property concerned. All other properties and subsequent WRITE statements are not affected.

Example

Changing the background color for the output of the data object `sum`. All the other outputs and spaces between the outputs have the background color that is set in the `FORMAT` statement.

```
DATA sum TYPE i.

FORMAT COLOR COL_NORMAL.

DO 10 TIMES.
  WRITE / sy-index.
  sum = sum + sy-index.
  WRITE sum COLOR COL_TOTAL.
ENDDO.
ULINE.
WRITE sum UNDER sum COLOR COL_GROUP.
```

27.2.1.6 List Elements

The *list_elements* additions serve to represent special list elements.

Syntax

```
...  {AS CHECKBOX}
   | {AS ICON}
   | {AS SYMBOL}
   | {AS LINE} ...
```

The output data object `dobj` must have certain properties. The additions cannot be used together, but they can be used conditionally with the additions *int_format_options* and *ext_format_options*.

Checkboxes

Syntax

```
...  AS CHECKBOX ...
```

This addition gives out a single-digit checkbox that is ready for input. For `dobj`, a character-type data type of length 1 is expected. If the first character in `dobj` is "X" or "x", the checkbox is shown as marked. If the first character is not "X" or "x", the checkbox is shown as empty. If `dobj` is an empty data object of the type `string`, the checkbox is not given out.

The user can select and deselect the checkbox in the list displayed on the screen. If the user selects the checkbox, the first character of the assigned field in the list is set to "X". If the user deselects it, it is set to blank. The change is stored in the list buffer and can be evaluated during the list results.

If the addition AS CHECKBOX is used, no length specification len is allowed after AT. Except for INPUT, NO-GAP, and UNDER, the other additions int_ format_options and ext_format_options given at the same time have no effect.

The addition AS CHECKBOX has the same effect as if the addition INPUT ON were specified simultaneously. The standard settings or a format INPUT OFF set by a FORMAT statement are overridden for the current WRITE statement. To switch off the input-readiness of the checkbox, the addition INPUT OFF must be used simultaneously.

Note
Whenever a list line contains only a checkbox with a blank, it will not be displayed unless the statement SET BLANK LINES ON was executed beforehand.

Example
Output of two checkbox fields and evaluation of the user inputs at the event AT LINE-SELECTION.

```
REPORT test NO STANDARD PAGE HEADING.

DATA: check1 TYPE c VALUE 'X',
      check2 TYPE c VALUE ' '.

START-OF-SELECTION.
  WRITE: / check1 AS CHECKBOX, 'Checkbox 1',
         / check2 AS CHECKBOX, 'Checkbox 2'.

AT LINE-SELECTION.
  READ: LINE 1 FIELD VALUE check1,
        LINE 2 FIELD VALUE check2.
```

Icons

Syntax

```
... AS ICON ...
```

This addition gives out icons. Be aware that not all icons are suitable for print lists. For dobj, data objects of the type c must be specified whose initial characters of the runtime environment can be interpreted as a coding of an icon. Such data objects can be declared by including the type group ICON or the general include programs <LIST> in the global declaration part of the program.

In the type group, a constant is declared for each icon that can be displayed. The names of the constants can be taken from the type groups or the output of the executable programs SHOWICON. This program also shows the corresponding output length and whether an icon can be printed or not.

If the content of dobj cannot be interpreted as an icon or the content is changed by concurrent use of other additions `int_format_options` and `ext_format_options`, blanks are given out instead of icons.

Notes

▶ None of the additions from `int_format_options` and `ext_format_options` are forbidden. When the additions are used, care must be taken that the content of dobj can be interpreted as an icon.

▶ The output length is determined, as always, either implicitly through the data type of dobj or through an explicit specification. Characters of the output area that do not have the icon are set to blanks.

Example
Displaying a traffic-light icon.

```
INCLUDE <list>.

WRITE icon_green_light AS ICON.
```

Symbols

Syntax

```
... AS SYMBOL ...
```

This addition gives out all the characters of the data object dobj as symbols. By including the type group SYM or the general include program <LIST> in the global declaration part of the program, constants of the length 1 are declared for each character that can be appropriately displayed as a symbol (that is, characters whose names show the meaning of the respective symbol). The names of the constants and the meaning and length of the symbols can be taken from the type group or from the output of the executable program SHOWSYMB.

Note
The output length is determined, as usual, either implicitly by the data type of dobj or by an explicit specification.

Example
Displaying a hand symbol.

```
INCLUDE <list>.

WRITE sym_left_hand AS SYMBOL.
```

Line elements

Syntax

```
... AS LINE ...
```

This addition gives out line elements of the output length 1. Line elements are corner elements, checkmarks, lines, and T-elements. For `dobj`, data objects of the type `c` must be specified whose content can be interpreted by the runtime environment as line elements. Such data objects can be declared in the global declaration part of the program by including the type group LINE or the general include program <LIST>.

The type group LINE declares the line element constants displayed in Table 27.3.

Constant	Meaning
line_space	Blank
line_top_left_corner	Top left corner
line_bottom_left_corner	Bottom left corner
line_top_right_corner	Top right corner
line_bottom_right_corner	Bottom right corner
line_horizontal_line	Horizontal line
line_vertical_line	Vertical line
line_left_middle_corner	T-element turned to the left
line_right_middle_corner	T-element turned to the right
line_bottom_middle_corner	T-element upside down
line_top_middle_corner	T-element
line_cross	Cross

Table 27.3 Constants for Line Elements

If `dobj` has a different content or the content is changed through concurrent use of other additions *int_format_options*, a blank is given out instead of a line element. The addition FRAMES OFF must not be given out simultaneously. The other *ext_format_options* and QUICKINFO are ignored during the output of line elements.

Note

The characters "-" and "|" and output with ULINE are linked with one another as a standard if, between them, there are no other characters. Here the system replaces the characters by the above line elements. A solitary character "|" is always replaced by a vertical line. Using the addition AS LINE, line elements are given out exactly as they are defined. Links only occur where real line elements meet each other. The system does not, however, execute any automatic extensions between the characters "-" or "|" and line elements given out explicitly using AS LINE.

Example

Output of four rectangles that belong together.

```
TYPE-POOLS line.

WRITE: /10 line_top_left_corner       AS LINE NO-GAP,
           line_top_middle_corner     AS LINE NO-GAP,
           line_top_right_corner      AS LINE,
       /10 line_left_middle_corner    AS LINE NO-GAP,
           line_cross                 AS LINE NO-GAP,
           line_right_middle_corner   AS LINE,
       /10 line_bottom_left_corner    AS LINE NO-GAP,
           line_bottom_middle_corner  AS LINE NO-GAP,
           line_bottom_right_corner   AS LINE.
```

27.2.1.7 Assigning a Quick Info Text

Syntax

```
... QUICKINFO info ...
```

A Quickinfo is assigned to the output. If the mouse cursor is placed on the output area of dobj, the content of info appears in a colored rectangle. For info, a character-type data object of the length 40 is expected.

The addition QUICKINFO has no effect on ready-for-input fields and line elements. If a list output is overwritten by another output, then no Quickinfo for the overwritten field appears, beginning with the position at which the overwriting starts.

Example

Additional information to output of date and time.

```
WRITE: (10) sy-datum QUICKINFO 'Date of list creation',
       (8)  sy-uzeit QUICKINFO 'Time of list creation'.
```

27.2.2   Creating Horizontal Lines

```
ULINE
```

Output of horizontal lines in lists.

Syntax

```
ULINE {[AT] [/][pos][(len)]} [NO-GAP].
```

This statement mainly has the same effect as the following WRITE statement:

WRITE line [[[AT] [/][pos][(len)]] [NO-GAP]].

In this case, line is a data object of type c and length 1,023, which is completely filled with "-" characters. In accordance with the predefined formatting rule for the character "-", these are joined together to form a continuous line and are replaced by the appropriate line element. The same applies for directly consecutive characters "-" and "|". In contrast to the WRITE statement, for ULINE, the characters are also replaced with the line element for an output length of 1.

The position and length of the line are determined by the rules for the WRITE statement (see Section 27.2.1). In the simplest case, ULINE produces the following output:

▶ A continuous horizontal line along a whole line, if no position and length are specified after AT. In contrast to the WRITE statement, the list cursor is positioned in the first position of the next line.

▶ A line of length len at the horizontal position pos if the position and length are specified after AT.

Note

If the statement FORMAT FRAMES OFF is used beforehand, the output of ULINE is not displayed as a continuous line, as this statement prevents the replacement of the "-" characters with line elements.

Example
Output of a horizontal line along the whole line after the first WRITE output and of two horizontal lines as parts of a frame.

```
WRITE 'A text in a frame'.
ULINE.
SKIP.
```

```
ULINE AT 10(10).
WRITE: /10 '|', 11(8) 'Text' CENTERED, 19 '|'.
ULINE AT /10(10).
```

27.2.3   Formatting Lists Section by Section

FORMAT

Certain format settings can be defined for all output statements of a list section.

Syntax

```
FORMAT [COLOR        {{{color [ON]}|OFF}|{= col}}]
       [INTENSIFIED  [{ON|OFF}|{= flag}]]
       [INVERSE      [{ON|OFF}|{= flag}]]
       [HOTSPOT      [{ON|OFF}|{= flag}]]
       [INPUT        [{ON|OFF}|{= flag}]]
       [FRAMES       [{ON|OFF}|{= flag}]]
       [RESET].
```

The settings defined with FORMAT apply from the current position of the list cursor onwards for all of the following output statements (WRITE and, with restrictions, ULINE) until they are redefined by a new FORMAT statement. Within a line, the areas between the individual outputs and between the start of the line and the first output are formatted. However, blank lines created with SKIP are not formatted.

The individual additions change only the corresponding setting and leave the others unchanged, with the exception of the RESET addition, which can change all settings.

At the start of the program, the standard settings are defined for the settings that can be defined with FORMAT. These are set automatically for each reporting and list event (with the exception of the attribute set by FRAMES). A list of the standard settings is located in the description of the RESET addition in Table 27.5.

For each individual WRITE output, the settings can be overridden by the use of the same additions in the WRITE additions. The settings that are defined with FORMAT or the standard settings then apply again.

Below is a description of the individual additions:

Select the color

Syntax

```
... COLOR { {{color [ON]}|OFF} | {= col} } ...
```

This addition sets the color of the output. If the attribute INVERSE is set to OFF (default setting), this sets the background color of the output. If the attribute INVERSE is set to ON, this sets the foreground color of the output.

You can specify the color either statically using color or dynamically using col. For color, use the syntax directly from Table 27.4. You do not need to specify ON. For col, a data object of type i is expected, which contains one of the values from Table 27.4. If col contains a different value, this is handled like the value 0.

Syntax of color	Value in col	Color
{ COL_BACKGROUND }	0	GUI-specific
{ 1	COL_HEADING }	1	gray-blue
{ 2	COL_NORMAL }	2	light gray
{ 3	COL_TOTAL }	3	yellow
{ 4	COL_KEY }	4	blue-green
{ 5	COL_POSITIVE }	5	green
{ 6	COL_NEGATIVE }	6	red
{ 7	COL_GROUP }	7	violet

Table 27.4 Syntax and Values for Colors in Lists

The OFF addition has the same effect as COL_BACKGROUND or the value 0 in col and is the default setting. In this setting, the color of the background corresponds to a line of the background color of the GUI window.

The COLOR addition does not affect lines that are made of line elements or windows that are ready for input.

Background color intensity

Syntax

```
... INTENSIFIED [{ON|OFF}|{= flag}] ...
```

This addition determines the intensity of the background color. For flag, a data object of type i is expected. If ON is specified or if the content of flag is not equal to 0, an intensive background color is used (default setting). If OFF is specified or if the content of flag is equal to 0, a light background color is used. An exception to this is the COL_BACKGROUND background color. In this case, INTENSIFIED OFF influences the foreground color. If neither ON, OFF nor flag are specified after INTENSIFIED, then the ON addition takes effect.

If the INPUT ON attribute is set at the same time, the INTENSIFIED OFF addition changes the foreground color of the fields that are ready for input. If the INVERSE ON setting is made at the same time, the INTENSIFIED OFF setting has no effect (with the exception of COL_BACKGROUND).

Switching between foreground and background color

Syntax

```
... INVERSE [{ON|OFF}|{= flag}] ...
```

This addition determines whether the COLOR addition sets the background or the foreground color. For flag, a data object of type i is expected. If ON is specified or the content of flag is not equal to 0, then the foreground—i.e. the output—is displayed in the selected color. An exception to this is the COL_BACKGROUND color. In this case, the foreground is displayed in white. If OFF is specified or if the content of flag is not equal to 0, the background is displayed in the selected color (default setting). If ON, OFF or flag are specified after INVERSE then the ON addition takes effect.

If the attribute INPUT ON is set at the same time, the addition INVERSE ON changes the background and foreground color of fields that are ready for input.

Example

Demonstration of the different combinations of the additions COLOR, INTENSIFIED and INVERSE. The program SHOWCOLO provides a similar result.

```
DATA col TYPE i VALUE 0.

DO 8 TIMES.
  col = sy-index - 1.
  FORMAT COLOR = col.
  WRITE: /  col                 COLOR OFF,
```

```
             'INTENSIFIED ON'   INTENSIFIED ON,
             'INTENSIFIED OFF'  INTENSIFIED OFF,
             'INVERSE ON'       INVERSE ON.
ENDDO.
```

Creating hot spots

Syntax

```
... HOTSPOT [{ON|OFF}|{= flag}] ...
```

This addition influences the display of the mouse pointer and the function of the mouse in the list displayed on the screen. For flag, a data object of type i is expected. If ON is specified or if the content of flag is not equal to 0, then the mouse pointer positioned on the list area that is formatted correspondingly changes its appearance to a hand, and a single click has the same effect as a double-click, that is the selection of the function key **F2**. If OFF is specified or if the content of flag is equal to 0, the function of the mouse does not change (default setting). If neither ON, OFF nor flag is specified after HOTSPOT, then the ON addition takes effect.

If the attribute INPUT ON is set, the HOTSPOT ON addition has no effect on line elements.

Example

Demonstration of a hotspot. Clicking once on the output creates a details list.

```
START-OF-SELECTION.
  FORMAT HOTSPOT.
  WRITE 'Click me!' COLOR 5.
  FORMAT HOTSPOT OFF.

AT LINE-SELECTION.
  WRITE 'Yeah!' COLOR 3.
```

Creating an input field

Syntax

```
... INPUT [{ON|OFF}|{= flag}] ...
```

This addition makes list areas ready for input. For flag, a data object of type i is expected. If ON is specified or the content of flag is not equal to 0, the relevant list area is displayed with a foreground and background color different from the rest of the list, and the user can overwrite the output. The screen cursor is positioned in the first field that is ready for input. If OFF is specified or the content of flag is equal to 0, the output is not made ready for input (default setting). If neither ON, OFF nor flag is specified after INPUT, the ON addition takes effect.

Within an area that is ready for input, icons are displayed empty and symbols are displayed as characters according to the code page. Line elements are not made ready for input. The "-" und "|" characters in a list area that is ready for input are not converted into line elements, however, and are displayed ready for input. The latter applies particularly to the ULINE statement.

The width of the list area that is ready for input is defined by the output length. If in Unicode systems the display of contents from the list buffer in a list area that is ready for input results in truncation, the indicator is placed outside the area. The number of characters that can be entered is limited by the output length. The content cannot be moved. In Unicode systems, the number of characters that can be entered depends on the space that the individual characters require.

The entries made by the user are saved in the list buffer and can be evaluated during a list event.

Note
If a list line exclusively contains an input field with blank characters exclusively, it is not displayed if the SET BLANK LINES ON statement was not executed beforehand.

Example
Output of a field ready for input and evaluation of the AT-LINE-SELEC-TION event. The evaluation is done only if the user clicks on the hotspot below the line that is ready for input.

```
DATA: input_field(100)  TYPE c,
      line_num           TYPE i.

START-OF-SELECTION.
  WRITE 'Input text:'.
  SET BLANK LINES ON.
  FORMAT INPUT.
  WRITE / input_field.
  FORMAT INPUT OFF.
  WRITE / '>>> OK <<<' COLOR 5 HOTSPOT.

AT LINE-SELECTION.
  IF sy-lisel = '>>> OK <<<'.
    line_num = sy-lilli - 1.
```

```
READ LINE line_num FIELD VALUE input_field.
WRITE:    'The input was:',
       /  input_field.
ENDIF.
```

Controlling the conversion to line elements

Syntax

```
... FRAMES [{ON|OFF}|{= flag}] ...
```

This addition determines whether the "-" and "|" characters are converted into line elements. For flag, a data object of type i is expected. If ON is specified or if the content of flag is not equal to 0, the conversion is made in the relevant list area (default setting). If OFF is specified or if the content of flag is equal to 0, the conversion does not take place. If neither ON, nor OFF, nor flag are specified after FRAMES, the ON addition takes effect.

In the FRAMES ON setting, the following points apply:

▶ If the "-" and "|" characters are given out directly next to each other or above each other, then they are replaced by line elements, resulting in continuous lines (frames). This applies particularly to lines that are given out using ULINE.

▶ A solitary "|" character is always replaced by a vertical line.

▶ Line elements that are explicitly given out with the AS LINE addition are not replaced by line elements, and they do not influence "-" and "|" characters that are next to each other.

In the FRAMES OFF setting, the "-" and "|" are not converted into line elements. You can explicitly give out line elements using the AS LINE addition.

Note
The FRAMES OFF addition is suitable for preventing unwanted results in print lists. This applies particularly to lists that are intended for archiving.

Example
Output of a frame with an without connecting the characters "-" and "|".

```
FORMAT FRAMES ON.
PERFORM frame.
FORMAT FRAMES OFF.
PERFORM frame.
```

```
FORM frame.
  SKIP.
  WRITE: /  '----',
         /  '|   |',
         /  '----'.
ENDFORM.
```

Setting all formatting settings

Syntax

```
... RESET ...
```

This addition sets all formatting settings for which the corresponding addition is not specified in the same FORMAT statement to the state OFF, apart from the setting of the FRAMES addition, which is set to ON. For settings whose addition is specified at the same time, the RESET addition has no effect.

Table 27.5 shows the effect of RESET compared with the default setting, with the setting at the program start and with the setting that is made for reporting and list events.

State	State after RESET	State after program start	State after reporting or list event
COLOR	OFF	OFF	OFF
INTENSIFIED	OFF	ON	ON
INVERSE	. OFF	OFF	OFF
HOTSPOT	OFF	OFF	OFF
INPUT	OFF	OFF	OFF
FRAMES	ON	ON	No change

Table 27.5 General Formatting Settings

Example

This FORMAT statement creates the default setting after the program starts.

```
FORMAT RESET
       INTENSIFIED ON.
```

27.2.4 Displaying Blank Lines

```
SET BLANK LINES
```

Controlling the output of blank lines.

Syntax

```
SET BLANK LINES {ON|OFF}.
```

This statement specifies whether the blank lines generated using WRITE are displayed. If the addition ON is specified, all the subsequent lines generated using WRITE statements are written into the list. If the addition OFF is specified (default), all subsequent lines that contain only blank characters after a line break are not written into the list.

Notes

▶ The suppression of blank lines does not depend on the formatting of the output. Particularly lines that contain only empty checkbox or input fields are also suppressed.

▶ Blank lines generated using SKIP are independent of the statement SET BLANK LINES. They do not contain any output.

Example
Output of a text file loaded from the presentation server as a list. Blank lines are included.

```
DATA: text_line(80) TYPE c,
      text_tab LIKE TABLE OF text_line.

CALL FUNCTION 'GUI_UPLOAD'
    EXPORTING
        filename    = 'Gone_with_the_Wind.txt'
        filetype    = 'ASC'
    TABLES
        data_tab = text_tab.

SET BLANK LINES ON.

LOOP AT text_tab INTO text_line.
  WRITE / text_line.
ENDLOOP.
```

27.2.5 Vertical Positioning of the List Cursor

The following statements change the vertical positioning of the list cursor.

27.2.5.1 Cursor Positioning in Specified Lines

```
SKIP
```

Positioning the list cursor in a particular line.

Syntax

```
SKIP { [n] | (TO LINE line} }.
```

Positioning of the list cursor below the current line or in any desired line.

Positioning the list cursor after the current line

Syntax

```
SKIP [n].
```

This statement positions the list cursor in relation to the current line. The new line is determined by the value of n. For n, a data object of type i is expected. If the value of n is smaller than or equal to 0, the statement is ignored. If n is not specified, the statement is executed as if n contains the value 1.

The cursor is positioned as follows:

▶ If the line of the current list cursor was set using an output statement (WRITE, ULINE), the list cursor is set to the first position of the line that is n lines under the current line.

▶ If the lines of the current list cursor was set using a positioning state-ment (BACK, NEW-LINE, NEW-PAGE, SKIP), the list cursor is set in the cur-rent position in the line that is n minus 1 lines under the current line.

Note the following special conditions.

▶ If the list cursor cannot be positioned on the current page, a new page is created which includes any page footers that the current page may have. The list cursor is positioned in the first position of the first line under the page header of the new page.

▶ The statement is only executed at the start of the page if this page is the first in a list level, or if it was generated using the statement NEW-PAGE.

Note

In most application cases, this variant of the statement SKIP works as if it creates n blank lines. You need to ensure, however, that these blank lines have no content that can be formatted by the FORMAT statement. Format-table blank lines can only be generated by the WRITE statement in combination with SET BLANK LINES ON.

Positioning the list cursor in any lines of a page

Syntax

```
SKIP TO LINE line.
```

This statement positions the list cursor in the first position of the on the current page whose number is determined by the value in line. For line, a data object of type i is expected. If the value of line is smaller than or equal to 0, or larger than the page length defined in sy-linct using the addition LINE-COUNT of the program-starting statement or NEW-PAGE, the addition TO LINE is ignored and the statement SKIP without additions is executed instead (see above).

Note
If the list cursor is positioned in the first list line using SKIP TO LINE and the list has a standard page header, the output in the first line is overwritten by the standard header. If, however, the cursor is positioned using SKIP TO LINE in the lines of page headers and page footers that are defined for TOP-OF-PAGE and END-OF-PAGE, the page headers or footers are overwritten.

Example
The first SKIP statement generates a blank line for the event TOP-OF-PAGE. The second SKIP statement positions the list cursor in this line.

```
REPORT ... NO STANDARD PAGE HEADING.

DATA sum TYPE i.

TOP-OF-PAGE.
  SKIP.
  ULINE.

START-OF-SELECTION.
  DO 10 TIMES.
    WRITE / sy-index.
    sum = sum + sy-index.
  ENDDO.

  SKIP TO LINE 1.
  WRITE: 'Numbers with sum' COLOR COL_HEADING,
         sum                COLOR COL_TOTAL.
```

27.2.5.2 Creating Blank Lines

```
WRITE
```

Generating a blank line.

Syntax

```
WRITE /.
```

This statement functions like the statement SKIP without additions.

Note
This is a special form of the WRITE statement in which no data object is specified.

27.2.5.3 Line Breaks and Fixed Lines When Scrolling Horizontally

```
NEW-LINE
```

Placing the list cursor in the next line and fixing the line.

Syntax

```
NEW-LINE [NO-SCROLLING|SCROLLING].
```

This statement sets the list cursor to the first position of the next line after the current line, provided that the current position of the list cursor results from a previous output statement. In the first line of a new page, and if the current list cursor was set with the statements SKIP, NEW-LINE, NEW-PAGE or BACK into the list line, NEW-LINE does not affect the list cursor.

The addition NO-SCROLLING has the effect that the first line of the current list level, which was written after the statement NEW-LINE using an output statement (WRITE, ULINE), cannot be moved horizontally. This applies to scrolling in the list displayed on the screen by the user as well as to scrolling with the statement SCROLL. Vertical mobility is not affected.

The addition SCROLLING undoes the addition NO-SCROLLING (default setting). The addition NO-SCROLLING can only be undone before an output statement is executed. Once a line has been frozen, you no longer can change this state.

Note

To freeze an area that covers several lines, use the statement `SET LEFT SCROLL-BOUNDARY`.

Example

The line with the output "Fixed Line" will not be moved during horizontal scrolling.

```
WRITE / 'Scrollable Line'.
NEW-LINE NO-SCROLLING.
WRITE: / 'Fixed Line',
       / 'Scrollable Line'.
```

27.2.5.4 Logical Positioning

```
BACK
```

Positioning the list cursor in the first unit of a logical unit.

Syntax

```
BACK.
```

This statement positions the list cursor on the first position of the first line in a logical unit. A list contains the following logical units.

▶ **A line block defined with `RESERVE`.**
If `BACK` is executed after the `RESERVE` statement, the list cursor is placed in the first line of the current line block.

▶ **The lines within a self-defined page header.**
If `BACK` is executed within the event block for `TOP-OF-PAGE` and is not placed after `RESERVE`, the list cursor will be positioned in the first line underneath the standard page header.

▶ **The lines of a page underneath the page header.**
If `BACK` is executed outside of the event block for `TOP-OF-PAGE` and not after `RESERVE`, the list cursor will be positioned in the first line underneath the page header.

Example

Output of a small input mask. The input fields are positioned after the description.

```
DATA: title(3)  TYPE c,
      sname(20) TYPE c,
      fname(20) TYPE c.
```

```
SKIP 5.

RESERVE 3 LINES.
WRITE: / 'Title',
       / 'Second name',
       / 'First name'.

BACK.
WRITE: /14 title INPUT,
       /14 sname INPUT,
       /14 fname INPUT.
```

27.2.6 Horizontal Positioning of the List Cursor

```
POSITION
```

Positioning the list cursor in a specific position.

Syntax

```
POSITION pos.
```

This statement places the list cursor at the position in the current line in the list buffer specified in pos. The program expects a data object of the type i for pos. If the value of pos is 0 or less or is greater than the page length in sy-linsz defined with the addition LINE-SIZE to the program initiating statement or NEW-PAGE, all subsequent output statements do not create any output until the list cursor is positioned within a line again.

Notes

▶ An output statement that follows POSITION and does not have its own position specification pos after AT writes to the specified position, regardless whether sufficient space is available in the line, and cuts off the output length accordingly if necessary.

▶ When an output position is specified within an existing output, please note that the position always refers to the characters stored in the list buffer. If characters that require more than one column in the list are displayed in a Unicode system, the output position displayed can differ from the specified output position, and the content displayed for output that has been partially overwritten can move, depending on the character used to overwrite.

Example

Definition and use of a macro `write_frame` to draw frames around `WRITE` output. The `POSITION` statement positions the list cursor for subsequent output.

```
DATA: x TYPE i, y TYPE i, z TYPE i.

DEFINE write_frame.
  x = sy-colno. y = sy-linno.
  WRITE: '|' NO-GAP, &1 NO-GAP, '|' NO-GAP.
  z = sy-colno - x.
  y = y - 1. SKIP TO LINE y.
  ULINE AT x(z).
  y = y + 2. SKIP TO LINE y.
  ULINE AT x(z).
  y = y - 1. x = sy-colno. SKIP TO LINE y. POSITION x.
END-OF-DEFINITION.

SKIP.
WRITE        'Demonstrating'.
write_frame 'dynamic frames'.
WRITE        'in'.
write_frame 'ABAP'.
WRITE        'output lists.'.
```

27.2.7   Fixed Area When Scrolling Horizontally

```
SET LEFT SCROLL-BOUNDARY
```

Setting the left margin for the movable area.

Syntax

```
SET LEFT SCROLL-BOUNDARY [COLUMN col].
```

This command sets the left-hand margin of the horizontally movable area of the current page. This applies to both user-activated scrolling through the list displayed on-screen and to scrolling activated by the `SCROLL` command. For the command to work properly, the list cursor has to be positioned in a page with an output command or with `SKIP`. The command has an effect only on this page. If the command is executed multiple times for one page, the last command is the one that takes effect.

If the addition `COLUMN` is not specified, all columns of the current page that are located to the left of the current position of the list cursor (sy-colno) are excluded from horizontal scrolling. If the addition COLUMN is specified, this applies to all columns in the current page that are located to the left of the position specified in col. col refers to the columns in the list displayed. A data object of the type i is expected for col. If the value in col is less than or equal to 0, or greater than the current list width, the command has no effect.

Notes

▶ Only the lower or upper limit of output data objects should be used as the margin of a movable area, because in Unicode systems only the positions for these in the list buffer and in the list displayed are guaranteed to match.

▶ To prevent an entire line from being horizontally movable, use the NEW-LINE NO-SCROLLING command.

Example

Output of a tabular list of airlines from the database table SCARR, in which the area for output from the key field is fixed.

```
DATA scarr_wa TYPE scarr.

SELECT *
       FROM scarr
       INTO scarr_wa.
  WRITE: / scarr_wa-carrid COLOR COL_KEY.
  SET LEFT SCROLL-BOUNDARY.
  WRITE: scarr_wa-carrname,
         scarr_wa-currcode,
         (20) scarr_wa-url.
ENDSELECT.
```

27.2.8 Page Breaks and Print Lists

```
NEW-PAGE
```

Creation of a new page.

Syntax

```
NEW-PAGE [page_options] [spool_options].
```

This statement allows you to create a new page in the current list and to write the subsequent list output into a print list. The additions *page_options* determine the general properties of the new page. The additions *spool_options* control the print list output.

The statement NEW-PAGE completes the current page. If on the current page an output was made with WRITE or ULINE, then a new page is created and the value in sy-pagno is increased by 1. Between the individual pages a blank line is inserted. The list cursor is set to the first position of the first line under the standard page header of the new page.

The new page is created independent of the current list cursor position underneath the last line of the current page in which an output occurred.

Notes

▶ With the NEW-PAGE statement, you cannot create empty pages.

▶ The list event END-OF-PAGE is not triggered. The event TOP-OF-PAGE is triggered before the first output on the new page.

27.2.8.1 Page-Related Additions

Syntax of *page_options*

```
...  [WITH-TITLE|NO-TITLE]
     [WITH-HEADING|NO-HEADING]
     [LINE-COUNT page_lines]
     [LINE-SIZE width]
     [NO-TOPOFPAGE] ...
```

These additions set properties of the list for all subsequent pages of the current list level, until they are set again in another NEW-PAGE statement. The additions overrule the identically named additions in the program introduction statement (see Section 3.2.1).

Influencing the standard page header

Syntax

```
...  [WITH-TITLE|NO-TITLE]
     [WITH-HEADING|NO-HEADING] ...
```

These additions determine which components of the standard page header are given out for the subsequent pages of the current list level. The standard page header consists of a standard heading and of column headings.

The additions WITH-TITLE and NO-TITLE switch the output of the standard title on or off for the subsequent pages. The predefined default setting for basic lists is WITH-TITLE and for detail lists NO-TITLE.

The additions WITH-HEADING and NO-HEADING switch the output of the column headings on or off for all subsequent pages. The predefined default setting for basic lists is WITH-HEADING and for detail lists NO-HEADING.

Note

For the basic list, these additions overrule the setting made in the program introduction statement. The addition NO STANDARD PAGE HEADING that you can use there is identical to the simultaneous use of NO-TITLE and NO-HEADING, except that the latter does not influence the system field sy-wtitl.

Defining the page length

Syntax

```
... LINE-COUNT page_lines ...
```

This addition determines the page length of the subsequent pages of the current list level in page_length and sets sy-linct to this value. For page_length, a data object of type i is expected. If the value of page_lines is less than or equal to 0 or greater than 60,000, then the page length is set to 60,000. For the basic list, the addition overrules the page length determined in the program introduction statement.

The page length determines how many lines including the page header and the page footer can be written onto a list page. If an output writes into a line outside the current page length or into the area reserved for the page footer of a basic list, a new page is automatically created.

Notes

The lines reserved in the program introduction statement for the page footer of the basic list cannot be changed with the addition LINE-COUNT of the NEW-PAGE statement. For detail lists, you cannot create a page footer.

Example

Demonstration of automatic page breaks on a basic list. The pages have two-line page headers and page footers defined after TOP-OF-PAGE and END-OF-PAGE. The page length is determined after NEW-PAGE. The program gives out five pages.

```
REPORT ... NO STANDARD PAGE HEADING LINE-COUNT 0(2).

TOP-OF-PAGE.
  WRITE sy-pagno.
  ULINE.
```

```
END-OF-PAGE.
  ULINE.
  WRITE 'Footer'.

START-OF-SELECTION.
  NEW-PAGE LINE-COUNT 6.
  DO 10 TIMES.
    WRITE / sy-index.
  ENDDO.
```

Defining the page width

Syntax

... LINE-SIZE width ...

This addition sets the page width of the current list level to the value in width and sets sy-linsz to this value. The line width determines the number of characters in the list buffer as well as the number of columns in the displayed list. For width, a data object of type i is expected. The value of width must not be negative. If the value of width is equal to 0 or greater than 1,023, the line width is set to a default width that depends on the window width of the current dynpro (sy-scols) but is at least as wide as the width of an SAP window in standard size. For the basic list, the addition overrules the page width determined in the program introduction statement.

The addition is effective only if no output has yet been sent to the current list level. The page width of a written list cannot be changed.

Note
The currently valid maximum value for the line width is stored in the constant slist_max_linesize of the type group SLIST. There, also a type slist_max_listline of type c and length slist_max_linesize is defined.

Example
Creation of a basic list and details lists with different page-width values. Of the standard page header, only the standard title is displayed.

```
REPORT ... NO STANDARD PAGE HEADING.

START-OF-SELECTION.
  NEW-PAGE WITH-TITLE LINE-SIZE 40.
  WRITE 'Basic list'.
```

```
AT LINE-SELECTION.
   NEW-PAGE WITH-TITLE LINE-SIZE 20.
   WRITE 'Secondary list'.
```

Controlling the list event

Syntax

```
... NO-TOPOFPAGE ...
```

This addition suppresses the event TOP-OF-PAGE on the new page and on all pages of the current list level that are automatically created up to the next NEW-PAGE statement. If the addition NO-TOPOFPAGE is not specified, the event TOP-OF-PAGE is triggered before the output to a new page.

Example

The program below creates six pages. The event TOP-OF-PAGE is triggered only on the first page.

```
REPORT ... NO STANDARD PAGE HEADING.

START-OF-SELECTION.
   ULINE.
   NEW-PAGE NO-TOPOFPAGE LINE-COUNT 2.
   DO 10 TIMES.
     WRITE / sy-index.
   ENDDO.

TOP-OF-PAGE.
   WRITE 'Basic list'.
```

27.2.8.2 Print List-Related Additions

Syntax of *spool_options*

```
... { PRINT ON [NEW-SECTION] spool_parameters }
  | { PRINT OFF } ...
```

The addition PRINT ON ensures that the subsequent list output is written into a print list for the SAP spool system. Use the additions *spool_parameters* to determine the print parameters and the archiving parameters of the spool request. The addition PRINT OFF closes the current print list. After the NEW-PAGE PRINT ON statement, no other NEW-PAGE statement is allowed to have the PRINT ON addition until the print list is closed with the PRINT OFF addition.

Every NEW-PAGE PRINT ON statement should be closed within the same processing block using NEW-PAGE PRINT OFF. Otherwise, the response can become undefined.

Initiating a print-list output

Syntax

```
... PRINT ON [NEW-SECTION] ...
```

The addition PRINT ON has the effect that all subsequent output statements are written into a print list. The print list is connected to a spool request. The number of the spool request is placed into sy-spono by the first output statement. During its creation, the print list is sent to the SAP spool system page by page.

In one internal mode, only one spool request can be managed simultaneously. If the current list is a screen list, its creation is interrupted and a new spool request is created. If a print list is already being created and the addition NEW-SECTION is not used, then no new spool request will be generated, but the output is appended to the current print list. The specified parameters *spool_parameters* apply for the next spool request. If a print list is already being created and the addition NEW-SECTION is used, there are two options:

▶ If the specified print parameters in *spool_parameters* correspond to the newly created list and the print parameter prnew in the structure pri_params is initial, no new spool request is generated and the output is appended to the current print list.

▶ If the specified print parameters in *spool_parameters* do not correspond to the newly created list or the print parameter prnew in the structure pri_params is not initial, the current spool request is closed and a new spool request is generated.

Note
Within a program, a print list started with NEW-PAGE PRINT ON must be closed with NEW-PAGE PRINT OFF before a new print list can be started. For this reason, a situation in which a new print list is started during the creation of another print list can occur only in programs that are called with SUBMIT TO SAP-SPOOL or for which the user on the selection screen chose **Execute and Print**.

Ending a print list output

Syntax

```
... PRINT OFF ...
```

The addition PRINT OFF closes the print list by sending the current page to the SAP spool system and releasing the respective spool request. For the subsequent output statements, you must distinguish between the following cases:

▶ The current print list was started by the NEW-PAGE PRINT ON statement, which interrupted a screen list: The subsequent output is again placed in the interrupted screen list.

▶ The current print list was started by the NEW-PAGE PRINT ON statement and the previous list was a print list: A new spool request is generated, and the subsequent output statements are placed in a new print list. If in the statement NEW-PAGE PRINT ON, you specify print parameters without the NEW-SECTION addition, these are used; otherwise the parameters of the previous spool request are used.

▶ The current spool request was generated using the SUBMIT TO SAP-SPOOL statement or by choosing **Execute and Print** on a selection screen: A new spool request with the same print parameters is generated.

Note
At the end of the program and at every list event AT LINE-SELECTION, AT PFnn and AT USER-COMMAND, the statement NEW-PAGE PRINT OFF is implicitly executed.

Print parameters

Syntax of *spool_parameters*

```
... PARAMETERS pri_params
    [ARCHIVE PARAMETERS arc_params]
    NO DIALOG ...
```

Use these additions to provide the spool request with print parameters and archiving parameters. The latter are necessary if you want to archive the print list using SAP ArchiveLink.

Use the addition PARAMETERS to pass the print parameters in a structure pri_params of data type PRI_PARAMS from the ABAP Dictionary. If archiving is specified in pri_params, you must pass the archiving parameters with the addition ARCHIVE PARAMETERS in a structure arc_params of data type ARC_PARAMS from the ABAP Dictionary.

Structures of the data types PRI_PARAMS and ARC_PARAMS must be filled exclusively with the function module GET_PRINT_PARAMETERS (see Section C.1.1). When calling the function module, you can set individual or all print parameters in the program and/or display a print dialog window. The function module creates in its output parameters a set of valid print and archiving parameters to be used as pri_params and arc_params.

The addition NO DIALOG suppresses the dialog window that by default appears when using the PRINT ON addition.

Notes

▶ Always use these additions and use them as described above. In particular, suppress the print dialog window that appears by default. When using the default print dialog window, inconsistent parameters may be passed to the program if the user leaves the window using **Exit**. Instead, display the print dialog window when you execute the function module GET_PRINT_PARAMETERS. This function module has an output parameter VALID, which signals the consistency of the generated print parameters (see Section C.1.1).

▶ Using the addition NO DIALOG without simultaneously passing print parameters is allowed only outside of ABAP Objects and results in a warning in the syntax check. The print parameters are then taken from the user master record, as far as possible.

▶ Apart from the additions shown here, there is a number of obsolete print parameters (see Section 42.15.2).

Example
Creating print lists during the list event AT LINE-SELECTION. The print parameters are determined by the function module GET_PRINT_PARAMETERS before the basic list is created.

```
REPORT ... NO STANDARD PAGE HEADING.

DATA: spfli_wa    TYPE spfli,
      sflight_wa TYPE sflight.

DATA: print_parameters TYPE pri_params,
      valid_flag(1)    TYPE c.

START-OF-SELECTION.
```

```
CALL FUNCTION 'GET_PRINT_PARAMETERS'
  IMPORTING
    out_parameters        = print_parameters
    valid                 = valid_flag
  EXCEPTIONS
    invalid_print_params = 2
    OTHERS                = 4.

IF valid_flag = 'X' AND sy-subrc = 0.
  SELECT carrid connid
         FROM spfli
         INTO CORRESPONDING FIELDS OF spfli_wa.
    WRITE: / spfli_wa-carrid, spfli_wa-connid.
    HIDE:    spfli_wa-carrid, spfli_wa-connid.
  ENDSELECT.
ELSE.
  ...
ENDIF.

AT LINE-SELECTION.
  NEW-PAGE PRINT ON PARAMETERS print_parameters
                   NO DIALOG.
  SELECT *
         FROM sflight
         INTO sflight_wa
         WHERE carrid = spfli_wa-carrid AND
               connid = spfli_wa-connid.
    WRITE: / sflight_wa-carrid, sflight_wa-connid,
             sflight_wa-fldate ...
  ENDSELECT.
  NEW-PAGE PRINT OFF.
```

27.2.9 Conditional Page Break

RESERVE

Page break depending on the lines that are still available.

Syntax

`RESERVE n LINES.`

This statement creates a page break if there is not enough space left on the current list page between the last output and the page end or page footer, as specified in n. A data object of type i is expected for n. No page break is triggered if the value of n is smaller than or equal to 0.

The page break triggers the list event END-OF-PAGE regardless of whether a page footer was defined in the statement introducing the program.

In addition, the statement RESERVE influences the behavior of the statement BACK (see Section 27.2.4).

Note

If the page length is greater than the value of n, you can define line blocks with the statement RESERVE that can only be displayed closed on one side.

Example

The three lines given out in the DO loop and the blank line that follows them form a line block and are not separated by page breaks.

```
REPORT ... NO STANDARD PAGE HEADING LINE-COUNT 10(2).

START-OF-SELECTION.
  DO 5 TIMES.
    RESERVE 4 LINES.
    WRITE: / '1', / '2', / '3'.
    SKIP.
  ENDDO.

END-OF-PAGE.
  ULINE.
  WRITE sy-pagno.
```

27.2.10 Saving Variables with List Lines

```
HIDE
```

Saving data objects with list lines.

Syntax

```
HIDE dobj.
```

This statement stores in the current list level the content of the variable dobj together with the current list line whose line number is contained in sy-linno. The data type of the variables dobj must be flat, and no field symbols can be specified that point to rows of internal tables. No class attributes can be specified. The stored values can be read as follows.

▶ For each user action in a displayed screen list that leads to a list result, all the row values stored using HIDE of the row on which the screen cursor is positioned at the time of the event are assigned to the respective variables.

▶ If a list row of an arbitrary list level is read or modified using the statements READ LINE or MODIFY LINE (see Section 27.3), all the values of this row stored using HIDE are assigned to the respective variables.

Notes

▶ The HIDE statement works whether the list cursor was set or not set. In particular, variables can be stored for empty list rows, that is, rows in which the list cursor was positioned using statements like SKIP.

▶ The HIDE statement should be executed immediately at the statement that has set the list cursor in the row.

▶ Outside of classes, constants and literals that cannot be read in list results and in the statement READ LINE can be specified for dobj.

Example

Storing square numbers and cubic numbers into a list of numbers. The example shows that arbitrary variables can be stored independently of the row content. In the real situation, one would more likely store only the number and execute the calculation, when required, in the event block for AT LINE-SELECTION.

```
REPORT ...

DATA: square TYPE i,
      cube   TYPE i.

START-OF-SELECTION.
  FORMAT HOTSPOT.
  DO 10 TIMES.
    square = sy-index ** 2.
    cube   = sy-index ** 3.
    WRITE / sy-index.
    HIDE: square, cube.
  ENDDO.

AT LINE-SELECTION.
  WRITE: square, cube.
```

27.2.11 Print List Page Margins

SET MARGIN

Defining the left and top margins for print lists.

Syntax

```
SET MARGIN macol [marow].
```

This statement determines the left margin of a print list to the columns specified in `macol` and the upper margin to the rows specified in `marow` and sets the system fields `sy-macol` and `sy-marow` to these values. For `macol` and `marow`, data objects of type `i` are expected, the values of which lie the current page width and page length. If `macol` or `marow` contain invalid values, the associated operand is ignored.

The set values apply for the current page and all subsequent pages until the next `SET MARGIN` statement. If there are several `SET MARGIN` statements on one page, the last statement always applies.

`SET MARGIN` has no effect on displaying screen lists. The set margins are only inserted in the list as blank characters or empty lines if a list page is sent to the SAP spool system. This applies for print lists created using `NEW-PAGE PRINT ON`, `SUBMIT TO SAP-SPOOL`, and by the selection of **Execute and Print** on the selection screen. `SET MARGIN` also applies if a screen list is printed while it is being displayed, through selection of **Print** (function code "PRI").

Note

For printers with an active list driver, margins can be defined in millimeters in the print dialog. When pages are sent from the spool system to the printer, the pages, including the margins set using `SET MARGIN`, are set up within these margins.

27.2.12   Controlling Print Lists

```
PRINT-CONTROL
```

Setting print formats and creating index entries for archiving.

Syntax

```
PRINT-CONTROL { { formats|{FUNCTION code}
                  [LINE line] [POSITION col] }
              | { INDEX-LINE index_line } }.
```

This statement formats areas of print lists or creates index entries in print lists to be archived.

The statement PRINT-CONTROLS only works for print lists created with NEW-PAGE PRINT ON, SUBMIT TO SAP-SPOOL, and through selection of **Execute and Print** on the selection screen. It does not work for a screen list that has been printed during display by selecting **Print** (function code "PRI").

27.2.12.1 Formatting Print Lists

Syntax

```
... formats|{FUNCTION code}
    [LINE line] [POSITION col] ...
```

This variant sets a print format starting from the line specified in line and the position specified in col for all subsequent output statements of the current page. If the additions LINE or POSITION are not specified, the current position of the list cursor (sy-linno, sy-colno) is used. For line and col, data objects of type i are expected whose values are within the current page width or page length. If line or col contain invalid values, the statement is ignored.

The possible print formats formats are listed in Table 27.6. The runtime environment converts these entries into printer-independent codes called print control. When a list is actually printed, the print control codes are translated into printer-specific control characters.

Formats	Print Control	Explanation
CPI cpi	CIcpi	characters per inch
LPI lpi	LIlpi	lines per inch
COLOR BLACK	CO001	color black
COLOR RED	CO002	color red
COLOR BLUE	CO003	color blue
COLOR GREEN	CO004	color green
COLOR YELLOW	CO005	color yellow
COLOR PINK	CO006	color pink
FONT font	FOfont	font

Table 27.6 Print formats of the PRINT-CONTROL statement. For cpi, lpi, font, left and siz, data objects of type i are expected.

Formats	Print Control	Explanation
LEFT MARGIN left	LMleft	left margin
SIZE siz	SIsiz	font size

Table 27.6 Print formats of the PRINT-CONTROL statement. For cpi, lpi, font, left and siz, data objects of type i are expected. (cont.)

There are more print control codes than print formats `formats` that can be specified in the statement PRINT-CONTROL. All print control codes can also be specified directly in `code` using the addition FUNCTION. `code` must be a flat character-type data object that contains a valid print control code. Invalid content is ignored. A list of valid print control codes and their assignment to printers is available in the spool administration (transaction SPAD).

Notes

▶ The statement PRINT-CONTROL should be used only for print formats that cannot also be set using the formatting options of the statements WRITE and FORMAT, or in the print dialog.

▶ The statement PRINT-CONTROL must be executed for every page to be formatted. If the additions LINE and POSITION are used, the source-text position of the statement PRINT-CONTROL in relation to the output statements becomes irrelevant.

27.2.12.2 Inserting Index Lines

Syntax

```
... INDEX-LINE index_line ...
```

This addition inserts the content of the data object `index_line` into the current print list as an index line. `index_line` must be a flat character-type data object. If the list cursor of an output statement has been set in the current list line, the index line is inserted after the end of the line.

An index line is sent to the spool system as a part of the print list and is displayed there, although not included in the print output. When archiving the list using SAP ArchiveLink, the index lines are stored in a description file.

When archiving, the spool system divides a list into a data file and a description file. The data file contains the actual print lists, and the description file contains the index lines. If the content of the index lines is structured according to a convention described in the SAP ArchiveLink documentation, index lines enable an effective search in archived lists.

Example

Inserting index lines in a list of square numbers. After every hundredth line, index lines for archiving are generated (DAIN lines) using the statement PRINT-CONTROL. The structure of the DAIN lines is defined at the start of the list in two additional index lines (DKEY lines). If the user selects **Execute and Print** on the selection screen and stores the list in the print dialog, the archived list can be searched by the indices.

```
PARAMETERS number TYPE i.

DATA: index      TYPE i,
      square     TYPE f,
      numb       TYPE i,
      num(4)     TYPE c,
      dkey(100) TYPE c, dain(100) TYPE c.

dkey      = 'DKEYIndex'.
dkey+44 = '0'.
dkey+47 = '3'.
PRINT-CONTROL INDEX-LINE dkey.

CLEAR dkey.

dkey ='DKEYNumber'.
dkey+44 = '3'.
dkey+47 = '4'.
PRINT-CONTROL INDEX-LINE dkey.

index = 0.
DO number TIMES.
  index = index + 1.
  IF index = 100.
    numb = sy-index / 100.
    WRITE numb TO num LEFT-JUSTIFIED.
    CONCATENATE 'DAIN' 'IDX' num INTO dain.
    PRINT-CONTROL INDEX-LINE dain.
    index = 0.
  ENDIF.
  square = sy-index ** 2.
  WRITE: / sy-index, square.
ENDDO.
```

27.3   Processing Lists in the List Buffer

The statements described in the following sections process lists that are already stored as screen lists in the list buffer. Print lists which are sent page by page to the SAP spool system cannot be processed in this manner.

27.3.1   Reading List Lines

```
READ LINE
```

Reading list lines in the list buffer.

Syntax

```
READ { {LINE line [{OF PAGE page}|{OF CURRENT PAGE}]
                  [INDEX idx]}
     | {CURRENT LINE} }
     [result].
```

This statement assigns the content of a row stored in the list buffer to the system field `sy-lisel` and allows other target fields to be specified in `result`. In addition, all values for this row stored with `HIDE` are assigned to the respective variables.

The row to be read is specified with the addition `LINE` or with `CURRENT LINE`.

▶ For the addition `LINE`, a data object of the type `i` is expected for `line`, which includes the line number based on the list page of a list level. The list level can be specified with the addition `INDEX`, where a data object (which contains the list index) of type `i` is expected for `idx`. The value of `idx` must be greater than or equal to 0. If the addition `INDEX` is not specified, then the list level 0 (the basic list itself) is selected during the creation of the basic list, and the list level at which the event was triggered (`sy-listi`) is selected during the processing of a list event. The list page can be specified either with `PAGE page` or with `CURRENT PAGE`. For `page`, a data object of the type `i` that contains the page number of an existing page of the list level is expected. No row is selected if no row is found for the specified values in `line`, `idx` and `page`. `CURRENT PAGE` indicates the topmost displayed page of the list, on which the last list event has taken place. No row is selected while creating the basic list. If no addition is specified for the page, then the current page (`sy-pagnc`) is selected during the creation of the basic list, and the page on which the event was triggered (sy-cpage) is selected during the processing of a list event.

▶ For the addition CURRENT LINE, the line on which the screen cursor was positioned during a preceding list event (sy-lilli) or the last row read with a preceding READ LINE statement is selected. No row is selected while creating the basic list.

Syntax

```
...  [LINE VALUE INTO wa]
     [FIELD VALUE dobj1 [INTO wa1] dobj2 [INTO wa2] ...] ...
```

The addition LINE VALUE assigns the formatted content of the complete list row in the list buffer to the data object wa. The addition FIELD VALUE assigns the output areas of single data objects dobj1, dobj2, ... that have been put out to the list buffer to these data objects, or—if specified— to the data objects wa1, wa2, ... For wa or wa1, wa2, ..., character-type (before Release 6.10 flat) data objects are expected. The list row or the data objects dobj1, dobj2, ... are treated as if they had the data type c, so that closing blanks are not accepted.

With data objects dobj1, dobj2, ... that have been put out multiple times to a row, only the first one is read out. If a data object dobj1, dobj2, ... is not found at all, the specification is ignored.

If the output area of a data object is to be read that was addressed in the WRITE-statement via a field symbol, and the same data object is no longer assigned to the field symbol, then the name of the data object and not the name of the field symbol must be specified.

Note

The content of the row or of single output areas is character-type and prepared according to the rules for the WRITE-statement. During the assignment, the conversion rules from Section A.2.2 apply. This fact can lead to incompatibilities with the target fields dobj1, dobj2, ... or wa1, wa2, ..., especially if these are numeric and the output contains separators. Due to this, the usage of READ LINE is mainly recommended for analysis of fields ready-for-input, whereas for other analyses, you can save values type-relatedly with HIDE.

Return values

sy-subrc	Relevance
0	The specified row is available and was read.
Not equal to 0	The specified row does not exist.

Example

This example reads all rows of the basic list after selecting a row. The content of the checkbox is assigned to the output data object `flag`. A target field `wa` with length 10 is used for the date, since this is the length of the output area and contains separators. If you assigned `date` to the output field, the area length would be reduced. The checked data is displayed in the details list.

```
DATA: date    TYPE d,
      flag(1) TYPE c,
      wa(10)  TYPE c.

START-OF-SELECTION.
  date = sy-datum.
  DO 10 TIMES.
    date = date + sy-index.
    WRITE: / flag AS CHECKBOX, (10) date.
  ENDDO.

AT LINE-SELECTION.
  DO.
    READ LINE sy-index FIELD VALUE flag
                                   date INTO wa.
    IF sy-subrc <> 0.
      EXIT.
    ELSEIF flag = 'X'.
      WRITE / wa.
    ENDIF.
  ENDDO.
```

27.3.2   Modifying List Lines

MODIFY LINE

Changing list lines in the list buffer.

Syntax

```
MODIFY { {LINE line [OF {PAGE page}|{CURRENT PAGE}]
                    [INDEX idx]}
       | {CURRENT LINE} }
       [source].
```

This statement overwrites a line saved in the list buffer with the content of the sy-lisel system field and permits additional modifications as specified in *source*. Furthermore, all values that are saved for this line using HIDE are assigned the relevant variables.

The line to be changed is specified with the LINE addition or with CURRENT LINE. The syntax and description of the additions are the same as for the READ LINE statement (see Section 27.3.1).

The first output of a data object in the list buffer with the WRITE statement defines the output length, which cannot be changed by the MODIFY statement. The MODIFY statement ignores perhaps any alignments that are specified for the output with CENTERED or RIGHT-JUSTIFIED.

Syntax of *source*

```
... [LINE VALUE FROM wa]
    [FIELD VALUE dobj1 [FROM wa1]
                dobj2 [FROM wa2] ...]
    [LINE FORMAT ext_format_options]
    [FIELD FORMAT dobj1 ext_format_options1
                  dobj2 ext_format_options2 ...] ...
```

These additions modify the list line after it was overwritten with the content of the sy-lisel system field.

▶ The LINE VALUE addition overwrites the whole list line with the content of wa. The FIELD VALUE addition overwrites the output areas of individual dobj1, dobj2, ... data objects that are given out in the list line with the current content of these objects, or—if it is specified—the content of the wa1, wa2, ... data objects. For wa or wa1, wa2, ..., character-type data objects (before Release 6.10 flat) are expected, and these are truncated on the right if they are too long. For data objects that are too short, the line or the output areas are filled from the right with blank characters. The FIELD VALUE specification overrides the LINE VALUE specification.

▶ For *ext_format_options*, one or more additions of the FORMAT statement (see Section 27.2.3) can be specified. The LINE FORMAT addition formats the whole list line accordingly; whereas FIELD FORMAT formats only the output areas of the dobj1, dobj2, … data objects that are given out in the list line. The FIELD FORMAT specification overrides the LINE FORMAT specification.

Of dobj1, dobj2, … data objects with the same name that are given out several times in a line, only the first one is processed. If there is no dobj1, dobj2, … data object at all, the specification is ignored.

Return values

sy-subrc	Meaning
0	The specified line is available and was changed.
Not equal to 0	The specified line is not available.

Notes

▶ We recommend that you fill the sy-lisel system field before you execute the MODIFY LINE statement with the content of the list line to be changed, and then change the line exclusively using the information in source, not by modifying sy-lisel. The sy-lisel system field is filled either using list events or with the READ LINE statement.

▶ For modifying icons and quick infos in list lines, you can use the LIST_ICON_PREPARE_FOR_MODIFY and LIST_MODIFY_QUICKINFO function modules.

Example

When you double-click on a line in the basic list, the background of the lines that are given out becomes yellow, and the background of the remaining list becomes green.

```
START-OF-SELECTION.
  DO 10 TIMES.
    WRITE / sy-index.
  ENDDO.

AT LINE-SELECTION.
  MODIFY CURRENT LINE FIELD FORMAT sy-index COLOR 3
                      LINE FORMAT COLOR 5.
```

27.3.3   Scrolling Lists

SCROLL LIST

Scrolls the screen list section vertically or horizontally.

Syntax

SCROLL LIST [*horizontal*] [*vertical*] [**INDEX** idx].

This statement scrolls the display area of a list stored in the list buffer to the position specified in *horizontal* and/or *vertical*. At least one of these additions must be specified in which all horizontal specifications refer to the columns of a displayed list. The corresponding section is displayed when the list is next displayed. The list level can be specified with the addition INDEX, where a data object (which includes the list index) of the type i is expected for idx. The value of idx must be greater than or equal to 0. If the addition INDEX is not specified, then the list level 0 (the basic list itself) is selected during the creation of the basic list, and the list level at which the event is triggered (sy-listi) is selected during the processing of a list event. If the list level specified in idx is not available, sy-subrc is set to the value 8.

Without using the statement SCROLL, a list is displayed during its initial display, beginning with the first column of the first row. If the user navigates from a details list back to a lower list level, the list is displayed with the section it had when it was last displayed. The SCROLL statement sets either a new first column or a new first row or both. Each SCROLL statement sets only the size specified in it, without changing the other positions.

Return values

sy-subrc	Relevance
0	Screen section was successfully scrolled.
4	Complete scrolling not possible because the list margin was reached.
8	Scrolling not possible because the specified list level does not exist.

Note

While scrolling through the list just created (sy-lsind), please note that a SCROLL statement has no effect prior to the first output statement, since the list does not yet exist in the list buffer.

Syntax of *horizontal*

```
... {TO COLUMN col} | {{LEFT|RIGHT} [BY n PLACES]} ...
```

These additions are used to scroll horizontally in the list.

▶ The addition TO COLUMN specifies the value from col for the first column in the screen segment. A type i data object is expected for col. If the value in col is 0 or smaller, it is processed as 1, and if it is greater than the current line width, it is treated as if it was of the same line width and sy-subrc is set to the value 4.

▶ The addition LEFT without BY n PLACES specifies the value of 1 for the first column in the screen segment. The addition LEFT with BY n PLACES specifies the current first column (sy-staco) minus the value of n as the first column in the display segment; a type i data object is required for n. If the result is 0 or less, it is processed as 1 and sy-subrc is set to 4.

▶ The addition RIGHT without BY n PLACES specifies the line length (sy-linsz) minus the window width (sy-scols minus 2) for the first column in the screen segment. If the result is 0 or less, it is processed as 1. The addition RIGHT with BY n PLACES specifies the current first column (sy-staco) plus the value in n for the first column in the display segment. A type i data object is expected for n. If the result is greater than the current line length, it is processed as if it were the same as the current line length and sy-subrc is set to 4.

Syntax of *vertical*

```
... {TO {{FIRST PAGE}|{LAST PAGE}|{PAGE pag}} [LINE lin]}
  | {{FORWARD|BACKWARD} [n PAGES]} ...
```

These additions are used to scroll vertically in the list.

▶ The addition TO FIRST PAGE defines the top page in the screen segment on the first page of the list.

▶ The addition TO LAST PAGE defines the top page in the screen segment on the last page of the list.

▶ The addition TO PAGE pag defines the top page in the screen segment on the page specified in pag; a type i data object is expected for pag. If the value in pag is 0 or less, it is processed as 1. If greater than the number of pages, it is processed as if it were the same and sy-subrc is set to 4.

▶ The addition `LINE` determines which line is displayed first on the pages selected with `PAGE`. Without the addition `LINE`, the list is displayed starting with the first line on the selected page. If the addition `LINE` is specified, the line on the selected page specified in `lin` is displayed under the page header. The page header itself is not counted. A type `i` data object is required for `lin`. If the value in `lin` is 0 or less, it is processed as 1, while if it is greater than the page length, it is processed as if it were the same and `sy-subrc` is set to 4.

▶ The additions `FORWARD` and `BACKWARD` without n `PAGES` move the current screen segment up or down by the current number of lines in the window (`sy-srows`). The page header of the top page displayed is always displayed first.

▶ The additions `FORWARD` and `BACKWARD` with n `PAGES` define the top page in the screen segment on the page derived by adding or subtracting the value in n from the current top page, where a type `i` data object is expected for n. If the resulting value is 0 or less or is greater than the number of pages, it is processed as 1 or as if it were the same as the number of pages, in which case the system enters a value of 4 for `sy-subrc`. The resulting page is displayed starting with the first line.

Example

By double-clicking the basic list, you can scroll down this list in the `AT LINE-SELECTION` event block to the page entered in a selection screen. The lines on the page retain their original position with reference to the page header by using `sy-staro`. However, you do not need to explicitly set the column to `sy-staco`, since this position is retained during vertical scrolling.

```
REPORT LINE-COUNT 100 LINE-SIZE 100
       NO STANDARD PAGE HEADING.

SELECTION-SCREEN BEGIN OF SCREEN 500 AS WINDOW.
PARAMETERS page TYPE i.
SELECTION-SCREEN END OF SCREEN 500.

START-OF-SELECTION.
  DO 10000 TIMES.
    WRITE sy-index.
  ENDDO.

TOP-OF-PAGE.
  ULINE.
  WRITE sy-pagno.
  ULINE.
```

```
AT LINE-SELECTION.
  CALL SELECTION-SCREEN 500 STARTING AT 10 10.
  SCROLL LIST TO COLUMN sy-staco
              TO PAGE page LINE sy-staro.
```

27.3.4   Reading List Attributes

DESCRIBE LIST

Reading the attributes of lists in the list buffer.

Syntax

```
DESCRIBE LIST { {NUMBER OF {LINES|PAGES} n}
              | {LINE linno PAGE page}
              | {PAGE pagno page_properties} }
              [INDEX idx].
```

This statement assigns the properties of a list stored in a list buffer to the variables n, page or to the variables specified in *page_properties*. The list level can be specified with the addition INDEX. A data object of the type i containing the list index is expected for idx. The value of idx must be greater than or equal to 0. If the addition INDEX is not specified, the list level 0 (the basic list itself) is selected during creation of the basic list, and the list level at which the event was triggered (sy-listi) is selected during the processing of a list event. If the list level specified in idx does not exist, the variables are not changed and sy-subrc is set to the value 8.

Return values

sy-subrc	Meaning
0	The list property was successfully specified.
4	The line specified in linno or the page specified in pagno does not exist.
8	The list level specified in idx does not exist.

Note
The statement DESCRIBE LIST should only be used for completed lists, because not all properties can be read in a list during its creation process.

27.3.4.1   Determining the Number of Lines or Columns

Syntax

```
... NUMBER OF {LINES|PAGES} n ...
```

The number of lines is stored in n when specifying LINES, the number of list pages is stored in n when specifying PAGES. A data object of the type i is expected for n. The number of lines is counted from the first to the last line described by an output statement and contains the page headers and page footers. The spaces automatically inserted between the list pages are not counted.

27.3.4.2 Determining the Page of a Line

Syntax

```
... LINE linno PAGE page ...
```

The corresponding page for the line number specified in linno is determined and stored in page. Data objects of the type i are expected for linno and page. If the line specified in linno does not exist, page is not changed and sy-subrc is set to 4. The page header and page footers are included in the line count but not the spaces automatically inserted between the list pages.

27.3.4.3 Determining the Attributes of a Page

Syntax of *page_properties*

```
... [LINE-SIZE width]
    [LINE-COUNT length]
    [LINES lines]
    [FIRST-LINE first_line]
    [TOP-LINES top_lines]
    [TITLE-LINES title_lines]
    [HEAD-LINES header_lines]
    [END-LINES footer_lines] ...
```

Different attributes are determined for the number of pages specified in pagno and are assigned to the specified variables. At least one addition must be specified after pagno. For pagno and all other variables, the data type i is expected. If the page specified in pagno is not available, the variables are not changed, and sy-subrc is set to 4. The meaning of the additions is given below:

▶ LINE-SIZE

The line length of the page defined with the addition LINE-SIZE of the statement at the start of the program or with NEW-PAGE is inserted after width.

▶ LINE-COUNT

The page length defined with the addition LINE-COUNT of the statement at the start of the program or with NEW-PAGE is inserted after length.

▶ LINES

The number of lines given out on the page including the page header and page footer is inserted after lines.

▶ FIRST-LINE

The line number of the first line of the page referring to the whole list is inserted after first_line. The page headers and page footers are included in the line count, but not the spaces automatically inserted between the list pages.

▶ TOP-LINES

The number of lines of the page's page header is inserted after top_lines. The standard page header and the lines that are given out during the event TOP-OF-PAGE are included in the count.

▶ TITLE-LINES

The number of lines of the standard header of the page's standard page header is inserted after title_lines.

▶ HEAD-LINES

The number of lines of the column headers of the page's standard page header is inserted after header_lines.

▶ END-LINES

The number of lines reserved with the addition LINE-COUNT of the statement at the start of the program for the page footer is inserted after footer_lines.

Example

Specification of properties of the list's last page that is currently displayed with two DESCRIBE statements during a list event.

```
AT LINE-SELECTION.
  DESCRIBE LIST: NUMBER OF PAGES last_page,
                 PAGE last_page LINES lines
                                FIRST-LINE first_line
                                TOP-LINES  top_lines.
```

27.4 Evaluating the Displayed List at the Cursor Position

```
GET CURSOR
```

The GET CURSOR statement can be used while processing dynpros (PAI) and after interactive list events. The following section describes the response in the event blocks after AT LINE-SELECTION, AT USER-COMMAND, and AT PFnn. The response during PAI processing of dynpros is described in Section 25.3.9.

Syntax

```
GET CURSOR { {FIELD field [field_properties]}
           | {LINE line [line_properties]} }.
```

Depending on the specification of FIELD or LINE, this statement will transfer into the variables field or line either the name of the output field or the number of the list line on which the screen cursor in the currently displayed list is positioned (after the user action). For field, a character-type (prior to Release 6.10 flat) variable is expected; for line, a variable of the type i is expected. With the additions field_properties and line_properties, further information on the cursor position can be read.

With the FIELD addition, only the names of global data objects of the ABAP program can be determined. If the cursor is positioned on the output of a data object that is not visible in the current context or literal, field will be initialized. The latter has no influence on the other additions and on sy-subrc.

Note
If the cursor is on the output area of a data object that was accessed in the WRITE statement using a field symbol, the name of the data object is assigned and not the name of the field symbol.

Return values

sy-subrc	Meaning
0	The cursor is on a field or a list row and the statement was executed successfully.
4	The cursor is not on any field or any list row.

Syntax of *field_properties*

```
... [VALUE val] [LENGTH len]
    [[DISPLAY|MEMORY] OFFSET off] [LINE lin] ...
```

The addition VALUE assigns the formatted content of the output area on which the cursor is positioned to the data object val. For val, a character-type (prior to Release 6.10 flat) variable is expected.

The addition LENGTH assigns the length of the output area on which the cursor is positioned to the data object len. For len, a variable of the type i is expected.

The addition OFFSET without an addition or with the addition DISPLAY (as of Release 6.20, Support Package 29) assigns the position of the cursor in the output area where it is positioned to the data object off. For off, a variable of the type i is expected.

The addition OFFSET with the addition MEMORY (as of Release 6.20, Support Package 29) assigns the offset of the character in the area of the data object in the list buffer (on whose output the cursor is positioned) to the data object off. If the cursor is positioned in a Unicode system on one of the characters ">" or "<" for characters cut off in the display, the position of the character in the list buffer that was overwritten by the character is assigned. For off, a variable of the type i is expected.

The addition LINE assigns the number of the list row on which the cursor is positioned to the data object lin. For lin, a variable of the type i is expected.

Syntax of *line_properties*

```
... [VALUE val] [LENGTH len]
    [[DISPLAY|MEMORY] OFFSET off] ...
```

The addition VALUE assigns the formatted content of the list line on which the cursor is positioned to the data object val. For val, a character-type (flat prior to Release 6.10) variable is expected.

The addition LENGTH assigns the line length set using the addition LINE-SIZE of the statement introducing the program or using NEW-PAGE (this is the line on which the cursor is positioned) to the data object len. For len, a variable of the type i is expected.

The addition `OFFSET` without an addition or with the addition `DISPLAY` (as of Release 6.20, Support Package 29) assigns the position of the cursor in the displayed line on which it is positioned to the data object `off`. For `off`, a variable of the type `i` is expected.

The addition `OFFSET` with the addition `MEMORY` (as of Releases 6.20, Support Package 29) assigns the position of the character in the list buffer line (on whose output the cursor is currently positioned) to the data object `off`. If the cursor in a Unicode system is on one of the characters ">" or "<" for characters cut off in the display, the position of the character in the list buffer that is overwritten by the character is assigned. For `off`, a variable of the type `i` is expected.

27.5 Display Attributes of Screen Lists

27.5.1 GUI Status of a Screen List

`SET PF-STATUS`

Setting the GUI status.

Syntax

`SET PF-STATUS status [dynpro_options] [IMMEDIATELY].`

During list processing, this statement sets the GUI status specified in `status` for the display window of the current list, and of all subsequent list levels until the next `SET PF-STATUS` statement.

The statement has mainly the same function as for dynpros (see Section 25.3.3). In `dynpro_options`, you can specify the additions `EXCLUDING` and `OF PROGRAM` that are described there.

In contrast to the screen layouts of dynpros, however, every list level is automatically linked to the GUI status that is set for it. If the user returns from the display of a higher list level to the display of a lower list level, the latter is redisplayed with the GUI status that was set for it.

The addition `IMMEDIATELY` only has an effect if it is used when creating a details list, that is, within an event block following an interactive list event. The effect of this addition is that `SET PF-STATUS` has an effect on the currently displayed list (`sy-listi`) and all subsequent list levels, and not only starting from the current details list (`sy-lsind`).

If the `status` data object is initial, the standard list status is set and the additions *dynpro_options* have no effect. The standard list status contains predefined list-specific functions whose function codes are handled by the runtime environment during the display of a screen list, and which do not lead to the call of event blocks in the ABAP program (see Table 4.1 and 4.2). If event blocks are also defined with AT LINE-SELECTION or AT PFnn, further function keys are automatically assigned function codes in the standard-list status, as follows.

▶ If AT LINE-SELECTION is used, the **F2** key and the double click function of the mouse is assigned the function code "PICK" and the function text **Select**. This function is then also automatically displayed in the application toolbar (see also Section 4.4.4).

▶ If AT PFnn is used, all the **Fnn** functions of the keyboard that are not handled by the runtime environment are assigned the function codes "PFnn", where nn is a number between 01 and 24 (see also Section 42.3.1).

If the standard list status is set, `sy-pfkey` receives the value "STLI".

Note
When setting the GUI status for the list dynpro, we recommended setting a GUI status for which a **List status** has been included as a **Template status** in the Menu Painter. Including this type of template status copies the list-specific functions of the standard list status into a self-defined GUI status.

Example
In the following program segment, double clicking the mouse or using the function key **F2** enables the selection of only a single line from the basic list. This function is then deactivated for the basic list and all subsequent list levels.

```
START-OF-SELECTION.
  SET PF-STATUS 'BASIC'.
  WRITE / 'Pick me!'.

AT LINE-SELECTION.
  SET PF-STATUS 'BASIC' EXCLUDING 'PICK' IMMEDIATELY.
  WRITE / 'Don't pick me!'.
```

27.5.2 Title of a Screen List

SET TITLEBAR

Setting the GUI-title of the list window.

Syntax

```
SET TITLEBAR title [dynpro_options].
```

When processing lists, this statement sets the GUI-title specified in `title` for the display window of the current list level and all subsequent list levels up to the next statement SET TITLEBAR.

The statement has for the most part the same syntax as for dynpros (see Section 25.3.4). In `dynpro_options`, the additions described there can be used for filling the placeholder of the title.

In contrast to the screens of dynpros, each list level remains automatically linked to the correspondingly set title. When returning from the display of a higher list level to that of a lower list level, the latter is again displayed with the correspondingly set title.

27.5.3 Setting the Cursor

SET CURSOR

The SET CURSOR statement can be used while processing the dynpros (PBO) and creating lists. The following section describes the response in the list processing. The response during the PBO processing of dynpros is described in Section 25.3.8.

Syntax

```
SET CURSOR { { FIELD field LINE line
                  [[DISPLAY|MEMORY] OFFSET off] }
         | { LINE line [[DISPLAY|MEMORY] OFFSET off] }
         | { col lin } }.
```

This statement positions the cursor in the next list displayed on the screen. This is either the current list or, if no detail list is created in an event block after an interactive list event, the previous list. The cursor can be positioned by entering a field after FIELD or a line after LINE, or by entering an absolute position using `col` and `lin`.

If the statement SET CURSOR is not specified, the cursor is positioned by default in the first field in the list that is ready for input or in the input field of the system toolbar.

The statement is ignored if the specified position is outside the display area of the list, or if it points to line elements.

Note
The exact position of the cursor is only visible in output areas that are ready for input. Otherwise the whole area in which the cursor is positioned is marked.

27.5.3.1 Positioning in Output Areas

Syntax

```
... FIELD field LINE line [[DISPLAY|MEMORY] OFFSET off] ...
```

The cursor is positioned in the list line specified in `line` in the output area of the data object whose name is contained in `field`. The entry is not case-sensitive.

▶ If OFFSET is not specified, the cursor is positioned in the first column of the output area.

▶ If OFFSET is specified without an addition or with the addition DISPLAY (as of Release 6.20, Support Package 29), the cursor is positioned in the column of the output area entered in `off`.

▶ If OFFSET is specified with the addition MEMORY (as of Release 6.20, Support Package 29), the cursor is positioned on the character of the output area that is in the list buffer at the position specified in `off`. If this character is cut off in the list display in a Unicode system, the cursor is positioned on the corresponding indicator (">" or "<").

The data object `field` must be character-type and flat. For `line` and `off`, data objects of type `i` are expected.

If the data object specified in `field` has been given out more than once in the visible area of the line, the cursor is positioned in the first output area. If the data object specified in `field` does not occur in the visible area of the line, the specification is ignored.

If you want the cursor to be positioned in the output area of a data object that is addressed in the WRITE statement using a field symbol, and if the same data object is no longer assigned to the field symbol, the name of

the data object, not the name of the field symbol, must be contained in
`field`.

Example
In the following output, the cursor is positioned in the output area ready
for input of the field `input`. Without the `SET CURSOR` statement, the cursor
would be positioned on the previous checkbox.

```
DATA: flag(1) TYPE c,
      inp(10) TYPE c.

SET BLANK LINES ON.
WRITE: / flag AS CHECKBOX, inp INPUT.
SET CURSOR FIELD 'inp' LINE sy-linno.
```

27.5.3.2 Positioning in List Lines

Syntax

```
... LINE line [[DISPLAY|MEMORY] OFFSET off] ...
```

The cursor is positioned in the list line specified in `line`.

▶ If `OFFSET` is not specified, the cursor is positioned in the first column of
the line.

▶ If `OFFSET` is specified without an addition or with the addition `DISPLAY`
(as of Release 6.20, Support Package 29), the cursor is positioned in the
column specified in `OFF`.

▶ If `OFFSET` is specified without an addition or with the addition `MEMORY`,
the cursor is positioned on the character in the position specified in `off`
in the list buffer. If this character is cut off in the list display in a Unicode system, the cursor is positioned on the corresponding indicator
(">" or "<").

For `line` and `off`, data objects of type `i` are expected.

Note
This variant of the `SET CURSOR` statement does not work with screen layouts of dynpros.

27.5.3.3 Specifying an Absolute Position

```
... col lin ...
```

The cursor is positioned in the column specified in `col` and the line specified in `lin` in the list window. For `col` and `lin`, data objects of type `i` are expected. The column numbering begins at 2.

27.5.4 Lists in a Dialog Box

```
WINDOW
```

Display of a details list in a modal dialog window.

Syntax

```
WINDOW STARTING AT col1 lin1
       [ENDING   AT col2 lin2].
```

This statement initiates the display of the currently created details list in a dialog box. It has an effect only in the event blocks for an interactive list event. In the case of several `WINDOW` statements in an event block, the last one is valid.

The upper left corner is determined for the column and the line by the values in `col1` and `lin1`. The values are based on the basic list window. The lower right corner is set automatically. The maximum lower right corner can either be specified in `col2` and `lin2` or is specified using the lower right corner of the window where the list event took place.

For `col1`, `lin1`, `col2` and `lin2`, data objects of type `i` are expected. The values of all data objects should lie within the basic list window, and the values of `col1` and `lin1` should be less than those of `col2` and `lin2`. Otherwise, the behavior is undefined.

If no GUI-Status is set with `SET PF-STATUS` and an event block is defined with `AT LINE-SELECTION` or `AT PFnn`, the system automatically uses a standard list status suitable for dialog windows without a menu and symbol bar. The standard list status includes pushbuttons for the predefined function codes "PICK" (only for `AT LINE-SELECTION`), "PRI", "%SC", "%SC+" and "RW" in the application bar (see Tables 4.2 and 4.3).

Note
If a GUI-Status is set with `SET PF-STATUS`, this should be created in the Menu Painter as a dialog window status; the list template should also be included.

Example

This example displays the details of an airline in a dialog box after selecting a line.

```
DATA: scarr_wa TYPE scarr,
      col      TYPE i,
      lin      TYPE i.

START-OF-SELECTION.
        SELECT carrid
        FROM scarr
        INTO scarr_wa-carrid.
  WRITE / scarr_wa-carrid.
  HIDE  scarr_wa-carrid.
 ENDSELECT.
 CLEAR scarr_wa-carrid.

AT LINE-SELECTION.
  col = sy-cucol + 40.
  lin = sy-curow + 2.
  WINDOW STARTING AT sy-cucol sy-curow
         ENDING   AT col lin.
  IF sy-lsind = 1 AND
     scarr_wa-carrid IS NOT INITIAL.
    SELECT SINGLE carrname url
          FROM scarr
          INTO (scarr_wa-carrname,scarr_wa-url)
          WHERE carrid = scarr_wa-carrid.
    WRITE: scarr_wa-carrname, / scarr_wa-url.
  ENDIF.
```

27.6 Calling and Exiting List Displays

A basic list is either displayed automatically or controlled by the program. A details list is always displayed automatically:

▶ In executable programs called with SUBMIT, the basic list created up to that point is displayed automatically after the event END-OF-SELECTION (see Section 10.2.1). At the start of the program, the standard list status is set automatically, which can be replaced by another GUI status in the program using SET PF-STATUS.

▶ In any programs that can contain dynpros as components, a display of the current basic list can be called during the processing of a dynpro sequence (program controlled).

▶ In any programs that can contain dynpros as components, the details list created in a processing block is automatically displayed when the processing block is terminated after AT LINE-SELECTION, AT USER-COMMAND, or AT PFnn. If no details list is created, the system continues to display the previous list level.

The following sections deal with the statements for calling the basic list during a dynpro sequence.

27.6.1   Calling the Basic List Display

```
LEAVE TO LIST-PROCESSING
```

Calling the list processor.

Syntax

```
LEAVE TO LIST-PROCESSING [AND RETURN TO SCREEN dynnr].
```

This statement can be executed during PBO and PAI processing. After processing the current dynpro, this statement interrupts the respective dynpro sequence, starts the list processor, and displays the basic list. The basic list consists of the list outputs of all PBO and PAI modules of the dynpro sequence executed to this point. The statement has no effect in the event blocks for reporting events and list events.

The list dynpro screen of the list processor replaces the screen presented in the pop-up level 0. Modal dialog windows that might be stacked on the display are hidden for the duration of the list display. The GUI status set in the dynpro sequence is used. List events initiated by user actions in the window of the list dynpro call the event blocks of the current main program. The details lists created there are displayed by the list processor in the basic list window (as long as the statement WINDOW is not used).

The user can exit the list processor or list display by selecting the functions **Back**, **End** or **Cancel** in the display of the list level 0, or using a program with the statement LEAVE LIST PROCESSING (see Section 27.6.2). By default, the interrupted dynpro sequence resumes in both cases with a PBO processing of the dynpro in which the list processor was called. Another dynpro can be specified in dynnr using the addition AND RETURN TO SCREEN to continue its PBO processing. For dynnr, a character-type data object of type n is expected that contains the number of a dynpro in the current main program.

Notes

▶ If the current dynpro is displayed in a dialog window, the list processor also displays the lists in this window.

▶ If the value 0 is specified in `dynnr`, the current dynpro sequence is closed after exiting the list processor.

27.6.2 Leaving the List Display

```
LEAVE LIST-PROCESSING
```

Leaving the list processor.

Syntax

```
LEAVE LIST-PROCESSING.
```

This statement leaves the list processor immediately. The runtime environment continues the processing with the PBO event of the dynpro from which the list processor was called using LEAVE TO LIST PROCESSING or the processing of the dynpro that was set using the AND RETURN TO SCREEN addition to this statement.

If the statement is not executed when the list is displayed by the list processor, it has no effect, except in the event blocks for reporting events. Here it branches to the end of the program and processing continues as described in Section 10.2.1.

When the list processor is exited, the list buffer of the dynpro sequence is initialized. New output statements describe a new basic list.

Example

This example shows the recommended procedure for displaying lists during dynpro sequences. A separate dynpro 500 is defined for calling the list processor. The screen of this dynpro does not contain any screen elements and it calls a single PBO module `call_list` but no PAI modules. The entire basic list, including the GUI status, is defined in the PBO module. When the screen is exited using LEAVE SCREEN, its processing is stopped and the list processor is started. The list events are handled in the same program. When the list processor is left, the dynpro sequence of dynpro 500 is ended, because the next dynpro 0 is specified when the list processor is called.

```
PROGRAM ... NO STANDARD PAGE HEADING.

...

MODULE call_list OUTPUT.
  SET PF-STATUS space.
  WRITE 'Basic List'.
  LEAVE TO LIST-PROCESSING AND RETURN TO SCREEN 0.
  LEAVE SCREEN.
ENDMODULE.

TOP-OF-PAGE.
  WRITE 'Header' COLOR COL_HEADING.
  ULINE.

TOP-OF-PAGE DURING LINE-SELECTION.
  WRITE sy-lsind COLOR COL_HEADING.
  ULINE.

AT LINE-SELECTION.
  WRITE 'Secondary List'.
  IF sy-lsind = 20.
    LEAVE LIST-PROCESSING.
  ENDIF.
```

28 Messages

28.1 Overview

Messages are repository objects maintained with the message maintenance tool in the ABAP Workbench and called with the `MESSAGE` statement in the ABAP program. Catching a message through the ABAP runtime environment depends on the context in which the message was sent.

28.1.1 Storing Messages

You create messages using message maintenance (transaction SE91) and store them in the database table T100. Table 28.1 shows the structure of database table T100.

Component	Meaning
SPRSL	Single-digit language key.
ARBGB	Max. 20-digit message class. The message class assigns messages to a specific area, such as an application area or a packet.
MSGNR	Max. 3-digit message number, the range between 900 and 999 is reserved for customers.
TEXT	Max. 73-digit short message text. You must create an explanatory long text when you maintain the message, if the short text itself is not sufficiently explanatory.

Table 28.1 Structure of Database Table T100

Within short and long texts, you can use placeholders, which can be replaced with the content of data objects using the `MESSAGE` statement. A maximum of four character-type placeholders is permitted. They are indicated by "&i" or "&" in short texts, and by "&Vi&" in long texts, where i is a number between 1 and 4. If "&" itself is to be displayed as part of the text, it must be specified as "&&" in short texts and as "<(>&<)>" in long texts.

28.1.2 Message Types

When sending a message using the `MESSAGE` statement, it must be classified using a one-digit message type. The message type specifies how the message is displayed and also the subsequent program flow. Valid message types are "A", "E", "I", "S", "W", and "X". The abbreviations stand for termination message, error message, information message, status message, warning, and exit message, respectively.

The system behavior after sending a message of a specific message type depends on the context. It is shown in Table 28.2.

Processing block	Message type					
	A	E	I	S	W	X
PAI module for PIA	1	2	3	4	5	6
PAI module for POH	1	7	3	4	7	6
PAImodule for POV	1	7	3	4	7	6
AT SELECTION-SCREEN for PAI	1	8	3	4	9	6
AT SELECTION-SCREEN for POH	1	7	3	4	7	6
AT SELECTION-SCREEN for POV	1	7	3	4	7	6
AT SELECTION-SCREEN ON EXIT	1	7	3	4	7	6
AT LINE-SELECTION	1	10	3	4	10	6
AT PFnn	1	10	3	4	10	6
AT USER-COMMAND	1	10	3	4	10	6
INITIALIZATION	1	11	3	4	11	6
START-OF-SELECTION	1	11	3	4	11	6
GET	1	11	3	4	11	6
END-OF-SELECTION	1	11	3	4	11	6
TOP-OF-PAGE	1	11	3	4	11	6
END-OF-PAGE	1	11	3	4	11	6
TOP-OF-PAGE DURING ...	1	10	3	4	10	6
LOAD-OF-PROGRAM	1	1	4	4	4	6
PBO module	1	1	4	4	4	6
AT SELECTION-SCREEN OUTPUT	1	1	4	4	4	6

Table 28.2 Message Handling

The numbers in the individual column contents of "A", "E", "I", "S", "W", and "X" have the following meaning.

1. The message is displayed in a dialog window. After exiting the dialog window, the program terminates, the system returns to the call position of the first program of the current call sequence and all internal sessions of the call sequence are deleted.

2. The PAI processing terminates and the system returns to the current screen layout without triggering the event PBO. By default, the message is displayed in the status bar of the current window. When sending the error message in a dialog module that is called in the dynpro flow logic outside a processing chain defined by CHAIN behind a FIELD statement, the only field that is ready for input is the input field specified behind FIELD. When sending the error message in a dialog mod-

ule that is called inside a processing chain defined by CHAIN, all input fields in the processing chain that are specified behind FIELD are made ready for input. After a user action, the PAI processing continues at the position described in Section 25.2.3.3.

3. The message is displayed in a dialog window. After exiting the dialog window, the program continues using the statement that follows MESSAGE.

4. The program continues using the statement that follows MESSAGE. By default, the message is displayed in the status bar of the current window when displaying the screen layout of the next dynpro.

5. The PAI processing is interrupted and the system returns to the current screen layout without triggering the event PBO. By default, the message is displayed in the status bar of the current window. The fields decribed under Number 2 are ready for input. If the user confirms the current field contents using the **Enter** key without entering new values, the program continues with the statement that follows MESSAGE. If the user enters one or more new values, the processing continues after a user action as described under Item 2.

6. The program terminates with the runtime error MESSAGE_TYPE_X, and the system displays its short dump which contains the message-ID and the short and long text of the message.

7. During the POH processing, the POV processing and the handling of a function code of the type "E", the sending of error messages or warnings is not allowed. An exception that cannot be handled is triggered.

8. The selection screen processing is interrupted and the system returns to the current selection screen without triggering the event AT SELEC-TION-SCREEN OUTPUT. By default, the message is displayed in the status bar of the current window. The input fields of the selection screen that have been specified using the additions of the statement AT SELEC-TION-SCREEN of the current event block (see Section 4.4.3) are ready for input. After a user action, the selection screen processing continues using the current selection screen event. Previous selection screen events are not triggered.

9. The selection screen processing is interrupted and the system returns to the current selection screen without triggering the event AT SELEC-TION-SCREEN OUTPUT. By default, the message is displayed in the status bar of the current window. The fields decribed under Item 8 are ready for input. If the user confirms the current field contents using the **Enter** key without entering new values, the program continues with the

statement that follows MESSAGE. If the user enters one or more new values, the processing continues after a user action as described under Item 8.

10. The event block of the current list event is interrupted and the display of the list level on which the list event was triggered remains. By default, the message is displayed in the status bar of the current window.

11. The program is interrupted and an empty screen with an empty GUI status is displayed. By default, the message is displayed in the status bar of the current window. The system returns to the call position of the program after a user action

In procedures, the message handling is executed according to the event block or dialog module in which the procedure was called. Exceptions from this rule occur when using the addition RAISING in the MESSAGE statement (see Section 28.2.3.2) and when handling a message during the call of a function module using the predefined exception error_message (see Section 11.2.3.1). During the update, all messages except those for type S cause the program to terminate and lead to a database rollback.

Notes

▶ You can use the function **Adjustment of Local Layout** in the toolbar of the GUI status to specify that error messages, warnings, and status messages are displayed in a dialog window instead of the status bar. The program flow continues as described above only after leaving the dialog box.

▶ A total of 50 characters can be displayed in a dialog window. Messages that contain more than 50 characters are wrapped. The display of a dialog window can contain a maximum of six rows, which corresponds to 300 characters. This covers the maximum length of a short message with 269 characters if it contains 73 characters and if four placeholders are replaced with 50 characters each (see Section 28.2.3.4). The first row is preceded by an icon specific to the message type. The maximum current width of the bar is used for the display of characters in the status bar. The truncation of characters is indicated by three dots (...) at the end of the bar.

▶ During the display of a message, the user can display a long text, if it exists. The push button **Help** and a double-click in the status bar can be used to display the message in a dialog box. If no long text is defined, it is generated with the content of the short text.

28.2 Sending Messages

MESSAGE

Sending a message.

Syntax

```
MESSAGE { msg | txt } [message_options].
```

This statement interrupts the program flow and either displays the short text of a message specified in `msg` in the logon language of the current user, or any text from `txt` as a news item. With the message-type it is specified how the text is displayed and how the program flow continues after the statement `MESSAGE` (see Section 28.1.2). With the statements `message_options`, you can change this behavior and replace the placeholders in messages.

System fields

Name	Relevance
sy-msgid	Contains the message-class after sending a message, and the value "00" after sending any text.
sy-msgno	Contains the message number after sending a message, and the value "001" after sending any text.
sy-msgty	Contains the identifier of the message type with which the message or text was sent.
sy-msgv1 to sy-msgv4	Contain the content of the data objects specified after the addition WITH after sending a message. After sending any text, they contain the first 200 characters of the data object text.

28.2.1 Specifying a Message

Syntax of *msg*

```
... tn
  | tn(id)
  | {ID mid TYPE mtype NUMBER num}
  | {oref TYPE mtype} ...
```

In `msg` a message is specified from the database table T100 (see Section 28.1.1). This occurs via direct specifications of `id` and `n`, via the content of the data objects `mid` and `num` for the message class and the message number; or via an object reference variable `oref` is specified whose dynamic type implements the interface IF_T100_MESSAGE. You have to specify one of the possible message types "A", "E", "I", "S", "W" or "X", either by direct specification of t or as content of the data object mtype.

If a message is not found, then the specified message type, the message class and the message number are used as short text in capital letters separated by a colon (:). The system fields of the statement MESSAGE are always supplied with the specified values.

28.2.1.1 Static Short Form

Syntax

```
... tn ...
```

With t and n you specify the one-digit message type and the three-digit message number directly in a row (static short form). The message class must be specified with the addition MESSAGE-ID at the statement that introduces the program.

Example
Display of the short text of the message with the number 014 from the message class SABAPDOCU as an information message.

```
REPORT rep MESSAGE-ID sabapdocu.
...

MESSAGE i014.
```

28.2.1.2 Static Long Form

Syntax

```
... tn(id) ...
```

For t and n the same applies as for the static short form. In the static long form, the message class is specified directly in brackets through id.

Notes

▶ The explicit specification of the message class overrides the addition MESSAGE-ID of the statement that introduces the program.

▶ The specification of the message class in brackets does not mean that the content of id is used. In fact, the message class is used that has the name that was specified directly with id.

Example

Same as example in Section 28.2.1.1, with explicit specification of the message class.

```
REPORT ...
...
MESSAGE i014(sabapdocu).
```

28.2.1.3 Dynamic Form

Syntax

```
... ID mid TYPE mtype NUMBER num ...
```

The message class, the message type and the message number are specified as content of the data objects `mid`, `mtype` and `num`. For `mid` and `mtype`, character-type data objects are expected that must contain the message class or the message type in capital letters. Invalid message types create an untreatable exception. For `num`, a data object of the type n and the length 3 is expected.

Note

The explicit specification of the message class overrides the addition MES-SAGE-ID of the statement that introduces the program.

Example

Same as example in Section 28.2.1.2, with dynamic specification of the message and the message type.

```
DATA: mid    TYPE sy-msgid VALUE 'SABAPDOCU',
      mtype TYPE sy-msgty VALUE 'I',
      num    TYPE sy-msgno VALUE '014'.
MESSAGE ID mid TYPE mtype NUMBER num.
```

28.2.1.4 Message of an Object

Syntax

```
... oref TYPE mtype ...
```

For `oref`, you can specify an object reference variable which, at the time of execution of the statement MESSAGE, points at an object whose class implements the system interface IF_T100_MESSAGE. This in turn contains the component interface IF_MESSAGE. For `mtype`, a character-type data object is expected which must contain the message type in capital letters.

The statement MESSAGE analyzes the components of the structured attribute T100KEY of the interface IF_T100_MESSAGE in the referenced object. The message class is taken from the component MSGID, the message number from the component MSGNO. If the components ATTR1 to ATTR4 contain the names of other attributes of the object, the placeholder "&1" to "&4" and "&" of the short text or "&V1&" to "&V4&" of the long text of the message are replaced by the content of these attributes. This replacement follows the rules of usage given by the additions WITH in message_options (see Section 28.2.3.4). If one of these components does not contain an attribute name, the character "&" is added to the content at the beginning and end, thus replacing the placeholder.

Notes

▶ With this variant, the additions WITH and INTO in message_options are not allowed.

▶ This variant is mainly designated to be used with exception objects. If an exception class implements the interface IF_T100_MESSAGE, then the components of the structure T100KEY are automatically filled according to the respective definition of the exception text when a class-based exception is raised.

▶ For compatibility reasons, this variant can still be used for classes that implement only the interface IF_MESSAGE. In this case, the interface methods GET_TEXT and GET_LONGTEXT are called automatically in the referenced object and their return value is used as a short text or long text of the messsage. In this case, the system fields sy-msgid and sy-msgno are not specifically filled. The root class of all exception classes, CX_ROOT, implements the interface IF_MESSAGE. In exception classes that do not implement the interface IF_T100_MESSAGE, the interface methods GET_TEXT and GET_LONGTEXT get the exception texts of exception objects stored in the OTR (Online Text Repository). These then can be issued by using the variant of the MESSAGE statement as a message.

Example

In a class c1, the interface IF_T100_MESSAGE is implemented and its attribute T100KEY is supplied with values. The statement MESSAGE displays the respective statement, in which a placeholder "&" is replaced with the content of the attribute text.

```
CLASS c1 DEFINITION.
  PUBLIC SECTION.
    INTERFACES if_t100_message.
```

```
      DATA text(10) TYPE c VALUE 'Hello!'.
      METHODS constructor.
ENDCLASS.

CLASS c1 IMPLEMENTATION.
  METHOD constructor.
    if_message~get_text( ).
  ENDMETHOD.
  METHOD if_message~get_text.
    if_t100_message~t100key-msgid = 'SABAPDOCU'.
    if_t100_message~t100key-msgno = '888'.
    if_t100_message~t100key-attr1 = 'TEXT'.
  ENDMETHOD.
  METHOD if_message~get_longtext.
  ENDMETHOD.
ENDCLASS.

DATA oref TYPE REF TO c1.

...

  CREATE OBJECT oref.

  MESSAGE oref TYPE 'I'.
```

28.2.2 Specifying any Text

Syntax of *txt*

```
... text TYPE mtype ... .
```

This variant sends a character string contained in text as a message of the message type specified in mtype. You can enter a character-type data object text which will be used as a short text for the message. Only the first 300 characters in text are taken into account. No long text can be defined for a message of this type.

For mtype, a character-type data object is expected, which must contain the message type in capital letters. Invalid message types generate an untreatable exception.

Notes

▶ In this variant, the additions WITH and INTO are not allowed in *message_options*.

▶ If field symbols or formal parameters of the type any or data are specified for text, these must be character-type when the statement is executed. The syntactically identical variant MESSAGE oref cannot be executed with generically typed field symbols or formal parameters.

▶ Because the system fields sy-msgid and sy-msgno are filled unspecifically when a character string is entered, this variant should only be used on rare occasions if the content of the system fields is not required for the identification of the message. Otherwise, in all cases in which messages are transferred (for example from function modules) or logged (for example in batch input) using these system fields, the language-independent access to the message text would be lost.

Example
Output of an exception text as an information message.

```
DATA: oref TYPE REF TO cx_sy_arithmetic_error,
      text TYPE string.
TRY.

  ...
  CATCH cx_sy_arithmetic_error INTO oref.

    text = oref->get_text( ).
    MESSAGE text TYPE 'I'.

ENDTRY.
```

28.2.3 Additions to MESSAGE

Syntax of *message_options*

```
... { {[DISPLAY LIKE dtype] [RAISING exception]}
    | [INTO text] }
    [WITH dobj1 ... dobj4] ...
```

These additions change the type of display, raise a non-class-based exception (see Section 15.4) in function modules or methods, assign the text of the message to a data object, and replace the placeholders in short- and long-texts of messages.

28.2.3.1 Changing the display of a Message

Syntax

```
... DISPLAY LIKE dtype ...
```

When you use this addition, the short text of the message is displayed in a dialog window for all message types specified in *msg* except "S" and "X". Instead of the corresponding icon, the icon of the message type specified in dtype is displayed. For dtype, a character-type data object is expected that must contain one of the values "A", "E", "I", "S" or "W" in capital letters.

Note
Use of this addition does not influence the behavior, determined by the message type (see Section 28.1.2), but only the type of display.

28.2.3.2 Raising an exception

Syntax

```
... RAISING exception ...
```

With this addition, the statement MESSAGE raises either a non-class-based exception exception (see Section 15.4) or sends a message. The addition only makes sense during the processing of methods and function modules in which the non-class-based exception exception is defined. Furthermore, the addition must not be used in the same processing block as the statement RAISE EXCEPTION for raising class-based exceptions.

Processing the MESSAGE-statement with the addition RAISING during the processing of a method or a function module whose caller assigns a return value to the exception exception with the addition EXCEPTIONS of the statement CALL (see Section 15.4.3) has the same effect as the statement RAISE (see Section 15.4.2). If no return value is assigned to the exception exception, then the addition RAISING is ignored and the message is processed according to its message type as described in Section 28.1.2).

The system fields of the statement MESSAGE are supplied in both cases and are available in the calling program after handling an exception raised with MESSAGE ... RAISING. This is especially pertinent when a function module was called through Remote Function Call (RFC).

Note
You can assign a return value to messages that are sent in function modules without the addition RAISING via the predefined exception error_ message (see Section 11.2.3.1).

Example
At the first call of the method, an information message is sent, at the second call an exception is raised instead and is handled after the call via the analysis of sy-subrc.

```
CLASS c1 DEFINITION.
  PUBLIC SECTION.
```

```
   CLASS-METHODS m1 EXCEPTIONS exc1.
ENDCLASS.

CLASS c1 IMPLEMENTATION.
  METHOD m1.
    MESSAGE 'Message in a Method' TYPE 'I' RAISING exc1.
  ENDMETHOD.
ENDCLASS.

...

  c1=>m1( ).
  c1=>m1( EXCEPTIONS exc1 = 4 ).

IF sy-subrc = 4.
  ...
ENDIF.
```

28.2.3.3 Assigning the Message Text

Syntax

```
... INTO text ...
```

With this addition, you assign the short text of the message to the variable `text`. The message type does not matter. The program flow is not interrupted and there is no message processing taking place as described in Section 28.1.2. For `text`, a character-type data object is expected.

The addition `INTO` cannot be specified at the output of a user-defined text (see Section 28.2.2).

Example
The short text of a message sent in a function module is stored in the data object `mtext` when handling the exception `error_message` (see Section 11.2.3.1) with the help of the respective system fields.

```
DATA mtext TYPE string.

CALL FUNCTION ... EXCEPTIONS error_message = 4.

IF sy-subrc = 4.
  MESSAGE ID sy-msgid TYPE sy-msgty NUMBER sy-msgno
          INTO mtext
          WITH sy-msgv1 sy-msgv2 sy-msgv3 sy-msgv4.
ENDIF.
```

28.2.3.4 Replacing placeholders

Syntax

```
... WITH dobj1 ... dobj4 ...
```

This addition replaces the placeholders "&1" and "&" of the short text or "&V1&" of the long text of the message with the first 50 characters of the content of the data objects `dobj1`, ..., `dobj4`. You can specify up to four character-type data objects. The position of a data object determines which placeholder will be replaced. The content of the first data object replaces the placeholders "&1", the first placeholder "&" and "&V1&."The content of the second data object replaces "&2", the second "&" and "&V2&" etc. Furthermore, the content of the data objects `dobj1`, ..., `dobj4` is assigned in sequence to the system fields `sy-msgv1` to `sy-msgv4`.

If you specify fewer data objects than placeholders, then the surplus placeholders are not replaced and not displayed in the short text. If a specified data object cannot be assigned to a placeholder, it will be ignored.

The addition `WITH` cannot be specified at the output of a user-defined text (see Section 28.2.2) or an object reference (see Section 28.2.1.4).

Note

If a short text contains placeholders of both forms "&i" and "&", then the content of a data object can replace two placeholders. The data object at the position `i` not only replaces "&i" but also the placeholder at position `i` "&". We recommend using only one form for placeholders in a short text.

Example

If the short text of the specified message in the table T100 contains the value "& & & &", then the text "This is not America" is put out as information message. If the short text was defined as "&4 &1 &3 &2", then the output is "America This not is".

```
MESSAGE i010 WITH 'This' 'is' 'not' 'America'.
```

Part 10
Processing External Data

29   Open SQL

29.1   Overview

29.1.1   Scope of Open SQL

Open SQL refers to the subset of ABAP statements that enable direct access to the data in the central database data of the SAP system. Open SQL statements implement in ABAP the Data Manipulation Language (DML) functionality of SQL, which is supported by all database systems.

29.1.2   Database Interface

The statements of Open SQL are converted to database-specific SQL in the Open SQL interface of the database interface. They are then transferred to the database system and executed there. Open SQL statements can be used to exclusively access database tables that are declared in the ABAP Dictionary. Access via views is also possible.

29.1.3   Database Access

Each Open SQL statement is synonymous with an access to the database. This applies particularly for SELECT statements that end in ENDSELECT. Data to be read and to be written is transported in packages between the database server and the application server. You can configure the size of the packages using profile parameters (for example, the standard value for Oracle is 65 KB). The number of characters that can be transported in one package depends on whether the system is a Unicode system or a non-Unicode system.

29.1.4   Client Handling

Open SQL works with automatic client handling. When client-specific database tables are accessed, the client identifier must not be explicitly specified or else it will be overwritten with the ID of the current client by the runtime environment. You can deactivate automatic client handling using the addition CLIENT SPECIFIED.

29.1.5   SAP Buffering

When database tables are accessed using Open SQL, SAP buffering normally takes effect if it is switched on for the relevant database table.

The following Open SQL statements bypass the SAP buffer and access the database tables directly:

▶ SELECT with the addition BYPASSING BUFFER

▶ SELECT with the addition FOR UPDATE

▶ SELECT with aggregate expressions in the column specification of the result set

▶ SELECT with JOIN expressions

▶ SELECT with IS [NOT] NULL in the WHERE or HAVING condition

▶ SELECT with single columns in the addition ORDER BY

▶ Access to Views in which multiple database tables are involved

29.1.6 LUW

When using the change statements (INSERT, UPDATE, MODIFY and DELETE), it is important to keep data storage consistent. The LUW concept is designed for this purpose. In application programs of an SAP system, the implicit database LUWs are normally not sufficient for consistent data storage. Instead, you need to program explicit SAP LUWs, which normally contain several database LUWs (see Section 33.3).

Significant changes from Release 6.10

▶ Columns of type RAWSTRING, SSTRING, or STRING can be accessed in the database tables.

▶ Almost all parts of an Open SQL statement can be dynamically specified as the content of data objects.

▶ From Release 6.20 on, you have the option of accessing databases other than the central SAP system database, using the CONNECTION addition. This addition is currently released for internal use only, and is therefore not mentioned further in this documentation.

29.1.7 Open SQL Statements

Statement	Section
SELECT	29.2
OPEN CURSOR, FETCH, CLOSE CURSOR	29.3
INSERT	29.4
UPDATE	29.5

Statement	Section
MODIFY	29.6
DELETE	29.7
COMMIT WORK	33.3.1
ROLLBACK WORK	33.3.2

Note
There are also obsolete forms of Open SQL statements and obsolete statements for accessing database tables, which do not belong in the scope of Open SQL. These obsolete forms are described in Section 42.16.

29.2   Reading Data from Database Tables

SELECT

SELECT is an Open SQL statement for reading data from one or several database tables into data objects.

Syntax

```
SELECT result
       FROM source
       INTO|APPENDING target
       [[FOR ALL ENTRIES IN itab] WHERE cond]
       [GROUP BY cols] [HAVING group_cond]
       [ORDER BY sort_args].

  ...
[ENDSELECT.]
```

The SELECT statement reads a result set whose structure is determined in result from the database tables specified in source, and it then assigns the data from the result set to the data objects specified in target. You can restrict the result set using the WHERE addition. The addition GROUP BY compresses several database rows into a single row of the result set. The addition HAVING restricts the compressed rows. The addition ORDER BY sorts the result set according to the sort arguments sort_args.

The data objects specified in target must match the result set result. This means that the result set is either assigned to the data objects in one step, or assigned by row, or assigned by packets of rows. If assignment is by row, the SELECT statement opens a loop which must be closed using

ENDSELECT. For every loop pass, the SELECT statement assigns a row or a packet of rows to the data objects specified in target. If the last row was assigned or if the result set is empty, then SELECT branches to ENDSELECT. A database cursor is opened implicitly to process a SELECT loop, and is closed again when the loop is ended. You can end the loop using the statements from Section 12.4.

Except for the INTO or APPENDING addition, the entries in the SELECT statement define which data should be read by the database and in which form. This requirement is translated in the database interface for the database system's programming interface and is then passed to the database system. The data are read in packets (see Section 29.1.3) by the database and are transported to the application server by the database server. On the application server, the data are transferred to the ABAP program's data objects in accordance with the data specified in the INTO and APPENDING additions.

System Fields
The SELECT statement sets the values of the system fields sy-subrc and sy-dbcnt.

sy-subrc	Relevance
0	The SELECT statement sets sy-subrc to 0 for every pass by value to an ABAP data object. Before leaving a SELECT loop via ENDSELECT, the SELECT statement sets sy-subrc to 0 if at least one line was transferred in the loop.
4	The SELECT statement sets sy-subrc to 4 if the result set is empty, that is, if no data was found in the database.
8	The SELECT statement sets sy-subrc to 8 if the FOR UPDATE addition is used in result, without the primary key being specified fully after WHERE.

After every value that is transferred to an ABAP data object, the SELECT statement sets sy-dbcnt to the number of rows that were transferred. If the result set is empty, sy-dbcnt is set to 0.

Notes
▶ Outside of classes, you do not need to specify the target area with INTO or APPENDING if a single database table or a single view is specified statically after FROM and if a table work area dbtab was declared with the TABLES statement for the corresponding database table or view. In this case, the system supplements the SELECT statement implicitly with the addition INTO dbtab.

- ▶ Although the WHERE condition is optional, you should always specify it for performance reasons, and the result set should not be restricted on the application server.
- ▶ SELECT loops can be nested. For performance reasons, you should check whether a join or a sub-query would be more effective.
- ▶ Within a SELECT loop you must not execute any statements that lead to a database commit (see Section 33.2.1) and consequently cause the corresponding database cursor to close.

Treatable Exceptions
See Section 29.9.

29.2.1 Determining the Structure of the Result Set

Syntax of *result*

```
... lines columns ...
```

The data in `result` define whether the resulting set consists of multiple rows (table-like structure) or a single row (flat structure). It specifies the columns to be read and defines their names in the resulting set. Note that column names from the database table can be replaced by alternative column names. For single columns, aggregate expressions can be used to specify aggregates. Identical rows in the resulting set can be excluded, and individual rows can be protected from parallel changes by another program.

The data in `result` consist of data for the rows `lines` and for the columns `columns`.

29.2.1.1 Specifying Lines

Syntax of *lines*

```
... { SINGLE [FOR UPDATE] }
  | { [DISTINCT] { } }        } ...
```

The data in `lines` specify that the resulting set has either multiple lines or a single line.

Single-lined result set

Syntax

```
... SINGLE [FOR UPDATE] ...
```

If SINGLE is specified, the resulting set has a single line. If the remaining additions to the SELECT statement select more than one line from the database, the first line found is entered into the resulting set. The data objects specified after INTO must not be internal tables, and the APPEND-ING addition must not be used.

An exclusive lock can be set on the database for this line using the FOR UPDATE addition when a single line is being read with SINGLE. Use the SELECT statement in this case only if all primary key fields in logical expressions linked by AND are checked to make sure they are the same in the WHERE condition. Otherwise, the resulting set is empty and sy-subrc is set to 8. If the lock causes deadlock, an exception occurs. If the FOR UPDATE addition is used, the SELECT command bypasses the SAP buffering.

Multiple-lined result set

Syntax

```
... [DISTINCT] { } ...
```

If SINGLE is not specified and if *columns* does not exclusively contain only aggregate expressions (see Section 29.2.1.2), the resulting set has multiple lines. All database lines that are selected by the remaining additions of the SELECT statement are included in the resulting list. If the ORDER BY addition is not used, the order of the lines in the resulting list is not defined. If the same SELECT statement is executed multiple times, the order may be different each time. A data object specified after INTO can be an internal table, and the APPENDING addition can be used. If no internal table is specified after INTO or APPENDING, the SELECT statement triggers a loop that has to be closed using ENDSELECT.

If multiple lines are read without SINGLE, the DISTINCT addition can be used to exclude duplicate lines from the resulting list. If the addition DIS-TINCT is used, the SELECT command bypasses the SAP buffering. The addition DISTINCT cannot be used in the following situations.

▶ If a column specified in *columns* has the type STRING, RAWSTRING, LCHAR or LRAW

▶ If the system tries to access pool or cluster tables and single columns are specified in *columns*.

Note
When SINGLE is being specified, the line to be read should be clearly specified in the WHERE condition for the sake of efficiency. When the data

is read from a database table, the system does this by specifying comparison values for the primary key. Note that, when specifying DISTINCT, you have to carry out sort operations for this in the database system.

29.2.1.2 Specifying Columns

Syntax of *columns*

```
...    *
   |  { {col1|agg( [DISTINCT] col1)}  [AS a1]
        {col2|agg( [DISTINCT] col2)}  [AS a2]   ... }
   |  (column_syntax) ...
```

The specifications in *columns* determine the columns that are used to make up the result set.

Static specification of all columns

Syntax

```
...    *  ...
```

If * is specified, the resulting set is built based on all columns in the database tables or views specified after FROM, in the order given there. The columns in the resulting set take on the name and data type from the database tables or views. Only one data object can be specified after INTO (see Section 29.2.3).

Note
If multiple database tables are specified after FROM, you cannot prevent multiple columns from getting the same name when you specify *.

Static specification of individual columns

Syntax

```
...  { {col1|agg( [DISTINCT] col1)}  [AS a1]
       {col2|agg( [DISTINCT] col2)}  [AS a2] ... } ...
```

A list of column labels col1, col2, ... is specified in order to build the resulting list from individual columns. An individual column can be specified directly or as an argument of an aggregate function *agg*. You can choose the order in which the column labels are specified in order to define the order of the columns in the result set. Only if a column of the type LCHAR or LRAW is listed does the corresponding length field also have to be specified directly before it (see Table 5.4). An individual column can be specified multiple times.

The addition AS can be used to define an alternative column name a1, a2, ... with a maximum of 14 digits in the resulting set for every column label col1, col2, ... The system uses the alternative column name in the additions INTO|APPENDING CORRESPONDING FIELDS and ORDER BY.

The following column labels are possible:

▶ If only a single database table or a single view is specified after FROM, the column labels in the database table—that is, the name of the components comp1, comp2, ...—can be specified directly for col1, col2, ... in the structure of the ABAP Dictionary.

▶ If the name of the component occurs in multiple database tables of the FROM addition, and if the desired database table or the view dbtab is only specified once after FROM, the names dbtab~comp1, dbtab~comp2, ... have to be specified for col1, col2, ... where. comp1, comp2, ... are the names of the components in the structure of the ABAP Dictionary.

▶ If the desired database table or view occurs multiple times after FROM, the names tabalias~comp1, tabalias~comp2, ... have to be specified for col1, col2, ... tabalias is the alternative table name of the database table or view defined after FROM; comp1, comp2, ... is the name of the component in the structure of the ABAP Dictionary.

Any number of specified column IDs can be listed as arguments of the following aggregate expressions, where the DISTINCT addition prevents any duplicated values during the calculation.

▶ MAX([DISTINCT] col1, col2, ...) determines the maximum value of the value in the column col1, col2, ... in the resulting set or in the current group.

▶ MIN([DISTINCT] col1, col2, ...) determines the minimum value of the content of the column col1, col2, ... in the resulting set or in the current group.

▶ AVG([DISTINCT] col1, col2, ...) determines the average value of the content of the column col1, col2, ... in the resulting set or in the current group. The data type of the column has to be numerical.

▶ SUM([DISTINCT] col1, col2, ...) determines the sum of the content of the column col1, col2, ... in the resulting set or in the current group. The data type of the column has to be numerical.

▶ COUNT(DISTINCT col1, col2, ...) determines the number of different values in the column col1, col2, ... in the resulting set or in the current group.

▶ COUNT(*) (or count(*)) determines the number of rows in the resulting set or in the current group. No column label is specified in this case.

If you are using aggregate expressions, all column labels that are not listed as parts of an argument of an aggregate function are listed after the addition GROUP BY (see Section 29.2.5). The aggregate functions evaluate the content of the groups defined by GROUP BY in the database system and transfer the result to the combined rows of the resulting set.

Note the following peculiarities when using aggregate expressions:

▶ If the addition FOR ALL ENTRIES is used in front of WHERE, or if cluster or pool tables are listed after FROM, no other aggregate expressions apart from COUNT(*) can be used.

▶ Columns of the type STRING or RAWSTRING must not be used with aggregate functions.

▶ When aggregate expressions are used, the SELECT statement bypasses the SAP buffering.

▶ Null values are not included in the calculation for the aggregate functions. The result is a null value only if all the rows in the column in question contain the null value.

▶ If only aggregate expressions are used after SELECT, the result set has one row and the addition GROUP BY is not necessary. If a non-table type target area is specified after INTO, the command ENDSELECT cannot be used as in the case with the addition SINGLE. If the aggregate expression count(*) is not being used, an internal table can be specified after INTO, and the first row of this table is filled.

▶ If aggregate functions are used exclusively without GROUP BY being specified at the same time, the resulting set also contains a row if no data is found in the database. If count(*) is used, the column in question contains the value 0. The columns in the other aggregate functions contain initial values. This row is assigned to the data object specified after INTO, and unless count(*) is being used exclusively, sy-subrc is set to 0 and sy-dbcnt is set to 1. If count(*) is used exclusively, the addition INTO can be omitted and if no data can be found in the database, sy-subrc is set to 4 and sy-dbcnt is set to 0.

The data type of a single column in the resulting list is the data type of the corresponding component in the ABAP Dictionary. The data type of aggregate expressions with the function MAX, MIN or SUM is the data type of the corresponding column in the ABAP Dictionary. Aggregate expressions with the function AVG have the data type FLTP, and those with COUNT have the data type INT4. The corresponding data object after INTO or APPENDING has to be selected accordingly. The corresponding data object after INTO or APPENDING has to be selected accordingly (see Table 29.1).

Note

If multiple database tables are specified after FROM, you can use alternative names when specifying single columns to avoid having multiple columns with the same name.

Example

Reading specific columns of a single row.

```
DATA wa TYPE spfli.
SELECT SINGLE carrid connid cityfrom cityto
       INTO CORRESPONDING FIELDS OF wa
       FROM spfli
       WHERE carrid EQ 'LH' AND connid EQ '0400'.

IF sy-subrc EQ 0.
  WRITE: / wa-carrid, wa-connid, wa-cityfrom, wa-cityto.
ENDIF.
```

Dynamic column entry

Syntax

```
... (column_syntax) ...
```

Instead of static data, a data object column_syntax in brackets can be specified, which, when the statement is executed, either contains the syntax shown with the static data or is initial. The data object column_syntax can be a character-type data object or an internal table with a character-type data type. The syntax in column_syntax, as with the ABAP editor, is not case-sensitive. When specifying an internal table, you can distribute the syntax over multiple rows.

If column_syntax is initial when the statement is executed, *columns* is implicitly set to * and all columns are read.

If columns are specified dynamically without the SINGLE addition, the resulting set is always regarded as having multiple rows.

Before Release 6.10, you could only specify for column_syntax an internal table with a flat character-type row type with a maximum of 72 characters. Also, before Release 6.10, if you used the DISTINCT addition for dynamic access to pool tables or cluster tables, this was ignored, but since Release 6.10, this causes a known exception.

Note
If column_syntax is an internal table with a header line, the table body and not the header line is evaluated.

Example
Read out how many flights go to and from a city. The SELECT statement is implemented only cnce in a sub-program. The column data, including the aggregate function and the data after GROUP BY, is dynamic. Instead of adding the column data to an internal l_columns table, you could just as easily concatenate it in a character-type l_columns field.

```
PERFORM my_select USING 'CITYFROM'.
ULINE.
PERFORM my_select USING 'CITYTO'.

FORM my_select USING l_group TYPE string.
  DATA: l_columns    TYPE TABLE OF string,
        l_container  TYPE string,
        l_count      TYPE i.
  APPEND l_group TO l_columns.
  APPEND 'count( * )' TO l_columns.
  SELECT (l_columns)
         FROM spfli
         INTO (l_ccntainer, l_count)
         GROUP BY (l_group).
    WRITE: / l_court, l_container.
  ENDSELECT.
ENDFORM.
```

29.2.2 Specifying Database Tables to Be Read

Syntax of *source*

```
... FROM { {dbtab [AS tabalias]}
         | join
         | {(dbtab_syntax) [AS tabalias]} }
         [UP TO n ROWS]
         [CLIENT SPECIFIED]
         [BYPASSING BUFFER] ...
```

Entries in *source* specify whether a single database table or view is accessed or if many database tables or views are accessed by a join expression. Optional additions execute the client handling, specify whether the SAP buffering is avoided, and determine the maximum number of rows to be read.

29.2.2.1 Specifying a Single Database Table or a Single View

Syntax

```
... dbtab [AS tabalias] ...
```

A database table or a view defined in the ABAP Dictionary can be specified for dbtab. An alternative table name tabalias can be assigned to the database table or the view using the addition AS. This name is valid only during the SELECT statement. In all other locations, it must be used instead of the actual name.

Note

If a database table or a view appears multiple times after FROM in a join expression, you must use the alternative name to avoid ambiguities.

Example

Reading from the database table SPFLI and assigning the alternative name s. In this case, the specification of the prefix s~ after ORDER BY can also be omitted, because only one database table is read and the column name carrid is unique. The prefix spfli~ can no longer be used when assigning the alternative name (see Section 29.2.1).

```
DATA wa TYPE spfli.
SELECT *
       FROM spfli AS s
       INTO wa
       ORDER BY s~carrid.
```

```
  WRITE: / wa-carrid, wa-connid.
ENDSELECT.
```

29.2.2.2 Defining Join

Syntax of *join*

```
... [(] {dbtab_left [AS tabalias_left]} | join
        { {[INNER] JOIN}|{LEFT [OUTER] JOIN} }
            {dbtab_right [AS tabalias_right]
                        ON join_cond} [)] ...
```

The *join* syntax represents a join expression that can be recursively nested. A join expression consists of left-hand and a right-hand sides, which are joined either by means of [INNER] JOIN or LEFT [OUTER] JOIN. Depending on the type of join, a join expression can be either an inner (INNER) or an outer (LEFT OUTER) join. Every join expression can be enclosed in round brackets. If a join expression is used, the SELECT statement bypasses the SAP buffering.

On the left-hand side, either a single database table a view dbtab_left or a join expression *join* can be specified. On the right-hand side, a single database table or a view dbtab_right as well as join conditions *join_cond* must be specified after ON. In this way, a maximum of 24 join expressions that join 25 database tables or views with one another can be specified after FROM.

AS can be used to specify an alternative table name tabalias for each of the specified database tables or for every view. A database table or a view can occur multiple times within a join expression and, in this case, have various alternative names.

The syntax of the join conditions *join_cond* is the same as that of the *cond* conditions after the addition WHERE (see Section 29.2.4), with the following differences:

▶ At least one comparison must be specified after ON.

▶ Individual comparisons may be joined using AND only.

▶ All comparisons must contain a column in the database table or the view dbtab_right on the right-hand side as an operand.

▶ The following language elements cannot be used: NOT, LIKE, IN.

▶ No sub-queries can be used.

▶ For outer joins, only equality comparisons (=, EQ) are possible.

- ▶ If an outer join occurs after FROM, the join condition of every join expression must contain at least one comparison between columns on the left-hand and the right-hand side.
- ▶ In outer joins, all comparisons that contain columns as operands in the database table or the view dbtab_right on the right-hand side must be specified in the corresponding join condition. In the WHERE condition of the same SELECT command, these columns are not allowed as operands.

Resulting set for an inner join

The inner join joins the columns of every selected line on the left-hand side with the columns of all lines on the right-hand side that jointly fulfill the *join_cond* condition. A line in the resulting set is created for every such line on the right-hand side. The content of the column on the left-hand side may be duplicated in this case. If none of the lines on the right-hand side fulfils the *join_cond* condition, no line is created in the resulting set.

Resulting set for an outer join

The outer join creates almost the same resulting set as the inner join, with the difference that at least one line is created in the resulting set for every selected line on the left-hand side, even if no line on the right-hand side fulfils the *join_cond* condition. The columns on the right-hand side that do not fulfill the *join_cond* condition are filled with null values.

Note

If a column name occurs in multiple database tables of a join expression, these database tables must be identified in all other additions of the SELECT statement by using the column selector ~.

Example

Join the columns CARRNAME, CONNID, FLDATE of the database tables SCARR, SPFLI and SFLIGHT by means of two inner joins. A list is created of the flights from p_cityfr to p_cityto. Alternative names are used for every table.

```
PARAMETERS: p_cityfr TYPE spfli-cityfrom,
            p_cityto TYPE spfli-cityto.

DATA: BEGIN OF wa,
        fldate   TYPE sflight-fldate,
        carrname TYPE scarr-carrname,
```

```
            connid    TYPE spfli-connid,
        END OF wa.

DATA itab LIKE SORTED TABLE OF wa
              WITH UNIQUE KEY fldate carrname connid.

SELECT c~carrname p~connid f~fldate
       INTO CORRESPONDING FIELDS OF TABLE itab
       FROM ( ( scarr AS c
         INNER JOIN spfli AS p ON   p~carrid   = c~carrid
                                AND p~cityfrom = p_cityfr
                                AND p~cityto   = p_cityto )
           INNER JOIN sflight AS f ON   f~carrid = p~carrid
                                    AND f~connid = p~connid ).

LOOP AT itab INTO wa.
  WRITE: / wa-fldate, wa-carrname, wa-connid.
ENDLOOP.
```

Example

Join the columns CARRID, CARRNAME and CONNID of the database tables SCARR and SPFLI using an outer join. The column CONNID is set to the null value for all flights that do not fly from p_cityfr. This null value is then converted to the appropriate initial value when it is transferred to the assigned data object. The LOOP loop returns all airlines that do not fly from p_cityfr.

```
PARAMETERS p_cityfr TYPE spfli-cityfrom.

DATA: BEGIN OF wa,
        carrid   TYPE scarr-carrid,
        carrname TYPE scarr-carrname,
        connid   TYPE spfli-connid,
      END OF wa,
      itab LIKE SORTED TABLE OF wa
              WITH NON-UNIQUE KEY carrid.

SELECT s~carrid s~carrname p~connid
       INTO CORRESPONDING FIELDS OF TABLE itab
       FROM scarr AS s
       LEFT OUTER JOIN spfli AS p
                  ON s~carrid = p~carrid
                  AND p~cityfrom = p_cityfr.

LOOP AT itab INTO wa.
  IF wa-connid = '0000'.
    WRITE: / wa-carrid, wa-carrname.
```

```
    ENDIF.
ENDLOOP.
```

29.2.2.3 Dynamically Specifying Database Tables

Syntax

```
... (dbtab_syntax) [AS tabalias] ...
```

Instead of static specifications, a data object dbtab_syntax can be specified in brackets. When executing the statement, it must contain the syntax displayed during the static specification. The data object dbtab_syn-
tax can be a character-type data object or an internal table with a
character-type data object. The syntax in dbtab_syntax is not case-sensitive as in the ABAP Editor. The syntax can be spread over many rows
when specifying an internal table.

The addition AS can be specified only if dbtab_syntax exclusively contains the name of a single database table or a view. The addition has the
same meaning for this database table or view as in a static specification.

When specifying the syntax in dbtab_syntax, the following restrictions
apply:

▶ Only a list of fields and no selection table can be specified in a join condition after the language element IN.

▶ No database table containing columns of the type RAWSTRING,
  SSTRING, or STRING must be used in a join expression.

Notes

If dbtab_syntax is an internal table with a header line, the header line
and not the table body is evaluated.

Prior to Release 6.10, you could specify only a flat, character-type data
object for dbtab_syntax, and this can contain only the name of a single
database table or a view in uppercase letters.

Example

Dynamic specification of the inner joins from the example above. The column specification after SELECT is also dynamic.

```
PARAMETERS: p_cityfr TYPE spfli-cityfrom,
            p_cityto TYPE spfli-cityto.

DATA: BEGIN OF wa,
        fldate   TYPE sflight-fldate,
```

```
          carrname TYPE scarr-carrname,
          connid   TYPE spfli-connid,
        END OF wa.

DATA itab LIKE SORTED TABLE OF wa
            WITH UNIQUE KEY fldate carrname connid.

DATA: column_syntax TYPE string,
      dbtab_syntax  TYPE string.

column_syntax = 'c~carrname p~connid f~fldate'.

dbtab_syntax = '( ( scarr AS c '
  & ' INNER JOIN spfli AS p ON p~carrid   = c~carrid'
  & ' AND p~cityfrom = p_cityfr'
  & ' AND p~cityto   = p_cityto )'
  & ' INNER JOIN sflight AS f ON f~carrid = p~carrid '
  & ' AND f~connid = p~connid )'.

SELECT (column_syntax)
       FROM (dbtab_syntax)
       INTO CORRESPONDING FIELDS OF TABLE itab.

LOOP AT itab INTO wa.
  WRITE: / wa-fldate, wa-carrname, wa-connid.
ENDLOOP.
```

29.2.2.4 Optional Additions after FROM

Maximum line number

Syntax

```
... UP TO n ROWS ...
```

This addition restricts the number of rows in the result set. A data object of the Type i is expected for n. A positive number in n indicates the maximum number of rows in the result set. If n contains the value 0, all selected rows are passed to the result set. If n contains a negative number, an exception that cannot be handled is raised.

If the addition ORDER BY is also specified, the rows of the hit list are sorted on the database server, and only the number of sorted rows is passed to the result set that is specified in n. If the addition ORDER BY is not specified, n is filled in the result set with any number of rows that meet the WHERE condition.

Client handling

Syntax

```
... CLIENT SPECIFIED ...
```

This addition switches off the automatic client handling of Open SQL. When specifying a single database table or a single view, the addition must be inserted directly after dbtab. When specifying a join expression, it must be inserted after the last addition ON of the join condition.

When using the addition CLIENT SPECIFIED, the first column of the client-dependent database tables can be specified in the WHERE condition to determine the client identifier. In the addition ORDER BY, the column can be sorted explicitly according to client identifier.

Buffer handling

Syntax

```
... BYPASSING BUFFER ...
```

This addition causes the SELECT statement to avoid the SAP buffering and to read directly from the database and not from the buffer on the application server.

29.2.3   Specifying the Target Area

Syntax of *target*

```
... { INTO
        { {[CORRESPONDING FIELDS OF] wa}|(dobj1, dobj2 ...)} }
    | { INTO|APPENDING
        [CORRESPONDING FIELDS OF] TABLE itab
        [PACKAGE SIZE n] } ...
```

target specifies the data objects to which the result set of a SELECT statement is assigned. You can either specify a single work area wa or a list of data objects dobj1, dobj2, ... after INTO, or you can specify an internal table itab after INTO or APPENDING. If the result set is empty, the objects remain unchanged.

Note

For the specification of target, there is no dynamic variant that corresponds to the other additions. Instead, you can work with dynamically created data objects (see the example for CREATE DATA in Section 9.2.3).

29.2.3.1 Specifying an Individual Work Area

Syntax

```
... INTO [CORRESPONDING FIELDS OF] wa ...
```

For wa, you can specify a data object that meets the prerequisites described in Section 29.8. If the result set consists of a single line, this line is assigned to wa. If the result set has multiple lines, SELECT must be followed by an ENDSELECT statement; the result set is assigned to the work area wa line-by-line and can be evaluated in the loop. After ENDSELECT, the work area wa contains the line that was assigned last.

The lines of the result set are assigned as follows, based on the column specification after SELECT:

Specifying * without the CORRESPONDING FIELDS addition

If all columns are read with * and CORRESPONDING FIELDS is not specified, the line of the result set is assigned left-justified and unconverted according to the structure of the result set. Non-affected parts of wa retain their original content. To enable type-dependent access to the components of the result set after the assignment, the work area wa must be structured the same way as the result set.

All other combinations

If the result set consists of a single column specified explicitly after SELECT or a single aggregate expression, wa can be an elementary data object or a structure. If the result set consists of multiple columns, it must be a structure and the following rules apply:

▶ If the CORRESPONDING FIELDS addition is not specified, wa must contain enough components, and the contents of the columns are assigned to the components of wa from left to right in the order specified after SELECT.

▶ If the CORRESPONDING FIELDS addition is specified, only those contents of columns for which there are identically named components in wa are assigned to them; alternative column names are taken into account. Columns and aggregate expressions that appear multiple times can only be assigned using alternative column names if CORRESPONDING FIELDS is specified. If a column name appears multiple times and no alternative column name was specified, the last column listed is assigned.

The assignment rules from Section 29.2.3.4 apply to the individual assignments.

Example

In this example, four columns of the result set are read into four correspondingly named components of a work area.

```
DATA wa TYPE spfli.

SELECT carrid connid cityfrom cityto
     FROM spfli
     INTO CORRESPONDING FIELDS OF wa.
  WRITE: / wa-carrid, wa-connid, wa-cityfrom, wa-cityto.
ENDSELECT.
```

29.2.3.2 Specifying a List of Data Objects

Syntax

```
... INTO (dobj1, dobj2 ...) ...
```

If the result set consists of several columns or aggregate expressions specified explicitly after SELECT, you can specify a list of elementary data objects dobj1, dobj2, ... in brackets and separated by commas after INTO. You must specify the same number of elementary data objects dobj1, dobj2, ... as there are columns in the result set. The contents of the columns in the result set are assigned to the data objects from left to right, according to the order specified after SELECT. The assignment rules from Section 29.2.3.4 apply to the individual assignments.

If the result set consists of one line, the columns are assigned from that line. If the result set contains multiple lines, SELECT must be followed by an ENDSELECT statement; the columns of the result set are assigned to the data objects line-by-line, and they can be evaluated in a loop.

Example

In this example, four columns of the result set are read into four individually specified columns of a structure. Unlike in the previous example, the runtime environment does not compare names here.

```
DATA wa TYPE spfli.

SELECT carrid connid cityfrom cityto
     FROM spfli
     INTO (wa-carrid, wa-connid, wa-cityfrom, wa-cityto).
  WRITE: / wa-carrid, wa-connid, wa-cityfrom, wa-cityto.
ENDSELECT.
```

29.2.3.3 Specifying Internal Tables

Syntax

```
... INTO|APPENDING [CORRESPONDING FIELDS OF] TABLE itab
                   [PACKAGE SIZE n] ...
```

If the result set consists of multiple lines, an internal table itab of any table type can be specified after INTO or APPENDING. The row type of the internal table must meet the prerequisites in Section 29.8.

The result set is inserted into the internal table itab line by line; a sorting process is executed in the case of a sorted table. If INTO is used, the internal table is initialized before the first line is inserted. Previous lines remain intact if APPENDING is used.

Before any assignment of a line of the result set, an initial row of the internal table itab is created and the line of the result set is assigned to this row. When assigning a line of the result set to a row of the internal table with or without CORRESPONDING FIELDS, the same rules apply as when assigning to an individual work area wa (see Section 29.2.3.1).

If the PACKAGE SIZE addition is not used, all lines of the result set are inserted in the internal table itab and the ENDSELECT statement must not be specified after SELECT.

If you specify the PACKAGE SIZE addition, all lines of the result set are processed in a loop, and this must be closed with ENDSELECT. The lines are inserted in the internal table itab in packages of n lines. For n a type i data object that contains the number of lines is expected. If the value of n is smaller than 0, an exception that cannot be handled occurs. If n is equal to 0, all lines of the result set are inserted in the internal table itab.

If INTO is used, the internal table is initialized before each loop pass, and in the SELECT loop it only contains the lines of the current package. If APPENDING is used, a further package is added to the existing rows of the internal table in each SELECT loop.

After ENDSELECT, the contents of itab is not defined if INTO is used; instead, the table either can contain the lines of the last package or it can be initial. If APPENDING is used, the content of itab retains the state of the last loop pass.

Note
In the case of an internal table with a unique key, an exception that cannot be handled occurs if an attempt is made to create a duplicate entry

Example

In this example, all columns of the result set are read into an internal table whose row type is a nested structure with the same construction as the result set. Note that, in practice, the column `carrid` exists twice in the result set with the same content, and, after the assignment, this content is stored redundantly in the columns `struc1-carrid` and `struc2-carrid` of the internal table.

```
DATA: BEGIN OF wa,
          struc1 TYPE scarr,
          struc2 TYPE spfli,
        END OF wa.

DATA itab LIKE SORTED TABLE OF wa
           WITH UNIQUE KEY table_line.

SELECT *
       FROM scarr
       INNER JOIN spfli ON scarr~carrid = spfli~carrid
       INTO TABLE itab.

LOOP AT itab INTO wa.
  WRITE: / wa-struc1-carrid,
           wa-struc1-carrname,
           wa-struc2-connid.
ENDLOOP.
```

29.2.3.4 Assignment Rules for Individual Columns

Table 29.1 shows the prerequisites for assigning individual columns of the result set to individual data objects. This applies to all forms of the SELECT statement, except when all columns in a work area wa are read with * and CORRESPONDING FIELDS is not specified at the same time. The table shows which data types of the result set (see Table 5.4) can be assigned to which ABAP data types.

Data type of the columns in the result set	ABAP data type
CHAR, CLNT, CUKY, LANG, SSTRING, STRING, UNIT, VARC	c, string
ACCP, NUMC	c, n
LCHR	c
RAW, RAWSTRING	x, xstring

Table 29.1 Assignment of the data types in the ABAP Dictionary to ABAP data types for which values can be assigned

Data type of the columns in the result set	ABAP data type
LRAW	x
CURR, DEC, INT1, INT2, INT4, PREC, QUAN	i, p, f
FLTP	f
DATS	d
TIMS	t

Table 29.1 Assignment of the data types in the ABAP Dictionary to ABAP data types for which values can be assigned (cont.)

The following rules apply to the assignment procedure:

▶ If the target field is of data type c or x, the content of the result field is inserted left-aligned into the target field. If the target field is too short, the result is truncated to the right. If the target field is too long, spaces or hexadecimal 0 are filled to the right.

▶ If the target field is of data type string or xstring, the content of the result field is inserted left-aligned into the target field. In result fields of the type STRING, closing blanks are adopted. The target field has the same length as the result field.

▶ If the target field is of data type n, the content of the result field is inserted right-aligned into the target field. If necessary, it is filled with zeros to the left. If the target field is too short, the result is truncated to the left.

▶ If the target field is of the numerical data type i, p or f, the value area must be big enough for the value of the result field.

▶ If the result field contains a null value, a type-specific initial value (see Table 5.2) is assigned to the target field.

As of Release 6.10, strings can be specified after INTO.

RELEASE

6.10

29.2.4 Restricting the Result Set

Syntax

```
... [FOR ALL ENTRIES IN itab] WHERE cond ...
```

The addition WHERE restricts the number of lines included in the result set by the statement SELECT by using a logical expression *cond*. The logical expression compares the content of columns in the database with the content of ABAP data objects or with the content of other columns. You can use the optional addition FOR ALL ENTRIES to compare the content of a column in the database with a component of all lines of a structured internal table `itab`.

The logical expression `cond` is true, false or unknown. The expression is unknown if one of the columns involved in the database contains a null value and is evaluated with another comparison as IS NULL. A line is only included in the resulting set if the logical expression is true.

Except for the columns of type STRING or RAWSTRING, all columns of the database tables or views listed after FROM can be evaluated in the WHERE condition. The columns do not necessarily have to be a part of the resulting set.

Notes

▶ The client identifier cannot be queried in the WHERE condition if the automatic client handling is not deactivated using the addition CLIENT SPECIFIED after FROM.

▶ The WHERE condition of the SELECT statement described here includes the WHERE conditions of the Open SQL statements DELETE, OPEN CURSOR and UPDATE.

▶ The logical expressions of the WHERE condition can also all be used after the addition HAVING and sometimes in the ON condition of a join expression after the addition FROM.

29.2.4.1 Logical Expressions in the WHERE Condition

The logical expression `cond` in the WHERE condition is similar to the general logical expressions for control statements (see Chapter 13). There are logical expressions with relational operators and other terms. Logical expressions can be linked to form an expression.

A single logical expression for a WHERE condition must always contain at least one column `col` from one of the database tables or views listed after FROM as an operand. You can specify the same column names (`comp`, `dbtab~comp`, `tabalias~comp`) for `col` as are listed in the specification of single columns after SELECT. You cannot specify aggregate expressions.

Comparisons with relational operators

Syntax of *cond*

```
... col operator f ...
```

The logical expression compares the content of the column `col`, corresponding to the relational operator *operator*, with the content of `f`. For `f`, another column of a database table specified behind `FROM`, an ABAP data object, or a scalar subquery (see Section 29.2.4.2) can be used. If `f` is another column, it must be specified via `dbtab~comp` or `tabalias~comp`.

Table 29.2 shows the possible relational operators.

Operator	Meaning
=, EQ	True, if the content of `col` is the same as the content of `f`.
<>, NE	True, if the content of `col` is different from the content of `f`.
<, LT	True, if the content of `col` is less than the content of `f`.
>, GT	True, if the content of `col` is greater than the content of `f`.
<=, LE	True, if the content of `col` is less than or equal to the content of `f`.
>=, GE	True, if the content of `col` is greater than or equal to the content of `f`.

Table 29.2 Relational Operators in the WHERE Condition

You should note the following when using these operators:

▶ If `f` is an ABAP data object, it is—if necessary—converted before the comparison to the data type that matches the type of the column `col` according to Table 5.4. The conversion is done according to the rules in Section A.2.

▶ If `f` is a column of a database table specified behind `FROM`, the types and lengths of both operators must be equal; otherwise, the result depends on the database system.

▶ In large/small comparisons with character-type columns the result can depend on the code page used by the database system.

Example
Reading overbooked flights.

```
DATA sflight_tab TYPE TABLE OF sflight.

SELECT carrid connid fldate
       FROM sflight
       INTO CORRESPONDING FIELDS OF TABLE sflight_tab
       WHERE seatsocc > sflight~seatsmax.
```

Checking interval relevance

Syntax of *cond*

```
... col [NOT] BETWEEN dobj1 AND dobj2 ...
```

This expression is true if the content of the column `col` lies (or does not lie) between the values of the data objects `dobj1` and `dobj2` (interval limits enclosed). You cannot define a column identifier for the interval limits.

Example

Readout of all flights within the next 30 days.

```
DATA sflight_tab TYPE TABLE OF sflight.
DATA date TYPE d.

date = sy-datum + 30.

SELECT carrid connid fldate
       FROM sflight
       INTO CORRESPONDING FIELDS OF TABLE sflight_tab
       WHERE fldate BETWEEN sy-datum AND date.
```

Comparing with character strings

Syntax of *cond*

```
... col [NOT] LIKE dobj [ESCAPE esc] ...
```

This expression is true if the value of the column `col` fits (does not fit) the pattern in the data object `dobj`. It is not possible to specify a column ID for `dobj`. The data types of the column `col` and the data object `dobj` must be character-type.

Mask characters can be used to create the pattern in `dobj`, where "%" represents any character string, even an empty one, and "_" represents any character. Capitalization is taken into account. Closing blank characters at the end of `dobj` are ignored. This is also valid in particular for data objects of the type `string` whose closing blank characters are otherwise taken into account in ABAP.

With the addition `ESCAPE`, an escape symbol can be defined. `esc` must be a flat character-like data object of the length 1, the content of which is used as an escape symbol. `esc` is always accessed like a data object of the data type `c` of the length 1. An escape symbol may only be placed before a mask character or before the escape symbol itself. In this case, they lose their special meaning. The addition `ESCAPE` cannot be used when accessing pool or cluster tables.

Notes

▶ The use of the wildcard characters "_" and "%" corresponds to the standard of SQL. In the rest of ABAP, the mask characters "+" and "*" are used in similar logical expressions, in particular when selection tables are used.

► You should not use patterns that are closed by mask characters to search for closing blanks. The semantics of searches of this type are dependent on the database system that is used and in general do not lead to the desired result.

Example
Full-text search in a text table.

```
PARAMETERS srch_str(20) TYPE c.
CONCATENATE '%' srch_str '%' INTO srch_str.

DATA text_tab TYPE TABLE OF dokt1.

SELECT *
       FROM dokt1
       INTO TABLE text_tab
       WHERE doktext LIKE srch_str.
```

Evaluating a value list

Syntax of *cond*

```
... col [NOT] IN (dobj1 dobj2 ...) ...
```

This expression is true if the value of the column `col` matches (does not match) the contents of a data object in a value list. The value list is specified as a list of elementary objects `dobj1`, `dobj2`, ... in parentheses and separated by commas.

Example
Reading the bookings in which the class does not lie in the value range (C – Business, F – First, Y – Economy) of the corresponding domain in the ABAP Dictionary.

```
DATA sbook_tab TYPE TABLE OF sbook.
SELECT *
       FROM sbook
       INTO TABLE sbook_tab
       WHERE class NOT IN ('C','F','Y').

IF sy-subrc = 0.
  "Error handling
ENDIF.
```

Evaluating a selection table

Syntax of *cond*

```
... col [NOT] IN seltab ...
```

This expression is true if the value of the column `col` is (or is not) in the result set described in the rows of the selection table `seltab`. Any internal table with a row type that corresponds to that of a selection table can be specified as the selection table `seltab` (see Section 26.4). This includes, in particular, ranges tables.

The selection table is evaluated in the same way as in logical expressions apart from the fact that in comparisons with the operators CP and NP the capitalization in the WHERE condition is taken into account whereas in other logical expressions it is not (see Section 13.5).

If the selection table is inital, the expression is true. If the selection table contains invalid values, an untreatable exception occurs.

Example
Reading of flights with a primary key that corresponds to the user entries on the selection screen.

```
DATA spfli_wa TYPE spfli.

SELECT-OPTIONS: s_carrid FOR spfli_wa-carrid
                         NO INTERVALS
                         NO-EXTENSION,
                s_connid FOR spfli_wa-connid
                         NO INTERVALS
                         NO-EXTENSION.

SELECT SINGLE *
       FROM spfli
       INTO spfli_wa
       WHERE carrid IN s_carrid AND
             connid IN s_connid.
```

Checking null values

Syntax of *cond*

```
... col IS [NOT] NULL ...
```

This expression is true if the value of `col` is (or is not) the null value. When using this expression, the SELECT statement bypasses the SAP buffering.

Note
All other logical expression of the WHERE condition are unknown if a participating column contains the null value.

Dynamic logical expression

Syntax of *cond*

```
... (cond_syntax) ...
```

A logical expression can be specified as a parenthesized data object cond_syntax that contains the syntax of a logical expression or is initial when the statement is executed.

It has been possible since Release 6.40 to specify all logical expressions dynamically, with the exception of the evaluation of a subquery (see Sections 29.2.4.2 and 29.2.4.3). Before Release 6.20 (Kernel Patch 1008), the evaluation of an internal table specified after FOR ALL ENTRIES in a logical expression was not possible (see Section 29.2.4.4). Up to Release 6.40, it was impossible to check a selection table (see Section 29.2.4.1).

In particular, the logical expression in cond_syntax can also be combined using AND or OR, or it can be negated using NOT. The data object cond_syntax can be a character-type data object or an internal table with a character-type data type. The syntax in cond_syntax is, as in the ABAP Editor, not case-sensitive. In the case of the specification of an internal table, the syntax can be spread across multiple rows.

The result of the logical expression cond_syntax is determined by the result of the contained logical expression. If cond_syntax is initial when the statement is executed, the logical expression is true.

Before Release 6.10, it was only possible to specify an internal table with a flat character-type row type with a maximum of 72 characters for cond_syntax. It was also impossible before Release 6.10 for the condition in cond_syntax to contain any named data objects as operands dobj. Only literals could be specified. Furthermore, before Release 6.10, a dynamic logical expression could only be used in the WHERE or HAVING condition of the SELECT statement, but not in the statements DELETE and UPDATE.

Note
If cond_syntax is an internal table with a header line, the table body is evaluated, and not the header line.

Example
Creating a dynamic comparison from user input. In the case of an incorrect syntax or incorrect semantics, exceptions are triggered which are handled using the common superclass.

```
PARAMETERS: column(8) TYPE c,
            value(30) TYPE c.

DATA spfli_wa TYPE spfli.

DATA cond_syntax TYPE string.

CONCATENATE column '= value'
            INTO cond_syntax SEPARATED BY space.

TRY.
    SELECT SINGLE *
           FROM spfli
           INTO spfli_wa
           WHERE (cond_syntax).
  CATCH cx_sy_dynamic_osql_error.
    MESSAGE 'Wrong WHERE condition!' TYPE 'I'.
ENDTRY.
```

Linking and negating logical expressions

Syntax

```
... cond1 AND cond2 AND cond3 ...
```

Link with the logical operator AND.

Syntax

```
... cond1 OR cond2 OR cond3 ...
```

Link with the logical operator OR.

Syntax

```
... NOT cond ...
```

Negation with the logical operator NOT.

Any number of logical expressions can be linked to a logical expression using AND or OR and the result of a logical expression can be negated using NOT. The same rules apply as for general logical expressions described in Section 13.6. Explicit use of parentheses is also possible.

For logical expressions of which the result is unknown, the following additional rules apply:

▶ The AND linking of two unknown expressions or one true expression with an unknown expression results in an unknown expression. The

AND linking of a false expression with an unknown expression results in a false expression.

▶ The OR linking of two unknown expressions or one false expression with an unknown expression results in an unknown expression. The OR linking of one true and one unknown expression results in a true expression.

▶ The negation of an unknown expression with NOT results in an unknown expression.

Note
The expressions specified dynamically as (cond_syntax) are also possible as logical expressions within a link or negation.

Example
Read flights from Frankfurt to Los Angeles or San Francisco.

```
DATA spfli_tab TYPE TABLE OF spfli.

SELECT *
       FROM spfli
       INTO TABLE spfli_tab
       WHERE cityfrom = 'FRANKFURT' AND
             ( cityto = 'LOS ANGELES' OR
               cityto = 'SAN FRANCISCO' ).
```

29.2.4.2 Subqueries

Syntax of *subquery*

```
... ( SELECT result
             FROM source
             [WHERE cond]
             [GROUP BY cols] [HAVING group_cond] ) ...
```

A subquery is a SELECT statement in parenthesis that can be used for a subquery in special logical expressions *cond* of the WHERE condition. The additions INTO and ORDER BY from the normal SELECT statement cannot be used.

A subquery with a single-column resulting set is known as a scalar subquery. This occurs when the specification of the expression *columns* in *result* (see Section 29.2.1) of the subquery is limited to one column or to an aggregate expression

Subqueries can be nested by using subqueries in the WHERE condition of a subquery. In nested subqueries, the columns specified in the WHERE conditions are searched inside out, though the columns of inner subqueries conceal columns with the same name in outer subqueries. A subquery that uses columns from the surrounding SELECT statement in its WHERE condition is known as a correlated subquery. It must be possible to assign the column uniquely to a database table or to a view in the surrounding SELECT statement. A correlated subquery is evaluated for each individual line of the resulting set in the surrounding SELECT statement.

A maximum of 10 SELECT statements are permitted within one ABAP statement, in other words the SELECT statement itself and a maximum of nine other subqueries. This restriction does not depend on whether the subqueries are nested or occur in different logical expressions of the WHERE condition.

Subqueries cannot be used when accessing pool tables or cluster tables.

29.2.4.3 Logical Expressions for Subqueries

Two special logical expressions *cond* are available for evaluating subqueries in the WHERE condition.

Using an Arbitrary Subquery

Syntax of *cond*

```
... [NOT] EXISTS subquery ...
```

This expression is true if the resulting set of the *subquery* subquery contains (does not contain) at least one line.

Using a Scalar Subquery

Syntax of *cond*

```
... col [NOT] IN subquery ...
```

This expression is true if the value of the col column is (not) contained in the resulting set of the scalar *subquery* subquery.

Comparison with Scalar Subqueries

Scalar subqueries can also be used as operands in comparisons with the relational operators from Table 29.2. If the resulting set of the subquery contains only one line, the *cond* comparison can be specified as usual:

Syntax

```
... col operator subquery ...
```

This expression is true if the relevant comparison of the value of `col` with the result of the scalar subquery `subquery` returns "true." Whether the resulting set contains only one line is checked when the statement is executed and does not depend on the addition `SINGLE` after the `SELECT` statement of the subquery. If the resulting set contains more than one line, an error occurs that cannot be handled.

If the resulting set of the subquery contains more than one line, the comparison `cond` must be specified as follows:

Syntax

```
... col operator {ALL|ANY|SOME} subquery ...
```

When using `ALL`, the expression is true if the comparison is true for all lines in the resulting set of the scalar `subquery` subquery. With the addition `ANY` or `SOME`, the expression is true if it is true for at least one line in the resulting set of the subquery.

Note

The matching operator (= or `EQ`), together with `ANY` or `SOME`, functions like the previous `IN` operator.

Example

Exporting the geographical longitude and latitude of a city from the database table SGEOCITY, which is the departure city of a flight in the database table SPFLI.

```
PARAMETERS: carr_id TYPE spfli-carrid,
            conn_id TYPE spfli-connid.

DATA: city  TYPE sgeocity-city,
      lati  TYPE p DECIMALS 2,
      longi TYPE p DECIMALS 2.

SELECT SINGLE city latitude longitude
       INTO (city, lati, longi)
       FROM sgeocity
       WHERE city IN ( SELECT cityfrom
                              FROM spfli
                              WHERE carrid = carr_id
                              AND connid = conn_id ).
```

29.2.4.4 Comparison with an Internal Table

If the addition FOR ALL ENTRIES is specified before the language element WHERE, then the components comp of the internal table itab can be used as operands in comparison with the relational operators from Table 29.2.

Syntax of *cond*

```
... col operator itab-comp ...
```

The internal table itab must have a structured line type and the component comp must be compatible with the column col.

The logical expression *cond* of the WHERE condition can comprise various logical expressions by using AND and OR. However, if FOR ALL ENTRIES is specified, there must be at least one comparison with a column of the internal table itab, specified either statistically or dynamically (as of Release 6.40). In a SELECT statement with FOR ALL ENTRIES, the addition ORDER BY can only be used with the addition PRIMARY KEY.

The whole logical expression *cond* is evaluated for each individual line of the internal table itab. The resulting set of the SELECT statement is the union of the resulting sets from the individual evaluations. Duplicate lines are automatically removed from the resulting set. If the internal table itab is empty, the whole WHERE statement is ignored and all lines in the database are put in the resulting set.

As of Release 6.10, the same internal table can be specified after FOR ALL ENTRIES and after INTO.

Note
The addition FOR ALL ENTRIES is only possible before WHERE conditions of the SELECT statement.

Example
Exporting all flight data for a specified departure city. The relevant airlines and flight numbers are first put in an internal table entry_tab which is then evaluated in the WHERE condition of the subsequent SELECT statement.

```
PARAMETERS p_city TYPE spfli-cityfrom.

TYPES: BEGIN OF entry_tab_type,
         carrid TYPE spfli-carrid,
         connid TYPE spfli-connid,
       END OF entry_tab_type.
```

```
DATA: entry_tab    TYPE TABLE OF entry_tab_type,
      sflight_tab TYPE SORTED TABLE OF sflight
                              WITH UNIQUE KEY
                                  carrid connid fldate.

SELECT carrid connid
       FROM spfli
       INTO CORRESPONDING FIELDS OF TABLE entry_tab
       WHERE cityfrom = p_city.

SELECT carrid connid fldate
       FROM sflight
       INTO CORRESPONDING FIELDS OF TABLE sflight_tab
       FOR ALL ENTRIES IN entry_tab
       WHERE carrid = entry_tab-carrid AND
             connid = entry_tab-connid.
```

29.2.5 Combining Lines

Syntax

```
... GROUP BY { {col1 col2 ...} | (column_syntax) } ...
```

The addition GROUP BY combines groups of rows that have the same content in their specified columns col1, col2, ... in the resulting set into a single row.

The use of GROUP BY has the prerequisite that after SELECT only individual columns, not all the columns, are specified using * (see Section 29.2.1). If GROUP BY is used, all columns that are specified directly after SELECT and not specified as an argument of an aggregate function must be listed there. Conversely, if GROUP BY is used, all the columns listed after SELECT that are not specified after GROUP BY must be specified as an argument of an aggregate function. The aggregate functions define how the content of these columns is determined in the combined row from the contents of all the rows of a group.

After GROUP BY, the same column identifiers col1, col2, ... must be specified as after SELECT. The specification can either be specified statically as a list col1, col2, ... or dynamically as a bracketed data object column_ syntax that—at the execution of the statement—contains the syntax of the static specification or is initial. For column_syntax, the same applies as for the dynamic column specification after SELECT.

If the content of `column_syntax` initial, either all the rows or no rows at all are grouped together. The columns after SELECT must then be listed either solely as arguments of aggregate functions or solely directly. If not, prior to Release 6.10 you could trigger a runtime error. As of Release 6.10, this would trigger an exception CX_SY_OPEN_SQL_DB that can be handled.

The columns listed after GROUP BY must not be of type STRING or RAW-STRING, and if GROUP BY is used, pool or cluster tables cannot be accessed.

29.2.6 Restricting Combined Lines

Syntax

```
... HAVING group_cond ...
```

The addition HAVING limits the number of lines to be grouped into groups in the resulting set by a logical expression `group_cond` for these lines. The syntax of the logical expression `group_cond` corresponds to the syntax of the logical expression `cond` of the WHERE condition. The comparisons of the logical expression evaluate the contents of line groups.

If a grouping is done using the addition GROUP BY, all the columns that are specified in the condition `group_cond` directly through their name `col` will be listed after GROUP BY. The direct specification of different columns leads to an exception CX_SY_OPEN_SQL_DB that can be handled. For any columns in the database tables or views listed after FROM, arbitrary aggregate expressions (see Section 29.2.1) can be specified in the comparisons of `group_cond`. This kind of aggregate expression is evaluated for each line group defined in GROUP BY and its result is used as an operand in the comparison. If such a column is also listed simultaneously as an argument of an aggregate function after SELECT, the aggregate expressions after SELECT and after HAVING can be different.

If the addition GROUP BY is not specified, or if the data object `column_syntax` in the dynamic column specification after GROUP BY is initial, the addition HAVING can only be specified if the entire resulting set is grouped into a line, if—in other words—you have only aggregate expressions after SELECT. In this case, solely aggregate expressions can be specified as operands in `group_cond`. These operands are evaluated for all lines of the resulting set.

The use of aggregate expressions as an operand in dynamic HAVING conditions is possible only as of Release 6.10.

Example
Reading the number of booked smoking or non-smoking seats for each flight date of a particular flight connection.

```
PARAMETERS: p_carrid TYPE sbook-carrid,
            p_connid TYPE sbook-connid.

TYPES: BEGIN OF sbook_type,
         fldate  TYPE sbook-fldate,
         smoker  TYPE sbook-smoker,
         smk_cnt TYPE i,
       END OF sbook_type.

DATA sbook_tab TYPE TABLE OF sbook_type.

SELECT fldate smoker COUNT( * ) AS smk_cnt
     FROM sbook
     INTO CORRESPONDING FIELDS OF TABLE sbook_tab
     WHERE connid = p_connid
     GROUP BY carrid fldate smoker
     HAVING carrid = p_carrid
     ORDER BY fldate smoker.
```

29.2.7 Sorting Result Set Lines

Syntax

```
... ORDER BY { {PRIMARY KEY}
            | { {col1|a1} [ASCENDING|DESCENDING]
                {col2|a2} [ASCENDING|DESCENDING] ... }
            | (column_syntax) } ...
```

The addition ORDER BY sorts the resulting set for the content of the specified columns. The order of the lines in the result set referring to all the columns that are not listed after ORDER BY is undefined, and it can be different in different executions of the same SELECT statement.

The addition ORDER BY can only be used with the addition PRIMARY KEY at the same time as the addition FOR ALL ENTRIES of the WHERE condition.

Note
If a sorted resulting set is assigned to a sorted internal table, the internal table is sorted again according to the sorting instructions.

29.2.7.1 Sorting According to Primary Key

Syntax

```
... PRIMARY KEY ...
```

If all columns are specified by the entry of * after SELECT, and a single database table is specified after FROM (rather than a view or a join expression), the addition PRIMARY KEY can be used to sort the resulting set in an ascending order according to the content of the primary key of this database table.

The addition PRIMARY KEY cannot be specified if a view or a join expression is statically specified after FROM. If a view or a join expression is specified after FROM in the dynamic specification dbtab_syntax, the data is sorted according to all the columns of the resulting set.

29.2.7.2 Sorting According to Any Column

Syntax

```
... { {col1|a1}  [ASCENDING|DESCENDING]
      {col2|a2}  [ASCENDING|DESCENDING] } ...
```

For any column specifications after SELECT, a list of columns can be entered after ORDER BY according to which the resulting set should be sorted. Only columns that are listed after SELECT can be entered. Columns can be specified directly using the column names col1, col2, ... or the alternative column names a1, a2, ... The latter is required if you want to sort by columns that are specified as aggregate expressions. In case a column name is not unique when accessing multiple database tables, the column must be identified using the column selector ~.

The additions ASCENDING and DESCENDING determine whether the rows are sorted in an ascending or descending order. If neither addition is specified, the sort is performed in an ascending order. The priority of sorting is based on the order in which the components col1, col2, ... or a1, a2, ... are specified.

Pooled and cluster tables cannot be sorted by all types of column. Columns specified after ORDER BY must not be of the type LCHAR, LRAW, STRING or RAWSTRING. If any columns are specified, the statement SELECT bypasses the SAP buffering.

29.2.7.3 Dynamic Column Specification

Syntax

```
... (column_syntax) ...
```

As an alternative to the static-column specification, a bracketed data object `column_syntax` can be specified. This syntax either contains the syntax of the list of columns or is initial when the statement is executed. The addition `PRIMARY KEY` cannot be specified in `column_syntax`. For `column_syntax`, the same applies as for the dynamic specification of columns after `SELECT`. If the content of `column_syntax` is initial, the addition `ORDER BY` is ignored.

Note

For performance reasons, sorting should only be performed in the database system if the sort is supported by an index.

Example

Selecting the database table SFLIGHT in a method, whereby the sort criterion is transferred as an input parameter. In this case, the user must enter the criterion in correct syntax on the selection screen. In a proper application, you would normally prepare an input help using a selection list.

```
TYPES sflight_table_type TYPE TABLE OF sflight.
CLASS handle_sflight DEFINITION.
  PUBLIC SECTION.
    CLASS-METHODS select_sort_sflight
          IMPORTING sort_crit   TYPE string
          EXPORTING sflight_tab TYPE sflight_table_type
          RAISING cx_sy_dynamic_osql_error.
ENDCLASS.

PARAMETERS p_sort(40) TYPE c.

DATA: s_sort      TYPE string,
      result_tab TYPE sflight_table_type.

TRY.
    s_sort = p_sort.
    handle_sflight=>select_sort_sflight(
      EXPORTING sort_crit = s_sort
      IMPORTING sflight_tab = result_tab ).
  CATCH cx_sy_dynamic_osql_error.
    MESSAGE 'Wrong sort criterium!' TYPE 'I'.
ENDTRY.
```

```
CLASS handle_sflight IMPLEMENTATION.
   METHOD select_sort_sflight.
      SELECT *
             FROM sflight
             INTO TABLE sflight_tab
             ORDER BY (sort_crit).
   ENDMETHOD.
ENDCLASS.
```

29.3   Reading Data from Database Tables Using a Cursor

Unlike the SELECT statement, generation of a result set when reading with a cursor occurs separately from the transfer of data from the result set to the data objects of the ABAP program.

29.3.1   Opening a Cursor

OPEN CURSOR

Opening a cursor for a selection.

Syntax

```
OPEN CURSOR [WITH HOLD] dbcur FOR
   SELECT result
          FROM source
          [[FOR ALL ENTRIES IN itab] WHERE cond]
          [GROUP BY cols] [HAVING group_cond]
          [ORDER BY sort_args].
```

This statement opens a database cursor for the selection defined after FOR, and links a cursor variable dbcur with this database cursor. For dbcur, a variable declared with the specific predefined data type cursor must be entered (see Section 5.2.4). A database cursor dbcur that has already been opened cannot be opened again. A line of the resulting set is always assigned to an opened database cursor as a cursor position. After the OPEN CURSOR statement, the database cursor is positioned in front of the first line of the resulting set.

After FOR, the syntax of a SELECT statement can be entered, containing all the additions of the normal SELECT statement (see Section 29.2) except for INTO and APPENDING. In the addition result, the addition SINGLE must also not be used after SELECT.

Only a limited number of database cursors can be open at the same time. An open database cursor can be closed using the statement CLOSE CUR-SOR. In addition, an open database cursor is closed for a database commit or a database rollback. If the addition WITH HOLD is specified, the database cursor is not closed at the event of a database commit or a database roll-back triggered explicitly for example in NATIVE SQL.

If a cursor variable dbcur of an open database cursor is assigned to another cursor variable, the latter is linked to the same database cursor at the same position. A cursor variable of an open database cursor can also be transferred to procedures that have been called externally, to enable the database cursor to be accessed externally.

Note
We recommended that you not assign cursor variables to each other, but rather to set them exclusively using the statements OPEN CURSOR and CLOSE CURSOR.

Treatable Exceptions
See Section 29.9.

29.3.2 Reading Data Using a Cursor

```
FETCH
```

FETCH is an Open SQL statement for importing data into data objects by using an opened database cursor.

Syntax

```
FETCH NEXT CURSOR dbcur {INTO|APPENDING} target.
```

This statement extracts the requested lines (by use of the addition INTO or APPENDING) from the resulting set of the database cursor (which is linked to the cursor variable dbcur) from the current cursor-position onwards and assigns these rows to the data objects specified in the resulting set.

The cursor-variable dbcur has to be a variable declared by the special pre-defined data type cursor, which was opened with the statement OPEN CURSOR or which had an opened cursor assigned to.

Syntax and meaning of the addition INTO or APPENDING target are com-pletely synonymous to the additions of the SELECT statement (see Sec-tion 29.2.3). If you specify non-table-type data objects after INTO, then one line is extracted. If an internal table is specified after INTO or APPEND-

ING, then either all lines are extracted or as many are extracted as are specified in the addition PACKAGE SIZE.

The statement FETCH moves the position of the database cursor which is linked to dbcur by the number of the extracted lines to the next line to be extracted. If you extract the last line of the resulting set in a FETCH statement, then every following FETCH statement in which dbcur is linked to the same database-cursor sets sy-subrc to 4 without influencing the data objects specified after INTO or APPENDING.

System Fields

The statement FETCH sets the values of the system fields sy-subrc and sy-dbcnt.

sy-subrc	Meaning
0	At least one line was extracted from the resulting set.
4	No line was extracted.

The statement FETCH sets sy-dbcnt after every line extraction to the number of the lines that have been extracted so far from the respective resulting set. If no line can be extracted, then sy-dbcnt is set to 0.

Note

Subsequent FETCH statements which access the same resulting set can have different additions INTO or APPENDING: The specification of work areas can be combined with the specification of internal tables. In doing so, the addition CORRESPONDING FIELDS is either not listed at all in all the FETCH statements or has to be listed in every statement. Moreover, the data types of all involved work areas wa or the line types of the internal tables itab have to be identical. The specification of a bracketed list of data objects after INTO can not be combined with the specification of work areas or internal tables, but every involved FETCH statement has to contain such a list.

29.3.3 Close Cursor

```
CLOSE CURSOR
```

Closing an open database cursor.

Syntax

```
CLOSE CURSOR dbcur.
```

This statement closes the database cursor and initializes the cursor variable dbcur with which the database cursor is linked. The cursor variable dbcur must be a variable declared using the special predefined data type cursor that was opered using the OPEN CURSOR statement or that was assigned an open cursor.

Notes

▶ Since only a limited number of database cursors can be open simultaneously, you should close all database cursors no longer required.

▶ Initializing a cursor variable using the CLEAR statement will not suffice to close a database cursor. If the value of the cursor variable in the program is known, the database cursor can be further processed using FETCH.

▶ Once a database cursor has been closed, it can no longer be accessed. Other cursor variables that were linked with the database cursor are not initialized but become invalid, and accessing them would raise an exception that can be handled.

Example

Reading of data of the catabase table SPFLI in packets of varying size with the help of two paralle. cursors. The packet sizes are determined by the first cursor through the aggregation function count(*) and are used when accessing the second cursor. Variable control of the addition PACKAGE SIZE is not possible within a single SELECT statement.

```
DATA: BEGIN OF count_line,
        carrid TYPE spfli-carrid,
        count  TYPE i,
      END OF count_line,
      spfli_tab TYPE TABLE OF spfli.

DATA: dbcur1 TYPE cursor,
      dbcur2 TYPE cursor.

OPEN CURSOR dbcur1 FOR
  SELECT carrid count(*) AS count
        FROM spfli
        GROUP BY carrid
        ORDER BY carrid.

OPEN CURSOR dbcur2 FOR
  SELECT *
        FROM spfli
        ORDER BY carrid.
```

```
DO.
  FETCH NEXT CURSOR dbcur1 INTO count_line.
  IF sy-subrc <> 0.
    EXIT.
  ENDIF.
  FETCH NEXT CURSOR dbcur2
    INTO TABLE spfli_tab PACKAGE SIZE count_line-count.
ENDDO.

CLOSE CURSOR: dbcur1,
              dbcur2.
```

29.4 Inserting Data into Database Tables

INSERT

`INSERT` is an Open SQL statement for inserting data into a database table.

Syntax

```
INSERT { {INTO target VALUES source}
       | {      target FROM   source} }.
```

The `INSERT` statement inserts one or more rows specified in *source* in the database table specified in *target*. The two variants with `INTO` and `VAL-UES` or without `INTO` with `FROM` behave almost identically, the difference being that you cannot specify any internal tables in `source` after `VALUES`.

System Fields

The `INSERT` statement sets the values of the system fields `sy-subrc` and `sy-dbcnt`.

sy-subrc	Meaning
0	At least one row was inserted.
4	At least one row could not be inserted, because the database table already contains a row with the same primary key or a unique secondary index.

The `INSERT` statement sets `sy-dbcnt` to the number of rows inserted.

Note

The inserted rows are finally included in the database table in the next database commit. Up until this point, they can still be removed by a database rollback.

Treatable Exceptions
See Section 29.9.

29.4.1 Specifying the Database Table

Syntax of *target*

```
... {dbtab|(dbtab_syntax)} [CLIENT SPECIFIED] ...
```

The entries in `target` determine, statically or dynamically, which database table or which view is accessed, and control the client handling.

29.4.1.1 Statically Specifying a Database Table or a View

Syntax

```
... dbtab ...
```

For `dbtab`, a database table defined in the ABAP Dictionary or a view defined in the ABAP Dictionary can be specified.

Only views that refer to a single database table and whose maintenance status in the ABAP Dictionary permits change access can be specified.

29.4.1.2 Dynamically Specifying a Database Table or a View

Syntax

```
... (dbtab_syntax) ...
```

Instead of a static specification, a bracketed data object `dbtab_syntax` can be specified, which must contain the name of the database table or the view when the statement is executed. A character-type data object can be specified for the data object `dbtab_syntax`. The syntax in `dbtab_syntax`, as in the ABAP Editor, is not case-sensitive.

Before Release 6.10, it was only possible to specify a flat character-type data object for `dbtab_syntax` which had to contain the name of the database table or the view in capital letters.

29.4.1.3 Client Handling

Syntax

```
... CLIENT SPECIFIED ...
```

This addition deactivates the automatic client handling of Open SQL. If the addition `CLIENT SPECIFIED` is used, the client identifier specified in source is taken into account. Without the addition CLIENT SPECIFIED, the ABAP runtime environment does not transfer the client identifier specified in source to the database system, but transfers the identifier of the current client instead.

As of Release 6.10, the client identifier specified in *source* remains unchanged during the automatic client handling. Before Release 6.10, it was overwritten with the current client identifier.

29.4.2   Specifying the Source

Syntax of *source*

```
... { {VALUES wa}
    | {FROM wa|{TABLE itab [ACCEPTING DUPLICATE KEYS]}}} }.
```

After FROM and VALUES, you can specify a non-table-type data object wa. After FROM, you can also specify an internal table itab. The content of the row(s) to be inserted is obtained from these data objects.

29.4.2.1   Specifying a Work Area wa

Syntax

```
... {VALUES wa}  |  {FROM wa} ...
```

If you specify a non-table-type work area wa, a row is formed from its content for insertion into the database table. The content of the row to be inserted is taken from the work area wa, regardless of its data type and without conversion from left to right, according to the structure of the database table or the view. The work area must meet the prerequisites from Section 29.8.

The new row is inserted into the database table if the latter does not already contain a row with the same primary key or the same unique secondary index. Otherwise, the row is not inserted and sy-subrc is set to 4.

If a view is specified in *target* that does not comprise all the columns of the database table, these columns are set to the type-dependent initial value or the null value in the inserted rows. The latter case only occurs if the attribute **Initial value** is not marked in the ABAP Dictionary for the relevant columns of the database table.

Notes

▶ The work area wa should always be declared with reference to the database table or the view in the ABAP Dictionary.

▶ If either the database table or the view is specified statically, you can omit the specification of the work area with `FROM wa` in the variant without `INTO` outside of classes, provided that a table work area `dbtab` is declared for the database table or view using the `TABLES` statement. In this case, the system implicitly adds the `FROM dbtab` addition to the `INSERT` statement.

29.4.2.2 Specifying an Internal Table itab

Syntax

```
... FROM TABLE itab [ACCEPTING DUPLICATE KEYS] ...
```

When you specify an internal table `itab`, several rows are created from its contents for insertion into the database table. A row for insertion into the database table is taken from each row of the internal table, using the same rules as for an individual work area `wa`. The row type of the internal table must meet the prerequisites from Section 29.8.

If a row with the same primary key or the same unique secondary key does not already exist in the database table for any of the rows to be inserted, all rows are inserted and `sy-subrc` is set to 0. If the internal table is empty, `sy-subrc` is also set to 0. The system field `sy-dbcnt` is always set to the number of rows actually inserted. If, for one or more of the rows to be inserted, a row with the same primary key or the same unique secondary key already exists and the `ACCEPTING DUPLICATE KEYS` addition is specified, the rows are not inserted and `sy-subrc` is set to 4. If, in this case, the addition `ACCEPTING DUPLICATE KEYS` is not specified, no rows are inserted. Prior to Release 6.10, this raises an exception that cannot be handled; as of Release 6.10, this raises the exception CX_SY_OPEN_SQL_DB that can be handled.

Example
In this example, a new airline is added to the database table SCARR.

```
DATA scarr_wa TYPE scarr.

scarr_wa-carrid   = 'FF'.
scarr_wa-carrname = 'Funny Flyers'.
scarr_wa-currcode = 'EUR'.
scarr_wa-url      = 'http://www.funnyfly.com'.

INSERT INTO scarr VALUES scarr_wa.
```

29.5 Changing Data in Database Tables

```
UPDATE
```

UPDATE is an Open SQL statement for changing data in a database table.

Syntax

```
UPDATE target source.
```

The statement UPDATE changes the content of one or more lines of the database table specified in *target*. The entries in *source* determine which columns of which lines are changed and how they are changed.

System fields

The statement UPDATE sets the values of the system fields sy-subrc and sy-dbcnt.

sy-subrc	Meaning
0	At least one line has been changed.
4	At least one line could not be changed, either because no appropriate line was found, or because the change would generate a line that leads to double entries in the primary key or a unique secondary index in the database table.

The statement UPDATE sets sy-dbcnt to the number of changed lines.

Note

The changes are definitively copied to the database table with the next database commit. Until then, they can still be undone using a database rollback.

Treatable Exceptions

See Section 29.9.

29.5.1 Specifying the Database Table

Syntax of *target*

```
... {dbtab|(dbtab_syntax)} [CLIENT SPECIFIED] ...
```

Entries in *target* statically or dynamically define which database table or view is accessed and also control the client handling.

For `dbtab`, `dbtab_syntax` and `CLIENT SPECIFIED`, the same rules are applicable as those used for the `INSERT` statement (see Section 29.4.1).

When individual columns are changed with `SET`, you can dynamically specify the database table or the view in `dbtab_syntax` only from Release 6.10 on.

29.5.1.1 Client Handling

Syntax

```
... CLIENT SPECIFIED ...
```

This addition deactivates the automatic client handling of Open SQL. If the addition `CLIENT SPECIFIED` is used, the client identifier specified in *source* is taken into account. When using the addition `CLIENT SPECI-FIED`, the first column of client-dependent database tables can be specified in the `WHERE` condition of *source* to determine the client identification. The client identification specified in *source* behind `FROM` is taken into account. Without the addition `CLIENT SPECIFIED`, the ABAP runtime environment does not transfer the client identifier specified behind `FROM` to the database system. Instead, it transfers the identifier of the current client.

As of Release 6.10, the client identifier specified in *source* remains unchanged during automatic client handling. Before Release 6.10, it was overwritten with the current client identifier.

29.5.2 Specifying Changes

Syntax of *source*

```
... { set_expression
    | {FROM wa|{TABLE itab}} } ...
```

The specifications in *source* define which rows and columns are changed. Either individual columns are changed using the addition *set_expression* or entire rows are overwritten using the addition `FROM`.

29.5.2.1 Changing Individual Columns

Syntax of *set_expression*

```
... SET { [col1 = f1 col2 = f2 ...]
          [col1 = col1 + f1 col2 = col2 + f2 ...]
          [col1 = col1 - f1 col2 = col2 - f2 ...]
          [(expr_syntax1) (expr_syntax2) ...] }
      [WHERE cond] ...
```

After the addition SET, the changes are specified in a list of change expressions. The addition WHERE uses a logical expression *cond* to determine in which rows of the database table the changes are executed. For the logical expression *cond*, the same process applies as for the WHERE condition of the statement SELECT (see Section 29.2.4), with the difference that no subqueries are to be evaluated in the database table that is to be changed. If no WHERE condition is specified, all the rows in the database table are changed. If a column of the type STRING or RAWSTRING is changed, the primary key must be fully specified in the WHERE condition.

Prior to Release 6.10, no dynamic logical expressions could be used in the WHERE condition of the statement UPDATE.

The content of primary key fields can only be changed if the respective database table is not linked with a search help, and if pool and cluster tables are not accessed. If a line to be created through the changes would cause double entries in the primary key or in a unique secondary index of the database table, no line is changed and sy-subrc is set to 4.

The syntax of the possible change expressions is specified below.

Assigning a value

Syntax

```
... col1 = f1 col2 = f2 ...
```

For col1, col2, ..., columns of the database table given in target or in the stated view dbtab can be specified through a column identifier comp1, comp2, ... or dbtab~comp1, dbtab~comp2, ... For f1, f2, ..., data objects of the ABAP program or a column identifier dbtab~comp1, dbtab~comp2, ... of another column in the database table can be used.

The statement UPDATE assigns the content of f1, f2, ... to the columns col1, col2, ... in all the rows defined by the WHERE condition. If the data types are not compatible, conversion is as follows:

▶ During the assignment of a data object, the content—if necessary—is converted according to the rules in Section A.2 into the ABAP data type that corresponds to the data type of the column (see Table 5.4). An error during the conversion causes an exception that cannot be handled.

▶ During the assignment of another column, the content—if necessary—is converted in the database system. The option of conversion and the rules for conversion depend on the database system concerned. An error during the conversion would (prior to Release 6.10) cause an exception that cannot be handled. Since Release 6.10, an error causes the exception CX_SY_OPEN_SQL_DB, which can be handled.

If for f1, f2, ... a column is specified, changes to this column that are made in the same UPDATE statement are not taken into consideration during the assignment.

If a column col1, col2, ... appears in several change-expressions, the last corresponding change-expression takes effect.

Adding a value

Syntax

```
... col1 = col1 + f1 col2 = col2 + f2 ...
```

For col1, col2, ... and f1, f2, ..., the same applies as for the assignment of a value. col1, col2, ... must have a numeric data type, however.

The statement UPDATE adds the value of f1, f2, ... to the content of the column col1, col2, ... in all the lines defined by the WHERE condition. Otherwise, the same rules apply as for the assignment of a value.

Subtracting a value

Syntax

```
... col1 = col1 - f1 col2 = col2 - f2 ...
```

For col1, col2, ... and f1, f2, ..., the same applies as for the assignment of a value. However, col1, col2, ... must have a numeric data type.

The statement UPDATE subtracts—in all the rows defined by the WHERE condition—the value of f1, f2, ... from the content of the column col1, col2, ... Otherwise, the same rules apply as for the assignment of a value.

Dynamically specifying change expressions

Syntax

```
... (expr_syntax1) (expr_syntax2) ...
```

A change-expression can be specified as a bracketed data object expr_syntax that—at the execution of the statement—either contains the syntax of one or several static change-expressions or is initial. The data object expr_syntax1, expr_syntax2, ... can be a character-type data object or an internal table with a character-type data type. The syntax in expr_syntax is—as in the ABAP Editor—independent of uppercase/lowercase lettering. In the specification of an internal table, the syntax can be split up into several lines.

If expr_syntax is initial at the execution of the statement, the change-expression is ignored.

Note
If expr_syntax is an internal table with a header line, not the header line but the table body is evaluated.

Example
Dynamic conversion of the content of an arbitrary column in an arbitrary database table of a previous currency in Euro.

```
PARAMETERS: table(30)  TYPE c,
            column(30) TYPE c,
            old_curr   TYPE sycurr.

DATA: set_expr  TYPE string,
      condition TYPE string.

CONCATENATE column ' = 'EUR''
            INTO set_expr.

CONCATENATE column ' = old_curr'
            INTO condition.

TRY.
    UPDATE (table)
           SET    (set_expr)
           WHERE  (condition).
  CATCH cx_sy_dynamic_osql_error.
    MESSAGE 'Error in update!' TYPE 'I'.
ENDTRY.
```

29.5.2.2 Overwriting Lines

Syntax

```
... FROM wa|{TABLE itab} ...
```

A data object `wa` that is not table-type or an internal table `itab` can be specified after `FROM`. The content of the data object determines which line or lines are to be updated and which values the line or lines will be overwritten with.

Specifying a work area wa

Syntax

```
... FROM wa ...
```

If you specify a non-table-type work area `wa`, the system will search for a row in the database table that, in its primary key, has the same content as the respective beginning part of the work area. The content of the work area is interpreted in its non-converted form and in accordance with the structure of the database table or the view. The content of the work area is assigned to this row. The assignment takes place without conversion from the left to the right in accordance with the structure of the database table or the view. The work area must fulfill the prerequisites set forth in Section 29.8.

If there is no row with the same content for the primary key in the database or if the change were to lead to a double entry in a unique secondary index, the line is not changed and `sy-subrc` is set to 4.

Notes

▶ The work area `wa` should always be declared in relation to the database table or the view in the ABAP Dictionary.

▶ If you have a static specification of the database table or the view, the specification of the work area using `FROM wa` can be omitted outside of classes, provided a table work area `dbtab` for the respective database table or the view is declared using the statement `TABLES`. The system expands the `UPDATE` statement implicitly to include the addition `FROM dbtab`.

Specifying an internal table itab

Syntax

```
... FROM TABLE itab ...
```

When an internal table itab is specified, the system processes all the rows of the internal table in accordance with the rules for the work area wa. The row type of the internal table must meet the requirements from Section 29.8.

If there is no row in the database with the same content of the primary key for a row in the internal table, or if the change would lead to a double entry in a unique secondary key, the respective row is not changed and sy-subrc is set to 4. If the internal table is empty, sy-subrc is set to 0. The system field sy-dbcnt is always set to the number of rows actually inserted.

Example

Reduction of the flight cost for all of today's flights of an airline carrier in the database table SFLIGHT by the percentage percent. The calculation of the new price is done in an internal table sflight_tab and the database table is changed accordingly.

```
PARAMETERS: p_carrid   TYPE sflight-carrid,
            percent(1) TYPE p DECIMALS 0.

DATA sflight_tab TYPE TABLE OF sflight.
FIELD-SYMBOLS <sflight> TYPE sflight.

SELECT *
       FROM sflight
       INTO TABLE sflight_tab
       WHERE carrid = p_carrid AND
             fldate = sy-datum.

IF sy-subrc = 0.
  LOOP AT sflight_tab ASSIGNING <sflight>.
    <sflight>-price =
      <sflight>-price * ( 1 - percent / 100 ).
  ENDLOOP.
ENDIF.

UPDATE sflight FROM TABLE sflight_tab.
```

29.6   Inserting or Changing Data in Database Tables

```
MODIFY
```

MODIFY is an Open SQL statement for inserting or changing data in a database table.

Syntax

```
MODIFY target FROM source.
```

The MODIFY statement inserts one or several lines specified in *source* in the database table specified in *target* or overwrites existing lines.

System fields

The MODIFY statement sets the values of the sy-subrc and sy-dbcnt system fields.

sy-subrc	Meaning
0	At least one line was inserted or changed.
4	At least one line could not be processed since there is already a line with the same unique name secondary index in the database table.

The MODIFY statement sets sy-dbcnt to the number of processed lines.

Note

The changes are transferred in final form to the database table with the next database commit. Up to that point, they can be reversed using a database rollback.

Treatable Exceptions

See Section 29.9.

29.6.1   Specifying the Database Table

Syntax of *target*

```
... {dbtab|(dbtab_syntax)} [CLIENT SPECIFIED] ...
```

Entries in *target* statically or dynamically define which database table or view is accessed and also control the client handling.

For dbtab, dbtab_syntax, and CLIENT SPECIFIED, the same rules are applicable as those used for the INSERT statement (see Section 29.4.1).

29.6.2 Specifying the Source

Syntax of *source*

```
... FROM wa|{TABLE itab} ...
```

A `wa` data object that is not table-type or an `itab` internal table can be specified after `FROM`. On the one hand the content of the data objects determines whether the line(s) is (are) inserted or changed, and on the other hand it determines which values are inserted or used for changes.

Specifying a work area wa

Syntax

```
... FROM wa ...
```

When you specify a `wa` work area that is not table-type, which meets the requirements from Section 29.8, a line is searched for in the database table that has the same content in the primary key as the corresponding beginning part of the work area.

▶ If such a line is not found, a new line is inserted according to the same rules as for the `INSERT` statement (see Section 29.4.2).

▶ If such a line is found, this line is overwritten according to the same rules as for the `UPDATE` statement (see Section 29.5.2).

If the change would lead to a double entry in a unique secondary index, then it is not executed and `sy-subrc` is set to 4.

Notes

▶ The `wa` work area should always be declared with reference to the database table or the view in the ABAP Dictionary.

▶ If the the database table or view is specified statically, then the specification of the work area using `FROM wa` can be ommitted outside of classes if a `dbtab` table work area is declared for the corresponding database table or for the view using the `TABLES` statement. The system enhances the `MODIFY` statement implicitly with the `FROM dbtab` addition.

Specifying an internal table itab

Syntax

```
... FROM TABLE itab ...
```

If an `itab` internal table is specified, the system processes all lines in the internal table according to the rules for the `wa` work area. The line type of the internal table has to meet the requirements from Section 29.8.

If the change to a line in the internal table were to lead to a double entry in a unique secondary index, the corresponding line is not inserted and `sy-subrc` is set to 4. If the internal table is empty, `sy-subrc` is set to 0. The `sy-dbcnt` system field is always set to the number of lines that were actually processed.

Example
Create or change a message in the database table T100. If there is no message with the number 100 in the MYMSGCLASS message class in English, it will be created. Otherwise only the text is changed.

```
DATA message_wa TYPE t100.

message_wa-sprsl = 'EN'.
message_wa-arbgb = 'MYMSGCLASS'.
message_wa-msgnr = '100'.

message_wa-text =  'Some new message ...'.

MODIFY t100 FROM message_wa.
```

29.7   Deleting Data in Database Tables

```
DELETE
```

`DELETE` is an Open SQL statement for deleting data in a database table.

Syntax

```
DELETE { {FROM target [WHERE cond]}
       | {target FROM source} }.
```

The statement `DELETE` deletes one or more rows from the database table specified in `target`. The rows that are to be deleted are specified either in a WHERE condition or with data objects in `source`.

System Fields
The statement `DELETE` sets the values of the system fields `sy-subrc` and `sy-dbcnt`.

sy-subrc	Meaning
0	A least one row was deleted.
4	At least one row could not be deleted, because it was not found in the database table.

The statement DELETE sets sy-dbcnt to the number of deleted rows.

Note
The rows are deleted finally from the database table in the next database commit. Until then, you can reverse the deletion in a database rollback.

Treatable Exceptions
See Section 29.9.

29.7.1   Specifying the Database Table

Syntax of *target*

```
... {dbtab|(dbtab_syntax)} [CLIENT SPECIFIED] ...
```

The entries in *target* determine statically or dynamically which database table or which view is accessed and control the client handling.

For dbtab, dbtab_syntax, and CLIENT SPECIFIED, the same rules are applicable as those used for the INSERT statement (see Section 29.4.1).

29.7.2   Specifying the Lines

Syntax

```
... { [WHERE cond]
    | {FROM wa|{TABLE itab}} } ...
```

Depending on the variant, the lines to be deleted are specified using either a WHERE condition or the content of a work area or an internal table.

29.7.2.1 Specifying the WHERE Condition

Syntax

```
... WHERE cond ...
```

The WHERE addition uses a logical expression *cond* to specify which rows in the database table are deleted. The same applies to the logical expression *cond* as for the WHERE condition of the SELECT statement (see Section 29.2.4). If there is no row in the database that satisfies the WHERE condition, no row is deleted and sy-subrc is set to 4. If no WHERE condition is specified, all rows are deleted.

As of Release 6.10, specifying the WHERE condition is optional. Prior to Release 6.10, you had to specify the WHERE condition in this variant of the DELETE statement and you could not use any dynamic logical expressions.

Example
Deleting all of today's airline's flights in which no seats are occupied from the database table SFLIGHT (see also the example in Section 29.7.2.2):

```
PARAMETERS p_carrid TYPE sflight-carrid.

DELETE FROM sflight
WHERE   carrid  = p_carrid AND
        fldate  = sy-datum AND
        seatsocc = 0.
```

29.7.2.2 Specifying a Line Using a Data Object

Syntax

```
... FROM wa|{TABLE itab} ...
```

After FROM, you can specify a data object wa that is not table-type or an internal table itab. The content of the data objects determines the row or rows to be deleted.

Specifying a work area wa

Syntax

```
... FROM wa ...
```

If you specify a work area wa that is not table-type, the database table is searched for a row whose primary key content is the same as that of the corresponding initial part of the work area. The content of the work area is not converted and is interpreted according to the structure of the database table or view. This row is deleted. The work area must meet the prerequisites from Section 29.8.

If there is no row in the database with the same content as the primary key, no row is deleted and sy-subrc is set to 4.

Notes

▶ The work area wa should be declared with reference to the database table or view in the ABAP Dictionary using the length of the primary key.

▶ If either the database table or view is specified statically, you do not have to specify the work area with FROM wa outside of classes if a table work area dbtab is declared for the relevant database table or view using the TABLES statement. The system then implicitly adds the FROM dbtab addition to the DELETE statement.

Specifying lines with an internal table itab

Syntax

```
... FROM TABLE itab ...
```

If an internal table itab is specified, the system processes all rows of the internal table according to the rules for the work area wa. The row type of the internal table must meet the prerequisites from Section 29.8 using the length of the primary key.

If, for a row of the internal table, there is no row in the database with the same content as the primary key, the corresponding row is ignored and sy-subrc is set to 4. If the internal table is empty, sy-subrc is set to 0. The system field sy-dbcnt is always set to the number of rows actually deleted.

Example

Deleting all of today's flights of an airline in which no seats are occupied from the database table SFLIGHT. The client field must be in the row structure of the internal table sflight_key_tab. Otherwise it would not cover the primary key of the database table and incorrect key values would be accepted as a result. This example has the same function as the one in Section 29.7.2.1, but it requires two database accesses. The deleted rows are recorded in the internal table.

```
PARAMETERS p_carrid TYPE sflight-carrid.

TYPES: BEGIN OF sflight_key,
         mandt  TYPE sflight-mandt,
         carrid TYPE sflight-carrid,
         connid TYPE sflight-connid,
         fldate TYPE sflight-fldate,
       END OF sflight_key.

DATA sflight_key_tab TYPE TABLE OF sflight_key.
```

```
SELECT carrid connid fldate
      FROM sflight
      INTO CORRESPONDING FIELDS OF TABLE sflight_key_tab
      WHERE carrid   = p_carrid AND
            fldate   = sy-datum AND
            seatsocc = 0.

DELETE sflight FROM TABLE sflight_key_tab.
```

29.8 Work Areas in Open SQL Statements

The Open SQL statements DELETE, INSERT, MODIFY, UPDATE and SELECT *
(without the CORRESPONDING FIELDS addition) as well as FETCH (if the
database cursor was opened with the preceding SELECT statement) work
with work areas wa or internal tables itab. The following prerequisites
apply in these statements for the work area or row type of the internal
table. If the prerequisites are ignored, a syntax error or an exception will
occur.

The first two points are minimum prerequisites that are replaced by
stricter requirements as of Release 6.10 in Unicode programs or in the
treatment of strings in database tables:

▶ The data type of the work area or row type of the internal table must
not be deep or contain deep components. This excludes strings as of
Release 6.10.

▶ The work area or rows of the internal table must be at least as long as
the database structure and the alignment must match. For the DELETE
statement, this prerequisite must only be met for the length of the primary key.

▶ If the work area or rows of the internal table are structured, the Unicode fragment view of the database structure must match that of the
work area or internal table in Unicode programs.

▶ If the work area or rows of the internal table are elementary, they must
be character-type and flat in Unicode programs. The columns of the database structure must also be character-type and flat.

▶ The work area contains strings as components or is itself a string, or if
columns of type SSTRING, STRING, or RAWSTRING

Note
The work area or row structure of the internal table should always be built
like the database structure. If you work in the Open SQL statement with
a single database table or one view, a data object built in the same way

can be declared with reference to the relevant structure in the ABAP Dictionary. If you work with more than one database table (in the `SELECT` statement), a data object built in the same way can be built as a nested structure which contains, as substructures, the structures of the single database tables or views in the sequence in which they are listed in the statement. No structure should be used in which all components lie on one level, as possible alignment gaps between the single database tables or views are not taken into account.

29.9 Treatable Exceptions in Open SQL Statements

The following errors in the database system trigger an exception which is defined in a sub-class of CX_SY_OPEN_SQL_ERROR:

▶ General error in the database system

▶ Statement cannot be processed because it is too big

▶ Conversion errors when assigning

▶ Violation of the length restriction for strings

▶ Inserting a line that is already present

▶ Using an invalid database cursor

The same applies if a dynamically specified part of an Open SQL statement contains errors. The corresponding runtime errors cannot be captured.

30   Native SQL

30.1   Overview

The term Native SQL refers to all statements that can be transferred to the Native SQL interface of the database interface.

Native SQL statements do not fall within the language scope of ABAP and do not follow the ABAP syntax. ABAP only contains statements for isolating program sections in which Native SQL statements can be listed. Database-specific SQL statements used in native SQL are mainly those that are transferred unchanged from the Native SQL interface to a database system and executed there. The full SQL language scope of the relevant database can be used and the addressed database tables do not have to be declared in the ABAP Dictionary. There is also a small set of SAP-specific Native SQL statements that are handled in a specific way by the native SQL interface.

The following ABAP statements are used for handling native SQL:

Statement	Section
EXEC SQL, ENDEXEC	30.2
EXIT FROM SQL	30.3

30.2   Including Native SQL

```
EXEC SQL
```

Including Native SQL statements.

Syntax

```
EXEC SQL [PERFORMING subr].
  ...
ENDEXEC.
```

These statements define an area in an ABAP program where one or more Native SQL statements are to be carried out. The area between EXEC and ENDEXEC is not completely checked by the syntax check. The statements entered there are passed to the Native SQL interface and processed there as follows.

- Almost all SQL statements that are valid for the program interface of the addressed database system can be included between EXEC and ENDEXEC, in particular the DDL statements. These SQL statements are passed from the Native SQL interface to the database system largely unchanged. The syntax rules are specified by the database system, in particular the case-sensitivity rules for database objects. If the syntax allows a separator between individual statements, you can include several Native SQL statements between EXEC and ENDEXEC. Generally, the semicolon (;) is used as the separator character.
- You can also include SAP-specific Native SQL language elements between EXEC and ENDEXEC. These statements are not passed directly from the Native SQL interface to the database, but are converted appropriately.

All Native SQL statements bypass the SAP buffering. The automatic client handling is not performed.

System fields
The statement ENDEXEC sets the system fields sy-subrc and sy-dbcnt.

sy-subrc	Meaning
0	The statements between EXEC and ENDEXEC were executed successfully.
4	The statements between EXEC and ENDEXEC were not executed.

The ENDEXEC statement sets sy-dbcnt to the number of table lines processed in the last Native SQL statement.

Note
Programs with Native SQL statements generally depend on the database system used and cannot be executed in all SAP systems. This is especially true for the examples in this section that were written for Informix database systems.

Example
Inserting two rows in the database table SCARR. If neither of these rows exists, sy-subrc is set to 0 by ENDEXEC and sy-dbcnt to 1. Otherwise, an exception is raised and handled.

```
DATA: exc_ref TYPE REF TO cx_sy_native_sql_error,
      error_text TYPE string.

TRY.
    EXEC SQL.
```

```
      INSERT INTO scarr
              (MANDT, CARRID, CARRNAME, CURRCODE, URL)
        VALUES ('000', 'FF', 'Funny Flyers', 'EUR',
              'http://www.ff.com');
      INSERT INTO scarr
              (MANDT, CARRID, CARRNAME, CURRCODE, URL)
        VALUES ('000', 'EF', 'Easy Flyers', 'EUR',
              'http://www.ef.com');
    ENDEXEC.
  CATCH cx_sy_native_sql_error INTO exc_ref.
    error_text = exc_ref->get_text( ).
    MESSAGE error_text TYPE 'I'.
ENDTRY.
```

30.2.1 Host Variables

Host variables are global or local variables declared in the ABAP program or variables used in operand positions by Native SQL statements. For identification purposes, the variable name has a colon (:) directly in front of it. Instead of specifying a variable itself, you also can specify a field symbol to which the variable is assigned. You cannot specify a dereferenced data reference variable.

You can use elementary fields and structures with elementary components as host variables. If a structure is listed in a native SQL statement after INTO, it is converted by the Native SQL interface as if its components were listed as individual fields separated by commas.

In a SELECT statement, you can specify the SAP-specific addition STRUCTURE between INTO and an individual host variable. With this addition, the host variable is treated like a structure, even if a non-typed formal parameter or a non-typed field symbol is specified. Otherwise, when several values are being passed, depending on the platform, either only the first value is passed or an exception occurs.

If you have assignments between host variables and fields in database tables, the Native SQL interface passes a description of type, size, and storage location of the used ABAP fields to the database system. The actual database accesses and conversions are usually executed directly by the corresponding operations of the database system. In some cases, however, the Native SQL interface executes extensive compatibility checks.

The conversion rules between ABAP data types and types of database columns are listed in the programming interface manuals of the appropriate database system for both write accesses (INSERT, UPDATE) as well as for read (SELECT) accesses. These conversion rules apply also for the input and output parameters of database procedures (see Section 30.2.3). Any combinations listed there are undefined and should not be used.

Example

Reading a row from the database table SPFLI using Native SQL and host variables. If a row was found, sy-subrc is set to 0; if not, it is set to 4. After INTO, the STRUCTURE addition could be specified. However, this is not necessary because wa can be statically recognized as a structure.

```
PARAMETERS: p_carrid TYPE spfli-carrid,
            p_connid TYPE spfli-connid.

DATA: BEGIN OF wa,
        cityfrom TYPE spfli-cityfrom,
        cityto   TYPE spfli-cityto,
      END OF wa.

EXEC SQL.
  SELECT cityfrom, cityto
         INTO :wa
         FROM spfli
         WHERE carrid = :p_carrid AND connid = :p_connid
ENDEXEC.
```

30.2.2   Cursor Processing

In Native SQL, as in Open SQL, statements for reading data using a database cursor can be specified (see Section 29.3).

Syntax

```
OPEN dbcur FOR SELECT ...
```

Opens a database cursor dbcur. For dbcur, a flat character-type host variable can be specified.

Syntax

```
FETCH NEXT dbcur INTO ...
```

Reads data using an opened database cursor dbcur.

Syntax

```
CLOSE dbcur
```

Closes an opened database cursor dbcur.

If no row can be read using FETCH, sy-subrc is set to 4 by ENDEXEC. The system field sy-dbcnt is set, after a FETCH statement, to the number of rows read up to that point using the respective cursor.

Example

Reading several rows from the database table SPFLI using cursor handling and host variables in Native SQL. If rows were found, sy-subrc was set to 0 and sy-dbcnt was increased by one for each row read.

```
PARAMETERS p_carrid TYPE spfli-carrid.

DATA:   connid   TYPE spfli-connid,
        cityfrom TYPE spfli-cityfrom,
        cityto   TYPE spfli-cityto.

EXEC SQL.
  OPEN dbcur FOR
    SELECT connid, cityfrom, cityto
          FROM spfli
          WHERE carrid = :p_carrid
ENDEXEC.

DO.
  EXEC SQL.
    FETCH NEXT dbcur INTO :connid, :cityfrom, :cityto
  ENDEXEC.
  IF sy-subrc <> 0.
    EXIT.
  ELSE.
    ...
  ENDIF.
ENDDO.

EXEC SQL.
  CLOSE dbcur
ENDEXEC.
```

30.2.3   Calling Database Procedures

You can define procedures in database systems as so-called "stored pro-cedures". Since the syntax for calling such procedures and the pertinent parameter transfer can vary widely for various database systems, a uniform command exists in Native SQL.

Syntax

```
EXECUTE PROCEDURE proc ( IN      p_in1    IN      p_in2 ...,
                         OUT     p_out1   OUT     p_out2 ...,
                         INOUT p_inout1 INOUT p_
inout2 ... )
```

This statement calls a procedure proc stored in the database system. For all formal parameters of the procedure, you must specify the actual parameters separated by commas. You must specify IN, OUT or INOUT before every actual parameter in order to indicate whether the parameter is an input, output or input/output parameter. You can use literals or host variables (see Section 30.2.1) labeled by a colon (:) for the actual parameters.

Example

Defining a selfunc procedure using database specific SQL-Statements (Informix). This involves calling the procedure using the SAP-specific Native SQL-statement EXECUTE PROCEDURE in a LOOP loop by means of a selection table and deleting the procedure using an SQL statement. In the case shown here, the procedure is a function whose return value output in EXECUTE PROCEDURE is copied to the host variable name.

```
DATA scarr_carrid TYPE scarr-carrid.
SELECT-OPTIONS s_carrid FOR scarr_carrid NO INTERVALS.
DATA s_carrid_wa LIKE LINE OF s_carrid.

DATA name TYPE c LENGTH 20.

TRY.
    EXEC SQL.
      CREATE FUNCTION selfunc( input CHAR(3) )
        RETURNING char(20);
        DEFINE output char(20);
        SELECT carrname
               INTO output
               FROM scarr
               WHERE mandt  = '000' AND
                     carrid = input;
        RETURN output;
        END FUNCTION;
    ENDEXEC.
```

```
      LOOP AT s_carrid INTO s_carrid_wa
                        WHERE sign = 'I' AND option = 'EQ'.
        TRY.
          EXEC SQL.
            EXECUTE PROCEDURE selfunc(
                                     IN  :s_carrid_wa-low,
                                     OUT :name )
          ENDEXEC.
          WRITE: / s_carrid_wa-low, name.
        CATCH cx_sy_native_sql_error.
          MESSAGE 'Error in procedure execution'
                                              TYPE 'I'.
        ENDTRY.
      ENDLOOP.
      EXEC SQL.
        DROP FUNCTION selfunc;
      ENDEXEC.
    CATCH cx_sy_native_sql_error.
      MESSAGE 'Error in procedure handling' TYPE 'I'.
  ENDTRY.
```

30.2.4   Defining the Database Connection

Working with Native SQL statements requires a defined connection to a
database system. When you start an SAP system, a standard link from the
database interface to the central database of the SAP system is started.
This connection will be defined as the current connection for Native SQL
statements and as a standard connection for Open SQL statements when
an ABAP program is started. Using the following SAP-specific Native SQL
statements, additional connections to other database systems can be
opened. These can then be accessed in Native SQL.

30.2.4.1 Opening a Connection

Syntax

```
CONNECT TO dbs [AS conn]
```

This Native SQL statement opens a connection to the database system
dbs and makes this the current connection. This means that all the subsequent Native SQL statements work with the database system named in
dbs. If a connection to the specified database system already exists, then
this is used; otherwise, a new connection is set up.

For dbs, you can specify a literal or a host variable that contains a name from the column CON_NAME in the database table DBCON (see Section 30.2.1). The database system listed there must be supported by SAP, and the technical data for the connection must be maintained. The column DBMS in the database table DBCON contains an abbreviation for the type of the database system.

Using the AS addition, a name conn can be assigned to the connection. For conn, a literal or a character-type host variable (see Section 30.2.1) can be specified. Its content is used as a name. The connection can then be selected using this name in the Native SQL statement SET CONNEC-TION.

30.2.4.2 Selecting the Connection

Syntax

```
SET CONNECTION {con|DEFAULT}
```

This Native SQL statement sets the current connection for all subsequent Native SQL statements. For con, you can specify a literal or a character-type host variable that must contain the name of a connection already opened. The name of the connection can be specified as the database system from the database table DBCON, as it is given in the Native SQL statement CONNECT TO, or as the name assigned there using the AS addition. With DEFAULT, the standard connection to the central database system of the current SAP system is set.

30.2.4.3 Ascertaining the Connection

Syntax

```
GET CONNECTION con
```

This Native SQL statement assigns the name of the current connection to con. If the connection has been set up using the Native SQL statement CONNECT TO and a name was given to it using AS, then this name is assigned. If the connection was set up without using a name assignment, the name of the database system from the database table DBCON is used. If the current connection is the standard connection to the central database of the SAP system, con is assigned the value "DEFAULT".

30.2.4.4 Closing the Connection

Syntax

```
DISCONNECT con
```

This Native SQL statement closes the connection con. If con is not the current connection, it is not affected. If con is the current connection, the standard connection to the central database of the SAP system is simultaneously set as the current connection for all following Native SQL statements.

For con, either a literal or a character-type host variable can be specified, and it must contain the name of a connection already opened. If a name was assigned while opening the connection using the Native SQL statement CONNECT TO with the addition AS, then this name must be used. Otherwise, the name of the database system from the DBCON database table must be used. The standard connection "DEFAULT" cannot be closed.

Example
Starting a connection to an Oracle database and importing all entries of a column in the database table SCARR.

```
PARAMETERS dbs TYPE dbcon-con_name.

DATA carrid_wa TYPE scarr-carrid.

DATA dbtype TYPE dbcon_dbms.

SELECT SINGLE dbms
       FROM dbcon
       INTO dbtype
       WHERE con_name = dbs.

IF dbtype = 'ORA'.
  TRY.
     EXEC SQL.
       CONNECT TO :dbs
     ENDEXEC.
     IF sy-subrc <> 0.
       RAISE EXCEPTION TYPE cx_sy_native_sql_error.
     ENDIF.
     EXEC SQL.
       OPEN dbcur FOR
         SELECT carrid
                FROM scarr
```

```
      ENDEXEC.
      DO.
        EXEC SQL.
          FETCH NEXT dbcur INTO :carrid_wa
        ENDEXEC.
        IF sy-subrc <> 0.
          EXIT.
        ELSE.
          WRITE / carrid_wa.
        ENDIF.
      ENDDO.
      EXEC SQL.
        CLOSE dbcur
      ENDEXEC.
      EXEC SQL.
        DISCONNECT :dbs
      ENDEXEC.
    CATCH cx_sy_native_sql_error.
      MESSAGE 'Error in Native SQL.' TYPE 'I'.
  ENDTRY.
ENDIF.
```

30.2.5 Implicit Cursor Processing

If the PERFORMING addition that is forbidden in classes is specified after
EXEC SQL, the Native SQL interface performs an implicit cursor edit.

Syntax

```
EXEC SQL PERFORMING subr.
  SELECT ... INTO {:wa1 :wa2 ...} ...
ENDEXEC.
```

Only a SELECT statement can be used as a Native SQL statement. The
Native SQL interface opens a cursor for the SELECT statement and reads
the appropriate data row by row. After each successful reading of a row,
the subr subroutine is called. The subr subroutine must be defined in the
same ABAP program and must not have any parameter interface.

When the host variables (see Section 30.2.1) specified in the SELECT
statement after INTO are global data objects of the ABAP program, they
can be evaluated in the subroutine. In the subroutine, sy-dbcnt contains
the number of rows read so far and sy-subrc contains the value 0. After
the ENDEXEC statement, sy-dbcnt contains the number of rows read alto-

gether so far, and `sy-subrc` is set to the value 4 since no more lines could be read using the implicit cursor.

Note
Implicit cursor processing using the PERFORMING addition is not allowed in ABAP objects since methods of global classes do not have any access to the global data and the subroutines of the calling ABAP program. Instead, explicit cursor processing (see Section 30.2.2) should be used.

Example
Reading several rows from the database table SCARR and calling the subroutine `evaluate` for each row read.

```
DATA wa TYPE spfli-carrid.

EXEC SQL PERFORMING evaluate.
  SELECT carrid FROM spfli INTO :wa
ENDEXEC.

FORM evaluate.
  WRITE / wa.
ENDFORM.
```

30.3   Leaving Native SQL

```
EXIT FROM SQL
```

Suspending implicit cursor processing.

Syntax

```
EXIT FROM SQL.
```

This statement is forbidden in classes and is only executed during the procession of subroutines that were called using the PERFORMING addition of the statement EXEC SQL. Otherwise it is ignored.

The statement has the effect that implicit cursor processing (see Section 30.2.5) is terminated after the current subroutine has finished. Processing of the called ABAP program is continued after ENDEXEC, whereby `sy-dbcnt` contains the number of rows read up until that point and `sy-subrc` is set to the value 4.

30.4 Treatable Exceptions in Native SQL

All exceptions triggered by the database interface appear via the exception in the ABAP program defined in the CX_SY_NATIVE_SQL_ERROR class. The corresponding runtime errors cannot be captured.

31 Data Clusters

31.1 Overview

This chapter deals with the procession of data clusters. A data cluster is a group of data objects grouped together for the purpose of storage in a storage medium, which can only be edited using ABAP statements.

The data objects are written to the storage medium using the statement EXPORT and are retrieved using the statement IMPORT. The statement DELETE can be used to delete a chosen storage memory, and FREE can be used to delete the ABAP Memory. The statement IMPORT DIRECTORY generates a list of all the data objects that have previously been exported to a database table. You can use the following storage media:

▶ Program-internal data buffer

▶ Cross-program data buffers

▶ ABAP Memory

▶ Database tables

You can use the following statements to process data clusters.

Statement	Section
EXPORT	31.2
IMPORT	31.3
IMPORT DIRECTORY	31.4
DELETE	31.5
FREE	31.6

In addition, the subclasses of class CL_ABAP_EXPIMP are system classes that expand the functionality of the above statements for special requirements (see Section B.1.7).

31.2 Creating Data Clusters

EXPORT

Storing a data cluster in a storage medium.

Syntax

```
EXPORT parameter_list TO medium [COMPRESSION {ON|OFF}].
```

This statement stores a data cluster defined using `parameter_list` in a storage area `medium`. You can use the COMPRESSION addition to specify whether the data is stored in the cluster in a compressed form. You can retrieve a data cluster from the storage area using the IMPORT statement and delete a data cluster using DELETE FROM.

All data objects are archived according to the current byte sequence (endian) and character-like data objects according to the character representation of the current text environment. The identification of the data cluster indicates which byte sequence and which character representation have been used during the export. When you import the data cluster using the IMPORT statement, this identification is evaluated and the data is converted to the current byte sequence and character representation.

31.2.1   Defining the Data Cluster

Syntax of *parameter_list*

```
... {p1 = dobj1 p2 = dobj2 ...}
  | {p1 FROM dobj1 p2 FROM dobj2 ...}
  | (ptab) ...
```

A data cluster can be defined statically by a list `p1 = dobj1 p2 = dobj2 ...` or `p1 FROM dobj1 p2 FROM dobj2 ...` and dynamically through the specification of a bracketed internal table `ptab`.

In the case of a static export, the content of the data object `dobj1`, `dobj2`, ... is stored under the name `p1`, `p2`, ... in the cluster. The name of a parameter `p1`, `p2`, ... can contain a maximum of 255 characters. The spellings `p1 = dobj1 p2 = dobj2 ...` and `p1 FROM dobj1 p2 FROM dobj2 ...` are synonymous. You can use all data types except reference types or those which contain reference types as components for the data object `dobj1`, `dobj2`, ... If a data object `dobj1`, `dobj2`, ... is an internal table with a header line, then the table body and not the header line is addressed.

In the dynamic case, the parameter list is specified in an index table `ptab` with two columns. These two columns can have any name and have to be character-type. In the first column of `ptab`, you have to specify the names of the parameters and in the second column the data objects. If the second column is initial, then the name of the parameter in the first column has to match the name of a data object. The data object is then stored under its name in the cluster. If the first column of ptab is initial, an uncatchable exception will be raised.

If the data cluster is too large for storage, an exception will occur.

Note
To export objects which are referenced by reference variables, use the statement CALL_TRANSFORMATION to serialize and export these objects if the class of these objects implements the interface IF_SERIALIZABLE_OBJECT (see the example in Chapter 40).

Obsolete short form
Outside of classes you can use the short form dobj1 dobj2 ... in the static variant. You can also use a single-column internal table for *parameter_list* in the dynamic form. In doing so, you ensure that all data objects are implicitly stored under their name in the data cluster.

31.2.2   Defining the Storage Medium

Syntax of *medium*

```
... { {DATA BUFFER xstr}
    | { {INTERNAL TABLE itab}
    | { {MEMORY ID id}
    | { {DATABASE        dbtab(ar) [FROM wa] [CLIENT cl] ID id
    }
    | { {SHARED MEMORY dbtab(ar) [FROM wa] [CLIENT cl] ID id
    }
    | { {SHARED BUFFER dbtab(ar) [FROM wa] [CLIENT cl] ID id
    }
    } ... .
```

The exported data cluster can be stored in a byte string xstr, in an internal table itab, in the ABAP Memory, in a database table dbtab, or in a shared memory area (specification SHARED MEMORY or BUFFER).

31.2.2.1   Storing Data in a Byte String

Syntax

```
... DATA BUFFER xstr ...
```

RELEASE
6.10

When specifying DATA BUFFER, the data cluster is written in the elementary data object xstr which has to be of the type xstring.

31.2.2.2 Storing Data in an Internal Table

Syntax

```
... INTERNAL TABLE itab ...
```

When specifying INTERNAL TABLE, the data cluster is stored in the internal table itab. The first column of itab has to be of the data type s, the second column of the type x. Depending on the width of the second column, the data is stored in multiple table rows if necessary. The first row contains the length occupied in the second row. As a table type, you can only use standard tables for itab.

31.2.2.3 Storing Data in the ABAP Memory

Syntax

```
... MEMORY ID id ...
```

When you specify MEMORY, the data cluster is written to the ABAP Memory with the stated identification id.

id is expected to be a flat character-type data object that contains an identification not longer than 55 characters. An already existing data cluster with the same identification id is completely overwritten. By the identification in id, a data cluster is identified in the memory and can be read again with the same identification.

Obsolete short form

The addition ID can be omitted outside of classes. However, this is prone to errors, as all EXPORT statements without identification overwrite the same data cluster.

Note

A data cluster in the ABAP Memory is available for all programs within a call sequence, whereby data can be handed over to called programs.

Example

Two fields with two different identifications "P1" and "P2" are written to the ABAP Memory with the dynamic variant of the cluster definition. After the execution of the statement IMPORT, the contents of the fields text1 and text2 are interchanged.

```
TYPES:
  BEGIN OF tab_type,
```

```
    para TYPE string,
    dobj TYPE string,
  END OF tab_type.

DATA:
  id(10)   TYPE c       VALUE 'TEXTS',
  text1    TYPE string VALUE 'IKE',
  text2    TYPE string VALUE 'TINA',
  line     TYPE tab_type,
  itab     TYPE STANDARD TABLE OF tab_type.

line-para = 'P1'.
line-dobj = 'TEXT1'.
APPEND line TO itab.

line-para = 'P2'.
line-dobj = 'TEXT2'.
APPEND line TO itab.

EXPORT (itab)     TO MEMORY ID id.

IMPORT p1 = text2
       p2 = text1 FROM MEMORY ID id.
```

31.2.2.4 Storing Data in a Database Table

Syntax

```
... DATABASE dbtab(ar) [FROM wa] [CLIENT cl] ID id ...
```

When specifying DATABASE, the data cluster with the identification id is stored in the database table dbtab and stored permanently at the next database-commit. For id, a flat character-type data object is expected that contains an identification of no more than 105 characters if the addition CLIENT is stated or no more than 108 characters if it is not stated. The database table has to be defined in the ABAP Dictionary with a fixated predetermined structure.

1. The first field must be a key field named MANDT of type CLNT for the client, if you want to store the data objects client-dependently. For a client-independent storage, this component does not apply.

2. The second field must be a key field named RELID of type CHAR and length 2. It stores the area ar specification.

3. After that, at least one key field of type CHAR of any name must follow. It stores the identifier specified in id in the length of the key field. If more than one key field is defined, the identifier is divided among

them according to the respective length of the key fields. If the total length of the key fields is not sufficient for the identifier, it is truncated on the right side.

4. The next field must be a key field named SRTF2 of type INT4. It contains the row numbers of a stored data cluster that can extend over several rows and is filled automatically by the system.

5. Then any number of components with freely chosen names and types may follow, and these are provided with values by the specification of FROM wa. The addition TO wa of the IMPORT statement reads these fields out again.

6. The last two components must be named CLUSTR and CLUSTD and must be of types INT2 and LRAW of any length. In CLUSTR, the current length of field CLUSTD of each line is stored, while CLUSTD contains the actual data cluster.

The double-digit area ar, which must be specified directly, splits up the rows of the database table into several areas, so that data clusters with the same identification id can occur multiple times in the data base table.

After FROM, a work area wa can be specified which has to have the same data type as the database table dbtab. When exporting, the current values of the components of wa situated between the fields SRTF2 and CLUSTR are written in all the rows occupied by the data cluster of the database table.

If the database table dbtab is client-specific, you can specify a flat character-type field cl after the addition CLIENT, which contains a client identifier. If you do not specify the addition, the current client is used. The row MANDT of every row occupied by the data cluster of the database table is filled with this client identification during the export.

Obsolete short form

If, outside of classes, the addition FROM wa is not specified and if instead a table work area is declared for the data base table dbtab with the statement TABLES, then, at the time of export, the current values of the components of the table work area dbtab, situated between the fields SRTF2 and CLUSTR, are written in the rows of the database table.

Note
The database table INDX delivered by SAP has the required structure and can be used as a pattern for creating your own database tables and for testing purposes. We strongly recommend using your own INDX-like database tables in productive systems.

Example

An internal table `itab` is exported under the name `tab` and the identification "TABLE" to the area "XY" of the data base table INDX delivered by SAP. The selectable components are supplied by the structure `wa_indx`.

```
TYPES:
  BEGIN OF tab_type,
    col1 TYPE i,
    col2 TYPE i,
  END OF tab_type.

DATA:
  wa_indx TYPE indx,
  wa_itab TYPE tab_type,
  cl      TYPE mandt VALUE '100',
  itab    TYPE STANDARD TABLE OF tab_type.

WHILE sy-index < 100.
  wa_itab-col1 = sy-index.
  wa_itab-col2 = sy-index ** 2.
  APPEND wa_itab TO itab.
ENDWHILE.

wa_indx-aedat = sy-datum.
wa_indx-usera = sy-uname.
wa_indx-pgmid = sy-repid.

EXPORT tab = itab
  TO DATABASE indx(xy)
  FROM wa_indx
  CLIENT cl
  ID 'TABLE'.
```

31.2.2.5 Storing Data in the Application Buffer of the Application Server

Syntax

```
... {SHARED MEMORY dbtab(ar) [FROM wa] [CLIENT cl] ID id}
  | {SHARED BUFFER dbtab(ar) [FROM wa] [CLIENT cl] ID id} ...
```

Specifying SHARED MEMORY or SHARED BUFFER causes the data cluster to be stored in application buffers in the application server's shared memory, to which all programs on the application server have access.

The two application buffers differ in respect to how the system behaves when reaching the memory limit. Both application buffers can be filled to an internal maximum limit, which can be adjusted via the profile parameters rsdb/esm/buffersize_kb (SHARED MEMORY) and rsdb/obj/buffersize (SHARED BUFFER). Before the maximum limit of the buffer of SHARED MEMORY is reached, you have to free some space with the statement DELETE FROM SHARED MEMORY before a new export. The buffer of SHARED BUFFER is automatically cleared by a displacement procedure when it reaches the maximum limit. This procedure deletes the least used data objects from the buffer.

When storing the data, the system creates a memory table in the application buffer, whose line structure is defined with dbtab. For dbtab, you have to specify a data base table from the ABAP Dictionary that has the same structure as the structure stored in the database table (see Section 31.2.2.4). The line area ar, the work area wa, the optional client cl and the identification id have the same significance for the memory table as if stored in a database table, with the exception that the length of the identification is limited in id to 59 or 62 characters depending on whether the addition CLIENT is specified or not.

Note
When storing something in the application buffer, you refer to a database table, although the data is not stored in the table itself, but in an accordingly created memory table.

31.2.3 Controlling Compression

Syntax

```
... COMPRESSION {ON|OFF} ...
```

This addition specifies whether or not the data in the data cluster are compressed. By default, and if you specify ON, the compression for the storage in a database is switched on. It is switched off if you specify OFF.

31.2.4 Treatable Exceptions During the Export of Data Clusters

If the data cluster being exported into the application buffer of the application server is larger than the entire buffer, or if the maximum internal buffer limit is reached because no objects have been deleted from the buffer, then for Release 6.20 and later, the exceptions defined in the classes CX_SY_EXPORT_BUFFER_NO_MEMORY and CX_SY_EXPORT_

NO_SHARED_MEMORY will be triggered. The respective runtime error of the first EXPORT_BUFFER_NO_MEMORY class can be captured. The runtime error of the second class cannot be captured.

31.3   Reading Data Clusters

```
IMPORT
```

Reading a data cluster from a storage medium.

Syntax

```
IMPORT parameter_list FROM medium [conversion_options].
```

Importing data objects specified in `parameter_list` from a data cluster stored in the memory area `medium`. If required, the data is automatically converted to the current byte sequence (endian) and character representation. You can use the additions `conversion_options` to make adaptations to the current platform.

Return values

sy-subrc	Meaning
0	The specified data cluster was found, and the content of the parameters in the data cluster was passed to the respective data objects.
4	The specified data cluster was not found.

31.3.1   Specifying the Data Objects to Be Read

Syntax of *parameter_list*

```
... (p1 = dobj1 p2 = dobj2 ...)
  | (p1 TO dobj1 p2 TO dobj2 ...)
  | (ptab) ...
```

A data cluster can be read statically by a list in the form p1 = dobj1 p2 = dobj2 ... or p1 TO dobj1 p2 TO dobj2 ... and dynamically through the specification of a bracketed internal table ptab.

In the static case, the contents of the cluster parameter p1, p2, ... are read and passed to the data objects dobj1, dobj2, ... The syntax styles p1 = dobj1 p2 = dobj2 ... and p1 TO dobj1 p2 TO dobj2 ... are the same. If a data object dobj1, dobj2, ... is an internal table with a header line, not the header line but the table body is addressed.

In the dynamic case, the parameter list is adopted from the two-column internal table `ptab` whose columns must be character-type. In the first column in `ptab`, the names of the parameter must be listed, and in the second, the data objects must be listed. If the first column of `ptab` is initial or an object name is listed twice, an exception that cannot be handled will be triggered.

If a parameter `p1`, `p2`, ... is specified and it is not stored in the data cluster, the specification will be ignored and the data object `dobj1`, `dobj2`, ... retains its current value. The data objects `dobj1`, `dobj2`, ... must have, in the standard version, the same data type as the parameters `p1`, `p2`, ... of the cluster. With internal tables, only the row type is relevant, and not the table type. The following exceptions apply.

▶ With data objects of the type `c`, different lengths are allowed. Then the appropriate conversion rule from Section A.2.2 applies.

▶ If, in structures, the data types of all components (except for the last one) match, and this component is of the type `c`, it can be extended or abbreviated according to the conversion rule from Section A.2.2. Alignment gaps in front of this component are considered to be a part of the component.

▶ If the structures otherwise have the same type, and the target structure at the highest level has more components than the source structure in the data cluster, the superfluous components are supplied with type-conform initial values. A substructure of the target structure must not have more components than the respective substructure in the source structure.

As of Release 6.10, when structures are exported, information is stored as to whether the structure contains components adopted using the statement `INCLUDE` (see Section 6.8) or adopted in the ABAP Dictionary from other structures. A structure into which data is imported must, since Release 6.10, also match the structure in the data cluster with regard to the components adopted using `INCLUDE`. For structures stored prior to Release 6.10 and for structures where all components of the uppermost hierarchy level were adopted using `INCLUDE`, the target structure does not need to be set up with the identical `INCLUDE` statements.

The additions specified under *conversion_options* (see Section 31.3.3) allow additional conversions and define other conversion rules. If structured data with character-type components are imported into Unicode systems and these components were exported in a multi-display, multi-processing (MDMP) system and vice versa, a special text language rule applies (see Section 31.3.4).

Note

The rule that a target structure at the highest level may have more components than the source structure can cause problems when dealing with structures defined in the ABAP Dictionary if a structure there is marked as enhanceable. Therefore, this situation triggers a warning message in the enhanced program check since Release 6.40.

Obsolete short form

Outside of classes, the abbreviated form `dobj1 dobj2 ...` can be used in the static variant and a single-column internal table for `parameter_list` in the dynamic form. In this case, the parameters are searched for implicitly in the cluster under the name of the specified data object.

31.3.2 Defining the Storage Medium

Syntax of *medium*

```
... { DATA BUFFER xstr }
  | { INTERNAL TABLE itab }
  | { MEMORY ID id }
  | { DATABASE      dbtab(ar) [TO wa] [CLIENT cl] ID id }
  | { SHARED MEMORY dbtab(ar) [TO wa] [CLIENT cl] ID id }
  | { SHARED BUFFER dbtab(ar) [TO wa] [CLIENT cl] ID id } ...
```

The data cluster to be imported can be taken from an elementary data object `xstr`, an internal table `itab`, the ABAP Memory (specification MEMORY), a database table `dbtab` (specification DATABASE), or a cross-program storage area (specification of SHARED MEMORY or BUFFER).

31.3.2.1 Importing from a Byte String

Syntax

```
... DATA BUFFER xstr ...
```

If DATA BUFFER is specified, the data cluster is taken from the elementary data object `xstr`, which must be of the type `xstring`. The data object must be filled with the same addition of the statement EXPORT.

31.3.2.2 Importing from an Internal Table

Syntax

```
... INTERNAL TABLE itab ...
```

If INTERNAL TABLE is specified, the data cluster is taken from the internal table itab. The first column of itab must have the data type s and the second one must have the type x. As a table type, only standard tables are allowed for itab. The internal table must have been filled with the same addition of the statement EXPORT.

31.3.2.3 Importing from the ABAP Memory

Syntax

```
... MEMORY ID id ...
```

If MEMORY is specified, the data cluster that was written to the ABAP Memory under the identification specified in id with the statement EXPORT is imported. For id, a flat, character-type data object is expected. This object contains the identification of the data cluster.

Obsolete Abbreviation

Outside of classes, the identification id can be omitted for storage in the ABAP Memory. Then the data cluster that was stored without specification of the ID with the statement EXPORT is read.

31.3.2.4 Importing from a Database Table

Syntax

```
... DATABASE dbtab(ar) [TO wa] [CLIENT cl] ID id ...
```

If DATABASE is specified, the data cluster written to the database table dbtab in the area ar and under the identification specified in id using the statement EXPORT is imported. The database table dbtab must be set up in the same way as described for the EXPORT statement. For id, a flat, character-type data object is expected that contains the identification of the data cluster, and the two-digit area ar must be specified directly.

After TO, a work area wa that has the same data type as the database table dbtab can be specified. During the import, the values of the database fields that are between the fields SRTF2 and CLUSTR are assigned to the components of wa with the same name.

If the database table `dbtab` is client-dependent, a flat, character-type field `cl` can be specified after the addition `CLIENT`. This field contains client identification. If the addition is not specified, the current client is used.

Obsolete Abbreviation

Outside of classes, the addition `TO wa` can be omitted. Instead, a table work area for the database table `dbtab` can be declared using the statement `TABLES`. Then, during the import, the values of the database fields that are between the fields SRTF2 and CLUSTR are assigned to the component with the same name in the table work area `dbtab`.

Example

The table that is imported into the internal table `itab` is the table exported under the name `tab` and the identification "TABLE" into the area "XY" of the database table INDX supplied by SAP (see Section 31.2.2). The components, which can be selected as required, are assigned to the structure `wa_indx`.

```
TYPES:
  BEGIN OF tab,
    col1 TYPE i,
    col2 TYPE i,
  END OF tab.

DATA:
  wa_indx TYPE indx,
  wa_itab TYPE tab,
  cl      TYPE mandt VALUE '100',
  itab    TYPE STANDARD TABLE OF tab.

IMPORT tab = itab
  FROM DATABASE indx(xy)
  TO wa_indx
  CLIENT cl
  ID 'TABLE'.

WRITE: wa_indx-aedat, wa_indx-usera, wa_indx-pgmid.
ULINE.
LOOP AT itab INTO wa_itab.
  WRITE: / wa_itab-col1, wa_itab-col2.
ENDLOOP.
```

Obsolete ID specification

```
... MAJOR-ID id1 [MINOR-ID id2] ...
```

You can replace the addition `ID` with these additions when you import database tables outside of classes. For the specification of `id1` and `id2`, the same rules apply as for `id`.

A data-cluster is imported whose identification in the first part matches the value of `id1`. If `MINOR-ID id2` is specified in addition, then the data-cluster is imported whose identification in the second part (at the positions after the number of characters specified in `id1`) is larger or equal to the value in `id2`. After the first correct identification is found, the search aborts.

Note
When you use `id2`, note that this data object must either contain only digits or only letters. Using mixed forms can lead to differing search results depending on the platform.

Example
If a data-cluster was exported with the identification "Sausage," then this sentence is found at the specification of `MAJOR-ID` "Sau". It is also found if you additionally specify `MINOR-ID` "ab" but it is not found if you specify `MINOR-ID` "yz".

31.3.2.5 Importing from Application Buffers of the Application Server

Syntax

```
... {SHARED MEMORY dbtab(ar) [TO wa] [CLIENT cl] ID id}
  | {SHARED BUFFER dbtab(ar) [TO wa] [CLIENT cl] ID id} ...
```

If `SHARED MEMORY` or `SHARED BUFFER` is specified, the data cluster is imported that was written into the area `ar` and under the identification specified in `id`, using the statement `EXPORT` to the respective application buffer of the application server. The system accesses a storage table of the application buffer whose row structure is defined by a database table `dbtab`. The set-up of this table is described in the statement `EXPORT`. For `id`, a flat, character-type data object is expected that contains the identification of the data cluster. The two-digit area `ar` must be specified directly.

For the optional specifications of the work area `wa` and the client `cl`, the same applies as for the import from a database table.

31.3.3 Conversion Additions

Syntax of *conversion_options*

```
... { { { {[ACCEPTING PADDING] [ACCEPTING TRUNCATION]}
        | [IGNORING STRUCTURE BOUNDARIES] }
      [IGNORING CONVERSION ERRORS
                [REPLACEMENT CHARACTER rc]] }
    | [IN CHAR-TO-HEX MODE] }
    [CODEPAGE INTO cp]
    [ENDIAN INTO endian] ...
```

These additions allow the reading of data stored in data clusters into non-type-related data objects. They also define appropriate conversion rules. Table 31.1 shows which of the additions may be used during the import from the various storage media. The column headings are abbreviations for the following storage medium: DATA BUFFER (B), MEMORY (M), SHARED MEMORY (SM), SHARED BUFFER (SB), DATA BASE (DB) and INTERNAL TABLE (IT).

Conversion addition	B	M	IT	DB	SM	SB
ACCEPTING PADDING	+	+	+	+	+	+
ACCEPTING TRUNCATION	+	+	+	+	+	+
IGNORING STRUCTURE BOUNDARIES	+	+	+	+	+	+
IGNORING CONVERSION ERRORS	+		+	+		
REPLACEMENT CHARACTER rc	+		+	+		
IN CHAR-TO-HEX MODE	+		+	+		
CODEPAGE INTO cp	+		+	+		
ENDIAN INTO endian	+		+	+		

Table 31.1 Assignment of the Conversion Additions to Storage Media

Note

With the storage medium SHARED BUFFER, the displayed additions are specified only after Release 6.40.

31.3.3.1 Conversion into Longer Data Objects

Syntax

```
... ACCEPTING PADDING ...
```

This addition enhances the rules from Section 31.3.1 for different data types of the source field and the target field dobj1, dobj2, ... in the data cluster:

▶ In addition to the data objects of the type c, the target field can also be longer than the source field for data objects of the type n, p or x.

▶ Source fields of the type b can be exported into target fields of the types s and i; source fields of the type s can be exported into target fields of the type i.

▶ Source fields of the type c can be exported into target fields of the type string; source fields of the type x can be exported into target fields of the type xstring.

▶ The above rules also apply if the component concerned is the last component of a source or target structure that is otherwise set up in the same manner.

▶ In a target structure, substructures can also have more components than the substructures of the source structure if the structure is otherwise set up in the same way. The superfluous components are supplied with type-related initial values.

Note

The rule that substructures in a target structure can have more components than the source structure can cause problems in relation to structures defined in the ABAP Dictionary. This is the case if the structure there is marked as enhanceable. Therefore, as of Release 6.40, this situation triggers a warning message in the enhanced program check.

Example
Without the addition ACCEPTING PADDING, the structure f1 in the data cluster could not be imported into the structure f2, because a substructure of f2 contains a superfluous component.

```
DATA: BEGIN OF f1,
        col1 TYPE string,
        BEGIN OF sub,
          col2 TYPE f,
        END OF sub,
        col3 TYPE i,
      END OF f1.

DATA: BEGIN OF f2,
        col1 TYPE string,
        BEGIN OF sub,
```

```
          col2 TYPE f,
          col3 TYPE xstring,
        END OF sub,
        col4 TYPE i,
      END OF f2.

EXPORT para = f1 TO MEMORY ID 'HK'.

...

IMPORT para = f2 FROM MEMORY ID 'HK' ACCEPTING PADDING.
```

31.3.3.2 Conversion into Shorter Data Objects

Syntax

```
... ACCEPTING TRUNCATION ...
```

This addition expands the rules in Section 31.3.1 for different data types of source field in the data cluster and source field dobj1, dobj2, ... in the data cluster. In the case of structures that otherwise have the same type but where the source structure at the highest level has more components than the target structure in the data cluster, superfluous components will be cut off. A substructure of the source structure must not have more components than the respective substructure in the target structure.

Example
Without the addition ACCEPTING TRUNCATION, the structure f1 in the data cluster could not be imported into the structure f2 since f2 contains fewer components.

```
DATA: BEGIN OF f1,
        col1 TYPE string,
        BEGIN OF sub,
          col2 TYPE f,
        END OF sub,
        col3 TYPE i,
        col4 TYPE xstring,
      END OF f1.

DATA: BEGIN OF f2,
        col1 TYPE string,
        BEGIN OF sub,
          col2 TYPE f,
        END OF sub,
        col3 TYPE i,
      END OF f2.
```

```
EXPORT para = f1 TO MEMORY ID 'HK'.

...

IMPORT para = f2 FROM MEMORY ID 'HK'
                    ACCEPTING TRUNCATION.
```

31.3.3.3 Conversion into Differently Built Structures

Syntax

```
    ... IGNORING STRUCTURE BOUNDARIES ...
```

This addition expands the rules from Section 31.3.1 for different data types of source field in the data cluster and target field dobj1, dobj2, ... in the data cluster. The rule expansion means that differences in the set-up of structures that result from substructures or from different adopted components of other structures with the statement INCLUDE (see Section 6.8) are of no importance whatsoever.

The components of source and target structure are viewed at the same level, independently of their set-up from substructures or from components adopted using INCLUDE. Source and target structures must both have the same number of components, and these must be of the same type. Possible alignment gaps that have resulted from substructures are of no importance.

This addition cannot be used together with the additions ACCEPTING PADDING and ACCEPTING TRUNCATION.

Example
Without the addition IGNORING STRUCTURE BOUNDARIES, the structure f1 in the data cluster could not be imported into the structure f2, since f1 and f2 are set up differently from substructures.

```
DATA: BEGIN OF incl_struc,
        cola TYPE string,
        colb TYPE i,
      END OF incl_struc.

DATA: BEGIN OF f1.
        INCLUDE STRUCTURE incl_struc.

DATA:   col1 TYPE string ,
          BEGIN OF sub,
            col2 TYPE f,
```

```
          col3 TYPE f,
        END OF sub,
        col4 TYPE i,
      END OF f1.

DATA: BEGIN OF f2,
        cola TYPE string,
        colb TYPE i,
        col1 TYPE string,
        BEGIN OF sub,
          col2 TYPE f,
        END OF sub,
        col3 TYPE f,
        col4 TYPE i,
      END OF f2.

EXPORT para = f1 TO MEMORY ID 'HK'.

...

IMPORT para = f2 FROM MEMORY ID 'HK'
                IGNORING STRUCTURE BOUNDARIES.
```

31.3.3.4 Preventing an Exception During the Conversion

Syntax

```
... IGNORING CONVERSION ERRORS [REPLACEMENT CHARACTER rc] ...
```

Through this addition, an exception that cannot be handled is suppressed. This is triggered if, during the import, there is a conversion to another code page and a character to be converted is not available in the target code page.

If the addition REPLACEMENT CHARACTER is specified, each inconvertible character will be replaced during the conversion by the character that is contained in rc. For rc, a character-type data object is expected that contains a single character. If the addition is not specified, the character "#" is used as a substitute character.

31.3.3.5 Reading Character-Like Fields as a Byte Sequence

Syntax

```
... IN CHAR-TO-HEX MODE ...
```

This addition has the effect that data that is stored in the data cluster under the data type x can be assigned to target fields of the type x. The contents of the source fields are not converted to the code page of the target system. Instead, they are placed into the target fields byte by byte and unconverted. A single source field or a structure component of the type c can be assigned to a single target field or to a structure component of the type x which has the same length in bytes. For target fields of the type c, the addition has no effect.

This addition cannot be used together with the previous conversion additions.

Note
With this addition, you should note that a program that uses this addition cannot be transported between systems in which the character representations require a different number of bytes. This addition is only meant for temporary programs, so that they can import byte strings stored incorrectly in fields of the type c and store them again for the correct type.

31.3.3.6 Ascertaining the Code Page of the Saved Data

Syntax

```
... CODEPAGE INTO cp ...
```

This addition assigns the identification of the code page for the exported data to the data object cp. This object must have a character-type data type. The identification of the code page is the content of the column CPCODEPAGE of the database table TCP00.

Note
The code page can be used in order to process data objects imported using CHAR-TO-HEX MODE. Conversions between code pages can be made using the system classes in Section B.1.2.

31.3.3.7 Ascertaining the Byte Sequence of the Saved Data

Syntax

```
... ENDIAN INTO endian ...
```

This addition assigns the identification of the byte sequence of the exported data to the data object endian which must have the data type ABAP_ENDIAN from the type group ABAP. The identification for Big endian is "B"; the identification for Little endian is "L".

Note

The byte sequence can be used in order to process data objects imported using `CHAR-TO-HEX MODE` since code pages in which a character takes up more than one byte can be dependent on the byte sequence.

Example

The target field `f2-col2` contains, after the import, the unconverted, binary content of `f1-col2`. The code page and the byte sequence in which the data is stored is available in `cp` and `en`. Normally, the data in such a case is exported and imported in different programs. You should note that this example only works in a system in which a character is displayed through two bytes since `f2-col2` is double the length of `f1-col2`.

```
TYPE-POOLS abap.

DATA: BEGIN OF f1,
        col1(10) TYPE c VALUE '1234567890',
        col2(10) TYPE c VALUE '1234567890',
      END OF f1.

DATA: BEGIN OF f2,
        col1(10) TYPE c,
        col2(20) TYPE x,
      END OF f2.

DATA: cp TYPE string,
      en TYPE abap_endian.

EXPORT para = f1 TO DATABASE indx(hk) ID 'HK'.

...

IMPORT para = f2 FROM DATABASE indx(hk) ID 'HK'
                 IN CHAR-TO-HEX MODE
                 CCDE PAGE INTO cp
                 ENDIAN INTO en.
```

31.3.4 Text Language Rule

The rule described in this section is only relevant if, in a Unicode system, structures defined in the ABAP Dictionary are imported from the database that were exported in an MDMP system and vice versa.

Character-type data can be stored in an MDMP system encoded according to different code pages. The character set ID stored in `EXPORT` is therefore not sufficient. For this reason, the statement `IMPORT FROM DATABASE`

is used as of Release 6.20 for evaluating the text language of database tables or structures defined in the ABAP Dictionary.

The following hierarchy applies for assigning the text language to a structure:

1. A component that is labelled as a text language in a substructure or in a table-type component with a structured-line type is only vald for this substructure or internal table.

2. A component labelled as a text language in a superordinate structure applies for this structure and for all other structures or table-type components nested in it that do not have any components of their own that can be identified as a text language.

3. If a component labelled as a text language is among the freely selected components of the INDX-type database table in which the data is stored, this determines the text language for all elementary fields, structures and internal tables in the corresponding data cluster that do not yet have their own language.

When importing from structures stored in the database, the text language determines the code page used to handle the character-type components of a structure as follows:

▶ **Importing MDMP data into a Unicode system**
The code page of the imported data is determined using the text language from the database tables TCP0C (table of text environments) and TCP0D (localization of the database). If no text language component is available, the character set ID stored during the export is used.

This rule is based on the assumption that the Unicode system has resulted from the conversion of an MDMP system. If it has not, this can lead to conversion errors.

▶ **Importing Unicode data into an MDMP system**
The imported data is handled according to the assignment of languages to code pages defined in the MDMP system, depending on the text language. If no text language component is available, the language of the current text environment is used.

Note
Structures and internal tables with a structured line type that are based on types defined in the ABAP program do not have a text language. The character set ID stored during the export is always used for these.

31.3.5 Treatable Exceptions During the Import from Data Clusters

If the data objects to be imported do not match the data type of the target fields, an exception defined by the class of CX_SY_IMPORT_ MISMATCH_ERROR is triggered. The respective runtime errors can be captured and assigned to the IMPORT_MISMATCH_ERRORS exception group (see Table D.9).

31.4 Reading the Table of Contents of a Data Cluster

IMPORT DIRECTORY

Import of a list of all data objects of a cluster in the database.

Syntax

```
IMPORT DIRECTORY INTO itab
  FROM DATABASE dbtab(ar) [TO wa] [CLIENT cl] ID id.
```

With this statement, a table of contents of all data objects of a data cluster written to the database table `dbtab` in the area `ar`, and under the ID specified in `id` using the statement EXPORT, is passed to the internal table `itab`. The database table `dbtab` must be set up as described for the statement EXPORT. For `id`, a flat character-type data object is expected that contains the ID of the data cluster, and the two-digit area `ar` must be specified directly. The additions TO and CLIENT have the same relevance as described in the statement IMPORT for importing data from the data cluster (see Section 31.3.2.4).

For `itab`, index tables whose row type matches the structure CDIR in the ABAP Dictionary are allowed. Table 31.2 shows the components of the structure CDIR and their relevance.

Component	Type	Relevance
NAME	CHAR(30)	Name of the parameter under which a data object was stored.
OTYPE	CHAR(1)	General type of the stored data object. The following values are possible: "F" for elementary flat data objects, "G" for strings, "R" for flat structures, "S" for deep structures, "T" for internal tables with flat row type and "C" for tables with a deep row type.

Table 31.2 Components of the Structure CDIR

Component	Type	Relevance
FTYPE	CHAR(1)	More exact type of the stored data object. For flat, elementary data objects and internal tables with a flat, elementary type, the data or type is returend in accordance with ("b", "C", "D", "F", "I", "N", "P", "s", "T", "X"). For elementary data objects of the type string or xstring and internal tables that have an elementary type string or xstring, "g" or "y" is returned. In the case of flat structures and internal tables with flat structured type, "C" is returned. In the case of deep structures and internal tables with deep, structured type, "v" is returned. In the case of a table that has an internal table as a type, "h" is returned.
TFILL	INT4	Filled length of the stored data object. For strings, the length of the content in bytes is returned; for internal tables, the number of rows is returned; for other data objects, the value 0 is returned.
FLENG	INT2	Length of the stored data object or of the stored table lines in bytes. For strings, the value 8 is returned.

Table 31.2 Components of the Structure CDIR (cont.)

Return values

sy-subrc	Meaning
0	The specified data cluster was found and a list of the imported data objects was passed to the internal table itab.
4	The specified data cluster was not found.

Example

Storing three data objects in a data cluster and reading the directory.

```
DATA: f1 TYPE d,
      f2 TYPE TABLE OF i,
      f3 TYPE spfli.

DATA itab TYPE STANDARD TABLE OF cdir.

DO 10 TIMES.
  APPEND sy-index TO f2.
ENDDO.

EXPORT par1 = f1
       par2 = f2
       par3 = f3 TO DATABASE indx(hk) ID
                                    'HK'.

IMPORT DIRECTORY INTO itab FROM DATABASE indx(hk) ID 'HK'.
```

The itab table contains the following data:

NAME	OTYPE	FTYPE	TFILL	FLENG
PAR1	F	D	0	8
PAR2	T	I	10	4
PAR3	R	C	0	92

31.5   Deleting a Data Cluster

```
DELETE
```

Deleting a data cluster from a storage medium.

Syntax

```
DELETE FROM { {MEMORY ID id}
            | {DATABASE       dbtab(ar) [CLIENT cl] ID id}
            | {SHARED MEMORY dbtab(ar) [CLIENT cl] ID id}
            | {SHARED BUFFER dbtab(ar) [CLIENT cl] ID id} }.
```

This statement deletes a data cluster that was stored in the ABAP memory, in a database table, or in an application buffer of the application server by the statement EXPORT. The data cluster to be deleted is identified by its ID id and, except in the case of the ABAP memory, by the name of a database table dbtab, an area ar and an optional client specification cl. The same rules apply to dbtab, ar, cl and id as apply when accessing the appropriate storage with the IMPORT statement.

Return Values

sy-subrc	Meaning
0	The specified data cluster was found and deleted.
4	The specified data cluster was not found.

Example
In this example, two fields are written to a data cluster in an application buffer of the application server, extracted, and then deleted. Accessing the same data cluster again sets sy-subrc to 4.

```
DATA: id(4) TYPE c       VALUE 'TEXT',
      text1 TYPE string VALUE 'Tina',
      text2 TYPE string VALUE 'Mike'.
```

```
EXPORT p1 = text1
       p2 = text2 TO SHARED BUFFER indx(XY) ID id.

IMPORT p1 = text2
       p2 = text1 FROM SHARED BUFFER indx(XY) ID id.

...

DELETE FROM SHARED BUFFER indx(XY) ID id.

IMPORT p1 = text2
       p2 = text1 FROM SHARED BUFFER indx(XY) ID id.
```

31.6 Deleting a Data Cluster in the ABAP Memory

FREE MEMORY

Deleting a data cluster in the ABAP Memory.

Syntax

FREE MEMORY ID id.

This statement has the same effect as the statement

DELETE FROM MEMORY ID id.

Obsolete short form

Outside of classes, you can omit the addition ID. Then, all data clusters are deleted from the ABAP Memory.

Note

You should refrain from using FREE MEMORY without the addition ID. While the statement EXPORT without the addition ID involves only one data cluster, in this case all clusters are involved. We recommend using the statement DELETE FROM, because here the addition ID is mandatory.

32 The ABAP File Interface

32.1 Overview

You can use the ABAP file interface to process files on the application server using ABAP statements. Function modules or global classes are available for files on the presentation server (see Section C.2).

32.1.1 Addressing Files

In all statements of the file interface, files are addressed directly using the name under which they are known on the current platform. A file therefore cannot be opened more than once within a program. The name of a file is normally composed of a path specification and the name of the file. The notation used depends on the operating system of the application server. If a file name is specified without a path specification, the directory stored in the profile parameter DIR_HOME is used automatically.

In writing cross-platform programs, we recommend that you use the transaction FILE to create logical file names and logical paths, which can be linked to every platform using actual names. The function module FILE_GET_NAME can be used to determine a logical file name for the actual name that is valid for the current platform. This name then can be used in statements of the file interface.

In Unicode programs, file names that contain blank characters are permitted. If the specified file name in a non-Unicode program contains blank characters, it is cut off after the first blank character. In Unicode programs, the blank characters are a part of the file name.

32.1.2 Authorizations for Accessing Files

File access authorizations can be viewed on three different levels: Operating system check, program-independent authorization check, and user and program authorization check for single files.

32.1.2.1 Operating System Check

From the perspective of the operating system of the application server, all file accesses are executed by the SAP system. As a consequence, the user of the operating system with the SAP system installed must have read-and-write access to all directories and files that are used by the ABAP file interface. If the user does not have an appropriate authorization, the statements of the file interface cannot be executed at all or only partly. If a statement cannot be executed due to a missing authorization in the operating system, the return value sy-subrc is set to a value that is not 0.

32.1.2.2 Program-Independent Authorization Check

If files are accessed using the statements OPEN DATASET, TRANSFER and DELETE DATASET, the system automatically checks the entries in the database table SPTH. The entries in the database table SPTH control general read-and-write access from ABAP programs to files and whether files should be included in a safety procedure.

In the database table SPTH, read-and-write access to generically specified files can be generally forbidden, regardless of authorization objects. For the remaining files (files for which read or write access is generally permitted in the database table SPTH), authorization checks can be performed based on authorization objects. For this, authorization groups for program-independent authorization checks can be defined in the database table SPTH. Table 32.1 shows the columns of the database table SPTH. If the check of the database table SPTH has a negative result, this leads to an untreatable exception.

Column	Meaning
PATH	Column for generic file names. The properties specified in the other columns of this line apply for all files of the application server for which the entry in this column is the most appropriate.
SAVEFLAG	If this column contains the value "X," the files specified in the column PATH are saved in a security procedure.
FS_NOREAD	If this column contains the value "X," the files specified in the column PATH cannot be accessed from ABAP. This setting overrides the settings in the columns FS_NOWRITE and FS_BRGRU and the authorization check using the authorization object S_DATASET (see Section 32.1.2.3).
FS_NOWRITE	If this column contains the value "X," no write access is permitted from ABAP to the files specified in the column PATH. This setting overrides the settings in the column FS_BRGRU and the authorization check using the authorization object S_DATASET (see Section 32.1.2.3).

Table 32.1 Columns of the Database Table SPTH Column Descriptions

Column	Meaning
FS_BRGRU	In this column, you can define a name of your choice for an authorization group. The files of several lines can then be grouped into authorization groups. When the database table SPTH is evaluated, an authorization check for the current user is performed against the authorization object S_PATH. This authorization object contains an authorization field RS_BRGRU and an authorization field ACTVT, which are used to permit user-specific access to the files specified in PATH. If no name is specified, no authorization check against the authorization object S_PATH is performed.

Table 32.1 Columns of the Database Table SPTH Column Descriptions (cont.)

Note

In contrast to the authorization check using the authorization object S_DATASET (see Section 32.1.2.3), the check against the authorization object S_PATH is independent of the ABAP program being used. This check is also not restricted to an individual file but includes all generically specified files in the column PATH instead.

32.1.2.3 User and Program Authorization Check for Single Files

Before a file is opened or deleted using the ABAP file interface, an authorization check is carried out automatically for the current user and the current program with the predefined authorization object S_DATASET. This authorization object has the authorization fields PROGRAM for the program name, FILENAME for the file to be opened, and ACTVT with the activities **Delete**, **Read**, **Write**, **Read with filter** and **Write with filter**. If the user does not have the appropriate authorization, this leads to a treatable exception (as of Release 6.10). To avoid this exception, the function AUTHORITY_CHECK_DATASET can be called before the relevant ABAP statement to check whether the authorization exists.

32.1.3 Locks

The database interface does not have an integrated lock mechanism to ensure that only one ABAP program accesses a file at any one time. If several programs simultaneously gain write access to a file, this will have unpredictable results.

To avoid this situation, SAP locks (see Section 33.5) can be assigned, or unique file names such as GUIDs can be used.

Note

If several computers of an application server access a file at the same time, conflicts may still arise even if SAP locks are used, for example if the operating system buffers data before it is written to a file.

32.1.4 The File Interface in Unicode Programs

As the content of files often reflects the file structure in the working memory, the file interface in a Unicode system must satisfy the following requirements.

▶ It must be possible to exchange files between Unicode and non-Unicode systems.

▶ It must be possible to exchange files between different Unicode systems.

▶ It must be possible to exchange files between different non-Unicode systems that work with different code pages.

For this reason, Unicode programs must always specify which code page is used to encode character-type data that is written to or read from text files.

Furthermore, it must also be possible to execute a Unicode program in both Unicode and non-Unicode systems. Some syntax rules for the file interface have therefore been changed to make programming file access in Unicode programs less prone to errors than in non-Unicode programs:

▶ A file must be opened explicitly before each read or write access. A file cannot be opened again once it is open. In non-Unicode programs, the first time a file is opened, it is opened implicitly using the standard settings. In non-Unicode programs, the statement for opening a file can be used on a file that is already open, although a file in a program can only be opened once.

▶ When opening the file, the access type and the type of data storage must be specified explicitly. In non-Unicode programs, a file is opened implicitly with the standard settings if not specified otherwise.

▶ If a file has been opened only with read access, it remains read-only. In non-Unicode programs, write access to the same file is also possible.

▶ If a file is opened as a text file, only the content of character-type data objects may be read or written. In non-Unicode programs, byte-type and numeric data objects are also permitted.

Essentially, instead of implicit programming with standard settings on which the developer has no influence, explicit programming is required in which all the important parameters must be specified. Mixed format files containing a combination of byte-type, character-type and numeric data are prone to errors and are forbidden.

SAP therefore recommends that you always follow the syntax rules for Unicode programs when using the file interface, even if you are not using a Unicode system.

32.1.5 File Size

As of Release 6.10, files larger than 2 GB can be edited on all platforms that support this file size. Only the operating system OS/390 is still excluded from this.

32.1.6 File Interface Statements

The ABAP file interface statements are listed below:

Statement	Section
OPEN DATASET	32.2
TRANSFER	32.3
READ DATASET	32.4
GET DATASET	32.5
SET DATASET	32.6
TRUNCATE DATASET	32.7
CLOSE DATASET	32.8
DELETE DATASET	32.9

32.2 Opening a File

`OPEN DATASET`

Opening a file on the application server.

Syntax

```
OPEN DATASET dset FOR access IN mode [position]
                                     [os_addition]
                                     [error_handling].
```

This statement opens the file specified in dset for the access specified in *access* in a storage mode specified in *mode*. For dset, a character-type data object is expected which contains the platform-specific name of the file (see Section 32.1.1).

Use the additions *position*, *os_addition* and *error_handling* to determine the position at which to open the file, to specify platform-specific additions, and to influence error handling.

In Unicode programs, the access and storage modes access and mode must be specified explicitly. If the additions are missing in non-Unicode programs, the file is opened implicitly as a binary file for read access.

In Unicode programs, the file must not yet be open in the current program; otherwise a treatable exception occurs. In non-Unicode programs, the file may already be open. The statement OPEN DATASET then does not reopen the file but moves the read or write position depending on the access mode. In this case, you should not change the access or storage mode.

Note

You can open up to 100 files per internal mode. The actual maximum number of simultaneously open files may be less, depending on the platform.

Return values

sy-subrc	Meaning
0	The file was opened.
8	The operating system could not open the file.

32.2.1   Definition of the Access Type

Syntax of *access*

```
... INPUT
  | OUTPUT
  | APPENDING
  | UPDATE ...
```

These additions are used to open the file for reading, writing, appending or changing. In Unicode programs, the specification of the access type is obligatory.

32.2.1.1 Opening a File for Reading

Syntax

```
... INPUT ...
```

The addition `FOR INPUT` opens the file for reading. By default, the file pointer is set at the start of the file. If the file specified does not exist, `sy-subrc` is set to 8.

In a Unicode program, it is not possible to obtain write access to a file that is open for reading. In a non-Unicode program, write access is also permitted.

32.2.1.2 Opening a File for Writing

Syntax

```
... OUTPUT ...
```

The addition `FOR OUPUT` opens the file for writing. If the specified file already exists, its content is deleted. If the file specified does not exist, it is created. Read access is also permitted.

32.2.1.3 Opening a File for Appending

Syntax

```
... APPENDING ...
```

The addition `FOR APPENDING` opens the file for appending. If the file specified already exists, it is opened and the file pointer is set at the end of the file. If the file specified does not exist, it is created. An attempted read access to a file opened with `FOR APPENDING` with the statement `READ DATASET` fails and returns the value 4 for `sy-subrc`.

32.2.1.4 Opening a File for Changing

Syntax

```
... UPDATE ...
```

The addition `FOR UPDATE` opens the file for changes to the existing content. By default, the file pointer is set to the start of the file. If the specified file does not exist, no file is opened and `sy-subrc` is set to 8.

32.2.2   Defining the Storage Type

Syntax of *mode*

```
...  {BINARY MODE}
   | {TEXT MODE ENCODING code}
   | {LEGACY BINARY MODE [endian] [codepage]}
   | {LEGACY TEXT MODE [endian] [codepage]} ...
```

These additions define whether the file is treated as a binary file or as a text file. By specifying LEGACY, files can be written in the format that is expected by a non-Unicode system, and files that have been created by a non-Unicode-system can be read. The byte order or the code page can be specified explicitly. In Unicode programs, the specification of the storage type is obligatory.

32.2.2.1   Opening a File as a Binary File

Syntax

```
... BINARY MODE ...
```

The addition IN BINARY MODE opens the file as a binary file. When writing in a binary file, the binary content of a data object is transferred unchanged into the file. When reading from a binary file, the binary content of the file is transferred unchanged into a data object.

The addition BINARY MODE has the same meaning in Unicode programs and non-Unicode programs.

32.2.2.2   Opening a File as a Text File

Syntax

```
... TEXT MODE ENCODING code ...
```

The addition IN TEXT MODE opens the file as a text file. The addition ENCODING defines how the characters are represented in the text file. When writing in a text file, the content of a data object is converted to the representation specified after *code* and transferred to the file. If the data type is character-type and flat, closing blanks are cut off. In the data type string, closing blanks are not cut off. The end-of-line marking of the relevant platform is appended to the transferred data by default. When reading from a text file, the content of the file is read until the next end-of-line marking, converted from the format specified after *code* into the current character format, and transferred to a data object.

The end-of-line marking depends on the operating system of the application server. In the MS Windows operating systems, the markings "CRLF" and "LF" are common, while under UNIX, only "LF" is used. If, when using Windows, an existing file is opened without the TYPE addition (see Section 32.2.4), the first end-of-line marking is searched for and used for the whole file. If a new file is created without the TYPE addition (see Section 32.2.4), the content of the profile parameter abap/NTfmode is used. If the profile parameter is not set, "CRLF" is used. If a file with the TYPE addition (see Section 32.2.4) is opened and a valid value is contained in attr, this value is used.

In Unicode programs, only the content of character-type data objects can be transferred to text files and read from text files. The addition ENCODING must be specified in Unicode programs and can only be omitted in non-Unicode programs.

Specifying the character representation

Syntax of *code*

```
... DEFAULT | UTF-8 | NON-UNICODE ...
```

The additions determine in which character representation the content of the file is handled.

▶ DEFAULT
  The designation DEFAULT corresponds to the designation UTF-8 in a Unicode system and to the designation NON-UNICODE in a non-Unicode system.

▶ UTF-8
  The characters in the file are handled according to the Unicode character representation UTF-8.

▶ NON-UNICODE
  In a non-Unicode system, the data is read or written without being converted. In a Unicode system, the characters in the file are handled according to the non-Unicode-code page that would be assigned to the current text environment according to the database table TCP0C at the time of reading or writing in a non-Unicode system (see Section 35.1.2).

If the addition ENCODING is not specified in non-Unicode programs, the addition NON-UNICODE is used implicitly.

32.2.2.3 Opening a File as a Legacy Binary File

Syntax

```
... LEGACY BINARY MODE [endian] [codepage] ...
```

The addition IN LEGACY BINARY MODE opens the file as a binary file, exactly as in the addition IN BINARY MODE, except that in this case the byte order and the code page with which the content of the file should be handled can also be specified.

Byte sequence

Syntax of *endian*

```
... { BIG | LITTLE } ENDIAN ...
```

This addition specifies that numerical data objects of type i, f or s are stored in the file in the byte order big-endian or little-endian. If conversion is needed when reading or writing a data object of this type, it is performed between this byte order and the byte order of the current platform. If the addition is not specified, the byte order of the current application server is used.

Notes

▶ The statement SET DATASET (see section 32.6) can be used to specify a different byte order for an open legacy file.

▶ The addition BIG|LITTLE ENDIAN replaces the use of the obsolete statement TRANSLATE NUMBER FORMAT (see Section 42.11.1) when accessing data.

Code page

Syntax of *codepage*

```
... CODE PAGE cp ...
```

This addition specifies that the representation of character-type data objects in the file is based on the code page specified in cp. When reading or writing a character-type data object, a conversion is performed between this code page and the current character representation if necessary. If the addition is not specified, the data is read or written in a non-

Unicode system without being converted. In a Unicode system, the characters in the file are handled according to the non-Unicode code page that would be assigned to the current text environment according to the entry in the database table TCP0C at the time of reading or writing in a non-Unicode system (see Section 35.1.2).

For the code page specification cp, a character-type data object is expected which, when the statement is executed, must contain the name of a non-Unicode code page from the column CPCODEPAGE of the database table TCP00. A Unicode code page cannot be specified.

Notes

▶ In Unicode systems, this addition allows the automatic conversion of file content to the current character representation when reading and writing files. This makes it possible to import files that have been stored in any non-Unicode system into Unicode systems.

▶ The statement SET DATASET (see Section 32.6) can be used to specify a different code page for an open legacy file.

▶ The addition CODE PAGE replaces the use of the obsolete statement TRANSLATE CODEPAGE (see Section 42.11.1) when accessing data.

32.2.2.4 Opening a File as a Legacy Text File

Syntax

```
... LEGACY TEXT MODE [endian] [codepage] ...
```

The addition IN LEGACY TEXT MODE opens the file as a legacy text file. As with legacy binary files, the byte order and the code page with which the content of the file should be handled can also be specified. The syntax and meaning of *endian* and *codepage* are the same as for legacy binary files (see Section 32.2.2.3).

In contrast to legacy binary files, the closing blanks in a legacy file are cut off when writing character-type flat data objects in a legacy text file. As for a text file, an end-of-line marking is also appended to the transferred data by default. In contrast to text files opened with the addition IN TEXT MODE, Unicode programs do not check whether the data objects used for reading or writing are character-type. Furthermore, the LENGTH additions of the statements READ DATASET and TRANSFER are used for counting in bytes in legacy text files and in the units of a character represented in the memory for text files.

Note

As with legacy binary files, text files that have been written in a non-Unicode system can be accessed in Unicode systems as legacy text files, and the content is converted accordingly.

Example

A file *test.dat* is created as a text file, filled with data, changed and exported. As every TRANSFER statement appends an end-of-line marking to the written content, the content of the file has two lines after the change. The first line contains "12ABCD". The second line contains "890". The character "7" was overwritten by the end-of-line marking of the first line.

```
DATA: file    TYPE string VALUE 'test.dat',
      result TYPE string.

OPEN DATASET file FOR OUTPUT
                  IN TEXT MODE ENCODING DEFAULT.
TRANSFER '1234567890' TO file.
CLOSE DATASET file.

OPEN DATASET file FOR UPDATE
                  IN TEXT MODE ENCODING DEFAULT
                  AT POSITION 2.
TRANSFER 'ABCD' TO file.
CLOSE DATASET file.

OPEN DATASET file FOR INPUT
                  IN TEXT MODE ENCODING DEFAULT.
WHILE sy-subrc = 0.
  READ DATASET file INTO result.
  WRITE / result.
ENDWHILE.
CLOSE DATASET file.
```

32.2.3 Specifying the Position

Syntax of *position*

```
... AT POSITION pos ...
```

This addition sets the file pointer at the position specified in pos. A numerical data object is expected for pos. As of Release 6.10, digits with a value greater than the value range of the data type i can also be entered.

The positioning is specified in bytes, and the start of the file is equal to the position 0. If pos contains the value -1, as of Release 6.10, the file pointer is positioned at the end of the file. For all other negative values and before Release 6.10, the behavior is undefined.

Please note the following special cases:

▶ If the file is opened for reading and the value of pos is greater than the length of the file, the file pointer is positioned outside the file. As long as the position is not changed, no data can be read. In a non-Unicode program, if a file is opened for reading and then is written in, the file is filled with hexadecimal 0 from the end of the file to the specified position, and the new content is written after that.

▶ If the file is opened for writing, the file is filled with hexadecimal 0 from the start of the file to the specified position at the time of the next writing, and the new content is written after that.

▶ If the file is opened for appending, the position specification is ignored and the file pointer remains positioned at the end of the file.

▶ If the file is opened for changing, and the value of pos is greater than the length of the file, the next time the file is written in it is filled with hexadecimal 0 from the end of the file to the specified position, and the new content is written after that.

The addition POSITION cannot be specified if the addition FILTER is specified at the same time (see Section 32.2.4).

Notes

▶ For file sizes larger than 2 GB, a data object pos of the data type i is not sufficient for positioning in the whole file, and f or p must be used instead.

▶ The positioning can be overwritten by the statement SET DATASET (see Section 32.6). In particular, SET DATASET should be used for positioning the file pointer at the end of the file instead of entering the value -1 in pos.

32.2.4   Operating System-Dependent Additions

Syntax of *os_addition*

```
... [TYPE attr]
    [FILTER opcom] ...
```

You can use these additions to make operating-system specific settings and to execute operating system statements.

32.2.4.1 File Settings

Syntax

```
... TYPE attr ...
```

The behavior of this addition depends on the operating system of the application server. If it is not an MS Windows operating system, a character-type field can be specified for `attr` that contains operating-system specific parameters for the file that is to be opened. These parameters are transferred to the operating system of the application server unchanged and without being checked for correctness.

If the operating system is an MS Windows operating system and the file is opened as a text file or as a legacy text file, the content of `attr` controls the end-of-line marking of the text file:

▶ If `attr` contains the value "NT," the end-of-line is marked by "CRLF".

▶ If `attr` contains the value "UNIX," the end-of-line is marked by "LF".

All other values of `attr` are ignored in MS Windows operating systems, and the end-of-line marking is opened in the same way as described in Section 32.2.2.

Example

Creating a file *test.dat*. The properties entered under TYPE are specific for the operating system OS/400.

```
OPEN DATASET 'test.dat'
  TYPE 'lrecl=80, blksize=8000, recfm=FB'
  FOR OUTPUT IN TEXT MODE ENCODING DEFAULT.
```

32.2.4.2 Operating System Statements

Syntax

```
... FILTER opcom ...
```

This addition can be used if the operating system of the application server supports pipes (UNIX and MS Windows). A character-type field can be specified for `opcom`, which contains an operating system statement that corresponds to the appropriate command-level syntax.

When the statement OPEN DATASET is executed, a process is started in the operating system for the specified statement. When the file is opened for reading, a channel (pipe) is linked with STDOUT of the process from which the data is read at the time of file reading. The file itself is linked with STDIN of the process. When the file is opened for writing, a channel (pipe) is linked to STDIN of the process to which data is transferred at the time of writing. The output of the process is diverted to this file.

The addition FILTER must not be used together with the addition AT POSITION or for the access type FOR UPDATE.

Note
When working with pipes, you need to ensure that the pipe only exists in the current work process. If a change of work process (see Section 33.2.1.1) takes place during the time that the file is open, the pipe is lost and an attempted read or write access leads to a treatable exception of the class CX_SY_PIPE_REOPEN.

Example
On a UNIX platform, a compress filter is started for writing, and an un-compress filter is started for reading. When the file is accessed for writing, the data is compressed, and when it is accessed for reading, the data is decompressed.

```
DATA file TYPE string VALUE '/usr/test.Z'.

OPEN DATASET file FCR OUTPUT IN BINARY MODE
                      FILTER 'compress'.

...

CLOSE DATASET file.

OPEN DATASET file FOR INPUT IN BINARY MODE
                      FILTER 'uncompress'.

...

CLOSE DATASET file.
```

32.2.5 Error Handling

Syntax of *error_handling*

```
...  [MESSAGE msg]
     [IGNORING CONVERSION ERRORS]
     [REPLACEMENT CHARACTER rc] ...
```

These additions allow the system to receive operating system messages, to suppress exceptions and to define a replacement character for unknown characters if an error occurs.

32.2.5.1 Receiving an Operating System Message

Syntax

```
... MESSAGE msg ...
```

If an error occurs when a file is opened, the corresponding operating system message is assigned to the data object msg. A character-type variable can be entered for msg.

Example

Issuing an operating system message after an attempt to open a file with an empty name.

```
DATA mess TYPE string.

OPEN DATASET '' FOR INPUT IN BINARY MODE MESSAGE mess.

IF sy-subrc = 8.
  MESSAGE mess TYPE 'I'.
ENDIF.
```

32.2.5.2 Suppressing Exceptions

Syntax

```
... IGNORING CONVERSION ERRORS ...
```

This addition can be used to suppress a treatable exception defined by the class CX_SY_CONVERSION_CODEPAGE. This exception can be triggered during reading or writing if a conversion between code pages takes place and a character cannot be converted to the target code page.

This addition is possible when opening text files, legacy text files or legacy binary files, but not when opening binary files.

Notes

▶ Each unconvertible character is replaced during the conversion either by the character "#" or by the character defined by the addition RE-PLACEMENT CHARACTER. The addition IGNORING CONVERSION ERRORS controls whether or not the user is notified of this by an exception.

▶ This setting can be changed in an opened file using the statement SET DATASET (see Section 32.6).

32.2.5.3 Defining Replacement Characters

Syntax

```
... REPLACEMENT CHARACTER rc ...
```

If a conversion between code pages takes place while data is being read or written, every character that cannot be converted to the target code page is replaced by the character specified in rc. For rc, a character-type data object with a single character is expected. If the addition is not specified, the character "#" is used as a replacement character.

This addition is possible when opening text files, legacy text files or legacy binary files, but not when opening binary files.

Notes

▶ If at least one character is replaced by a replacement character during reading or writing, the exception defined in the class CX_SY_ CONVERSION_CODEPAGE is triggered after the conversion if this is not suppressed by the addition IGNORING CONVERSION ERRORS.

▶ The replacement character of an opened file can be changed using the statement SET DATASET (see Section 32.6).

32.2.6 Treatable Exceptions When Opening Files

If the system tries to open a file that is not valid or permitted, it will trigger an exception that is defined by a sub-class of CX_SY_FILE_ACCESS_ ERROR. The corresponding runtime errors can be captured and summarized in the exception group FILE_ACCESS_ERRORS (see Table D.8).

If the FILTER addition is used although the operating system does not support pipes, the exception defined by the class CX_SY_PIPES_NOT_ SUPPORTED is triggered. The corresponding runtime error DATASET_ NO_PIPE belongs to the exception group FILE_ACCESS_ERRORS.

If no more files can be opened, the exception defined in the class CX_SY_ TOO_MANY_FILES is triggered. The corresponding runtime error DATASET_TOO_MANY_FILES belongs to the exception group FILE_ ACCESS_ERRORS.

If an invalid code page is specified, this triggers an exception that is defined by the class CX_SY_CODEPAGE CONVERTER_INIT. The corresponding runtime error CONVT_CODEPAGE_INIT can be captured.

32.3 Writing a File

Output to a file on the application server.

Syntax

```
TRANSFER dobj TO dset [LENGTH len]
                      [NO END OF LINE].
```

This statement passes the content of the data object dobj to the file specified in dset. For dobj, you can specify data objects with elementary data types and flat structures. In Unicode programs, dobj must be character-type if the file was opened as a text file (this restriction does not apply to legacy text files).

dset is expected to be a character-type data object that contains the platform-specific name of the file (see Section 32.1.1). The content is written to the file from the current file pointer. After the transfer, the file pointer is positioned after the data that was added. You can use the addition LENGTH to restrict the number of characters or bytes transferred.

In a Unicode program, the file for writing, appending, or changing must be open. Otherwise, a treatable exception occurs.

If the file is closed in a non-Unicode program, the file is implicitly opened using the statement

OPEN DATASET dset **FOR OUTPUT IN BINARY MODE.**

This means, the file is opened as a binary file for writing. If the system accesses an invalid file, a treatable exception is raised.

32.3.1 The Influence of the Access Type

The access type (see Section 32.2.1) defined in the statement OPEN DATASET has the following effect on the transfer:

▶ In Unicode programs, you cannot write in a file opened for reading while using FOR INPUT. In non-Unicode programs, TRANSFER writes in a file opened for reading using FOR INPUT in exactly the same way as a file opened for changing using FOR UPDATE.

▶ In a file opened for writing using FOR OUTPUT, the system writes to the file from the current file pointer onwards. If the file pointer is positioned after the current start of the file, the file is pre-filled with hexadecimal 0 from the start of the file to the file pointer.

▶ In a file opened for appending using FOR APPENDING, the system writes into the file from the current file pointer which is always at the end of the file.

▶ In a file opened for changing, using FOR UPDATE, the system writes into the file from the current file pointer onwards. If the file pointer is positioned after the end of the file, the file is pre-filled with hexadecimal 0 between the end of the file and the file pointer position.

Note

If, prior to Release 6.10 parts of a file were to be overwritten, it was only possible to write to a file opened for reading. This is not allowed in Unicode programs; as of Release 6.10 and later, you can open a file for changing instead. This is the recommended procedure for non-Unicode programs as well.

32.3.2 The Influence of the Storage Type

The transfer depends on the storage type used when the file is opened using the statement OPEN DATASET (see Section 32.2.2). If the specified storage type requires a conversion, it is carried out before the writing process.

If the file was opened as a text file or as a legacy text file, the closing blank characters are deleted for all data objects except for those of the data type string. A platform-specific end-of-line mark is then added to the remaining content of the data object or to the result of the conversion, and the final result is written byte-by-byte into the file.

As of Release 6.40, the appending of the end-of-line separator can be prevented using the addition NO END OF LINE.

If the file was opened as a binary file or as a legacy binary file, the content of the data object or the result of the conversion is written byte-by-byte into the file.

Note

Only character-type data objects should be written to text files. Only byte-type data objects should be written to binary files. To store numerical data objects or mixed structures, we recommend that you assign them to character-type or byte-type typed field symbols (see Section 17.2.2) using the CASTING addition of the statement ASSIGN and save these field symbols.

Example

The binary data from the database table SPFLI is transferred to a binary file *flights.dat*. The structure of the table rows transferred contains both character-type and numerical fields. Since the type-specific storage of mixed structures in files is not possible, the binary content of the structure is directly accessed using a typed field symbol <hex_container>. To attain the same result, you could also transfer the structure wa directly, but we recommend using the field symbol because it explicitly transfers a binary data type to a binary file. This type of storage is only recommended for short-term storage within the same system because the byte-type content depends on the byte sequence and the current system code page. For long-term storage or for exchanging between systems, the data should be converted to character-type containers and stored as a text file.

```
DATA: file TYPE string VALUE 'flights.dat',
      wa TYPE spfli.

FIELD-SYMBOLS <hex_container> TYPE x.

OPEN DATASET file FOR OUTPUT IN BINARY MODE.

SELECT *
      FROM spfli
      INTO wa.
  ASSIGN wa TO <hex_container> CASTING.
  TRANSFER <hex_container> TO file.
ENDSELECT.

CLOSE DATASET file.
```

32.3.3 Restricting the Number of Transferred Characters or Bytes

Syntax

```
... LENGTH len ...
```

This addition determines how many characters or how many bytes of the data object dobj are written to the file. len is expected to be a data object of type i that contains the number of characters or bytes. In text files, the content of len specifies the number of characters that are read from the storage. For binary files, legacy text files and legacy binary files, len specifies the number of bytes that are written to the file. The first len characters or bytes are transferred and alignment gaps are included in the structures. If the addition LENGTH is not specified, all characters or bytes are transferred.

If the value of `len` is less than or equal to 0, no characters or bytes are transferred. If the file is opened as a (legacy) text file, however, an end-of-line separator is inserted into the file by default. If the value of `len` is greater than the number of characters or bytes in `dobj`, hexadecimal 0 or blank characters are transferred to the file instead of the missing bytes or characters, depending on whether the file was opened as a (legacy) text file or as a (legacy) binary file.

32.3.4 Preventing the Appending of an End-of-Line Marking

Syntax

```
... NO END OF LINE ...
```

This addition has the effect that, in text files or legacy text files, no end-of-line marking is appended to the data transferred.

32.3.5 Treatable Exceptions When Writing in Files

If a general error occurs when the file is written, an exception occurs that is defined by a sub-class of CX_SY_FILE_ACCESS_ERROR. The corresponding runtime errors can be captured and summarized in the exception group FILE_ACCESS_ERRORS (see Table D.8).

If, when opening the file, the addition `FILTER` is specified and the file is accessed in a written way after a change of the work process, the exception defined by the class CX_SY_PIPE_REOPEN is triggered. The corresponding runtime error cannot be caught.

If at least one character had to be replaced because it could not be converted in the code page specified when opening the file and because the exception was not suppressed by the addition `IGNORING CONVERSION ERRORS`, then this triggers the exception defined by the class CX_SY_CONVERSION_CODEPAGE. The corresponding runtime error CONVT_CODEPAGE belongs to the exception group CONVERSION_ERRORS (see Table D.3).

If the file is opened in non-Unicode programs using `TRANSFER`, then the exceptions listed for the statement `OPEN DATASET` can also occur.

32.4 Reading a File

Reading from a file on the application server.

Syntax

```
READ DATASET dset INTO dobj [ MAXIMUM LENGTH mlen ]
                            [[ACTUAL] LENGTH alen ] .
```

This statement exports data from the file specified in `dset` into the data object `dobj`. For `dobj`, variables with elementary data types and flat structures can be specified. In Unicode programs, `dobj` must be character-type if the file was opened as a text file.

For `dset`, a character-type data object is expected that contains the platform-specific name of the file (see Section 32.1.1) onwards. The content is read from the file starting from the current file pointer. After the data transfer, the file pointer is positioned after the section that was read. Using the `MAXIMUM LENGTH` addition, the number of characters or bytes to be read from the file can be limited. Using `ACTUAL LENGTH`, the number of characters or bytes actually used can be determined.

In a Unicode program, the file must be opened in an arbitrary access type; otherwise, an exception that cannot be handled will be triggered. If the file has not yet been opened in a non-Unicode program, it will be implicitly opened as a binary file for read access using the statement

OPEN DATASET dset **FOR INPUT IN BINARY MODE**.

If a non-existing file is accessed, an exception that can be handled is triggered.

Return values

sy-subrc	Meaning
0	Data was read without reaching the end of the file.
4	Data was read and the end of the file was reached, or there was an attempt to read after the end of the file.

32.4.1 The Influence of the Access Type

Files can be read independently of the access type (see Section 32.2.1). Whether data can be read or not depends solely on the position of the file pointer. If the latter is at the end of the file or after the file, no data can be read and `sy-subrc` will be set to 4.

32.4.2 The Influence of the Storage Type

The import function depends on the storage type in which the file was opened with the statement `OPEN DATASET` (see Section 32.2.2).

If the file was opened as a text file or as a legacy text file, the data is normally read from the current position of the file pointer to the next end-of-line marking, and the file pointer is positioned after the end-of-line marking. If the data object `dobj` is too short for the number of read characters, the superfluous characters and bytes are cut off. If it is longer, it will be filled with blanks to the right.

If the file was opened as a binary file or as a legacy-binary file, as much data is read by default as fits into the data object `dobj`. If the data object `dobj` is longer than the number of exported characters, it is filled with hexadecimal 0 on the right.

If the specified storage type makes conversion necessary, this is executed before the assignment to the data object `dobj`. Afterwards, the read data is placed byte by byte into the data object.

Note
The data from the text files should be imported solely into character-type data objects and data from binary files should be imported solely into byte-type data objects. To evaluate imported data as numeric data objects or mixed structures, we recommend that you export these into binary containers and then assign these using the `CASTING` addition of the `ASSIGN` statement in accordance with the typed field symbols (see Section 17.2.2). If the file is opened as a (legacy) text file when such data is being imported, there is the danger that an end-of-line marking is contained in the binary representation of a number and that the number can therefore not be read.

Example
Importing the binary file *flights.dat* written from the example in Section 32.3.2). The data is written in a binary form into a byte-type typed field symbol `<hex_container>`. Through the assignment of the structured data area `wa` to the field symbol, this adopts the length of the data area, and a corresponding number of bytes for the loop process are imported. It would be possible to import directly into the structure `wa` with the same result, but the use of the field symbol is recommended. The reason is that

in this way the data is explicitly transferred from a binary file into a binary data type.

```
DATA: file TYPE string VALUE 'flights.dat',
      wa   TYPE spfli.

FIELD-SYMBOLS <hex_container> TYPE x.

OPEN DATASET file FOR INPUT IN BINARY MODE.

ASSIGN wa TO <hex_container> CASTING.

DO.
  READ DATASET file INTO <hex_container>.
  IF sy-subrc = 0.
    WRITE: / wa-carrid,
             wa-connid,
             wa-countryfr,
             wa-cityfrom,
             wa-cityto,
             wa-fltime,
             wa-distance.
  ELSE.
    EXIT.
  ENDIF.
ENDDO.

CLOSE DATASET file.
```

32.4.3 Restricting the Number of Imported Characters or Bytes

Syntax

`... MAXIMUM LENGTH mlen ...`

This addition determines the maximum number of characters or bytes are read from the file. For `mlen`, a data object of the type `i` is expected. It contains the number of characters or bytes. In the case of text files, the content of `mlen` determines how many characters are written to the memory. In the case of binary, legacy-text, and legacy-binary files, `mlen` determines how many bytes are read from the file.

The first `mlen` characters or bytes are read from the current position of the file pointer and the file pointer is positioned after the read file. If the file is opened as a (legacy) text file and there is an end-of-line marking within the specified length, the data is read only up to this position and the file pointer is positioned after the end-of-line marking.

If the value of `mlen` is equal to 0, no data is read. If the value of `mlen` is negative, the addition will be ignored and importing takes place in the same way as described in Section 32.4.2.

Example

The following program section has the same functionality as the example in Section 32.4.2. Here data is imported not into a byte-type field symbol but into a byte-type data object `hex_container`. The number of bytes to be imported is determined by the typed field symbol `<spfli>`. This symbol is used in each loop process to access the imported data component by component.

```
DATA: file TYPE string VALUE 'flights.dat',
      hex_container(1000) TYPE x,
      len TYPE i.

FIELD-SYMBOLS <spfli> TYPE spfli.

DESCRIBE FIELD <spfli> LENGTH len IN BYTE MODE.

OPEN DATASET file FOR INPUT IN BINARY MODE.

ASSIGN hex_container TO <spfli> CASTING.

DO.
  READ DATASET file INTO hex_container
                    MAXIMUM LENGTH len.
  IF sy-subrc = 0.
    WRITE: / <spfli>-carrid,
             <spfli>-connid,
             <spfli>-countryfr,
             <spfli>-cityfrom,
             <spfli>-cityto,
             <spfli>-fltime,
             <spfli>-distance.
  ELSE.
    EXIT.
  ENDIF.
ENDDO.

CLOSE DATASET file.
```

32.4.4 Determining the Number of Imported Characters or Bytes

Syntax

```
... [ACTUAL] LENGTH alen ...
```

This addition assigns the number of characters or bytes to be read from the file to the data object `alen`.

For `alen`, a variable of the type `i` is expected. For text files, the system determines how many characters were written to the memory area. With binary, legacy-text and legacy-binary files, the system determines how many bytes were read from the file.

Note

The optional addition `ACTUAL` was introduced for Release 6.10 in order to be better able to distinguish the addition `LENGTH` —which was also available prior to Release 6.10—from the addition `MAXIMUM LENGTH`. As of Release 6.10, the addition `ACTUAL` should always be used.

32.4.5 Treatable Exceptions When Reading Files

If a general error occurs when reading a file, an exception occurs that is defined by a sub-class of CX_SY_FILE_ACCESS_ERROR. The corresponding runtime errors can be captured and summarized in the exception group FILE_ACCESS_ERRORS (see Table D.8).

If, when opening a file, the addition `FILTER` is specified and a file is accessed in a reading way after a change of the work process, an exception defined by the class of CX_SY_PIPE_REOPEN is triggered. The corresponding runtime error cannot be caught.

If at least one character had to be replaced because it could not be converted in the current system code page and because the exception was not suppressed by the addition `IGNORING CONVERSION ERRORS` when opening the file, then the exception defined by the class CX_SY_CONVERSION_CODEPAGE is triggered. The corresponding runtime error CONVT_CODEPAGE belongs to the exception group CONVERSION_ERRORS (see Table D.3).

If the file is opened in non-Unicode programs using `READ DATASET`, then the exceptions listed for the statement `OPEN DATASET` can also occur.

32.5 Determining the Attributes of an Opened File

```
GET DATASET
```

Determining the attributes of an opened file.

Syntax

```
GET DATASET dset [POSITION pos] [ATTRIBUTES attr].
```

With the POSITION addition, this statement determines the current position of the file pointer in the file specified in dset and gets additional file attributes using the ATTRIBUTES addition.

dset must be a character-type data object that contains the platform-specific name of the file (see Section 32.1.1). The file must be open; otherwise an exception that can be handled is raised.

Note

If no additions are specified, the statement can be used to determine with the aid of a TRY control structure whether or not the file is open.

32.5.1 Determining the Position of the File Pointer

Syntax

```
... POSITION pos ...
```

This addition assigns the current position of the file pointer to the data object pos, which must be numeric variable. The position is specified in bytes; the start of the file corresponds to position 0.

The POSITION addition cannot be specified for files that were opened using the FILTER addition of the OPEN DATASET statement; otherwise an exception that can be handled is raised.

Note

In the case of files larger than 2 GB, a data object pos of the data type i is not sufficient for including all possible positions of the file pointer.

Example

After the first literal is saved the position of the file pointer is assigned to the variable pos, which is then used to position the file pointer before the read access.

```
DATA: file TYPE string VALUE 'test.dat',
      pos  TYPE I,
      text TYPE string.

OPEN DATASET file FOR OUTPUT
               IN TEXT MODE ENCODING DEFAULT.
TRANSFER '1234567890' TO file.
GET DATASET file POSITION pos.
TRANSFER 'ABCDEFGHIJ' TO file.
CLOSE DATASET file.

OPEN DATASET file FOR INPUT
               IN TEXT MODE ENCODING DEFAULT
               AT POSITION pos.
READ DATASET file INTO text.
CLOSE DATASET file.
```

32.5.2 Determining Other Attributes

Syntax

```
... ATTRIBUTES attr ...
```

This addition places the attributes with which the file was opened using the OPEN DATASET statement into the data object attr. The data type of attr must be dset_attributes, which is defined in the type group DSET as follows:

dset_attributes is a structured type with two substructures: fixed and changeable. The components of the substructure fixed take in attributes of the file that cannot be changed using the SET DATASET statement (see Table 32.2). The components of the substructure changeable include attributes of the file that can be changed using the SET DATASET statement (see Table 32.3).

Component	Meaning
indicator	Structure whose components mode, access_type, encoding and filter contain the value "X" in attr if the identically-named components of the structure fixed are significant for the current file.
mode	Storage type. Possible values in attr are "T," "LT," "B," and "LB" for text files, legacy text files, binary files and legacy binary files. The corresponding addition of the OPEN DATASET statement is IN mode.

Table 32.2 Components of the Structure dset_attributes-fixed

Component	Meaning
access_type	Access type. Possible values in attr are "I," "O," "A," and "U" for files that were opened for reading, writing, appending, and editing. The corresponding addition of the OPEN DATASET statement is FOR access.
encoding	Character representation. Possible values in attr are "NON-UNI-CODE" and "UTF-8." The corresponding addition of the OPEN DATASET statement is ENCODING code.
filter	Contains the filter command in attr if the file was opened with the FILTER addition of the OPEN DATASET statement.

Table 32.2 Components of the Structure dset_attributes-fixed (cont.)

Component	Meaning
indicator	Structure whose components repl_char, conv_errors, code_page and endian contain the value "X" in attr if the identically-named components of the structure changeable are significant for the current file.
repl_char	After opening the file, this component contains the replacement character in attr that was specified using the REPLACEMENT CHARACTER addition of the OPEN DATASET statement.
conv_errors	After opening the file, this component contains the value "I" in attr if it was opened using the addition IGNORING CONVERSION ERRORS of the statement OPEN DATASET, otherwise it contains the value "R."
code_page	After opening the file, this component contains the code page in attr that was specified using the CODE PAGE addition of the OPEN DATASET statement. If this addition is not used, the content of attr initial.
endian	After opening the file, this component contains the value "B" in attr if the BIG ENDIAN addition of the OPEN DATASET statement was used or "L" if the LITTLE ENDIAN addition was used. If no addition is used, the content of attr is initial.

Table 32.3 Components of the Structure dset_attributes-changeable

For some of the components, constants are defined in the type group DSET as comparison values.

Note
The determinable attributes do not represent the attributes of the file in the operating system, but the attributes with and by which the file is opened and handled in ABAP.

Example

In this example, the system first checks whether the file *test.dat* was opened using the FILTER addition. Only if this is not the case is the current file position determined using GET DATASET.

```
TYPE-POOLS dset.

DATA: dset TYPE string VALUE 'test.dat',
      attr TYPE dset_attributes,
      pos  TYPE i.

OPEN DATASET dset FOR INPUT IN BINARY MODE
                  FILTER 'uncompress'.

...

GET DATASET dset ATTRIBUTES attr.
IF attr-fixed-indicator-filter <> 'X'.
  GET DATASET dset POSITION pos.
ELSE.
  ...
ENDIF.

CLOSE DATASET dset.
```

32.5.3 Treatable Exceptions When Determining File Attributes

If the system accesses a closed file, or if you want to determine the position of the file pointer for a file that was opened using the addition FILTER, exceptions that are defined by sub-classes of CX_SY_FILE_ACCESS_ERROR are triggered. The corresponding runtime errors can be captured and summarized in the exception group FILE_ACCESS_ERRORS (see Table D.8).

32.6 Changing the Attributes of an Opened File

SET DATASET

Changing the attributes of an opened file.

Syntax

```
SET DATASET dest [POSITION {pos|{END OF FILE}}]
                 [ATTRIBUTES attr].
```

With the addition POSITION, this statement determines the position of the file pointer in the file specified in dset. With the addition ATTRIBUTES, it sets additional attributes for the file (see Section 32.1.1). At least one of these two additions must be specified.

For dset, a character-type data object is expected that contains the platform-specific name of the file. The file must already be open; otherwise a treatable exception occurs.

32.6.1   Defining the Position of the File Pointer

Syntax

```
... POSITION {pos|{END OF FILE}} ...
```

This addition sets the file pointer in the file either on the position specified in pos or, if END OF FILE is specified, at the end of the file. For pos, a numerical data object is expected.

The positioning is specified in bytes and the start of the file is equal to the position 0. If the value of pos is -1, the file pointer is set to the end of the file. Other negative values are not permitted.

Note the following special cases:

▶ If the file is open for reading and the value of pos is greater than the length of the file, the file pointer is positioned outside of the file. Unless the position is changed, no data can be read. If write changes are then made to the file in a non-Unicode program, the file is filled before with hexadecimal 0s from the end of the file to the specified position.

▶ If the file is opened for writing, and the value of pos is greater than the length of the file, the next time the file is written in it is filled with hexadecimal 0s from the end of the file to the specified position.

▶ If the file is opened for appending, the position specification is ignored and the file pointer remains positioned at the end of the file.

▶ If the file is opened for changing, and the value of pos is greater than the length of the file, hexadecimal 0s are added at the next write access from the end of the file to the specified position.

The addition POSITION cannot be specified for files that have been opened with the addition FILTER of the statement OPEN DATASET. Otherwise, this leads to a treatable exception.

Notes

▶ For file sizes greater than 2 GB, a data object `pos` of the data type `i` is not sufficient for entering all the possible positions of the data pointer.

▶ For reasons of compatibility, you can use the spelling `END-OF-FILE` instead of `END OF FILE`. The valid spelling `END OF FILE` was introduced with Release 6.40 for reasons of uniformity.

Example

During writing, the file is read from the start of the file until the first end-of-line marker, and then the new content is written starting from the end of the file onwards. Without the explicit setting of the data pointer after reading, the last `TRANSFER` statements of the file would be overwritten after the first end-of-line marker.

```
DATA: file TYPE string VALUE 'test1.dat',
      pos  TYPE i,
      text TYPE string.

OPEN DATASET file FOR OUTPUT
                  IN TEXT MODE ENCODING DEFAULT.

TRANSFER: 'Line1' TO file,
          'Line2' TO file,
          'Line3' TO file.

SET DATASET  file POSITION 0.
READ DATASET file INTO text.
SET DATASET  file POSITION END OF FILE.

TRANSFER: 'Line4' TO file,
          'Line5' TO file,
          'Line6' TO file.

CLOSE DATASET file.
```

32.6.2 Changing Further Attributes

Syntax

```
... ATTRIBUTES attr ...
```

Using this addition changes some of the attributes that were determined when the file was opened with the statement `OPEN DATASET`. For `attr`, a data object of the type `dset_changeable_attributes` from the type group DSET must be specified (see Table 32.4). The structure `dset_changeable_attributes` corresponds to the substructure `changeable` of the structure `dset_attributes`. Data objects of the structure `dset_attributes` can be filled using the statement `GET DATASET`.

Component	Meaning
indicator	Structure with the components `repl_char`, `conv_errors`, `code_page` and `endian`. If these components contain the value "X" in `attr`, the values are used in the components with the same names in the structure `dset_changeable_attributes` when changing.
repl_char	In this component of `attr`, a single-digit character-type replacement character can be specified to overwrite the replacement character specified when the file was opened using the addition `REPLACEMENT CHARACTER` of the statement `OPEN DATASET`.
conv_errors	In this component of `attr`, the value "I" or "R" can be specified to overwrite the setting made when the file was opened using the addition `IGNORING CONVERSION ERRORS`. The value "I" suppresses the exceptions with "R" the exceptions are triggered.
code_page	In this component of `attr`, a code page from the column CPCODEPAGE of the database table TCP00 can be specified to overwrite the code page specified when the file was opened using the addition `CODE PAGE` of the statement `OPEN DATASET`.
endian	In this component of `attr`, the value "B" or "L" can be specified to overwrite the setting made when the file was opened using the additions `BIG ENDIAN` and `LITTLE ENDIAN` of the statement `OPEN DATASET`. The value "B" sets the byte order to big endian, the value "L" sets it to little endian.

Table 32.4 Components of the Structure dset_changeable_attributes

For some components, the possible input values are defined as constants in the type group DSET.

The values entered in `attr` must comply with the syntax rules for the relevant additions of the statement `OPEN DATASET`, otherwise this leads to a treatable exception.

▶ The components `repl_char` and `conv_errors` can only be used when making changes if the file is opened as a text file, legacy text file or legacy binary file, but not if it is opened as a binary file.

▶ The components `code_page` and `endian` can only be used when making changes if the file is opened as a legacy text file or a legacy binary file.

Note
The changeable attributes do not affect the attributes of the file in the operating system, but rather the attributes with which the file is opened in ABAP and which affect the way this file is handled in ABAP.

Example

Depending on the non-changeable attributes of the file *test.dat*, some of its changeable attributes are reset.

```
TYPE-POOLS dset.

DATA: dset TYPE string VALUE 'test.dat',
      attr TYPE dset_attributes.

OPEN DATASET dset FOR INPUT IN LEGACY TEXT MODE.

...

GET DATASET dset ATTRIBUTES attr.

IF attr-fixed-mode = 'T' OR
   attr-fixed-mode = 'LT'.
  CLEAR attr-changeable.
  attr-changeable-indicator-conv_errors = 'X'.
  attr-changeable-conv_errors = 'I'.
  IF attr-fixed-mode = 'LT'.
    attr-changeable-indicator-code_page = 'X'.
    attr-changeable-code_page = '1100'.
  ENDIF.
  SET DATASET dset ATTRIBUTES attr-changeable.
ENDIF.

CLOSE DATASET dset.
```

32.6.3 Treatable Exceptions When Changing File Attributes

If an invalid code page is specified, this triggers an exception that is defined by the class CX_SY_CODEPAGE_CONVERTER_INIT. The corresponding runtime error CONVT_CODEPAGE_INIT cannot be captured.

If the specified replacement character does not exist in the specified target code page, the exception defined by the class CX_SY_CONVERSION_CODEPAGE is triggered. The corresponding runtime error CONVT_CODEPAGE belongs to the exception group CONVERSION_ERRORS (see Table D.3).

If the file is not opened in the correct mode, or if an error occurs when the file pointer is positioned, an exception defined by a sub-class of CX_SY_FILE_ACCESS_ERROR is triggered. The corresponding runtime errors can be captured and summarized in the exception group FILE_ACCESS_ERRORS (see Table D.8).

32.7   Changing the Size of a File

Changing the size of the file on the application server.

Syntax

```
TRUNCATE DATASET dset AT {CURRENT POSITION}|{POSITION pos}.
```

This statement sets the end of file of the file specified in dset to the value specified after AT and can thus change the size of the file. When shortened, the file is truncated after the new end of file; when extended, the file is filled with hexadecimal null from the previous to the new end of file.

For dset, a character-type data object is expected which contains the platform-specific name of the file. The file must be opened for writing, adding or changing and must not contain the FILTER addition of the OPEN DATASET statement; otherwise, a non-catchable exception will be triggered.

With the CURRENT POSITION addition, the end of file is set to the current file pointer. With the POSITION pos addition, the end of the file is set to the position specified in pos. For pos, a numeric data object is expected whose contents cannot be negative. The positioning is specified in bytes, whereby the start of file is synonymous with the position 0.

Return values
The statement always sets sy-subrc to the value 0 or triggers an exception.

Note
The TRUNCATE statement does not change the position of the current file pointer. If the file is open for adding, the file pointer is only set to the end of the file prior to the next write access.

Example
After the first TRUNCATE statement, the file contains the value "FF", and after the second, it contains the value "FF00".

```
DATA: name TYPE string VALUE 'test.dat',
      hex  TYPE xstring.

hex = 'FFFF'.
```

```
OPEN DATASET name FOR OUTPUT IN BINARY MODE.

TRANSFER hex TO name.
SET DATASET name POSITION 0.
READ DATASET name INTO hex.

TRUNCATE DATASET name AT POSITION 1.
SET DATASET name POSITION 0.
READ DATASET name INTO hex.

TRUNCATE DATASET name AT POSITION 2.
SET DATASET name POSITION 0.
READ DATASET name INTO hex.

CLOSE DATASET name.
```

32.8   Closing a File

CLOSE DATASET

Closing a file on the application server.

Syntax

CLOSE DATASET dset.

This statement closes the file specified in dset. dset must be a character-type data object that contains the platform-specific name of the file (see Section 32.1.1). If the file is already closed or does not exist, the statement is ignored and the return value sy-subrc is set to 0.

If the operating system buffers data before it is written to a file and there is still data in the buffer, this data is written to the file before closing.

Note
An opened file that was not explicitly closed using CLOSE DATASET is automatically closed when the program is left.

Return values
If a file was opened without the FILTER addition, sy-subrc always contains the value 0.

If a file was opened using the FILTER addition, sy-subrc contains the return value of the filter program. This return value is returned by the operating system. This value is generally 0 if the statement was executed successfully.

Treatable exceptions

If the file cannot be closed, for example because there is no more storage space to write buffered data, the exception defined by the class CX_SY_FILE_CLOSE is triggered. The corresponding runtime error DATASET_CANT_CLOSE belongs to the exception group FILE_ACCESS_ERRORS (see Table D.8).

This exception is also triggered if a file is opened with the FILTER addition for writing or appending and if the return value of the filter program does not equal 0.

32.9 Deleting a File

```
DELETE DATASET
```

Deleting a file on the application server.

Syntax

```
DELETE DATASET dset.
```

This statement deletes the file specified in dset. dset is expected to be a character-type data object that contains the platform-specific name of the file (see Section 32.1.1). The file can be opened or closed.

Return values

sy-subrc	Meaning
0	File deleted.
4	File could not be deleted.

Treatable exceptions

If no authorization to delete the file is available, the exception defined in the class CX_SY_FILE_AUTHORITY is triggered. The corresponding runtime error OPEN_DATASET_NO_AUTHORITY can be captured and assigned to the exception group FILE_ACCESS_ERRORS (see Table D.8).

33 Data Consistency

33.1 Overview

When external data is changed by application programs, the data must remain consistent after changes have been made. This is particularly critical for processing of data in the database. The time span during which a consistent data status is transferred to another consistent status is known as a LUW (Logical Unit of Work). If an error occurs during a LUW, it is possible to reset all the changes made up to this point and regenerate the data in its original consistent status (rollback). When a new consistent status has been reached, this new status can be set and a new LUW can be opened (commit).

In an SAP system, there are two types of LUWs:

▶ Database LUWs that are realized by the database system (see Section 33.2)

▶ SAP LUWs that are realized using special ABAP proramming techniques (see Section 33.3)

Accordingly, there are two significant lock types:

▶ Database locks that are realized by the system (see Section 33.4)

▶ SAP locks that are set using special ABAP proramming techniques (see Section 33.5)

Finally, the authorizations of a user for accessing data whose check has an ABAP statement are important for data consistency.

Statements connected with data consistency

Statement	Section
COMMIT WORK	33.3.1
ROLLBACK WORK	33.3.2
SET UPDATE TASK LOCAL	33.3.3
AUTHORITY-CHECK	33.6

33.2 Database LUW

A database LUW is a non-separable sequence of database operations that ends in a database commit. The database LUW is either executed completely by the database system or not executed at all. After a database

LUW has been successfully completed, the database returns to a consistent status and a new database LUW is opened. If an error is discovered within a database LUW, all database changes made since the start of the database LUW can be canceled using a database rollback. The database is subsequently restored to the same status as before the start of the LUW.

Note
A database commit closes all opened database cursors. In Open SQL, this particularly affects `SELECT` loops and the statement `OPEN CURSOR`.

33.2.1   Database Commit

Database commits are triggered either implicitly or explicitly in an SAP system.

33.2.1.1   Implicit Database Commits

The implicit database commits in an SAP system occur because the SAP system is logged on to the database system via its work processes. A work process can only execute a single database LUW and cannot interfere with the database LUWs belonging to other work processes. Since an ABAP program can be executed by different work processes during its runtime, the database LUW for the current work process must be completed each time an action takes place that leads to a change of the work process. As a result, a database commit is performed implicitly in the following situations.

▶ Completion of a dialog step
    The program waits for a user action and does not occupy a work process during this time. The next free work process is assigned to the program in the next dialog step.

▶ Calling a function module via a synchronous or asynchronous Remote Function Call
    The current work process hands over control to a different work process or system.

▶ Completion of a function module accessed with a synchronous Remote Function Call in a separate work process
    The calling program is assigned a new work process.

▶ Execution of a `RECEIVE` statement in a callback routine specified in an asynchronous RFC
    The current work process is interrupted so that the data can be received from the other application server.

- Interruption of the current work process with a `WAIT` statement
  After the interruption, the program is assigned the next free work process.

- Sending error and information messages and warnings
  These messages interrupt the current dialog step (see above).

33.2.1.2 Explicit Database Commits

Database commits can be triggered explicitly in ABAP programs in the following ways:

- Use of the corresponding database-specific Native SQL statement
- Calling the function module DB_COMMIT. This function module, which has no parameters, encapsulates the corresponding Native SQL statement
- Executing the Open SQL statement `COMMIT WORK` (see Section 33.3.1)

33.2.2 Database Rollback

Database rollbacks are triggered implicitly or explicitly in a SAP system.

33.2.2.1 Implicit Database Rollbacks

The following exceptions trigger an implicit database rollback:

- Occurrence of a runtime error
- Program termination through the sending of a message

  Termination and Exit messages always lead to a termination of the program. Other message types can also lead to a program termination in certain contexts (see Section 28.1.2).

33.2.2.2 Explicit Database Rollbacks

You have the following opportunities to trigger explicit database rollbacks in ABAP programs:

- Use of the according database-specific Native SQL statement
- Execution of the Open SQL statement `ROLLBACK WORK` (see Section 33.3.1)

33.3 SAP LUW

Since, as a rule, an application program is processed by several work processes in succession, and every change of the work process is linked with an implicit database commit (see Section 33.2.1), an application program is not automatically linked with a single database LUW. This applies in particular to dialog-oriented applications, in which a single database LUW is assigned to a single dialog step.

To ensure the data consistency of application programs executed across different work processes, application statements are not directly executed in an SAP LUW, but are first registered and then executed by a single work process within a single database LUW.

Two techniques are available for bundling the change statements in a database LUW:

▶ **Bundling via function modules (update)**
Through the statement CALL FUNCTION ... IN UPDATE TASK, an update function module is registered for a subsequent execution in an update work process (see Section 11.2.3).

▶ **Bundling via function modules (transactional RFC)**
Through the statement CALL FUNCTION ... IN BACKGROUND TASK DESTINATION, a remote-compatible function module is registered for a subsequent asynchronous execution via the RFC interface (transactional RFC, see Section 39.2.3).

▶ **Bundling via subroutines**
Through the statement PERFORM ... ON COMMIT, a subroutine is registered for subsequent execution in a different work process (see Section 11.2.4).

The Open SQL statements COMMIT WORK and ROLLBACK WORK control an SAP LUW.

Note
A function module can be classified either as an update function module or as remote-compatible but not as both at the same time. The update helps to realize SAP LUWs within an SAP system, while the transactional RFC creates LUWs in distributed systems.

33.3.1   SAP Commit

```
COMMIT WORK
```

Ending an SAP LUW and storing the changes.

Syntax

```
COMMIT WORK [AND WAIT].
```

The statement COMMIT WORK completes the current SAP LUW and opens a new one, storing all change requests for the current SAP LUW in the process. In this case, COMMIT WORK performs the following actions:

1. It executes all subroutines registered using PERFORM ON COMMIT.

2. It triggers an internal event in the Object Services that ensures changes in persistent objects will be registered as the last update function module as well as the subsequent initialization of persistent object attributes.

3. It initiates the processing of all registered update function modules in the update work process.

   This executes all high-priority update function modules registered using CALL FUNCTION ... IN UPDATE TASK in the order of their registration and in a common database LUW. If you do not specify the addition AND WAIT, the program does not wait until the update work process has executed it (asynchronous updating). If you specify the addition AND WAIT, however, the program processing after COMMIT WORK will not continue until the update work process has executed the high-priority update function modules (synchronous updating).

   If all high-priority update function modules are completed successfully, the statement executes the low-priority update function modules together in a common database LUW.

   In parallel, it also executes the individual function modules registered using CALL FUNCTION ... IN BACKGROUND TASK DESTINATION in a separate database LUW for each destination (see Section 39.2.3).

4. It handles all SAP locks set in the current program according to the value of the formal parameter _SCOPE of the corresponding lock function modules (see Section 33.5).

5. It triggers a database commit that also terminates the current database LUW.

The completion of the statement COMMIT WORK triggers the event TRANSACTION_FINISHED of the system class CL_SYSTEM_TRANSACTION_STATE, where the parameter KIND has the value of the constant CL_SYSTEM_TRANSACTION_STATE=>COMMIT_WORK.

If the statement COMMIT WORK is executed in specially called programs, be aware of the following:

▶ In a program executed using batch input, or if you have called the program using the USING addition of the statement CALL TRANSACTION, COMMIT WORK terminates the batch input processing when this is set correspondingly.

▶ In a program called using CALL DIALOG, COMMIT WORK does not trigger the processing of subroutines or updated function modules registered using PERFORM ... ON COMMIT and CALL FUNCTION ... IN UPDATE TASK. Therefore, COMMIT WORK does not complete the current SAP LUW. The SAP LUW is completed until the COMMIT WORK statement is executed in the calling program.

You cannot execute the COMMIT WORK statement during the updating procedure or during the execution of subroutines registered using PERFORM ... ON {COMMIT|ROLLBACK}.

Return values

sy-subrc	Meaning
0	You have specified the AND WAIT addition, and the updating of the update function modules was successful.
4	You have specified the AND WAIT addition, and the updating of the update function modules was not successful.

The COMMIT WORK statement always sets sy-subrc to 0 if the AND WAIT addition is not specified.

Note

The COMMIT WORK statement closes all database cursors. Open SQL statements that access a database cursor later (SELECT loop and FETCH) raise an exception that cannot be handled.

33.3.2 SAP Rollback

```
ROLLBACK WORK
```

Ending an SAP LUW without storing the changes.

Syntax

```
ROLLBACK WORK.
```

The statement ROLLBACK WORK closes the current SAP LUW and opens a new one. In doing so, all change requests of the current SAP LUW are canceled. To do this, ROLLBACK WORK carries out the following actions:

1. Executes all subroutines registered with PERFORM ON ROLLBACK.

2. Deletes all subroutines registered with PERFORM ON COMMIT.

3. Raises an internal event in the Object Services that makes sure that the attributes of persistent objects are initialised.

4. Deletes all update function modules registered with CALL FUNCTION . . . IN UPDATE TASK from the database table VBLOG and deletes all transactional Remote Function Calls registered with CALL FUNCTION . . . IN BACKGROUND TASK from the database table ARFCSSTATE of the ARFCS-DATA (see Section 39.2.3).

5. Removal of all SAP locks set in the current program in which the formal parameter _SCOPE of the lock function module was set to the value 2.

6. Triggers a database rollback which also ends the current database LUW.

After the completion of the statement COMMIT WORK, the event TRANSACTION_FINISHED of the system class CL_SYSTEM_TRANSACTION_STATE is raised, in which the parameter KIND has the value of the constant CL_SYSTEM_TRANSACTION_STATE=>ROLLBACK_WORK.

33.3.3 Local Updating

```
SET UPDATE TASK LOCAL
```

Activating a local update function.

Syntax

```
SET UPDATE TASK LOCAL.
```

This statement specifies that the high-priority update function modules—registered during the current SAP LUW using CALL FUNCTION . . . IN UPDATE TASK—are registered in the ABAP Memory instead of the VBLOG database table. In addition, it specifies that the current work process and not the update work process runs these modules during the current database LUW when the COMMIT WORK statement is executed. This statement has no effect on low-priority update function modules.

At the beginning of every SAP LUW, the local update function is deactivated. If you wish to use it, you must reactivate it again before the first update function module is registered.

Return values

sy-subrc	Meaning
0	The local update function was activated.
1	The local update function was activated because the program had already registered at least one update function module for the normal updating procedure in the current SAP LUW.

Notes

▶ The local update function performs a synchronous update according to the COMMIT WORK statement, independent of the addition AND WAIT.

▶ The occurrence of a database rollback during the local update affects all previous change statements.

33.4   Database Locks

When accessing database tables using SQL statements, the database system sets implicit physical database locks to the addressed lines that are realized using explicit lock flags for the addressed data records. These locks remain until the end of the database LUW. The units that are actually locked depend on the database system. The modifying statements (INSERT, UPDATE, MODIFY and DELETE) set exclusive locks. The SELECT read statement sets shared locks if the DB_SET_ISOLATION_LEVEL function module sets the so-called isolation level to "Committed Read". In the "Uncommitted Read" standard setting, SELECT does not set a lock (Oracle databases are the exception). The SELECT statement also sets an exclusive lock using the FOR UPDATE addition.

The implicit locks of the database system do not suffice for setting SAP LUW locks. You should use SAP locks for this purpose.

33.5   SAP Locks

SAP locks must be maintained for the duration of SAP LUWs. For this reason, various work processes and, if applicable, changing application servers must be able to handle these locks.

SAP locks are based on lock objects. The ABAP Dictionary defines these objects; they permit locks of single or several lines of one database table or locks of lines of several database tables linked by foreign key dependencies.

The creation of a lock object generates two lock function modules whose names consist of the prefixes ENQUEUE_ and DEQUEUE_ and the name of the lock object.

33.5.1 Imposing SAP Locks

SAP locks are set or released when calling lock function modules. The function locks access a central lock table in the memory of a special application server work process. Every SAP system contains exactly one such table (administered by transaction SM12). An enqueue function module sets an SAP lock by writing a corresponding entry in the lock table. If you cannot set a lock because corresponding lock entries already exist in the lock table, the function module terminates with the FOREIGN_LOCK exception.

The most important entry parameters of an enqueue function module are:

Parameter	Meaning
MODE_dbtab	Type of lock for the dbtab database table of the lock object. Possible entry values include "S" for a shared lock, "E" for an exclusive lock, and "X" for an expanded exclusive lock that can be requested only once (unlike a regular exclusive lock within a program).
key_fields	For all key fields of the lock object, you can specify values that define the rows to be locked. If you have not specified a value for a key field, all corresponding rows are locked.
_SCOPE	Definition of the lock duration with respect to an SAP LUW. Possible entry values include "1" for handling the lock in the same program, "2" for transferring the lock to the update, and "3" for handling the lock in the program and in the update.

Note
You can check an SAP lock by trying to set a corresponding lock and handling the FOREIGN_LOCK exception in the process.

33.5.2 Lifting SAP Locks

You can release SAP locks by deleting the corresponding entry in the lock table.

When you set an SAP lock using the ENQUEUE function module, the value transferred to the _SCOPE entry parameter determines the lock duration. Depending on the formal parameter _SCOPE, you can release an SAP lock as follows:

- ▶ If _SCOPE is set to the value 1, the lock is not linked to the current SAP LUW. You can release the lock either by calling the DEQUEUE function module whose formal parameter _SCOPE can have any value, or by terminating the program.

- ▶ If _SCOPE is set to the value 2, the lock is linked to the current SAP LUW. In case CALL FUNCTION ... FOR UPDATE TASK has registered at least one update function module, the statements COMMIT WORK or ROLLBACK WORK release the lock upon completion of the SAP LUW. When using COMMIT WORK, the update releases the lock after processing the update function modules. This type of lock may persist beyond the end of a program until the update procedure has been completed.

- ▶ If _SCOPE is set to 3, both the update and the program must release the lock. The update releases the lock as if _SCOPE had a value of 2. The program releases the lock as if _SCOPE had a value of 1. The entire release procedure is specified by the last user who released the lock.

If you want to release an SAP lock using the DEQUEUE function module independent of the update, you must transfer a value to the formal parameter _SCOPE that is greater than or equal to the value transferred to the parameter of the same name for the ENQUEUE function module.

Besides the _SCOPE parameter, the entry parameters of a DEQUEUE function module correspond to those of the ENQUEUE function module. You can then use the additional parameter _SYNCHRON to specify whether the release of the lock should be delayed until the program processing continues.

33.6 Authorization Check

AUTHORITY-CHECK

Checking a user authorization.

Syntax

```
AUTHORITY-CHECK OBJECT auth_obj
                ID id1 {FIELD val1}|DUMMY
                [ID id2 {FIELD val2}|DUMMY]
                ...
                [ID id10 {FIELD val10}|DUMMY].
```

This statement checks whether an authorization is entered in the user master record of the current user (sy-uname) for the authorization object entered in the field `auth_obj` and whether this is sufficient for the request specified in the statement. A flat character-type field that contains the name of an authorization object is expected for `auth_obj`.

With `id1`, `id2`, ..., you must have at least one and can have a maximum of 10 authorization fields listed for the authorization object specified. With `id1`, `id2`, ..., flat character-type fields are expected that contain the name of the authorization fields in uppercase letters. If an authorization field is specified that does not appear in the authorization object, no check can be executed, and `sy-subrc` is set to 4. For each specified authorization field, you either must specify with `FIELD` a value to be checked in a flat character-type field `val1`, `val2`, ... or the language element `DUMMY`.

The authorization check is successful if one or more authorizations are created for the authorization object in the user master record and if—for at least one of the authorizations—each of the value sets defined there for the authorization fields specified using `FIELD` includes the value `val1`, `val2`, ... to be checked. Authorization fields that are not included in the statement or that have `DUMMY` specified for them are not checked. If the check is successful, `sy-subrc` is set to 0. Otherwise, it is set to a value not equal to 0 (see below).

Note

The authorization fields of an authorization object are fields for data and a field with the name ACTVT for activities. Activities are represented by abbreviations with two digits defined in the ACTVT column of the database table TACT or have a customer-specific definition in TACTZ. Possible activities are assigned to the authorization field ACTVT in the authorization object. In the user master record, authorizations for data and activities in the form of operands of logical expressions are stored as value sets. Here, masking characters can be used for generic authorizations.

Return values

sy-subrc	Meaning
0	Authorization successful. An authorization for the authorization object was found in the user master record. Its value sets include the specified values.
4	Authorization check not successful. Although one or more authorizations were found for the authorization object in the user master record, their value sets do not include the specified values, or wrong authorization fields were specified, or too many authorization fields were specified.
12	No authorization was found for the authorization object in the user master record.

sy-subrc	Meaning
24	Incorrect authorization fields or an incorrect number of authorization fields was found. This return value is no longer set since Release 6.20. To Release 4.6 it is set only if the profile parameter auth/new_buffering has a value less than 3.

Example

Check as to whether the current user has the authorization required for displaying the airline that he enters on the selection screen. The used authorization object is called S_CARRID and includes the authorization fields CARRID for the name of an airline and ACTVT for the activity. The abbreviation "03" stands for the "Display" activity and is one of the activities that are assigned to the authorization object S_CARRID.

```
PARAMETERS carr TYPE spfli-carrid.

AT SELECTION-SCREEN.
  AUTHORITY-CHECK OBJECT 'S_CARRID'
    ID 'CARRID' FIELD carr
    ID 'ACTVT'  FIELD '03'.

  IF sy-subrc <> 0.
    MESSAGE 'No authorization' TYPE 'E'.
  ENDIF.
```

Part 11
Program Parameters

34 Parameters in the SAP Memory

34.1 Overview

34.1.1 SPA/GPA parameters

The SAP Memory is a user-specific memory area of the application server, which is accessed by all main sessions of a user session simultaneously. ABAP programs have access to SPA/GPA parameters stored in the SAP Memory (also called SET/GET parameters).

Each SPA/GPA parameter is identified by an ID of up to 20 characters. SPA/GPA parameters can be created either explicitly using the statement SET PARAMETER or implicitly in a PAI event. They are then available to any program and any session throughout the whole duration of a user session.

One example of a program that uses SPA/GPA parameters is user maintenance (transaction SU01). In this transaction you can enter user-specific parameters on the **Parameters** tab, which then are set when the user logs on to the SAP system and are evaluated by other programs.

34.1.2 Administrating SPA/GPA parameters

The names of SPA/GPA parameters are administrated in the database table TPARA. In the Object Navigator of the ABAP Workbench, the names of SPA/GPA parameters are created in the database table TPARA in upper case and are linked to packages. The database table TPARA acts as a reservation table for SPA/GPA parameters. If you use SPA/GPA parameters in a program, you should ensure that the name of the parameter is contained in the PARAMID column of the database table TPARA. The SPA/GPA parameters of other applications should not be unintentionally overwritten.

Note

If a name exists in the database table TPARA, this does not automatically mean that the corresponding parameter also exists in the SAP Memory. SPA/GPA parameters are created only during execution of an ABAP program.

34.1.3   SPA/GPA parameters and dynpro fields

When defining input fields, you can link screen fields to SPA/GPA parameters by entering the name of an SPA/GPA parameter from the database table TPARA as an attribute PARAMETER ID. If the corresponding parameter GET PARAMETER is set and no other value is assigned to the input field, the input field is filled with the value of the SPA/GPA parameter when the screen is sent. If the corresponding attribute SET PARAMETER is set, the content of the input field is assigned to the SPA/GPA parameter at the PAI event. If the parameter does not yet exist in the SAP Memory, it is implicitly created at the PAI event. In selection screens, you can create this link by using the MEMORY ID addition of the statements PARAMETERS and SELECT-OPTIONS (see Sections 26.3.3.4 and 26.4.3.4).

Notes

▶ A data transport between a dynpro field and an SPA/GPA parameter in the SAP Memory only takes place if a global data object with the same name as the dynpro field is declared in the corresponding ABAP program.

▶ If the PAI event is triggered using a function of type "E" (compare Section 25.2.2.1), no values are assigned to the SPA/GPA parameters that are linked to the dynpro and no parameters are created in the SAP Memory.

34.1.4   Statements for SPA/GPA Parameters

Statement	Section
SET PARAMETER	34.2
GET PARAMETER	34.3

34.2   Setting Parameters

SET PARAMETER

Sets a parameter value in the SAP memory.

Syntax

```
SET PARAMETER ID pid FIELD dobj.
```

This statement sets the content of the SPA/GPA parameter specified in `pid` to the content of the data object `dobj`. For `pid`, a flat character-type field is expected that can contain a maximum of 20 characters and not exclusively blank characters. `pid` is case-sensitive. For `dobj`, a flat, (character-type, as of Release 6.10) field is expected, whose binary content is transferred in an unconverted format.

If the SPA/GPA parameter specified in `pid` does not yet exist in the SAP memory for the current user, it is created. If the SPA/GPA parameter has already been created for the current user, its value is overwritten.

In a program, you can only create SPA/GPA parameters or assign values to them if a name for them exists in the table TPARA. The extended program check reports an error, if it can be statically determined that a name specified in `pid` is not contained in the database table TPARA.

Note
For a SPA/GPA parameter specified in `pid` to match a name in the database table TPARA, it must be entered uppercase.

Example
If the user selects a flight connection displayed in the basic list, the SPA/GPA parameters CAR and CON are set to the ID of the airline and the connection number, when the event AT LINE-SELECTION takes place. The names of both parameters are defined in the table TPARA for this purpose. In the initial dynpro of the transaction DEMO_TRANSACTION, two input fields are linked with these SPA/GPA parameters and are displayed with the selected values as start values.

```
DATA: carrier     TYPE spfli-carrid,
      connection  TYPE spfli-connid.

START-OF-SELECTION.
  SELECT carrid connid
       FROM spfli
       INTO (carrier, connection).

    WRITE: / carrier HOTSPOT, connection HOTSPOT.
    HIDE:  carrier, connection.
  ENDSELECT.

AT LINE-SELECTION.
  SET PARAMETER ID: 'CAR' FIELD carrier,
                    'CON' FIELD connection.
  CALL TRANSACTION 'DEMO_TRANSACTION'.
```

34.3   Reading Parameters

```
GET PARAMETER
```

Reads a parameter SPA/GPA in the SAP memory.

Syntax

```
GET PARAMETER ID pid FIELD dobj.
```

This statement sets the content of the data object `dobj` to the content of the SPA/GPA parameter specified in `pid`. A flat character-type field that contains no more than 20 characters and does not consist solely of blanks is expected for `pid`; it is also case-sensitive. A flat and (as of Release 6.10) character-type field into which the binary content of the SPA/GPA parameter is transferred unconverted is expected for `dobj`.

If the SPA/GPA parameter specified in `pid` has not yet been created in the SAP Memory for the current user, the data object `dobj` is initialized and `sy-subrc` is set to 4.

In a program, only those SPA/GPA parameters can be read for which there is a name in the table TPARA. The extended program check reports an error, if it can be statically determined that an ID specified in `pid` is not in the database table TPARA.

Return values

sy-subrc	Meaning
0	The SPA/GPA parameter specified in `pid` exists for the current user in the SAP Memory and its value has been transferred to the target field.
4	The SPA/GPA parameter specified in `pid` does not exist for the current user in the SAP Memory.

Notes

▶ An SPA/GPA parameter that is readable with `GET PARAMETER` can previously either have been created in the SAP Memory using the `SET PARAMETER` statement or automatically during the event PAI of a dynpro or selection screen.

▶ For an SPA/GPA parameter specified in `pid` to match a name in the database table TPARA, it must be specified in uppercase.

Example

In this example, the current value of the SPA/GPA parameter RID is read from the SAP Memory to the data object `prog`. In the screens dynpro of the ABAP Workbench, this parameter is linked with the input fields for a program name. When an ABAP Workbench tool, in which an ABAP program is processed, is first called, the parameter is created at the event PAI and assigned the name of the program specified there. If in the same user session, no dynpro is processed that sets the parameter RID and no corresponding `SET PARAMETER` statement has been executed beforehand, RID is not found in the SAP Memory.

```
DATA: para TYPE tpara-paramid VALUE 'RID',
      prog TYPE sy-repid.

GET PARAMETER ID para FIELD prog.

IF sy-subrc <> 0.
  MESSAGE 'Parameter not found' TYPE 'I'.
ENDIF.
```

35 Language Environment

35.1 Overview

ABAP programs can be configured so that they can be executed in different language environments without adapting the source text. The language environment of a program determines the language of the used text pool, which text environment is used, and how country-specific output is formatted in lists.

35.1.1 Text Pools

You can store headings, labels of input fields on selection screens and other texts as text elements in test pools for different languages. From which text pool an ABAP program takes its texts depends on the logon language or (as of Release 6.20) a secondary language, or it can be set using the statement SET LANGUAGE.

35.1.2 Text Environment

The text environment is part of the runtime environment of an ABAP program. It affects all operations that depend on the character set, which include:

▶ Statements that work with character-type data objects
▶ Data transfer between the application server and the presentation server
▶ Data transfer between external storage systems and the application server
▶ Data transfer with RFC
▶ Data output on the screen in the SAP GUI
▶ Printing

The text environment is made up of a language, a locale, and a code page. The code page of the text environment must be a system code page. All programs of an internal session work in a common text environment, which can be changed during program execution.

35.1.2.1 Text environment in Unicode systems.

Locale

The locale attributes that belong to a country and a language are defined in Unicode systems in an ICU library (International Components for Unicode) that exists on the application server and that is independent of its operating system.

Code page

In Unicode systems, UTF-16 is the only system code page and therefore the code page of every text environment. There is a special feature whereby the non-Unicode code page is used for conversions that would be assigned to the current text environment in a non-Unicode system. This only applies for specific statements, such as reading and writing legacy files (see Sections 32.2.2.3 and 32.2.2.4).

35.1.2.2 Text environment in non-Unicode systems

Locale

The locale attributes of a country or language in a non-Unicode system depend on the operating system of the application server. Every operating system has predefined locales for every language.

Code page

The code page of the text environment is always a non-Unicode code page. In non-Unicode single-code-page systems, there is only one system code page. Only text environments with this code page can be set. In MDMP systems, there are multiple system code pages. All text environments that contain one of these code pages can be set. The code page of the current text environment is the active system code page of an internal session.

Database table TCP0C

The possible text environments of non-Unicode systems are predefined in the database table TCP0C. This system table is supplied by SAP and its content normally should not be changed. In Unicode systems, the entries in TCP0C are only used for setting the code page in the special cases mentioned above.

Table 35.1 shows the columns of the table TCP0C. The text environment depends on four key fields and is defined in the columns LOCALE (Locale) and CHARCO (code page).

Name	Key	Meaning
PLATFORM	X	Operating system of the application server
LANGU	X	Language key
COUNTRY	X	Country key
MODIFIER	X	Locale key (is not used)
LOCALE		Operating system locale
CHARCO		SAP code page number
CHARCOMNLS		Obsolete

Table 35.1 Columns of the System Table TCPOC

The SAP code page number specified in the column CHARCO identifies a non-Unicode code page. Before Release 6.10, the assignment of SAP code page numbers to code pages could be defined using the transaction SPAD and as of Release 6.10 can be defined using the transaction SCP.

35.1.2.3   Setting the text environment

When an internal session is opened, the text environment is set implicitly according to the logon language of the current user. During the execution of an ABAP program, the text environment of the current internal session can be set using the statement SET LOCALE.

The system field sy-langu always contains the single-character abbreviation for the language of the current text environment of an internal session. The possible abbreviations are stored as language keys in the column SPRAS of the database table T002.

35.1.3   Country Identification for List Processing

The country identification specifies the format in which the decimal separators and date specifications are displayed in lists. A list of possible country identifications are defined in the database table T005X. When opening an internal session, the format for the decimal separators and date specifications is read from the default settings in the **Fixed values** of the current user's master record. The format can be changed using the statement SET COUNTRY.

35.1.4 Statements for the Language Environment

Statement	Section
SET LANGUAGE	35.2
SET LOCALE	35.3
GET LOCALE	35.4
SET COUNTRY	35.5

35.2 Setting the Text Pool of a Language

`SET LANGUAGE`

Sets the language for text elements.

Syntax

`SET LANGUAGE lang.`

This statement loads the list headings and text symbols of the text pool of the language specified in `lang`. `lang` must be a character-type (and prior to Release 6.10, a flat) data object that contains a language key of length 1. The possible language keys are contained in the column SPRAS of the database table T002. The loaded text elements are only valid for the current program and not for the programs called within it. If `lang` contains a space, the behavior is undefined.

If there is no text pool for the specified language, the system loads the text pool in the secondary language which, as of Release 6.20, is specified in the profile parameter `zcsa/second_language`. If no secondary language is set, no new text pool is loaded and `sy-subrc` is set to 4. The program then continues to use the text elements from the previous text pool.

If list headings and text symbols are missing in a text pool loaded with SET LANGUAGE, but existed in the previously loaded text pool, these are initialized as of Release 6.20. Prior to Release 6.20, they retained their previous value.

Return values

sy-subrc	Meaning
0	The text pool of the specified language or secondary language (as of Release 6.20) has been loaded.
4	The text pool of neither the specified language nor the secondary language (as of Release 6.20) could be loaded.

Notes

When calling a program, the text pool of the logon language is loaded by default. If this text pool does not exist, as of Release 6.20, the text pool is loaded in the secondary language. If this text pool also does not exist, all text elements remain initialized.

Example

Output of the text symbol text-010 in different languages. Prior to Release 6.20, output for a language only occurs if the text pool exists in that language. As of Release 6.20, output occurs for every language, if the text pool exists in the secondary language.

```
DATA langu LIKE sy-langu.

SELECT spras FROM t002
       INTO  langu.
  SET LANGUAGE langu.
  IF sy-subrc = 0.
    WRITE: / langu, text-010.
  ENDIF.
ENDSELECT.
```

35.3   Setting the Text Environment

SET LOCALE

Sets the text environment.

Syntax

SET LOCALE LANGUAGE lang [**COUNTRY** cntry] [**MODIFIER** mod].

This statement defines the text environment for all programs of the current internal session for the languages specified in lang and sets sy-langu to the value of lang. For lang, a character-type (and before Release 6.10 flat) data object must be specified. This must contain a language key with a maximum length of one character, whose value must be contained in the column SPRAS of the database table T002. If the data object lang only contains blanks, the logon language of the current user is used and the additions COUNTRY and MODIFIER are ignored.

The text environment is country-specific. By default, the country key is used that is corresponding to the language specified in lang in the database table TCP0D. The country key can also be explicitly specified using the addition COUNTRY. For cntry, a character-type (before Release 6.10 flat) data object has to be specified that contains a country key with a maximum of three characters. The addition MODIFIER is currently not required and should be omitted. If it is specified, it must be as a character-type (and before Release 6.10 flat) data object with a maximum of eight characters.

The statement SET LOCALE has different effects depending on whether the system is a Unicode system or a non-Unicode system.

Setting the text environment in Unicode systems

In a Unicode system, a language key must be entered in lang and a country key can be entered in cntry, for which local properties are defined in the ICU library of the application server (see Section 35.3.2.1). The keys of possible languages are contained in the SPRAS column of the database table T002. The locale of the text environment is set accordingly and influences how internal tables and extracts are sorted using the statement SORT with the addition AS TEXT (see Sections 22.4.3 and 23.4).

The code page of a Unicode system is always UTF-16 and is not influenced by the statement SET LOCALE. After SET LOCALE has been executed, however, the non-Unicode code page that would be set by the statement in a non-Unicode system (see below), is used for converting specific statements such as reading and writing legacy files (see Sections 32.2.2.3 and 32.2.2.4).

Setting the text environment in non-Unicode systems

In a non-Unicode system, the language key specified in lang must, together with the operating system of the application server (system field sy-opsys) and the country key taken implicitly from the database table TCP0D or set explicitly, produce a valid key for the database table TCP0C. This key is used to extract the name of the operating system specific Locale from the column LOCALE and the number of the non-Unicode code page from the column CHARCO (see Table 35.1). If no entry exists for the specified key in the table TCP0C, a treatable exception occurs.

The code page specified by the key in TCP0C must be released as a system code page for the current SAP system. Otherwise a treatable exception will occur. This results in different consequences for single code page systems and MDMP systems:

▶ In a single-code-page system, only one code page is released as a system code page. With SET LOCALE, only the language and the locale can be changed and not the code page of the text environment.

▶ In an MDMP system, multiple code pages are released as system code pages. SET LOCALE can be used to change the language, the locale, and the code page of the text environment. If the code page found in TCP0C is released, the SET LOCALE statement sets this code page as the active system code page.

A non-Unicode code page can be released as a system code page by entering the SAP code page number in the database table TCPDB, which is maintained using the executable program RSCPINST. If the database table TCPDB is empty, it is handled as if it contains a single entry with the number 1100.

Notes

▶ The text environment of an internal session should only be changed for the following purposes:

  ▷ Processing character-type data objects that are in a different language than the logon language of the current user. The language is important for the statements SORT ... AS TEXT, TRANSLATE ... TO UPPER CASE and for comparisons that ignore upper/lower case.

  ▷ In a non-Unicode system, characters from an East-Asian language (Chinese, Japanese, Korean) are processed. If the text environment is not set correctly, double-byte characters are not correctly recognized.

  ▷ In Unicode systems, and legacy files are read and written (see Sections 32.2.2.3 and 32.2.2.4).

▶ When setting the text environment, the addition COUNTRY should not be used. Instead the implicitly set country key should be used, if possible.

▶ After processing in a changed text environment, the text environment should be reset to the previous text environment.

▶ Instead of the SET LOCALE statement, the four function modules whose names begin with SCP_MIXED_LANGUAGES_ can be used to set or change the current text environment, and to reset it to the original text environment.

▶ When changing the system code page in MDMP systems, you need to ensure that a compatible code page is also installed on the presentation server. Otherwise, it may not be possible to display all the characters on the screen.

▶ The addition MODIFIER is intended for setting different locales for a language within a country, for example, for sorting according to different sort criteria. The SAP standard system does not yet support such locales.

Treatable Exceptions

If in a Unicode system an invalid language is specified, an exception defined by the class CX_SY_LOCALIZATION_ERROR is raised which is connected to the not catch able runtime error TEXTENV_UNICODE_LANGU_INVALID.

If in a non-Unicode system no entry is found in the database table TCP0C for the specified key, or if the code page deposited there is not released as a system-code page, or if the text environment cannot be set for different reasons, the exception defined by the class CX_SY_LOCALIZATION_ERROR is triggered. The associated catchable runtime errors, TEXTENV_KEY_INVALID, TEXTENV_CODEPAGE_NOT_ALLOWED and, TEXTENV_INVALID are grouped together in the exception group LOCALIZATION_ERRORS (see Table D.10).

Example

Effect of the locale of the text environment on sortings: In Unicode and non-Unicode systems, "ch" is interpreted as a single letter in a Spanish (or, for example Czech) text environment, and is sorted in a different way than in an English text environment. In a Spanish text environment in a Unicode system, a double "ll" is sorted as two separate letters "l". In non-Unicode systems, however, Spanish locales can be used, (for example Spanish_Spain.1252 on Windows NT), which interpret "ll" as a single character and sort it differently. The last SET LOCALE statement can be used to reset the text environment to the logon language.

```
DATA text_tab TYPE HASHED TABLE OF string
             WITH UNIQUE KEY table_line.

INSERT: 'polo'    INTO TABLE text_tab,
        'pollo'   INTO TABLE text_tab,
```

```
              'chunky'  INTO TABLE text_tab,
              'crunchy' INTO TABLE text_tab.
SET LOCALE LANGUAGE 'E'.
SORT text_tab AS TEXT.
PERFORM write_text_tab.

SET LOCALE LANGUAGE 'S'.
SORT text_tab AS TEXT.
PERFORM write_text_tab.

SET LOCALE LANGUAGE ' '.

FORM write_text_tab.
  FIELD-SYMBOLS <line> TYPE string.
  LOOP AT text_tab ASSIGNING <line>.
    WRITE / <line>.
  ENDLOOP.
  SKIP.
ENDFORM.
```

Example

Effect of the code page of the text environment on the statement TRANS-LATE ... TO UPPER CASE: In Unicode systems, the content of text that is coded according to UTF-16 ("00E400F600FC") is converted in the same way in all text environments ("00C400D600DC"). In non-Unicode single code page systems the program triggers an exception, because different code pages belong to the language keys "E" and "R" (SAP code page numbers 1,100 and 1,500). In MDMP systems in which the code pages 1,100 and 1,500 are released, the binary content of text ("E4F6FC" in code page 1,100) is converted differently. In a text environment with the code page 1,100, the characters are interpreted as umlauts. In a text environment with the code page 1,500, these are Cyrillic characters. When converting to upper case, the system searches in the code page for the appropriate character according to the text environment, and the binary content is converted accordingly. The result for code page 1,100 is "C4D6DC", and for code page 1,500 is "C4A6AC".

```
DATA text(3) TYPE c.

FIELD-SYMBOLS <hex> TYPE x.

ASSIGN text TO <hex> CASTING.
text = 'äöü'.
WRITE / <hex>.
```

```
SET LOCALE LANGUAGE 'E'.
TRANSLATE text TO UPPER CASE.
WRITE / <hex>.

text = 'äöü'.
SET LOCALE LANGUAGE 'R'.
TRANSLATE text TO UPPER CASE.
WRITE / <hex>.

SET LOCALE LANGUAGE ' '.
```

35.4 Determining the Text Environment

GET LOCALE

Determines the current text environment.

Syntax

GET LOCALE LANGUAGE lang **COUNTRY** cntry **MODIFIER** mod.

The parameters of the current text environment, consisting of language key, country key and identifier for a specific locale are assigned to the variables lang, cntry and mod. The data objects lang, cntry and mod must have character-like (before Release 6.10 flat) data types.

Notes

▶ The ascertained parameters can be used to restore the current text environment, after a change with the SET LOCALE statement.

▶ The statement GET LOCALE currently initializes the variable mod currently in all text environments.

Example

Determining the current text environment and restoring it after a possible change in a called procedure.

```
DATA: lang  TYPE tcp0c-langu,
      cntry TYPE tcp0c-country,
      mod   TYPE tcp0c-modifier.

GET LOCALE LANGUAGE lang COUNTRY cntry MODIFIER mod.

CALL ...

SET LOCALE LANGUAGE lang COUNTRY cntry.
```

35.5 Setting Country Identification

```
SET COUNTRY
```

Determining the display of decimal separators and date output in lists.

Syntax

```
SET COUNTRY cntry.
```

This statement specifies the predefined output formats for the decimal format (selection of decimal separators and thousand separators) and the date format in all programs of the current internal session for all subsequent outputs in lists. A character-type (prior to Release 6.10 flat) data object is has to be specified for `cntry`.

If the value specified in `cntry` exists as a country key in the column COUNTRY of the database table T005X, the output of numbers and dates is formatted according to the entries in columns XDEZP and DATFM. Tables 35.2 and 35.3 list the possible values in these columns and their meanings, whereat MM stands for the month, DD for the day, and YYYY for the year, in Table 35.3.

Value	Decimal separator	Thousand separator
"X"	"."	","
" "	","	"."
"Y"	","	" "

Table 35.2 Possible Values of the Column XDEZP of the Database Table T005X

Value	Date format
"1"	DD.MM.YYYY
"2"	MM/DD/YYYY
"3"	MM-DD-YYYY
"4"	YYYY.MM.DD
"5"	YYYY/MM/DD
"6"	YYYY-MM-DD

Table 35.3 Possible Values of the Column DATFM of the Database Table T005X

If cntry contains a blank at the first position, the decimal and date formats of the predefined **Fixed values** are taken from the user master record of the current user. If the content of cntry is not found in the database table T005X, and cntry does not contain a blank at the first position, sy-subrc is set to 4 and the decimal separator is displayed as a dot, the thousand separator as a comma and the date is displayed using the format MM/DD/YYYY.

Return values

sy-subrc	Meaning
0	The specified country key was found in the database table T005X or a blank was specified.
4	The specified country key could not be found in the database table T005X.

Note

The country names that belong to the country identification code in Table T005X can be found in Table T005T.

Example

Display of all formats for decimal numbers and date specifications currently contained in the table T005X.

```
DATA: dat TYPE sy-datum VALUE '20020127',
      num TYPE p DECIMALS 2 VALUE '1234567.89',
      t005x_wa TYPE t005x,
      t005x_tab TYPE SORTED TABLE OF t005x
                WITH NON-UNIQUE KEY xdezp datfm.

SELECT *
      FROM t005x
      INTO TABLE t005x_tab.

DELETE ADJACENT DUPLICATES FROM t005x_tab.

LOOP AT t005x_tab INTO t005x_wa.
  SET COUNTRY t005x_wa-land.
  WRITE: / num, dat.
ENDLOOP.
```

36 Date and Time Information

36.1 Overview

This section describes the capabilities for accessing and editing the current values of time and date in ABAP programs.

36.1.1 System Fields for Date and Time

Table 36.1 lists the system fields for date and time.

System field	Content
sy-datlo	Date in the current user's time zone.
sy-datum	Local date of the SAP system.
sy-dayst	Indicator for summer time. During summer time, "X," otherwise " ".
sy-fdayw	Factory calendar weekday. "1" for Monday, ..., "5" for Friday.
sy-timlo	Time in the current user's time zone.
sy-tzone	Time difference from the UTC reference time in seconds, ignoring summer time.
sy-uzeit	Local time of the SAP system.
sy-zonlo	User's time zone.

Table 36.1 System Fields for Date and Time

The values of all system fields in Table 36.1 are implicitly set when the program is started, every time a screen layout of a dynpro is sent, and when the internal mode is changed. The GET TIME command explicitly updates the system fields, except for sy-dayst, sy-fdayw and sy-tzone.

With the exception of sy-datlo and sy-timlo, all system fields refer to the local date and time of the current SAP system. The ABAP runtime environment clock is synchronized with the database server clock at regular intervals in order to calculate the local time of the SAP system. During the synchronization, the ABAP runtime environment clock is set to the database server clock. Because this happens on all application servers in an SAP system, the ABAP runtime environment clock on an application server is synchronous with the clocks on all other application servers and with the database system clock, and therefore shows the local time of the entire SAP system. The time zone on which the local time of an SAP system is based refers to is the only entry in the database table TTZCU.

The content of `sy-zonlo` is taken from the user master record of the current user. The values of `sy-datlo` and `sy-timlo` are calculated from `sy-datum` and `sy-uzeit` and from the time zone of the SAP system for the time zone in `sy-zonlo`. If the user master record does not contain a time zone, or if it contains an invalid or an inactive time zone, `sy-datlo` and `sy-timlo` are set to the values of `sy-datum` and `sy-uzeit`. All valid time zones are defined in the table TTZZ.

36.1.2 Time Stamps

The system fields from Section 36.1.1 do not completely satisfy many requirements for determining specific points in time. They represent local times and the values are only measured in seconds. For more exact date and time determination, time stamps are available.

36.1.2.1 Internal Format of Time Stamps

A time stamp represents date and time in the form YYYYMMDDH-HMMSS. YYYY is the year, MM the month, DD the day, HH the hour, MM the minutes and SS the seconds. There is a short form and a long form. In the long form, the form specified above additionally contains seven decimal places for fractions of seconds, which allow an accuracy of up to 100 ns. The achievable maximum time resolution may be less precise, depending on the operating system of the application server.

A valid time stamp must contain values whose date and time specifications before the decimal separator correspond to valid values for the data types d and t (see Table 5.2). Time stamps in this form are always considered as UTC time stamps when processed with the corresponding ABAP statements. Use the statement GET TIME STAMP to create a time stamp that represents the current UTC reference time.

36.1.2.2 Data Types for Time Stamps

For the short and long form of time stamps, the data types TIMESTAMP and TIMESTAMPL are available in the ABAP Dictionary. The respective ABAP types are p of length 8 without decimal paces (short form) and p of length 11 with seven decimal places (long form). Time stamps are stored in the format stated above in data objects of these types, where the decimal places before the decimal separator represent the date and the time and the decimal places in the long form represents the fractions of seconds.

Note

In programs for which the program attribute **Fixed point arithmetic** is not set, take notice of the rules applying for the data type p.

36.1.2.3   Using Time Stamps

Time stamps can be used to log points in time and to compare them. They are not suited for direct calculations or for date and time output.

For calculations and display, you can convert time stamps into date and time fields of local time zones using the CONVERT TIME STAMP statement, or vice versa using the CONVERT DATE statement. For output to lists, use the addition TIME ZONE of the WRITE statement. As of Release 6.20, the system class CL_ABAP_TSTMP provides methods for adding, subtracting, converting and comparing time stamps (see Section B 1.6).

Notes

▶ When assigning time stamps in the long form to time stamps in the short form, unwanted rounding effects are possible.

▶ Direct comparisons of time stamps in the long form with the short form are only possible, if the program attribute **Fixed point arithmetic** is set. Otherwise, you must use the system class CL_ABAP_TSTMP for comparisons as well.

36.1.2.4   Rules for Time Stamps

The conversion of the UTC reference time of a time stamp into the local time zone of an SAP system or a user is based on the set of rules stored in database tables. The names of all respective database tables start with TTZ. The following database tables whose content you can maintain using the transaction STZBD are relevant for time stamps:

▶ The database table TTZZ contains in column TZONE a list of possible time zones. The entries in the columns ZONERULE and DSTRULE refer to the rules for the time difference of the time zone from the UTC reference time in table TTZR and to the rules for summer time in the tables TTZD, TTZDF and TTZDV.

▶ The database table TTZR contains in column ZONERULE a list of possible rules for the time difference between time zones and the UTC reference time. The columns UTCDIFF and UTCSIGN contain the time differences to UTC and their algebraic signs without consideration of summer time.

- The database table TTZD contains in column DSTRULE a list of all possible summer time rules. Column DSTDIFF contains the time difference between summer and winter time.

- The database table TTZDF contains in column DSTRULE a list of fixed summer time rules. Column YEARACT contains year dates for every rule for which the rule applies. The columns DATEFROM, TIMEFROM, DATETO and TIMETO contain date and time for beginning and end of the summer time.

- The database table TTZDV contains in column DSTRULE a list of variable summer time rules. Column YEARFROM contains year numbers for every rule, saying from which year on the rule applies. The columns MONTHFROM, WEEKDFROM, WEEKDCFROM, TIMEFROM, MONTHTO, WEEKDTO, WEEKDCTO and TIMETO contain month, week, day and time for beginning and end of the summer time.

For a correct set of rules, all rules listed in TTZZ for the time difference between time zones and the UTC reference time in TTZR and all rules listed for the summer time in TTZD must be contained. If the time difference between summer and winter time in TTZD is not equal to 0, the respective summer time rule must be contained in at least one of the tables TTZDF or TTZDV. While TTZDF contains fixed date specifications of the conversion, the date in TTZDV is variable, because a day in a particular week of a month is specified. The system always checks TTZDF first for the summer time rule and then TTZDV.

36.1.2.5 Notes for Summer Time

If in a time zone a summer time rule with a summer time difference not equal to 0 is defined, take notice of the following:

- If during summer time a new year starts (in the Southern Hemisphere), then the year specified in the database tables TTZDF or TTZDV (see Section 36.1.2) identifies the beginning of summer time, while the end lies in the following year.

- The time specified for the beginning of summer time in the database tables TTZDF and TTZDV identifies the time at which, in the ending winter time, the clock is put forward by the difference between winter and summer time. The first second of summer time is the time you get when you add the summer time difference to the specified point in time.

At the beginning of summer time, a time interval of the length of the summer time difference is created. You can formulate a date and time specification for that interval, but it does not exist as a local time and cannot be assigned to a UTC reference time. Such a local time specification is treated in the CONVERT DATE statement as an invalid time specification (see Section 36.5).

▶ The time specified in the data base tables TTZDF or TTZDV for the end of summer time identifies the time at which, in the ending summer time, the clock is put backward by the difference between summer and winter times. The first second of the winter time is the time you get when you subtract the summer time difference from the specified point in time.

At the end of summer time, a time interval of a length of the summer time difference is created, and this is run through twice as a local time (the double hour). If you formulate a date and time specification for this interval, the statement CONVERT DATE treats it as a time specification for summer time, by default.

36.1.3 Statements for Date and Time

Statement	Section
GET TIME	36.2
GET TIME STAMP	36.3
CONVERT TIME STAMP	36.4
CONVERT DATE	36.5

36.2 Supplying System Fields for Date and Time

GET TIME

Sets the system fields for date and time.

Syntax

GET TIME [FIELD tim].

Without the addition FIELD, the system fields sy-datlo, sy-datum, sy-timlo, sy-uzeit, and sy-zonlo from Table 36.1 are set to the current value. The content of the system fields sy-dayst, sy-fdayw and sy-tzone is not updated.

Using the addition `FIELD`, the current time is transmitted in the format HHMMSS into the variable `tim` and none of the system fields are updated. The return value of the statement is of the data type t. For `tim`, a (prior to Release 6.10 flat) data object must be specified, into which the return value can be converted according to Table A.8.

Note
Except for `GET TIME`, the system fields are updated after starting a program, after sending a screen, and after changing the internal mode (see Section 36.1.1).

36.3   Creating Current Time Stamp

```
GET TIME STAMP
```

Creates the UTC time stamp.

Syntax

```
GET TIME STAMP FIELD time_stamp.
```

This statement assigns a time stamp for the current UTC reference time of the SAP system to the variable `time_stamp`. The data object `time_stamp` either must have the data type TIMESTAMP or TIMESTAMPL from the ABAP Dictionary corresponding to ABAP type p of length 8 or p of length 11 with seven decimal places. Depending on the data type of `time_stamp`, the time stamp is created either in short or long form (see Section 36.1.2).

Note
The accuracy of the decimal places of the long form depends on the hardware (processor) of the application server. The maximum resolution of 100 ns is not always reached. On some platforms, only a resolution of milliseconds can be reached.

Example
Determining the current time stamp in the long form and using it to log the point in time, at which a row is inserted into a database table.

```
DATA: BEGIN OF wa,
        ...
      time_stamp TYPE timestampl,
        ...
      END OF wa.
```

```
...
GET TIME STAMP FIELD wa-time_stamp.
INSERT dbtab FROM wa.
```

36.4 Converting Time Stamp Into Local Time

CONVERT TIME STAMP

Converts a time stamp into a local date and a local time.

Syntax

```
CONVERT TIME STAMP time_stamp TIME ZONE tz
        INTO [DATE dat] [TIME tim]
        [DAYLIGHT SAVING TIME dst].
```

This statement interprets a time stamp specified in `time_stamp` as a UTC reference time, converts it to the local date and local time of the time zone specified in `tz` and assigns the result to the `dat`, `tim` and `dst` variables. At least one of the two additions `DATE` or `TIME` must be specified.

The `time_stamp` data object either must have the data type TIMESTAMP, or TIMESTAMPL from the ABAP Dictionary and the corresponding ABAP type `p` of length 8 or `p` of length 11 with seven decimal places containing one valid time stamp in short or long form (see Section 36.1.2). If `time_stamp` does not contain a valid time stamp, the content of `dat` and `tim` is not changed, and sy-subrc is set to 12.

For `tz`, a data object of the type TIMEZONE from the ABAP Dictionary must be specified, which contains a time zone from the TZONE column of the TTZZ database table in uppercase. If `tz` is initial, no local time is calculated. Instead, the UTC reference time is assigned to `dat` and `tim` and `sy-subrc` is set to 4. If the specified time zone is not found in the database table TTZZ, the content of `dat` and `tim` remains unchanged and `sy-subrc` is set to 8. If the set of rules for the specified time zone are not complete (see Section 36.1.2.4), this results in an untreatable exception.

The return values for `dat` and `tim` are of data type `d` or `t`. For `dat` and `tim`, suitable data objects have to be specified, into which the return values can be converted according to Tables A.2 and A.8. If the time stamp contained in `time_stamp` is available in long form, then the fractions of seconds in the decimal places are ignored.

A dst variable of type c of length 1 must be specified after the optional DAYLIGHT SAVING TIME addition. If the time stamp contained in time_stamp for the time zone specified in tz lies in the summer time, then dst is set to "X." Otherwise it is set to " ".

Return values

sy-subrc	Meaning
0	Time stamp was converted into the local time of the specified time zone and assigned to the target fields.
4	Time stamp was assigned to the target fields without conversion into the local time.
8	Time stamp could not be converted since the specified time zone is not available in database table TTZZ.
12	Time stamp could not be converted since time_stamp contains an invalid value.

Notes

▶ A current UTC time stamp can be created using the GET TIME STAMP statement. The current user-related local time zones can be found in the system field sy-zonlo (see Table 36.1).

▶ Since Release 6.20, it is now possible to use the return value for the summer time in dst to differentiate between duplicate local time specifications. These might occur if UTC time stamps are converted into local time during the double hour in the changeover between summer and winter time (see Section 36.1.3).

Example

For the "BRAZIL" time zone available in database table TTZZ, a shift of -3 hours compared to the UTC reference time is entered in the database table TTZR. The end of the summer time is defined in the database table TTZDV as the second Sunday in March at 02:00, which in the year 2003 corresponds to March 9th. With these settings in the set of rules, the two following conversions both result in the same local time of "01:30:00" where the first conversion shows that the time is still in the summer time (since Release 6.20).

```
DATA: time_stamp TYPE timestamp,
      dat        TYPE d,
      tim        TYPE t,
      tz         TYPE ttzz-tzone,
      dst(1)     TYPE c.
```

```
tz = 'BRAZIL'.

time_stamp = 20030309033000.
CONVERT TIME STAMP time_stamp TIME ZONE tz
       INTO DATE dat TIME tim DAYLIGHT SAVING TIME dst.
WRITE: /(10) dat, (8) tim, dst.

time_stamp = 20030309043000.
CONVERT TIME STAMP time_stamp TIME ZONE tz
       INTO DATE dat TIME tim DAYLIGHT SAVING TIME dst.
WRITE: /(10) dat, (8) tim, dst.
```

36.5 Converting Local Time Into a Time Stamp

CONVERT DATE

Converts a local date and a local time into a time stamp.

Syntax

```
CONVERT DATE dat [TIME tim [DAYLIGHT SAVING TIME dst]]
       INTO TIME STAMP time_stamp TIME ZONE tz.
```

This statement interprets a date specified in dat, a time specified in tim, and a daylight saving time selection specified in dst as a local date and time specification for the time zone specified in tz, converts it to the UTC reference time, and assigns the result to the time_stamp variable as a time stamp.

For dat and tim data objects of the data type d or t are expected. Data objects of other types are converted to d or t, according to the rules in Appendix A. If the TIME addition is not specified, the system implicitly uses the initial time "000000" for tim. If dat or tim contain invalid values (see Table 5.2), time_stamp is not changed and sy-subrc is set to 12.

For tz, a data object with type TIMEZONE from the ABAP Dictionary must be specified that contains a time zone from the column TZONE of the database table TTZZ in uppercase. If tz is initial, the time specified in dat and tim is adopted as the UTC reference time and sy-subrc is set to 4. If the specified time zone is not found in the database table TTZZ, time_stamp remains unchanged and sy-subrc is set to 8. If the set of rules for the specified time zone is not complete (see Section 36.1.2.4), an untreatable exception is raised.

The data object `time_stamp` must either have the data type TIMESTAMP or TIMESTAMPL from the ABAP Dictionary and accordingly be of ABAP type `p` with length 8 or `p` with length 11 and have seven decimal places (see Section 36.1.2). If `time_stamp` is of data type TIMESTAMPL for the long form, the second fractions in the decimal places are initialized during assignment.

The DAYLIGHT SAVING TIME addition can be specified after TIME. For `dst` you must specify a data object of the type `c` with the length 1 that must have the value "X" or " ". If `dst` has the value "X", the value of `tim` is interpreted as the time specification in daylight saving time. If `dst` has the value " ", the value of `tim` is interpreted as the time specification in winter time. If `dst` has a different value or the specified value does not suit the value in `tim` and `dat`, `time_stamp` remains unchanged and `sy-subrc` is set to 12. If the DAYLIGHT SAVING TIME addition is not specified, the value of `dst` is implicitly set to "X" in daylight saving time and " " in winter time for specifications in `tim` and `dat`. In the extra hour that arises when switching from daylight saving time to wintertime, it is set to "X," and the specification in `tim` and `dat` is interpreted as the time specification in daylight saving time (see Section 36.1.3).

Return values

sy-subrc	Meaning
0	Local time of specified time zone was converted to time stamp and assigned to the target field.
4	Time specification was converted to time stamp without time shift and assigned to the target field.
8	Time specification could not be converted, because the specified time zone is not in the database table TTZZ.
12	Time specification could not be converted, because `dat`, `tim`, or `dst` contain invalid or inconsistent values.

Notes

▶ Current user-specific local time specifications and the corresponding local time zone are contained in the system fields `sy-datlo`, `sy-timlo`, and `sy-zonlo` (see Table 36.1).

▶ As of Release 6.20, specifying daylight saving and winter time after DAYLIGHT SAVING TIME enables you to create different UTC time stamps from matching local time specification within the extra hour when switching from daylight saving to winter time.

Example

For the time zone "BRAZIL", the settings described in the example for Section 36.4 apply to the set of rules for time stamps. By specifying the daylight saving and winter time (as of Release 6.20) two different UTC time stamps — "20030309033000" and "20030309043000" — are created from one local time specification. Without the addition DAYLIGHT SAVING TIME, the UTC time stamp "20030309033000" is created.

```
DATA: time_stamp TYPE timestamp,
      dat TYPE d,
      tim TYPE t,
      tz   TYPE ttzz-tzone.

tz = 'BRAZIL'.

dat = '20030309'.
tim = '013000'.

CONVERT DATE dat TIME tim DAYLIGHT SAVING TIME 'X'
        INTO TIME STAMP time_stamp TIME ZONE tz.
WRITE: / time_stamp.

CONVERT DATE dat TIME tim DAYLIGHT SAVING TIME ' '
        INTO TIME STAMP time_stamp TIME ZONE tz.
WRITE: / time_stamp.
```

Part 12
Program Processing

37 Testing and Checking Programs

37.1 Overview

When creating a program, the statements of this section can be used for testing purposes or can be incorporated for checking completed programs. However, productive programs can only contain statements that do not hinder the program flow. These are ASSERT and BREAK-POINT with the ID addition, as well as SET EXTENDED CHECK.

The following statements are dealt with in this section:

Statement	Section
ASSERT	37.2.1
BREAK-POINT	37.2.2
GET RUN TIME	37.3.1
SET RUN TIME CLOCK RESOLUTION	37.3.2
SET RUN TIME ANALYZER	37.4
SET EXTENDED CHECK	37.5

37.2 Checkpoints

Checkpoints define positions in a program at which the state of the program can be tested during program execution. The effects of checkpoints are either conditional or unconditional. Conditional checkpoints are implemented by assertions (as of Release 6.20, Support Package 29), unconditional checkpoints by break points. You can activate and deactivate assertions as well as break points from outside the program by assigning them to a checkpoint group (also as of Release 6.20, Support Package 29).

37.2.1 Defining Assertion

ASSERT

Defines an assertion (as of Release 6.20, Support Package 29).

Syntax

```
ASSERT [ [ID group [SUBKEY sub]]
         [FIELDS dobj1 dobj2 ...]
         CONDITION ] log_exp.
```

This statement defines a conditioned checkpoint (assertion). For `log_exp`, you can specify any logical expression (see Chapter 13). When the program reaches an active assertion, the logical expression is evaluated and the program execution continues with the next statement after ASSERT, but only if the result of `log_exp` is true. If an assertion is inactive, the logical condition `log_exp` is not evaluated, and the program execution continues with the next statement after ASSERT.

The logical expression is started with the addition CONDITION. It must be specified before `log_exp`, if one of the other additions is specified. Otherwise, it can be omitted.

37.2.1.1 Activating the assertion

Without the addition ID, the assertion is always active. When using the addition ID, the activation and the behavior of the statement are controlled from outside the program by means of a checkpoint group.

The addition ID assigns the assertion to a checkpoint group `group`. You must specify the name of the checkpoint group directly, and the group must exist in the repository. To administer a checkpoint group, use the transaction SAAB. It contains the activation settings of the checkpoints assigned to it, whereas assertions and breakpoints are dealt with separately.

The activation settings of a checkpoint group activate or deactivate the assigned assertions and breakpoints within determinable validity areas. Possible validity areas are user, application server, SAP system, etc.

37.2.1.2 Program behavior for an assertion

If the result of `log_exp` is false, an untreatable exception is triggered and the program terminates with the runtime error ASSERTION_FAILED, for an always active assertion without the addition ID.

For an assertion activated from the outside, the activation mode specified in the checkpoint group determines how the program execution is continued. The possible settings are:

▶ Creating an entry in a special log and continuing the program execution with the statement after ASSERT. By default, an existing entry of the same ASSERT statement is overwritten. You use the transaction SAAB to evaluate the log.

- Switching to the ABAP Debugger. This setting takes effect only during dialog processing. For background processing and update, one of the other two settings must be specified as an alternative.

- Triggering an untreatable exception and terminating the program with the runtime error ASSERTION_FAILED.

The addition SUBKEY only takes effect, if the statement ASSERT writes entries into a log. When specifying SUBKEY, the content of sub is stored in the log as a subkey. Existing log entries of the same ASSERT statement are only overwritten, if the subkey has the same content. For sub, you must specify a character-type data object, of which the first 200 characters are evaluated. If you do not specify SUBKEY, the subkey is initial.

After the addition FIELDS, you can specify a list dobj1, dobj2, ... of any (before Release 6.40 flat) data objects other than reference variables. If the statement ASSERT writes entries into a log, the content of the data objects dobj1, dobj2, ... is also included into the log. If an untreatable exception is triggered, the content of the first eight specified data objects is displayed in the corresponding short dump. If you switch to the ABAP debugger, the FIELDS addition has no effect.

Notes

- Assertions are used to verify certain assumptions on the state of a program at a certain position and to guarantee that they are kept. Compared to the implementation using an IF statement (for example, an exit message), the statement ASSERT is shorter, its meaning is clear, and it can be activated from outside.

- The log into which assertions use to write is not the system log, to which breakpoints write during background processing.

- The size of each of the data objects stored in the log with the FIELDS addition is limited by the profile parameter abap/aab_log_field_size_limit. The value of the profile parameter specifies the size in bytes. The preset value is 1,024. A value of 0 means no restriction. When a log entry is created, the content of each data object is truncated at this length, whereas complete rows are removed in internal tables.

37.2.2 Setting Breakpoint

```
BREAK-POINT
```

Sets static breakpoint.

Syntax

```
BREAK-POINT [ {ID group}
             | {log_text} ].
```

This statement defines an unconditional checkpoint (breakpoint). If the program reaches an active breakpoint during dialog processing, the program execution is interrupted and the system switches to the ABAP Debugger. An inactive breakpoint will be ignored and the program execution will continue with the statement following BREAK-POINT.

37.2.2.1 Activating the Breakpoint

Without the ID addition, the breakpoint is always active. If the ID addition is used, activation from outside the program will be controlled by a checkpoint group.

The ID addition assigns the breakpoint to a checkpoint group group (as of Release 6.20, Support Package 29). The same rules apply to the checkpoint group and its activation settings as to the activation of assertions (see Section 37.2.1.1).

37.2.2.2 Behavior during background processing and updating

During background processing and during updating, program execution will not be interrupted. If the ID addition is specified, a breakpoint will always be inactive during breakpoint processing and during the updating process.

If a breakpoint is always active—meaning that the ID addition is not specified—the entry "Breakpoint reached" is written into the system log during background processing and during the update task. After the entry, the program name and the point where the breakpoint took place in the program are also recorded.

In log_text, a supplementary text for the system log can be specified. During dialog processing, the specification of log_text has no effect. During background processing and during the update, the content of log_text in the system log is inserted between the words "Breakpoint" and "reached." For log_text, a flat, character-type data object with a length of 40 characters is expected. The specification of a data object of the type string is ignored.

Notes

▶ A breakpoint in SELECT loops (see Section 29.2) can cause an exception through the loss of the database cursor, because a database commit could be triggered during debugging,

▶ In the ABAP Editor and in the ABAP Debugger, dynamic breakpoints can be set and managed without changing the source code. These are effective, at maximum, until the end of a user session.

▶ A breakpoint that is always active is used solely as a test help and is not allowed in productive programs. The BREAK-POINT statement without the ID addition therefore causes an error in the enhanced program check.

▶ BREAK, followed by a user name, is not a statement but rather a predefined macro (see Section 4.5.2.1).

▶ In HTTP sessions (BSP), the system will stop at the BREAK-POINT statement only if, before execution, additional dynamic http breakpoints are set in the editor of an BSP page. Otherwise, only one entry is written into the system log.

▶ In system programs, system modules, system subroutines, and system function modules whose name begins with %_, the BREAK-POINT statement will only be executed if system debugging is switched on (via the entry of "/hs" in the input field of the standard toolbar or via the menu **Settings**).

37.3   Runtime Measurement

The following statements allow you to measure the runtime of a program and make corresponding settings. Alternatively, you can also use a class for runtime measurements with CL_ABAP_RUNTIME as of Release 6.40.

37.3.1   Relative Program Runtime

```
GET RUN TIME
```

Determines the relative runtime of a program.

Syntax

```
GET RUN TIME FIELD rtime.
```

At the first execution of GET RUN TIME after the creation of an internal mode, the value 0 is placed into the variable rtime. At each further execution in the same internal mode, the program runtime that has elapsed since the first execution, in microseconds, is placed into the variable rtime. The return value of the statement is of the data type i.

Notes

▶ To measure the runtime of program sections, a GET RUN TIME statement can be executed before and after the required section and then the difference of the results can be created. The sequence of statements set within limits is called a measuring section, and the time duration determined for it is called measuring interval.

▶ Using the statement SET RUN TIME CLOCK RESOLUTION, the measuring precision can be defined before the first execution of GET RUN TIME, which is used to determine the runtime.

▶ The maximum resolution of the command GET RUN TIME is a microsecond. Shorter measuring intervals cannot be determined reliably.

▶ The value area of the return value of the statement must be taken into account You should not make measuring sections too large (not greater than 1000 s), and no measuring sections should be created through access to external data or through screen calls.

▶ As of Release 6.40, the class CL_ABAP_RUNTIME provides methods for generating objects whose method GET_RUNTIME can be used to execute several runtime measurements with different resolutions in an internal mode (see Appendix B.1.11).

▶ The runtime of the program sections can also be determined using the tool runtime analysis, instead of the GET RUN TIME statement.

Example

Determining the calculation time for calculating the tangent of 1. Since the runtime of the statement is less than a microsecond, the runtime of several executions in an inner loop is measured. The execution time for the loop itself is also measured in order to deduct it as an offset. These measurements are executed several times in an outer loop and the mean value is created using division by n0. Through division by ni, the runtime of an individual statement is determined.

```
DATA: t0    TYPE i,
      t1    TYPE i,
      t2    TYPE i,
      t3    TYPE i,
      t4    TYPE i,
      tm    TYPE f,
```

```
       no    TYPE i VALUE 100,
       ni    TYPE i VALUE 1000,
       res   TYPE f.
DO no TIMES.
  GET RUN TIME FIELD t1.
  DO ni TIMES.
    res = TAN( 1 ).
  ENDDO.
  GET RUN TIME FIELD t2.
  GET RUN TIME FIELD t3.
  DO ni TIMES.
  ENDDO.
  GET RUN TIME FIELD t4.
  t0 = t0 + ( ( t2 - t1 ) - ( t4 - t3 ) ).
ENDDO.

tm = t0 / ni / no.
```

37.3.2   Setting Time Resolution

`SET RUN TIME CLOCK RESOLUTION`

Sets the precision of measurements for runtime measurement.

Syntax

`SET RUN TIME CLOCK RESOLUTION {HIGH|LOW}.`

This statement specifies the precision with which the GET RUN TIME statement is measured. You can only execute it in a program before the GET RUN TIME statement is executed for the first time, otherwise an uncatchable exception occurs.

When you specify HIGH, the system uses the highest level of precision of the current application server's operating system. The following operating systems support highly precise measurement in single processors and multi-processors:

▶ AIX

▶ SINIX

▶ SUN-OS

▶ OS/400

▶ Windows NT

For the operating systems OSF/1 and HP-UX, high precision measurement is only reliable for single processors, since the time registers for multi-processors cannot be reconciled. This means that false values may occur when you change processors.

If you specify `LOW`, the system uses the lowest precision of measurement of all supported platforms.

Without the above `SET RUN TIME CLOCK RESOLUTION` statement, `GET RUN TIME` implicitly uses the high precision measurement.

Notes

▶ When using highly precise measurement, the measured measurement intervals should be smaller than a second, otherwise, inaccuracies due to variations in load distribution can result.

▶ To execute several measurments with different levels of precision within an internal mode, the class CL_ABAP_RUNTIME is available since Release 6.40 (see Appendix B.1.11).

37.4 Measuring Section for Runtime Analysis

```
SET RUN TIME ANALYZER
```

Sets the measuring section for runtime analysis.

Syntax

```
SET RUN TIME ANALYZER {ON|OFF}.
```

This statement influences the measurement of a program with the runtime analysis tool. If you activate the setting **Particular units** in the runtime analysis, done using **Restrictions · Program units**, the runtime analysis only measures the runtime of statements that occur between `SET RUNTIME ANALYZER ON` and `SET RUNTIME ANALYZER OFF`.

Notes

▶ This statement should only be used in the test phase of a program, in order to enable a runtime measurement independent of a source text later.

▶ You can switch the runtime analysis on and off in the transaction SE30, by selecting **System · Utilities · Runtime analysis** or by entering "/RON" and "/ROFF" in the input field of the standard toolbar.

▶ As of Release 6.10, you can start and stop the runtime analysis on a program-controlled basis, by calling the static methods ON and OFF the class CL_ABAP_TRACE_SWITCH either before or after the SET RUNTIME ANALYZER statements.

Return value

The statement SET RUNTIME ANALYZER always sets the return value sy-subrc to 0.

Example

If you execute the method m0 when the runtime analysis is switched on, only the runtime from callup and execution of the method m2 is measured.

```
METHOD m0.
  me->m1( ).
  SET RUN TIME ANALYZER ON.
  me->m2( ).
  SET RUN TIME ANALYZER OFF.
  me->m3( )..
ENDMETHOD.
```

37.5 Deactivating the Extended Program Check

SET EXTENDED CHECK

Activates and de-activates the extended program check.

Syntax

SET EXTENDED CHECK {ON|OFF}.

This statement uses the addition OFF to deactivate the extended program check for the following statements and uses the addition ON to reactivate it. A deactivated extended program check should be reactivated within the same program. The extended program reports a statement SET EXTENDED CHECK OFF without the following statement SET EXTENDED CHECK ON and the superfluous statements SET EXTENDED CHECK ON. By default, the extended program check is switched on.

Notes

▶ This statement may only be used for warnings and errors that the program author can explicitly exclude as such.

▶ For individual statements, the extended program check can also be deactivated using pseudo comments (see Section 2.5).

▶ In this case, deactivation of the extended program check can be overridden by selecting **Display hidden messages (pseudo comments)**.

Example

The statement SELECT SINGLE reads a single line from the database table TDOKUIMGR. Although this table has several key fields, the entry in the NODE_ID column of the WHERE condition is unique. The warning in the extended program check that the specified key may not be unique is therefore deactivated.

```
...

SET EXTENDED CHECK OFF.

SELECT SINGLE ref_object
       FROM   tdokuimgr
       INTO   docu_object
       WHERE  node_id = node_key.

SET EXTENDED CHECK ON.

...
```

38 Dynamic Program Development

38.1 Overview

In addition to static program development in the ABAP Workbench, you also can edit and generate ABAP programs with language elements. This type of program development is called dynamic program development. The following statements are available for that purpose[1]:

Statement	Section
GENERATE SUBROUTINE POOL	38.2
READ REPORT	38.3
SYNTAX-CHECK	38.4
INSERT REPORT	38.5
READ TEXTPOOL	38.6
INSERT TEXTPOOL	38.7
EDITOR-CALL FOR REPORT	38.8

Notes

These statements do not carry out authorization checks or other checks. Instead these must be programmed manually. You can use the following special function modules in addition to the statement AUTHORITY-CHECK for the required checks (see Section 33.6).

▶ The function module RS_ACCESS_PERMISSION carries out all authorization checks that are also carried out when the ABAP Editor is called.

▶ The function module TR_SYS_PARAMS and other function modules of the function group STR9 determine the changeabilty of repository objects.

38.2 Dynamic Subroutine Pool

```
GENERATE SUBROUTINE POOL
```

Creation of temporary subroutine pools.

---

1 Those are partly the same statements that are used internally by the ABAP Workbench for creating programs. The current section describes only those variants that are released for external use.

Syntax

```
GENERATE SUBROUTINE POOL itab NAME prog [error_handling].
```

This statement generates a temporary subroutine pool. The source code of the subroutine pool is taken from the internal table itab. The generated subroutine pool is stored internally in the current internal mode. The 8-digit name of the temporary subroutine pool is assigned to the variable prog.

The line type for itab must be character type (prior to Release 6.10 flat). A source-code line in itab may contain a maximum of 255 characters. The data object prog must also be character-type (prior to Release 6.10 flat). In an internal mode, a maximum of 36 temporary subroutine pools can be created.

If the source text contained in itab has a syntax error, the subroutine pool is not generated and prog is initialized. The syntax errors of the subroutine pool can be handled using the additions error_handling.

Subroutines defined in the source code of the subroutine pool can be called from all programs that are loaded in the same internal mode in which the subroutine pool has been generated. This is done by specifying the program name prog using the statement PERFORM (see Section 11.2.4.1). At the first call of a subroutine in the subroutine pool this is loaded into the internal mode, whereupon the event LOAD-OF-PROGRAM is initialized.

Notes

▶ If the creating program is a Unicode program, the corresponding syntax rules also apply for the generated subroutine pool.

▶ The source code in the internal table itab must contain a complete ABAP program, including the statement that introduces the program (see Chapter 3).

▶ In a temporary subroutine pool, the same global declarations and processing blocks can be defined as in the static subroutine pool of the repository (see Table 3.1).

▶ Temporarily generated subroutine pools can be executed in the ABAP Debugger in single steps.

▶ A temporary subroutine pool generated for an internal mode cannot be explicitly deleted. It remains available from its generation up to the point where the whole internal mode is deleted.

Return values

sy-subrc	Meaning
0	Generation was successful.
4	Source code contains a syntax error.
8	A generation error occurred.

Treatable exceptions

If no further subroutine pool can be created in an internal mode, the exception defined by the class CX_SY_GENERATE_SUBPOOL_FULL is triggered. No exception group is assigned to the corresponding catchable runtime error GENERATE_SUBPOOL_DIR_FULL. Since Release 6.20, the specification of a source-code line that is too wide leads to an exception, defined by the class CX_SY_GEN_SOURCE_TOO_WIDE. The related runtime error is not catchable.

38.2.1 Additions for Error Exceptions

Syntax of *error_handling*

```
... [MESSAGE mess]
    [INCLUDE incl]
    [LINE lin]
    [WORD wrd]
    [OFFSET off]
    [MESSAGE-ID mid]
    [SHORTDUMP-ID sid] ...
```

With these additions, syntax and generation errors can be analyzed. Syntax errors can appear either in the source code contained in itab or in the include programs included there with INCLUDE. Generation errors can appear if the program contains errors in its declarative statements which are not recognized during the static syntax check.

38.2.1.1 Receive error message

Syntax

```
... MESSAGE mess ...
```

If the subroutine pool contains one or several syntax errors, the text of the error message of the first syntax error is assigned to the variable mess. mess must be a character- type (prior to Release 6.10 flat) data object.

If a generation error occurs (see Section 38.2.1.7), `mess` is also supplied with an appropriate error message. If the subroutine pool can be generated, the content is not changed by `mess`.

38.2.1.2 Recognizing Include programs

Syntax

```
... INCLUDE incl ...
```

If, in the subroutine pool, one or several include programs are included, and one of them contains the first syntax error of the subroutine pool, the name of this include program is assigned to the variable `incl`. `incl` must be a character-type (prior to Release 6.10 flat) data object. If the first syntax error in the source code occurs in `itab`, the internal name is assigned to `incl` that would have been returned if generation had been successful in `prog`. This name always begins with "%_".

If a generation error occurs (see Section 38.2.1.7), `incl` is also supplied with the name of the corresponding include program. If the subroutine pool can be generated, the content of `incl` is not changed.

38.2.1.3 Recognizing line numbers

Syntax

```
... LINE lin ...
```

If the subroutine pool contains one or more syntax errors, the line number of the first syntax error from the program in which it occurs (either the source code in `itab` or an Include program included there) is assigned to the variable `lin`. The data type i is expected for `lin`.

If a generation error occurs (see Section 38.2.1.7), `lin` is also supplied with the corresponding line number. If the subroutine pool can be generated, the content of `lin` is not changed.

38.2.1.4 Recognizing incorrect language elements

Syntax

```
... WORD wrd ...
```

If the subroutine pool contains one or several syntax errors, the first incorrect language element is assigned to the variable `wrd`. `wrd` must be a character-type (prior to Release 6.10 flat) data object.

If a generation error occurs (see Section 38.2.1.7), `wrd` is also supplied with the corresponding language element. If the subroutine pool can be generated, the content of `wrd` is not changed.

38.2.1.5 Recognizing the position in a line

Syntax

```
... OFFSET off ...
```

If the subroutine pool contains one or several syntax errors, the offset of the first incorrect language element, in relation to the line in the source code, is assigned to the variable `off`. The data type `i` is expected for `off`.

If there is a generation error (see Section 38.2.1.7), `off` is also supplied with the appropriate offset. If the subroutine pool can be generated, the content of `off` is not changed.

38.2.1.6 Recognizing an error message ID

Syntax

```
... MESSAGE-ID mid ...
```

If the subroutine pool contains one or several syntax errors, the key under which the first error message is stored in the database table TRMSG is assigned to the variable `mid`.

If there is a generation error (see Section 38.2.1.7), `mid` is also supplied with the corresponding key. If the subroutine pool can be generated, the content of `mid` is not changed.

The key of the database table TRMSG consists of the component SPRAS of length 1, KEYWORD of length 20, and MSGNUMBER of length 4. The component MSGNUMBER is used to adopt a three-digit ID. The fourth position can contain an empty character or a letter. If you have error messages with multiple parts that occupy more than one line in the database table TRMSG, all the parts have the same three-digit ID, while the fourth position marks a part of the message.

In Unicode systems, `mid` must have the data type TRMSG_KEY, which exists since Release 6.10 and is from the ABAP Dictionary. It is made up of the components SPRAS of length 1, KEYWORD of length 20, and MSGNUMBER of length 3. In non-Unicode programs, an appropriately created structure or a flat character-type data object can be specified.

Note
The return value in mid only contains the three-digit ID of a syntax error message. In order to read all parts of an error message from the table TRMSG using SELECT, the key component MSGNUMBER must be specified generically in the WHERE condition: with LIKE, for example, using the wildcard character "%" (see Section 29.2.4.1).

38.2.1.7 Determining the ID of a runtime error during generation

Syntax

```
... SHORTDUMP-ID sid ...
```

If the subroutine pool does not contain any statically recognizable syntax errors, but an exception still occurs during generation, the ID of the runtime error to which the exception is allocated is assigned to the variable sid. sid must be a character-type (prior to Release 6.10 flat) data object. If the subroutine pool can be generated, the content of sid is not changed.

Notes

▶ An exception during generation terminates these, but does not cause a runtime error. The exception cannot be handled as described in Chapter 15.

▶ The IDs of runtime errors are part of the key column ERRID in the database table SNAPT in which texts are assigned to them.

Example
Dynamic creation and generation of a subroutine pool that implements the event block LOAD-OF-PROGRAM and two subroutines. Depending on the return value sy-subrc, a subroutine is called or a message is issued.

```
DATA: prog TYPE string,
      tab  TYPE STANDARD TABLE OF string,
      mess TYPE string,
      sid  TYPE string.

APPEND 'PROGRAM subpool.'                      TO tab.
APPEND 'DATA spfli_tab TYPE TABLE OF spfli.'   TO tab.
APPEND 'LOAD-OF-PROGRAM.'                       TO tab.
APPEND '   SELECT *' &
       '           FROM spfli' &
       '           INTO TABLE spfli_tab.'       TO tab.
```

```
APPEND 'FORM loop_at_tab.'                        TO tab.
APPEND '  DATA spfli_wa TYPE spfli.'              TO tab.
APPEND '  LOOP AT spfli_tab INTO spfli_wa.'       TO tab.
APPEND '    PERFORM evaluate_wa USING spfli_wa.'  TO tab.
APPEND '  ENDLOOP.'                               TO tab.
APPEND 'ENDFORM.'                                 TO tab.
APPEND 'FORM evaluate_wa USING l_wa TYPE spfli.'  TO tab.
APPEND '  WRITE: / l_wa-carrid, l_wa-connid.'     TO tab.
APPEND 'ENDFORM.'                                 TO tab.

GENERATE SUBROUTINE POOL tab NAME prog
         MESSAGE mess
         SHORTDUMP-ID sid.

IF sy-subrc = 0.
  PERFORM ('LOOP_AT_TAB') IN PROGRAM (prog) IF FOUND.
ELSEIF sy-subrc = 4.
  MESSAGE mess TYPE 'I'.
ELSEIF sy-subrc = 8.
  MESSAGE sid TYPE 'I'.
ENDIF.
```

38.3   Reading an ABAP Program

READ REPORT

Reads the source code of a program from the repository.

Syntax

READ REPORT prog **INTO** itab [**MAXIMUM WIDTH INTO** wid].

This statement reads the source text of the program specified in prog from the repository and inserts its rows into the internal table itab. The previous content of itab is deleted. If the program cannot be loaded, the content of itab remains unchanged.

For prog, you have to specify a flat character-type data object that contains the name of the program to be read; whether it is in uppercase or lowercase is irrelevant. The internal table itab must be a standard table with character-type (before Release 6.10 flat) row type. When the row length of the internal table is fixed, it must be long enough for the longest program line. Before Release 6.10 program lines that are too long, are cut off to the right, since Release 6.10, a treatable exception occurs.

If you use the addition MAXIMUM WIDTH, the number of characters of the longest imported source text row is assigned to the variable wid, for which the data type i is expected.

Return values

sy-subrc	Meaning
0	The program has been imported.
4	The specified program has not been found in the repository.
8	The specified program is a system program protected against read access.

Treatable Exceptions

If the line length of the internal table is not sufficient for the longest line in the source code an exception defined by the class CX_SY_READ_SRC_LINE_TOO_LONG is raised. The corresponding runtime error is not catchable.

Example

After the import of a program into the internal table itab, further lines are attached to the source code. After that, a temporary subroutine-pool is generated from the changed program and one of its subroutines called.

```
DATA prog(30) TYPE c.

DATA itab TYPE TABLE OF string.

prog = ...

READ REPORT prog INTO itab.

IF sy-subrc = 0.
  APPEND 'FORM subr.'  TO itab.
  ...
  APPEND 'PERFORM ...' TO itab.
  APPEND 'ENDFORM.'    TO itab.
  GENERATE SUBROUTINE POOL itab NAME prog.
  PERFORM ('SUBR') IN PROGRAM (prog).
ENDIF.
```

38.4   Checking Syntax

SYNTAX-CHECK

Checks the syntax of a source code.

Syntax

```
SYNTAX-CHECK FOR itab MESSAGE mess LINE lin WORD wrd
              check_options
              [error_handling].
```

This statement executes a syntax check for the content of the internal table itab. The internal table itab must be a standard table with character-like row type.

If the internal table does not contain a syntactically correct ABAP source text, then:

▶ The error message of the first syntax error is assigned to the variable mess. mess must be a character-like (before Release 6.10 flat) data object.

▶ The row number of the first syntax error in reference to the program in which it occurs (either the source text in itab or an include program included there) is assigned to the variable lin. For lin, the data type i is expected.

▶ The first defective language element is assigned to the variable wrd. wrd must be a character-like (before Release 6.10 flat) data object.

Use the additions in check_options to set the attributes of the syntax check. Use the additions in error_handling to find out further attributes of the first syntax error to be encountered.

Return values

sy-subrc	Meaning
0	The internal table itab contains a syntactically correct ABAP program.
4	The internal table itab contains an ABAP program with syntax errors.
8	Other errors occurred.

38.4.1 Determining the Attributes of the Syntax Check

Syntax of check_options

```
... [PROGRAM prog]
    [DIRECTORY ENTRY dir] ...
```

Use the following additions to determine the program attributes used for the syntax check.

- Use the addition PROGRAM to specify in prog the name of an existing ABAP program to use its program attributes for the syntax check. prog must be a character-like (before Release 6.10 flat) data object, whose content is not case-sensitive. If the specified program is not found, standard attributes specified below are used instead.

- After the addition DIRECTORY ENTRY, you must specify a data object dir, whose data type corresponds to the structure of the database table TRDIR from the ABAP Dictionary. In the components of this structure, you can specify the desired program attributes. Invalid contents are replaced implicitly by internally defined standard values.

In non-Unicode programs, you should specify one of these two additions, and in Unicode programs you must do so. If you specify neither PROGRAM nor DIRECTORY ENTRY, the system assumes an executable program as the program type. The other program attributes are set to general standard values. If both additions PROGRAM and DIRECTORY ENTRY are specified, the program attributes are determined by the structure dir.

Notes

- We recommend using the addition PROGRAM, because the components of the structure dir and their valid values are only of system-internal importance. If the addition DIRECTORY ENTRY is nevertheless used in application programs, the content of structure dir should be set by getting the appropriate entry from the database table TRDIR and should be modified only by purposeful conversion of single components.

- Important program attributes for the syntax check are the program type and whether the program is a Unicode program.

38.4.2   Additions for Error Handling

Syntax of *error_handling*

```
...   [INCLUDE incl]
      [OFFSET off]
      [MESSAGE-ID mid] ...
```

A found syntax error can be analyzed with these additions. Such a syntax error can appear either in the source code given in itab or in the include programs included there with INCLUDE. The additions have the same meaning as in the statement GENERATE SUBROUTINE POOL (see Section 38.2.1). Further additions of the statement SYNTAX-CHECK are allowed for internal purposes only.

Example

Syntax check for a source text in `itab`. By importing the program attributes of the current program from the database table TRDIR into the
structure `dir`, it can be used after the DIRECTORY ENTRY. By setting the
component `dir-uccheck`, the first syntax check is executed as for a non-
Unicode program and the second as for a Unicode program. The first syntax check does not find an error in a non-Unicode system and finds an error in a Unicode system, because the program is not Unicode-enabled.
The second syntax check always finds the error that in the statement DE-
SCRIBE, the addition BYTE or CHARACTER MODE is missing.

```
DATA: itab TYPE STANDARD TABLE OF string,
      mess TYPE string,
      lin  TYPE i,
      wrd  TYPE string,
      dir  TYPE trdir.

APPEND 'PROGRAM test.'                   TO itab.
APPEND 'DATA dat TYPE d.'                TO itab.
APPEND 'DATA len TYPE i.'                TO itab.
APPEND 'DESCRIBE FIELD int LENGTH len.' TO itab.

SELECT SINGLE *
       FROM trdir
       INTO dir
       WHERE name = sy-repid.

dir-uccheck = ' '.
SYNTAX-CHECK FOR itab MESSAGE mess LINE lin WORD wrd
             DIRECTORY ENTRY dir.

IF sy-subrc = 4.
  MESSAGE mess TYPE 'I'.
ENDIF.

dir-uccheck = 'X'.
SYNTAX-CHECK FOR itab MESSAGE mess LINE lin WORD wrd
             DIRECTORY ENTRY dir.

IF sy-subrc = 4.
  MESSAGE mess TYPE 'I'.
ENDIF.
```

38.5 Creating or Overwriting an ABAP Program

```
INSERT REPORT
```

Creates or overwrites an ABAP program in the repository.

Syntax

```
INSERT REPORT prog FROM itab [MAXIMUM WIDTH INTO wid]
                             [attributes].
```

This statement places the contents of itab as a source code into the ABAP program specified in prog in the Repository. If a program with the specified name already exists, its source code is overwritten. Otherwise a new program with the name specified in prog and the source code from itab is created in the Repository. With the additions in attributes the program attributes of the program in the Repository can be determined since Release 6.10.

The row type of itab must be character-type (before Release 6.10 flat). A source-code line in itab can contain a maximum of 255 characters (maximum of 72 characters before Release 6.10). prog must be a character-type flat data object, which may contain no more than 30 characters, and the content of which can be either upper or lower case.

If you use the MAXIMUM WIDTH addition, the number of characters of the longest source-code line in itab is assigned to the variable wid, which must be of data type i.

Return values

sy-subrc	Meaning
0	The program specified in prog was successfully created or overwritten.
4	An error occurred when creating or overwriting the program specified in prog.

Notes

▶ The INSERT REPORT statement must only be used with extreme caution, because it can completely overwrite existing programs without warning. You can prevent any unintentional overwriting by checking whether the specified name already exists in the NAME column of the system table TRDIR.

▶ If you use `INSERT REPORT` to create a new program, this program is not assigned to a package, so that it is not connected to the correction or transport systems. You must either assign the program to a package in the ABAP Workbench or it is only suitable for temporary tasks in the current system.

▶ When creating a program the name of the program should comply with the naming conventions of the ABAP Workbench, if it is to be processed using the Workbench's tools.

Treatable Exceptions

If a line in the source code contains more than 255 characters, the exception defined by class CX_SY_WRITE_SRC_LINE_TOO_LONG is triggered. The assigned runtime error is not catchable.

38.5.1 Determine Program Attributes

Syntax of *attributes*

```
...{ [KEEPING DIRECTORY ENTRY]
   | { [PROGRAM TYPE pt]
       [FIXED-POINT ARITHMETIC fp]
       [UNICODE ENABLING uc] }
   | [DIRECTORY ENTRY dir] } ...
```

With these additions the program attributes of the program given in `prog` can be affected in the repository. The attributes are stored in the system table TRDIR. Further additions of the statement `INSERT REPORT` are allowed only for internal purposes.

If none of the additions are specified, the following default values are set when a new program is created.

▶ The **Original language** is set to the system language stored in the profile parameter `zcsa/system_language`.

▶ The **Creation date** and the date of the last change, along with the corresponding time, are set to the current values.

▶ The **Program author** and the last changer are set to the current user.

▶ The **Program status** is set to active. The program is compiled when it is first executed.

▶ The **Program type** is set to **Executable program**.

▶ The **Application** is set to the value of the current program.

▶ No **Logical database** is connected with the program.

- Fixed point arithmetic is activated.
- The setting for the Unicode check is adopted from the current program.

If none of the additions are specified, an existing program's attributes remain intact if it is overwritten, but with the following exceptions.

- Date and time of the last change are set to the current value.
- The last changer is set to the current user.
- The version number is increased by one.
- The setting for the Unicode check is activated, if the current program is a Unicode program and a non-Unicode program is overwritten. The setting remains active, if the current program is a non-Unicode program and a Unicode program is overwritten.

38.5.1.1 Keeping previous attributes

Syntax

```
... KEEPING DIRECTORY ENTRY ...
```

This addition is only effective when a program is overwritten. The statement behaves as if no additions had been specified (see Section 38.4.1), with the exception that the setting for the Unicode check remains intact in the overwritten program.

Note
With this setting, the source codes of non-Unicode programs can be overwritten from Unicode programs, without the Unicode check being implicitly activated.

38.5.1.2 Determine Program Type

Syntax

```
... PROGRAM TYPE pt ...
```

This addition specifies the program type of the created or overwritten program according to the content of pt. pt must be a data object of data type c and length 1 that contains a valid program type ID. Table 38.1 lists the IDs of all program types from Table 3.1, which must be in uppercase.

ID	Program Type
1	Executable program
F	Function group or function pool
I	Include program
J	Interface pool
K	Class pool
M	Module pool
S	Subroutine pool
T	Type group or type pool

Table 38.1 IDs for ABAP Program Types

38.5.1.3 Specifying Fixed Point Arithmetic

Syntax

```
... FIXED-POINT ARITHMETIC fp ...
```

This addition specifies the attribute **Fixed point arithmetic** for the created or overwritten program, according to the content of fp. fp must be a data object of the data type c and length 1 that either has the value "X" or " ". The value "X" sets the **Fixed point arithmetic** attribute, the value " " deactivates it.

38.5.1.4 Specifying Unicode Check

Syntax

```
... UNICODE ENABLING uc ...
```

This addition specifies the setting of the **Unicode check** for the created or overwritten program according to the content of uc, which must be a data object of the data type c and length 1 that has the value "X" or " ". The value "X" activates the Unicode check while the value " " deactivates it.

Note

With this addition, the source codes of non-Unicode programs can be overwritten from Unicode programs without the Unicode check being implicitly activated. You can also create Unicode programs from non-Unicode programs.

38.5.1.5 Setting all Program Attributes

RELEASE
6.10

Syntax

```
... DIRECTORY ENTRY dir ...
```

This addition specifies the program attributes for the created or overwritten program, according to the content of dir. dir must be a structure of the data type TRDIR from the ABAP Dictionary. In the component of this structure, you can specify the desired program attributes. Invalid contents result in invalid program attributes. Most program attributes are obtained from dir, the exceptions being the creation and change dates, and the corresponding times, program authors or last changer, and the last version number. The latter are set to the values described in Section 38.4.1.

Note

When using the DIRECTORY ENTRY addition, it is strongly recommended that you only set the contents of the structure dir by reading the attributes of an existing program from the database table TRDIR.

Example

Partial conversion of a program to Unicode. A non-Unicode program is imported and, by means of an example, the DESCRIBE FIELD statement is converted to the syntax for Unicode systems. The source code of the program is then overwritten with the modified source code and the Unicode check is activated in the program attributes.

```
DATA: itab TYPE TABLE OF string,
      prog TYPE sy-repid,
      uc   TYPE trdir-uccheck.

FIELD-SYMBOLS  <line> TYPE string.

prog = ...

SELECT SINGLE uccheck
       FROM   trdir
       INTO   (uc)
       WHERE name    = prog AND
             uccheck = ' '.

IF sy-subrc = 0.
  READ REPORT prog INTO itab.
  LOOP AT itab ASSIGNING <line>.
    TRANSLATE <line> TO UPPER CASE.
    IF <line> CS 'DESCRIBE FIELD' AND
       <line> CS 'LENGTH' AND
```

```
      <line> NS 'MODE'.
        REPLACE '.' IN <line> WITH ' IN CHARACTER MODE.'.
      ENDIF.
      ...
    ENDLOOP.
    SYNTAX-CHECK FOR itab ...
    IF sy-subrc = 0.
      INSERT REPORT prog FROM itab UNICODE ENABLING 'X'.
    ENDIF.
  ENDIF.
ENDIF.
```

38.6   Reading a Text Pool

READ TEXTPOOL

Reads the text elements of a program from the repository.

Syntax

READ TEXTPOOL prog **INTO** itab **LANGUAGE** lang.

This statement reads the text elements of the text pool of the language specified in `lang` and the program specified in `prog` from the repository and places them into the internal table `itab`. The previous content of `itab` is deleted. If the text elements cannot be read, then the content of `itab` remains unchanged.

For `prog`, you must specify a flat character-like data object containing the name of the program of text elements to be read, with the name case-independent. The internal table can have any table type and its row type must correspond to the structure TEXTPOOL from the ABAP Dictionary.

For `lang`, you must specify a flat character-like data object that contains a language key of up to one character, whose value must be contained in the SPRAS column of the database table T002. If `lang` contains a blank, the behavior is undefined.

After a successful read, `itab` contains in the ENTRY column the texts of the text symbols, the selection texts, the list headings and the title from the program attributes. Every text element that exists for the specified language occupies one row of the internal table and is identified uniquely by the columns ID and KEY. The column LENGTH contains the length of the text element. Table 38.2 shows the possible values of the columns ID and KEY and their meaning.

ID	KEY	ENTRY
H	001 to 004	List heading: Column headings
I	Text symbol identifier	Text symbol text
R		Program title
S	Name of a parameter or selection criterion	Selection text
T		List Title: Titlebar

Table 38.2 IDs for Text Elements

Return values

sy-subrc	Meaning
0	At least one text element has been read.
4	The program specified in prog or the language specified in lang does not exist or there is no text pool in the specified language.

38.7 Creating or Overwriting a Text Pool

`INSERT TEXTPOOL`

Inserts or overwrites text elements of a program from the repository.

Syntax

```
INSERT TEXTPOOL prog FROM itab LANGUAGE lang.
```

This statement places the contents of table itab into the repository as a text pool of the language specified in lang for the ABAP program specified in prog. If a text pool for the specified language already exists, all its text elements are overwritten. Otherwise, a new text pool is created for this language.

For prog, you must specify a flat character-type data object that contains the name of the program of the text elements to be read, whereat it can be uppercase or lowercase.

For lang, you must specify a character-type, flat data object that contains a language key with the maximum length of 1 character, whose value must be contained in the column SPRAS of the database table T002. If an invalid language is specified in lang, no text pool is created or overwritten. If lang contains a blank, the behavior is undefined.

The internal table can be of any table type and its row type must correspond to the TEXTPOOL structure in the ABAP Dictionary. If a non-existent program is specified in prog, no text pool is created or overwritten.

In the internal table itab, the ENTRY column can contain the texts of the text symbols, the selection texts, the list headings, and the title for the program attributes. In the LENGTH column, you can specify the corresponding lengths. The individual text elements are identified using the entries in the columns ID and KEY, whose valid values are shown in Table 38.2.

If the columns ID or KEY of the internal table contain invalid values or duplicate entries exist, an inconsistent text pool is created. If the internal table is empty, all text elements of an existing text pool are deleted or a text pool without text elements is created. If the length specified in LENGTH is shorter than the text length in ENTRY, it is automatically set to the text length in the text pool.

Notes

▶ The specification of the text length in the LENGTH field defines the maximum length of the text element that is available in the ABAP Workbench when translating the text pool into other languages and should be set sufficiently large.

▶ The INSERT TEXTPOOL statement should only be used with caution, because it completely overwrites existing text pools.

Return Values
The INSERT TEXTPOOL statement always sets sy-subrc to the value 0.

Example
Prototype of a translation tool for text elements. The text pools of a source and a target language are imported into internal tables. For each text element of the source language, a selection screen is displayed as a translation template. After the translation has been completed, the text pool of the target language is overwritten with the correspondingly changed internal table.

```
PARAMETERS: program TYPE sy-repid,
            langu1  TYPE spras DEFAULT sy-langu,
            langu2  TYPE spras.

SELECTION-SCREEN BEGIN OF SCREEN 500 AS WINDOW.
SELECTION-SCREEN COMMENT /1(83) source.
SELECTION-SCREEN BEGIN OF LINE.
PARAMETERS target TYPE textpool-entry.
```

```
SELECTION-SCREEN END OF LINE.
SELECTION-SCREEN END OF SCREEN 500.

DATA: text1 TYPE SORTED TABLE OF textpool
             WITH UNIQUE KEY id KEY,
      text2 TYPE SORTED TABLE OF textpool
             WITH UNIQUE KEY id KEY,
      wa1 TYPE textpool,
      wa2 TYPE textpool.

READ TEXTPOOL program: INTO text1 LANGUAGE langu1,
                       INTO text2 LANGUAGE langu2.

LOOP AT text1 INTO wa1.
  CLEAR wa2.
  READ TABLE text2 INTO wa2
          WITH TABLE KEY id  = wa1-id
                         key = wa1-key.
  source = wa1-entry.
  target = wa2-entry.
  CALL SELECTION-SCREEN 500 STARTING AT 1 1.
  IF sy-subrc = 0.
    IF target IS NOT INITIAL.
      wa2-id = wa1-id.
      wa2-key = wa1-key.
      wa2-entry = target.
      wa2-length = wa1-length.
      DELETE TABLE text2
            WITH TABLE KEY id  = wa1-id
                           key = wa1-key.
      INSERT wa2 INTO TABLE text2.
    ENDIF.
  ELSE.
    EXIT.
  ENDIF.
ENDLOOP.
```

INSERT TEXTPOOL program FROM text2 LANGUAGE langu2.

38.8 Calling the ABAP Editor

EDITOR-CALL FOR REPORT

Calls the ABAP editor for a program.

Syntax

```
EDITOR-CALL FOR REPORT prog [DISPLAY-MODE].
```

This statement starts the ABAP editor for the source code of the program specified in `prog`. `prog` has to be a character-type data object, which contains the name of a program in capital letters that exists in the repository. Otherwise you will get a corresponding status message.

The ABAP editor starts by default in change-mode. The addition `DISPLAY-MODE` causes the ABAP editor to start in display mode.

After starting the ABAP editor, it provides the full functionality, as if called from the ABAP Workbench. You can navigate forward to branch to other tools. After returning from the ABAP Editor, the current program continues after the statement `EDITOR-CALL`.

Note
This statement bypasses the authority checks that are performed when calling the ABAP editor via transaction code.

Part 13
External Programming Interfaces

39   Remote Function Call

39.1   Overview

39.1.1   RFC Interface

When a function module is called that is defined in system (other than a calling program), this is referred to as a remote function call (RFC). The RFC interface facilitates this kind of program communication by supporting function calls between different SAP systems (or Web application servers) or between an SAP system and an external system. An RFC client calls the function module, and an RFC server provides and executes the function module. The RFC interface provides the following services.

▶ Calling and controlling the communication routines that are needed to communicate with the remote system.

▶ Log-on and log-off to and from the remote system and authorization checks for the function groups used.

▶ Converting actual parameters into the format required in the remote system and vice versa. This includes any platform-dependent conversions (for example for differing code pages or byte sequences). The conversion supports all ABAP data types.

▶ Handling any communication errors and, if required (see Section 39.1.4), forwarding them to the caller.

If two SAP systems are in communication with each other, two ABAP programs communicate via the RFC interface. If an SAP system and an external system are communicating, an ABAP program communicates with a program in another programming language (C, C++, Visual Basic, Java or .NET).

RFC libraries are available for communication with programs in other languages for all the operating systems supported by SAP, such as MS Windows, UNIX (RS/6000, SUN Solaris, HP-UX), Linux, z/OS (OS/390) and AS400:

▶ Java Connector (JCo) for Java

▶ .NET Connector for .NET (C#, VB.NET)

▶ RFC Software Development Kit (SDK) for C and C++

The following additions of the CALL FUNCTION statement cause a remote function call:

▶ DESTINATION (synchronous RFC)
If the DESTINATION addition is specified without either of the following two additions, the calling program waits until the remotely called function is ended.

▶ STARTING NEW TASK (asynchronous RFC, or aRFC)
The STARTING NEW TASK addition continues processing of the calling program as soon as the remotely-called function is started, without waiting for it to end. The results can be stored in callback routines.

▶ IN BACKGROUND TASK (transactional RFC, or tRFC)
The IN BACKGROUND TASK addition pre-marks the remotely called function for execution and starts it with the COMMIT WORK command.

39.1.2 RFC Destination

When a function module is called via the RFC interface, the calling program has to specify the connection parameters in the form of a destination. The destination determines the connection type, the partner program, and the target system. It is administrated using the transaction SM59 and handles many different connection types, such as TCP/IP and R/3 connections. With synchronous RFC, you have to explicitly specify the destination. A destination can also be specified for asynchronous and transactional RFC. If a destination is not specified in these cases, the function module is called via the RFC interface in the same system. The following conditions apply, depending on the execution type:

▶ For synchronous and asynchronous calls, the call parameter values are transferred directly to the function module. For transactional calls, the call parameter values are temporarily stored in the database until they are executed.

▶ With asynchronous calls, it is not possible to connect to external systems (**TCP/IP connections** in the transaction SM59).

▶ For synchronous calls, the results of the called function are transferred directly. For asynchronous calls, the RECEIVE command can be used to receive the results in callback routines. For transactional calls, the results cannot be transferred.

▶ With synchronous and asynchronous calls, the server of the called function module has to be available.

In order to call a function module via the RFC interface, the function module has to be marked in its attributes as **Remote-enabled**, and its interface parameters can only be transferred using value transfer. Its table parameters are likewise implicitly transferred by value transfer. Remote-enabled function modules can be called in the system in which they are defined either using the RFC interface or as normal function modules using the `CALL FUNCTION` command without any of its additions (`DESTINATION`, `STARTING NEW TASK` and `IN BACKGROUND TASK`). To call them via the RFC interface, either the special destination "NONE" (see below) has to be specified, or an asynchronous or transactional RFC without a destination has to be executed.

All possible destinations are stored in the RFCDES database table whose content is administrated with the transaction SM59. When a function module is remotely called from within an ABAP program, the destination after the `DESTINATION` addition in the `CALL FUNCTION` statement is specified as a key value of the RFCDEST column in the RFCDES database table. The corresponding row of the database table contains all the parameters specified in transaction SM59 for communicating with external systems.

There are two predefined destinations that do not have to be maintained with the transaction SM59:

▶ Destination "NONE" causes the function module to be started on the same application server as the calling program, but via the RFC interface and in its own context (see Section 39.1.3). This destination can be used for all types of calls.

▶ Destination "BACK" can be used in a remotely called function module and refers back to the caller. It can only be used in function modules that are called synchronously. The destination "BACK" can be used to call every remote-enabled function module of the calling system in all three execution types. With synchronous callbacks, the corresponding function group in the internal mode of the calling program is loaded if it does not already exist there. The existing RFC connection is used for the callback.

Besides the destinations created in transaction SM59 and the two pre-defined destinations, destinations can also be specified directly in the form "hostname_sysid_sysnr", where "hostname" is the name of the application server, "sysid" is the name of an SAP system, and "sysnr" is the system number, as they are displayed in transaction SM51 for example.

39.1.3   RFC Context

Every remote call of a function module that uses an RFC interface defines its own context in the target system. The function group of the function module is loaded into an internal mode of the context and is kept there. As a result, when function modules with the same destination and function group are called repeatedly, the global data belonging to this function group can all be accessed at the same time. When functions are called in an external system, the RFC library API simulates this behavior. A connection and its context are kept in the context until they are explicitly closed or until the calling program is closed. The function module RFC_ CONNECTION_CLOSE or the API functions RfcAbort and RfcClose are used to explicitly close a connection.

39.1.4   RFC Exceptions

With external function calls, the EXCEPTIONS addition of the CALL FUNC- TION statement can be used to assign return values to the exceptions defined in the interface of the called function module (see Section 11.2.3.1). Class-based exceptions (see Section 15.2) cannot be propagated to the caller from a remotely called function module, and have the effect of an exception that cannot be handled.

In addition to the exceptions defined in the interface of the called function module, an external function call can also trigger the following predefined exceptions:

▶ The SYSTEM_FAILURE exception is the response to a runtime error that occurs when the remotely called function module is executed.

▶ The COMMUNICATION_FAILURE exception occurs when the connection to the partner system cannot be established or if the connection is lost during the communication.

Note
We strongly recommend that you assign a return value to both these exceptions for every RFC and that you handle this return value; otherwise, a runtime error will occur in the exception situations in question.

39.1.5   RFC System Fields

Identical to any call of a function module, the RFC initializes the system field sy-subrc in the calling program or sets it to the value specified during the error handling (see Section 11.2.3.1). Additionally, RFC initializes the system fields sy-msgid, sy-msgno, sy-msgty and sy-msgv1 to sy- msgv4 in the calling program at every remote call of a function module. If an error or termination message is sent during the execution of a remotely called function module through the statement MESSAGE (see

Chapter 28), then the exception SYSTEM_FAILURE is triggered in the calling program, to which you can assign a return value at the time of calling. If the exception occurs, then these system fields are supplied with the properties of the message (see Section 28.2).

39.1.6 RFC—Authorization

At a remote call of a function module, an automatic authorization check is executed if the profile parameter `auth/rfc_authority_check` is set to 1. The authorization check uses the authorization object S_RFC to check whether the user specified in the destination has an RFC authorization for the function group of the called function module.

At the remote call of a function module within the same system, the automatic authorization check is executed only if client and user ID differ. Across systems, the automatic authorization check is executed only outside of trusted systems. To specify a system as a trusted system, use transaction SMT1.

The automatic authorization check is executed via the implicit call of the function module AUTHORITY_CHECK_RFC. If the authorization is missing, the function module triggers one of the exceptions USER_DONT_EXIST or RFC_NO_AUTHORITY defined in its interface and causes a runtime error. We recommend calling the function module AUTHORITY_CHECK_RFC explicitly before a remote call to be able to treat a possible exception. If the authorization exists, the function module does not return an explicit result but, like all successfully executed function modules, sets `sy-subrc` to 0.

39.1.7 RFC Restrictions

Calling an RFC is different from the normal calling of function modules, insofar the following restrictions apply:

▶ At every call via synchronous and asynchronous RFC, a database commit is issued (see Section 33.2.1.1). For this reason, synchronous or asynchronous RFC must not be used between Open SQL statements that open or close a database cursor.

▶ Within a remotely called function module, you cannot use statements that close the current context and, in doing so, the connection (see Section 39.1.3). These are the statements `LEAVE PROGRAM` or `SUBMIT` without the `RETURN` addition.

- Dynpros and selection screens called in a remotely called function module are displayed in the calling system with synchronous RFC, providing that the calling program is executed in the dialog processing and that the user specified in the destination has the authorization for dialog. The screen data is transferred from the RFC interface to the calling system. In this case, lists can be displayed with `LEAVE TO LIST-PROCESSING` that are written in a remotely called function module (see Section 27.6.1).

- As RFC only performs a pass by value, you can never access interim results if an exception occurs (neither with synchronous RFC).

- When transferring character-type data, there usually is a conversion between the participating code pages. At the transfer between MDMP systems and Unicode systems, the allocation might not be clear. With structures defined in the ABAP Dictionary, the text language is evaluated since Release 6.20.

- Information messages and warnings are treated like status messages.

39.1.8 Statements of the RFC Interface

Statement	Section
`CALL FUNCTION ... DESTINATION`	39.2.1
`CALL FUNCTION ... STARTING NEW TASK`	39.2.2
`RECEIVE`	39.2.2
`WAIT`	39.2.2
`CALL FUNCTION ... IN BAKGROUND TASK`	39.2.3

39.2 Calling Remote Functions

`CALL FUNCTION ... DESTINATION`

Calling a function module or a function in an external system using the RFC interface.

With remote calls, you can differentiate between the following forms of executing the called function module:

- Synchronous (see Section 39.2.1)
- Asynchronous (see Section 39.2.2)
- Transactional (see Section 39.2.3)

39.2.1 Synchronous Remote Function Call

Syntax

```
CALL FUNCTION func DESTINATION dest parameter_list.
```

Synchronous call of a remote-enabled function module specified in func using the RFC interface. Use the addition DESTINATION to specify the destination (see Section 39.1.2) in dest. For func and dest, character-type data objects are expected. After terminating the remotely called function, the calling program is continued after the statement CALL FUNCTION.

Parameter Transfer

Syntax of *parameter_list*

```
... [EXPORTING   p1 = a1 p2 = a2 ...]
    [IMPORTING   p1 = a1 p2 = a2 ...]
    [CHANGING    p1 = a1 p2 = a2 ...]
    [TABLES      t1 = itab1 t2 = itab2 ...]
    [EXCEPTIONS [exc1 = n1 exc2 = n2 ...]
                [system_failure = ns [MESSAGE smess]]
                [communication_failure = nc [MESSAGE cmess]]
                [OTHERS = n_others]] ...
```

These additions are used to assign actual parameters to the formal parameters of the function module and return values to exceptions that are not class-based (see Section 15.4). The additions have the same meaning as in the general function module call (see Section 11.2.3.1), with two differences: Only tables with flat row types can be passed when using the addition TABLES, and a header—if there is one—cannot be passed. As of Release 4.6C, the additions EXPORTING, IMPORTING and CHANGING enable you to pass tables with deep row types, deep structures and strings.

In addition, you can add an optional addition MESSAGE after EXCEPTIONS for the specific exceptions SYSTEM_FAILURE or COMMUNICATION_FAILURE described in Section 39.1.4. If one of these exceptions is triggered, the first row of the corresponding short dump is displayed in the field smess or cmess, which must be flat and character-type.

Note
Internal tables are passed considerably faster when using the addition TABLES instead of other additions because a binary format instead of an XML format is used internally.

39.2.2 Asynchronous Remote Function Call

Syntax

```
CALL FUNCTION func STARTING NEW TASK task
             [DESTINATION {dest|{IN GROUP {group|DEFAULT}}}]
             parameter_list
             [{PERFORMING subr}
             |{CALLING meth} ON END OF TASK].
```

Asynchronous call of a remote-enabled function module specified in func using the RFC interface. Use either the addition DESTINATION to specify a single destination in dest (see Section 39.1.2) or use IN GROUP to specify a group of application servers. The latter supports parallel processing of several function modules. The calling program is continued after the CALL FUNCTION statement as soon as the remotely called function has been started in the target system, without waiting for its processing to be completed. Use PERFORMING and CALLING to specify callback routines for the takeover of events when the remotely called function is terminated. For func and dest, character-type data objects are expected.

If no destination is specified, the destination "NONE" is used implicitly. When using the destination "NONE," a new main mode is opened for the current user session. The asynchronous RFC does not support communication with external systems or programs in other programming languages.

For task, you must specify a character-type data object which contains a task identifier for the called remote function module, which can be up to eight characters long and chosen at will. This task ID should be unique for each call; it is passed to the callback routines to identify the function. Every task ID defines its own RFC connection with its own context, so that the global data of the respective function group can be accessed for repeated calls of function modules of the same task ID, provided that the connection still stands (see Section 39.2.2.1).

Note

You cannot exceed the maximum number of six main modes in the dialog processing. Otherwise, an error message is triggered.

Parameter Transfer

Syntax of *parameter list*

```
...  [EXPORTING   p1 = a1 p2 = a2 ...]
     [CHANGING    p1 = a1 p2 = a2 ...]
     [TABLES      t1 = itab1 t2 = itab2 ...]
     [EXCEPTIONS  [exc1 = n1 exc2 = n2 ...]
                  [system_failure = ns [MESSAGE smess]]
                  [communication_failure = nc [MESSAGE cmess]]
                  [OTHERS = n_others]] ...
```

These additions are used to assign actual parameters to formal parameters of the function module and return values to exceptions that are not class-based (see Section 15.4). The additions have the same meaning as in the synchronous RFC (see Section 39.2.1), except that values with IMPORTING cannot be imported and actual parameters specified by CHANGING can be transferred but cannot be imported.

Parallel processing

Syntax

```
...  DESTINATION IN GROUP {group|DEFAULT} ...
```

If you specify IN GROUP as the destination, you can execute several function modules in parallel on a predefined group of application servers of the current SAP system.

For group, you must specify a data object of type RZLLI_APCL from the ABAP Dictionary, which either contains the name of an RFC server group created in transaction RZ12 or is initial. When specifying DEFAULT or if group is initial, all currently available application servers of the current SAP system are used as the group. Within a program, you are only allowed to use one single RFC server group. At the first asynchronous RFC with the addition IN GROUP, the specified RFC server group is initialized. At each asynchronous RFC with the group specified, the best suited application server is automatically determined and the called function module is executed on this server.

If the function module cannot be executed on any of the application servers because not enough resources are available at present, a predefined exception RESOURCE_FAILURE is triggered to which, in addition to the other RFC exceptions described in Section 39.1.4, a return value can be assigned. With this exception, the addition MESSAGE is not allowed.

Notes

▶ The parallel processing of function modules with the addition IN GROUP uses the available resources optimally and should be chosen over self-programmed parallel processing with explicitly specified destinations.

▶ An application server used as a part of an RFC server group for parallel processing must have at least three dialog work processes, one of which is currently free. Other resources, such as requests in the queue, the number of system messages etc. are considered as well and must not exceed certain threshold values.

▶ To guarantee that only application servers with sufficient resources are accessed, we recommend that you use the addition DEFAULT with explicitly defined RFC server groups.

▶ The function modules of function group SPBT provide service functions for parallel processing. These functions include initialization of RFC server groups, determination of the used destination, and temporary removal of an application server from an RFC group.

Callback Routines

Syntax

```
... {PERFORMING subr}|{CALLING meth} ON END OF TASK ...
```

Use this addition to specify either a subroutine subr or, as of Release 6.20 (Kernel Patch 623), a method meth as the callback routine executed after terminating the asynchronously called function module. For subr, you must directly specify a subroutine of the same program. For meth, you can enter the same specifications as for the general method call (see Section 11.2.2.1).

The specified subroutine subr can have exactly one USING parameter (see Section 4.2.3.1) of type clike. The method meth must be public and can have only one non-optional input parameter p_task of the type clike. At the call, the RFC interface fills this parameter with the task ID of the remotely called function which was specified at the call in task. In the subroutine subr or in the method meth, you can use the statement RECEIVE to receive the results of the remote function (see Section 39.2.2.1). In the callback routine, you are not allowed to execute statements that interrupt the program execution or terminate an SAP LUW. Statements for list output (see Chapter 27) are not executed.

In order to execute the callback routine, the calling program must still exist in its internal mode when the remote function is terminated. It is then executed at the next change of the work process (see Section 33.2.1.1). If the program was terminated or lies on the stack as a part of a call chain, the callback routine is not executed. Use the statement WAIT to stop the program execution until certain or all callback routines have been executed (see Section 39.2.2.2).

Note

A callback routine is not executed if the asynchronous call of a function module was stopped with an exception.

39.2.2.1 Receiving Results

```
RECEIVE
```

Receiving the results of an asynchronously called function module.

Syntax

```
RECEIVE RESULTS FROM FUNCTION func
                           parameter_list
                           [KEEPING TASK].
```

You can use this statement in a callback routine specified in an asynchronous RFC (see Section 39.2.2) to receive output parameters of an asynchronously called function func and to assign return values to exceptions in the parameter list parameter_list.

Use the addition KEEPING TASK to keep the asynchronous RFC connection and thus the context of the called function module. At a new call with the same task identifier, the same global data of the function group is addressed. Without the KEEPING TASK addition, an asynchronous RFC connection is closed after the execution of the remote function or after receiving the results.

Notes

▶ You should use the addition KEEPING TASK only if you need the context of the called function module for other function calls.

▶ If a function module is started several times in a row using asynchronous RFC, the sequence of the execution is not fixed but depends on the system availability.

▶ The RECEIVE statement triggers a database commit.

Parameter Transfer

Syntax of *parameter_list*

```
...  [IMPORTING   p1 = a1 p2 = a2 ...]
     [CHANGING    p1 = a1 p2 = a2 ...]
     [TABLES      t1 = itab1 t2 = itab2 ...]
     [EXCEPTIONS  [exc1 = n1 exc2 = n2 ...]
                  [system_failure = ns [MESSAGE smess]]
                  [communication_
failure = nc [MESSAGE cmess]]
                  [OTHERS = n_others]] ...
```

With these additions, the specified formal parameters of the function module specified in func are passed to the current parameter of the callback routine in the calling program. Return values are assigned to non-class-based exceptions (see Section 15.4). The meaning of the additions is the same as in synchronous RFC (see Section 39.2.1), but values are only adopted by current parameters specified using CHANGING and not passed on by them. In particular, return values can be assigned to the special exceptions SYSTEM_FAILURE and COMMUNICATION_FAILURE described in Section 39.1.4. If no exception occurs, RECEIVE sets the content of sy-subrc to 0.

39.2.2.2 Interrupting the Program

```
WAIT
```

Interruption of the program after calling an asynchronous function module.

Syntax

```
WAIT UNTIL log_exp [UP TO sec SECONDS].
```

This variant of the statement WAIT is designed only for use by an asynchronous RFC with callback routines (see Section 39.2.2). It interrupts the program execution for as long as the result of the logical expression log_exp is incorrect. For log_exp, an arbitrary logical expression can be specified (see Chapter 13).

If the result of log_exp is incorrect, the program waits until a callback routine of a previous function that was called asynchronously was executed and then checks the logical expression again. If the result of the logical expression is true or if the callback routines of all functions called asynchronously beforehand have been executed, the program execution is continued with the statement following the statement WAIT.

With the specification UP TO, the program interruption is limited to no longer than the number of seconds specified in sec. For sec, a data object of type f is expected that must contain the positive number. At the end of the specified time, by the latest, the program execution is continued with the statement following the statement WAIT.

Return Values

sy-subrc	Meaning
0	The logical condition log_exp was fulfilled.
4	No asynchronous function calls exist.
8	With the specification of the addition UP TO, the maximum time was exceeded.

Notes

▶ The statement WAIT causes a change in the work process, which is linked to rolling out and rolling in all loaded programs. For this reason, the time in sec should not be less than one second, so as not to load the system with a too-frequent change of the work process.

▶ Each time the statement WAIT is used, a database commit is issued (see Section 33.2.1.1). For this reason, WAIT must not be used between Open SQL statements that open or close a database cursor.

▶ There is also a variant of the statement WAIT that can be used independently of the asynchronous RFC. It is described in Section 14.4.

39.2.3 Transactional Remote Function Call

Syntax

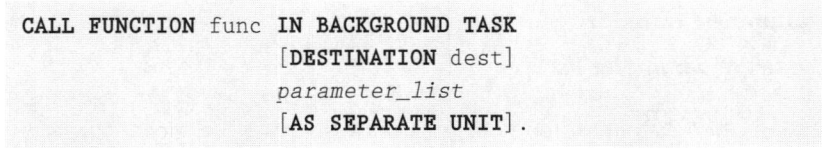

```
CALL FUNCTION func IN BACKGROUND TASK
                [DESTINATION dest]
                parameter_list
                [AS SEPARATE UNIT].
```

Transactional call of a remote-enabled function module specified in func using the RFC interface. Use the addition DESTINATION to specify a single destination in dest (see Section 39.1.2). If you do not specify the destination, the destination "NONE" is used implicitly. For func and dest, character-type data objects are expected.

For transactional calls, the name of the called function is registered together with the destination and the actual parameters for the current SAP LUW passed in the `parameter_list` in the database tables ARFC-SSTATE and ARFCSDATA of the current SAP system. This occurs under a unique transaction ID (short TID, stored in a structure of type ARFCTID from the ABAP Dictionary, to be displayed with transaction SM58). After the registration, the program execution is resumed after the `CALL FUNC-TION` statement.

The function modules registered for the current SAP LUW are started at the `COMMIT WORK` statement (see Section 33.3.1) in the sequence in which they were registered. The statement `ROLLBACK WORK` deletes all previous registrations of the current SAP LUW (see Section 33.3.2).

Use the addition `AS SEPARATE UNIT` to execute the respective function module in an individual context in which the global data of the function group is not influenced by the previous calls. Every function module registered with the addition `AS SEPARATE UNIT` receives its own transaction ID. Without the `AS SEPARATE UNIT` addition, the description from Section 39.1.3 applies to the context of the called function modules, so that access to the global data of a function group is shared, provided that several calls of function modules of the same function group use the same destination.

If the specified destination is not available for `COMMIT WORK`, an executable program called RSARFCSE is started in the background processing. By default, the program tries every 15 minutes up to 30 times to start the function modules registered for an SAP LUW in their destination. To change these parameters, use transaction SM59. If the destination does not become available within the given time, this is noted in the database table ARFCSDATA as an entry "CPICERR". The entry in the database table ARFCSSTATE is deleted by default after eight days.

Parameter Transfer

Syntax of *parameter list*

```
...  [EXPORTING  p1 = a1 p2 = a2... ]
     [TABLES     t1 = itab1 t2 = itab2 ...]  ...
```

These additions are used to assign actual parameters to the formal parameters of the function module. The additions have the same meaning as in the synchronous RFC (see Section 39.2.1), except that the values with `IMPORTING` and `CHANGING` cannot be adopted, and return values cannot be assigned to non-class-based exceptions (see Section 15.4).

Notes

▶ Use the function module ID_OF_BACKGROUNDTASK to find out the transaction ID (TID) of the current SAP LUW after a transactional RFC.

▶ The transactional RFC (tRFC) is designed to realize LUWs in distributed environments (a typical application is ALE). Keep in mind that the execution of the function modules within a transaction ID is predefined, but the sequence of the LUWs in the RFC servers does not necessarily correspond to the sequence of the SAP LUWs in the RFC client. To extend the serialization to the RFC servers, extend the tRFC to queued RFC (qRFC). To do this, call the function module TRFC_SET_QUEUE_NAME before a transactional RFC.

39.2.4 Remote Function Call Example

Parallel asynchronous processing of the function module RFC_SYSTEM_INFO using asynchronous remote function calls. Ten calls take place, each of which runs with a different task name name in a separate work process. In the callback routine rfc_info, the completed function modules are counted and information about the target system is received.

By using the GROUP DEFAULT addition, the execution is spread across all application servers in the current system. If no free work process is available after at least one successful call, the execution of the program is interrupted until all function modules that were started up to this point are completed. This interruption is limited to a maximum of five seconds.

After all function modules have been started, the system waits until all callback routines have been executed. The internal table task_list filled there is then displayed. The output shows the order in which the individual tasks were completed and on which application server they were executed.

```
TYPES: BEGIN OF task_type,
         name    TYPE string,
         dest    TYPE string,
       END OF task_type.

DATA: snd_jobs   TYPE i,
      rcv_jobs   TYPE i,
      exc_flag   TYPE i,
      info       TYPE rfcsi,
      mess       TYPE c LENGTH 80,
      indx       TYPE c LENGTH 4,
      name       TYPE c LENGTH 8,
```

```
        task_list TYPE STANDARD TABLE OF task_type,
        task_wa   TYPE task_type.

DO 10 TIMES.
  indx = sy-index.
  CONCATENATE 'Task' indx INTO name.
  CALL FUNCTION 'RFC_SYSTEM_INFO'
    STARTING NEW TASK name
    DESTINATION IN GROUP DEFAULT
    PERFORMING rfc_info ON END OF TASK
    EXCEPTIONS
      system_failure        = 1  MESSAGE mess
      communication_failure = 2  MESSAGE mess
      resource_failure      = 3.
  CASE sy-subrc.
    WHEN 0.
      snd_jobs = snd_jobs + 1.
    WHEN 1 OR 2.
      MESSAGE mess TYPE 'I'.
    WHEN 3.
      IF snd_jobs >= 1 AND
         exc_flag = 0.
        exc_flag = 1.
        WAIT UNTIL rcv_jobs > = snd_jobs
             UP TO 5 SECONDS.
      ENDIF.
      IF sy-subrc = 0.
        exc_flag = 0.
      ELSE.
        MESSAGE 'Resource failure' TYPE 'I'.
      ENDIF.
    WHEN OTHERS.
      MESSAGE 'Other error' TYPE 'I'.
  ENDCASE.
ENDDO.

WAIT UNTIL rcv_jobs >= snd_jobs.

LOOP AT task_list INTO task_wa.
  WRITE: / task_wa-name, task_wa-dest.
ENDLOOP.

FORM rfc_info USING name.
  task_wa-name = name.
  rcv_jobs = rcv_jobs + 1.
  RECEIVE RESULTS FROM FUNCTION 'RFC_SYSTEM_INFO'
```

```
      IMPORTING
        rfcsi_export = info
      EXCEPTIONS
        system_failure       = 1 MESSAGE mess
        communication_failure = 2 MESSAGE mess.
   IF sy-subrc = 0.
     task_wa-dest = info-rfcdest.
   ELSE.
     task_wa-dest = mess.
   ENDIF.
   APPEND task_wa TO task_list.
ENDFORM.
```

40 ABAP and XML

With the `CALL TRANSFORMATION` statement (see Section 40.4), you can convert ABAP data into the XML format and vice versa. Transformation programs of the following types are called: XSL transformations or Simple Transformations (as of Release 6.40).

40.1 XSL Transformations

An XSL transformation is a program in the repository that is written in XSLT (Extensible Stylesheet Language Transformation program) and used for the transformation of XML documents. When calling an XSL transformation using the `CALL TRANSFORMATION` statement, you can also directly convert ABAP data into XML and vice versa. For this purpose, a serialization or de-serialization is carried out implicitly.

In the case of transformations that use ABAP data as a source, the ABAP data is first serialized into a canonical XML representation (asXML, see 40.2), which then serves as the actual source for the XSL transformation. In the case of transformations that expect ABAP data as a result, the result of the XSL transformation is de-serialized into the ABAP data. As a prerequisite for de-serialization is the result must take the form of a canonical XML representation.

As of Release 6.10, the ABAP runtime environment contains an XSLT processor for executing the transformations. It supports almost all XSLT statements and provides enhancements (so-called extension instructions) such as the possibility to call ABAP methods from XSLT programs.

40.1.1 XSL Transformations in the Repository

XSL transformations that can be called with a `CALL TRANSFORMATION` statement must exist in the repository as XSLT programs. To create and edit XSLT programs in the Object Navigator in the ABAP Workbench, choose **Edit Object · More ... · Transformation** (or **XSLT program** before Release 6.40 and **XSL transformation** before Release 6.20) and choose XSLT program.

SAP delivers the identity transformation under the name ID. If you perform an identity transformation from XML to XML, the result is a copy of the source document. If you perform an identity transformation from ABAP to XML, this results in a canonical XML representation (asXML) of the ABAP data (explicit serialization). An identity transformation from

XML to ABAP transforms a canonical XML representation to ABAP data (explicit de-serialization).

40.2   Canonical XML Representation

The canonical XML representation is the format of an XML document that results from a serialization of ABAP data or that is required for a de-serialization. This format is also referred to as asXML (ABAP Serialization XML). The canonical XML representation supports all ABAP data types.

The asXML format is significant in the following cases:

▶ If you have written any XSL transformations of ABAP data into an XML format, the asXML format of the serialization result must be known.

▶ If you want to create external XML documents that can be de-serialized into ABAP data, they must be in an asXML format.

Note
The asXML format of serialized ABAP data or objects can be created and examined using the predefined identity transformation ID.

40.2.1   General asXML Format

The following lines show the general format of the canonical XML representation[1] without the XML header; line breaks and indents are included for clarification purposes only. A detailed example can be found in Section 40.5.

```
<asx:abap version = "1.0"
          xmlns:asx = "http://www.sap.com/abapxml">
  <asx:values>
    <bn1>...</bn1>
    ...
    <bnn>...</bnn>
  </asx:values>
  <asx:heap>
    ...
  </asx:heap>
</asx:abap>
```

The root element of an asXML documents is abap in the namespace (XML Namespace) http://www.sap.com/abapxml. The optional attribute ver-

---

1   The asXML format is a general format that cannot be completely defined with an XML pattern. The reason for this is that various ABAP types are referred to.

sion currently always has the value "1.0" and is intended for future enhancements of asXML. The root element `abap` must contain the sub-element `values` of the same namespace. The sub-elements `bni` of `values` represent the ABAP data objects that are specified as `e1`, `e2`, ... in the `source` addition to the `CALL TRANSFORMATION` statement or as `f1`, `f2`, ... in the `result` addition (see Section 40.4). The names of the elements `bn1`, `bn2`, ... are the names specified there in uppercase. The text contents of the elements `<bn1>...</bn1>` (or `<bn1 ... />`,), ... represent the contents of all named data objects with the exception of reference variables. The latter are represented by elements without text contents but with a special attribute (see Section 40.2.3.1). The optional element `heap` contains the contents of referenced anonymous data objects and objects (see Sections 40.2.3.2 and 40.2.3.3).

With the exception of the special cases in Table 40.1, the names of the element `bn1`, `bn2`, ... contain only capital letters. The names `bn1`, `bn2`, ... (or components of structures or objects, see Sections 40.2.2.2 and 40.2.2.3) specified in the `source` and `result` additions to the `CALL TRANSFORMATION` statement can only be used as (uppercase) names for XML elements if they consist solely of the characters "a" to "z", "A" to "Z", "0" to "9", or "_"; the first character must be a letter or "_". Other characters are replaced according to Table 40.1.

Character in the ABAP name	Replacement character in the XML name
ASCII character other than "a" to "z," "A" to "Z," "0" to "9," or "_" and character "0" to "9" as first character.	"_--hex(c)," where hex(c) is the two-digit hexadecimal representation of the ASCII code of the character c.
"/"	"_"
"xml" as the first three characters in any combination of uppercase and lowercase	"x-ml" in a corresponding combination of uppercase and lowercase

Table 40.1 Replacement Rules for Charaters in ABAP Names

40.2.2 asXML Format for Named Data Objects with the Exception of Reference Variables

Named data objects, except for reference variables, are represented as the text contents of the elements `<bn1>...</bn1>`, ... The representation of named data objects in `<bn1>...</bn1>`, ... depends on the relevant ABAP data type.

40.2.2.1 Elementary Data Types

The asXML representation of elementary data objects with predefined ABAP types from Table 5.2 corresponds to the canonical representation of XML pattern data types (http://www.w3.org/TR/xmlschema-2/#built-in-datatypes, see Table 40.2), where date and time are represented according to ISO-8601, and binary data is represented using Base 64 encoding.

ABAP type	ABAP example	XML pattern type	XML example
c	" Hi"	string	" Hi"
d	"20020204"	date	"2002-02-04"
f	-3.140...0E+02	double	"-3.14E2"
i, b, s	-123	int, unsignedByte, short	"-123"
n	"001234"	string (pattern [0-9]+)	"001234"
p	-1.23	decimal	"-1.23"
string	" Hello "	string	" Hello "
t	"201501"	time	"20:15:01"
x	"ABCDEF"	base64Binary	"q83v"
xstring	"456789AB"	base64Binary	"RweJqw=="

Table 40.2 Canonical XML Representation (asXML) of Predefined ABAP Types

40.2.2.2 Structures

In asXML, the components of an ABAP structure are represented as a sequence of sub-elements of the structure element. The content of each sub-element corresponds to the canonical representation of the component value. The name of each sub-element is the name of the corresponding component. In the case of serialization, the sub-elements are represented in the order of the components in the structure. When the asXML representation of a structure is de-serialized, the order of the sub-elements is irrelevant and excess XML elements are ignored. Components of the structure for which there is no sub-element remain initial.

40.2.2.3 Internal Tables

In asXML, the rows of an internal table are represented as a a sequence of sub-elements of the table element. The content of each sub-element corresponds to the canonical representation of the row value. The name of a sub-element is irrelevant. If the canonical XML representation is created by serialization and the row type refers to the ABAP Dictionary, the name there is used; otherwise, the name `item` is used. Any table kind is allowed. During serialization, no information about the table kind is transferred to the XML document. If the target field of an XSL transformation is a sorted table, the rows are sorted accordingly during de-serialization.

40.2.3 asXML Format for Reference Variables and Referenced Objects

Anonymous data objects and instances of classes (objects) are addressed in ABAP exclusively by means of references in reference variables. The corresponding asXML format is made up of sub-elements of `values` for named reference variables (see Section 40.2.3.1) and of sub-elements of `heap` (see Sections 40.2.3.2 and 40.2.3.3) for the referenced objects. The link between the reference elements and the object elements is set up by means of an XML reference mechanism, whereby a referenced object in the same XML document is identified with a key. The dynamic type of the reference variables for the object elements under `heap` is specified when serialization takes place, so that de-serialization is unambiguous.

40.2.3.1 Named Reference Variables

A named reference variable is the only attribute of the corresponding sub-element of `values` that is displayed without textual content. An attribute of a reference variable has the name `href` and the content "#key", where `key` is the unique key of an object in the element `heap`. An element of an initial reference does not have a `href` attribute or any other content. During serialization, the ABAP runtime environment sets the key `key`; any key is possible for de-serialization.

40.2.3.2 Anonymous Data Objects

An anonymous data object that is a sub-element of `heap` is displayed as follows:

```
<asx:heap xmlns:nspace ...>
  <type id = "key" attr="...">...</type>
</asx:heap>
```

The value of a sub-element of this kind is displayed in the asXML display for named data objects (see Table 40.2) or for named reference variables (see Section 40.2.3.1). If the anonymous data object itself is a non-initial reference variable, it references a further element of heap according to the rules above. The element name type is the data type of the data object (or the dynamic type of the reference variables) specified as the XML schema type name from the name range nspace (see Table 40.3). Attributes attr may define technical characteristics of the type. The mandatory attribute attri contains the unique key key of the element, which is used to reference it from the display of the corresponding reference variables in values or heap.

The XML schema type name is constructed according to the following hierarchy:

1. If the data type of the data object is defined in the ABAP Dictionary, the XML schema type name is the name of the data type from the ABAP Dictionary in the corresponding name range (see Table 40.3).

2. If the data type is an elementary ABAP type, the XML schema type name is specified in Table 40.4.

3. If the data type is defined as a component of a global or local class or interface, the XML schema type name comprises the name of the class or interface and the name of the data type separated by a period (.). The corresponding name range (see Table 40.3) indicates whether the data type is a component of a global or local class or of an interface.

4. If the data type is a generic reference type defined with REF TO data or REF TO object, the XML schema type name is refData or refObject. Both of these have the name range http://www.sap.com/abapxml/types/built-in.

5. Otherwise, the XML schema type name is the name of a data type defined with TYPES and the corresponding name range (see Table 40.3) indicates where the data type is defined.

Before an XML schema type name can be constructed, the data type of the data object must have a name that can be used statically. If the data type only exists as a property of a data object and therefore only has a technical name (compare Section 6.1.4), a treatable exception takes place during serialization.

Table 40.3 indicates the name ranges for the XML schema type names; types in the first column stand for http://www.sap.com/abapxml/types. The name ranges indicate where a data type is defined. Characters other than "a" to "z," "A" to "Z," "0" to "9," "_" or "-" are displayed as "!hex(c)" in the names prg, cpool, fpool, tpool, meth, func, form and class, where hex(c) is the two-character hexadecimal display of the ASCII code for the character "c".

Name range	Location of definition
types/dictionary	ABAP Dictionary
types/program/prg	ABAP program prg
types/class-pool/cpool	Class pool cpool
types/type-pool/tpool	Type group tpool
types/function-pool/fpool	Function group fpool
types/function/func	Function module func
types/program.form/prg/frm	Subroutine frm in program prg
types/function-pool.form/fpool/frm	Subroutine frm in function group fpool
types/method/class/meth	Method meth of a global class class
types/program.method/prg/class/meth	Method meth of a local class class in program prg
types/class-pool.method/cpool/class/meth	Method meth of a local class class in a class pool cpool
types/function-pool.method/fpool/class/meth	Method meth of a local class class in function group fpool

Table 40.3 Name ranges for XML schema type names, whereby types in the first column stands for http://www.sap.com/abapxml/types

The following table lists the XML schema type names for elementary ABAP types. These are slightly different from the canonical XML schema data types from Table 40.2, since the data type of anonymous data objects must be specified in full. The name ranges nspace for the elementary ABAP types for anonymous data objects are either xsd="http://www.w3.org/2001/XMLSchema" for general schema types or abap="http://www.sap.com/abapxml/types/built-in" for special ABAP schema types for which some technical attributes must be specified.

ABAP type	XML schema type name	Attributes
c	abap:string	maxLength
d	abap:date	–
f	xsd:double	–

Table 40.4 XML Schema Type Names for Elementary ABAP Types

ABAP type	XML schema type name	Attributes
i, b, s	xsd:int, xsd:unsigned Byte, xsd:short	—
n	abap:digits	maxLength
p	abap:decimal	totalDigits, fractionDigits
string	xsd:string	—
t	abap:time	—
x	abap:base64Binary	maxLength
xstring	xsd:base64Binary	—

Table 40.4 XML Schema Type Names for Elementary ABAP Types (cont.)

The attribute maxLength defines the length for ABAP types with a generic length. The XML schema type abap:digits restricts the value range for an element to digits. The XML schema type abap:decimal specifies the length and fractional portions via the attributes totalDigits and frac-tionDigits. The length specification totalDigits defines the number of places between 1 and 31. In ABAP programs, the length of data objects of the type p is specified in bytes and the number of decimal places is calculated from 2×len-1 (see Table 5.2). This means that the value of total-Digits is always odd in serialization. During de-serialization, an even value of totalDigits is implicitly increased by one.

Instances of Classes

The instance of a class (object) as a sub-element of heap is displayed as follows:

```
<asx:heap xmlns:nspace ...>
   <class id = "key">
     <part classVersion = "...">
       <name>...</name>
     </part>
     ...
   </class>
 </asx:heap>
```

The element name class is the XML schema type name of the class for the object (or the dynamic type of the reference variables) from the name range nspace (see Table 40.5) in block capitals. The mandatory attribute id contains the unique key key of the element, which is used to reference it when the corresponding reference variables are displayed in values.

The sub-elements `<part>`...`</part>` contain the values of the instance attributes for individual object parts as sub-elements `<name>`...`</name>`. The individual object parts are defined by the classes in the current inheritance hierarchy that can be serialized (see below).

The name range for the class name indicates where the class is defined. Table 40.5 lists the possible name ranges; `classes` in the first column stands for `http://www.sap.com/apapxml/classes`. The substitution rule for the name ranges in Table 40.3 also applies to the names `prg`, `cpool` and `fpool`.

Name range	Location of definition
classes/global	Class library
classes/program/prg	Program prg
classes/class-pool/cpool	Class pool cpool
classes/function-pool/fpool	Function group fpool

Table 40.5 Name ranges for class names, whereby classes in the first column stands for http://www.sap.com/abapxml/classes

The values of the values of a class instance that can be serialized (instance attributes or output parameters for a special method, see below) are displayed as the content or as an attribute of `<name>`...`</name>` in the asXML display for named data objects (see Table 40.2) or for reference variables, wherein `name` is the name of an instance attribute or an output parameter in block capitals. If the object is an interface attribute, the name is preceded by the name of the interface separated by a period (.) in order to distinguish it from another class attribute of the same name. The substitution rules from Table 40.1 apply for the names.

The values of a class instance that can be serialized are defined by implementing the system interface IF_SERIALIZABLE_OBJECT in the class (see Section B.2). If the class does not implement the interface IF_SERIALIZABLE_OBJECT, the element `class` does not contain any sub-elements. All the instance attributes of a class in which the interface IF_SERIALIZABLE_OBJECT is implemented are serialized and de-serialized to the interface by default. You can change this behavior by declaring special utility methods (see below). Static attributes are neither taken into account during serialization nor during de-serialization (with the exception of the special constant SERIALIZABLE_CLASS_VERSION, see below).

Standard Behavior

If the class implements the interface IF_SERIALIZABLE_OBJECT, the element `<class>...</class>` contains at least one subelement `<part>...</part>`. These sub-elements correspond to individual object parts that can be serialized and contain the presentations of the instance attributes for the corresponding object part in an asXML format. An object part is defined by the class in which instance attributes are declared or in which an interface containing instance attributes is integrated. A object class that can be serialized contains an object part for itself as well as object parts for all superclasses in the current path in the inheritance tree, up to and including the class that implements the interface IF_SERIALIZABLE_OBJECT. The name `part` is the name of the class in question. If it is a local class, its name is preceded by the prefix `local` separated by a period (.) to distinguish it from a global class of the same name. Object parts of superclasses in which the interface IF_ SERIALIZABLE_OBJECT is not implemented cannot be serialized and do not have a corresponding sub-object `part`. This means that a class in which the interface IF_SERIALIZABLE_OBJECT is not implemented (neither in the class itself nor in a superclass) creates a blank XML element `class` during serialization.

During serialization, the XML elements `part` of the object parts are created from the superclasses to the subclasses and the XML elements of the instance attributes are created as standard in the order in which they are declared in the class.

De-serialization creates an object in the corresponding class but the instance constructor is not executed. All instance attributes have their initial values or the start values specified with the `VALUE` addition for the `DATA` statement after the object creation. The values of the corresponding XML elements are entered in the instance attributes by default; the order of the object parts and attributes is irrelevant. Instance attributes without a corresponding XML element retain their value. Excess XML elements are ignored if they do not belong to a name range; otherwise, they create a treatable exception. When an element without `part` sub-elements is de-serialized, the system does not create an object but initializes the target reference variable.

If a class implements the interface IF_SERIALIZABLE_OBJECT, you can declare the private constant SERIALIZABLE_CLASS_VERSION of the type `i` in each object part; that is, each class involved in the inheritance tree. During serialization, the value of the constant is assigned to the attribute `classVersion` of the XML element `part`. A treatable exception is created during de-serialization by default if the value of the attribute does not match the value of the constant in the class specified. An object can only be de-serialized if the values match or if there is neither an attribute nor a constant. You can change this system behavior by declaring special utility methods.

Modified Behavior

By default, all the instance attributes for an object part are serialized as standard regardless of their visibility, and the version of the class is checked. To change this behavior, you can declare and implement the instance methods SERIALIZE_HELPER and DESERIALIZE_HELPER in the relevant class for each object part. These methods can only be declared as private instance methods in classes that implement the interface IF_SERIALIZABLE_OBJECT. If you declare one of the methods, you must also declare the other and the interface must be defined as follows for the syntax check:

▶ The method SERIALIZE_HELPER can only have output parameters, and the method DESERIALIZE_HELPER can only have input parameters with non-generic typing.

▶ There must be an input parameter of the method DESERIALIZE_HELPER with the same name for each output parameter of the method SERIALIZE_HELPER with the same typing. Additional input parameters for the method DESERIALIZE_HELPER must be optional.

▶ The method SERIALIZE_HELPER must not have an output parameter with the name SERIALIZABLE_CLASS_VERSION, and the method DESERIALIZE_HELPER can have an optional input parameter of this name that is of type `i`. This parameter is supplied with the value of the attribute `classVersion` of the element `part` during de-serialization, and the standard check on the version (see above) is skipped.

If the methods SERIALIZE_HELPER and DESERIALIZE_HELPER are declared in an object part, the instance attributes of the object part are not serialized and de-serialized. Instead, the method SERIALIZE_HELPER is executed during serialization and the values of all the output parameters are written in the asXML format as sub-elements to the corresponding element `part` in the specified order. Here, the name of a sub-element is the name of the corresponding output parameter in block capitals. The method DESERIALIZE_HELPER is called during de-serialization and the values of the sub-elements for the corresponding element `part` are transferred to the input parameters of the method with the same names. The order in which they appear is irrelevant and excess XML elements are ignored.

40.3 Simple Transformations

Simple Transformations (ST) is an SAP programming language for describing transformations between ABAP data and XML formats. ST is restricted to the two modes of serialization (ABAP to XML) and de-serialization (XML to ABAP) of ABAP data, which are most important for data integration. Like in the more general XSLT, transformations from ABAP to ABAP and XML to XML are not possible in ST.

In comparison with XSLT, the main advantages of ST programs are as follows:

▶ ST programs are declarative and thus easier to read.
▶ ST programs only have serial access to the XML data and are therefore very efficient even with large data volumes.
▶ ST programs describe serialization and de-serialization simultaneously; that is, ABAP data serialized in XML with ST can also be de-serialized with the same ST program.

Simple Transformations that can be called using CALL TRANSFORMATION must be in the repository. In the Object Navigator of the ABAP Workbench, you can create and edit ST programs by choosing **Edit Object · More · Transformation** followed by **Simple Transformation**.

A detailed description of the language ST goes beyond the scope of this ABAP reference. For more information, please turn to the corresponding online help. You can find an introductory example in Section 40.6.

40.4 Calling an XSL or ST Transformation

CALL TRANSFORMATION

Calling an XSLT or ST program.

Syntax

```
CALL TRANSFORMATION transformation
                    [PARAMETERS parameters]
                    [OBJECTS objects]
```

```
[OPTIONS options]
SOURCE source
RESULT result.
```

This statement calls the specified XSL transformation (XSLT) or a simple transformation (ST, as of Release 6.40). The source of the transformation is specified after SOURCE, and the result is stored as specified after RESULT. Use PARAMETERS and OBJECTS to pass parameters to the transformation. Possible transformation types are:

▶ From XML to XML (only for XSLT)

▶ From XML to ABAP (for XSLT and ST)

▶ From ABAP to XML (for XSLT and ST)

▶ From ABAP to ABAP (only for XSLT)

The last two types are available only as of Release 6.20.

Treatable Exceptions

The common superclass of all exception classes for CALL TRANSFORMA-TION is CX_TRANSFORMATION_ERROR (as of Release 6.40). The corresponding runtime errors cannot be caught.

Exceptions with XSL-Transformations

All exception classes for XSL transformations are subclasses of CX_XSLT_EXCEPTION.

If an error occurs when passing an XML document or if another error is reported by the XSLT processor, an exception defined by the class CX_XSLT_RUNTIME_ERROR is triggered. If the calling of an ABAP method from the XSLT program leads to an error, an exception defined by the class CX_XSLT_CALL_ERROR is triggered, whereby the attribute PREVI-OUS points to the exception object of the original error.

If an XML document does not have the asXML format during the de-serialization, an exception defined by the class CX_XSLT_FORMAT_ERROR is triggered, where the attribute TREE_POSITION contains the error position. If, during serialization or de-serialization, invalid values or data types occur, exceptions defined by the classes CX_XSLT_SERIALIZATION_ERROR or CX_XSLT_DESERIALIZATION_ERROR are triggered, where the attribute PREVIOUS (if required) points to the exception object of the original error. The attribute TREE_POSITION contains the error position during de-serialization.

Exceptions with Simple Transformations

All exception classes for simple transformations are subclasses of CX_ST_ERROR.

40.4.1 Specifying the Transformation

Syntax of *transformation*

```
... trans | (name) ...
```

The name of the transformation can be specified either directly as `trans` or as a content of a character-type data object `name` in brackets. The specified transformation must exist as a XSLT program or as a simple transformation in the repository.

40.4.2 Transformation Source

Syntax of *source*

```
... { XML sxml }
  | {{bn1 = e1 bn2 = e2 ...}|(stab)} ...
```

40.4.2.1 Transformation of an XML Document

When you specify `XML sxml`, the XML document contained in `xsml` is transformed in such a way that `sxml` can have one of the following forms:

- ▶ Data object of type `string` and `xstring` or as a standard table with flat character-type row type
- ▶ Interface reference variable of type IF_IXML_ISTREAM which points to an iXML input stream (only for XSLT)
- ▶ Interface reference variable of type IF_IXML_NODE which points to an iXML nodeset (only for XSLT)
- ▶ Class reference variable of type CL_FX_READER, which points to an XML reader (only for ST)

Note

The interfaces IF_IXML_ISTREAM and IF_IXML_NODE are components of the "Stream" and "DOM" packages of the iXML Library delivered by SAP.

40.4.2.2 Transformation of ABAP Data

Use `bn1 = e1, bn2 = e2, ...` or `(stab)` to specify the ABAP data `e1, e2, ...` to be transformed.

▶ When calling an XSLT program, the ABAP data are serialized into the canonical XML representation, which is then used as source of the XSL transformation. Use `bn1, bn2, ...` to specify the names of the XML elements meant to represent the ABAP data objects in the canonical XML presentation.

▶ When calling a simple transformation, the names `bn1, bn2, ...` are used in the transformation to access the ABAP data in a written way.

Instead of using a static parameter list, you also can pass the data objects dynamically as value pairs in the columns of an internal table `stab` which has the type ABAP_TRANS_SRCBIND_TAB from the ABAP type group.

The following data objects cannot be serialized and trigger a treatable exception:

▶ Data objects of type `n`, whose current content does not exclusively consist of numbers.

▶ Data objects of type `p`, whose current content does not represent a valid packed number.

▶ Data objects of type `d` and `t`, whose current content contains leading or trailing blanks and at the same time uses the separators ("-" or ":") according to ISO-8601 for the presentation.

▶ Data reference variables pointing to data objects, whose data type has only a technical name (see Section 40.2.3).

Data reference variables pointing to data objects that were not created with `CREATE DATA` are treated as initial reference variables during the serialization.

40.4.3 Result of a Transformation

Syntax of *result*

```
... { XML rxml }
  | {{bn1 = f1 bn2 = f2 ...}|(rtab)} ...
```

40.4.3.1 Transformation into an XML Document

When you specify XML rxml, a transformation into an XML is executed; the document is then placed into rxml, where rxml can be one of the following:

▶ A data object of type string and xstring or a standard table with a flat, character-type row type.

▶ An interface reference variable of type IF_IXML_OSTREAM which points to an IXML output stream (only for XSLT).

▶ An interface reference variable of type IF_IXML_DOCUMENT which points to an IXML document (only for XSLT),

▶ A class reference variable of type CL_FX_WRITER, which points to an XML writer (only for ST).

Notes

▶ The interfaces IF_IXML_OSTREAM and IF_IXML_DOCUMENT are components of the "Stream" and "DOM" packages of the iXML Library delivered by SAP.

▶ If you use the data type xstring for rxml, then the result is stored in the UTF-8 character representation. This is helpful, if the resulting XML-document is to be stored in a file (see Chapter 32).

40.4.3.2 Transformation into ABAP Data

Use bn1 = f1, bn2 = f2, ... or (rtab) to specify the ABAP target fields f1, f2, ... into which you want the XML data to be transformed.

▶ When calling an XSLT program, the result of the XSL transformation into ABAP data objects is de-serialized, provided that it is a canonical XML representation. You should use bn1, bn2, ... to specify the names of the XML elements that represent the ABAP data objects in the canonical XML representation, and use f1, f2, ... to specify the ABAP data objects of the appropriate data type into which you want to de-serialize them.

▶ When calling a simple transformation, in the transformation, the names bn1, bn2, ... are used for write access to the ABAP data.

Instead of using a static parameter list, the data objects can also be passed dynamically as value pairs in the columns of the internal table rtab, which has the type ABAP_TRANS_RESBIND_TAB of the ABAP type group.

An XML element must be convertible into the respective ABAP data objects, where instead of the usual conversion rules (see Appendix A) the following restrictions apply:

▶ De-serialization into too short data objects of data types c or n must never lead to a loss of data, except when for data type c only leading and trailing blanks are concerned and for data type n only leading zeros.

▶ Data must never be lost due to the de-serialization into a data object of data type p with too few decimal places.

▶ Data must never be lost due to the de-serialization into a too short data object of data type x.

▶ Structures cannot be converted into elementary data objects.

If an XML element cannot be converted into the ABAP data object, a treatable exception is triggered.

When de-serializing into a reference variable, this variable must be the same as or more general than the dynamic type of the object stored in the XML document. The allocated ABAP objects or instances of a class are created during the de-serialization.

40.4.4 Parameters for an XSL Transformation

Syntax of *parameters*

```
... {p1 = e1 p2 = e2 ...}|(ptab) ...
```

Use this addition to pass ABAP data objects e1, e2, ... as parameters p1, p2, ... to an XSL transformation. In Release 6.10, the data objects e1, e2, ... must be character-type, as of Release 6.20 all elementary data objects and object references are allowed.

Instead of using a static parameter list, you also can pass the parameters dynamically as value pairs in the columns of the internal table ptab which has the type ABAP_TRANS_PARMBIND_TAB from the ABAP type group.

The specified parameters must be defined in the XSL transformation as input parameters as follows:

```
<xsl:param name="..." type="..."/>
```

For the attribute name, enter the parameter name in uppercase. For the optional attribute type, specify one of the type indicators string, number, `boolean`, `xstring`, `nodeset` or `object(...)`, where you must enter the name of a global ABAP class in the brackets after `object`.

If no type is specified in the XSL transformation, the data types of elementary parameters are mapped to XSL types according to Table 40.6.

ABAP Data Type	XSL Parameter Type
`c, d, n, string`	`string`
`i, s, b, f, p`	`number`
`x, xstring`	`string`, where the content is presented to the base of 64

Table 40.6 Mapping of ABAP Data Types on XSL Parameter Types

If during the XSL transformation the XSL types shown in Table 40.6 are specified explicitly, you must enter the matching elementary ABAP parameters which can be converted into the XSL type:

▶ The XSL type `boolean` expects ABAP parameters of the type `c` with the length 1. A space is interpreted as "false" and a different character is interpreted as "true."

▶ The XSL type `xstring` expects ABAP parameters of the type `x` or `xstring` and the display of the content is hexadecimal.

▶ The XSL types `nodeset` and `object` expect an object reference variable pointing to a class instance. The type `nodeset` expects appropriate object properties.

If a parameter does not match the XSL type, an untreatable exception is triggered. If a parameter defined in the XSL transformation is not passed, it is set to the default value in the transformation. A specified parameter that is not defined in the XSL transformation is ignored.

Note

The XSL types `string`, `number`, `boolean` and `nodeset` are XSL standard types, whereas `xstring` and `object` are special SAP extensions. The type `xstring` allows a hexadecimal display of byte chains instead of the presentation to the base of 64. The type `object` enables you to call ABAP methods from the XSL program.

40.4.5 Passing External Objects to an XSL Transformation

Syntax of *objects*

```
... {o1 = e1 o2 = e2 ... }|(otab) ...
```

You can use this addition to pass object references e1, e2, ... as external objects o1, o2, ... to an XSL transformation where you can call their methods.

Instead of using a static parameter list, you can also pass the objects dynamically as value pairs in the columns of the internal table otab which has the type ABAP_TRANS_OBJBIND_TAB from the ABAP type group.

Note

As of Release 6.20, the addition OBJECTS is obsolete and external objects are treated as parameters. Therefore, object references should be passed with the addition PARAMETERS (see Section 40.4.4).

40.4.6 Controlling the Transformation

Syntax of *options*

```
... a1 = e1 a2 = e2 ...
```

You can use this addition to specify the values e1, e2, ... for additional control options a1, a2, ... of the transformation. The values e1, e2, ... must be of the type c or string.

For a1, a2, ... you can specify the following values:

▶ XML_HEADER to control the output of the XML header in case of a transformation to XML and in case of storage in a data object of the type c, string or in an internal table.

Possible values	Meaning
no	No output of an XML header
without_encoding	Output of an XML header without specification of the encodings
full	Default setting, output of an XML header with specification of the encoding

▶ DATA_REFS to control the output of data references in case of a transformation from ABAP to XML.

Possible values	Meaning
no	Default for ST, no output of data references

Possible values	Meaning
heap	Default for XSLT and only possible there; output of referenced data as sub-elements of the asXML elements `<asx:heap>`.
embedded	Output of referenced data with the reference

▶ INITIAL_COMPONENTS to control the output of initial structure components in case of a transformation from ABAP to XML.

Possible values	Meaning
include	Default setting, output of initial components of structures
suppress	No output of initial components of structures

40.5 Example of an XSL Transformation

This example shows the serialization of data objects in a string `xmlstr` using the identical transformation ID. A date field `date`, a time field `time`, and a data reference variable `dref1` are serialized. The data reference variable points to an anonymous object reference variable, which in turn points to an object of the class `c2`. Objects serialized in this way can be stored persistently, for example in a data cluster. After the objects are imported from where they are stored, they are de-serialized into further data objects. Following de-serialization, `dref2` points to another anonymous reference variable, such as `dref1`. This anonymous data object and the instance of the class `c2` to which it points are generated during the de-serialization.

```
PROGRAM xmltst.

CLASS c1 DEFINITION.
  PUBLIC SECTION.
    INTERFACES if_serializable_object.
  PROTECTED SECTION.
    DATA carriers TYPE TABLE OF scarr.
ENDCLASS.

CLASS c2 DEFINITION INHERITING FROM c1.
  PUBLIC SECTION.
    METHODS constructor.
  PRIVATE SECTION.
    DATA lines TYPE i.
    METHODS: serialize_helper
```

```
                EXPORTING count TYPE i,
            deserialize_helper
                IMPORTING count TYPE i.
ENDCLASS.

CLASS c2 IMPLEMENTATION.
  METHOD constructor.
    super->constructor( ).
    SELECT * UP TO 2 ROWS
          FROM  scarr
          INTO  TABLE carriers.
  ENDMETHOD.
  METHOD serialize_helper.
    count = LINES( carriers ).
  ENDMETHOD.
  METHOD deserialize_helper.
    lines = count.
  ENDMETHOD.
ENDCLASS.

DATA: oref   TYPE REF TO object,
      dref1  LIKE REF TO oref,
      xmlstr TYPE string,
      date   TYPE d,
      time   TYPE t,
      dref2  LIKE dref1.

...

CREATE DATA dref1 LIKE oref.
CREATE OBJECT dref1->* TYPE c2.

CALL TRANSFORMATION id
                SOURCE xmldat = sy-datum
                       xmltim = sy-uzeit
                       ref    = dref1
                RESULT XML xmlstr.

EXPORT obj = xmlstr TO DATABASE indx(hk)
                ID 'OBJECT'.

...

IMPORT obj = xmlstr FROM DATABASE indx(hk) ID 'OBJECT'.

CALL TRANSFORMATION id
                SOURCE XML xmlstr
                RESULT xmldat = date
```

```
                        xmltim = time
                        ref    = dref2.
```

The XML document generated in the serialization has the content
described below. In this description, line breaks and indents have been
added. The element values contains the asXML representations of the
three transferred data objects (see Section 40.2). In the names X-MLDAT
and X-MLTIM, "xml" has been replaced according to Table 40.1. The
attribute href of the element REF uses the key "d1" to refer to the representation of the corresponding anonymous data object in the element
heap. This uses the key "o3" to refer to the representation of the instance
of the class c2, which is also in the element heap. This representation is
divided into the object parts for the classes c1 and c2. The object part for
c1 contains the representation of the double-line structured internal
table carriers. The object part for c2 contains the representation for the
output parameter count of the method SERIALIZE_HELPER.

```
<?xml version="1.0" encoding="iso-8859-1" ?>
<asx:abap xmlns:asx="http://www.sap.com/
abapxml" version="1.0">
  <asx:values>
    <X-MLDAT>2003-04-15</X-MLDAT>
    <X-MLTIM>14:57:53</X-MLTIM>
    <REF href="#d1" />
  </asx:values>
  <asx:heap
      xmlns:xsd="http://www.w3.org/2001/XMLSchema"
      xmlns:abap="http://www.sap.com/abapxml/types/built-in"
      xmlns:cls="http://www.sap.com/abapxml/classes/global"
      xmlns:dic="http://www.sap.com/abapxml/types/dictionary">
    <abap:refObject href="#o3" id="d1" />
    <prg:C2
      xmlns:prg=http://www.sap.com/abapxml/classes/program/
        XMLTST id="o3">
      <local.C1>
        <CARRIERS>
          <SCARR>
            <MANDT>000</MANDT>
            <CARRID>AA</CARRID>
            <CARRNAME>American Airlines</CARRNAME>
            <CURRCODE>USD</CURRCODE>
            <URL>http://www.aa.com</URL>
          </SCARR>
          <SCARR>
```

```
        <MANDT>000</MANDT>
        <CARRID>AB</CARRID>
        <CARRNAME>Air Berlin</CARRNAME>
        <CURRCODE>DEM</CURRCODE>
        <URL>http://www.airberlin.de</URL>
      </SCARR>
    </CARRIERS>
  </local.C1>
  <local.C2>
    <COUNT>2</CCUNT>
  </local.C2>
  </prg:C2>
  </asx:heap>
</asx:abap>
```

40.6   Simple Transformation Example

Serialization of a nested structure. In the following ABAP program section, a nested structure `struc1` is serialized to `xml_string` with the Simple Transformation ST_TRAFO and de-serialized with the same transformation.

```
DATA: BEGIN OF struc1,
        col1(10) TYPE c VALUE 'ABCDEFGHIJ',
        col2     TYPE i VALUE 111,
        BEGIN OF struc2,
          col1 TYPE d VALUE '20040126',
          col2 TYPE t VALUE '084000',
        END OF struc2,
      END OF struc1.

DATA: xml_string TYPE string,
      result LIKE struc1.

TRY.

    CALL TRANSFORMATION st_trafo
      SOURCE para = struc1
      RESULT XML xnl_string.

    ...

    CALL TRANSFORMATION st_trafo
      SOURCE XML xml_string
      RESULT para = result.

  CATCH cx_st_error.
```

```
...
```

ENDTRY.

The Simple Transformation ST_TRAFO has the following form:

```
<?sap.transform simple?>
<tt:transform template="temp"
    xmlns:tt="http://www.sap.com/transformation-templates"
    version="0.1">

  <tt:root name="PARA"/>

  <tt:template name="temp">
    <X>
      <X1>
        <tt:value ref="PARA.COL1" />
      </X1>
      <X2>
        <tt:value ref="PARA.COL2" />
      </X2>
      <X3>
        <X1>
          <tt:value ref="PARA.STRUC2.COL1" />
        </X1>
        <X2>
          <tt:value ref="PARA.STRUC2.COL2" />
        </X2>
      </X3>
    </X>
  </tt:template>

</tt:transform>
```

The transformation consists of a template `temp` that defines the structure
of the XML document and establishes relationships between value nodes
and components of the structure. The result of the transformation is as
follows (line breaks and indentations were inserted for clarification purposes):

```
<X>
  <X1>ABCDEFGHIJ</X1>
  <X2>111</X2>
  <X3>
    <X1>2004-01-26</X1>
    <X2>08:40:00</X2>
```

```
  </X3>
</X>
```

The conversion of the elementary data types is the same as for asXML (see Table 40.2). The reverse transformation generates the same content in the structure `result` as in `struc1`.

41 OLE Interface

You can use ABAP to process automation objects whose functions are available on the presentation server in the form of an OLE Automation server. Only automation objects for Windows are supported. Typical applications that offer an automation interface are Microsoft Office products Excel and Word, in which public classes and methods are found using the path **Tools · Macro · Visual Basic Editor · Object Browser**.

All automation applications that can be used by ABAP are contained in the database table TOLE, which is maintained using the transaction SOLE. This table contains the names of the classes and components supported by the ABAP runtime environment. It also contains type information for adapting different data formats. CREATE OBJECT and CALL METHOD should not be confused with the ABAP Objects statements using the same syntax. The automation command set consists of the following ABAP statements:

Statement	Section
CREATE OBJECT	41.1
CALL METHOD	41.2
GET PROPERTY	41.3
SET PROPERTY	41.4
FREE OBJECT	41.5

The statements of the automation command set are transferred from the ABAP runtime environment to the SAP GUI on the presentation server which is responsible for the actual communication with the automation server. The transfer is not direct; the statements are first buffered in an automation queue and transferred at once to the SAP GUI in a flush call. By default, a flush is triggered by the next ABAP statement that does not belong to the automation command set.

Note
For processing automation objects, you can use the more general interfaces SAP Desktop Office Integration (DOI) and Control Framework (CFW). The statement of the automation command set should only be used to access automation applications for which there is no such wrapping.

41.1 Creating an Automation Object

CREATE OBJECT

Creating an automation object.

Syntax

```
CREATE OBJECT ole class [NO FLUSH] [QUEUE-ONLY].
```

This statement creates the automation object ole of the automation class class. The object ole must have the type ole2_object which is defined in the ABAP Dictionary in the type group OLE2. When specifying the automation class class, a character-like data object is expected which contains the name of the class.

The system automatically executes an authorization check if the column AUTH_CHK of the database table TOLE contains the value "X" for the class. The authorization status can be checked with the function module AUTHORITY_CHECK_OLE.

When the addition NO FLUSH is used, the call is collected in the automation buffer until the function module FLUSH—provided for this purpose—is called, until the FREE OBJECT statement is passed, or until a change of screen is performed. The call is only then transferred to the automation server on the presentation server for asynchronous execution. Without this addition, the flush is executed, and the transfer takes place as soon as a statement that does not belong to the automation command set is reached. Note that, in the ABAP Debugger, the return values of the individual automation statements are not available until after the transfer to the presentation server.

The effect of the addition QUEUE-ONLY is that, during the flush, the created object is not transferred as a return value using methods called by CALL METHOD OF to the specified ABAP data object rc. The precondition is that the automation buffer only contains the statements CREATE OBJECT, CALL METHOD and GET PROPERTY with the addition QUEUE-ONLY. When executing the program in the ABAP Debugger, the return values are passed by default.

Return values

sy-subrc	Meaning
0	Automation object was created.
1	Communication to SAP GUI with errors.
2	Function call in SAP GUI with errors.
3	Problems with memory allocation on the presentation server.

Note

An automation object `ole` created using `CREATE OBJECT ole` must also be released by using `FREE OBJECT ole` in order to avoid memory bottlenecks and terminations of the application to be controlled.

Example

In this example, the automation object `app` is created, with access to all methods and attributes of the class APPLICATION in the MS Excel Library. This class contains methods with which, for example, an Excel document can be opened or copied.

```
TYPE-POOLS ole2.

DATA app TYPE ole2_object.

CREATE OBJECT app 'Excel.Application' NO FLUSH.
```

41.2 Calling an Automation Method

```
CALL METHOD OF
```

Calling an automation method.

Syntax

```
CALL METHOD OF ole meth [= rc]
                [EXPORTING p1 = f1 p2 = f2 ...]
                [NO FLUSH] [QUEUE-ONLY].
```

With this statement you call the method `meth` of the automation object `ole`. The automation object must be created with the special statement `CREATE OBJECT` for automation objects. The name of the method has to be specified in a character-type data object `meth`.

The return value of the external method `meth` can be stored in a data object `rc`. This data object expects, according to the called method, a character-type data type of the length 8 or a data type of the type `ole2_object` from the Type group OLE2 to be able to accept the addressed object.

With the addition `EXPORTING`, you can assign actual parameters `f1`, `f2`, ... to the input parameters `p1`, `p2`, ... of the automation method. The data type of the data objects `f1`, `f2`, ... depends on the requirements of the automation method.

The additions `NO FLUSH` und `QUEUE-ONLY` are described in the statement `CREATE OBJECT` (see Section 42.1).

Return values

sy-subrc	Meaning
0	Successful processing of the method `meth`.
1	Communication error to SAP GUI.
2	Error when calling the method `meth`.
3	Error when setting a property.
4	Error when reading a property.

Example

Depending on the selection on the selection screen, you can open the Excel-file Table.xls in the directory *C:\temp*, start the application Word, and then close both applications again by use of this source text. The used automation methods are listed in the following table.

Application	Method	Parameter	Function
Excel	Open	File Name and Path	Open
Excel	Quit	–	Exit
Word	AppShow	–	Start
Word	AppClose	–	Exit

```
TABLES
  sscrfields.
TYPE-POOLS
  ole2.

DATA:
  excel TYPE ole2_object,
  word  TYPE ole2_object,
```

```
    book   TYPE ole2_object,
    rc     TYPE c LENGTH 8.

SELECTION-SCREEN:
  BEGIN OF SCREEN 100 AS WINDOW TITLE title,
    BEGIN OF LINE,
      PUSHBUTTON   2(12) button_1
                   USER-COMMAND word_start,
      PUSHBUTTON  20(12) button_2
                   USER-COMMAND excel_start,
    END OF LINE,
    BEGIN OF LINE,
      PUSHBUTTON   2(12) button_3
                   USER-COMMAND word_stop,
      PUSHBUTTON  20(12) button_4
                   USER-COMMAND excel_stop,
    END OF LINE,
  END OF SCREEN 100.

START-OF-SELECTION.
  button_1 = 'Start Word'.
  button_2 = 'Start Excel'.
  button_3 = 'Stop  Word'.
  button_4 = 'Stop  Excel'.
  CALL SELECTION-SCREEN 100 STARTING AT 10 10.

AT SELECTION-SCREEN.
  CASE sscrfields-ucomm.
    WHEN 'WORD_START'.
      CHECK word-handle <> -1.
      CHECK word-header = space.
      CREATE OBJECT   word  'Word.Basic'.
      CALL METHOD  OF word  'AppShow'.
    WHEN 'EXCEL_START'.
      CHECK excel-handle = 0.
      CHECK excel-header = space.
      CREATE OBJECT   excel 'Excel.Application'.
      SET PROPERTY OF excel 'Visible' = 1.
      GET PROPERTY OF excel 'Workbooks' = book.
      CALL METHOD  OF book  'Open' = rc
         EXPORTING #1 = 'C:\temp\Table.xls'.
    WHEN 'WORD_STOP'.
      CALL METHOD OF word 'AppClose'.
      FREE OBJECT word.
      CLEAR: word-handle, word-header.
```

```
    WHEN 'EXCEL_STOP'.
      CALL METHOD OF  excel 'Quit'.
      FREE OBJECT excel.
      CLEAR: excel-handle, excel-header.
    WHEN OTHERS.
      LEAVE PROGRAM.
  ENDCASE.
```

41.3   Reading the Attributes of an Automation Object

GET PROPERTY

Reading the attribute of an automation object.

Syntax

```
GET PROPERTY OF ole attr = dobj [NO FLUSH] [QUEUE-ONLY].
```

The content of the attribute `attr` of an automation object `ole` is assigned to data object `dobj`. The automation object must have been created using the special `CREATE OBJECT` statement for automation objects. For the typing of `ole` and for the meaning of the `NO FLUSH` and `QUEUE-ONLY` additions, the description of the `CREATE OBJECT` statement applies (see Section 42.1). The typing of the `dobj` data object depends on the properties of the automation attribute `attr`.

Return values

sy-subrc	Meaning
0	Object attributes successfully passed.
1	Error in communication with SAP GUI.
2	Error in function call in SAP GUI.
3	Error when setting an attribute.
4	Error when reading an attribute.

Example

In this example, the attribute "Visible" of an Excel table which was created at runtime is read. This attribute specifies whether the table processing is visible or runs in the background. The variable `vis` is typed as an integer because Excel passes an integer value.

```
TYPE-POOLS
  ole2.

DATA:
  vis TYPE i,
  app TYPE ole2_object.

CREATE OBJECT   app 'Excel.Application'.
GET PROPERTY OF app 'Visible' = vis.
WRITE vis.
```

41.4   Setting the Attributes of an Automation Object

> **SET PROPERTY**

Setting the attributes of an automation object.

Syntax

> **SET PROPERTY OF** ole attr = dobj [**NO FLUSH**].

The attribute `attr` of an automation object `ole` is set according to the content of the data object `dobj`. The automation object must have been generated with the specific statement `CREATE OBJECT` for automation objects. For the typing of `ole` and the meaning of the `NO FLUSH` addition, the description in the statement `CREATE OBJECT` applies (see Section 42.2). The typing of the data object `dobj` depends on the properties of the automation attribute `attr`.

Return values

sy-subrc	Meaning
0	Successful transfer of object properties
1	Error in communication to the SAP GUI
2	Error in function call in the SAP GUI
3	Error when setting a property
4	Error when reading a property

Example

Calling the Office application Excel and displaying an empty Excel table by assigning the value 1 to the attribute "Visible".

```
TYPE-POOLS
  ole2.

DATA app
  TYPE ole2_object.

CREATE OBJECT app 'Excel.Application'.
SET PROPERTY OF app 'Visible' = 1.
```

41.5   Releasing an Automation Object

FREE OBJECT

Releasing the memory space of an automation object.

Syntax

FREE OBJECT ole [**NO FLUSH**].

This statement releases the memory occupied for the object `ole` on the application server. The automation object must have been created with the special statement `CREATE OBJECT`. After the release, the object is still available on the presentation server, but can no longer be processed in the ABAP program. For the typing of `ole` and for the meaning of the addition `NO FLUSH`, the same description applies as for `CREATE OBJECT` (see Section 42.1).

The transfer of the statement `FREE OBJECT` to the presentation server causes the transfer of the entire automation queue collected using the addition `NO FLUSH`.

Note
An automation object `ole` created using `CREATE OBJECT ole` must also be released using `FREE OBJECT ole` to avoid memory bottlenecks and terminations of the application to be controlled.

Return values

sy-subrc	Meaning
0	Successful memory release
1	Error during communication to SAP GUI
2	Error during function call in SAP GUI

Example

```
TYPE-POOLS
  ole2.

DATA
  app TYPE ole2_object.

CREATE OBJECT app 'Excel.Application' NO FLUSH.
...
FREE OBJECT app NO FLUSH.
```

Part 14
Obsolete Statements

42 Obsolete Statements

42.1 Overview

The statements described in this chapter are obsolete and are only still available for reasons of compatibility with versions prior to Release 4.6, Release 6.20 or Release 6.40. You may still come across these statements in old programs, but you should not use them any longer.

Most of the obsolete statements listed here are syntactically forbidden in ABAP Objects or in Unicode programs. As a result, they can now only be used outside of classes or non-Unicode programs. There are replacement constructions for all obsolete statements that improve the efficiency and readability of programs.

Apart from the obsolete statements listed in this chapter, there are also obsolete variants and additions for non-obsolete statements. These cannot be used in ABAP Objects and Unicode programs either. They are detailed in the description of the corresponding statements.

42.2 Obsolete Syntax

The following syntax forms are obsolete. They are forbidden within ABAP Objects, and outside of classes they cause the syntax check to issue warnings.

▶ Outside of classes, separators (blank characters, commas, colons, periods or the end of a line) can be omitted after literals or offset/length specifications.

▶ Outside of classes, the operators for offset and length can be omitted in offset/length specifications. A single plus sign directly after a field name, a plus sign that directly follows a parenthetical expression, or an empty parenthetical expression after a plus sign, offset value or field name, are all interpreted as not existing.

▶ Outside of classes, a character literal can extend across several program lines. The numner of blank characters inserted depends on the line length of the editor.

42.3   Obsolete Modularization

42.3.1   Obsolete Event Block

```
AT PF
```

Introduction of an event block for function key selection in lists.

Syntax

```
AT PFnn.
```

This statement defines an event block whose event is triggered by the ABAP runtime environment during the display of a list, provided that the screen cursor is positioned on a list line and a function is selected with the function code "PFnn," where nn stands for a number between 01 and 24. In the standard list status, these function codes are assigned to the function keys on the input device.

Note

Instead of `AT PFnn` you should always use `AT USER-COMMAND`, and the desired function keys should be assigned your own function codes.

42.4   Obsolete Declarations

42.4.1   Obsolete Interface Work Areas

Apart from the interface work areas declared with the statements `TABLES` and `NODES`, which are still needed for specific purposes, the following declarations should no longer be used.

42.4.1.1   Common Data Area

```
COMMON PART
```

Declaration of a common data area.

Syntax

```
DATA BEGIN OF COMMON PART [name].
  ...
  DATA ...
  ...
DATA END OF COMMON PART [name].
```

DATA statements with the additions BEGIN OF COMMON PART and END OF COMMON PART define a global interface work area that can be used jointly by the programs of a program group. All data objects declared between these statements using DATA are part of the interface work area.

The COMMON PART addition can only be used in the global declaration section of an ABAP program. Several common data areas can be declared in a program, but they cannot be nested. Every common data area must be given a unique name using the name addition. You can only omit the name addition if there is just one common data area in a program.

In all programs of a program group that access the data of a common data area, this data area must be declared with the same name and exactly the same structure; otherwise an exception that cannot be handled is raised.

Note
The declaration of common data areas for different programs is usually carried out in an include program, which is then integrated in all the programs involved. As the use of common data areas in otherwise independent programs can be very problematic with regard to both the maintainability and the functions, common data areas should no longer be used in this way. The parameter interfaces of procedures are available for exchanging data between programs.

Example
In this example, a common data area struc is declared in the include program part. By incorporating the include program, the three programs param, sum and disp have shared access to the data area struc if they are part of a program group. The latter is accomplished by loading the programs sum and disp into the program group of param using external subroutine calls. The subroutine display in the program disp gives out the input values in the program param and the result of the summation in the subroutine summing.

```
* INCLUDE part.
DATA:
  BEGIN OF COMMON PART struc,
    f1 TYPE i,
    f2 TYPE i,
    s  TYPE i,
  END OF COMMON PART struc.

PROGRAM param.
INCLUDE part.
```

```
PARAMETERS:
  p1 TYPE i DEFAULT 20,
  p2 TYPE i DEFAULT 90.
f1 = p1.
f2 = p2.
PERFORM summming IN PROGRAM sum.

PROGRAM sum.
INCLUDE part.
FORM summing.
  s = f1 + f2.
  PERFORM display IN PROGRAM disp.
ENDFORM.

PROGRAM disp.
INCLUDE part.
FORM display.
  WRITE: / f1, f2, s.
ENDFORM.
```

42.4.1.2 Additional Table Work Area

TABLES *

Declaration of an additional table work area.

Syntax

TABLES `*table_wa.`

This statement declares an additional table work area `*table_wa` whose data type, like that of a TABLES statement of the flat, structured data type `table_wa` described in Section 6.9.1, is copied from the ABAP Dictionary.

The additional table work area can be used like the normal table work area. This applies in particular to obsolete short forms of Open SQL statements (see Section 42.16.4).

Note
The statement TABLES is forbidden in ABAP Objects. For declaring as many work areas as you want, you can use the addition TYPE to refer to the data types in the ABAP Dictionary.

Example
Declaration of a normal and an additional table work area and its use in obsolete short forms of the SELECT statement.

```
TABLES: scarr, *scarr.
SELECT SINGLE *
       FROM scarr
       WHERE carrid = 'LH'.

SELECT SINGLE *
       FROM *scarr
       WHERE carrid = 'UA'.
```

42.4.2 Obsolete Declarations of Internal Standard Tables

OCCURS

Definition of a standard table with the addition OCCURS.

42.4.2.1 Table Types and Table Objects of Any Row Type

In the following variants of the statements TYPES and DATA, internal tables are defined by entering the addition OCCURS. The initial memory requirement n, which is optional in the valid form of the statement TYPES or DATA, must be specified. Normally, 0 can be entered as a value for n.

Table types

Syntax

```
TYPES dtype { {TYPE [REF TO] type}
            | {LIKE [REF TO] dobj} } OCCURS n.
```

This statement cannot be used in ABAP Objects. The statement has exactly the same function as the following statement (see Section 6.3.5) and is replaced by the following:

```
TYPES dtype {{ TYPE STANDARD TABLE OF [REF TO] type }
            |{ LIKE STANDARD TABLE OF [REF TO] dobj }}
            WITH NON-UNIQUE DEFAULT KEY
            INITIAL SIZE n.
```

Table objects

Syntax

```
DATA itab { {TYPE [REF TO] type}
          | {LIKE [REF TO] dobj} } OCCURS n
          [WITH HEADER LINE].
```

This statement is forbidden in ABAP Objects. It has exactly the same function as the following statement (see Section 6.4.6) and is replaced by this:

```
DATA itab {{ TYPE STANDARD TABLE OF [REF TO] type }
          |{ LIKE STANDARD TABLE OF [REF TO] dobj }}
          WITH NON-UNIQUE DEFAULT KEY
          INITIAL SIZE n.
          [WITH HEADER LINE].
```

42.4.2.2 Table Objects with Structured Row Type

The following statement sequence mixes the declaration of a structure with that of an internal table.

Syntax

```
DATA BEGIN OF itab OCCURS n.
  ...
DATA END OF itab [VALID BETWEEN intlim1 AND intlim2].
```

This sequence of statements declares an internal table itab as a structured standard table with a header line. The declarations between the statements DATA BEGIN OF and DATA END OF define the components of the row type for itab (compare Section 6.4.5). The data object n that has to be specified as a numeric literal or numeric constant determines the initial memory requirement (see Section 6.4.6).

The VALID BETWEEN addition of the DATA END OF statement is only important if the internal table is to be processed using the obsolete form of the statement PROVIDE (see Section 42.12.3). As intlim1 and intlim2, you can specify columns from the internal table of the data type d, i, n or t. These columns are used implicitly as interval limits in their obsolete form of the statement PROVIDE.

Note

In classes, no internal tables with header lines can be declared. For this reason, the above sequence of statements is not allowed in ABAP Objects. The following sequence of statements replaces the above statements (with the exception of the addition VALID BETWEEN); here the role of the header line is adopted by the work area wa:

```
DATA BEGIN OF wa.
    ...
DATA END OF wa.

DATA itab LIKE TABLE OF wa.
```

The last statement is an abbreviated form of the complete declaration of `itab`, where the table type and key are supplemented with standard values (see Section 6.4.6).

42.4.3 Obsolete Declarations of Special Internal Tables

The following obsolete statements declare special standard tables with header lines.

42.4.3.1 Internal Tables for HR Info Types

```
INFOTYPES
```

Declaration of an internal table for HR info types.

Syntax

```
INFOTYPES nnnn [NAME name]
               [OCCURS n]
               [MODE N]
               [VALID FROM intlim1 TO intlim2]
               [AS PERSON TABLE].
```

If you do not use the additions MODE and AS PERSON TABLE, then this statement is a short form of the following statement sequence:

```
DATA BEGIN OF {pnnnn|ppnnnn|name} OCCURS { 10 | n}.
  INCLUDE TYPE pnnnn.
DATA END OF {pnnnn|ppnnnn|name}
    VALID BETWEEN { begdat|intlim1 }
              AND { enddat|intlim2 }.
```

For nnnn you must specify the four-digit numeric key of an info type of the SAP-R/3-Enterprise-Component Human Resources (HR). Each info type is represented in the component HR through a special structure Pnnnn in the ABAP dictionary. Each info type contains the character-type components BEGDAT and ENDDAT. Info types enable the application to process employee-related data effectively. The statement PROVIDE is especially helpful for this purpose (see Section 22.7).

Without the addition NAME, an internal table pnnnn or ppnnnn with the structure of the info type "Pnnnn" and a header line is created. The name ppnnnn is used if the addition AS PERSON TABLE is specified (since Release 6.20), if not, then pnnnn is specified. With the addition NAME, you can specify a name `name` with a maximum length of 20 digits. This name is then used for the internal table instead of `pnnnn` or `ppnnnn`.

Without the addition `OCCURS`, the initial memory requirement (see Section 6.4.6) of the internal table is set to 10 rows. With the addition `OCCURS` you can specify a numeric literal or a numeric constant n to determine a different initial memory requirement.

If the addition `MODE N` is not specified, then the properties of the internal table are saved in an internal system table, which can be accessed via special logical databases. The programming of such logical databases is reserved to the component Human Resources which delivers two logical databases PNP and PCH for info types. If, in an executable program linked to one of these databases, the statement `INFOTYPES` is listed without the addition `MODE N`, then the internal table is filled from the logical database PNP at the event `GET pernr` and filled from the logical database PCH at the event `GET object`. If the addition `MODE N` is specified, then the table is not linked to logical databases and is not filled at the `GET` events.

Without the addition `VALID FROM`, the components BEGDAT and ENDDAT of the info type Pnnnn are specified as interval limits for the obsolete form of the statement `PROVIDE`. With the addition `VALID FROM`, you can specify other flat character-type components `intlim1` and `intlim2` of the info type as interval limits.

Note
It is not allowed to declare internal tables with header lines in classes, and for this reason, the statement `INFOTYPES` is not allowed in ABAP Objects. To declare an internal table of the same structure, you should use the allowed statements from Chapter 6.

42.4.3.2 Ranges Tables

```
RANGES
```

Declaration of a ranges table.

Syntax

```
RANGES rtab FOR dobj [OCCURS n].
```

This statement is a short form of the following statement sequence:

```
DATA: BEGIN OF rtab OCCURS {10|n},
        sign(1)   TYPE c,
```

```
       option(2) TYPE c,
       low        LIKE dobj,
       high       LIKE dobj,
    END OF sel.
```

An internal table `rtab` with the structure of a selection table and a header line is declared. Without the addition OCCURS, the initial memory requirement (see Section 6.4.6) of the ranges-table is set to 10 rows. With the addition OCCURS, you can specify a numeric literal or a numeric constant n to determine a different initial memory requirement.

Note
It is not allowed to declare internal tables with header lines. Due to this, the statement RANGES is not allowed in ABAP Objects. To declare a ranges-table in ABAP Objects, you can use the addition TYPE|LIKE RANGE OF (see Section 6.3.6 and 6.4.7).

42.4.4 Obsolete Note for the Extended Program Check

FIELDS

Addressing a data object.

Syntax

```
FIELDS dobj.
```

This statement addresses a data object `dobj` of the program. A warning from the extended program check can be avoided if the data object `dobj` is only dynamically addressed in the program but not statically.

Note
For data objects for which static read access is possible but not write access, this statement forbidden in ABAP Objects can be replaced with the pseudo comment "#EC NEEDED. In other cases, the warning of the extended program check can be switched off using the statement SET EX-TENDED CHECK (see Section 37.5).

42.5   Obsolete Object Creation

ASSIGN LOCAL COPY

Creation of a local data object.

Syntax

```
ASSIGN LOCAL COPY
  OF { {[INITIAL] mem_area}
     | {INITIAL LINE OF {itab|(itab_name)}} }
  TO <fs> casting_spec.
```

This variant of the ASSIGN statement can only be used in subroutines and function modules. The field symbol <fs> must be declared locally in the procedure.

Like the normal statement ASSIGN (see Section 17.2), the statement ASSIGN LOCAL COPY assigns a memory area mem_area to the field symbol <fs>. In contrast to the normal statement ASSIGN, however, the field symbol does not reference the memory area specified in mem_area after the successful assignment. Instead, an anonymous data object is created in the local data area of the procedure. After the successful execution of the statement, the field symbol points to the new data object. The new data object is treated as follows.

▶ The size of the memory area of the new data object conforms to either the data in mem_area or the line type of an internal table if LINE OF is specified. The internal table can be specified directly as itab or as the content of a flat character-type field itab_name.

▶ The data type with which the newly created data object is to be handled conforms to the data in casting_spec as is the case when using the normal ASSIGN.

▶ The initial content of the new data object is copied from the memory area specified in mem_area when specifying mem_area without the addition INITIAL. Otherwise, it is initialized according to the type.

The limitation of the memory area range_spec, which can occur in the normal ASSIGN statement implicitly and (as of Release 6.10) explicitly, can occur only implicitly in the obsolete variant following the same rules that apply to the normal ASSIGN.

Syntax of *mem_area*

```
... { {dobj[+off][(len)]}
    | (name)
    | {oref->(attr_name)}
    | {class|(class_name)}=>{attr|(attr_name)}
    | {dref->* } } ...
```

The specifications in `mem_area` are a subset of the specifications in the normal ASSIGN statement. They have the same function except for the following restrictions:

▶ If the addition INITIAL is used before `mem_area`, the data object name must be character-like and flat.

▶ If the addition INITIAL is used before `mem_area`, the data reference dref cannot be typed generically when using the dereferencing operator ->*.

Syntax of *casting_spec*

The specification of `casting_spec` corresponds to that of the normal ASSIGN (see Section 17.2.2) with the limitation that, if the addition INITIAL is used before `mem_area` and an internal table is specified, no explicit specifications can be made. This means that the field symbol copies the data type of the data object in `mem_area` or the line type of the internal table.

Note

As of Release 4.6, the creation of a local data object with the statement ASSIGN LOCAL COPY is replaced with the statement CREATE DATA with subsequent dereferencing in the normal ASSIGN statement.

Example

Prior to release 4.6, a typical use of the statement ASSIGN LOCAL COPY was the creation of a local copy of a global data object.

```
DATA g_dobj TYPE i.

...

CLEAR g_dobj.

PERFORM subroutine.

...

FORM subroutine.
  FIELD-SYMBOLS <l_dobj> TYPE ANY.
```

```
   ASSIGN LOCAL COPY OF g_dobj TO <l_dobj>.
   <l_dobj> = <l_dobj> + 1.
   WRITE: / g_dobj, <l_dobj>.
ENDFORM.
```

The following subroutine shows how the same functions can be universally implemented with a data reference as of Release 4.6.

```
FORM subroutine.
   DATA dref TYPE REF TO data.
   FIELD-SYMBOLS <l_dobj> TYPE ANY.
   CREATE DATA dref LIKE g_dobj.
   ASSIGN dref->* TO <l_dobj>.
   <l_dobj> = g_dobj.
   <l_dobj> = <l_dobj> + 1.
   WRITE: / g_dobj, <l_dobj>.
ENDFORM.
```

42.6   Obsolete Program Call

CALL DIALOG

Calling a dialog module.

Syntax

```
CALL DIALOG dialog [ {AND SKIP FIRST SCREEN}
                   | {USING bdc_tab [MODE mode]} ]
                     [EXPORTING p1 FROM a1 p2 FROM a2 ...]
                     [IMPORTING p1 TO a1 p2 TO a2 ...].
```

The statement CALL DIALOG calls the dialog module whose name is contained in the character-like data object dialog. The data object dialog must contain the name in uppercase. If the dialog module specified in dialog is not found, an exception that cannot be handled is raised.

When calling the dialog module, the assigned ABAP program is loaded in a new internal mode. The mode of the calling program is still available. In contrast to CALL TRANSACTION, the called program runs in the same SAP LUW as the calling program.

After loading the ABAP program, the event LOAD-OF-PROGRAM is triggered and the dynpro defined as the initial dynpro of the dialog module is called. The dialog module is terminated when the corresponding dynpro sequence terminates upon reaching the next dynpro with dynpro number 0, or when the program is exited using the statement `LEAVE PROGRAM`.

Note

Dialog modules are the only language resource that can be used to open a new mode without changing the SAP LUW. Be especially aware of the following:

▶ The statements `COMMIT WORK` and `ROLLBACK WORK` cause database commits or database rollbacks in the called program. However, the procedures registered with `CALL FUNCTION IN UPDATE TASK` and `PERFORM ON {COMMIT|ROLLBACK}` are not executed until the corresponding statements in the calling program are executed.

▶ In the called program, SAP locks are adopted by the caller.

Additions

Syntax

```
... AND SKIP FIRST SCREEN ...
```

Under the same conditions as for the statement `CALL TRANSACTION`, this addition surresses the display of the screen picture of the initial dynpro. If the called dialog module has input parameters for the obligatory input fields of the initial screen, they also can be filled using a parameter transfer instead of SPA/GPA parameters.

Syntax

```
... USING bdc_tab [MODE mode] ...
```

This addition controls the called program as in the statement `CALL TRANSACTION` using the specification of a batch input folder in an internal table `bdc_tab` of the line type BDCDATA. In this case, only `MODE` can be used as an addition for the control of the batch input processing.

If a message is sent in the called program, this message is available in the system fields `sy-msgid`, `sy-msgty`, `sy-msgno`, `sy-msgv1`, ..., `sy-msgv4` after the call.

Syntax

```
... EXPORTING p1 FROM a1 p2 FROM a2 ...
... IMPORTING p1 TO a1 p2 TO a2 ...
```

These additions can be used to assign the appropriate actual parameters a1, a2, ... to the formal parameters p1, p2, ... The formal parameters of a dialog module are always optional. They can have all data types except for reference types.

When loading the called program, the values of the actual parameters are assigned to the global data objects of the called program that are defined as formal parameters. If this data is associated with dynpro fields of the same name, they are not overwritten by possible SPA/GPA parameters.

If you specify IMPORTING, the system field sy-subrc is implicitly adopted by the called dialog module and unknown formal parameters are ignored by the system.

Note
Outside of classes, the additions FROM a1, FROM a2, ... and TO a1, TO a2, ... in the parameter lists can be omitted if the formal parameters and actual parameters have the same names.

Example
Calling a dialog module DEMO_DIALOG_MODULE which is associated with the program SAPMDEMO_TRANSACTION.

```
DATA spfli_wa TYPE spfli.
spfli_wa-carrid = 'LH'.
spfli_wa-connid = '0400'.

CALL DIALOG 'DEMO_DIALOG_MODULE'
  EXPORTING
    spfli-carrid FROM spfli_wa-carrid
    spfli-connid FROM spfli_wa-connid
  IMPORTING
    spfli_wa     TO spfli_wa.
```

42.7 Obsolete Exiting of a Program

`LEAVE`

Leaving a program depending on the program call.

Syntax

`LEAVE.`

This statement is only executed if the system field sy-calld is not initial, otherwise it is ignored.

LEAVE exits a program called using `CALL TRANSACTION`, `CALL DIALOG` or `SUBMIT ... AND RETURN` and returns to the calling position. In the case of programs called using `CALL DIALOG`, the output parameters of the dialog module are transferred to the caller.

LEAVE does not exit a program if it was started using `LEAVE TO TRANSACTION` or if a transaction code from a dynpro or if the program is processed in the batch input.

If a program was called using `SUBMIT` without the `AND RETURN` additions, `LEAVE` functions in the same way as in the calling program.

Note
The `LEAVE` statement without an addition exits a program, depending on how it was called. Therefore, `LEAVE` should only be used with additions that uniquely control the behavior.

42.8   Obsolete Program Flow Control

42.8.1   Obsolete Relational Operators

The left-hand side of the following table shows relational operators that from now on can be used only outside of ABAP Objects in logical expressions. This applies to logical expressions in control statements and in Open SQL. The right-hand side shows which operators replace the obsolete operators.

Obsolete operator	Valid operator
`><`	`<>`, `NE`
`=<`	`<=`, `LE`
`=>`	`>=`, `GT`

42.8.2   Obsolete Branching

`ON CHANGE OF`

Conditional execution of a statement block.

Syntax

```
ON CHANGE OF dobj [OR dobj1 [OR dobj2] ...].
  statement_block
ENDON.
```

The statements ON CHANGE OF and ENDON define a control structure that can contain a statement block *statement_block*. After ON CHANGE OF, any number of data objects dobj1, dobj2, ... of any data type and linked by OR can be added.

The first time a statement ON CHANGE OF is executed, the statement block is executed if at least one of the specified data objects is not initial. The statement block is executed for each additional execution of the same statement ON CHANGE OF if the content of one of the specified data objects has been changed since the last time the statement ON CHANGE OF was changed.

Each time the statement ON CHANGE OF is executed, the content of all the specified data objects is saved in an internal program-global auxiliary variable. The auxiliary variable is linked to this statement and cannot be accessed in the program. The auxiliary variables and their contents are retained longer than the lifetime of procedures. An auxiliary variable of this type can only be initialized if its statement ON CHANGE OF is executed while the associated data object is initial.

Note
This control structure, which is forbidden in ABAP Objects, is particularly prone to errors and should be replaced by branches with explicitly declared auxiliary variables.

Example
In a SELECT loop, a statement block should only be executed if the content of the column CARRID has changed.

```
DATA spfli_wa TYPE spfli.
SELECT *
      FROM spfli
      INTO spfli_wa
      ORDER BY carrid.
  ...
  ON CHANGE OF spfli_wa-carrid.
    ...
  ENDON.
  ...
ENDSELECT.
```

The following section of a program shows how the ON control structure can be replaced by an IF control structure with an explicit auxiliary variable carrid_buffer.

```
DATA: spfli_wa TYPE spfli,
      carrid_buffer TYPE spfli-carrid.

CLEAR carrid_buffer.

SELECT *
       FROM spfli
       INTO spfli_wa
       ORDER BY carrid.
  ...
  IF spfli_wa-carrid <> carrid_buffer.
    carrid_buffer = spfli_wa-carrid.
    ...
  ENDIF.
  ...
ENDSELECT.
```

42.9   Obsolete Assignments

42.9.1   Obsolete Assignment of a Percentage Subfield

MOVE PERCENTAGE

Assignment of a percentage of the source field.

Syntax

MOVE source **TO** destination **PERCENTAGE** perc [**LEFT**|**RIGHT**].

This statement assigns the subfield of the data object source that begins from the first position onwards and whose length corresponds to the percentage of the total length of source specified in perc to the data object destination. By default, and if LEFT is specified, destination is left-aligned; if RIGHT is specified, it is right-aligned.

The data type of the data objects source and destination must be character-type, otherwise the addition PERCENTAGE is ignored. For perc, a data object of type i is expected. If the value of perc is smaller than or equal to 0, nothing is assigned. If the value of perc is greater than or equal to 100, the entire content of source is assigned.

Note

This variant of the statement MOVE, which is forbidden in ABAP Objects, can be replaced by subfield accesses with a specified offset/length.

42.9.2 Obsolete Conversion

`PACK`

Conversion of character sequences into a packed number.

Syntax

```
PACK source TO destination.
```

This statement converts the content of the data object `source` to the data type p of length 16 without decimal places. In contrast to the conversion rules in Section A.2, a decimal separator in `source` is ignored. This assigns the converted content to the data object `destination`.

The data type of `source` must be character-type, flat, and its content must be interpretable as a numeric value. The data type of `destination` must be flat. If `destination` has the data type p, the interim result is assigned to it from left to right. Surplus characters are cut off on the left, and the decimal places are determined by the data type of `destination`. If `destination` does not have the data type p, the interim result is converted to the data type of `destination` according to the rules in Section A.2.7.

Notes

▶ The function of the statement `PACK` is based on the second half-byte of the code corresponding to a character in most character representations of the BCD representation for the corresponding numeric value. This conversion is generally known as "packing."

▶ If the source field contains a number without a decimal separator, and the target field has `dobj2` of data type p with sufficient length and without decimal places, the result of the `PACK` statement (which is forbidden in ABAP Objects) corresponds to the result of the statement `MOVE`.

Treatable Exceptions

If `source` cannot be interpreted as a number or if there is an overflow in the conversion, the exceptions defined in the classes CX_SY_CONVERSION_NO_NUMBER or CX_SY_CONVERSION_OVERFLOW are triggered. The assigned runtime errors CONVT_NO_NUMBER, BCD_FIELD_OVERFLOW or CONVT_OVERFLOW can be treated.

42.9.3 Obsolete Temporary Storage of Data Objects

```
LOCAL
```

Assignment of a data object to temporary storage.

Syntax

```
LOCAL dobj.
```

The statement LOCAL saves the current content of a data object dobj in an internal temporary storage area. It can be used only in subroutines or function modules. At the end of the procedure, the value in temporary storage is reassigned to the data object dobj. If LOCAL is executed in a procedure for a data object several times, only the first execution is taken into account.

For dobj, all data objects possible in write positions can be specified (see Section 2.2.5). If dobj is an internal table, the procedure should not be called within a LOOP loop via the table.

After LOCAL, changeable formal parameters of the procedure, field symbols or dereferenced data references are also possible. When formal parameters are specified, the assigned actual parameter is set to the value in temporary storage at the end of the procedure. With field symbols, the field reference and the content of the referenced fields are stored.

Note

The statement LOCAL serves, in particular, to protect global variables of the framework program declared with DATA from unwanted changes during a procedure. Instead of using LOCAL, you should avoid accessing the global data of the framework program in procedures.

Example

When executing the following program section, the value of the global variable text is stored twice, temporarily, and in separate places: once by specifying the name in subr1 and a second time in subr2 by specifying the formal parameter para to which text will be transferred by reference. After coming back from subr2, text once again has the value that is set in subr1. After return from subr1, text assumes the value set in the framework program.

```
DATA text TYPE string VALUE 'Global text'.

WRITE / text.
```

```
PERFORM subr1.

WRITE / text.

FORM subr1.
  LOCAL text.
  text = 'Text in subr1'.
  WRITE / text.
  PERFORM subr2 USING text.
  WRITE / text.
ENDFORM.

FORM subr2 USING para TYPE string.
  LOCAL para.
  para = 'Text in subr2'.
  WRITE / text.
ENDFORM.
```

42.10   Obsolete Calculation Statements

42.10.1 Addition of Field Sequences in the Memory

ADD

Addition of fields at relative memory positions.

Syntax

```
ADD { { dobj1 THEN dobj2 UNTIL dobj
      { {TO result} | {GIVING result [ACCORDING TO sel]} } }
    | { dobj FROM pos1 TO pos GIVING result } }
    [RANGE range].
```

These variants of the ADD statement add sequences of data objects that are stored in the memory in equal distances from one another.

In the variant with THEN and UNTIL, the sequence is defined by the distance between the data objects dobj1 and dobj2. At all storage locations whose distances to dobj1 are multiple values of this distance—up to and including the position dobj—numeric data objects of identical type must be stored. The content of all these data objects is added. In the variant with TO, the total is added to the content of the data object result, and the result is assigned to it. In the variant with GIVING, the sum is directly assigned to the data object result. The data object result must be a numeric variable. If you use the addition ACCORDING, a data object of the sequence is added to the sum only if its position in the sequence fulfills the condition in the selection table `sel`. For the components `low` and `high` of the selection table, the data type `i` is expected.

In the variant with `TO` and `FROM`, the sequence is formed by data objects directly adjacent in the storage, whose first data object is `dobj` and which must all have the same numeric data type. For `pos1` and `pos`, data objects of type `i` are expected whose values define a subset of the sequence. The contents of the data objects of the subsequence are added and assigned to the data object `result`. The data object `result` must be a numeric variable. If `pos1` or `pos` contain negative values or if `pos1` is greater than `pos`, the statement is not executed and `result` remains unchanged.

In both variants, an untreatable exception occurs if addresses are accessed that do not contain suitable data objects.

In Unicode programs, all data objects of the sequence must lie within one structure. If this cannot be recognized statically in the syntax check, you must specify a structure `range` with the addition `RANGE`. If, during the execution of the statement, the data objects of the sequence are not part of the specified structure, an untreatable exception is triggered.

In non-Unicode programs, the sequence of the data objects can extend over the entire data area of the current program. Only if the first data object of the sequence is specified as a field symbol do the area boundaries defined at the same time using the addition *range_spec* of the statement `ASSIGN` (see Section 17.2.3) specify the allowed area of the sequence.

Note
The function of these variants of the `ADD` statement depends on the structure of the working memory. They are not allowed in ABAP Objects and can be replaced by `DO` and `WHILE` loops in the additions `VARYING` or `VARY`, if required.

Treatable Exceptions
The treatable exceptions that can be triggered with the statement `ADD` (see Section 20.2) may also occur in this case.

Example
The components of the structure `numbers` entered on the selection screen are added and the sum is assigned to the variable `sum`.

```
DATA: BEGIN OF numbers,
        one   TYPE ɔ VALUE 10,
```

```
       two   TYPE p VALUE 20,
       three TYPE p VALUE 30,
       four  TYPE p VALUE 40,
       five  TYPE p VALUE 50,
     END OF numbers,
     sum     TYPE i.

SELECT-OPTIONS position FOR sum.

ADD numbers-one THEN numbers-two
                UNTIL numbers-five
                ACCORDING TO position
                GIVING sum.
```

42.10.2 Adding Component by Component

ADD-CORRESPONDING

Adding the components of structures with the same name.

Syntax

ADD-CORRESPONDING struc1 **TO** struc2.

You must specify structures for struc1 and struc2. All components of the same name in struc1 and struct2 are added in pairs and the result is assigned to the respective component of struct2.

The name comparison is executed in the same way as for the MOVE-COR-RESPONDING statement. For each component pair with the same name comp, internally the statement

ADD struc1-comp **TO** struc2-comp.

is executed and, if necessary, the required conversions are performed.

Note
This statement is not allowed in ABAP Objects. It is error-prone, because—especially in complex structures—it cannot be guaranteed in a simple manner that components of the same name actually have the data types and contents required for a numeric operation.

Treatable Exceptions
The treatable exceptions that can be triggered with the statement ADD (see Section 20.2) may also occur in this case.

Example

The components x and y exist in both structures and are added. After the addition, the results are stored in `struc2-x` and `struc2-y`.

```
DATA: BEGIN OF struc1,
        x TYPE i,
        y TYPE i,
        z TYPE i,
      END OF struc1,
      BEGIN OF struc2,
        a TYPE i,
        b TYPE i,
        x TYPE p,
        y TYPE p,
      END OF struc2.

...

ADD-CORRESPONDING struc1 TO struc2.
```

42.10.3 Subtracting Component by Component

`SUBTRACT-CORRESPONDING`

Subtracting components of structures with the same name.

Syntax

`SUBTRACT-CORRESPONDING struc1 FROM struc2.`

For `struc1` and `struc2`, structures must be specified. For all identically named components in `struc1` and `struc2`, the component in `struc1` is subtracted in pairs from the component in `struc2`, and the result is assigned to the component of `struc2`.

The name comparison is executed as by the assignment `MOVE-CORRESPONDING`. For each identically named component pair `comp`, the statement

`SUBTRACT struc1-comp FROM struc2-comp.`

is executed internally. If required, the associated conversions are also executed.

Note

This statement is not allowed in ABAP Objects. The statement is prone to errors, because you cannot easily ensure that the corresponding components have the data type and content required for a numeric operation in complex structures.

Treatable exceptions

The treatable exceptions that can be triggered with the statement SUB-TRACT (see Section 20.3) may also occur here.

42.10.4 Multiplying Component by Component

```
MULTIPLY-CORRESPONDING
```

Multiplying components of structures with the same name.

Syntax

```
MULTIPLY-CORRESPONDING struc1 BY struc2.
```

Structures must be specified for struc1 and struc2. All components with the same name in struc1 and struc2 are multiplied in pairs, and the result is assigned to the appropriate component of struc1.

The name comparison is executed in the statement MOVE-CORRESPOND-ING. For each component pair comp with the same name, the statement

```
MULTIPLY struc1-comp BY struc2-comp.
```

is executed internally, and the corresponding conversions are executed if necessary.

Note

This statement is forbidden in ABAP Objects. It is prone to errors because, particularly in complex structures, it is not easy to ensure that the components with the same name have the data types and content required for a numerical operation.

Treatable Exceptions

The treatable exceptions that can be triggered with the statement MULTI-PLY (see Section 20.4) may also occur here.

42.10.5 Dividing Component by Component

```
DIVIDE-CORRESPONDING
```

Dividing components of structures with the same name.

Syntax

```
DIVIDE-CORRESPONDING struc1 BY struc2.
```

Structures must be specified for `struc1` and `struc2`. For all components of the same name in `struc1` and `struc2`, the components of `struc1` are divided by the components in `struc2` in pairs, and the result is assigned to the relevant component in `struc1`.

The names are compared, as in the statement `MOVE-CORRESPONDING`. For each component pair with the same name `comp`, the statement

```
DIVIDE struc1-comp BY struc2-comp.
```

is executed internally, and—if necessary—the appropriate conversions are carried out.

In complex structures, the names of the field pairs in question have to be completely identical at all hierarchical levels.

Note
This statement is not allowed in ABAP Objects. It is error-prone because, particularly in complex structures, it is not easy to check that the components of the same name have the data type and content necessary for a numeric operation.

Treatable Exceptions
The treatable exceptions that can be triggered with the statement `DIVIDE` (see Section 20.5) may also occur here.

42.10.6 Obsolete Calculations During List Creation

When lists are being created, minimum, maximum, and sum of values given out with `WRITE` can be calculated implicitly.

```
MINIMUM
```

Determining the minimum of output values.

Syntax

```
MINIMUM dobj.
```

For each WRITE statement that writes the content of the dobj data object to a list in any list level after the MINIMUM statement is executed, the minimal value of all values given out since the MINIMUM statement was executed is determined using WRITE and assigned to a MIN_dobj data object.

The MINIMUM statement declares the global data object MIN_dobj with the same type as dobj. For dobj, you can specify all data objects that can be written to a list with the WRITE statement. The MINIMUM statement must not be listed within a procedure and it may be listed in a program only once.

MAXIMUM

Determining the maximum of output values.

Syntax

```
MAXIMUM dobj.
```

For every WRITE statement which, after the execution of the statement MAXIMUM, writes the content of the data object dobj to a list on any list level, implicitly the maximum value of all output values of dobj since the execution of MAXIMUM with WRITE is determined and assigned to a data object MAX_dobj.

The statement MAXIMUM declares the global data object MAX_dobj with the same type as dobj. For dobj you can specify all data objects that can be written to a list using WRITE. The statement MAXIMUM must not be positioned within a procedure and may occur only once in every program.

SUMMING

Determining the sum of output values.

Syntax

```
SUMMING dobj.
```

For every WRITE statement that, after the execution of the SUMMING statement, writes the content of the data object dobj onto a list of any list level, the total of all values of dobj given out with WRITE since the execution of SUMMING is determined implicitly and assigned to a data object SUM_dobj.

The SUMMING statement declares the global data object SUM_dobj with the same type as dobj. For dobj, you can specify numeric data objects. You are allowed to execute the SUMMING statement only once in a program. It may be located within a procedure, but the declared data object SUM_dobj is not local.

If the content of dobj in a WRITE statement after the execution of the SUMMING statement cannot be interpreted as a number, or if the addition results in an overflow, then an untreatable exception occurs.

Note
The statements MINIMUM, MAXIMUM and SUMMING are forbidden in ABAP Objects. The implicit handling of global fields during the creation of lists can lead to errors, particularly in interactive list processing.

Example
Implicit determination of minimum, maximum and sum of a list of flight distances.

```
PARAMETERS p_carrid TYPE spfli-carrid.

DATA spfli_wa TYPE spfli.

MINIMUM spfli_wa-distance.
MAXIMUM spfli_wa-distance.
SUMMING spfli_wa-distance.

SELECT carrid connid distance
       FROM spfli
       INTO CORRESPONDING FIELDS OF spfli_wa
       WHERE carrid = p_carrid.
  WRITE: / spfli_wa-carrid, spfli_wa-connid,
           spfli_wa-distance.
ENDSELECT.

ULINE.

WRITE: min_spfli_wa-distance,
       max_spfli_wa-distance,
       sum_spfli_wa-distance.
```

Without using the implicit statements MINIMUM, MAXIMUM and SUMMING, you can get the same result using explicitly calculated help fields.

```
PARAMETERS p_carrid TYPE spfli-carrid.

DATA: spfli_wa     TYPE spfli,
      min_distance TYPE spfli-distance VALUE +99999,
      max_distance TYPE spfli-distance VALUE -99999,
      sum_distance TYPE spfli-distance.

SELECT carrid connid distance
      FROM spfli
      INTO CORRESPONDING FIELDS OF spfli_wa
      WHERE carrid = p_carrid.
  WRITE: / spfli_wa-carrid, spfli_wa-connid,
           spfli_wa-distance.
  IF spfli_wa-distance < min_distance.
    min_distance = spfli_wa-distance.
  ENDIF.
  IF spfli_wa-distance > max_distance.
    max_distance = spfli_wa-distance.
  ENDIF.
  sum_distance = sum_distance + spfli_wa-distance.
ENDSELECT.

ULINE.

WRITE: min_distance,
       max_distance,
       sum_distance.
```

42.11 Obsolete Character-String Processing

42.11.1 Obsolete Translation

TRANSLATE

Translating character strings and character formats.

Syntax

```
TRANSLATE dobj { codepage | number_format }.
```

Translation of the content of a data object to another code page or to another number format.

Syntax of codepage

```
... [FROM CODE PAGE cp1] [TO CODE PAGE cp2] ...
```

The character-like content of a data object dobj is translated from code page cp1 to code page cp2. If dobj does not have a character-like data type, no translation takes place. If dobj is a structure, only the components with character-like data type are translated. Apart from strings, no deep data objects can be specified for dobj.

When specifying the code pages cp1, cp2, ... data objects of data type n with the length 4 are expected. Upon the execution of the statement, these must contain an SAP code page number of the column CPCODE-PAGE in the database table TCP00.

At least one of the additions FROM CODE PAGE or TO CODE PAGE must be specified. If one of the additions is not included, the code page of the current system is used instead of the missing code page cp1 or cp2.

Syntax of *number_format*

```
... [FROM NUMBER FORMAT nf1] [TO NUMBER FORMAT nf2] ...
```

The platform-dependent numeric content of a data object dobj is translated from the number format nf1 to the number format nf2. If dobj is not of data type i or f, the translation does not take place. If dobj is a structure, only the components of the data type i or f are translated. Apart from strings, no deep data objects can be specified for dobj.

When specifying the number formats nf1, nf2, ..., data objects of data type n with the length 4 are expected, which—upon the execution of the statement—must contain either the value "0000" for the platforms HP, SINIX, IBM, or "0101" for the platform DEC-OSF.

At least one of the additions FROM NUMBER FORMAT or TO NUMBER FORMAT must be specified. If one of the additions is not used, the number format of the current platform is used instead of the missing number format nf1 or nf2.

These variants of the TRANSLATE statement are not allowed in Unicode programs. Their functionality is replaced with methods of the following conversion classes (see Section B.1.2):

▶ CL_ABAP_CONV_IN_CE
Reading data from a byte-like data object and converting from an external format to the system format.

▶ CL_ABAP_CONV_OUT_CE
Converting data from the system format to an external format and writing in a byte-like data object.

▶ CL_ABAP_CONV_X2X_CE

Converting data from an external format to another external format.

When opening legacy files in the ABAP file interface, you can directly convert when reading and writing files (see Section 32.2.2).

Example

Translating the components of a structure. The character-like component `text` is translated from the code page "1100" (HP-UX) to the code page "0100" (IBM-EBCDIC). The numeric component `num` is converted from the number format "0000" (for platforms by HP, IBM, or Siemens for example) to the number format "0101" (for platforms provided by DIGITAL for example).

```
DATA: BEGIN OF struc,
        text(80) TYPE c VALUE 'I know You know',
        num       TYPE i VALUE  2505,
      END OF struc.

TRANSLATE struc FROM CODE PAGE '1100'
                TO   CODE PAGE '0100'.

TRANSLATE struc FROM NUMBER FORMAT '0000'
                TO   NUMBER FORMAT '0101'.
```

42.11.2 Obsolete Replacement

REPLACE

Pattern-based replacement of characters in a string.

Syntax

```
REPLACE sub_string WITH new INTO dobj
        [IN {BYTE|CHARACTER} MODE]
        [LENGTH len].
```

This statement searches through a byte string or character string `dobj` for the subsequence specified in `sub_string` and replaces the first byte or character string in `dobj` that matches `sub_string` with the contents of the data object `new`.

The optional addition IN {BYTE|CHARACTER} MODE determines whether byte or character string processing will be executed. If the addition is not specified, character-string processing is executed (see Section 21.1.2). Depending on the processing type, the data objects `sub_string`, `new` and dobj must be byte or character type. The storage areas for sub_string and new must not overlap; otherwise the result is undefined. In character-string processing, the closing blanks in the data objects dobj, sub_string and new of the type c, d, n or t are taken into consideration.

If sub_string is an empty string, the position in front of the first character or byte of the search area is found, and the contents of new are inserted before the first character.

If the addition LENGTH is not specified, all the data objects involved are evaluated in their entire length. If the addition LENGTH is specified, only the first len bytes or characters of sub_string are used as a search pattern. For len, a data object of the type i is expected.

If the length of the interim result is longer than the length of dobj, data objects of fixed length will be cut off to the right. If the length of the interim result is shorter than the length of dobj, data objects of fixed length are filled to the right with blanks or with hexadecimal 0. Data objects of variable length are adapted.

Return Values

sy-subrc	Meaning
0	The search pattern in sub_string was replaced in the target field dobj with the content of new.
4	The earch pattern in sub_string could not be replaced in the target field dobj with the contents of new.

Note

This variant of the statement REPLACE will be replaced, beginning with Release 6.10, with the new variant described in Section 21.4.

Example

After the replacements, text1 contains the complete content "I should know that You know," while text2 has the cut-off content "I should know that."

```
DATA:
  text1      TYPE string VALUE 'I know You know',
  text2(18)  TYPE c      VALUE 'I know You know',
  sub_string TYPE string VALUE 'know',
  new        TYPE string VALUE 'should know that'.

REPLACE sub_string WITH new INTO text1.
REPLACE sub_string WITH new INTO text2.
```

42.11.3 Complement on Nine of a Date

`CONVERT DATE`

Conversion of a date for sorting in descending order.

Syntax

```
CONVERT { {DATE dat1 INTO INVERTED-DATE dat2}
        | {INVERTED-DATE dat1 INTO DATE dat2} }.
```

Both variants of this statement convert the numbers in a character-type data object `dat1` into their complement on nine (the difference to the number nine) and assign the result to the data object `dat2`. The data objects `dat1` and `dat2` must have a flat character-type data type with the length 8. You can specify the same data object for `dat2` as for `dat1`.

Note

These forms of the `CONVERT` statement are not allowed in ABAP Objects. They were previously used for sorting by date fields in internal tables and extracts for changing the sort sequence. They have now been replaced by the `ASCENDING` and `DESCENDING` additions of the `SORT` statement. If necessary, the complement on nine can be formed using the following `TRANSLATE` statement:

```
dat2 = dat1.
TRANSLATE dat2 USING '09182736455463728190'.
```

Example

After the following program section, the internal table `sflight_tab` is sorted in descending order according to the FLDATE column.

```
DATA
  sflight_tab  TYPE TABLE OF sflight.
FIELD-SYMBOLS
  <sflight_wa> TYPE sflight.

SELECT * FROM sflight INTO TABLE sflight_tab.

LOOP AT sflight_tab ASSIGNING <sflight_wa>.
  CONVERT DATE <sflight_wa>-fldate
    INTO INVERTED-DATE <sflight_wa>-fldate.
ENDLOOP.

SORT sflight_tab BY fldate.
```

```
LOOP AT sflight_tab ASSIGNING <sflight_wa>.
  CONVERT INVERTED-DATE <sflight_wa>-fldate
    INTO DATE <sflight_wa>-fldate.
ENDLOOP.
```

The last nine lines can be replaced with a single line:

```
SORT sflight_tab BY fldate DESCENDING.
```

42.12   Obsolete Processing of Internal Tables

42.12.1   Obsolete Key Specification When Reading Rows

`READ TABLE`

There are obsolete forms of key specification when reading individual lines from internal tables.

Syntax

```
READ TABLE itab obsolete_key result.
```

This statement has the same function as the general `READ` statement described in Section 22.2.1. As well as the additions listed there for specifying the individual rows to be read, the search key can also be specified in three obsolete forms outside of ABAP Objects.

Syntax of *obsolete_key*

```
...{ { }
   | { WITH KEY dobj }
   | { WITH KEY = dobj [BINARY SEARCH]} } ...
```

These three forms can all be replaced by the permitted forms discussed in Section 22.2.1.

42.12.1.1 Implicit Search Key

Syntax

```
READ TABLE itab ...
```

If the search key is not specified explicitly, the internal table `itab` must be a standard table with a header line. The first found line in the internal table is read for which the values in the columns of the standard key match the values in the corresponding components of the header line.

Key fields in the header line that contain only blank characters are handled as if they match all values. If all the key fields in the header line only contain blank characters, the first entry in the table is read.

In Unicode programs, the standard key of the internal table must not contain any byte-type components when the implicit search key is used.

Note
The statement READ TABLE itab ... is not the same as the statement READ TABLE itab FROM itab ... In the latter, the table key and not the search key of the header field is used for the search. Also, with this statement, key fields that contain blank characters do not match all fields of the internal table.

Example
In the following READ statement (in contrast to the example in Section 22.2.1.1) in general no entry is found as the whole standard key is compared. Note, in particular, the components deptime and arrtime that belong to the standard key of the internal table are of type t and contain the value "000000" instead of blank characters as an initial value in the header line. Only table entries that contain exactly these values are read.

```
DATA: spfli_tab TYPE STANDARD TABLE OF spfli
                WITH NON-UNIQUE KEY carrid connid
                WITH HEADER LINE.

FIELD-SYMBOLS <spfli> TYPE spfli.

SELECT *
      FROM spfli
      INTO TABLE spfli_tab
      WHERE carrid = 'LH'.

spfli_tab-carrid = 'LH'.
spfli_tab-connid = '0400'.

READ TABLE spfli_tab ASSIGNING <spfli>.
```

42.12.1.2 Search Key with Casting

Syntax

```
READ TABLE itab WITH KEY dobj ...
```

If a single data object is specified directly after the addition WITH KEY, the internal table itab must be a standard table. The first line found in the internal table is read, whose left-aligned content matches the content of the data object `dobj`. For the data object `dobj`, only flat data types are allowed. In the search, the start of table rows that are longer than the data object `dobj` are handled as if they have the same data type `dobj` (casting).

Example

To use the addition `WITH KEY dobj` for evaluating specific key fields, a structure must be created that corresponds to the relevant starting part of the line type. In contrast to the example in Section 22.2.1, in the following program section the client column `mandt` of the table `spfli_tab` must be taken into account in the search key.

```
DATA: spfli_tab TYPE STANDARD TABLE OF spfli
                WITH NON-UNIQUE KEY carrid connid.

DATA: BEGIN OF key_struc,
        mandt  TYPE spfli-mandt  VALUE '000',
        carrid TYPE spfli-carrid VALUE 'LH',
        connid TYPE spfli-connid VALUE '0400',
      END OF key_struc.

FIELD-SYMBOLS <spfli> TYPE spfli.

SELECT *
      FROM spfli
      INTO TABLE spfli_tab
      WHERE carrid = 'LH'.

READ TABLE spfli_tab WITH KEY key_struc
                     ASSIGNING <spfli>.
```

42.12.1.3 Search Key for the Entire Table Line

Syntax

```
READ TABLE itab WITH KEY = dobj [BINARY SEARCH] ...
```

If the addition `WITH KEY` is followed by a single data object after an equals sign, the first line found in the internal table `itab` is read, whose whole content corresponds to the content of the data object `dobj`. It must be possible to convert the data object `dobj` to the line type of the internal table. If the data type of `dobj` does not correspond to the line type of the internal table, a conversion is performed for the comparison according to the rules in Section 13.2.1.2.

Note

This statement has the same function as the specification of the pseudo component table_line as a free key (see Section 22.5) and is replaced by this.

READ TABLE itab **WITH KEY** table_line = dobj
                    [BINARY SEARCH] ...

Example

Obsolete determination of whether a line in an internal table exists with an elementary line type. The comment lines show the general valid syntax with the pseudo component table_line.

```
DATA itab TYPE TABLE OF i.

DO 10 TIMES.
  APPEND sy-index TO itab.
ENDDO.

READ TABLE itab WITH KEY = 4
               TRANSPORTING NO FIELDS.
* READ TABLE itab WITH KEY table_line = 4
*              TRANSPORTING NO FIELDS.

IF sy-subrc = 0.
  ...
ENDIF.
```

42.12.2 Obsolete Assignment to Table Lines

```
WRITE TO
```

Writing formatted values into table lines.

Syntax

```
WRITE dobj TO itab[+off][(len)] INDEX idx
      [int_format_options].
```

This variant of the statement WRITE TO has the same effect as the variant in Section 16.4, with the difference that the edited content is written to the row in the internal table itab in which idx is specified. The internal table must be a standard table. The same requirements apply for the row type as for the variable destination in Section 16.4.

For idx, a data object of the data type i is expected. It must be a data type which, when the statement is executed, contains the index of the row to be overwritten. If the value of idx is less than or equal to 0, an exception that cannot be handled will result. If the value of idx is greater than the number of table rows, no row will be overwritten and sy-subrc will be set to 4.

After the table name itab, offset and length specifications off and len can be made. These refer to the specified table row.

Return values

sy-subrc	Meaning
0	The data object specified in source_name and the row specified in idx were found and the statement was executed.
4	The data object specified in source_name or the row specified in idx were not found and the statement was not executed.

Note

This form of the statement WRITE TO is now only possible outside of ABAP Objects and is replaced via access to table lines by field symbols or data references. The following rows show the implementation with a field symbol:

FIELD-SYMBOLS ⟨line⟩ **LIKE LINE OF** itab.

READ TABLE itab **INDEX** idx **ASSIGNING** ⟨line⟩.
WRITE dobj **TO** ⟨line⟩[+off][(len)][*int_format_options*].

Example

Formatted writing of the current date into the first row of the internal table itab. The first statement WRITE TO uses the obsolete form; the second statement WRITE TO represents the recommended variant.

```
DATA line(80) TYPE c.
DATA itab     LIKE TABLE OF line.

FIELD-SYMBOLS <line> LIKE LINE OF itab.

APPEND line TO itab.

WRITE sy-datum TO itab INDEX 1 DD/MM/YYYY.

READ TABLE itab INDEX 1 ASSIGNING <line>.
WRITE sy-datum TO <line> DD/MM/YYYY.
```

42.12.3 Obsolete Form of the PROVIDE Statement

```
PROVIDE
```

Short form of the special join for internal tables.

Syntax

```
PROVIDE {*|{comp1 comp2 ...}} FROM itab1
        {*|{comp1 comp2 ...}} FROM itab2
        ...
        BETWEEN extlim1 AND extlimu.
    ...
ENDPROVIDE.
```

This form of the `PROVIDE` statement is a short form of the variant described in Section 22.7. It can only be used outside of classes. The ABAP compiler distinguishes the long from the short form by the language elements `FIELDS` to be specified explictly before the component specifications.

In principle, the short form of the `PROVIDE` statement works like the permitted variant since Release 6.20. Unlike the permitted variant, however, fewer additions are allowed here. In the short form, you cannot specify a table several times. The internal tables must have headers, and the additions that have to be specified in the long form are enhanced in the short form by the runtime environment as described below.

For the `PROVIDE` loop to function correctly, the same conditions apply as for the form valid since Release 6.20. However, exceptions are now raised if one of the involved tables is not sorted or if there are overlapping intervals.

42.12.3.1 Interval limits BOUNDS

The columns for interval limits to be specified in the long form as `intlim1` and `intlim2` using `BOUNDS` are attributes of the relevant tables in the short form and must be specified when they are declared.

This is done using the `VALID BETWEEN` addition that can be specified after `DATA END OF` if an internal table is declared with the obsolete `OCCURS` addition to the `DATA BEGIN OF` statement (see Section 42.4.2). If an internal table is declared using the `INFOTYPES` statement, these are usually the BEGDA and ENDDA columns (see Section 42.4.3). If no columns are specified for the interval limits in the declaration, the short form of `PROVIDE` uses the first two columns of the internal table.

42.12.3.2 Work area INTO

In the short form, the headers of the internal table are implicitly used for the work areas that have to be specified as wa in the new form using the INTO addition.

42.12.3.3 VALID flag

For the data objects to be specified as flag with the addition VALID in the new form, a data object itab_valid of type c and length 1 is created implicitly for each table itab in the short form.

42.12.3.4 WHERE condition

No conditions can be specified in the short form.

42.12.3.5 INCLUDING GAPS addition

In the short form, you cannot force the system to pass the PROVIDE loop for every interval.

Note
The short form of the PROVIDE statement is especially useful with internal tables declared using INFOTYPES or with internal tables that have the structure of Infotypes (see Section 42.4.3).

System fields
The system fields sy-tabix and sy-subrc are not filled by the short form for PROVIDE – ENDPROVIDE.

Example
The example has the same result as the example for the new form of PROVIDE in Section 22.7. Here, the tables itab1 and itab2 have headers, and the columns col1 and col2 are defined as interval limits of type i using the VALID addition to the DATA END OF statement.

```
DATA: BEGIN OF itab1 OCCURS 0,
        col1 TYPE i,
        col2 TYPE i,
        col3 TYPE string,
      END OF itab1 VALID BETWEEN col1 AND col2.

DATA: BEGIN OF itab2 OCCURS 0,
        col1 TYPE i,
        col2 TYPE i,
```

```
            col3 TYPE string,
         END OF itab2 VALID BETWEEN col1 AND col2.
itab1-col1 = 1.
itab1-col2 = 6.
itab1-col3 = 'Itab1 Int1'.
APPEND itab1 TO itab1.

itab1-col1 = 9.
itab1-col2 = 12.
itab1-col3 = 'Itab1 Int2'.
APPEND itab1 TO itab1.

itab2-col1 = 4.
itab2-col2 = 11.
itab2-col3 = 'Itab2 Int1'.
APPEND itab2 TO itab2.

PROVIDE col3 FROM itab1
        col3 FROM itab2
             BETWEEN 2 AND 14.
  WRITE: / itab1-col1, itab1-col2,
           itab1-col3, itab1_valid.
  WRITE: / itab2-col1, itab2-col2,
           itab2-col3, itab2_valid.
  SKIP.
ENDPROVIDE.
```

42.13   Contexts

42.13.1   Overview

Contexts are repository objects defined abstractly in the Context Builder in the ABAP Workbench (transaction SE33) that are used to derive the values of additional fields from key fields. ABAP programs work with instances of contexts.

A context comprises fields and modules. The fields of a context are subdivided into key fields and derived fields. The modules describe how the values of the derived fields are created from the key fields. Modules are based on foreign key dependencies between database tables and function modules defined in the ABAP Dictionary or on other contexts. Viewed from a technical perspective, contexts are special ABAP programs (context programs) generated by the Context Builder.

An ABAP program can create one or more instances of a context. It can supply the key fields for each instance with values, and it can query the fields derived. Each context has a cross-transaction buffer on the application server, and the buffer's attributes are defined in the Context Builder. When an instance is queried for values, the system first searches the corresponding buffer for a record with the corresponding key fields. Only if no values have yet been recorded for this key are they derived from the modules and written to the buffer.

Note

Although contexts can be compared with highly specialized classes, they are not a part of ABAP Objects. Contexts were introduced with Release 4.0 for high-performance access to commonly required derived data. Since the introduction of ABAP Objects with Release 4.5, development of contexts has been discontinued. Since Release 6.40, contexts can be replaced with Shared Objects.

The ABAP statements for processing contexts are:

Statement	Section
CONTEXTS	42.13.2
SUPPLY	42.13.3
DEMAND	42.13.4

42.13.2 Creating Instances of Contexts

`CONTEXTS`

Declaring the data type for context instances.

Syntax

`CONTEXTS con.`

This statement can be specified in the global declaration section of a program or in the locale declaration section of a procedure. It creates a structured data type, local to the program, which can be used to create an instance of the context `con`. For `con`, you can specify the name of a context defined in the current SAP system. The name of the created data type is made up of the prefix `context_` and the name `con` of the specified context.

If you use the data type context_con, created using CONTEXTS, after the TYPE addition to the DATA statement, this creates an instance of the context con to which the declared data object points. The data object must not be declared as a component of a structure. The content of the created data object is interpreted as a reference. After value is assigned to another data object of the same data type, this data object points to the same context instance.

In addition to the data type context_con, another structured data type context_t_con is created. For each field of the context, this data type contains an identically-named component with its relevant data type.

Note

Data objects declared with the data type context_con should only be used in the statements SUPPLY and DEMAND.

42.13.3 Providing Contexts with Key Values

```
SUPPLY
```

Filling key fields of context instances.

Syntax

```
SUPPLY key1 = f1 key2 = f2 ... TO CONTEXT context_ref.
```

This statement fills the key fields key1, key2, ... of a context instance with the values of data objects f1, f2, ... For context_ref, you must specify a data object that points to a context instance (see Section 42.13.2). For key1, key2, ..., you can specify the names of key fields of the respective context. For f1, f2, ..., you must specify data objects whose data type is suited for the respective key field key1, key2, ...

The SUPPLY statement overwrites only the specified key fields with new values. If not all key fields are specified, the previous values are kept. The values of all fields of the context instance derived from a changed key field are rendered invalid by the SUPPLY statement.

42.13.4 Querying Contexts

```
DEMAND
```

Querying fields of context instances.

Syntax

```
DEMAND val1 = f1 val2 = f2 ...
       FROM CONTEXT context_ref
       [MESSAGES INTO itab].
```

This statement assigns the values of derived fields `val1`, `val2`, ... of a context instance to the data objects `f1`, `f2`, ... For `context_ref`, you must specify a data objects that points to a context instance (see Section 42.13.2). For `val1`, `val2`, ..., you can specify the names of derived fields of the corresponding context. For `f1`, `f2`, ..., you must specify data objects whose data type conforms with the corresponding context field `val1`, `val2`, ...

If the context instance contains valid derived values for the current key, these are assigned directly. Otherwise, the cross-transaction buffer of the context is searched for the corresponding data record, which is then transferred to the context instance and from there to the data objects `f1`, `f2`, ... Only if no corresponding data is found here, the values in the modules of the context are derived and placed in the buffer, the context instance and the data objects `f1`, `f2`, ...

If not all required values can be derived because not enough key fields are known, processing is stopped. The derived values are initialized and the module sends the message specified in the context for this purpose.

The `MESSAGES` addition is used for handling messages that may be sent by the modules of a context. If the `MESSAGES` addition is not specified, each message is sent according to its definition in the context as described in Section 28.1.2. If the `MESSAGES` addition is specified, the messages are not sent; instead, for each message, a row is attached to the internal table `itab` specified after `INTO`. The row type of the internal table must refer to the structure SYMSG in the ABAP Dictionary. The columns `msgty`, `msgid`, `msgno`, and `msgv1` to `msgv4` contain the message type, message class, message number, and content of any possible placeholders (see Chapter 28). The internal table `itab` is initialized at the start of the `DEMAND` statement.

Note
The structured type `context_t_con` created with `CONTEXTS` can be used to create suitable fields.

Return values

sy-subrc	Meaning
0	The MESSAGES addition is not specified or the internal table specified after MESSAGES is empty.
Unequal to 0	The internal table specified after MESSAGES contains messages.

Example

In this example, an instance of the context demo_travel is created, the key fields are supplied, and the derived values are requested.

```
CONTEXTS demo_travel.

PARAMETERS: p_carrid TYPE context_t_demo_travel-carrid,
            p_connid TYPE context_t_demo_travel-connid.

DATA: context_ref TYPE context_demo_travel,
      fields      TYPE context_t_demo_travel.

SUPPLY carrid = p_carrid
       connid = p_connid
       TO CONTEXT context_ref.

DEMAND cityfrom = fields-cityfrom
       cityto   = fields-cityto
       fltime   = fields-fltime
       FROM CONTEXT context_ref.

WRITE: / fields-cityfrom, fields-cityto, fields-fltime.
```

42.14 Obsolete Statements in the Flow Logic of Dynpros

42.14.1 Checking Values in the Flow Logic

```
FIELD ... VALUES | SELECT
```

Comparison of a dynpro field with a value list or with database content.

```
FIELD f { value_list | db_query }.
```

This statement can be used in the event block at PAI of the dynpro flow logic. It compares the content of dynpro field f either with entries in a value list value_list or with the results of a database access db_query.

These types of input checks in the dynpro flow logic are executed after the automatic input checks and before the self-programmed input checks in the ABAP program. The specified value list or the result set of the database accesses overrule the automatic input help of the ABAP Dictionary. They are themselves overruled by the events POH and POV. The additions VALUES and SELECT have no influence on the effect of the FIELDS statement on the data transport from the dynpro to the ABAP program.

Note

The variants *value_list* and *db_query* are supported only for reasons of compatibility. You should replace them by checks within the ABAP program.

42.14.1.1 Comparing with a Value List

Syntax of *value_list*

```
VALUES ([[NOT] val1], [[NOT] val2], ...
        [[NOT] BETWEEN vali AND valj], ...).
```

A value list is specified by entries after the addition VALUES which must be in brackets and separated by commas.

The content of the dynpro field f can be compared with single values val1, val2, ... and with value ranges [vali, valj]. You can negate the result of each of the comparisons using the NOT operator. The comparison fields val must be included in inverted commas and specified in uppercase. The content must be part of the value ranges of the data types CHAR or NUMC of the ABAP Dictionary.

If a comparison is not true, an error message appears in the status bar of the current window and the corresponding input field is input-enabled again.

Example

Checking the input field for an airline carrier.

```
PROCESS AFTER INPUT.
  FIELD carrier
        VALUES ('AA', NOT 'BA', BETWEEN 'QF' AND 'UA').
```

42.14.1.2 Comparing with a Database Selection

Syntax of *db_query*

```
SELECT *
       FROM dbtab
       WHERE col1 = f1 AND col2 = f2 ...
       [INTO wa]
       WHENEVER [NOT] FOUND
         SEND {ERRORMESSAGE|WARNING} [num [WITH p1 ... p4]]
```

During the execution of the FIELD statement, the addition SELECT looks for a line of the database table dbtab, whose primary key fields col1, col2, ... match the dynpro fields f1, f2, ... The database table dbtab must be defined in the ABAP Dictionary. In the WHERE condition, all primary key fields of the database table that are specified in AND comparisons must be specified with an equal sign (=).

Depending on whether the addition NOT is specified or not, an error or warning message is sent if no or one entry was found in the database table. In both cases, the input field for the dynpro field f is again input-enabled. The message class of the message to be sent must be two characters long and is taken from the first two places of the value specified after the addition MESSAGE-ID of the program-introducing statement of the respective ABAP program. If no message class is specified there, a standard message is sent. The message number can be specified as a number literal num. If the message contains placeholders, they can be filled with up to four values p1, ..., p4 as in the MESSAGE statement with the WITH addition: The placeholders can be specified either as text literals or as dynpro fields.

If a row is found, its content can be assigned to a table work area wa whose structure must match the row type of dbtab. Such a table work area is declared in the dynpro by copying dynpro fields from the ABAP Dictionary.

Note

Without the addition INTO, you can compare the addition SELECT to a subquery in Open SQL. When you specify the addition INTO, you can also use the above SELECT syntax as a stand-alone statement in the dynpro flow logic, that is, without the FIELD statement. However, the use of a SELECT dynpro statement is obsolete. Replace it by the respective Open SQL statement in the ABAP program.

Example

Check whether for the dynpro fields `carrier` and `connect` a row with identical primary key exists in the database table SPFLI. The corresponding ABAP program must contain an appropriate `MESSAGE-ID` addition in the program-introducing statement.

```
PROCESS AFTER INPUT.
  FIELD connect
    SELECT *
           FROM spfli
           WHERE carrid = carrier AND connid = connect
           WHENEVER NOT FOUND SEND ERRORMESSAGE 107
           WITH carrier connect.
```

42.14.2 Processing Step Loops

Step loops are the predecessors of table controls and are defined without individual descriptions in the Screen Painter. A step loop contains screen elements that, unlike table controls, can occupy several lines and that are grouped together in one group which can be repeated several times within the step loop on the screen. The attributes of the screen elements of the first group determine the attributes of the entire step loop. For this reason, the fields of a group can only be created once in the dynpro and the ABAP program.

Processing of step loops and table controls is based on the step loop technique whose main features are the statements `LOOP ... ENDLOOP` in the dynpro flow logic. These statements cause a loop pass via the step-loop rows displayed on the screen and a data transport between the ABAP program and the dynpro for all like-named data objects.

In the Screen Painter, you can also determine whether the size of the step loop is fixed or variable. For each screen, you can define more than one fixed step loop, but only one variable step loop. If the user changes the vertical size of the window, this also changes the vertical size of the variable step loop, whereby the PAI event is triggered.

Independent step loops are obsolete and are replaced by table controls, which are based on step loops but encapsulate them. Accordingly, the listed variants of the `LOOP` statement are obsolete in the dynpro flow logic. The `LOOP` statement of the dynpro flow logic should only be used with the `WITH CONTROL` addition to which it assigns a table control.

LOOP

Processing a step loop in a loop.

Syntax

```
LOOP [AT itab CURSOR top_line [INTO wa] [FROM n1] [TO n2]].
  ...
ENDLOOP.
```

Definition of a loop in the dynpro flow logic. The loop sequentially processes the listed groups of the corresponding step loop by executing a loop pass for each group. The statement block between LOOP and END-LOOP can contain the keywords FIELD, MODULE and CHAIN (as well as the obsolete ones SELECT and VALUES) of the flow logic. Nesting of loops is not possible. Loops can either be executed with or without reference to an internal table.

If step loops are defined in a screen, a loop must be defined for each step loop both in the the PBO processing block and in the PAI processing block. The assignment of loops to step loops is derived from the alignment of the step loops on the screen; the lines are valuated with primary priority and the columns with secondary priority.

System Fields
Within a loop pass, the system field sy-stepl contains the line number of the displayed group, counted from the uppermost visible line. The system field sy-loopc contains the number of group lines displayed on a screen.

42.14.2.1 Loops That Do Not Refer to an Internal Table

Syntax

```
LOOP.
  ...
ENDLOOP.
```

If the AT itab addition is not specified, the contents of the dynpro fields belonging to the current group of the step loop are transported during a loop pass from (at event PBO) or to (at event PAI) data objects with the same name in the ABAP program.

Note

For step loop fields that are defined with reference to the ABAP Dictionary, the data objects with the same name in the ABAP program must be declared using `TABLES`, as is the case with normal dynpro fields. Otherwise, no data transport will take place.

Example

In the layout of the dynpro screen, there are two dynpro fields `wa-col1` and `wa-col2` that are grouped together to a group of a step loop. The dynpro flow logic contains the following statements:

```
PROCESS BEFORE OUTPUT.
  ...
  LOOP.
    MODULE tab_out.
  ENDLOOP.
  ...
PROCESS AFTER INPUT.
  ...
  LOOP.
    MODULE tab_in.
  ENDLOOP.
  ...
```

Loops are run on the step loop and, in the loops for PBO and PAI, the dialog modules `tab_out` and `tab_in` are called. The following program section shows how the respective ABAP program fills the step loop fields in the PBO module `tab_out` from an internal table `itab`. It also shows how, in the PAI module `tab_in`, it modifies the internal table in accordance with the user specifications in the step loop.

```
DATA: BEGIN OF wa,
        col1 TYPE i,
        col2 TYPE i,
      END OF wa,
      itab LIKE STANDARD TABLE OF wa.

...

MODULE tab_out OUTPUT.
  IF itab IS INITIAL.
    DO 40 TIMES.
      wa-col1 = sy-index.
      wa-col2 = sy-index ** 2.
      APPEND wa TO itab.
```

```
      ENDDO.
    ENDIF.
    READ TABLE itab INTO wa INDEX sy-step1.
ENDMODULE.

...

MODULE tab_in INPUT.
   MODIFY itab FROM wa INDEX sy-step1.
ENDMODULE.
```

42.14.2.2 Loop That Refers to an Internal Table

Syntax

```
LOOP AT itab CURSOR top_line [INTO wa] [FROM n1] [TO n2].
   ...
ENDLOOP.
```

If the addition AT itab is specified, an internal table itab of the corresponding ABAP program is sequentially processed parallel to the processing of the step loop. For each group of the step loop, a line in the internal table is processed. The internal table itab must be an index table.

A scroll bar will continue to be generated for the display of the corresponding step loop. This bar allows you to scroll between the lines of the internal table itab and to display the corresponding lines in the step loop. Each scrolling action triggers the event PAI. For the scrolling to function correctly, the addition AT itab must be specified both in the PBO as well as in the PAI processing block.

The additions CURSOR, INTO, TO and FROM can only be specified in the PBO, not in the PAI processing block.

▶ The addition CURSOR controls at which line of the internal table processing will begin at the time of PBO, that is, the content of which line will be displayed first in the step loop. For top_line, you must specify a global data object of the ABAP program with the type i. If the content of top_line is less than 1 or the value of n1, it is implicitly set to 1 or to the value of n1. If it is larger than the number of lines in the internal table or than the value of n2, the step loop will not be displayed. For each PAI event, top_line is set to the index of the first displayed table line.

▶ With the addition INTO, you specify a work area wa to which the current line of the internal table is assigned at the time of PBO. If the addition wa is not specified, an internal table with a header line must be used; this is then used implicitly instead of wa. The content of wa or of the header line is transported after the assignment to the fields of the same name in the current group of the step loop. The work area wa must be a global data object of the ABAP program that matches the line type of the internal table. At the time of PAI, in contrast, only the work area wa or the header line of the internal table is supplied through the contents of the step loop fields. The content of the internal table is not modified automatically.

▶ With the additions FROM and TO, you can limit the internal table lines to be processed. Sequential processing of the table begins with the line whose index is contained in n1 and ends with the line whose index is contained in n2. If the additions are not specified, processing begins with the first line and ends with the last line. For n1 and n2, global data objects of the ABAP program with the type i must be specified. The value of n2 must be larger than the value of n1, and it must lie within the number of lines in the internal table. If the value of n1 is less than or equal to 0, it will be implicitly set to 1.

Example

In the layout of a dynpro screen, there are two dynpro fields wa-col1 and wa-col2 belonging to a group of a step loop. The dynpro flow logic contains the following statements:

```
PROCESS BEFORE OUTPUT.
  ...
  MODULE tab_init.
  LOOP AT itab CURSOR top_line INTO wa.
  ENDLOOP.
  ...

PROCESS AFTER INPUT.
  ...
  MODULE get_first_line.
  LOOP AT itab.
    MODULE tab_in.
  ENDLOOP.
  ...
```

Parallel loops are executed through the step loop and the internal itab table. At PBO, no dialog module is called in the loop. Instead, the module tab_init is called beforehand to edit the internal table itab. At PAI, the module tab_in is called in the loop to modify the internal table in accordance with the user specifications in the step loop. But first, the module `get_first_line` is called in order to store the index of the first displayed table line in the help variable `line`. This is necessary because the content of `cur` will be changed when the user scrolls further. The following program section shows the dialog modules of the corresponding ABAP program:

```
DATA: BEGIN OF wa,
        col1 TYPE i,
        col2 TYPE i,
      END OF wa,
      itab LIKE TABLE OF wa.

DATA: cur  TYPE i,
      line TYPE i,
      idx  TYPE i.
...

MODULE tab_init OUTPUT.
  IF itab IS INITIAL.
    DO 40 TIMES.
      wa-col1 = sy-index.
      wa-col2 = sy-index ** 2.
      APPEND wa TO itab.
    ENDDO.
  ENDIF.
ENDMODULE.
...

MODULE get_first_line INPUT.
  line = cur.
ENDMODULE.

MODULE tab_in INPUT.
  idx = sy-step1 + line - 1.
  MODIFY itab FROM wa INDEX idx.
ENDMODULE.
```

42.15 Obsolete Statements in List Processing

42.15.1 Obsolete Formatting Statements

The following formatting statements are not allowed in ABAP Objects because they have been replaced by the statements FORMAT and WRITE.

42.15.1.1 Weak Background Colors

```
DETAIL
```

Setting the weak color palette for the background colors of a list line.

Syntax

```
DETAIL.
```

This statement has the same meaning as the following statement and is replaced by it:

```
FORMAT INTENSIFIED OFF.
```

42.15.1.2 Intensified Background Colors

```
SUMMARY
```

Setting the intensified color palette for the background colors of a list line.

Syntax

```
SUMMARY.
```

This statement is synonymous with the following statement and is replaced by it:

```
FORMAT INTENSIFIED ON.
```

42.15.1.3 Input Fields

```
INPUT
```

Making fields on lists ready for input.

Syntax

```
INPUT.
```

This statement has the same meaning as the following statement, which replaces it

```
FORMAT INPUT ON.
```

42.15.2 Obsolete Print Parameters

In the statements for creating print lists NEW-PAGE PRINT ON and SUBMIT
... TO SAP-SPOOL, either the print dialog window is displayed or print
parameters have to be transferred. Print parameters are transferred using
the additions [SPOOL] PARAMETERS and ARCHIVE PARAMETERS. The following print parameters are obsolete.

42.15.2.1 Printing in the Current Program

```
NEW-PAGE PRINT ON
```

Creating a print list in a program.

Syntax

```
NEW PAGE PRINT ON ... obsolete_parameters.
```

Instead of the additions PARAMETERS and ARCHIVE PARAMETERS, the obsolete print parameter additions obsolete_parameters listed in Table 42.1
can still be specified outside of ABAP Objects.

42.15.2.2 Printing in the Called Program

```
SUBMIT TO SAP-SPOOL
```

Creating a print list in a called program.

Syntax

```
SUBMIT ... TO SAP-SPOOL ... obsolete_parameters.
```

Instead of the additions SPOOL PARAMETERS and ARCHIVE PARAMETERS, the
obsolete print parameter additions obsolete_parameters in Table 42.1
can still be specified outside of ABAP Objects.

42.15.2.3 Table of Obsolete Print Parameter Additions

The obsolete_parameters additions have been completely replaced by
the additions [SPOOL] PARAMETERS and ARCHIVE PARAMETERS. The structures transferred in this process are filled using the function module GET_
PRINT_PARAMETERS. The second column in the table lists the corresponding input parameter of this function module for every obsolete
addition.

Obsolete addition	Input parameter
ARCHIVE MODE arcmode	ARCHIVE_MODE
COPIES cop	COPIES
COVER PAGE flag (only for SUBMIT)	COVER_PAGE
COVER TEXT text	LIST_TEXT
DESTINATION dest	DESTINATION
DATASET EXPIRATION days	EXPIRATION
DEPARTMENT dep	DEPARTMENT
IMMEDIATELY flag	IMMEDIATELY
KEEP IN SPOOL flag	RELEASE
LAYOUT layout	LAYOUT
LINE-COUNT line	LINE_COUNT
LINE-SIZE col	LINE_SIZE
LIST AUTHORITY auth	AUTHORITY
LIST DATASET dsn	DATA_SET
LIST NAME name	LIST_NAME
NEW LIST IDENTIFICATION flag	NEW_LIST_ID
RECEIVER user	RECEIVER
SAP COVER PAGE mode	SAP_COVER_PAGE

Table 42.1 Obsolete Print Parameters

42.15.3 Obsolete Creation of a Spool Task

```
NEW-SECTION
```

Redirects the list output into a print list.

Syntax

```
NEW-SECTION.
```

This statement is identical to the statement below and is replaced by it:

```
NEW-PAGE PRINT ON NEW-SECTION.
```

Note

This statement is not allowed in ABAP Objects, because it is replaced by the addition of the NEW-PAGE statement and does not allow the specification of print parameters.

42.16 Obsolete Database Accesses

42.16.1 Obsolete Reading of a Row

```
READ TABLE dbtab
```

Directly reading a line in a database table.

Syntax

```
READ TABLE dbtab [WITH KEY key]
                 [SEARCH {FKEQ|FKGE|GKEQ|GKGE}]
                 [VERSION vers].
```

This variant of the statement READ reads a row from the database table dbtab and assigns the content to the respective table work area. For dbtab, you can specify the name of a database table that begins with "T" and is not longer than five characters. The table work area must be declared with the statement TABLES for the datbase table dbtab.

Without the addition WITH KEY, the row to be read is determined by the content of the components of the table work area which correspond to the primary key fields of the database table dbtab. With the addition WITH KEY, the key is determined through the content of the data object key for which a flat character-type data type is expected.

The content of the table work area or of the data object key is taken from the database table as a search key (left-aligned with the length of the key components); then a matching entry is searched in the database table. The addition SEARCH determines how the row is searched:

▶ Without the addition SEARCH and with SEARCH FKEQ, the first row in the database table is searched that matches the withdrawn search key.

▶ With SEARCH GKEQ, you search generically for the first row in the database table that matches the withdrawn search key. The search key treats blanks as if they match all values.

▶ With SEARCH FKGE, the first row of the database table is searched that is larger or equal to the withdrawn search key.

- With SEARCH GKGE, you search generically for the first row of the database table that is larger or equal to the withdrawn search key. The search key treats blanks as if they match all values.

If the addition VERSION is specified, then not the database table dbtab is read but the table whose name is composed of "T" and the content of vers. For vers, you have to specify a data object of the type c with a maximum length of four characters. The content of the rows is still assigned to the table work area dbtab on whose type it is also cast onto.

The statement is not executed if the database table does not exist or does not comply with the naming conventions stated above.

In Unicode-programs, all components of the table work area which correspond to primary key fields of the database table dbtab must be character-type.

Return values

sy-subrc	Meaning
0	A table entry was read.
4	No table entry was found for the specified search key.

Note

This form of the READ statement is not allowed in ABAP Objects. It must be replaced with the SELECT statement.

Example

Reading a row from the database table T100 or another database table that starts with "T."

```
TABLES t100.

PARAMETERS p TYPE c LENGTH 4 DEFAULT '100T'.

t100-sprsl = 'E'.
t100-arbgb = 'BC'.
t100-msgnr = '010'.

READ TABLE t100 SEARCH FKEQ VERSION p.
IF sy-subrc = 0.
  ...
ENDIF.
```

The Open SQL syntax to be used instead reads:

```
PARAMETERS p TYPE c LENGTH 5 DEFAULT 'T100T'.
```

```
DATA dref TYPE REF TO data.
FIELD-SYMBOLS <fs> TYPE ANY.

CREATE DATA dref TYPE (p).
ASSIGN dref->* TO <fs>.

SELECT SINGLE *
       FROM (p)
       INTO <fs>
       WHERE sprsl = 'E' AND
             arbgb = 'BC' AND
             msgnr = '010'.

IF sy-subrc = 0.
  ...
ENDIF.
```

42.16.2 Obsolete Sequential Reading of Several Rows

```
LOOP AT dbtab
```

Sequential reading of several lines of a database table in a loop.

Syntax

```
LOOP AT dbtab [VERSION vers].
  ...
ENDLOOP.
```

The statements LOOP and ENDLOOP define a loop around a statement block. For dbtab, you can specify a database table that begins with "T" and has a maximum length of five characters. For the database table dbtab, a table work area must be declared with the TABLES statement.

In each loop run, the statement LOOP reads a line from the database table dbtab and assigns its content to the table work area. The lines to be read are determined by the content of the components of the table work area, which correspond with the primary key fields of the database table dbtab. Before the first loop run, the content of these components is taken as the search key, reading from the left, and the database table is searched generically for suitable entries. In the search key, blank characters are treated as if they agree with all values.

If the addition VERSION is specified, the database table dbtab is not read; instead, the table with a name made up of "T" and of the content of vers is read. For vers, a data object with a maximum of four characters of type c must be specified. The content of the row is still assigned to the table work area of `dbtab` and its type is cast.

The loop is not executed if the database table does not exist or if it does not comply with the naming conventions outlined above.

In Unicode programs, all components of the table work area that correspond with the primary key fields of the database table `dbtab` must be character-like.

Note
This form of the `LOOP` loop is not allowed in ABAP Objects. It must be replaced with the `SELECT` statement.

Example
Sequential reading of rows from the database table T100.

```
TABLES t100.

t100        = space.
t100-sprsl = 'E'.
t100-arbgb = 'BC'.
t100-msgnr = '1'.

LOOP AT t100.
  ...
ENDLOOP.
```

The Open SQL syntax to be used instead reads:

```
DATA wa TYPE t100.

SELECT *
      FROM t100
      INTO wa
      WHERE sprsl = 'E'  AND
            arbgb = 'BC' AND
            msgnr LIKE '1%'.
  ...
ENDSELECT.
```

42.16.3 Obsolete Reading of Several Rows into an Internal Table

REFRESH FROM TABLE

Reading several lines of a database table into an internal table.

Syntax

```
REFRESH itab FROM TABLE dbtab.
```

The variant of the statement REFRESH initializes the internal table itab, reads several rows from the database table dbtab, and adds their contents to the internal table itab. The row contents are cast to the row type of the internal table.

For dbtab, the name of a database table that begins with "T" and covers a maximum of five characters can be specified. For the database table dbtab, a table work area must be declared using the statement TABLES. The internal table itab must be an index table.

Which rows are read is determined by the content of the components in the table work area. These are contents that match the primary key fields of the database table dbtab. The content of these components is taken, left-aligned, as a search key, and the system makes a generic search for suitable entries in the database table. Blanks in the search key are treated as if they matched all values.

The statement is not executed if the database table does not exist or if it does not match the specified name conventions.

In Unicode programs, all components of the table work area that match primary key fields of the database table dbtab must be character-type.

Note

This form of the READ statement is not allowed in ABAP Objects. It must be replaced by the SELECT statement.

Example

Reading several rows from the database table T100 into an internal table itab.

```
TABLES t100.
DATA itab TYPE STANDARD TABLE OF t100.

t100-sprsl = 'E'.
t100-arbgb = 'BC'.

REFRESH itab FROM TABLE t100.
```

The Open SQL syntax to be used instead is:

```
DATA itab TYPE STANDARD TABLE OF t100.
```

```
SELECT *
      FROM t100
      INTO TABLE itab
      WHERE sprsl = 'E' AND
            arbgb LIKE 'BC%'.
```

42.16.4 Obsolete Short Forms in Open SQL

SELECT, INSERT, UPDATE, MODIFY, DELETE

Short forms with an implicit work area.

Syntax

```
{ {SELECT result FROM}
| INSERT
| UPDATE
| MODIFY
| DELETE } { dbtab | *dbtab } [VERSION vers] ...
```

This statement is a short form of the following Open SQL statements from Chapter 29 for accessing a single database table dbtab:

SELECT *result* **FROM** dbtab **INTO** { dbtab | *dbtab } ...

INSERT dbtab **FROM** { dbtab | *dbtab } ...

UPDATE dbtab **FROM** { dbtab | *dbtab } ...

MODIFY dbtab **FROM** { dbtab | *dbtab } ...

DELETE dbtab **FROM** { dbtab | *dbtab } ...

In the short form, the explicit specification of a work area is omitted. A table work area or *dbtab is used implicitly as a work area which has to be declared with TABLES. If *dbtab is used instead of the database table name dbtab, dbtab is accessed, but the additional table work area is used (see Section 41.4.1).

With the VERSION addition, you can specify the database table dynamically in the short form of the MODIFY and DELETE statements if its name begins with "T" and includes no more than five characters. The database table is acessed whose name is made up of "T" and the content of vers. For vers, a data object with four digits at most of type c must be specified. The line contents are still assigned to the table work area of dbtab or dbtab* whose type is cast. The statement is not excecuted if the database table is not available or if it does not correspond to the naming convention specified above.

Note

The short forms and the VERSION addition are not allowed in ABAP Objects. Explicit work areas must be used instead. Rather than using the VERSION addition, you should, in Open SQL, dynamically specify the database table at its operand position.

Example

```
TABLES t100.
DATA vers(4) TYPE c.

...

vers = '100'.

...

t100-sprsl = 'E'.
t100-arbgb = 'BC'.
t100-msgnr = '100'.
DELETE t100 VERSION vers.
```

The Open SQL syntax to be used instead is:

```
DATA: wa TYPE t100,
      dbtab(5) TYPE c.

...

dbtab = 'T100'.

...

wa-sprsl = 'E'.
wa-arbgb = 'BC'.
wa-msgnr = '100'.
DELETE (dbtab) FROM wa.
```

42.17 Obsolete External Programming Interface CPC-I

```
COMMUNICATION
```

Implementation of a program-to-program communication.

Syntax

```
COMMUNICATION comstep ID id [cpic_options].
```

This statement allows cross-system communication between two ABAP programs or between an ABAP program and a program written in another programming language. The entire communication takes place in individual communication steps, for which the statement COMMUNICATION is executed multiple times using the corresponding *comstep* additions. The CPI-C interface, defined by IBM as a communication standard in accordance with the Systems Application Architecture (SAA) standard, is the basis of the communication for both partner programs involved. It makes the following functions available in the form of the CPI-C starter set:

▶ Creating, accepting and terminating a connection
▶ Sending and receiving data

Coordination of the individual communication steps, logging of any errors that occur in the database table TCPIC, and any data conversion that may be needed all take place in each individual program. The parameters that determine the physical partner system of a connection are maintained in the database table TXCOM.

After initializing the connection, the system writes an eight-figure connection number in the data object id. Individual connections can be identified using this number. As is standard, 2^{16} connections are possible for each calling program. Only flat character-like data types are valid for id; the length should not be less than eight characters.

The internal mode in the calling program cannot be changed during the communication. If the statement NEW-PAGE is first specified, screen outputs are ignored and list outputs are diverted to the SAP spool system. Messages of the types "I," "S," and "W" are ignored, and those of the types "A" and "E" cause a program termination.

Note
The statement COMMUNICATION is no longer supported in ABAP Objects. It should not be used outside of ABAP Objects either, because the more efficient statement CALL FUNCTION ... DESTINATION is now available for the communication between programs (see Chapter 39).

42.17.1 Connection Steps

Syntax of *comstep*

```
... {INIT DESTINATION dest}
  | ALLOCATE
```

```
|   ACCEPT
|   {SEND BUFFER buf}
|   {RECEIVE BUFFER buf DATAINFO dat STATUSINFO stat}
|   DEALLOCATE ...
```

There are different alternatives for specifying `comstep`, each of which is responsible for a connection step.

42.17.1.1 Initializing the connection

Syntax

```
... INIT DESTINATION dest ...
```

The connection between the programs is initialized by specifying `dest`. A flat character-like data object of the length 8 is expected for `dest`. When executing the statement, the data object contains a value from the column SDEST of the database table TXCOM.

On initialization, the system automatically executes an authorization check on the authorization object S_CPIC. The authorization can be checked before the connection is established using the function module AUTHORITY_CHECK_CPIC.

42.17.1.2 Establishing the connection

Syntax

```
... ALLOCATE ...
```

Establishment of a connection to the partner program identified in the previous addition DESTINATION. At the same time, a start request is passed to the partner program.

42.17.1.3 Accepting the connection

Syntax

```
... ACCEPT ...
```

This addition can be used to accept the established connection in a called partner program. After the authentication, the called program is in receive status.

42.17.1.4 Sending data

Syntax

```
... SEND BUFFER buf ...
```

Sending data to the partner program. A data object can be specified for buf, for which all flat elementary types are permitted and for which the memory requirement of 32 KB must not be exceeded. On the execution of the statement COMMUNICATE, the content of buf is passed to the partner program.

Note
Information loss can occur if, for example, the communication partners have different number formats. This can be avoided by using only character-like types for transferring the data. Furthermore, the data is only completely transferred if the sending buffers and the receiving buffers have the same structure and length.

42.17.1.5 Receiving data

Syntax

```
... RECEIVE BUFFER buf DATAINFO dat STATUSINFO stat ...
```

Receiving data from the partner program. A data object can be specified for buf, for which all flat elementary types are permitted and the memory requirement of 32 KB cannot be exceeded. On the execution of the statement COMMUNICATE, the content of buf is received by the partner program.

After the execution of the statement, the data object dat contains information about whether the data is sent completely, and the content of the data object stat indicates whether the current program is in send or receive mode. Only byte-like data objects are allowed for dat and stat; the length should not be less than 4 bytes. The code for the values in dat and stat can be extracted from the include program RSCPICDF. Here, data objects with a descriptive name and start values are declared which can be compared with dat and stat.

42.17.1.6 Terminating the connection

Syntax

```
... DEALLOCATE ...
```

The connection is terminated and all memory areas are released.

42.17.2 Other Additions

Syntax of *cpic_options*

```
... [ RETURNCODE rc ]
    [ LENGTH leng ]
    [ RECEIVED rec ]
    [ HOLD ] ...
```

42.17.2.1 Receiving a return value

Syntax

```
... RETURNCODE rc ...
```

This addition can be specified in all connection steps. The data type `i` is expected for `rc`. The meaning of the return values is coded in the include program RSCPICDF. Here, data objects with descriptive names and start values are declared that can be compared with `rc`. Table 42.2 contains a list of possible return values.

rc	Data Object from RSCPICDF
0	CM_OK
1	CM_ALLOCATE_FAILURE_NO_RETRY
2	CM_ALLOCATE_FAILURE_RETRY
3	CM_CONVERSATION_TYPE_MISMATCH
6	CM_SECURITY_NOT_VALID
8	CM_SYNC_LVL_NOT_SUPPORTED_PGM
9	CM_TPN_NOT_RECOGNIZED
10	CM_TP_NOT_AVAILABLE_NO_RETRY
11	CM_TP_NOT_AVAILABLE_RETRY
12	CM_DEALLOCATED_ABEND
13	CM_DEALLOCATED_NORMAL
14	CM_PARAMETER_ERROR
15	CM_PRODUCT_SPECIFIC_ERROR
16	CM_PROGRAM_ERROR_NO_TRUNC
18	CM_PROGRAM_ERROR_NO_TRUNC

Table 42.2 CPI-C Return Values

rc	Data Object from RSCPICDF
19	CM_PROGRAM_ERROR_TRUNC
26	CM_RESOURCE_FAILURE_NO_RETRY
27	CM_RESOURCE_FAILURE_RETRY
28	CM_UNSUCCESSFUL

Table 42.2 CPI-C Return Values (cont.)

The same return values are also written in the system field `sy-subrc`.

42.17.2.2 Specifying length

Syntax

```
... LENGTH leng ...
```

This addition can only be specified in the connection steps `SEND` and `RECEIVE`. As a result, the data buffer `buffer` is only sent or received in the length `leng`. A data object of the data type `i` is expected for the length specification `leng`.

42.17.2.3 Evaluating the number of bytes

Syntax

```
... RECEIVED rec ...
```

This addition can only be specified in the connection step `RECEIVE`. The data object `rec` contains the number of bytes received by the partner program. Only byte-like data objects of the length 4 are allowed for `rec`.

42.17.2.4 Hold Internal Mode

Syntax

```
... HOLD ...
```

This addition can only be specified using the connection step `RECEIVE`. It prevents the internal mode being changed during the receiving process to avoid the possible loss of the database cursor. In this case, the current work process waits until the data transfer is complete.

Example

In the simplest case, an ABAP program calls a subroutine in an ABAP program of another SAP system. To do so, the calling program must log on to the other system by specifying the type of the CPI-C service, the log-on data, the program names, the subroutine names, and the type of error handling in effect. The log-on is achieved by sending a special structure to the other system.

The following example illustrates the communication between two ABAP programs P1 and P2 without requesting return values. First, the calling program P1 establishes the connection and sends a structure `connect` with the data required. Once P2 has authorized the connection, P1 sends the actual application data in buffer `b`. Once this data has been received, P2 sends a confirmation to P1. After that, P1 terminates the connection and the content of the buffer ("Answer"), and the length of the received data are output in `rec` ("6").

```
PROGRAM p1.

DATA:
  d    TYPE c LENGTH 8,
  id   TYPE c LENGTH 8,
  b    TYPE c LENGTH 100,
  l    TYPE i,
  dat  TYPE xstring,
  stat TYPE xstring,
  rec  TYPE xstring,

  BEGIN OF connect,
    header   TYPE c LENGTH 12 VALUE 'CONNCPIC1',
    client   TYPE c LENGTH  3 VALUE '001',
    user     TYPE c LENGTH 12 VALUE 'BONDJ',
    password TYPE c LENGTH  8 VALUE '007',
    language TYPE c LENGTH  1 VALUE 'E',
    corr     TYPE c LENGTH  1 VALUE 'X',
    program  TYPE c LENGTH 40 VALUE 'P2',
    routine  TYPE c LENGTH 30 VALUE 'CPIC_START',
  END OF connect.

  d = ...

COMMUNICATION INIT
  DESTINATION d
  ID id.

COMMUNICATION ALLOCATE
  ID id.
```

```
COMMUNICATION SEND
  BUFFER connect
  ID id.
                              ---------▶
                                        PROGRAM p2.
                                        DATA:
                                            id   TYPE c LENGTH 8,
                                            b    TYPE c LENGTH 100,
                                            dat  TYPE xstring,
                                            stat TYPE xstring.
                                        FORM cpic_start.
                                          COMMUNICATION ACCEPT
                                             ID id.
                              ◀---------
b = 'Request'.
COMMUNICATION SEND
  BUFFER b
  LENGTH 7
  ID id.
                              ---------▶
                                        COMMUNICATION RECEIVE
                                          BUFFER     b
                                          DATAINFO   dat
                                          STATUSINFO stat
                                          ID         id.
                                        CLEAR b.
                                        b = 'Answer'.
                                        COMMUNICATION SEND
                                          BUFFER b
                                          ID id.
                                        ENDFORM.
                              ◀---------
CLEAR b.
COMMUNICATION RECEIVE
  BUFFER     b
  DATAINFO   dat
  STATUSINFO stat
  RECEIVED   rec
  ID         id.
WRITE: / b, rec.
  COMMUNICATION DEALLOCATE ID id.
```

42.18 Obsolete Call of a Text Editor

`EDITOR-CALL`

Calling a text editor.

Syntax

```
EDITOR-CALL FOR itab [TITLE title]
                     [{DISPLAY-MODE}|{BACKUP INTO jtab}].
```

This statement transfers the content of the internal table `itab` to a text editor and starts this text editor. The internal table has to be a standard table with a character-type line type.

The text editor has a line width of 72 characters. The content of the table rows is converted according to the rules in Section A.2 line by line into a field of the type `c` with the length 72 and transferred to the text editor. If you leave the text editor via the function **Save**, then the prior content of the table is deleted and the content of each row of the editor is attached from top to bottom to the internal table. During this process, a conversion takes place of the type `c` of the length 72 into the row type of the internal table if necessary.

The optional additions have the following effects.

▶ You can specify the character-type data object `title` after the addition `TITLE`. The first 50 characters of `title` are displayed in the header line of the text editor.

▶ If you specify the addition `DISPLAY-MODE`, the text editor is started in the display mode.

▶ If you specify the addition `BACKUP INTO`, then the content of the internal table `itab` is assigned to an internal table `jtab` before calling the text editor. You can choose any table-type for `jtab`. The row types have to be compatible or convertible.

Return Values

sy-subrc	Meaning
0	You left the text editor via the function **Save** after changing the content.
2	You left the text editor via the function **Save** without changing the content.
4	The text editor was not left via the function **Save**.

Note

This statement is replaced by the direct use of the class CL_GUI_TEXTEDIT for the respective GUI-Control.

Example

Calling a text editor for a text table. The processing in the IF-ENDIF statement block is only executed if the content of the table was actually changed, which is not guaranteed by sy-subrc equals 0 alone.

```
TYPES text(255) TYPE c.

DATA: text_tab TYPE TABLE OF text,
      back_tab LIKE text_tab.

EDITOR-CALL FOR text_tab BACKUP INTO back_tab.

IF sy-subrc = 0 AND
   text_tab <> back_tab.
 ...
ENDIF.
```

Part 15
Appendix

A   Conversion Rules for Assignments

A.1   Overview

The following sections describe the rules for type conversion in assignments. Conversion always takes place if data objects are not compatible, meaning that not all of their attributes, such as type or length, match. For every assignment between incompatible data objects, an appropriate conversion rule must be found to carry out the assignment. If such a rule exists for two data types, they are convertible. A basic rule for all conversions is that the content of the source field must show a meaningful value for the data type of the target field. A detailed description of conversion rules are available for:

Conversion rule	Section
Elementary data types	A.2
Structures	A.3
Internal tables	A.4
Reference variables	A.5

The conversion rules explained here generally apply to all statements in which the contents of data objects are changed. Exceptions to these rules are explained for each individual statement. Differences between Unicode programs and non-Unicode programs are also explained individually.

A.2   Conversion Rules for Elementary Data Types

The programming language ABAP contains 10 predefined elementary data types. It supports automatic type conversion and length adjustment for all of these data types except d (date) and t (time), for which conversion makes no sense. The conversion tables of this section define the conversion rules for assignments between elementary data types for all possible combinations of source-target fields.

In all conversions, it must be possible to create a valid value for the data type of the target field from the content of the source field; otherwise the system triggers an exception that is defined in one of the subclasses of the class CX_SY_CONVERSION_ERROR. The corresponding runtime errors

are catchable and are grouped in the exception group CONVERSION_
ERRORS (see Table D.3).

A.2.1 Presenting Numeric Values in Character-Like Fields

The values of data objects of character-type data types can be assigned to
data objects of the numeric types i, p and f, if they contain the valid representation of a number. The following character strings represent valid
numbers:

▶ **Mathematical Notation**
An uninterrupted sequence of numbers that may contain a maximum
of one period symbol (.) as a decimal separator. An arbitrary number of
blanks may be in front of and behind the sequence of digits. There can
be specified exactly one algebraic sign "+" or "-" in front of the digit sequence. The position of the algebraic sign is arbitrary. We recommend
placing it directly in front of the digit sequence.

▶ **Commercial Notation**
Like the mathematical notation, with the difference that exactly one algebraic sign "+" or "-" can be specified after the digit sequence. The position of the algebraic sign is arbitary. We recommend assigning it directly after the digit sequence.

▶ **Scientific Notation**
An uninterrupted sequence of a mantissa and an exponent. The mantissa is an uninterrupted sequence of a algebraic sign "+" or "-" and a
digit sequence that can have a maximum of one period (.) as a decimal
separator. The exponent is an uninterrupted sequence of the character
"E" or "e", an algebraic sign "+"or "-", and a digit sequence. The numeric value is the value of the mantissa multiplied by 10 to the power
of the value given after the character "E" or "e".

There can be an arbitary number of blanks in front of the number. If
there is a blank after the number, this terminates the number. Any following characters will be ignored. Parts of the notation that are not
required, such as the algebraic sign or the specification of the exponent, can be omitted.

Note
The three different notations have an intersection that can be interpreted
in each notation with the same result, namely an uninterrupted sequence
of numbers with a maximum of one decimal separator. For a common, interpretable intersection of the mathematical notation with the scientific

notation, an algebraic sign can be placed directly in front of this digit sequence. To avoid unexpected results it is recommended to avoid using blanks between algebraic sign and digit sequence.

A.2.2 Conversion Table for Source-Field Type c

Target	Conversion
c	The characters of the source field are inserted in the target field, left-aligned. Trailing blanks in the source field are not transferred. If the target field is longer than the number of transferred characters, it is filled with blank characters to the right. If the target field is shorter, the number is truncated from the right.
d	The same conversion rules apply as to a field of type c of length 8. If the source field does not contain a valid date in the first eight characters, in the format YYYYMMDD, an invalid date is created in the target field.
f	The source field must contain a number in scientific notation. Exception: A source field that contains only blank characters is interpreted as the number zero. Mathematical or commercial notations are not allowed, unless they can be interpreted as scientific notation. If the mantissa contains more than 17 digits, surplus digits are rounded. If the number lies within the value range of data type f, it is converted into the internal representation of a floating point number, otherwise a treatable exception is raised.
i, b, s	The source field must contain a number in mathematical or commercial notation. Exception: A source field that contains only blank characters is interpreted as the number zero. Scientific notation is not allowed, unless it can be interpreted as mathematical notation. Decimal places are rounded commercially to whole-numbered values. If the number lies within the value range of data types i, b or s, it is converted into the internal representation of an integral number; otherwise, a treatable exception is raised. Prior to Release 6.10, an exception is also raised when the source field has been specified as the text field literal '-2147483648'.
n	The characters in the source field that represent digits are inserted in the target field, right-aligned. Other characters are ignored. If the target field is longer than the number of digits in the source field, it is filled to the left with the character "0." If the target field is shorter, the number is truncated from the left.
p	The source field must contain a number in mathematical or commercial notation. Exception: A source field that contains only blank characters is interpreted as the number zero. Scientific notation is not allowed, unless it can be interpreted as a mathematical notation. Decimal places are rounded commercially to the number of decimal places in the target field. If the number lies within the value range of the data type of the target field, it is converted into the internal representation of a packed number. Otherwise a treatable exception is raised.

Table A.1 Conversion rules for source field of type c

Target	Conversion
string	The characters in the source field are inserted in the target field, left-aligned. Trailing blanks in the source field are not transferred. The length of the target field is determined by the number of transferred characters.
t	The same conversion rules apply as to a field of type c with the length 6. Exception: Trailing blanks are transferred, and if the target field is longer than the number of characters transferred, the field is filled to the right with the "0" character.
x	The characters in the source field are interpreted as the representation of the value of a half-byte in hexadecimal representation. As long as the valid characters "0" to "9" and "A" to "F" appear, the corresponding half-byte value is transferred to the memory of the target field, left-aligned. If the target field is longer than the number of transferred half-bytes, it is filled to the right with the hexadecimal 0. If it is too short, the number is truncated to the right. The first invalid character terminates the conversion from the position of this character and the half-bytes of the target field not filled up to that point are filled with the hexadecimal 0.
xstring	Like with conversion to a field of type x half bytes are copied into the destination field. The length of the destination field results from the amount of valid characters in the source field. If the number of valid characters in the destination field is odd, the last remaining half byte is filled with hexadecimal 0.

Table A.1 Conversion rules for source field of type c (cont.)

Note

In ABAP, the trailing blanks in source fields of type c are ignored, by default (compare Section 21.1.4). An assignment from source type c to the target type t is an exception to this rule.

A.2.3 Conversion Table for Source-Field Type d

Target	Conversion
c	Content is handled in the same way as a source field of type c (see Section A.2.2).
d	The content of the source field is transferred unconverted.
f	If the source field contains a valid date in the format YYYYMMDD, this is used to calculate the number of days since 01.01.0001, and this value is then converted to the internal representation of a floating point number. If the source field contains an invalid date, the target field receives the value 0.

Table A.2 Conversion rules for source field of type d

Target	Conversion
i, b, s	If the source field contains a valid date in the format YYYYMMDD, this is used to calculate the number of days since 01.01.0001, and this value is converted to the internal representation of an integer. If the source field contains an invalid date, the target field receives the value 0. If the value range for the data types b and s is not sufficient, this leads to an untreatable exception.
n	The characters of the source field are transferred left-aligned into the target field. Trailing blanks from the source field are copied. If the target field is longer than the source field, the field is filled from the right with "0" characters. If the target field is shorter, the values are cut off from the right.
p	If the source field contains a valid date in the format YYYYMMDD, the number of days since 01.01.0001 is calculated and this value is converted to the internal representation of a packed number. If the value range of the target field is too small, this leads to a treatable exception. If the source field contains an invalid value, the target field receives the value 0.
string	Content is handled in the same way as a source field of type c (see Section A.2.2).
t	Not supported. This leads to a syntax error or an untreatable exception.
x	The content of the source field is first converted to the data type i (see above), and then to the type x (see Section A.2.5).
xstring	The content of the source field is first converted to the data type i (see above), and then to the type xstring (see Section A.2.5).

Table A.2 Conversion rules for source field of type d (cont.)

Note

The conversion rules are designed to complement the way that data objects of type d exhibit character-type behavior when assigned to character-type data objects and exhibit numeric behavior when assigned to numeric data objects. The latter is the basis for date calculations in arithmetic expressions. Only date entries in the format YYYYMMDD are valid data for data objects of type d. The conversion rules, however, allow the assignment of date fields that contain invalid data. The latter is not recommended.

A.2.4 Conversion Table for Source-Field Type f

Target	Conversion
c	The value of the floating point number is formatted in scientific notation (see Section A.2.1) and is copied into the target field aligned to the right. The exponent is always displayed with an algebraic sign and at least two digits. If the target field is shorter than the complete notation, the mantissa is rounded. If the target field is not long enough to include at least one digit of the mantissa apart from the exponent and the algebraic sign (for a negative value), the target field is filled with the "*" character. If the target field is longer than the complete notation, it is filled with blank characters from the left.
d	The content of the source field is first converted to the data type i (see below), and then to the type d (see Section A.2.5).
f	The content of the source field is transferred unconverted.
i, b, s	The value of the floating point number is rounded to an integer. If this number lies within the value range for the data type i, b, or s, it is converted to the internal representation of an integer. If the number is not within this range, it leads to a treatable exception.
n	The value of the floating point number is rounded up to the nearest integer. The absolute value is transferred as a character string right-aligned to the target field. If the target field is longer than the character string, the field is filled with zeros from the left. If the target field is too short, the value is cut off from the left.
p	The value of the floating point number is rounded to the number of decimal places in the target field. If this number is within the value range for the data type of the target field, it is converted to the internal representation of a packed number. Otherwise, a treatable exception occurs.
string	The value of the floating point number is formatted in scientific notation (see Section A.2.1) and transferred to the target field without gaps. The exponent is always displayed with an algebraic sign and at least two digits, and the mantissa with 16 decimal places. Depending on the algebraic sign and the length of the exponent, the resulting length of the target field is between 22 and 24.
t	The content of the source field is first converted to the data type i (see above), and then into the type t (see Section A.2.5).
x	The content of the source field is first converted to the data type i (see above), and then to the type x (see Section A.2.5).
xstring	The content of the source field is first converted to the data type i (see above), and then to the type x (see Section A.2.5).

Table A.3 Conversion rules for source field of type f

A.2.5 Conversion Table for Source Field of Types i, b, or s

Target	Conversion
c	The value of the integer is formatted in the commercial notation and transferred right-justified and without decimal separators into the target field. With negative values, the character "-" is placed in the last position. With positive values, a blank character is placed in the last position. If the target field is longer than the numeric string, including the algebraic sign, the places to the left are filled with blank characters. If the target field is too short, positive numbers are moved one place to the right. If the target field is still too short, (and with negative values) the integer is cut off on the left and the "*" character is placed in the first position of the target field.
d	If the value of the integer is between 1 and 3.652.060, it is interpreted as the number of days since 01.01.0001, and the resulting date is put in the target field in the format YYYYMMTT. If the value lies outside this range, the target field is filled with the character "0."
f	The value of the integer is converted into the internal representation of a floating point number.
i, b, s	If the content is assigned to the same data type, it is not converted when it is transferred. Otherwise the value of the integer is converted into the internal representation of i, b, s. If the value range of data type b or s is exceeded, a treatable exception occurs.
n	The absolute value of the integer is transferred into the target field as a right-justified character string. If the target field is longer than the character string, the spaces to the left are filled with zeros. If it is too short, the values to the left are cut off.
p	The value of the integer is converted into the internal representation of a packed number. If the value range of the target field is too small, a treatable exception results.
string	The value of the integer is formatted in the commercial notation and transferred without any gaps and decimal separators into the target field. With negative values the character "-" is placed in the last position. With positive values a blank character is placed in the last position. The resulting length of the target field is determined by the number of digits plus the algebraic sign.
t	The value of the integer is divided by the number of seconds in a day (86,400) and the whole number of the divide remainder is interpreted as the number of seconds since midnight. The resulting time is put in the target field in the format HHMMSS.

Table A.4 Conversion rules for source fields of types i, b, and s

Target	Conversion
x	The contents of 4, 2 or 1 bytes of the integer are put right-justified in big-endian sequence into the target field. If the target field is longer than 4, 2 or 1, the left side of the integer is filled with hexadecimal 0. If the target field is too short, the places on the left are cut off.
xstring	The contents of 4, 2 or 1 bytes of the integer are put in big-endian sequence into the target field. The length of the target field is always 4, 2 or 1.

Table A.4 Conversion rules for source fields of types i, b, and s (cont.)

A.2.6 Conversion Table for Source-Field Type n

Target	Conversion
c	Content is handled in the same way as a source field of type c (see Section A.2.2).
d	Content is handled in the same way as a source field of type c (see Section A.2.2).
f	Content is handled in the same way as a source field of type c (see Section A.2.2).
i, b, s	Content is handled in the same way as a source field of type c (see Section A.2.2).
n	The characters from the target field are positioned right-aligned in the target field. Trailing blanks are copied. If the target field is longer than the characters transferred, the field is filled with "0" characters from the left. If the target field is shorter, the characters are cut off from the left.
p	Content is handled in the same way as a source field of type c (see Section A.2.2).
string	Content is handled in the same way as a source field of type c (see Section A.2.2).
t	Content is handled in the same way as source field of type c.
x	The content of the source field is first converted to the data type i (see above), and then to the type x. (see Section A.2.5).
xstring	The content of the source field is first converted to the data type i (see above) and then to the type xstring (see Section A.2.5).

Table A.5 Conversion table for source field of type n

Note

The conversion rules are designed to match the way that data objects of type n exhibit character-type behavior when assigned to character-type data objects, and numeric behavior when assigned to numeric data objects. Valid data for data objects of type n is in the form of pure character strings. When assigning valid data to numeric data objects, the numeric value of the character string is assigned to the target object. The conversion rules, however, also allow assignment of numeric text fields that contain invalid data. The latter is not recommended.

A.2.7 Conversion Table for Source-Field Type p

Target	Conversion
c	The value of the packed number is prepared as a numerical value and transferred to the target field, left-aligned. The character "-" is set at the last position for a negative value, and a blank is set for a positive value. If the target field is longer than the sequence of digits, including the algebraic sign, the field is filled with blanks to the left. If it is too short, the number representation is moved to the right, in the case of positive values. If the target field is still too short (and in the case of negative values), the field is cut off to the left and the character "*" is set to the first position of the target field.
d	The content of the source field is converted first into the data type i (see below) and then into the type d (see Table A.3).
f	The value of the packed number is converted to the internal representation of a floating point number.
i, b, s	The value of the packed number is commercially rounded to an integer. If this number lies within the value area for data type i, b, or s, it is converted into the internal representation of an integer. Otherwise, an exception that can be handled will be triggered.
n	The value of the packed number is commercially rounded to an integer. The absolute value of this number is transferred as a digit sequence, right-aligned, into the target field. If the target field is longer than the digit sequence, the field is filled to the left with zeroes. If it is too short, it is cut off at the left.
p	The value of the packed number is commercially rounded to the number of decimal places of the target field. If this number lies within the value area for the data type of the target field, it is converted to the internal representation of this packed number. Otherwise, an exception that can be handled will be triggered.
string	The value of the packed number is prepared in commercial notation and transferred without gaps to the target field. The character "-" is set at the last position for a negative value, and a blank is set for a positive value. The resulting length of the target field is determined by the number of digits, in addition to the positions for the algebraic sign and the decimal separator.
t	The content of the source field is converted first into the data type i (see above) and then into the type t (see Section A.2.5).

Table A.6 Conversion table for source field of type p

Target	Conversion
x	The content of the source field is converted first into the data type i (see above) and then into the type x (see Section A.2.5).
xstring	The content of the source field is converted first into the data type i (see above) and then converted into the type x (see Section A.2.5).

Table A.6 Conversion table for source field of type p (cont.)

A.2.8 Conversion Table for Source-Field Type string

Target	Conversion
c	The content is treated in the same way as a source field of type c (see Section A.2.2), with the difference that trailing blanks are transferred. If the length of the source field is 0, the target field is filled with blank characters.
d	The content is treated in the same way as a source field of type c (see Section A.2.2), with the difference that trailing spaces are transferred. If the length of the source field is 0, the target field is filled with the character "0".
f	The content is treated in the same way as a source field of type c (see Section A.2.2). If the length of the source field is 0, the value 0 is assigned to the target field.
i, b, s	The content is treated in the same way as a source field of type c (see Section A.2.2). If the length of the source field is 0, the value 0 is assigned to the target field.
n	The content is treated in the same way as a source field of type c (see Section A.2.2). If the length of the source field is 0, the target field is filled with the character "0".
p	The content is treated in the same way as a source field of type c (see Section A.2.2). If the length of the source field is 0, the value 0 is assigned to the target field.
string	No conversion. After the assignment, the internal reference of the target field points to the same string as the source field. A new string is only created in the memory if a change request for the content of the source field or target field is submitted.
t	The content is treated in the same way as a source field of type c (see Section A.2.2), wherein trailing blanks are transferred. If the length of the source field is 0, the target field is filled with the character "0."

Table A.7 Conversion rules for source field of type string

Target	Conversion
x	The content is treated the same way as a source field of type c (see Section A.2.2). If the length of the source field is 0, the target field is filled with hexadecimal 0.
xstring	The content is treated the same way as a source field of type c (see Section A.2.2). If the length of the source field is 0, the length of the target field is also 0 after the assignment.

Table A.7 Conversion rules for source field of type string (cont.)

Note

In ABAP, the trailing spaces in source fields of type string are taken into account, and in data objects of type c they are ignored by default (compare Section 21.1.4).

A.2.9 Conversion Table for Source-Field Type t

Target	Conversion
c	The content is treated in the same way as a source field of type c (see Section A.2.2).
d	Not supported. Leads to a syntax error or to an untreatable exception.
f	If the source field only contains digits, the content is interpreted as date specification in the HHMMSS format. Out of it the value HH*3600+MM*60+SS is calculated and this value is converted to the internal representation of a floating point number. If the source field does not only contain digits, the target field receives the value 0.
i, b, s	If the source field only contains digits, the content is interpreted as a date specification in the HHMMSS format. Out of it the value HH*3600+MM*60+SS is calculated, and this value is then converted into the internal representation of an integer. If the source field does not contain only digits, the target field receives the value 0. If the value range for the data types b and s does not suffice, an untreatable exception occurs.
n	The characters in the source field are inserted in the target field, left-aligned. Trailing blanks in the source field are transferred. If the target field is longer than the source field, it is filled to the right with the character "0." If the target field is shorter, the number is truncated to the right.

Table A.8 Conversion rules for source field of type t

Target	Conversion
p	If the source field only contains digits, the content is intepreted as a date specification in the HHMMSS format. Out of it the value HH*3600+MM*60+SS is calculated and this value is converted into the internal representation of a packed number. If the value range of the target field is too small, a treatable exception occurs. If the target field does not only contain digits, the target field receives the value 0.
string	The content is treated in the same way as a source field of type c (see Section A.2.2).
t	The content of the source field is transferred without conversion.
x	The content of the source field is first converted into data type i (see above) and then into type x (see Section A.2.5).
xstring	The content of the source field is first converted into data type i (see above) and then into type xstring (see Section A.2.5).

Table A.8 Conversion rules for source field of type t (cont.)

Note

The conversion rules are designed in such a way that, when data objects of type t are assigned to character-like data objects, they behave as character-like data objects. When assigned to numeric data objects, they behave as numeric data objects. The latter serves as the basis for calculating time in arithmetic expressions. If the content of data objects of type t are date specifications in the HHMMSS format, wherein the values only correspond to valid time (which means HH is 00 to 23, MM and SS are 00 to 59), the value assigned to a numeric data object corresponds to the number of seconds since midnight. The conversion rules also allow assignments from time fields that contain invalid data. This, however, is not recommended.

A.2.10 Conversion Table for Source-Field Type x

Target	Conversion
c	The values of each half-byte in the source field are converted into the hexadecimal characters "0" to "9" and "A" to "F", and transferred to the target field, left-aligned. If the target field is longer than the number of characters transferred, it is filled to the right with blank characters. If it is too short, the number is truncated to the right.
d	The content of the source field is first converted into data type i (see below) and then into type d (see Section A.2.5).

Table A.9 Conversion rules for source field of type x

Target	Conversion
f	The content of the source field is first converted into data type i (see below) and then into type f (see Section A.2.5).
i, b, s	Only the last four bytes in the source field are converted. If the source field is shorter than four bytes, it is extended to the left with the hexadecimal 0 until it reaches a length of four bytes. The content of these bytes is interpreted as a number stored in big endian order, of type i. The hexadecimal values from "00000000" to "7FFFFFFF" are assigned to the numbers from +0 to +2 147 483 647 and the hexadecimal values from "80000000" to "FFFFFFFF" are assigned to the numbers from -2 147 483 648 to -1. The number obtained in this way is converted into the internal representation of an integer. If the value range of the data types b and s is not sufficient, an untreatable exception is raised.
n	The content of the source field is first converted into data type i (see above) and then into type n (see Section A.2.5).
p	The content of the source field is first converted into data type i (see above) and then into type p (see Section A.2.5).
string	The values of each half-byte in the source field are converted into the hexadecimal characters "0" to "9" and "A" to "F" and transferred to the target field, left-aligned. The resulting length of the target field is specified by the number of characters transferred.
t	The content of the source field is first converted into data type i (see above) and then into type t (see Section A.2.5).
x	The bytes in the source field are inserted in the target field, left-aligned. If the target field is longer than the number of bytes transferred, it is filled to the right with the hexadecimal 0. If the target field is shorter, the number is truncated to the right.
xstring	The bytes in the source field are inserted in the target field, left-aligned. The resulting length of the target field is specified by the number of bytes transferred.

Table A.9 Conversion rules for source field of type x (cont.)

A.2.11 Conversion Table for Source-Field Type xstring

Target	Conversion
c	The content is treated in the same way as a source field of type x (see Section A.2.10). If the length of the source field is 0, the target field is filled with blank characters.
d	The content is treated in the same way as a source field of type x (see Section A.2.10). If the length of the source field is 0, the target field is filled with the character "0."

Table A.10 Conversion rules for source field of type xstring

Target	Conversion
f	The content is treated in the same way as a source field of type x (see Section A.2.10). If the length of the source field is 0, the value 0 is assigned to the target field.
i, b, s	The content is treated in the same way as a source field of type x (see Section A.2.10). If the length of the source field is 0, the value 0 is assigned to the target field.
n	The content is treated in the same way as a source field of type x (see Section A.2.10). If the length of the source field is 0, the target field is filled with the character "0."
p	The content is treated in the same way as a source field of type x (see Section A.2.10). If the length of the source field is 0, the value 0 is assigned to the target field.
string	The content is treated in the same way as a source field of type x (see Section A.2.10). If the length of the source field is 0, the length of the target field is also 0 after the assignment.
t	The content is treated in the same way as a source field of type x (see Section A.2.10). If the length of the source field is 0, the target field is filled with the character "0."
x	The content is treated the same way as a source field of type x (see Section A.2.10). If the length of the source field is 0, the target field is filled with the hexadecimal 0.
xstring	The content is treated in the same way as a source field of type x (see Section A.2.10). If the length of the source field is 0, the length of the target field is also 0 after the assignment.

Table A.10 Conversion rules for source field of type xstring (cont.)

A.3   Conversion Rules for Structures

A structure is a data type for data objects that consist of individual components. You can differentiate between the following types of structure:

▶ Flat structures contain only components of the elementary types c, n, d, t, f, i, p, and x or other structures consisting of these types.

▶ Deep structures contain components with deep data types, namely strings, internal tables, data references, or object references.

▶ Nested structures are structures that contain structures other than components.

▶ Non-nested structures indicate structures that do not contain further structures.

In assignments between structures, you first must differentiate between flat and deep structures. Deep structures can only be assigned to each other if they are compatible. For flat structures, there are conversion rules that allow assignments between flat incompatible structures and between single fields and flat structures.

A.3.1 Conversion Between Flat Structures

A.3.1.1 Structures Outside of Unicode Programs

Outside of Unicode programs, the flat structures involved are regarded as single fields of type c (Casting), whose length is determined by the length of their components and possible alignment gaps. In this case, the assignment between the structures takes place according to the conversion rules for the data type c (see Section A.2.2). Most significantly, when assigning a shorter structure to a longer one, the components at the end of the target structure are not initialized according to their type, but are filled with blanks.

Note
Assignments of this type are only advisable, if the structures involved contain only character-like components.

A.3.1.2 Flat Structures in Unicode Programs

When converting flat structures in Unicode programs, you must pay attention to the Unicode fragment view for the corresponding structures.

Unicode fragment view

The Unicode fragment view splits a structure into fragments. A fragment is a grouping of structure components of the same or similar data types. In nested structures, the elementary components on the lowest nesting depth are taken into account when forming fragments. The following parts of a structure are each grouped to form one fragment:

▶ Consecutive flat character-like components of the types c, n, d, and t, between which there are no alignment gaps, form character-like fragments.

▶ Consecutive flat byte-like components of the type x, between which there are no alignment gaps, form byte-like fragments.

▶ Consecutive numeric components of the types i, b, s, or f, between which there are no alignment gaps, each form a separate fragment.

▶ Each individual numeric type p component forms a separate fragment.

▶ Each alignment gap is regarded as a fragment.

Notes

▶ In nested structures, you should note that alignment gaps can arise before and after aligned substructures.

▶ When transferring structure components with INCLUDE (see Section 6.8), an additional alignment gap can arise before the components transferred.

▶ In deep structures, each deep component (reference) forms a separate fragment.

Example

In Figure A.1, the sections F1 to F6 show the individual Unicode fragments of the flat structure struc in a Unicode program, in which character-like fields are represented with 2 bytes per character:

```
BEGIN OF struc,
  a TYPE c LENGTH 3,
  b TYPE n LENGTH 4,
  c TYPE d,
  d TYPE t,
  e TYPE f,
  f TYPE x LENGTH 2,
  g TYPE x LENGTH 4,
  h TYPE i,
  i TYPE i,
  j TYPE i,
  k TYPE i,
END OF struc.
```

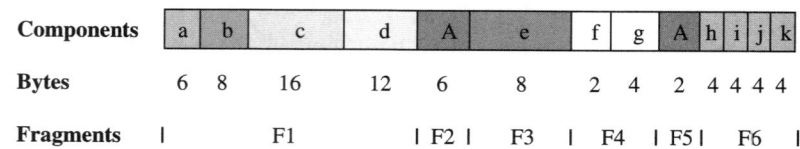

Figure A.1 Unicode fragment view of a structure. The alignment gaps are marked with "A".

Conversion rule

The following rules apply when converting a flat structure to another flat structure in Unicode programs:

1. When assigning structures with the same fragment view, the structure is assigned without being converted.

2. When assigning structures of different lengths where the length of the fragment view exactly matches the shorter structure, the assignment is made at the length of the shorter structure without conversion. If the target structure is longer than the source structure, the components of the target structure that are positioned after the common fragments are filled with type-specific initial values and alignment gaps are set to hexadecimal 0. If the target structure is shorter than the source structure, the components of the source structure that are positioned after the common fragments are cut off.

3. When assigning structures of different lengths whose fragment views match until the second to the last fragment in the shorter structure, and in which the next fragment is byte-like in one and character-like in the other, the parts in which the fragments are the same are assigned without conversion. The characters in the next fragment in the source structure are assigned to the corresponding fragment in the target structure without conversion and left justified. If this fragment in the target structure is larger than in the source structure, the right hand side is filled with blanks or with hexadecimal 0, depending on the data type. If it is shorter, the objects are cut off on the right. The remaining components after this fragment are either cut off or filled with type-specific initial values.

No conversion rule is defined for any other cases and therefore assignment is not possible.

Note
If a syntax error occurs due to an impermissible assignment between flat structures, you can display the fragment views for the corresponding structures when displaying the syntax error in the ABAP Editor by choosing the pushbutton with the information icon.

Examples
Assigning struc1 to struc2 and vice versa is not allowed in Unicode programs because the fragment views are not the same (unlike struc2-b, struc1-x only fills one byte).

```
DATA:                    DATA:
  BEGIN OF struc1,         BEGIN OF struc2,
    a(1) TYPE c,             a(1) TYPE c,
    x(1) TYPE x,             b(1) TYPE c,
  END OF struc1.          END OF struc2.
```

Assignments of `struc3` to `struc4` and vice versa are allowed, because the fragment view of the shorter structure `struc3` is the same as the fragment view in the first part of the longer structure `struc4`.

```
DATA:                    DATA:
  BEGIN OF struc3,         BEGIN OF struc4,
    a(2) TYPE c,             a(8) TYPE c,
    n(6) TYPE n,             i    TYPE i,
    i    TYPE i,             f    TYPE f,
  END OF struc3.           END OF struc4.
```

Assignments of `struc5` to `struc6` and vice versa are also not allowed, because the fragment views in the two structures do not match due to the alignment gaps before `struc5-b` and before `struc6-struc0-b`.

```
DATA:                    DATA:
  BEGIN OF struc5,         BEGIN OF struc6,
    a(1) TYPE x,             a(1) TYPE x,
    b(1) TYPE x,             BEGIN OF struc0,
    c(1) TYPE c,               b(1) TYPE x,
  END OF struc5.             c(1) TYPE c,
                           END OF struc0,
                         END OF struc6.
```

Assignment of `struc7` to `struc8` and vice versa are possible, because the fragment view is the same until the second to the last fragment `p` in the shorter structure `struc7`:

```
DATA:                    DATA:
  BEGIN OF struc7,         BEGIN OF struc8,
    a    TYPE i,             a    TYPE i,
    p(8) TYPE p,             p(8) TYPE p,
    c(1) TYPE c,             c(5) TYPE c,
  END OF struc7.             o(8) TYPE p,
                         END OF struc8.
```

A.3.2 Conversion Between Flat Structures and Single Fields

A.3.2.1 Conversion Outside of Unicode Programs

Outside of Unicode programs, the structure involved is regarded as a single field of type c (Casting), whose length is determined by the length of its components and possible alignment gaps. In this case, the assignment between the structure and the single field takes place according to the conversion rules between data type c and the data type of the single field (see Section A.2).

Note
Assignments of this type are only advisable if the corresponding structure only contains character-like components. If you assign a single field to a structure that does not only contain character-like components, the content of these components will usually then no longer match the data type, so that it will no longer be possible to evaluate them individually.

A.3.2.2 Conversion in Unicode Programs

The following rules apply in Unicode programs when converting a flat structure to a single field and vice versa:

▶ If a structure is purely character-like, it is processed during conversion like a data object of the type c (Casting). The single field can have any elementary data type.

▶ If the structure is not purely character-like, the single field must be of type c and the structure must begin with a character-like fragment that is at least as long as the single field. The assignment takes place only between this fragment and the single field. The character-like fragment of the structure is treated like a data object of the type c (Casting) in the assignment. If the structure is the target field, the remaining character-like fragments are filled with blanks and all other components with the initial value that corresponds to their type.

No conversion rule is defined for any other cases, so that assignment is not possible.

Note
If a syntax error occurs due to an impermissible assignment between flat structures and single fields, you can display the fragment view of the involved structure when displaying the syntax error in the ABAP Editor by choosing the pushbutton with the information icon.

A.4 Conversion Rules for Internal Tables

Internal tables can only be assigned to internal tables. Whether assignment is possible depends exclusively on row type, and is independent of table type, table key, and number of rows. Internal tables can be assigned to each other if and only if their row types are compatible or if there is a conversion rule for the corresponding row types. This applies to both Unicode programs and non-Unicode programs.

When assigning an internal table to another, the rows of the target table are deleted. A new row is created in the target table for each row in the source table. They are then filled with the row contents in the source table. The rows are stored according to the table category. For assignments to a sorted table, the content is automatically sorted and hash tables are stored according to the hash algorithm.

The content of the individual rows in the source table is assigned to the rows in the target table according to the same rules as for assignments between individual data objects of corresponding row types. The same basic rule as for all conversions applies here: Converting the content of single rows in the source table must lie within the value range of the row type in the target table.

Note

In internal tables with compatible or convertible row types, untreatable exceptions can occur during assignment, if for example several entries in the source table with the same key are transferred to a target table with a unique key.

A.5   Assignments Between Reference Variables

The content of a reference variable can only be assigned to another reference variable; data references can only be assigned to data reference variables, and object references can only be assigned to object reference variables. No conversion takes place in this type of assignment. After the successful assignment, the target reference variable points to the same object as the source reference variable or the target reference variable adopts the dynamic type of the source reference variable.

A.5.1   Static and Dynamic Type

Each reference variable has a dynamic and a static type.

▶ The dynamic type is set at program runtime. It is the data type of the data object or the class of the object to which the reference variable points. It determines the components contained in the object. The dynamic type of an initial data reference variable is the predefined generic type `data`. The dynamic type of an initial object reference variable is the predefined generic type `object`.

▶ The static type is set at the declaration of the reference variable. In data references, the static type is either a non-generic data type (as of Release 6.10) or the predefined generic type `data`. In object references, the static type is either a class or an interface, so that an object reference can also be referred to as a class reference or an interface reference.

The static type of a reference variable is always less specific or the same as the dynamic type. This basic rule applies to all assignments between reference variables.

A.5.2 Up Cast and Down Cast

In an assignment between reference variables, the target variable adopts the dynamic type of the source variable. An assignment is possible if and only if the static type of the target variable is less specific or the same as the dynamic type of the source variable.

A.5.2.1 Up Cast

If the static type of the target variable is less specific or the same as the static type of the source variable, an assignment is always possible. The name "Up Cast" derives from the fact that you move up in the inheritance tree. Because the target variable can adopt more dynamic types in comparison to the source variable, this assignment is also called "Widening Cast." An Up Cast can occur in all ABAP statements in which the content of a data object is assigned to another data object. These are for example assignments with the normal assignment operator (=), insertion of rows in internal tables or transfer of actual parameters to formal parameters.

A.5.2.2 Down Cast

If the static type of the target variable is more specific than the static type of the source variable, you must check at runtime before the assignment is executed, whether it is less specific or the same as the dynamic type of the source variable. The name "Down Cast" derives from the fact that you move down in the inheritance tree. Because the target variable can adopt less dynamic types in comparison to the source variable, this assignment is also called "Narrowing Cast." A Down Cast can only occur with the special assignment operator ?= (Casting Operator) or the statement MOVE . . . ?TO . . . (see Section 16.2). If the precondition is not fulfilled, a treatable exception occurs.

A.5.3   Assignments Between Data Reference Variables

Data reference variables are either completely typed (as of Release 6.10) or typed with the generic type `data`.

A.5.3.1   Up Cast in Data References

An up cast in data references is possible in the following cases.

▶ The static types of the source variable and the target variable are identical. If the static type is elementary, the types are considered equal if all technical attributes of the types are the same. If the static type is not elementary, the types are equal only if both data types are declared with reference to exactly the same data type, as is the case with object references. The data type is determined here by the names of the type, using `TYPE REF TO`, or by the name of the data object, using `LIKE REF TO`.

▶ The static type of the source variable is fully typed (since Release 6.10), and that of the target variable is generic.

A.5.3.2   Down Cast in Data References

Down cast in data references is only possible if the static type of the source variable is generic and that of the target variable is completely typed. The syntax check precludes that the static types of the source variable and the target variable are both completely typed, but not identical.

Example

Assigning from `dref1` to `dref2` is an up cast. Assigning from `dref2` to `dref1` is a down cast, which in the example shown leads to an exception. If the statement `CREATE DATA` had the addition `TYPE i`, the down cast would also have been successful.

```
DATA: dref1 TYPE REF TO i,
      dref2 TYPE REF TO data.

CREATE DATA dref1.
dref2 = dref1.
CREATE DATA dref2 TYPE string.

TRY.
  dref1 ?= dref2.
  CATCH cx_sy_move_cast_error.
  ...
ENDTRY.
```

A.5.4   Assignments Between Object Reference Variables

Object reference variables are either class references or interface references.

A.5.4.1   Up Cast in Object References

An up cast in object references is possible in the following cases.

▶ If both static types are classes, the class of the target variable must be of the same class or a superclass of the source variable.

▶ If both static types are interfaces, the interface of the target variable must be of the same interface or a component interface of the source variable.

▶ If the static type of the target variable is an interface and that of the source variable is a class, the class of the source variable must implement the interface of the target variable.

▶ If the static type of the target variable is a class and the static type of the source variable is an interface, the class of the target variable must be the generic type or the root class `object`.

A.5.4.2   Down Cast in Object References

For all other cases, not listed under the up cast, assignment can only be programmed using a down cast.

Example
Declaration of interfaces and classes, creation of an object in the subclass and access to the components of the object. In the statement CREATE OBJECT, an up cast occurs implicitly from `c2` to `iref`. The interface reference `iref` can only be used to access the components declared in the interface `i2`. The method `m1` of the object cannot be called using `iref`. After assigning the object reference to the class reference `cref` using a down cast, `m1` can be accessed dynamically but not statically.

```
INTERFACE i1.
  DATA a1 TYPE ...
ENDINTERFACE.

INTERFACE i2.
  INTERFACES i1.
  ALIASES a1 FOR i1~a1.
  DATA a2 TYPE ...
ENDINTERFACE.
```

```
CLASS c1 DEFINITION.
  PUBLIC SECTION.
    INTERFACES i2.
ENDCLASS.

CLASS c2 DEFINITION INHERITING FROM c1.
  PUBLIC SECTION.
    METHODS m1.
ENDCLASS.

...

DATA: iref TYPE REF TO i2,
      cref TYPE REF TO c1.

...

CREATE OBJECT iref TYPE c2.

... iref->a1 ...
... iref->a2 ...

...

TRY.
  cref ?= iref.
  CALL METHOD cref->('M1').
  CATCH cx_sy_move_cast_error
        cx_sy_dyn_call_illegal_method.
    ...
ENDTRY.
```

B   Language-like Classes and Interfaces

This appendix lists the global classes and interfaces (system classes) that are available in the class library for supporting the ABAP language. The interfaces of the classes and their exact functions are documented in the system.

B.1   Auxiliary Classes

B.1.1   Run Time Type Services (RTTS) Classes

The RTTS are implemented through a hierarchy of type classes that contain the methods for RTTC (Run Time Type Creation, as of Release 6.40) and RTTI (Run Time Type Identification). With the help of these system classes it is possible:

▶ To determine type information of existing instances and type names of the ABAP type system at runtime.

▶ To define new data types at runtime.

B.1.1.1   Concept

The properties of the types are represented by the attributes of type objects. For each type there is exactly one type object. The attributes of the type object contain information on the properties of the type. For each kind of type (elementary type, table, class and so on), there is a type class with special attributes for special type properties. The class hierarchy of the type classes corresponds to the hierarchy of the type kinds of the ABAP type system.

In addition, type classes for complex types, references, classes, and interfaces have special methods to determine references to part types. With these methods, you can navigate through a combined type to all part types.

Type objects can only be created through the methods of type classes. To get a reference to a type object of a type, you can use the static methods of the class CL_ABAP_TYPEDESCR or call methods of the special type classes.

B.1.1.2   Hierarchy of the Type Classes

Table B.1 shows the Hierarchy of System Classes for the RTTS.

```
CL_ABAP_TYPEDESCR
    CL_ABAP_DATADESCR
        CL_ABAP_ELEMDESCR
        CL_ABAP_REFDESCR
        CL_ABAP_COMPLEXDESCR
            CL_ABAP_STRUCTDESCR
            CL_ABAP_TABLEDESCR
        CL_ABAP_OBJECTDESCR
            CL_ABAP_CLASSDESCR
            CL_ABAP_INTFDESCR
```

Table B.1 Hierarchy of the System Classes for the RTTS

There is a description class for every type possible in ABAP (for example elementary type, internal table, class and so on) with special attributes for the type properties. Instance attributes and constants for general type information are available in the shared superclass CL_ABAP_TYPEDESCR. Static methods for creating description objects are also defined in this class.

B.1.2   Classes for Converting External Data Formats

The following system classes make it possible to convert character strings between different code pages and to convert numeric data between different number representations. They replace the obsolete variants of the statement TRANSLATE (see Section 42.11.1).

Data in a format that does not fit the current platform—that is, character strings not in the current codepage or numeric data not in the current byte order (endian)—must be stored in the ABAP program in containers of type x or xstring. The following three classes allow you to convert such data.

▶ CL_ABAP_CONV_IN_CE
A byte-like data object can be read with this class, and its content can be converted from an external format to the current format and can be assigned to data objects of the corresponding data types.

▶ CL_ABAP_CONV_OUT_CE
With this class, a data object of an ABAP data type can be read and its content can be converted from the current format to a different format and can be assigned to a byte-like data object.

▶ CL_ABAP_CONV_X2X_CE
A byte-like data object can be read with this class, and its content can be converted from an external format to another format and can be assigned to another byte-like data object.

B.1.3   Class for Extreme Values of Data Objects

The class CL_ABAP_EXCEPTIONAL_VALUES contains two static methods, GET_MIN_VALUE and GET_MAX_VALUE, which can determine the minimum and maximum values of their value range for data objects of built-in ABAP types (see Table 5.2).

B.1.4   Class for the Properties of Characters

The class CL_ABAP_CHAR_UTILITIES contains static methods and static attributes to determine the properties of single characters and the coding of special characters such as carriage return or return on the current platform.

B.1.5   Classes for Mathematical Operations

B.1.5.1   General operations

The class CL_ABAP_MATH currently contains just one static method, ROUND_F_TO_15_DECS, to round off a variable of the data type f to 15 decimal places. This method helps to avoid rounding errors, that can occur if floating point numbers are used in calculations and assignments, because their internal representation as binary fractions.

Example
In the first assignment from float to pack a rounding error occurs which can be avoided by using the method ROUND_F_TO_15_DECS.

```
DATA: float TYPE f VALUE '1.005',
      pack  TYPE p DECIMALS 2.

CLASS cl_abap_math DEFINITION LOAD.

pack = float.
WRITE / pack.

float = cl_abap_math=>round_f_to_15_decs( float ).

pack = float.
WRITE / pack.
```

B.1.5.2   Random numbers

The class CL_ABAP_RANDOM calls the pseudo random number generator "Mersenne Twister' for different numeric types. For the one-dimensional case, the following special classes generate random numbers for the different numeric types:

- CL_ABAP_RANDOM_INT for type i
- CL_ABAP_RANDOM_FLOAT for type f
- CL_ABAP_RANDOM_PACKED for type p
- CL_ABAP_RANDOM_PACKED_DECn with n = 1 to 14 for type p with n decimal places.

B.1.6 Class for Time Stamps

The class CL_ABAP_TSTMP contains static methods to convert time stamps according to their time length in seconds and to execute calculations with time stamps.

B.1.7 Classes for Data Clusters

Table B.2 shows the hierarchy of the system classes for data clusters. The superclass CL_ABAP_EXPIMP is an abstract class with no components of its own.

```
CL_ABAP_EXIMP
    CL_ABAP_EXPIMP_MEM
    CL_ABAP_EXPIMP_SHMEM
    CL_ABAP_EXPIMP_SHBUF
    CL_ABAP_EXPIMP_DB
    CL_ABAP_EXPIMP_CONV
```

Table B.2 Tabelle B.2: Hierarchy of the system classes for data clusters

These subclasses extend the functionality of the statements for data clusters (see Chapter 31). They allow you to access data clusters in the individual storage media, of which only parts of the identifier id or of the area ar are specified, by determining the complete key. In addition, you can delete data clusters generically using partly specified keys.

The methods of the class CL_ABAP_EXPIMP_CONV convert the Release-dependent internal format of data clusters (as of Support Package 29).

B.1.8 Class for Transactions

The class CL_SYSTEM_TRANSACTION_STATE contains static methods that return the status of the current SAP LUW.

B.1.9 Class for Formatting Lists

The methods of the class CL_ABAP_LIST_UTILITIES can be used for the calculation of output lengths, for the conversion of values from the list buffer, and for the calculation of required output lengths on lists.

The return values of these methods can be used to program the correct column alignment in lists, even when using East Asian characters that need more than one column in the presented list in Unicode systems.

B.1.10 Classes for Compressing Data

The methods of the classes

▶ CL_ABAP_GZIP

▶ CL_ABAP_GZIP_BINARY_STREAM

▶ CL_ABAP_GZIP_TEXT_STREAM

▶ CL_ABAP_UNGZIP_BINARY_STREAM

▶ CL_ABAP_UNGZIP_TEXT_STREAM

make it possible to compress or decompress texts in text fields or text strings, or binary data in byte fields or byte strings using "GZIP" (since Support Package 29).

B.1.11 Class for Runtime Measurements

The static methods CREATE_HR_TIMER and CREATE_LR_TIMER of the class CL_ABAP_RUNTIME can be used to generate objects for runtime measurements. The objects contain a method GET_RUNTIME that performs a runtime measurement in the same way as the statement GET RUN TIME (see Section 37.3.1).

An object generated using CREATE_HR_TIMER performs a measurement with high precision, and an object generated using CREATE_LR_TIMER performs a measurement with a lower level of measurement precision.

In contrast to the statement GET RUN TIME, these objects can be used to carry out different measurements with different levels of precision and parallel measurements for each internal mode.

Because the execution of the method GET_RUNTIME is approximately 2 microseconds slower than the execution of the statement GET RUN TIME, in some circumstances this method may not be suitable for the measurement of very short periods of time.

B.1.12 Class for Weak References

An object of the class CL_ABAP_WEAK_REFERENCE represents a weak reference to an object. Unlike normal object references, a weak reference does not prevent the referenced object from being deleted when the Garbage Collector is executed.

A weak reference to an existing object is created by transferring an object reference to the instance constructor for CL_ABAP_WEAK_REFERENCE. You can then use the functional method GET to retrieve the reference afterwards. If the object was deleted in the meantime, the return value is initial.

Note
A different type of reference retains objects until the available memory becomes limited. The class CL_ABAP_SOFT_REFERENCE is available for these soft references, but this class is currently still implemented like the class CL_ABAP_WEAK_REFERENCE.

B.2 Interface for the Serialization of Objects

To transform classes to XML using the statement CALL TRANSFORMATION or to generate classes from XML documents, their classes must implement the interface IF_SERIALIZABLE_OBJECT.

The system interface IF_SERIALIZABLE_OBJECT is not an interface in the common sense. Implementing this interface displays the serialization of a class to the runtime environment and allows the declaration of certain other components according to fixed rules (see Section 40.2.3.3).

B.3 Shared Objects

Shared objects are objects in the shared memory. An area is the pattern for area instance versions in the shared memory. An area class of the same name is assigned to each area. Areas are created and controlled using the transaction SHMA. Area classes of the same name are generated when creating areas. The instances of these area classes serve as area handles. The methods of an area handle are used for accessing the area. The following classes and interfaces are available for using them:

▶ CL_ABAP_MEMORY_AREA
  Common superclass for all area classes.

▶ CL_SHM_AREA
  Common superclass for all area classes for area handles of area instance versions in the shared objects memory.

- CL_IMODE_AREA
  Predefined area class that can be used to process the current internal mode like an area instance.

- IF_SHM_BUILD_INSTANCE
  This interface must be implemented by the class that is to implement the optional area constructor for an area.

B.4 Object Services

Object Services provide a persistence service and a transaction service for applications written in ABAP Objects. The services are realized by global classes and interfaces with the prefixes CL_OS_ and IF_OS_. The persistence service allows you to work with persistent objects, while the transaction service makes object-oriented transactions possible. Both techniques are based on the classic methods of persistent data management, that is database tables and SAP LUW concept, yet they encapsulate these for the object-oriented user.

Persistent classes form the basis of working with Object Services. The attributes of persistent classes are mapped to columns in the database table (object relational mapping). The instances of persistent classes are persistent objects that are not dealt with directly. Instead, they are handled via objects of the Object Service, which are known as class actors or agents. The properties of persistent objects still exist as line content of the assigned database table after program runtime. In the simplest case, an object corresponds to a row in a database table.

The classes and interfaces of Object Services are documented in the SAP Library.

B.5 JavaScript Integration

In the SAP runtime environment (Kernel), a JavaScript (JS) Engine is integrated in which you can execute JavaScript programs on the application server of the SAP system, either in normal or in debugging mode (Server Side Scripting). The built-in JavaScript engine supports the JavaScript version 1.5.

The API of the JavaScript Engine is encapsulated in the global class CL_JAVA_SCRIPT. As a result, JavaScript programs can be compiled, debugged, and executed in ABAP programs. You can link script variables with data objects of an ABAP program using proxies (binding).

The attributes and methods of the class CL_JAVA_SCRIPT are documented in the SAP Library, and there are comprehensive examples in the ABAP example library (Transaction ABAPDOCU).

C   Language-like Function Modules

This appendix describes a group of function modules which are necessary for supporting the ABAP language.

C.1   Function Modules for Print Parameters

C.1.1   GET_PRINT_PARAMETERS

The function module GET_PRINT_PARAMETERS is needed to fill structures that must be specified in the additions [SPOOL] PARAMETERS and ARCHIVE PARAMETERS of the statements NEW-PAGE PRINT ON and SUBMIT report TO SAP SPOOL, in order to provide print parameters and archiving parameters for a spool request.

Print and archiving parameters can be set via input parameters or a print dialog box. The function module gets any parameters that have not been set from the system, with some values being taken from the user master record. Dependent parameters are set automatically. If the function module cannot create a record of valid print or archiving parameters, it generates an exception.

Name	Meaning
Print parameters	
IN_PARAMETERS	Entire structure of type PRI_PARAMS.
ARCHIVE_MODE	Archiving mode: if "1" print only if "2" archive only if "3" print and archive
AUTHORITY	Defines the authorization necessary to display the spool request.
COPIES	Number of prints.
COVER_PAGE	If checked with an "X", a cover page with the input values of the selection screen is given out.
DATA_SET	Spool file.
DEPARTMENT	Name of department for the SAP cover page.
DESTINATION	Name of a printer or fax machine.

Table C.1 Input parameters of GET_PRINT_PARAMETERS

Name	Meaning
EXPIRATION	Number of days during which a spool request should be kept in the spool system before it is deleted.
IMMEDIATELY	If checked with an "X", the spool request is sent to the output device as soon as it is completed.
LAYOUT	Page format of the output. Possible values depend on DESTINATION.
LINE_COUNT	Number of list lines per page. It has the same effect as the addition `LINE-COUNT` in a program introductory statement. It is not possible to enter 0 (unlimited number of lines). The maximum number of lines depends on LAYOUT.
LINE_SIZE	Number of characters per list line. This field has the same effect as the addition `LINE-SIZE` in a program introductory statement. The maximum number of characters depends on LAYOUT.
LIST_NAME	Name of the spool request. It need be set only if it is not being printed immediately.
LIST_TEXT	Description text on the spool request. It appears on the standard cover page. It is displayed in the output controller instead of LIST_NAME.
NEW_LIST_ID	If "X" is specified, a new spool request is created; if " " is specified, it tries to append itself to an existing spool request. For this to be possible, DESTINATION, COPIES, LAYOUT, and LIST_NAME must match.
RECEIVER	The name of the recipient on the SAP cover page.
RELEASE	If "X" is specified, the spool request is deleted after output; if " " is specified, it is deleted in accordance with EXPIRATION.
SAP_COVER_PAGE	If checked with "X,", a SAP cover page is given out. If "D" is specified, the printer setting is adopted. If " " is specified, no SAP cover page is given out.
TYPE	Type of the spool request.
Archiving parameters	
IN_ARCHIVE_PARAMETERS	Entire structure of type ARC_PARAMS.
ARCHIVE_ID	Target archive of the archiving request.
ARCHIVE_INFO	Information identifier of the archiving request.
ARCHIVE_TEXT	Description text of the archiving request.

Table C.1 Input parameters of GET_PRINT_PARAMETERS (cont.)

Name	Meaning
AR_OBJECT	Document type of the archiving object.
SAP_OBJECT	Object type of the SAP object.
Control parameters	
MODE	Possible values are "PARAMS", "PARAMSEL," "DISPLAY," "CURRENT," and "BATCH" (see Table C.2).
NO_DIALOG	If "X" is specified, no print dialog window is displayed.
REPORT	Default value for the name of the spool request. If nothing is specified, `sy-repid` is used. It is even overwritten by LIST_NAME. If MODE is the same as BATCH, the name of the program to be started must be specified in REPORT.

Table C.1 Input parameters of GET_PRINT_PARAMETERS (cont.)

Name	Meaning
BATCH	Print parameters are determined for a background job. The corresponding program must be specified in REPORT. On the print dialog box, the Save button appears instead of the Print button.
CURRENT	During a print process, the print parameters are set in accordance with the current print parameters. Outside of a print process, they are set in accordance with standard settings.
DISPLAY	The print parameters are displayed in the print dialog box and cannot be changed.
PARAMS	The user can change the print parameter on the print dialog box and select Print or Cancel.
PARAMSEL	A selection cover page checkbox appears in the print dialog box. If it contains an "X," a cover page with the selections of the selection screen is given out.

Table C.2 Meaning of the values for MODE

Name	Meaning
OUT_PARAMETERS	Print parameter in a structure of type PRI_PARAMS. Either complete or empty.
OUT_ARCHIVE_PARAMETERS	Archiving parameter in a structure of type ARC_PARAMS. Either complete or empty.

Table C.3 Output parameters of GET_PRINT_PARAMETERS

Name	Meaning
VALID	If "X" is specified, print and archiving parameters are fully available. If " " is specified, the parameter structures are empty. VALID is " ," if the print dialog box is closed with Cancel.

Table C.3 Output parameters of GET_PRINT_PARAMETERS (cont.)

C.1.2 SET_PRINT_PARAMETERS

The function module SET_PRINT-PARAMETERS can be used to fill the input fields of the print dialog box with standard values if it is called with the functions **Execute + Print** on a selection screen or with **Print** on a displayed list.

Apart from MODE, NO_DIALOG and REPORT, SET_PRINT_PARAMETERS has the same input parameters as the function module GET_PRINT_ PARAMETERS (see Table C.1), and it has no output parameters.

There is also an additional input parameter called FOOT_LINE. This can be used to pre-set the output of a footer line when printing a displayed list.

C.2 Function Modules for Files on the Presentation Server

With the function modules GUI_UPLOAD and GUI_DOWNLOAD, files can be loaded from and saved on the presentation server.

These function modules replace the function modules UPLOAD, WS_ UPLOAD, DOWNLOAD and WS_DOWNLOAD since Release 6.10. The latter can no longer be used in a Unicode program.

The interface of the new function modules GUI_UPLOAD and GUI_ DOWNLOAD makes it possible to process Unicode-based data on the presentation server.

Instead of the function modules GUI_UPLOAD and GUI_DOWNLOAD, the static methods GUI_UPLOAD and GUI_DOWNLOAD of the global class CL_GUI_FRONTEND_SERVICES can also be used. This class contains further methods for handling files on the presentation server, such as DIRECTORY_CREATE for creating a directory.

C.3 Function Modules for Calling Logical Databases

The function module LDB_PROCESS allows you to call logical databases from any program. Several logical databases can be called at the same time and any one logical database can be called numerous times.

When a logical database is called using the function module LDB_PRO-CESS, the selection screen of the logical database is not displayed. It is rather filled using the interface parameters of the function module. The logical database does not trigger a GET event in the calling program; instead, the data read is transferred to so-called call-back routines during the call. A call-back routine is a subroutine in the calling program or another program that is executed on the appropriate event.

The logical database does not have to be adapted for this, with the following exceptions: A logical database can be called several times consecutively only if the subroutine LDB_PROCESS_INIT is included in the database program. The subroutine LDB_PROCESS_CHECK_SELECTIONS must be used instead of the subroutine PAI to check the input values of the selection screen.

The input and table parameters of LDB_PROCESS are listed in Table C.4 and Table C.5.

Name	Meaning
LDBNAME	Name of the logical database to be called.
VARIANT	Name of a variant to fill the selection screen of the logical database. The variant must be assigned to the database program of the logical database. Data is transferred in the same way as with the addition WITH SELECTION-TABLE in a program call using SUBMIT.
EXPRESSIONS	In this parameter, additional selections can be transferred for the nodes of the logical database, which are provided in the selection include for free selections. The data type of the parameters RSDS_TEXPR is defined in the type group RSDS. Data is transferred in the same way as with the addition WITH FREE SELECTION in a program call using SUBMIT.

Table C.4 Input parameters of LDB_PROCESS

Name	Meaning
FIELD_SELECTION	In this parameter, a list of necessary fields can be transferred for the nodes of the logical database, which is provided in the selection include for field selections. The data type of the parameter is the internal table RSFS_FIELDS from type group RSFS. The component TABLENAME contains the names of the node and the deep component FIELDS contains the names of the fields to be read.

Table C.4 Input parameters of LDB_PROCESS (cont.)

Name	Meaning
CALLBACK	In this table parameter, the names of nodes and events are assigned to call-back routines. The parameter determines the nodes in the logical database for which data is read, when this data should be transferred, and which call-back routine it should be transferred to. The data type of the parameter is the flat structure LDBCB from the ABAP Dictionary.
SELECTIONS	In this table parameter, input values for selection criteria and parameters of the selection screen can be transferred to the logical database. The data type of the parameter corresponds to the structure RSPARAMS in the ABAP Dictionary. Data is transferred in the same way as with the addition WITH SELECTION-TABLE in a program call using SUBMIT.

Table C.5 Table parameters of LDB_PROCESS

The depth at which the logical database is read is determined by the node name transferred to the parameter CALLBACK. For each node for which data is requested, there are two points in time when a call-back routine can be executed. These points correspond with GET and GET LATE in executable programs. The name of the corresponding call-back routine and the desired points in time are specified for each node in the table parameter CALLBACK.

D Predefined Treatable Exceptions

D.1 Overview

Since Release 6.10, predefined treatable exceptions are based on predefined exception classes with the prefix CX_SY_. Before Release 6.10 there were only catchable runtime errors.

D.2 Predefined Exception Classes

Table D.1 shows the hierarchy of the predefined exception classes. Exceptions of subclasses can be treated by specifying the superclass in the statement CATCH and can be declared in the definition of procedures.

CX_SY_ROOT
CX_STATIC_CHECK
CX_DYNAMIC_CHECK
CX_SY_ARITHMETIC_ERROR
CX_SY_ZERODIVIDE
CX_SY_ARITHMETIC_OVERFLOW
CX_SY_ARG_OUT_OF_DOMAIN
CX_SY_PRECISION_LOSS
CX_SY_ASSIGN_ERROR
CX_SY_ASSIGN_CAST_ERROR
CX_SY_ASSIGN_CAST_ILLEGAL_CAST
CX_SY_ASSIGN_CAST_UNKNOWN_TYPE
CX_SY_ASSIGN_OUT_OF_RANGE
CX_SY_CODEPAGE_CONVERTER_INIT
CX_SY_CONVERSION_ERROR
CX_SY_CONVERSION_OVERFLOW
CX_SY_CONVERSION_NO_NUMBER
CX_SY_CONVERSION_CODEPAGE
CX_SY_CONVERSION_BASE_64 (6.20)
CX_SY_CONVERSION_ILLEGAL_DATE_TIME (6.20)

Table D.1 Hierarchy of predefined exception classes. All classes, except for those flagged as being from Release 6.20, are available since Release 6.10.

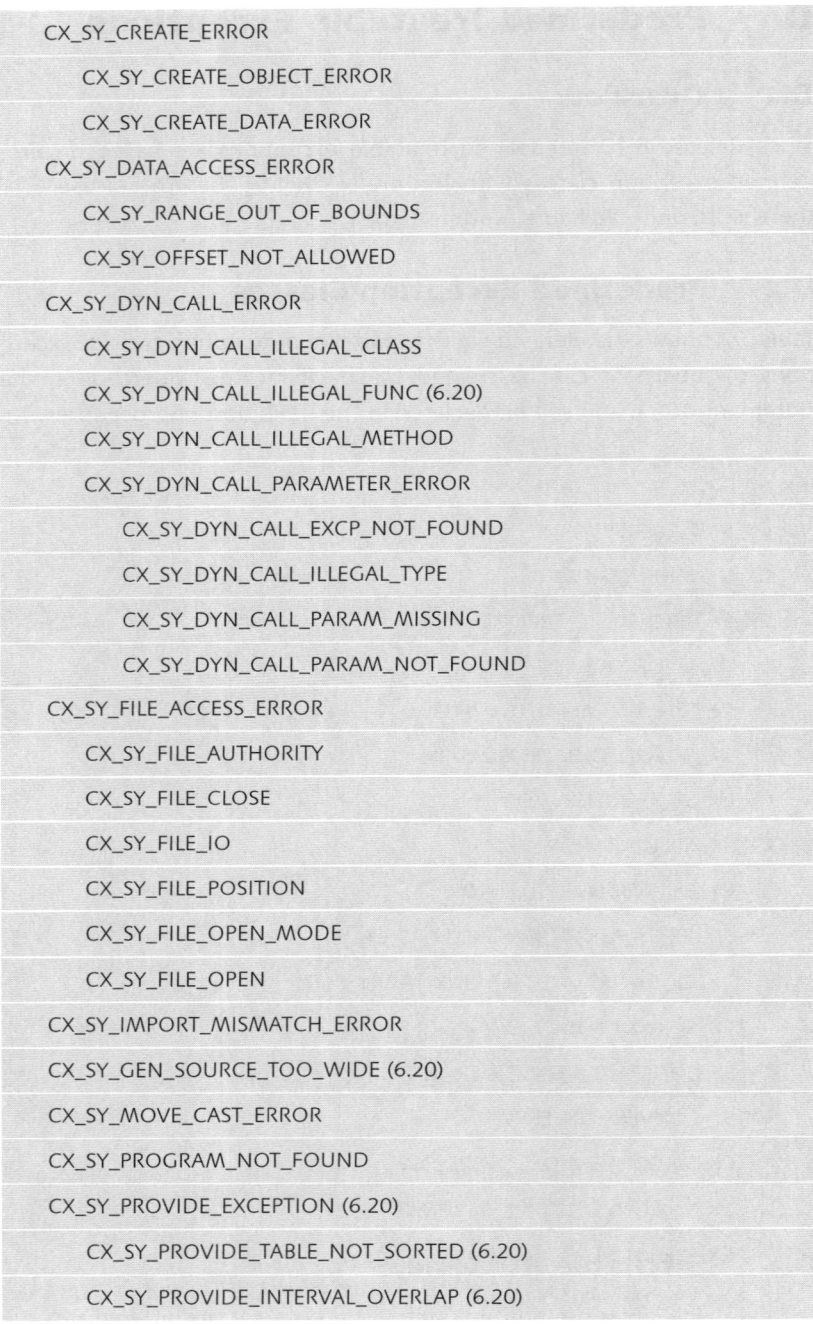

CX_SY_CREATE_ERROR

    CX_SY_CREATE_OBJECT_ERROR

    CX_SY_CREATE_DATA_ERROR

CX_SY_DATA_ACCESS_ERROR

    CX_SY_RANGE_OUT_OF_BOUNDS

    CX_SY_OFFSET_NOT_ALLOWED

CX_SY_DYN_CALL_ERROR

    CX_SY_DYN_CALL_ILLEGAL_CLASS

    CX_SY_DYN_CALL_ILLEGAL_FUNC (6.20)

    CX_SY_DYN_CALL_ILLEGAL_METHOD

    CX_SY_DYN_CALL_PARAMETER_ERROR

        CX_SY_DYN_CALL_EXCP_NOT_FOUND

        CX_SY_DYN_CALL_ILLEGAL_TYPE

        CX_SY_DYN_CALL_PARAM_MISSING

        CX_SY_DYN_CALL_PARAM_NOT_FOUND

CX_SY_FILE_ACCESS_ERROR

    CX_SY_FILE_AUTHORITY

    CX_SY_FILE_CLOSE

    CX_SY_FILE_IO

    CX_SY_FILE_POSITION

    CX_SY_FILE_OPEN_MODE

    CX_SY_FILE_OPEN

CX_SY_IMPORT_MISMATCH_ERROR

CX_SY_GEN_SOURCE_TOO_WIDE (6.20)

CX_SY_MOVE_CAST_ERROR

CX_SY_PROGRAM_NOT_FOUND

CX_SY_PROVIDE_EXCEPTION (6.20)

    CX_SY_PROVIDE_TABLE_NOT_SORTED (6.20)

    CX_SY_PROVIDE_INTERVAL_OVERLAP (6.20)

Table D.1 Hierarchy of predefined exception classes. All classes, except for those flagged as being from Release 6.20, are available since Release 6.10. (cont.)

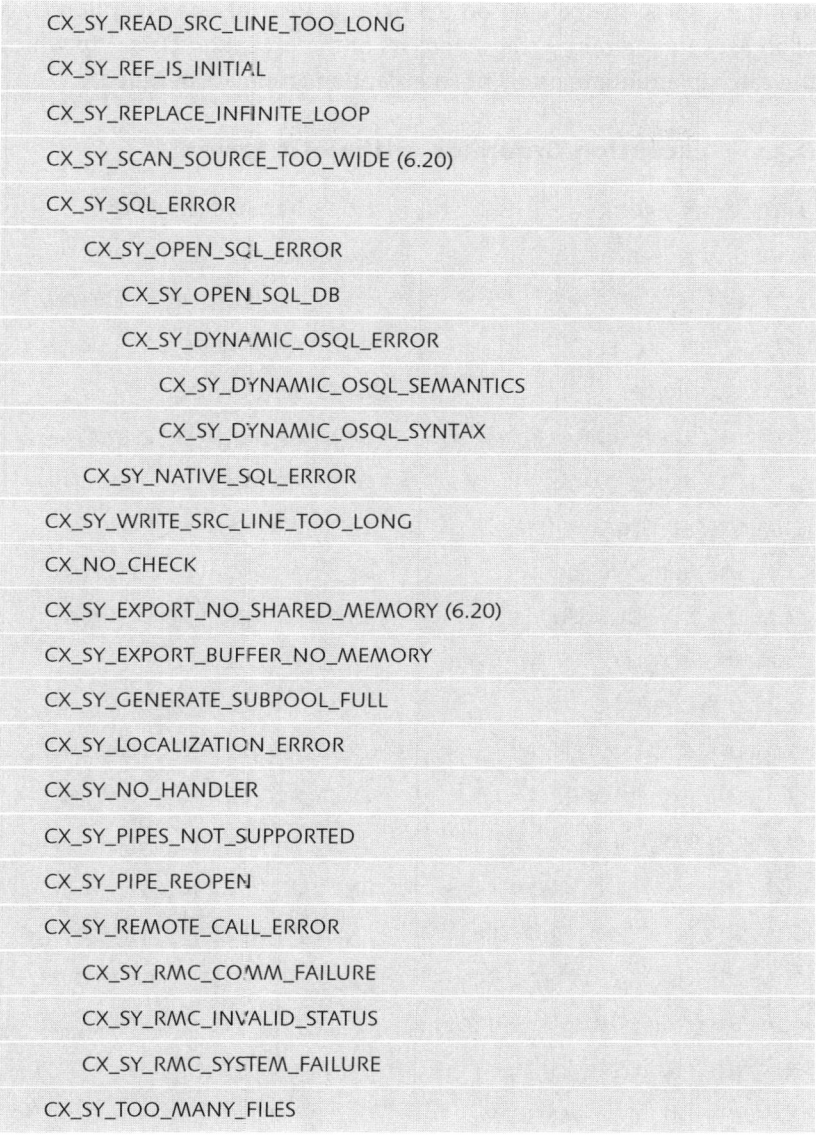

CX_SY_READ_SRC_LINE_TOO_LONG

CX_SY_REF_IS_INITIAL

CX_SY_REPLACE_INFINITE_LOOP

CX_SY_SCAN_SOURCE_TOO_WIDE (6.20)

CX_SY_SQL_ERROR

    CX_SY_OPEN_SQL_ERROR

        CX_SY_OPEN_SQL_DB

        CX_SY_DYNAMIC_OSQL_ERROR

            CX_SY_DYNAMIC_OSQL_SEMANTICS

            CX_SY_DYNAMIC_OSQL_SYNTAX

    CX_SY_NATIVE_SQL_ERROR

CX_SY_WRITE_SRC_LINE_TOO_LONG

CX_NO_CHECK

CX_SY_EXPORT_NO_SHARED_MEMORY (6.20)

CX_SY_EXPORT_BUFFER_NO_MEMORY

CX_SY_GENERATE_SUBPOOL_FULL

CX_SY_LOCALIZATION_ERROR

CX_SY_NO_HANDLER

CX_SY_PIPES_NOT_SUPPORTED

CX_SY_PIPE_REOPEN

CX_SY_REMOTE_CALL_ERROR

    CX_SY_RMC_COMM_FAILURE

    CX_SY_RMC_INVALID_STATUS

    CX_SY_RMC_SYSTEM_FAILURE

CX_SY_TOO_MANY_FILES

Table D.1 Hierarchy of predefined exception classes. All classes, except for those flagged as being from Release 6.20, are available since Release 6.10. (cont.)

D.3   Catchable Runtime Errors

The following tables present the catchable runtime errors ordered according to exception groups. The exception classes assigned since Release 6.10 will be displayed for each exception group and for each catchable runtime error in the column on the right. In general, the exception class of an exception group is the superclass of the exception classes to which the catchable runtime errors of an exception group are assigned.

D.3.1 Exception Group for Arithmetic Errors

ARITHMETIC_ERRORS	CX_SY_ARITHMETIC_ERROR
ADDF_INT_OVERFLOW	CX_SY_ARITHMETIC_OVERFLOW
BCD_FIELD_OVERFLOW	CX_SY_CONVERSION_OVERFLOW
BCD_OVERFLOW	CX_SY_ARITHMETIC_OVERFLOW
BCD_ZERODIVIDE	CX_SY_ZERODIVIDE
COMPUTE_ACOS_DOMAIN	CX_SY_ARG_OUT_OF_DOMAIN
COMPUTE_ASIN_DOMAIN	CX_SY_ARG_OUT_OF_DOMAIN
COMPUTE_ATAN_DOMAIN*	CX_SY_ARG_OUT_OF_DOMAIN
COMPUTE_BCD_OVERFLOW	CX_SY_ARITHMETIC_OVERFLOW
COMPUTE_COS_DOMAIN	CX_SY_ARG_OUT_OF_DOMAIN
COMPUTE_COS_LOSS	CX_SY_PRECISION_LOSS
COMPUTE_COSH_DOMAIN*	CX_SY_ARG_OUT_OF_DOMAIN
COMPUTE_COSH_OVERFLOW	CX_SY_ARITHMETIC_OVERFLOW
COMPUTE_EXP_DOMAIN	CX_SY_ARG_OUT_OF_DOMAIN
COMPUTE_EXP_RANGE	CX_SY_ARITHMETIC_OVERFLOW
COMPUTE_FLOAT_DIV_OVERFLOW	CX_SY_ARITHMETIC_OVERFLOW
COMPUTE_FLOAT_MINUS_OVERFLOW	CX_SY_ARITHMETIC_OVERFLOW
COMPUTE_FLOAT_PLUS_OVERFLOW	CX_SY_ARITHMETIC_OVERFLOW
COMPUTE_FLOAT_TIMES_OVERFLOW	CX_SY_ARITHMETIC_OVERFLOW
COMPUTE_FLOAT_ZERODIVIDE	CX_SY_ZERODIVIDE
COMPUTE_INT_ABS_OVERFLOW	CX_SY_ARITHMETIC_OVERFLOW
COMPUTE_INT_DIV_OVERFLOW	CX_SY_ARITHMETIC_OVERFLOW
COMPUTE_INT_MINUS_OVERFLOW	CX_SY_ARITHMETIC_OVERFLOW
COMPUTE_INT_PLUS_OVERFLOW	CX_SY_ARITHMETIC_OVERFLOW
COMPUTE_INT_TIMES_OVERFLOW	CX_SY_ARITHMETIC_OVERFLOW

Table D.2 Exception group ARITHMETIC_ERRORS. The runtime errors marked with an asterisk no longer exist from Release 6.40 onwards and should therefore not be caught.

ARITHMETIC_ERRORS	CX_SY_ARITHMETIC_ERROR
COMPUTE_INT_ZERODIVIDE	CX_SY_ZERODIVIDE
COMPUTE_LOG_ERROR	CX_SY_ARITHMETIC_OVERFLOW, CX_SY_ARG_OUT_OF_DOMAIN
COMPUTE_LOG10_ERROR	CX_SY_ARITHMETIC_OVERFLOW, CX_SY_ARG_OUT_OF_DOMAIN
COMPUTE_MATH_DOMAIN*	CX_SY_ARG_OUT_OF_DOMAIN
COMPUTE_MATH_LOSS*	CX_SY_PRECISION_LOSS
COMPUTE_MATH_OVERFLOW*	CX_SY_ARITHMETIC_OVERFLOW
COMPUTE_POW_DOMAIN	CX_SY_ARG_OUT_OF_DOMAIN
COMPUTE_POW_RANGE	CX_SY_ARITHMETIC_OVERFLOW
COMPUTE_SIN_DOMAIN	CX_SY_ARG_OUT_OF_DOMAIN
COMPUTE_SIN_LOSS	CX_SY_PRECISION_LOSS
COMPUTE_SINH_DOMAIN*	CX_SY_ARG_OUT_OF_DOMAIN
COMPUTE_SINH_OVERFLOW	CX_SY_ARITHMETIC_OVERFLOW
COMPUTE_SQRT_DOMAIN	CX_SY_ARG_OUT_OF_DOMAIN
COMPUTE_TAN_LOSS	CX_SY_PRECISION_LOSS
COMPUTE_TANH_DOMAIN*	CX_SY_ARG_OUT_OF_DOMAIN

Table D.2 Exception group ARITHMETIC_ERRORS. The runtime errors marked with an asterisk no longer exist from Release 6.40 onwards and should therefore not be caught. (cont.)

D.3.2   Exception Group for Conversion Errors

CONVERSION_ERRORS	CX_SY_CONVERSION_ERROR
BCD_FIELD_OVERFLOW	CX_SY_CONVERSION_OVERFLOW
BCD_OVERFLOW	CX_SY_ARITHMETIC_OVERFLOW
CONVT_CODEPAGE	CX_SY_CONVERSION_CODEPAGE
CONVT_NO_NUMBER	CX_SY_CONVERSION_NO_NUMBER
CONVT_OVERFLOW	CX_SY_CONVERSION_OVERFLOW

Table D.3 Exception group CONVERSION_ERRORS

D.3.3 Exception Group for Errors When Creating Data Objects

CREATE_DATA_ERRORS	CX_SY_CREATE_ERROR
CREATE_DATA_ILLEGAL_DECIMALS	CX_SY_CREATE_DATA_ERROR
CREATE_DATA_ILLEGAL_INIT_SIZE	CX_SY_CREATE_DATA_ERROR
CREATE_DATA_ILLEGAL_LENGTH	CX_SY_CREATE_DATA_ERROR
CREATE_DATA_LEN_NOT_ALLOWED	CX_SY_CREATE_DATA_ERROR
CREATE_DATA_NOT_ALLOWED_TYPE	CX_SY_CREATE_DATA_ERROR
CREATE_DATA_UNKNOWN_TYPE	CX_SY_CREATE_DATA_ERROR

Table D.4 Exception group CREATE_DATA_ERRORS

D.3.4 Exception Group for Errors When Creating Instances of Classes

CREATE_OBJECT_ERRORS	CX_SY_CREATE_ERROR
CREATE_OBJECT_CLASS_ABSTRACT	CX_SY_CREATE_OBJECT_ERROR
CREATE_OBJECT_CLASS_NOT_FOUND	CX_SY_CREATE_OBJECT_ERROR
CREATE_OBJECT_CREATE_PRIVATE	CX_SY_CREATE_OBJECT_ERROR
CREATE_OBJECT_CREATE_PROTECTED	CX_SY_CREATE_OBJECT_ERROR

Table D.5 Exception group CREATE_OBJECT_ERRORS

D.3.5 Exception Group for Errors When Accessing Data Objects

DATA_ACCESS_ERRORS	CX_SY_DATA_ACCESS_ERROR
DATA_LENGTH_0	CX_SY_RANGE_OUT_OF_BOUNDS
DATA_LENGTH_NEGATIVE	CX_SY_RANGE_OUT_OF_BOUNDS
DATA_LENGTH_TOO_LARGE	CX_SY_RANGE_OUT_OF_BOUNDS
DATA_OFFSET_LENGTH_NOT_ALLOWED	CX_SY_OFFSET_NOT_ALLOWED
DATA_OFFSET_LENGTH_TOO_LARGE	CX_SY_RANGE_OUT_OF_BOUNDS
DATA_OFFSET_NEGATIVE	CX_SY_RANGE_OUT_OF_BOUNDS
REFI_WRONG_SECTION	CX_SY_RANGE_OUT_OF_BOUNDS

Table D.6 Exception group CREATE_DATA_ACCESS_ERRORS

DATA_ACCESS_ERRORS	CX_SY_DATA_ACCESS_ERROR
STRING_LENGTH_NEGATIVE	CX_SY_RANGE_OUT_OF_BOUNDS
STRING_LENGTH_TOO_LARGE	CX_SY_RANGE_OUT_OF_BOUNDS
STRING_OFFSET_LENGTH_TOO_LARGE	CX_SY_RANGE_OUT_OF_BOUNDS
STRING_OFFSET_NEGATIVE	CX_SY_RANGE_OUT_OF_BOUNDS
STRING_OFFSET_TOO_LARGE	CX_SY_RANGE_OUT_OF_BOUNDS

Table D.6 Exception group CREATE_DATA_ACCESS_ERRORS (cont.)

D.3.6 Exception Group for Errors in Dynamic Method Calls

DYNAMIC_CALL_METHOD_ERRORS	CX_SY_DYN_CALL_ERROR
DYN_CALL_METH_CLASS_ABSTRACT	CX_SY_DYN_CALL_ILLEGAL_CLASS
DYN_CALL_METH_CLASS_NOT_FOUND	CX_SY_DYN_CALL_ILLEGAL_CLASS
DYN_CALL_METH_CLASSCONSTRUCTOR	CX_SY_DYN_CALL_ILLEGAL_METHOD
DYN_CALL_METH_CONSTRUCTOR	CX_SY_DYN_CALL_ILLEGAL_METHOD
DYN_CALL_METH_EXCP_NOT_FOUND	CX_SY_DYN_CALL_EXCP_NOT_FOUND
DYN_CALL_METH_NO_CLASS_METHOD	CX_SY_DYN_CALL_ILLEGAL_METHOD
DYN_CALL_METH_NOT_FOUND	CX_SY_DYN_CALL_ILLEGAL_METHOD
DYN_CALL_METH_PARAM_KIND	CX_SY_DYN_CALL_ILLEGAL_TYPE
DYN_CALL_METH_PARAM_LITL_MOVE	CX_SY_DYN_CALL_ILLEGAL_TYPE
DYN_CALL_METH_PARAM_MISSING	CX_SY_DYN_CALL_PARAM_MISSING
DYN_CALL_METH_PARAM_NOT_FOUND	CX_SY_DYN_CALL_PARAM_NOT_FOUND
DYN_CALL_METH_PARAM_TAB_TYPE	CX_SY_DYN_CALL_ILLEGAL_TYPE
DYN_CALL_METH_PARAM_TYPE	CX_SY_DYN_CALL_ILLEGAL_TYPE
DYN_CALL_METH_PARREF_INITIAL	CX_SY_DYN_CALL_PARAM_MISSING
DYN_CALL_METH_PRIVATE	CX_SY_DYN_CALL_ILLEGAL_METHOD
DYN_CALL_METH_PROTECTED	CX_SY_DYN_CALL_ILLEGAL_METHOD
DYN_CALL_METH_REF_IS_INITIAL	CX_SY_REF_IS_INITIAL

Table D.7 Exception group DYNAMIC_CALL_METHOD_ERRORS

D.3.7 Exception Group for Errors When Accessing Files

FILE_ACCESS_ERRORS	CX_SY_FILE_ACCESS _ERROR
DATASET_CANT_CLOSE	CX_SY_FILE_CLOSE
DATASET_CANT_OPEN	CX_SY_FILE_OPEN
DATASET_NO_PIPE	CX_SY_PIPES_NOT_SUPPORTED
DATASET_NO_POSITION	CX_SY_FILE_POSITION
DATASET_NOT_OPEN	CX_SY_FILE_OPEN_MODE
DATASET_READ_ERROR	CX_SY_FILE_IO
DATASET_READ_ONLY	CX_SY_FILE_OPEN_MODE
DATASET_SEEK_ERROR	CX_SY_FILE_POSITION
DATASET_TOO_MANY_FILES	CX_SY_TOO_MANY_FILES
DATASET_WRITE_ERROR	CX_SY_FILE_IO
EXPORT_DATASET_CANNOT_OPEN	CX_SY_FILE_OPEN
EXPORT_DATASET_WRITE_ERROR	CX_SY_FILE_IO
OPEN_DATASET_NO_AUTHORITY	CX_SY_FILE_AUTHORITY
OPEN_PIPE_NO_AUTHORITY	CX_SY_FILE_AUTHORITY

Table D.8 Exception group FILE_ACCESS_ERRORS

D.3.8 Exception Group for Errors When Accessing Data Clusters

IMPORT_MISMATCH_ERRORS	CX_SY_IMPORT_MISMATCH_ERROR
CONNE_IMPORT_WRONG_COMP_DECS	CX_SY_IMPORT_MISMATCH_ERROR
CONNE_IMPORT_WRONG_COMP_LENG	CX_SY_IMPORT_MISMATCH_ERROR
CONNE_IMPORT_WRONG_COMP_TYPE	CX_SY_IMPORT_MISMATCH_ERROR
CONNE_IMPORT_WRONG_FIELD_DECS	CX_SY_IMPORT_MISMATCH_ERROR
CONNE_IMPORT_WRONG_FIELD_LENG	CX_SY_IMPORT_MISMATCH_ERROR
CONNE_IMPORT_WRONG_FIELD_TYPE	CX_SY_IMPORT_MISMATCH_ERROR
CONNE_IMPORT_WRONG_OBJECT_TYPE	CX_SY_IMPORT_MISMATCH_ERROR
CONNE_IMPORT_WRONG_STRUCTURE	CX_SY_IMPORT_MISMATCH_ERROR

Table D.9 Exception group IMPORT_MISMATCH_ERRORS

IMPORT_MISMATCH_ERRORS	CX_SY_IMPORT_MISMATCH_ERROR
IMPORT_ALIGNMENT_MISMATCH	CX_SY_IMPORT_MISMATCH_ERROR
IMPORT_WRONG_END_POS	CX_SY_IMPORT_MISMATCH_ERROR

Table D.9 Exception group IMPORT_MISMATCH_ERRORS (cont.)

D.3.9 Exception Group for Errors in the Language Environment

LOCALIZATION_ERRORS	CX_SY_LOCALIZATION_ERROR
TEXTENV_CODEPAGE_NOT_ALLOWED	CX_SY_LOCALIZATION_ERROR
TEXTENV_INVALID	CX_SY_LOCALIZATION_ERROR
TEXTENV_KEY_INVALID	CX_SY_LOCALIZATION_ERROR

Table D.10 Exception group LOCALIZATION_ERRORS

D.3.10 Exception Group for Errors with Remote Function Calls

REMOTE_CALL_ERRORS	CX_SY_REMOTE_CALL_ERROR
RMC_COMMUNICATION_FAILURE	CX_SY_RMC_COMM_FAILURE
RMC_INVALID_STATUS	CX_SY_RMC_INVALID_STATUS
RMC_SYSTEM_FAILURE	CX_SY_RMC_SYSTEM_FAILURE

Table D.11 Exception group REMOTE_CALL_ERRORS

D.3.11 Catchable Runtime Errors That Are Not Assigned to Any Group

ASSIGN_CASTING_ILLEGAL_CAST	CX_SY_ASSIGN_CAST_ILLEGAL_CAST
ASSIGN_CASTING_UNKNOWN_TYPE	CX_SY_ASSIGN_CAST_UNKNOWN_TYPE
ASSIGN_FIELD_NOT_IN_RANGE	CX_SY_ASSIGN_OUT_OF_RANGE
CONVT_CODEPAGE_INIT	CX_SY_CODEPAGE_CONVERTER_INIT
DATASET_OFFSET_TOO_LARGE	CX_SY_FILE_POSITION
DYN_CALL_METH_NOT_IMPLEMENTED	CX_SY_DYN_CALL_ILLEGAL_METHOD

Table D.12 Catchable runtime errors not assigned to any exception group

EXPORT_BUFFER_NO_MEMORY	CX_SY_EXPORT_BUFFER_NO_MEMORY
GENERATE_SUBPOOL_DIR_FULL	CX_SY_GENERATE_SUBPOOL_FULL
MOVE_CAST_ERROR	CX_SY_MOVE_CAST_ERROR
PERFORM_PROGRAM_NAME_TOO_LONG	CX_SY_PROGRAM_NOT_FOUND
REPLACE_INFINITE_LOOP	CX_SY_REPLACE_INFINITE_LOOP

Table D.12 Catchable runtime errors not assigned to any exception group (cont.)

E   Glossary

Note

When you see a term set in italics within a glossary definition, this indicates that there is an entry for that term elsewhere in the glossary.

ABAP: Advanced Business Application Programming.

ABAP Compiler: The ABAP Compiler creates a *byte code* when generating a program from the *source code*. This byte code is stored in the *database*.

ABAP data type: → *Data type*

ABAP Debugger: Tool with which *ABAP programs* are executed line by line or section by section. In this way it is possible to process the contents of *data objects* and to check the program logic. See also *breakpoint*.

ABAP Dictionary: Persistent storage for *data types* that are visible in all *Repository objects*. In addition, the *database tables*—among other things —of the *central database*, *views*, and *lock objects* in the ABAP Dictionary are managed. The objects of the ABAP Dictionary are maintained using the homonymous tool in the *ABAP Workbench*. Call using transaction code SE11.

ABAP Editor: *ABAP Workbench* tool for creating *ABAP programs*. Call using *transaction code* SE38.

ABAP keyword: *ABAP word* that initiates an *ABAP statement*.

ABAP language element: (Token) Component of an *ABAP statement*. Either an *ABAP word*, *operator*, or parentheses.

ABAP memory: Memory area within every *main session*, which the programs with the statements EXPORT and IMPORT (see Chapter 31) can access. This memory area is maintained via a succession of program calls (*call sequence*).

ABAP Objects: Component of the ABAP programming language that allows object-oriented programming on the basis of *classes* and *interfaces*.

ABAP program: *Repository object* that contains ABAP source text and has a *program type*. The ABAP program is assigned additional *components* such as *dynpros* or the *GUI status*.

ABAP runtime environment: Hardware, operating system, and database-independent platform (virtual machine) of an *ABAP program*. At the same time processes of the ABAP runtime environment control the execution of an ABAP program by calling the *processing blocks* of the program.

ABAP statement: A complete sentence of the ABAP programming language. Consists of *ABAP language elements* and *operands* and ends with a period (see Section 2.1).

ABAP Unit: Test tool integrated in the *ABAP runtime environment* since Release 6.40 that is used for checking the functions of code sections in a program (module tests). Individual tests are implemented as *test methods* of local *test classes* in ABAP programs. The tests of a test class use the same *fixture*. Tests of several ABAP programs can be grouped into *test tasks*.

ABAP word: *ABAP language element*, either an *ABAP keyword* or an addition to an ABAP keyword.

ABAP Workbench: Development environment for *ABAP programs* and their components. Contains tools for editing and managing of all *Repository objects*. Accessed using *forward navigation*, the *Object Navigator*, *transaction codes*, or *SAP Easy Access*.

Absolute type name: *Type name* which is structured like a path that uniquely specifies the *context* of a *data type*, a class or an *interface* (see Section 6.1.4). The *RTTS* can determine the absolute type name of any *object*.

Abstract: Term in *ABAP objects*. An abstract *class* cannot be instanced (see Section 7.2.1). An abstract *method* can only be implemented in *subclasses* of its class (see Section 7.4.1).

Activatable checkpoint: *Checkpoint* that can be assigned to a *checkpoint group* by the addition ID of the statement ASSERT or BREAK-POINT. The behavior of an activatable checkpoint is controlled either by group-specific or program-specific activation settings. Program-specific settings apply for all activatable checkpoints of a program and overwrite the settings of the respective checkpoint group.

Actual parameter: *Data object* whose content is transferred to a *formal parameter* as an argument when a *procedure* is called (see Section 11.2).

Additional program group: *Program group* in an *internal session*. This is cre-

ated when a *function group* or a *class pool* is loaded in the internal session by means of an external procedure call. The function group or class pool is the *main program* in the additional program group (see Figure 11.2). An additional program group and its data is retained for the entire duration of the internal session.

Aggregate: Grouping of data from several lines in a *database table*. Can be determined by means of *aggregate functions* in the SELECT statement.

Aggregate expression: Specification of a column in the SELECT statement by means of an *aggregate function* (see Section 29.2.1).

Aggregate function: Function that determines a value from the values in several lines of a column in a *database table*. The value is calculated in the *database system*. The specification of a column in a database table as an argument for an aggregate function constitutes an *aggregate expression*, which can be used in the SELECT statement.

Alias name: Name of an *interface component* in a *class* or *compound interface* declared with the ALIASES statement (see Section 7.4.3).

Alignment: Some *data types*, such as *numeric data types* or *references* have specific alignment requirements that depend on the respective platform. *Fields* in the memory that have one of these *types* must begin at addresses that can be divided by 4 or 8. In *Unicode systems*, *data objects* of *character-like data types* are also located in storage addresses that can be divided by 2 or 4, depending on the *Unicode character representation*. In a *structure* or *substructure*, the *component* with the highest alignment requirement determines the alignment of the entire structure.

Alignment gap: Bytes inserted in a *structure* before *components* with alignment requirements to obtain the necessary *alignment*.

Anonymous data object: *Data object* that cannot be addressed using a name. Anonymous data objects are created in ABAP by the CREATE DATA statement and can be addressed using *reference variables*. See also *Named Data Object* and *Literal*.

Append structure: *Structure* of the *ABAP Dictionary* that is appended to another structure or a *database table* so as to add further *components*. Structures and database tables delivered by SAP can be extended by means of append structures in customer systems.

Application server: Software layer of a *SAP system* in which the application programs are executed. An SAP system can contain several application servers. These communicate with the *presentation server*, the *database server*, and with each other. The most important components of an application server are its *work processes*. The number of work processes and the r type are defined when the SAP system is started.

Application toolbar: Part of a *window*. Contains *pushbuttons* defined in the *Menu Painter* tool. Part of the GUI status set with SET PF-STATUS. A named pushbutton in the *ABAP Workbench*.

Archiving: Storing *print lists* with the *SAP ArchiveLink* tool. Print lists stored in the *SAP spool system* can be archived. During archiving, print lists

from the spool system are copied exactly in the formatting stored there.

Archiving parameters: *Parameters* that must be passed to a *spool request*, if you want to archive its data using *SAP ArchiveLink* (see Section 10.2.3 and 27.2.8).

Area: *Repository object* for storing *shared objects*. An area is the template for *area instance versions* in the *shared memory*. To each area, an identically named *area class* and any *root data class* is assigned. Areas are created and administered using the *transaction* SHMA.

Area class: *Final global class*, whose *instances* are used as *area handles*. The *attributes* of the instances of an area class represent the properties of an *area*. The *methods* of an area class are used to access the area. All area classes are *subclasses* of CL_ABAP_MEMORY_AREA. When creating areas, area classes of identical names are generated as subclasses of CL_SHM_AREA. A special predefined area class is CL_IMODE_AREA, whose instance represents the area handle for the *internal session* of a program.

Area handle: *Instance* of an *area class*. An area handle allows an *ABAP program* to access an *area instance version* in the *shared memory* and the *shared objects* stored there. An area handle is generated by static methods of its area class and is attached to an area instance version in the process. Every attached area handle sets an *area lock* to the respective area instance version.

Area instance: Number of all *area instance versions* with identical area instance name. An area instance is a unique attribute of an *area*, which is divided into versions.

Area instance version: Attribute of an *area* in the *Shared Objects Memory*. In an area instance version, *shared objects* are stored in the form of instances of shared *memory-enabled classes*, wherein there is at least one instance of the *root data class* of the area. Creating and accessing area instance versions is done exclusively using *area handles*. Every area instance version has a name. Area instance versions with identical names form an *area instance*.

Area lock: Write, read, or update lock for an *area instance version* in the *Shared Objects Memory*. Area locks are set by attaching *area handles* to area instance versions.

Area root class: Global *shared memory capable class* that must be assigned to an *area* during its definition. A non-blank *area instance version* contains at least one *instance* of the area root class (root object). The attribute ROOT of a belonging *area handle* points to this instance of the area root class. The root object contains *references* to the remaining *shared objects* of the area instance version.

aRFC: → *asynchronous Remote Function Call*

Arithmetic expression: Formulation of a calculation. The result of an arithmetic expression is a numerical value. Arithmetic expressions appear only in the statement COMPUTE (see Section 19.3).

Arithmetic operator: Links two numeric *operands* of an *arithmetic expression*. Arithmetic operators are +, -, *, /, DIV, MOD and ** (see Section 19.3.1).

ASCII: Abbreviation of American Standard Code for Information Interchange. 7-bit *character set* according to ISO-646 norm. Extended to 8-bit character sets by *ISO-8859*.

Assertion: Conditional *checkpoint* defined by the ASSERT statement. When the program reaches an active assertion, it evaluates the corresponding condition. If the condition is violated, the program terminates with a runtime error, branches to the *ABAP Debugger*, or creates a log entry. If the assertion is assigned to a *checkpoint group*, the behavior is controlled by the corresponding activation settings, otherwise the program terminates. See also *activatable checkpoint*.

Assignment: Transfers the content of a *data object* to another data object. If the data objects are *compatible*, the content is copied unchanged. If the data objects are incompatible and there is a suitable *conversion rule*, the content is converted. Typical statement: MOVE.

Assignment operator: *Operator* for assigning the content of a *data object* to a *variable*. Assignment operators are the equals sign (=) and the *Casting Operator* (?=) (see Section 16.2).

Asynchronous remote function call: *Remote Function Call* that does not wait until processing of the function called remotely is completed (see Section 39.2.2).

Asynchronous update: Execution of high priority *update function modules* whereat the calling program does not wait for completion. An asynchronous update is started by a `CCMMIT WORK` without the addition `AND WAIT` (see Section 33.3.1).

asXML: ABAP Serialization XML. Short name for the *canonical XML representation* of ABAP data.

Attribute: *Data object* declared within a *class* or an *interface*. There are *instance attributes* and *static attributes*.

Authorization: Entry in the *user master record* or part of an *authorization profile*. An authorization consists of fully specified or generic values for the *authorization fields* of an *authorization object*. The combination tells which activities a user can use to access which data. Authorizations are maintained directly using *transaction code* SU03 or are generated using the profile generator from role management (transaction PFCG).

Authorization assignment: Creation of *authorizations* in the *user master record*, either from *authorization profiles* or by entering individual values.

Authorization check: Checks whether the current program user has the corresponding *authorization*. The system compares a value for checking with the corresponding entries in the *user master record* for each *authorization field* in an *authorization object*. The responsible ABAP statement is `AUTHORITY-CHECK` (see Section 33.6).

Authorization field: Smallest unit of an *authorization object*. An authorization field represents either data such as a *key field* of a *database table* or activities such as reading or changing. Activities are specified as short forms, which are stored in database table TACT and specifically in TACTZ.

Authorization group: *Program attribute* that allows the combining of different programs in groups for common *authorization checks*. The group name is the *authorization field* of the *authorization object* S_DEVELOP, for which in the statement `SUBMIT` an *authorization check* is executed implicitly, in order to find out whether the current user is authorized to execute the program.

Authorization object: *Repository object* on which *authorizations* are based. An authorization object consists of up to 10 *authorization fields*. The combination of authorization fields that represent data and activities is used for *authorization assignment* and *authorization check*. Authorization objects are combined organizationally in authorization classes and are maintained by *transaction code* SU21.

Authorization profile: Combination of several individual *authorizations* or further authorization profiles. Can be entered in the *user master record* instead of individual authorizations. Authorization profiles are maintained directly using *transaction* code SU02 or are generated using the profile generator from role management (transaction PFCG).

Background job: → *Background request*

Background processing: Execution of *ABAP programs* with determined setting in the background, that is, without on-screen user dialog. In contrast to *dialog processing*, the execution flow is fixed when the program is started. An executable program is scheduled in the *ABAP editor* or after calling **System • Services • Reporting** using menu **Program • Execute • Background** for automatic execution or is called in the background using SUBMIT VIA JOB (see Section 10.2.4). For background processing, at least one background *work process* must be set up.

Background request: *Job* used to start one or more *ABAP programs* in *background processing*. A background request consists of single *background tasks*.

Background task: Subunit of a *background task*.

BAdI: → *Business Add-In*

BAdI Builder: Tool of the *ABAP Workbench* for creation and maintenance of *Business Add-Ins*. Call using *transaction code* SE18.

BAPI: → *Business Application Programming Interface*

Basic list: *List of list level* 0. After calling a program, *output statements* by default write to the basic list.

Batch input: Data transfer technique that allows you to transfer datasets automatically to *dynpros* belonging to *transactions*, and thus to an *SAP system*. Batch input is controlled by a *batch input session* (see Section 10.3).

Batch input session: Groups a series of transaction calls together with input data and user actions. A batch input session can be used to execute a *dialog transaction* in *batch input*, where some or all the *screens* are processed by the session. Batch input sessions are stored in the *database* as *database tables* and can be used within a program as *internal tables* when accessing *transactions* (see Section 10.3).

BCD: Abbreviation of Binary Coded Decimals. Code for displaying decimal numbers that displays each decimal digit in 4 bits. See also *packed number*.

Big endian: *Byte sequence* in which the highest value byte is at the first storage position.

Bit expression: Formulation of a binary operation. The result of a bit expression is a byte-like value. Bit expressions are only used in the COMPUTE statement (see Section 19.4).

Bit operator: Links two *operands* of a *bit expression*. Bit operators are BIT-NOT, BIT-AND, BIT-OR or BIT-XOR (see Section 19.4.1).

Boolean operator: Connects or negates *logical expressions*. Boolean operators are AND, OR, and NOT (see Section 13.6).

Bound data type: *Data type* that only exists as a property of a *data object*. See also *Stand-Alone Data Type*.

Branch: Also *selection*. *Control structure* that can comprise several statement blocks defined by keywords IF—ELSEIF—ELSE—ENDIF, CASE—WHEN—ENDCASE, TRY—CATCH—CLEANUP—ENDTRY and are executed according to conditions.

Breakpoint: Unconditional *checkpoint* that is either set interactively in the *ABAP Editor* or *ABAP Debugger* or is defined by the BREAK-POINT statement. When a program reaches an active breakpoint, it accesses branches to the ABAP Debugger or creates a log entry. You can deactivate a breakpoint defined by a BREAK-POINT statement using the corresponding activation settings by assigning it to a *checkpoint group*. See also *Activatable Checkpoint*.

BSP: → *Business Server Pages*

Business Add-In (*BAdI*): Location in a program delivered by SAP, at which industries, partners, and customers can insert their own logic without having to modify the original object. Some expansions can only have a maximum of one implementation, and others can be extended by any number of customers at the same time. The expansions are implemented in special *classes*. Business Add-Ins replace *function module exits* as of Release 4.6. Business Add-Ins are edited in the *BAdI Builder*.

Business Application Programming Interface (BAPI): Predefined *interface* to data and processes in an SAP application. Stored in the Business Object Repository with the basic functions Create *Objects*, Query Object Properties, and Change Object Properties. BAPIs are implemented using *function modules* with the naming convention BAPI_<business_object_name>_<method_name> that can be called remotely and that must not run a user dialog. The BAPI Explorer, which lists the function modules for each application, can be accessed with the *transaction code* BAPI.

Business Server Pages: *User interface* of an Internet application of the *Web Application Server* encoded in HTML. Business Server Pages can include server-side scripts written in ABAP or JavaScript. When a script written in ABAP is compiled, the system generates an ABAP objects class whose methods implement the functions of the script is generated on the *application server*. This means that all language

tools available in *ABAP objects* can also be used in Business Server Pages and, most importantly, that the database can be accessed with *Open SQL*. Business Server Pages are created using the *Web Application Builder*.

Byte chain: Content of a *byte-like data object*. Also *byte sequence*.

Byte code: Result of generating an *ABAP program* using the *ABAP Compiler*. The statements in the byte code are connected to C functions. When the ABAP program is executed, the byte code is loaded into the PXA and interpreted by the ABAP *runtime environment* (Virtual Machine), which accesses the corresponding C functions.

Byte field: *Data object* of type x.

Byte-like data object: *Data object* that can be interpreted as byte-like if it contains the appropriate content. This only applies to data objects of *byte-like data types* x and xstring.

Byte-like data type: *Data types* whose *data objects* contain uncoded bytes. The corresponding *built-in data types* are x and xstring. The corresponding *generic data type* is xsequence.

Byte order: Determines the order in which a number of the *data types* i and f or a character in a *Unicode system* is stored in the memory. A distinction is made between *big* and *little endian*. In the former, the system writes the byte with the highest level to the first position in the memory, and in the latter it writes the byte with the lowest level to the first position. The byte order on the current *application server* can be derived from the static attribute

ENDIAN in the system class CL_ABAP_CHAR_UTILITIES.

Byte sequence → *Byte Chain*

Byte string: *Data object* of the type `xstring`.

Calculation expression: Right hand side of a COMPUTE statement. Calculates a value. Either an *arithmetic expression* or a *bit expression*.

Calculation type: Property of an *arithmetic expression* subject to the *numeric data types* involved. The calculation type determines the procedure used to evaluate an arithmetic expression. There are different procedures for the calculation types `i`, `p`, and `f` (see Section 19.3.4).

Call sequence: This sequence is created if you can return from the called program to the calling program at the call of an *ABAP-Program* with SUBMIT ... AND RETURN or CALL TRANSACTION. For this purpose, the data of the *internal session* of the caller remains on a stack. The programs of a call sequence have collective access to the *ABAP Memory*. A call sequence can be left completely using the statement LEAVE TO TRANSACTION (see Chapter 10).

Canonical XML representation: Format of an *XML* document, which is created during the *serialization* of ABAP-data or which is the prerequisite for a *de-serialization* (see Section 40.1.3). The short form is *asXML*.

Cast, casting: Handling a *Data object* under the assumption of a certain *Data type*. Explicit casting is possible with the statement ASSIGN (see Section 17.2.2) and with the *assignments*

between *reference variables* (see Section A.5). An implicit casting sometimes takes place during the handling of *operands* at certain *operand positions* (see Section 2.2.5.3).

Casting operator: Special *assignment operator* (?=) for *assignments* between *reference variables*, for which it is not checked if the assignment is possible until runtime. Necessary for *down cast* (see Section A.5.2).

Catchable runtime error: Exceptional circumstances in the runtime environment which can be handled with CATCH SYSTEM-EXCEPTIONS (see Section 15.3). Since Release 6.10 replaced by *class-based exceptions* (see Chapter 15).

CATT: Computer Aided Test Tool. Allows storing of application process flows for test purposes.

Chained statement: Abbreviated diction for multiple *ABAP-statements* with the same beginning section. The beginning section is noted once and concluded with a colon (:). The remaining parts follow, (see Section 2.4) separated by commas.

Character: Encoded element of a *character set*. Letter, number or special character.

Character-like data object: *Data object* that can be interpreted as *character-like* if its content is appropriate. Besides data object of the *character-like data types* `c`, `d`, `n`, `t` and `string`, in *Unicode systems* also *structures* with purely *flat* character-like *components* and, in non-Unicode systems, any kind of flat structures and *byte-like data objects* can be character-like.

Character-like data type: *Data type*, whose *data objects* contain *characters* encoded according to the current *code page*. The respective *predefined data types* are c, d, n, t and string. The relevant *generic data type* is clike.

Character literal: Generic term for *text field literals* and *string literals*.

Character representation: Binary coding of characters. To assign a *character set* to a character representation, you use *code pages*. The ISO-8859 code-pages are *single-byte* character representations, in which every character is encoded in up to one byte. SJIS and BIG5 are *double-byte* character representations for Japanese and traditional Chinese fonts. The *Unicode character representations* enclose all characters world-wide and can be encoded by 1, 2, or 4 bytes, depending on the *UTF* representation.

Character sequence: → *Character string*

Character set: Defined set of characters. For example, *ASCII*, *EBCDIC* or *Unicode*. Character sets are mapped onto *character representations* by means of *codepages*.

Character string: Content of a *character-type data object*.

Checkbox: *Screen element* linked to a *dynpro field*, into which the user can enter the values "X" or " " by selection.

Checkpoint: Generic term for *assertions* and *breakpoints*. The statements ASSERT and BREAK-POINT for defining checkpoints are not operative but equip the program for test purposes. Checkpoints are either always active or can be activated by assigning them to a *checkpoint group*. Deactivated checkpoints are ignored during program execution.

Checkpoint group: *Repository object*, in which the activation settings of the allocated *checkpoints* are determined. To create checkpoint groups and maintain the activation settings, use *transaction* SAAB.

Check table: *Database table* whose *primary key* appears as a *foreign key* in a *foreign key table*.

Class: Template for *objects* in *ABAP Objects*. Defined with CLASS—END-CLASS, either globally in a *class pool* or locally in another *ABAP program* (see Section 7.2). The definition of a class comprises a *declaration section* for the declaration of the *class components* and an *implementation part* for the implementation of the *methods*.

Class-based exception: *Treatable exception*, which is represented by an *exception* object of an *exception class*. Class-based exceptions replace *catchable runtime errors* and non-class-based exceptions (see Chapter 15).

Class Builder: Tool in the *ABAP Workbench* for creating and maintaining global classes. Can be accessed with the *transaction code* SE24.

Class component: *Component* of a *class*. Declared in the *declaration section* of the class. Possible class components are *attributes*, *methods*, and *events* (see Section 7.2.1).

Class component selector: Character =>. Each visible *static component* comp of a *class* class can be addressed via class=>comp.

Class library: Storage location for all global *classes* and *interfaces* defined in the *Class Builder*.

Class pool: *ABAP program* that contains the definition of exactly one global class and is loaded via usage of the class. Does not support its own dynpros, and the only possible *processing blocks* are *methods*.

Class reference variable: *Object reference variable* of the *static type* of a *class*.

Client: Area in an *SAP system* with independent application data. Identified by means of the *client identifier*, which is specified at *logon* to a SAP system.

Client handling: Processing the application data in a *client*. *Open SQL* statements work with automatic client handling that always accesses the current client (see Section 29.1.4).

Client identifier: Three-character identifier of a client. First column in client-specific *database tables*. *Open SQL* statements contain an implicit WHERE condition for the current client by default (see Section 29.1.4).

Cluster: Grouping of different data in a common storage area. Either as a *data cluster* in various storage media for *data objects* or as a *table cluster* for *database tables* (*cluster tables*).

Cluster table: *Database table* defined in the *ABAP Dictionary*, whose characteristic on the *database* is not only assigned to one table defined in the ABAP Dictionary. Several cluster tables are assigned to a *table cluster* in the database. The intersection of the *key fields* of the cluster tables forms the

primary key of the table cluster. The remaining columns of the cluster tables are stored in compressed form in a single column VARDATA of the table cluster. You can access cluster tables only via *Open SQL*, and only without using *joins*.

Code Inspector: Tool for checking *Repository objects* as regards performance, security, syntax, and compliance with naming conventions (as of Release 6.40). Can be accessed using the *transaction code* SCI.

Code page: Mapping of a selected amount of characters (*character set*) onto bit sequences (*character representation*). For example, Latin1 (*ISO-8859–1*) represents a code page that contains all the characters required for Western European languages, while a *Unicode character representation* can display all the characters required across the globe. The way in which characters are displayed in an *internal session* is determined by the active *system code page* of the *text environment* in the internal session. Each code page supported by SAP is assigned an SAP code page number in the *database table* TCP00.

Column selector: Character ~. A column col of a *database table* dbtab can be addressed via dbtab ~ col in a SELECT statement. This type of addressing is necessary, if the name of one column occurs in different database tables at the time of access.

Comment line: Line in a program introduced with an asterisk * in the first position. Comment lines are ignored by the *ABAP Compiler* when generating a program (see Section 2.5).

Commercial notation: Displays a number as a sequence of digits, with a possible decimal separator if applicable, displaying the algebraic sign after the digits (see Section A.2.1).

Compatible: Two non-*generic data types* are compatible if all their characteristics are the same. Any *data type* is compatible with a generic data type if the generic data type includes its characteristics. *Data objects* are compatible if their data types are compatible. Conversion does not take place when *assigning* compatible data objects.

Complex selection: → *Selection criterion*

Component: Subunit of a *structure*, a *class*, or an *interface*.

Component interface: *Interface* included in a *compound interface* by means of an INTERFACES statement (see Section 7.4.3). A component interface can be a self-compound interface.

Component selector: Defined characters that can be used to address *components* of upper units. There is a *structure component selector* (-), a *class component selector* (=>), an *interface component selector* (~), and an *object component selector* (->).

Compound interface: *Interface* in which at least one *component interface* is included in its declaration with INTERFACES (see Section 7.4.3). Also called *nested interface*.

Constant: *Named data object* whose value cannot be changed during the runtime of an *ABAP program* (see Section 6.6).

Constructor: A special *method* in a *class* that sets a defined initial value for the status (*attributes*) of the class or its *objects*. There is an *instance constructor* for *instance attributes* and a *static constructor* for *static attributes*.

Context: 1. Contexts are obsolete *Repository objects* made up of of *key fields* to be entered, relationships between these fields, and further fields that can be derived from them. They are defined abstractly in the *Context Builder* in of the *ABAP Workbench* and used during runtime as temporary *objects*. Contexts can be edited with the statements CONTEXTS, DEMAND, and SUPPLY (see Section 42.13).
2. Environment of an *object*. Determines its visibility and lifetime. Possible contexts are *procedures*, *instances* of *classes*, classes and *framework programs*.

Context Builder: Tool in the *ABAP Workbench* for editing *contexts*. Can be accessed by means of the *transaction code* SE33.

Control: Software component of the *ABAP runtime environment* used to handle complex *screen elements*. Table control and tabstrip control are platform-independent controls that are handled directly using *dynpro* and *ABAP statements* (see Chapter 25). In addition, there are platform-independent *GUI controls* that are accessed in ABAP by the *classes* of the *Control Framework*.

Control element: Element of the *user interface* at which a *user action* can be executed. Most control elements can be linked to a *function code*.

Control framework: CFW; class hierarchy whose *classes* begin with the prefix

CL_GUI_. The common *super-class* is CL_GUI_OBJECT. The classes in the Control Framework wrap *GUI controls* and screen containers for these controls.

Control-level processing: *Control structures* defined in LOOP loops using *internal tables* or extracts with the key word AT (see Section 22.2.3 and 23.6).

Control statement: Statement used to define a *control structure*.

Control structure: Means of structuring a *processing block* into *statement blocks*. The possible control structures are *sequence*, *branch*, and *loop*. Control structures can be nested, so that closed statement blocks can contain other control structures. See Chapter 14.

Conversion Exit: → *Conversion Routine*

Conversion routine: A conversion routine CONV (also known as *conversion exit*) is represented by two *function modules*, which follow the naming convention CONVERSION_EXIT_ CONV_INPUT|OUTPUT where CONV is the name of the conversion routine. Statements leading to an interruption of the program flow or terminating an *SAP-LUW* must not be executed in the function modules. A conversion routine can be assigned to a *domain* in the *ABAP Dictionary*. If a *dynpro field* refers to a domain with a conversion routine or if a conversion routine is assigned to it in its attributes, the function module ..._INPUT is automatically executed with each entry in the corresponding screen. The function module ..._OUTPUT is automatically executed when values are displayed in this screen and the corresponding converted content is used. If a data object refers to a

domain of this type, the function module ..._OUTPUT is executed when the *data object* is output in a *list* and the converted content is output. Conversion routines could not be debugged before Release 6.40.

Conversion rule: Rule for converting content during *assignments* between *convertible data objects* (see Appendix A).

Convertible: Two different *data types* are convertible if a *conversion rule* exists for them. Two *data objects* are convertible if their data types are convertible and their content allows the corresponding conversion.

CPI-C: Standardized *interface* for cross-system communication of programs (see Section 42.17.1).

Cross-transaction application buffer: Application buffer in the *shared memory*. Cross-transaction application buffers are accessed via specifying SHARED BUFFER or SHARED MEMORY as a medium with the statements for *data-clusters*. Both forms differ in the way the system behaves when it reaches its memory limit.

Cursor: A cursor determines a position. First, the term cursor means the position of a pointer in a display window. Second, a *list-cursor* determines the output position in a *list*. There is also a *database-cursor* to read data from *database tables*. In the basic sense, the *file pointer* can be seen as a cursor as well.

Currency field: Component of a *structure* or *database table* of the type CURR, defined in the *ABAP Dictionary*. A currency value must be linked to a *currency key* of a structure or database table, which determines the amount of decimal places.

Currency key: Component of a structure or database table of the type CUKY, defined in the ABAP Dictionary. A currency key can be linked to a currency field of a structure or database table. The currency key can have a 3-digit currency abbreviation from the database table TCURX and determines the amount of decimal places for the currency field.

Custom control: Area on a *screen* in which you can display *GUI Controls*.

Customer exit: Option prepared by SAP to extend delivered standard programs without modification of the original program at the customer site. For potential customer requirements that are not part of the standard, SAP installs blank containers, which can be filled with own functionalities by the customer. Customer exits are administered by SAP in the *transaction* SMOD. The customer selects in transaction CMOD the extensions that she/he wants to process, groups them together as enhancement projects, processes the components and activates the according projects. See also *Function module exit*.

Data area: Memory area of an *ABAP program* in which data is stored. The data area covers a static area for *data objects* of fixed length and a dynamic area for data objects of variable length (*data types* string, xstring and *internal tables*). The internal *references* to the dynamic area lie in the static area.

Database: Organizational unit of *files*, among which logical dependencies exist. The files of the database of the *SAP system* are stored on the *database*

server and are administered by the *database system*.

Database commit: Ending of a *database LUW*, whereat changed sets are written to the *database*. Until database-commit, all changes are temporary and only visible to the executing program. After that, the changes are visible to all users of the database. In the *SAP system*, database commits are triggered implicitly, as well as through explicit requests (see Section 33.2.1).

Database connection: Connection of an *ABAP-program* to a *database system*. Open SQL instructions always access the central *database* of the *SAP systems* via a standard connection. In *Native SQL*, you can open additional connections (see Section 30.2.4).

Database cursor: Pointer to the result set of a database selection. The database cursor is always assigned to a row of the result set. In *Open SQL*, the cursor handling is implicit, except for the statements OPEN CURSOR, FETCH and CLOSE CURSOR (see Section 29.3).

Database field: Smallest logical unit of the *structure* of a *database table*. The properties of a database field are determined by a *data element*.

Database interface: *Interface* of the *database* of a *SAP system* which is integrated into the *ABAP runtime environment*. The statements of *Open SQL* and *Native SQL* access the database via the database interface. The database interface is accordingly divided into an *Open SQL interface* and a *Native SQL interface*. The database interface is responsible for data transport between *application server* and *database server*, automatic *client handling* and *SAP buffering*.

Database lock: Physical locks for rows in *database tables*, imposed by the *database system*. A database lock persists until the end of the current *database LUW* (see Section 33.4).

Database LUW: Indivisible sequence of database operations that are concluded by a *database commit*. The database LUW is either executed completely or not at all by the *database system*. If an error is detected within a database-LUW, it is possible to cancel all database changes since begin of the database-LUW with the help of *database rollback*. (see Section 33.2)

Database program: *ABAP program* of a *logical database*, which provides data to other programs in a *table work area* and, in doing so, triggers the *reporting event* GET with the statement PUT. The functionality of a database program is implemented in *subroutines* which are called by the *ABAP runtime environment* during the execution of an *executable program* or the *function module* LDB_PROCESS. The execution time of the individual subroutines is assigned to certain *reporting events* and *selection screen events*.

Database rollback: Ending of a *database LUW*, whereat all changing database operations are cancelled until the LUW begins. In the *SAP system*, database rollbacks are triggered either implicitly, as well as through explicit requirements (see Section 33.2.2).

Database server: Software layer of a *SAP-system* on which the *database system* runs.

Database system: System to store extensive amounts of data in a *database*. Besides the database, a database system consists of a database manage-

ment system that administers the database and offers access via a programming interface.

Database table: Display format for data in a *relational database*. The columns or *database fields* of the database tables of the *SAP system* are defined in the *ABAP Dictionary*. Each database table has a unique *primary index* and can possess additional secondary indices. Between individual database tables, *foreign key dependencies* can exist. The definition of a database table is in general instantiated as a *transparent table* in the *database* of the SAP system. Besides transparent tables, there are also SAP-specific instances such as *cluster tables* and *pool tables*. All database tables defined in the ABAP Dictionary can be referenced as *data type* (just as flat structures) and you can access them with *Open SQL*.

Data cluster: Grouping of *data objects* for transient and persistent storage in a selectable storage medium. A data cluster can be processed using the statements IMPORT and EXPORT (see Chapter 3).

Data element: *Elementary data type* in the *ABAP Dictionary*. Describes, in addition to the properties, the semantic meaning of a (*database*) field (for example heading for tabular displays or documentation text). The properties, such as *data type*, length, and so on, are either defined directly in the data element or copied from a *domain*.

Data object: *Instance* of a data type. Exists in the *internal mode* of an *ABAP program*. Is created either as a named, statically declared data object (statement DATA and similar, see Section 6.4) during loading of a program, a *class* or a *procedure*, or dynamically as an *anon-*

ymous *data object* at runtime (statement CREATE DATA, see Section 6.4). In addition, the *literals* defined as part of the source code count also as data objects. The data type of a data object is always complete (not *generic*) and can be *bound* or *independent*.

Data reference: *Reference* that points to a *data object*.

Data reference variable: *Reference variable* for *data references* (see Section 6.4.4). The *static type* of a data reference variable is a *data type*.

Data type: Property of a *data object*. ABAP interprets the content of a data object in according to its data type. Data types only exist either *bound* as a property of data objects or *independently*. Independent data types can be defined globally in the *ABAP Dictionary* or locally using TYPES in an *ABAP program* (see Section 6.3). The *generic data type* of all data types is data.

Date field: Data object of type d, that combines a date specification in the YYYYMMDD format. At calculations the content of date fields is converted into the number of days since 01.01.0001. For combined date/time specification of higher accuracy time stamps are available.

DCL: Data Control Language. Subset of *SQL*. The statements of DCL execute authorization checks and consistency checks on *relational databases*. In the *SAP basis*, the functionality of DCL is mapped via logical constructs like *authorization objects* and *SAP locks*.

DDL: Data Definition Language. Subset of *SQL*. The statements of DDL create and delete the *objects* of a relational database. In the *SAP Basis*, the

functionality of DDL is integrated into the *ABAP Dictionary* tool of the *ABAP Workbench*.

Deadlock: Blocked access to shared files (e.g. a *database*) due to an incorrect locking concept (prevents competing access) or an incorrect application of a locking concept.

Debugger: → *ABAP Debugger*

Decimal comma: A comma to display the *decimal point separator*.

Decimal number: Number in the decimal numbering system. It consists of *decimal places*, which can contain the decimal numbers 0–9 and can additionally contain a *decimal separator* and an algebraic sign.

Decimal place: Position in a *decimal number*.

Decimal point: A point to display the *decimal point separator*.

Decimal separators: Separators between the integer part and the decimal part of a *decimal number*. Within an *ABAP program*, the *decimal point* is always used. The display of the decimal separator in the output depends on entries in the *user master record* and can be set using the statement SET COUNTRY (see Section 35.5). See also *decimal comma* and *decimal point*.

Declaration part: Part of the definition in a *class* in which the *class components* are declared (see Section 7.2.1).

Deep: Description for *data types* in which the contents of their *data objects* are *references* that point to the actual content (*strings*, *reference variables*, and *internal tables*). A *structure* is deep if it contains at least one deep *component*.

Default value: Value that appears in an *input field* when a *screen* is called and can be overwritten by the user. A default value is usually set before the screen is called in the corresponding *ABAP program*.

Dereferencing operator: The special *operator* ->* is used for dereferencing *data reference variables* at *operand positions* (see Section 2.2.5).

Descriptive function: *Built-in function* that supplies properties of *data objects* (see Section 5.4).

De-serialization: Transformation of an *XML* document to ABAP data, either by accessing an *XSLT program* or by means of a *simple transformation*. If you use *XSLT*, the XML document must display a *canonical XML representation* (*asXML*).

Destination: The destination contains the connection parameters for *remote function calls*. It contains the connection type, the target system and the partner program. Connections that affect *SAP systems* exclusively can be agreed as *trusted systems*. RFC destinations are managed using the *transaction* SM59.

Details list: *List* of a *list level* greater than 0. List output in *event blocks* in *interactive list processing* writes to details list.

Development class: → *Package*

Dialog box: Also modal dialog box. Display of the *window* of a *dynpro sequence* called with CALL SCREEN, where the previous window remains

visible, although it is inactive (see Section 25.3.1). Up to nine dialog boxes can be stacked over a window (see *pop-up level*). Amodal dialog boxes, where the previous window remains active, can be implemented in the *SAP GUI* as *GUI controls* only.

Dialog module: 1. Obsolete *repository object*. Predecessor of *function modules*. Similar to a *transaction code*, linked with an *initial dynpro* of a *dynpro sequence* of any *ABAP program*. Can contain *formal parameters* that have to be declared in the ABAP program as global data. You can assign different dialog modules to an ABAP program. You call it via CALL DIALOG (see Section 42.6). You maintain dialog modules via the transaction code SE35.
2. *Processing block* without a local *data area* that can be defined in *ABAP programs* that support their own *dynpros* (*executable programs*, *function groups*, *module pools*) and that is called from the *dynpro* flow logic. Begins with MODULE and ends with ENDMODULE (see Section 4.3).

Dialog processing: Execution of programs in the foreground. In contrast to *background processing*, the flow of execution is not predefined at program start, but can be controlled by the user during program flow. For dialog processing, dialog *work processes* must be set up.

Dialog program: Outdated description for a *module pool* and its *dynpros*.

Dialog step: State of a *user session* between a *user action* on the user interface of a *dynpro* and the sending of a new *screen*. During a dialog step, the *SAP system* does not react to user actions. The current user session is assigned a *work process* of the *applica-*

tion server, which executes the program logic of the dialog step. Generally, the dialog step is made up of the logic programmed for the points *PAI* of the current dynpro and *PBO* of the following dynpro.

Dialog transaction: The *transaction code* of a dialog transaction is linked to a *dynpro* of an *ABAP program*. When the transaction is called, the respective program is loaded and the dynpro is called after the *event* LOAD-OF-PRO-GRAM.

Dictionary: → *ABAP Dictionary*

DML: Data Manipulation Language. Subset of *SQL*. The statements of DML read and change the contents of *relational database tables*. In ABAP, the DML is mapped by *Open SQL*.

Domain: *Repository object* in the *ABAP Dictionary* that describes properties of *data elements*, such as *data type*, *value range*, and so on. A domain can be linked with an arbitrary number of data elements.

Double-byte code: Display of a character in 2 bytes. It was used even before the introduction of *Unicode* for displaying Asian characters.

Double click: Selecting a *screen element* by double-clicking with the mouse. In the *user interface* of the *SAP-system*, double-clicking with the mouse always has the same effect as selecting *function key* F2.

Down cast: Also called *Narrowing Cast*. Assignment between reference variables, wherein the *static type* of the target variables is more specific than the static type of the source variable (see Section A.5.2). Only possible in

assignments with the *casting operator* (?=) or MOVE... ?TO. Compare *Up Cast*.

Dropdown list box: A list of values for an *in/output field*. Entries can only be selected from this *list*. The actual value is assigned to an entry in the dropdown list box. The program uses the assigned value and not the entry.

Dynamic selections: *Components* on the *selection screen* of a *logical database*. Offers the user the possibility of making dynamic selection conditions, in addition to the statically predefined *parameters* and *selection criteria*, for specific nodes in the logical database, which can be evaluated in the *database program*. Dynamic selections are declared in the logical database with the addition DYNAMIC SELECTIONS to the statement SELECTION-SCREEN (see Section 26.2.4).

Dynamic type: In a *reference variable*, the *data type* or the *class* of the *object*, to which the reference variable points. The dynamic type is always more specific than or the same as the *static type*.

Dynpro: Dynamic program, component of an *executable program* of a *function group*, or of a *module pool*. Consists of a *screen* and a *dynpro flow logic*, contains *dynpro fields* and is created with the tool *screen painter*.

Dynpro event: An *event* during *dynpro-processing*. Either *PAI*, *PBO*, *POH* or *POV* (see Section 25.2.1).

Dynpro field: A *data object* in the working memory of a *dynpro*. With *PAI*, the content of a dynpro field is transferred to a *data object* of the same name in the *ABAP program*. With *PBO*, the dynpro field is provided with the content of the data object in the ABAP program. All dynpro fields, except for the *OK field*, are linked with a *screen element*.

Dynpro flow logic: Procedural part of a *dynpro* with its own programming language, similar to ABAP. The dynpro flow logic is executed on the *application server*. Separated into *processing blocks*, PROCESS AFTER INPUT, PROCESS BEFORE OUTPUT, PROCESS ON HELP REQUEST and PROCESS ON VALUE REQUEST, which react to the *dynpro events PAI, PBO, POH* and *POV* and call *dialog modules* of the corresponding *ABAP-program*.

Dynpro number: A unique number that identifies a *dynpro* in an *ABAP program* through a four-digit number.

Dynpro sequence: The sequence for processing *dynpros*, whose flow is determined by the respective *next dynpro*. The first dynpro in a screen *dynpro sequence* is the *initial dynpro*. Dynpro sequences are called with *transaction codes* or CALL SCREEN (see Section 25.3.1). A dynpro sequence always belongs to a single *pop-up level* and is executed in a single *window*. A dynpro sequence is ended when the next screen with the *dynpro number* 0 is called.

EBCDIC: Abbreviation for Extended Binary Coded Decimal Interchange Code. 8-bit *character set* which is based on *BCD*. EBCDIC incorporates basically the same characters as *ASCII*.

Edit mask: Template for formatting the output of *data objects* in a *list*. An edit mask is a character string consisting of placeholders for the characters of the data object to be output, and specific

characters for formatting the output (see Section 27.2.1).

Elementary data object: *Data object* with an *elementary data type*.

Elementary data type: *Data type* of fixed or variable length that is neither *structured* nor a *table type* or *reference type*. In particular, the non-*generic* pre-defined *data types* are elementary (see Table 5.1).

Endian: → *Byte order*

Error message: *Message* of the *message type* E. Error messages during the PAI processing of *dynpros* make *input fields* on *screens* ready for input, again (see Section 28.1.2).

Escape character: Character that cancels special characters that are assigned to specific characters, for example *wildcard characters*.

EVA: Possible process flow in program execution. The EVA principle dictates that a program is executed in the order input, processing, and then output of the results. See also *Reporting*.

Event: Either a *component* of a *class* or an *interface* defined using [CLASS-] EVENTS (see Section 7.4.2), or an event of the *ABAP runtime environment*. An event can trigger the execution of a *processing block*, without actually knowing the processing block. Events in classes trigger *event handlers*, event handlers of the ABAP runtime environment trigger *event blocks*.

Event block: *Processing block* without a local *data area*, which can be defined in every *ABAP program* except for *subroutine pools*, *class pools*, and *interface pools*, and which is processed at the start of the corresponding event of the *ABAP runtime environment*. It starts with an *event keyword* and ends at the start of the next processing block.

Event handler: *Method* that can handle an *event* that has been triggered by `RAISE EVENT` in the same method or in a different method (see Section 7.4.1).

Event keyword: *ABAP keyword* that introduces an *event block* (see Section 4.4).

Exception: Error situation during execution of an *ABAP program*. Exceptions are *treatable* (statements `TRY`, `CATCH`) or untreatable. An untreated exception results in a *runtime error*. An exception is triggered either by the *ABAP runtime environment* due to error situations that are not foreseeable by the static *program check*, or by the `RAISE EXCEPTION` statement. Before Release 6.10, exceptions could be defined only in interfaces of function modules and methods. As of Release 6.10, there are class-based exceptions, which include the *catchable runtime errors* (see Chapter 15).

Exception class: Special *class* that is the basis for *treatable exceptions*. If an *exception* occurs, an *object* of an exception class is generated. There are predefined exception classes for exceptions of the runtime environment (see Section D.3), and self-defined exception classes for custom applications.

Exception group: Grouping together of several *catchable runtime errors* in an organizational unit (see Section D.3). The catchable runtime errors of an exception group, together with `CATCH-ENDCATCH`, can be treated by specifying the group name.

Exception object: *Instance* of an *exception class*. Created when a *treatable exception* occurs (as of Release 6.10) and contains information on exceptional circumstances. Can be propagated across call levels (see Chapter 15).

Exclusive lock: *Lock* that does not allow other users to set simultaneous locks for the data locked in that way. The *Open SQL* statements `INSERT`, `DELETE`, `MODIFY` and `UPDATE`, `SELECT` with the addition `FOR UPDATE` as well as all respective *Native SQL* statements set the corresponding *database locks* to the addressed rows. As an *SAP lock*, an exclusive lock is set by an appropriately parameterized call of a *lock function module* (see Section 33.5).

Executable program: *ABAP program* that can be executed using the `SUBMIT` statement (see Section 10.2). An executable program can be started via **System • Services • Reporting** or other services such as *report transactions*, in which a `SUBMIT` is always executed internally. An executable program can have its own dynpros, can be linked to a logical database and can be processed in *background processing*.

Exit message: *Message* of *message type* X. Exit messages terminate the running program and create a *short dump* (see Section 28.1.2).

Extended program check: Complete check of the ABAP source text for all statically recognizable errors. Programs with errors in the extended program check can be executed, but usually result in *exceptions*. Call in the *ABAP Editor* via **Program • Check • Extended Program Check** or via *transaction code* SLIN.

External data type: *Predefined data type* of the *ABAP Dictionary* (see Section 5.2.3).

External procedure call: Call of a *procedure* of a different *ABAP program* of the same SAP system (see Section 11.2). At the first external call of one of its procedures, the required program is loaded into the *internal session* of the calling program. Except for *class pools*, the *event* LOAD-OF-PROGRAM is then triggered. See also *Program Group*.

External session: → *Main session*

Extract: Short for *Extract dataset*.

Extract dataset: Structured unnamed dataset of an *ABAP program*. Consists of rows that are organized as *field groups*. Not part of the ABAP type concept for *data types* and *data objects* (see Chapter 23).

Field: Other name for *elementary data object*.

Field exit: Obsolete *customer exit*, which can be linked in customer systems with *data elements* in the *ABAP Dictionary*. If a *dynpro* field is defined with reference to such a data element, during the data transport from the *dynpro* to the *ABAP program* at the event *PAI* a *function module* named FIELD_EXIT_dtel is called, where dtel is the name of the data element. In the function module, the value of the *dynpro* field can be changed. The function module of a field exit cannot be debugged at present.

Field group: Row structure of an *extract dataset*. Consists of program-global *fields* of a program. Defined using the FIELD-GROUPS statement (see Section 6.11).

Field help: Direct help that appears when the user presses the **F1** key on a *field* of a *screen*.

Field selection: Property of a node of a *logical database*. If a node is defined for field selection, you can control from outside the logical database, which *fields* of the node are to be read out. Field selections are declared with the addition FIELD SELECTION of the SELECTION-SCREEN statement in the logical database (see Section 26.2.4).

Field symbol: Symbolic name for a *data object*, to which you can assign actual memory areas at program runtime. A field symbol can be used as a placeholder for data objects at operand positions. A field symbol is *typed* either *generically* or fully. Field symbols are declared using the FIELD-SYMBOLS statement (see Section 6.10) and memory areas are assigned to them with ASSIGN (see Section 17.2).

File: Storage of data under a name in a persistent storage medium. Use the statements of the ABAP file interface (see Chapter 32) to edit files on the *application server*. For files on the *presentation server*, use *function modules* or *methods* of a global *class* (see Section C.2). The files of the *database server* are part of the *database* and are maintained by the *database system*.

File pointer: Current position for writing to a reading from a *file*.

Final: Term in *ABAP Objects*. A final *class* can not have any *subclasses* (see Section 7.2.1). A final *method* cannot be *redefined* (see Section 7.4.1).

Fixed point arithmetic: Calculation with *packed numbers* (data type p). Is calculated with an internal accuracy of

31 or—if not sufficient—63 *decimal places*. *Fractional portions* are arithmetically rounded, if necessary. Decimal places before the *decimal point* are never lost, if the program is completed successfully (see Section 19.3.4). As a *program attribute*, the fixed point arithmetic determines whether for numbers of type p the decimal point is considered or not.

Fixed value: *Value range* to be defined for a *domain* for *data elements* in the *ABAP Dictionary*.

Fixture: Test configuration from which a unique test behavior results. A fixture comprises test data, test objects, resources and connections. In *ABAP Unit*, a fixture is realized through the methods [class_]setup and [class_]teardown of test classes.

Flat: Name of a *data type*, for which the content of its *data objects* represents the actual work data. All *elementary data types* except string and xstring are flat. A *structure* is flat if it contains only flat *components*. See also *deep*.

Floating point arithmetic: Calculation with *floating point numbers*. Is executed directly on the platform of the *application server*. Can lead to rounding errors, because floating point numbers are not internally represented in the decimal system (see Section 19.3.4).

Floating point function: *Mathematical function* that expects a *floating point number* as an argument and delivers a floating point number as a *return value* (see Table 5.10).

Floating point number: Content of a *data object* of data type f. The position of the decimal point is part of the data,

which consist of the value (mantissa) and an exponent. Calculations with floating point numbers are executed using *floating point arithmetic*.

Foreign key: One or more columns of a *database table* (*foreign key table*) that are *primary keys* of another database table (*check table*).

Foreign key relationship: Relationship between a *foreign key table* and a *check table*. A *foreign key* table usually only contains entries where the content of the foreign key also occurs in the check table as content of the *primary key*.

Foreign key table: *Database table* that contains *foreign keys*.

Formal parameter: *Parameter* of the *interface* of a *procedure*. Formal parameters have names and are either *generic* or completely typed. Depending on their *typing* assignment they can be used like *data objects* in the procedure. The formal parameters make up a substantial part of the *signature* of a procedure. Formal parameters are either positional parameters (for *subroutines*) or keyword parameters (for *methods* and *function modules*). At the call of a procedure formal parameters are supplied with *actual parameters*.

Forward navigation: Procedure used to go to the respective tool of a *repository object* within the *ABAP Workbench*. To do this the *cursor* must be positioned on the object name and the *object* must be selected.

Fractional portion: Fractional portions contain the fractional part of a number and are noted independent of the number system to the right of the separator. These are the *decimal places* (for *decimal numbers*) that come after the *decimal separator*.

Frame: *Screen element* used to group other screen elements and in which no *user actions* are possible. A frame is not linked to a *dynpro field*.

Framework program: Description of a program used as an organizational framework for subunits (*processing blocks* or *include programs*).

Friend: Term in *ABAP Objects*. The additions FRIENDS of the statement CLASS define other *classes* or *interfaces* as friends of the class and thus grant them access to their *protected* and *private components*. In addition, friends of a class can create *instances* of the class without restrictions (see Section 7.2.1).

Functional method: *Method* with any number of *input parameters* but only one *return value*. It can be used in *operand positions* in some statements.

Function Builder: *ABAP Workbench* tool which can be used to create and maintain *function modules*. Call using *transaction code* SE37.

Function code: *Sequence* of up to 20 characters that can be assigned to specific *control elements* of the *user interface*. When selecting one of these control elements, the *dynpro event PAI* is triggered and the function code is transferred to the *ABAP program* using the *system field* sy-ucomm or the *OK field* of the *dynpro*.

Function group: An *ABAP program* which is the only program that can contain *function modules* and which is usually loaded via a function module. It supports its own *dynpros*.

Function key: *Control element* of the *user interface*. Certain keys or key combinations on an input device. In the *function key setting* a *function code* can be assigned to a function key.

Function key setting: Assigning *function codes* to *function keys*. Part of the *GUI status* set using SET PF-STATUS. Created with the *Menu Painter* tool.

Function module: A *procedure* that can only be defined in *function group* and outside of *classes*. It can be called from any program. Begins with FUNCTION and ends with ENDFUNCTION (see Section 4.2.2).

Function module exit: *Customer exit* for *ABAP programs* in the form of empty or partially implemented *function modules* delivered with the SAP standard system. Included in the ABAP program using the statement CALL CUSTOMER-FUNCTION (see Section 11.2.3). The function module *interfaces* are predefined by SAP. The implementation can be empty or partially predefined. The customer must fully implement and activate them using the *transaction* CMOD. As of Release 4.6, function module exits can be replaced by *BAdIs*.

Function pool: → *Function group*

Garbage Collector: Deletes *objects* that are no longer referenced by *object variables* or *data reference variables*. The Garbage Collector is called periodically by the *ABAP runtime environment*. It tracks *reference variables* of deleted objects. See also *weak reference*.

Generic data type: *Data type* that does not set all attributes of a *data object*. Generic data types can only be used for the *typing* of *formal parameters* and *field symbols*.

Global declaration section: Area following the opening statement of an *ABAP program*, in which *data types*, *classes*, and *data objects* that are visible in the whole program can be declared (see Figure 1.1).

GUI: Graphical User Interface. Graphic part of the *user interface*. The GUI is displayed in a *window*.

GUI control: Stand-alone software component of the *presentation server*. Examples of GUI controls are Picture Control, Text Edit Control, and Tree Control. GUI controls are installed with *SAP GUI* and are accessed in ABAP via *classes* of the *Control Framework*.

GUID: Global Unique Identifier. The *function module* GUID_CREATE can be used to generate 16-character byte-type GUIDs, 22-character case-sensitive character-type GUIDs, and 32-character character-type GUIDs in upper case.

GUI status: Groups together the *menu bar*, *tool bar*, and *application toolbar* of a window together with the *function key settings*. A GUI status is set using the statement SET PF-STATUS (see Section 25.3.2), and is created using the *Menu Painter* tool.

GUI title: Text that can be displayed in the *title bar* of a window. A GUI title is set using the statement SET TITLEBAR (see Section 25.3.4), and created using the *Menu Painter* tool.

Hash algorithm: Distributed memory management. The data in a distributed memory is stored without order in the memory. The memory position of an

entry is calculated using the hash algorithm on the basis of a unique key.

Hashed table: *Table type* of an *internal table*. The lines of a hashed table are stored internally according to a *hash algorithm*, and can only be accessed using their unique *table key* (see Section 6.3.5). The corresponding *generic data type* is hashed table.

Header line: Obsolete work area of an *internal table*, whose type is the *line type* and which has the same name as the internal table (see Section 6.4.6).

Icon: Graphic element of the *GUI* for use on *pushbuttons*, and also as a *status icon* on *screens* or *lists*.

Implementation section: Part of the definition of a *class*, in which the *methods* of the class are implemented (see Section 7.2.2).

Include program: *ABAP program* that does not generate independently, but which is integrated into other ABAP programs using the INCLUDE statement (see Section 4.5.1).

Index: Selected columns of a *database table* that are sorted in order and stored as a copy in the *database system*, and which refer to the actual lines. For the database tables of the *SAP system* that are defined in the *ABAP Dictionary*, there is always a *primary index*, and additional *secondary indices* can also be created.

Index table: General term for *internal tables* that are administrated using a logical index (*standard table* and *sorted table*). The corresponding generic data type is index table.

INDX-type: A *database table* that has the necessary structure for storing *data clusters* in database tables. In the *shared memory*, it is called INDX-type, with reference to the database table INDX supplied by SAP.

Information message: *Message* of the *message type* I. Information messages are normally displayed in a *dialog box* (see Section 28.21).

Info type: Special *structure* in the *ABAP Dictionary*. The INFOTYPES statement (see Section 42.4.3) creates special *internal tables* of this structure, which can be processed in a PROVIDE *loop* (see Section 22.7).

Inheritance: General/specific relationship between *classes*. Inheritance means that new *subclasses* are derived by adopting all *components* of *superclasses*. A subclass can be made more specific by declaring new components and *redefining methods*.

Inheritance hierarchy: A hierarchical relationship between *superclasses* and *subclasses* in *inheritance*. In *single inheritance*, the inheritance hierarchy forms an *inheritance tree*.

Inheritance tree: An *inheritance hierarchy* in *single inheritance*. A unique path leads from each *subclass* to a *root class*.

Initial dynpro: First *dynpro* in a *dynpro sequence*. In a *dialog transaction*, the *dynpro* that is linked to the *transaction code*. For *dynpro* sequences called using CALL SCREEN, the initial *dynpro* is the *dynpro* specified in this command.

Initial value: An initial value is specified in the runtime environment for each *data type*. The initial values of the *elementary data types* can be found in

Table 5.2. The initial value of *reference types* is the *null reference*. The initial value of an *internal table* is an empty table without lines. The initial value of *structured types* results from the initial values of the individual *components*. The statement CLEAR with no additions sets a *data object* to its appropriate initial value for its type (see Section 18.2).

Input help: List of values that is displayed when pressing **F4** for a selected field on the *screen*.

Input help button: Single-digit *pushbutton* with an *icon*, which is displayed to the left of an *input field* on a *dynpro* if an *input help* is defined for that field. Selecting the pushbutton has the same effect as pressing **F4** for the field.

Input/Output field: *Screen element* that is linked to a *dynpro field*. Displays the content of the *dynpro field* and enables it to be changed using buttons of the keyboard or another input device that is not a *function keys*.

Input/Output Parameter: Also CHANGING *parameter*. *Formal parameter* of a *procedure*. When a call is made, the value of an *actual parameter* is transferred to the input/output parameter. At the end of procedure, the value of the input/output parameter is transferred to the actual parameter.

Input parameter: Also IMPORTING *parameter*. *Formal parameter* of a *procedure*, to which the value of an *actual parameter* is transferred at the time of a call.

Instance: Concrete entity of an abstract type. The instance of a data type is a *data object*. The instance of a *class* is simply described as an *object*. See also *instantiation*.

Instance attribute: *Attribute* of a *class* that is declared using DATA. The instance attribute is only valid in the *context* of an *instance* of the class. The content of the instance attributes determines the status of the *objects* of a class.

Instance component: Superordinate concept for *instance attribute*, *instance event*, and *instance method*. The instance components of a *class* can only be addressed in *instances* of the *class*.

Instance component selector: → *object component selector*

Instance constructor: *Constructor* that is declared under the name constructor as an *instance method* in the *public visibility area* of a *class*, and which is automatically executed at the instantiation of the class, after the generation of the *object* (see Section 7.4.1).

Instance event: *Event* of a *class* that is declared using EVENTS. Instance events usually display status changes of *objects*.

Instance method: *Method* of a *class* that is declared using METHODS, which can only be used in an *instance* of the class. Instance methods can access all *attributes* and *events* in its own class (see Section 7.4.1).

Instancing: Creation of an *instance*. *Data objects* as instances of *data types* are created implicitly during loading of a *context*, or explicitly with CREATE DATA (see Section 9.2). *Objects* as instances of *classes* are only created

explicitly with CREATE OBJECT (see Section 9.3).

Interactive list processing: *List processing* that takes place after *user actions* on lists. The relevant *event key words* are AT LINE-SELECTION, AT USER-COMMAND (see Section 4.4.4), and AT PFnn (see Section 42.3.1).

Interface: 1. Transition between two *contexts*. *Procedures* have a *parameter interface*. In *classes*, interfaces are defined by the *components* of the different *visibility sections*. In special cases, interface work areas act as an interface between the programs in a *program group*, and the global data of the ABAP program or the *interface work areas* can act as an interface between *ABAP programs* and *dynpros*. **2.** Template for the *public interface* of *classes*. Defined with INTERFACE—ENDINTERFACE, either globally in an *interface pool*, or locally in another *ABAP program* (see Section 7.3). An interface contains the declaration of *interface components*, but does not contain method implementations. Can be implemented in classes using INTERFACES, a practice which enhances the external interface of the class by adding the interface components (see Section 7.4.3).

Interface component: *Component* of an *interface*. Declared in the *declaration section* of an interface. Possible interface components are *attributes*, *methods*, and *events* (see Section 7.3.1).

Interface component selector: Character ~. A *component* comp of an *interface* ifac can be addressed in an implementing *class* or a *compound interface* via ifac~comp.

Interface pool: *ABAP program* that contains the definition of exactly one global *interface* and is loaded using the interface. An interface pool does not support any of its own *dynpros*.

Interface reference variable: *Object reference variable* of the *static type* of an *interface*.

Interface work area: Specific data objects that can act as a cross-program interface between programs and *dynpros*, and between programs and *logical databases*. Interface work areas are declared using the statements TABLES, NODES (see Section 6.9) and the addition COMMON PART of the statement DATA (see Section 42.4.1). All programs in a *program group* access the data of an interface work area together.

Internal procedure call: Call of a *processing block* (*procedure*) of the same program. The required program does not have to be reloaded into the *internal session*, again (see Chapter 11).

Internal session: Memory area in the *main session* in which the data and *objects* of an *ABAP program* are stored during the execution of the program. An internal session is created when an ABAP program is called, and exists for as long as the *main program* of its *main program group* is being executed.

Internal table: *Data object* that consists of a sequence of rows of the same *data type*. An internal table has a *table type*, which specifies the *line type*, the *table category*, and a *table key*. The corresponding *generic data type* is any table (see Chapter 22).

Internet Transaction Server (ITS): *Interface* between the *SAP system* and the Internet. The ITS is based on the

data interface between *ABAP programs* and *dynpros*. It enables users to communicate with an SAP system directly from the Internet by converting the *screens* to HTML files, thus enabling them to be edited in a Web browser.

Introductory statement: The first statement of every independent *ABAP program* (see Chapter 3).

ISO-8859: Standard for 8-bit *character sets* whose first 128 characters are identical to *ASCII*. The corresponding *code pages* ISO-8859–1, –9, –14, and –15 (Latin1, –5, –8, and –9) contain the Western European characters, ISO-8859–2 (Latin2) covers most Eastern European characters, ISO-8859–3 (Latin3) contains characters for Esperanto and Maltese, ISO-8859–4, –10, and –13 (Latin4, –6, and –7) contain the Northern European (Baltic, Greenland, and Lapp) characters. Also covered are: Cyrillic (ISO-8859–5), Arabic (ISO-8859–6), Greek (ISO-8859–7), Hebrew (ISO-8859–8), and Thai (ISO-8859–11).

Iteration: → *loop*

iXML Library: Part of the *class library* accessible via *interfaces*, which is used for handling *XML* documents. The iXML Library provides services such as an XML parser, an XML renderer, an XML DOM (Document Object Model), and input/output streams. The interfaces of the iXML Library all begin with the prefix IF_IXML.

Job: Closed chain of programs executed chronologically by particular control commands, especially as *background requests*.

Join: Combination of multiple *database tables* in which every two of the tables involved are linked using conditions between one or more columns. Joins can be realized statically as *views* in the *ABAP Dictionary*, or dynamically as *Join expressions* in the SELECT statement.

Join expression: A link between two or more *database tables* in the SELECT statement (see Section 29.2.2), realized using the *language element* JOIN.

Key field: Individual *component* of a *table key*

Layout Editor: A *Screen Painter tool* for the graphic design of *screens*.

Line element: Predefined output element in a *list*. Line elements can be corners, crosses, horizontal and vertical lines, and T-sections. Line elements are either output explicitly using WRITE, or set by the system in automatic line connections (see Section 27.2.1).

List: Medium for structured and formatted output of data. List output is internally stored in a *list buffer* and displayed by default on a *list dynpro* or sent to the *SAP spool system* as a *print list*.

Listbox: → *Dropdown listbox*

List buffer: Memory area for recording *list output*. Subdivided into *list levels*. For each *screen dynpro* sequence, the list buffer contains a hierarchy of a *basic list* and up to 20 *details lists* (see Section 27.1.2).

List creation: Formatted output of contents in a *list* in the *list buffer* or in a *print list* (see Section 27.2).

List cursor: Current cursor position for output in a *list* in the *list buffer*. Defined by the contents of the system fields sy-colno (position) and sy-linno (line) and refers to the current page in the list. In non-*Unicode systems*, the horizontal position also corresponds to the column in the list displayed. In Unicode systems, this is only certain for the top and bottom limits of the individual items output, since a character can occupy more columns in the list than positions in the list buffer.

List Dynpro: *Dynpro* used to display *lists*. The list dynpro is a component of the *list processor* and is accessed either implicitly during processing of an *executable program* or explicitly with a LEAVE TO LIST-PROCESSING statement (see Section 27.6.1).

List event: *Event* in the *ABAP runtime environment* that occurs during *list processing*. The corresponding *event keywords* are TOP-OF-PAGE, END-OF-PAGE, and AT LINE-SELECTION, AT-USER-COMMAND (see Section 4.4.4) and the obsolete AT PFnn (see Section 27.5.1).

List header: Heading of a *list*, composed of the list title in the *title bar* and of possible column headings. These can be maintained as part of the *text elements* of an *ABAP program* for the *standard page header*.

List index: Identifier of a list in the *list buffer*. The value of the list index can be 0 for the *basic list* and 1 to 20 for the *details lists* (see Section 27.1.2).

List level: Position of a *list* in the *list buffer*. A *basic list* has the *list index* 0, the list index of a *details list* is greater than 0. Content of the *system field* sy-lsind (see Section 27.1.4).

List processing: Processing of a *screen list*, which is encapsulated in the *ABAP runtime environment*. In this processing, the *dynpro event PAI* is passed in the form of *list events* to the *ABAP program*.

List processor: System program for *list processing* that contains the *list dynpro* for displaying *screen lists*.

List status: *GUI status* that contains special functions for handling a displayed *list*.

Literal: *Data object* defined in the *source code* of a program and fully qualified by its value. Possible literals are *numeric literals*, *text field literals* and *string literals* (see Section 6.3.1). See also *anonymous data object* and *named data object*.

Little endian: *Byte order* in which the lowest value byte is stored at the first storage place.

Locale: Part of the *text environment*. Defines language-dependent and country-dependent characteristics of characters, such as the sort sequence or uppercase/lowercase conversion. In Non-*Unicode systems*, the locale attributes depend on the operating system of the *application server* and in Unicode systems, they are defined in a library which is independent of any operating system.

Local update: *Update* in the current *work process* (see Section 33.3.3).

Lock: Locks protect data from being accessed by several users at the same time as a *shared lock* or as *exclusive locks* (see Section 33.5).

Lock function module: Special *function module* for setting and removing *SAP locks*. To create a *lock object*, a function module with the prefix ENQUEUE_ is created to set the lock and a function module with the prefix DEQUEUE_ is created to remove the lock (see Section 33.5).

Lock object: A *repository object* defined in the *ABAP Dictionary* that serves as the basis for *SAP locks*. Linked *database tables* to which a common *lock* is to be applied are specified in a lock object using *foreign key relationships*. When a lock object is created, two *lock function modules* are automatically generated (see Section 33.5).

Logical database: Special *ABAP program*, which provides other ABAP programs with data from the nodes of a hierarchical tree structure. Is linked either in the *program attributes* of an *executable program* to this program or is called using *function module* LDB_ PROCESS. A logical database uses a hierarchical structure with nodes to link a *database program* written in ABAP and an own *standard selection screen*. You edit logical databases in the *Logical Database Builder*.

Logical Database Builder: Tool of the *ABAP Workbench*, used to create and maintain *logical databases*. Call via *transaction code* SE36.

Logical expression: Formulation of a condition. The result of a logical expression is either true or false. Is used in *control statements* or other statements for conditions (see Chapter 13).

Logon: Time when a user logs on to the *SAP-System* with specification of *user name*, *password*, and the *logon* *language*. Each logon starts a *user session*.

Logon language: Language with which a user logs on to an *SAP system*. The logon language is fixed throughout the entire *user session*. See also *message*, *text element*, and *text environment*.

Loop: Also *iteration*. *Control structure* that consists of a *statement block* which is defined using keywords (DO – ENDDO, WHILE – ENDWHILE, LOOP – ENDLOOP, PROVIDE – ENDPROVIDE, SELECT – ENDSELECT) and can be executed on a multiple basis (see Section 14.3).

LUW: Logical Unit of Work. Span of time between two consistent states on the *database*. See *SAP-LUW* and *database LUW*.

Macro: Summary of a statement sequence for program-internal reuse. Defined between DEFINE and END-OF-DEFINITION (see Section 4.5.2).

Main mode: Also called *external mode*. Memory area for a *user session* in a *SAP System*. In *dialog processing*, a user session can manage up to six main modes, each of which is linked to its own *window*.

Main program: The first program of a *program group*. The first program (*executable program*, *module pool*, or *function group*) that is loaded by a program call into an *internal mode* is the main program of the *main program group*. The program (function group or class pool) — in which an *additional program group* is created when it is loaded — is the main program of the additional program group (see Figure 11.2).

Main program group: First *program group* of an *internal mode*. It is created

when the internal mode is called through a program call. The first program in an internal mode is the *main program* of the main program group (see Figure 11.2). The runtime of the main program in the main program group determines its lifespan and the entire internal mode.

Matchcode object: The predecessor of *search helps* in the *ABAP Dictionary*.

Mathematical function: *Built-in function* that calculates numeric values. There are *floating point functions* and *overloaded functions* (see Section 5.4.1).

Mathematical notation: Representation of a number as a digit sequence with possible *decimal separators* where the algebraic sign is specified in front of the digits (see Section A.2.1).

MDMP system: Abbreviation for multi-display, multi-processing system. In a MDMP system, there are several non-*Unicode system-code pages*. The system code page active for an *internal mode* depends on its current *text environment*. See also *Single Codepage System*.

Measuring interval: Execution duration of a limited *measuring section*.

Measuring section: A statement sequence delimited by GET RUN TIME in the program text, whose runtime is to be measured.

Memory Extract: Contains information on all *data objects* and *instances* of an *internal mode* and their memory consumption (as of Release 6.20). Is created in the *ABAP Debugger*, with the *static method* WRITE_MEMORY_CONSUMPTION_FILE of the *system* *class* CL_ABAP_MEMORY_UTILITIES, or via input of "/hmusa" in the *input field* of the *toolbar*. The evaluation takes place using the *Memory Inspector*.

Memory Inspector: Tool for displaying and analyzing memory snapshots (since Release 6.20, Support Package 29). You call this tool using the *transaction code* S_MEMORY_INSPECTOR.

Menu: Graphic *control element* that offers the user several options in the form of *menu entries*.

Menu bar: Part of a *window*. Contains *menus* for operating the program. Part of the *GUI status* set using SET PF-STATUS. Created using the *Menu Painter*.

Menu entry: Textual *control element* of a *menu* that is linked to a *function code* and can be selected simply by clicking it.

Menu Painter: Tool of *ABAP Workbench* for creating the *GUI status* and its components. Call through *transaction code* SE41.

Message: Text that can be displayed during the processing of *dynpros* with the statement MESSAGE. Messages are always displayed in the *logon language*, which cannot be changed during a *user session*. Message texts are organized in *message classes* and *message numbers* and are processed in the *transaction message maintenance*. When a message is displayed with the statement MESSAGE, it is classified with a *message type* that defines the display type (see Chapter 28).

Message class: Identifier that groups *messages* in an application area (see Section 28.1.1).

Message Maintenance: Tool of *ABAP Workbench* for creating and maintaining *messages*. Call using *transaction code* SE91.

Message number: Number that identifies the *messages* of a *message class* (see Section 28.1.1).

Message type: Determines in the MESSAGE statement the representation of the *message* and the remaining program flow. There are the message types *information message*, *status message*, *error message*, *warning*, *termination message*, and *exit message* (see Section 28.1.2).

Method: *Procedure* that is declared as a *component* of a *class* or of an *interface*. There are *instance methods* and *static methods*. A method can only be implemented in the *implementation part* of its class between METHOD and ENDMETHOD (see Section 7.4.1).

Mode: → *External and internal mode*.

Modification group: Grouping of several *screen elements* of a *dynpro* under a three-digit abbreviation in order to be able to modify its display properties together. The assignment of screen elements to modification groups takes place in the *Screen Painter* or in selection screens in the *ABAP program* (addition MODIF ID). A screen element can be assigned to up to four modification groups (see Section 25.3.6).

Module pool: *ABAP program* that can be started via *transaction codes*. Usually contains *dynpros* and *dialog modules*.

Multibyte code: Display of a character in more than one byte.

Multiple selection: *Selection criteria* with which the *selection table* is filled with more than one row (see Section 26.4).

Named data object: *Data object* that can be addressed via a name. Named data objects are *constants*, *variables*, and *text symbols* (see Chapter 6). See also *anonymous data object* and *literal*.

Named includes: Combination of *components* of a *structure* under one name. Instead of an offset/length access, subareas of a structure can be addressed by this name (see Section 6.8).

Narrowing Cast: → *Down cast*

Native SQL: Statements that can be listed in the *ABAP programs* between the statements EXEC SQL and ENDEXEC. Database-specific *SQL statements* and some SAP-specific statements are possible. Native SQL statements are not fully checked by the *syntax check* and are handled by the *Native SQL interface* of the *database interface* (see Chapter 30).

Native SQL interface: Part of the *database interface* that is responsible for *Native SQL statements*. The Native SQL interface handles all Native SQL statements that are listed between EXEC and ENDEXEC. The manufacturer-specific *SQL statements* listed there are transferred further, unchanged, to the *database system* of the current *database connection*. Only the SAP-specific Native SQL statements are handled in the Native SQL interface prior to transfer.

Nested interface: → *Compound Interface*

Next dynpro: Each *dynpro* has a *next dynpro*. Thus, each dynpro is part of a *dynpro sequence*. Next dynpros can be set statically in the *Screen Painter* or with SET SCREEN or LEAVE TO SCREEN in the *ABAP program* (see Section 25.3.14 and 25.3.15). If a dynpro links to a next dynpro with the *screen number* 0, it is the last dynpro of the dynpro sequence.

Null reference: *Initial value* of a *reference variable*. The null reference points to no object.

Null value: *Initial value* of an empty column in a row of a *database table*. Null values can be processed using *Native SQL* statements, but they have no equivalent as the content of *data objects* in ABAP. Only the WHERE addition allows a special condition IS NULL for null values. Changing *Open SQL* statements (INSERT, UPDATE, MODIFY) generally do not create null values, provided that you are not processing a *view* that does not comprise all columns of a database table. Depending on the *database system*, you can also display empty *strings* as null values. Furthermore null values can arise from database tables, if the columns are appended to filled tables. When reading with the Open SQL statement SELECT, null values can be created by *aggregate functions* or an outer *join*, but they are converted to initial values of the correct type when passed to data objects.

Numeric data object: *Data object* that can be interpreted numerically if the content is appropriate. In addition to data objects of the *numeric data types* i, f and p, *byte-like* and *character-like data objects* can also be numeric.

Numeric data type: *Data types*, whose *data objects* contain numeric values in a platform-specific code. The corresponding *predefined data types* are i, f, and p. The corresponding *generic data type* is numeric.

Numeric literal: A *literal* that is defined by a sequence of numbers in the source code and an optional algebraic sign (see Section 6.1.3). The data type is I, if the value lies between $-2^{31}+1$ and $2^{31}-1$ otherwise it is p.

Object: *Instance* of a *type*. Either an instance of a *class* or as a *data object* instance of a *data type*. Exists in the *internal session* of an *ABAP program* or as a *shared object* in the *shared memory* (see Chapter 9). There are also persistent *objects* in the *database*.

Object component selector: Character -〉. Also *instance component selector*. Each visible *component* comp of a *data object* or an *instance* of a *class* can be addressed via ref-〉comp, if ref is a *reference variable* that points to the *object*.

Object Navigator: Development environment for central processing of *repository objects*. All *objects* belonging to a particular category are displayed in the navigation area as a tree structure and can be processed by *forward navigation* in the tool area. Call using *transaction code* SE80.

Object reference: *Reference* that points to an *instance* of a *class*. See also *weak reference*.

Object reference variable: *Reference variable* for *object references*. Object reference variables are differentiated into *class reference variables* and *interface reference variables* (see Section 6.4.4).

Object Services: Since Release 6.10 *interfaces* and *classes* of the *class library* with the prefixes IF_OS_ and CL_OS_. The Object Services provide Persistence Services and Transaction Services with which *persistent objects* and object-oriented *transactions* are managed.

Object type: Description of an *object* in *ABAP Objects*. Either a *class* for the entire object or *interface* for part of an object. The assigned *generic data type* is object.

Offset: Position specification for a character or a byte in a *character-* or *byte-type data object* where counting begins with 0.

Offset/Length specification: Access to sub-areas of *data objects* (see Section 2.2.5).

OK field: Twenty-digit *dynpro field* that is not linked to a *screen element*. When a *user action* is carried out on a *control element* that is linked to a function code, the *function code* is placed in the OK field is transferred to PAI to a *data object* of the same name.

OLE automation: OLE (object linking and embedding) automation allows various software applications to use automation objects to communicate with each other, exchange data, and control each other. A software application can make automation objects available to other applications (clients) by means of an automation interface. A client can use the corresponding object interface to create and control these kinds of objects (see Chapter 41).

OO transaction: As of Release 6.10. The *transaction code* of a OO transaction is linked to a *method* of a local or global *class*. When the transaction is called, the corresponding program is loaded, for *instance methods* an *object* of the class is generated and the method is executed. OO transactions can be linked using the Transaction Service of the *Object Services*.

Open SQL: Open SQL is the umbrella term for a subset of *SQL* that is realized through *ABAP statements* that includes the *DML* partial quantity. Independent of platform, the statements of Open SQL access the database of the *SAP system* via the Open SQL interface of the *database interface* With Open SQL, data in *database tables*, which are defined in the *ABAP Dictionary*, can be read (SELECT) and changed (INSERT, UPDATE, MODIFY, DELETE). See Chapter 29.

Open SQL interface: Part of the *database interface* that is responsible for *Open SQL* commands. The Open SQL interface converts all Open SQL commands that access the central *database* of the *SAP system* to manufacturer-specific SQL and forwards this to the *database system*.

Operand: Component of an *ABAP statement*. Specified either directly or as a *data object*, *formal parameter*, *field symbol*, *dereferenced data reference*, *predefined function* or *functional method* (see Section 2.2.2).

Operand position: Position in an *ABAP statement* at which an *operand* is specified. The system differentiates between read and write positions. An operand position is typed with an *operand type*.

Operand type: The *Data type* with which a operand position is typed. The operand type can be complete or generic. An *operand* must suit the operand type. Depending on the statement, *type conversions* or *castings* take place for incompatible operands.

Operator: *ABAP language element* that forms an expression in combination with *operands*. When the statement is executed, an operation is executed for two operands connected with one operator and the result is processed further in the statement. There are *arithmetic*, *bit*, *Boolean*, *relational*, and *assignment operators* (see Section 2.2.1).

Output field: → *In-/Output field*

Output parameter: *Formal parameter* of a *procedure* whose value is passed to the *actual parameter* after the procedure has been completed.

Output statement: Statement for describing a *list*. Output statements are WRITE and ULINE. In addition, there are statements for positioning the *list cursor* (see Section 27.2).

Overloaded function: *Mathematical function* that expects a *numeric data object* as argument. The *data type* of the argument determines the data type of the function (see Table 5.9).

Package: Ordering criterion for managing *Repository objects* that are grouped together into packages by topic. Packages are linked to the Correction and Transport System and are Repository objects themselves. As of Release 6.10, they replace *development classes* and are an enhancement of their concept for requirements in the environment of the *SAP Web Application Server*.

Packed number: Content of a *data object* of the *data type* p in *BCD format*. The number of the *decimal places* is the property of the data type and not, as with *floating point numbers,* a property of the data itself.

Page footer: Reserved rows at the bottom of a page in a *list*. The page footer is defined in the *introductory statement* and can be filled during the *event* END-OF-PAGE (see Section 4.4.4).

Page header: Rows at the start of a page in a *list* that are excluded from vertical scrolling. Headers can be filled with the content of the *standard page header* during the *event* TOP-OF-PAGE (see Section 4.4.4).

PAI: Process After Input, a *dynpro event*. Triggered by *user action* on the *GUI*. With PAI, the contents of *dynpro fields* are transferred to *data objects* of the same name in the *ABAP program* (see Section 25.2.1).

Parameter: A component of a *selection screen*, defined by PARAMETERS, on which it is displayed as an *input field* and which is represented internally as an *elementary data object* (see Section 26.3). Parameters are also components of the *parameter interface* of a procedure.

Parameter interface: *Interface* of a *procedure*. Consists of *formal parameters* and specifies the possible *exceptions* of the procedure.

Parameter transaction: A special *transaction code*, in which a *dialog transaction* is linked with parameters. The dialog transaction is called when you call a parameter transaction, and the *input fields* of the *initial dynpro* of the dialog transaction are filled with parameters.

The *screen* of the initial dynpro can be inhibited by specifying all mandatory input fields as parameters of the *transaction*, and provided that the *next dynpro* is not the initial dynpro itself.

Pass by reference: A way of passing data from *actual parameters* to *formal parameters* (defined in the *interface* of a *procedure*) during call of the procedure. When you pass by reference, no local *data object* is specified for the actual parameter, but the procedure receives a reference to the actual parameter during call and works with the actual parameter itself. *Input parameter* that have been passed by reference must not be changed in the procedure.

Pass by value: A way to pass data, defined in the *interface* of a *procedure* from *actual parameters* to *formal parameters* when calling the procedure. When passing data, a local *data object* is created as a duplicate of the actual parameter and the procedure receives the value of the actual parameter at calling time. Changed formal parameters are only transferred to the actual parameter if the procedure was concluded without error. Also see *pass by reference*.

Password: Character ID of a user which is necessary for the *logon* to *SAP systems* and which is only known to the user. Makes the authorized use of SAP systems possible, together with the *username*.

PBO: Process Before Output, a *dynpro event*. Triggered by the *ABAP runtime environment*, before a screen is sent to the *presentation server*. After PBO processing, dynpro fields receive the contents of *data objects* of the same name of the *ABAP program* (see Section 25.2.1).

Persistent class: A special *class*, the *attributes* of which are linked to *database tables* via object-relational mapping. Since Release 6.10 they can be created using the Mapping Assistant of the *Class Builder*. The *objects* of persistent classes are managed by *Object Services*.

Persistent object: An object in a *persistent class*, the *attributes* of which are saved as database content after the runtime of an *ABAP program*. Persistent objects are managed by *object services*.

Platform: The current system environment of a *SAP system*, consisting of the *application server*'s *operating system*, the *database system*, the *text environment* and the communication interface.

POH: Process On Help Request, a *Dynpro-event*. Triggered when requesting the *field help* (F1) for an *input field* on the *screen* (see Section 25.2.1).

Pool table: A *database table* defined in the *ABAP Dictionary* whose *database* instance is assigned to more than one table defined in the ABAP Dictionary. Multiple pool tables are assigned to a *table pool* in the database. The *key fields* of a pool table have to be character-type fields. The table pool's *primary key* consists of the fields TABNAME for the name of a pool table, and VARKEY for the concatenated content of the key fields in the corresponding pool table. The non-key fields of the pool table are stored in compressed format in one single column, called VARDATA, of the table pool. The only way to access pool tables is by using *Open SQL*. *Joins* cannot be created.

Pop-up level: Hierarchical level of a *window*. The first window of a *logon* procedure to a *SAP system* has the popup level 0. You create larger popup levels by stacking modular *dialog boxes* using the CALL SCREEN or the CALL SELECTION-SCREEN command (see Section 25.3.1 and 26.5.4). The maximum pop-up level is 9.

Posting: Technique for bundling of the changing data base accesses of an *SAP LUW* in a posting *work process* or in a *data base LUW*. Realized through *posting function modules*, which are marked for posting. The *transaction* SM13 manages the posting.

POV: Process on Value Request, a *Dynpro-event*. Triggered when requesting the *input help* (F4) for an *input field* on the *screen* (see Section 25.2.1).

Predefined data type: *Data type* that the *ABAP runtime environment* makes available to an *ABAP program*. The predefined *elementary data types* are: b, c, d, f, i, n, p, s, string, t, x and xstring.
There are also *generic data types* and *ABAP Dictionary* data types.

Predefined function: Function predefined in ABAP that can be used before operand positions in some commands (only in COMPUTE before Release 6.10). There are two types: *mathematical functions* and *descriptive functions* (see Section 5.4).

Presentation server: *Software layer* of the *SAP system* that displays the *SAP GUI*, evaluates *user actions*, and sends these to the *application server*.

Primary index: Unique *index* of a *database table* defined in the *ABAP Dictio-*

nary. The index consists of from the *key fields* of the *primary key*.

Primary key: *Table key* that is determined when you define a *database table* and which distinctively defines a table row.

Print: Sending of lists to the SAP spool system. See print list.

Print dialog box: *Dialog box* for entering *print parameters*. A print dialog box is created using the NEW PAGE PRINT ON (see Section 27.2.8), SUBMIT TO SAP SPOOL (see Section 10.2.3) commands, and the *function module* GET_PRINT_ PARAMETERS (see Section C.1.1). You can pre-allocate values for the *input fields* using the function module SET_ PRINT_PARAMETERS (see Section C.1.1).

Print list: List that is not stored in the *list buffer* as a *screen list*, but is send page by page directly from the central memory to the *SAP-spool system*. When it is created, a print list is linked to exactly one *spool request*. Only one print list can be created at one time in an *internal mode*. The commands used to create a print list are NEW PAGE PRINT ON|OFF (see Section 27.2.8) and SUBMIT TO SAP-SPOOL (see Section 10.2.3).

Print parameters: *Parameters* that must be passed to a *spool request* (see Section 10.2.3 and 27.2.8). Print parameters can be enhanced through *archiving parameters*.

Private: Term in *ABAP objects*. A private *component* of a *class* can be accessed only by the class itself. Only the class itself can create *objects* of a class with private instantiation (see Section 7.2.1).

Procedure: *Processing block* with a data interface and local *data area*. Possible procedures include *methods*, *function modules*, and *subroutines* (see Section 4.2).

Processing block: Modularization unit of an *ABAP program* that cannot be split or nested. Processing blocks are *procedures*, *dialog modules*, and *event blocks*. They contain commands that are structured into *command blocks* by *control structures*.

Profile parameters: Define pre-settings of *SAP systems*. Profile parameters are created and displayed through the *transaction* code RZ11.

Program attribute: Attribute of an *ABAP program* defined in the *ABAP Editor*. Program attributes are used to administer the program and influence how it is handled in *syntax checks* and in the *ABAP runtime environment*. Examples of important program attributes are: *program type*, the linked *logical database* in the case of *executable programs*, and (as of Release 6.10) whether a program is a *Unicode program*.

Program check: The ABAP program check includes the *syntax check* and the *extended program check*.

Program constructor event: An *ABAP runtime environment event* that occurs exactly once in the *internal mode* when any *ABAP program* (except *class pools*) is loaded. The corresponding *event keyword* is LOAD-OF-PROGRAM (see Section 4.4.1).

Program group: An organizational unit of programs in the *internal session*. There is always a *main program group* and it is possible to have several *addi-*

tional program groups. Each program group has a *main program*. If an external call of a *subroutine* in a program belonging to a program group causes the *framework program* of the subroutine to be loaded, this is added to the program group. Loading a *function group* as a result of an external call from *function modules* and loading *class pools* leads to the creation of an additional program group (see Figure 11.2). All programs of a program group share the *interface work areas* declared with TABLES, NODES and COMMON PART. Within a program group, CALL SCREEN can only be used to call the *dynpros* of the main program (see Section 25.3.1).

Program type: Property of an *ABAP program*. Defines which *processing blocks* are contained in a program and how the *ABAP runtime environment* executes the program. Program types include *executable program*, *class pool*, *function group*, *interface pool*, *module pool*, *subroutine pool*, *type group* (see Table 3.1), and *include program*. The program type is maintained in the *ABAP Editor* in the *program attributes*, or by the relevant tool.

Protected: A term in *ABAP Objects*. A protected *component* of a *class* can only be accessed by the class itself or its subclasses. Only the class itself and its subclasses can create *objects* from a protected class that can be instantiated (see Section 7.2.1).

Pseudo comment: Special comment behind the " character in a program line. A pseudo comment begins with the expression #EC and takes out the content of this line from the assigned test of the *extended program check* (see Section 2.5).

Pseudo component: table_line expression that can be specified in the statements for *internal tables* instead of a *component*. The entire line of the internal table is then interpreted as the only component (see Section 22.5).

Pseudo reference: super expression that can be specified in the implementation of a redefined *instance method* or an *instance constructor* instead of a *reference variable*. The implementation of the *method* can then be called in the direct *superclass* (see Section 7.4.1).

Public: Term in *ABAP Objects*. A public *component* of a *class* can be accessed at any point in which the class is known. *Objects* can be generated by a class that can be publicly instantiated at every point at which a class is known (see Section 7.2.1).

Push button: *Control element* of the *GUI* that is linked with a *function code*, and can be selected by clicking on it. Pushbuttons can be defined as *screen elements* and in *symbol* and *application tool bars* in the *SAP GUI*.

Pushbutton bar: Description for application tool bar used in the *ABAP Workbench*.

PXA: Program Execution Area, a program memory for managing the byte codes of all programs running concurrently at any one time on an *application server*. This memory is shared by all users of the application server and there is only one on each server. The byte-code of a once executed program remains buffered in the PXA as long as possible to prevent reload from the *database* in the event the program is executed again.

qRFC: → *queued Remote Function Call*

Quantity field: Component of a *structure* or *database table* of the type QUAN, defined in the *ABAP dictionary*. A quantity field must be linked to a unit key of a structure or database table, which determines the unit of the quantity field.

Queued Remote Function Call: Enhancement of the *transactional Remote Function Call* by the possibility to determine the call order (see Section 39.2.3).

Quick Info: Display of information on elements of the *GUI* in the form of a short text whenever the mouse pointer is passed over the element concerned.

Radio button: *Screen element* that is linked to a *dynpro field*, and in which the user can enter the value "X" or " " by selection. Radio buttons are grouped together in *radio button groups*.

Radio button group: Group of *radio buttons* that belong together. Within a radio button group, one radio button can be selected.

Ranges table: *Internal table* with the same structure as a *selection table*. Declaration with the addition TYPE RANGE OF of the statements DATA and TYPES, or the statement RANGES (see Section 6.3.6).

Redefinition: Term in *ABAP Objects*. An *instance method* in a *subclass* can be implemented again without changing the *interface* for a redefinition (see Section 7.4.1).

Reference: Content of *reference variables*. Made up of the address of a *data object* (*data reference*) or the *instance* of a *class* (*object reference*) and additional administration information, such as the *data type* of a referenced data object.

Reference type: → *static type*

Reference variable: *Data object* that contains a *reference*. Reference variables are differentiated by *data reference variables* and *object reference variables*. Reference variables have a length of 8 bytes and are opaque, which means the reference cannot be accessed directly. These are typed with the addition REF TO that defines their *static type*. The static type is always more general or the same as the *dynamic type*.

Relational database: A *database* whose data is managed according to the *relational data model*; that is, in *database tables*.

Relational data model: In the relational data model, data in two-dimensional tables (relations) is displayed with a fixed number of columns and an arbitrary number of rows. The sequence of rows and columns is not of importance.

Relational operator: Links two *operands* of a *logical expression*. Relational operators for all data types are: =, <>, <, >, <=, >=. There are additional relational operators for special data types.

Relative type name: *Type name* given when defining a *data type*, a *class*, or an *interface*. The actual *type* described by a relative type name depends on the *context*, because local definitions cover global definitions. See also *absolute type name*.

Remote Function Call: Call of a *function module* that runs in a different system (*destination*) than the calling program. Possibilities include connections between different *SAP systems* or connections between a SAP and a third-party system. A specially programmed function, whose *interface* simulates a function module, is called in external systems instead of a function module. There are *synchronous*, *asynchronous*, and *transactional function calls*. The system is called up using the *RFC interface*.

Remote user: User that is logged on to a *SAP system* from the outside via *Remote Function Call*. The logon data and the *authorization* can be declared in the *destination*.

Report: Reading and displaying data— for example, in a *list*. Outdated term for an *executable program* that solely executes *reporting*.

Reporting: Classic application area of *executable programs* in which the program run implements the EVA principle by displaying a *selection screen*, reading data (often via a *logical database*), and the formatted display of data of a *list*.

Reporting event: Event of the *ABAP runtime environment* that occurs in *executable programs* when these are started using a SUBMIT or a *report transaction*. Reporting events implement the *EVA* principle of *reporting* when used with a *logical database*. The *event key words* assigned to the reporting events are INITIALIZATION, START-OF-SELECTION, GET, and END-OF-SELECTION (see Section 4.4.2).

Report transaction: *Transaction* whose *transaction code* is linked with the *selection screen* of an *executable program* (see Section 26.5.2), and is called internally using the statement SUBMIT.

Repository: Part of the central *database* that solely contains cross-client *repository objects*.

Repository object: Repository objects are development objects such as, programs or *classes*. They are edited using tools of the *ABAP Workbench*. Each repository object is assigned to a *package*.

Return value: Numerical value for many *ABAP statements* that is entered in the *system field* sy-subrc when the statement is executed. The value 0 usually means processing has been completed successfully. The result for *functional methods* and *predefined functions*. The *formal parameter* defined by the addition RETURNING of the statement [CLASS-]METHODS for functional methods (see Section 7.4.1).

RFC: → *Remote Function Call*

RFC client: Instance of a system that calls services by *RFC*.

RFC interface: Interface for *Remote Function Calls* (*RFC*). The RFC interface consists of an interface for *ABAP programs* and call interfaces for non-ABAP programs (see Section 39.1.1).

RFC server: Instance of a system that makes available services that can be called up by *RFC*.

RFC server group: Group of multiple *application servers* of a SAP system, which are available for the parallel processing of asynchronous *Remote Function Calls* (*RFC*). RFC server groups are created via the *transaction* RZ12.

Roll area: A delimited memory area in the *application server* reserved for each *internal session*. The changeable parts of a program are managed in the roll area, while the unchangeable parts of a program are stored in the *PXA*.

Root class: A *superclass* shared by all *subclasses* in an *inheritance tree* in *single inheritance*. In *ABAP Objects*, all *classes* are subclasses of the predefined *abstract* root class `object`.

Row type: Common data type of the rows in an *internal table* (see Section 6.3.5).

RTTC: → *Run Time Type Creation*

RTTI: → *Run Time Type Identification*

RTTS: → *Run Time Type Services*

Runtime Analysis: Tool for analyzing the execution of program parts or individual statements and for measuring their runtime. Call using *transaction code* SE30.

Runtime error: A runtime error is caused by *exceptions* that are not handled during the execution of a program. This leads to a program termination. Every runtime error triggers a *database rollback* and is by default documented in a *short dump*. See also *exception*.

Run Time Type Creation: Abbreviation *RTTC*. Creating *data types* during runtime of the program. Realized since Release 6.40 via methods of *type classes RTTS*.

Run Time Type Identification: Abbreviation *RTTI*. Identification of *data types* during program runtime. Implemented by means of description methods in *type classes*. Since Release 6.40, constitutes the *RTTS* together with the *RTTC*.

Run Time Type Services: Abbreviation *RTTS*. Combination of *RTTC* and *RTTI* in a class hierarchy. The RTTS methods get information on *data types* or *classes* of *objects*, or create new data types in the form of *type objects*. The RTTSs are implemented as a hierarchy of *type classes* from which type objects can be created (see Section B.1.1).

SAP ArchiveLink: A service to link between applications in the *SAP system* and archived documents.

SAP Basis: Prior to Release 6.10, SAP Basis was the central platform for all SAP applications written in ABAP. It consists of the components presentation, *ABAP Workbench*, kernel, and administration services. SAP Basis guarantees that the applications are independent of the hardware, the operating system, and the *database*. *ABAP programs* can be executed only in a SAP Basis. An installed SAP Basis without any application components is the smallest possible SAP system. The functions of the SAP Basis were integrated into the *SAP Web Application Server* from Release 6.10.

SAP buffering: Buffering of data from *database tables* defined in the *ABAP Dictionary* on the *application server*. The definition determines whether and how a database table is buffered. Buffering generally leads to greatly enhanced performance (by a factor of between 50 and 500) and is administrated by the *database interface*. Buffering usually becomes effective when *Open SQL* commands are used for database access. However, some variants do not use the buffering process (see Section 29.1.5).

SAP Character Set: *Character set* supported by SAP. As of Release 6.10, this also includes the *Unicode character set*.

SAP Easy Access: *Menu* that contains all the functions required by a user and is assigned by the system administrator through roles in the *user master record*. It can be enhanced individually through **Favorites**.

SAP GUI: Software component of the *SAP system* on the *presentation server*. Implements the SAP-specific *GUI* of the *application server* applications and supports further functions on the presentation server, such as *GUI controls* and *OLE automation*.

SAP lock: Logical *lock* that is based on *lock objects* (see Section 33.5).

SAP LUW: Interrelated sequence of programming units whose execution, for example in *dialog steps* or in *Remote Function Calls,* can be distributed across several *work processes*, but whose database changes are executed within one single *database LUW*. SAP LUWs are implemented by bundling techniques, in which *update function modules* or *subroutines* are registered in different work processes but executed by one single work process. An SAP LUW is completed by the *Open SQL* statement COMMIT WORK. Changes within one SAP LUW can be undone by the Open SQL statement ROLLBACK WORK (see Section 33.3).

SAP memory: Memory area of *application server*, which all *main sessions* of a *user session* access jointly. *ABAP programs* have access to *SPA/GPA parameters* stored in the SAP memory (see Chapter 34).

SAP NetWeaver: Open, integration and application platform, enabling business processes to be standardized beyond system boundaries and to access all available information (*http://www.sap.com/solutions/netweaver*). The integration platform comprises components for the integration of people, information and processes. The application platform is the *SAP Web Application Server*, which provides a standardized environment for ABAP and J2EE applications.

SAP spool system: *Application server* process for managing sequential data streams, which are output as lists on a printer or stored with *SAP ArchiveLink*. *ABAP programs* can create *spool requests* during the process of creating lists. Pages of lists are selected as parts of a *print list*.

SAP system: A client/server system based on the *SAP Web Application Server ABAP* and containing at least three software layers: presentation server, application server, and database server.

SAP Web Application Server: Application platform of *SAP NetWeaver* for all SAP application components, which replaces *SAP Basis* as of Release 6.10. The SAP Web Application Server supports HTTP (HyperText Transfer Protocol) and this enables the use of Web services and other Web applications. An open development environment is available for the programming of applications. Former SAP Basis functions for all existing SAP applications are integrated. As of Release 6.30 the SAP Web Application Server contains a SAP Web Application Server Java for creating J2EE applications, in addition to the SAP Web Application Server ABAP. Both parts of the SAP Web Application

Server can access a persistence layer independent of the operating and database system, and they can call one another up.

SAP Web Application Server ABAP: Component of the *SAP Web Application Server* for application programming in ABAP. See also *SAP Web Application Server Java*.

SAP Web Application Server Java: Component of the *SAP Web Application Server* for application programming in Java (since Release 6.30), based on J2EE. See also *SAP Web Application Server ABAP*.

Scientific notation: Representation of a number with mantissa and exponent. The value of the number is created by multiplication of the mantissa by 10 to the power of the exponent (see Section A.2.1).

Screen: Part of a *window* that contains *screen elements*. For a user, the visible part of a *dynpro*. The screen is created using the *Layout Editor* of the *Screen Painter*.

Screen element: Graphic element on a *screen*. Screen elements are *check boxes*, *radio buttons*, *custom controls*, *dropdown list boxes*, *pushbuttons*, *input/output fields*, *frames*, *subscreens*, *table controls*, *tabstrip controls*, *text fields*, and *status icons*.

Screen list: *List* that is displayed on the screen in the *list dynpro*. A screen list is stored in the *list buffer* during its creation. See also *print list*.

Screen Painter: Tool from the *ABAP Workbench* to create *dynpros*. Contains a text editor to write the *dynpro flow logic* and contains a *layout editor* to configure the *screen layout*. You call it via *transaction code* SE51.

Scroll bar: Part of the *GUI*. Automatically created whenever a *screen* or a *screen element* is too large for the area available in the window.

Search help: A *repository object* maintained in the *ABAP Dictionary*. It supplies *input fields* on *Dynpros* with single- or multi-column *input helps*. Search helps can be linked in the Dictionary with *components* from *structures*, *data elements*, and *check tables*. A search help enables you to search for entry values with assigned data, without you having to know the exact spelling of the value.

Secondary index: *Index* of *data base tables* defined in the *ABAP Dictionary*. This index can be created in addition to the *primary index*. The creation of secondary indices can improve the performance when accessing *data bases* that evaluate the data base indices.

Selection: → *Branch*

Selection criteria: Components of a *selection screen*, defined with SELECT-OPTIONS. Displayed on the selection screen via two *input fields* for interval boundaries and a pushbutton for *multiple selection*. Displayed internally via a *selection table* (see Section 26.4).

Selection include: *Include program* within a *logical database*. The *standard selection screen* of the logical database is defined in this include program (see Section 26.2.4).

Selection option: The *relational operator* assigned to a *selection criterion*.

Selection screen: A special *dynpro* that can be defined without the use of the *Screen Painter* by using the statements SELECTION-SCREEN, PARAMETERS or SELECT-OPTIONS in the *global declaration section* of *executable programs*, *function groups*, and *module pools*. Selection screens are processed by the *ABAP runtime environment*, which triggers *selection screen events*. There are *standard selection screens* and *standalone selection screens* (see Chapter 26).

Selection screen event: *Event* of the *ABAP runtime environment* that occurs during the *selection screen processing*. The corresponding *event key word* is AT SELECTION-SCREEN (see Section 4.4.3).

Selection screen processing: Processing of a selection screen, encapsulated in the *ABAP runtime environment*, in which the *dynpro events* PAI and PBO are passed to the *ABAP program* in form of *selection screen events* (see Section 26.2.4).

Selection screen variant: → *variant*

Selection table: A global *internal table* with a *heading line*, the columns SIGN, OPTION, LOW and HIGH, and the name of a *selection criterion*. It is used for the internal storage of a selection condition. Declared with the statement SELECT-OPTIONS (see Section 26.4); it can be evaluated in *logical expressions* (see Section 13.5).

Selection text: Part of the *text elements* of an *ABAP program*. A selection text can be assigned to every *parameter* or *selection criterion* defined with PARAMETERS or SELECT-OPTIONS. It is then displayed on the *selection screen* in the respective *input fields*.

Selection view: If you want a node of a *logical database* to have *dynamic selections*, in a selection view you can determine the node *fields*, for which the user can define dynamic selections. Selection views can be edited via **Extras • Selection Views** in the *Logical Database Builder*.

Self reference: *Object reference variable* called me that is predefined as a local data object and available in each *instance method* and points to its own object. The *static type* of me is the *class* in which the instance method is implemented.

Sequence: *Control structure* which consists of a *statement block* that is not defined by keywords and is executed once without a condition (see Section 14.1).

Serialization: Transformation of ABAP data into an *XML* document, either by calling a *XSLT program* or a *simple transformation*. When using *XSLT*, the system first generates a *canonical XML representation* (*asXML*) (see Chapter 40).

SET/GET parameter: → *SPA/GPA parameter*

Shared lock: *Lock* that allows other users to set further shared locks but no simultaneous *exclusive locks* for the locked data. The *Open SQL* statement SELECT without the addition FOR UPDATE, as well as the corresponding *Native-SQL* statement, do not set a corresponding database lock for the addressed lines, by default (see Section 33.4). A shared lock is set as a *SAP lock* via a correspondingly parameterized call of a *lock function module* (see Section 33.5).

Shared memory: Memory area on an *application server* that all *ABAP programs* of this server access together. Either *data clusters* or *shared objects* (as of Release 6.40) can be stored in the shared memory.

Shared-memory-enabled class: *Class* whose *instances* can be stored as *shared objects* in *area instance versions* of the *shared memory*. Shared memory-enabled classes are defined using the addition SHARED MEMORY ENABLED of the statement CLASS. A special shared-memory-enabled class is the area root class.

Shared object: *Object* of a *shared memory-enabled class* that is stored in an *area instance version* of the *shared memory*. A shared object is generated with the addition AREA HANDLE of the statement CREATE OBJECT. *References* to shared objects are possible in other shared objects of the same area instance version and in the internal session of an ABAP program included via area handler.

Shared objects memory: Part of the *shared memory* in which *shared objects* are stored in *area instance versions*.

Short dump: Error log that is displayed and saved after a *runtime error* or an *exit message*. Call using *transaction code* ST22.

Signature: In a procedure, the name, the entirety of *formal parameters* of the *interface*, and the remaining properties.

Simple transformation: Abbreviation *ST*. SAP-specific programming language for transformations between *XML* formats and ABAP data and vice versa. *Serializations* and *de-serializations* can

be carried out with simple transformations. The simple transformation is called with the statement CALL TRANSFORMATION (see Chapter 40).

Single-byte code: Display of a character in exactly one byte.

Single code-page system: System with only one *system code page*. Either a *Unicode system* with *UTF 16* or a non-*Unicode system* with a non-Unicode code page. The *text environment* for an *internal mode* can only be set with this code page in a single code page system. See also *MDMP* system.

Single inheritance: *Inheritance* in which a *class* can have several *subclasses* but only one direct *superclass* in contrast to a *multiple inheritance*. See also *inheritance hierarchy*.

Soft reference: *Reference* to an *object* that is not contained in the reference when the available memory is insufficient. The *class* CL_ABAP_SOFT_REFERENCE is planned but not yet implemented for soft references. See also *weak reference*.

Sorted table: *Table category* of an *internal table* that is managed by a logical index and is always sorted according to its *table key* (see Section 6.3.5). The corresponding *generic data type* is sorted table.

Source code: Linear list of *ABAP statements* and comments. Created and maintained using the ABAP Editor.

Source-code modularization: Decomposition of the *source code* of a program into its individual parts. *Include programs* and *macros* are used for source code modularization (see Section 4.5).

SPA/GPA parameter: Also *SET/GET parameter*. Data objects in the *SAP memory* that can be accessed in *ABAP programs*. SPA/GPA parameters are set using SET PARAMETER and read with GET PARAMETER. *Input fields* on *dynpros* can be linked with SPA/GPA parameters and be pre-assigned values when the dynpro is called. User input in such fields remains stored in the corresponding SPA/GPA parameters. The names of SPA/GPA parameters are managed in the *database table* TPARA (see Chapter 34).

Spool request: Output request to the *SAP spool system*. In *ABAP programs*, spool requests can be opened with the statements NEW-PAGE PRINT ON and SUBMIT TO SAP-SPOOL (see Section 10.2.3 and 10.2.3). During a spool request, the system processes the *print list* of the current program. When the spool request is opened, the system determines *print parameters* that can no longer be changed. An *internal mode* cannot manage more than one spool request at a time.

SQL: Structured Query Language. To a large extent, the standardized language for accessing *relational databases*. Divided into *DML*, *DDL*, and *DCL*. SQL is the programming interface of the *database* of the *SAP system*. In ABAP, the DML part is mapped by *Open SQL*. The entire scope of the SQL statements of the installed *database system* is available as *Native SQL*.

ST: → *simple transformations*

Stand-alone data type: *Data type* that is defined with the statement TYPES in the *ABAP program* (see Section 6.3) or in the *ABAP Dictionary*. Compare with *bound data type*.

Stand-alone selection screen: *Selection screen* that is defined between the statements SELECTION-SCREEN {BEGIN|END} OF SCREEN (see Section 26.2.1). Stand-alone selection screens can be defined in all programs that can contain *dynpros*. See also *standard selection screen*.

Standard key: *Table key* of an *internal table* whose *key fields* are all table fields with *byte-type* data types and *character-type data types*. If the *row type* contains *substructures*, these are accounted for their elementary *components* (see Section 6.3.5)

Standard list status: A predefined *GUI status* for a *list* (see Section 27.5.1).

Standard page header: *List headers* maintained as *text elements* in an *ABAP program*. The standard page header consists of a standard header and column headings.

Standard selection screen: *Selection screen* that is defined outside of the statements SELECTION-SCREEN BEGIN|END OF SCREEN (see Section 26.2.1). A standard selection screen has the *dynpro number* 1000 and is only possible in *executable programs* and *logical data bases*. When linking an executable program with a logical data base, the two selection screens are grouped into one selection screen. When their program is executed, standard selection screens are automatically called by the *ABAP runtime environment* with the statement SUBMIT (see Section 10.2.1). See also *stand-alone selection screen*.

Standard table: *Table category* of an *internal table* that is managed by a logical index and has no unique *table key* (see Section 6.3.5). The corresponding *generic data type* is [standard] table.

Start value: Value specified when a data object is declared. The data object is filled with this value when it is created. The start value is set with the VALUE addition in the DATA statement (see Section 6.4). If the VALUE addition is not used, the system uses the type-specific *initial value* (see Table 5.2.).

Statement block: Structural unit within *control structures* that consists of one or more sequential statements. The statements of a statement block are processed sequentially. Statement blocks again can contain control structures.

Static attribute: *Attribute* declared with CLASS-DATA of a *class*. The attribute is valid independent of the *instance* of a class. The content of the static attribute determine the instance-dependent state of a class (see Section 6.5).

Static component: Generic term for *static attribute*, *static event*, and *static method*. The static components of a *class* can be addressed using the name of the class.

Static constructor: *Constructor* that is declared under the name class_ constructor as a *static method* in the *public visibility section* of a *class*. Is automatically executed in an *internal session* prior to the first use of the class (see Section 7.4.1).

Static event: *Event* of a class declared using CLASS-EVENTS. This is an event of a *class* that can be triggered independently of an *instance* of the class (see Section 7.4.2).

Static method: *Method* of a *class* that is declared with CLASS METHODS and which can be used independent of a class *instance*. Static methods can only access *static attributes* and *static events* of their own class (see Section 7.4.1).

Static type: Also called *reference type*. *Data type* of a *reference variable*. Determines which *objects* a reference variable can point to. For *object reference variables*, the static type is a *class* or an *interface* for *data reference variables*, the static type is a data type. The static type is always a mere general type or the same as the *dynamic type* (see Section 6.5.1).

Status bar: Part of a *window*. Displays *status messages* and system information.

Status icon: *Icon* that is displayed as a *screen element* of a *screen* and is linked to a *dynpro field*. The same-named *data object* in the *ABAP program* must be of the ICONS data type in the *ABAP Dictionary*.

Status message: Message of *message type* S. Status messages are displayed in the *window* of the subsequent *dynpro* in the *status bar* (see Section 28.12).

Step: → *background task*

Step loop: Repeated display of a group of *screen elements* on a *dynpro*. Step loops are processed with the *step-loop technique* are the predecessors of *table controls* (see Section 42.14.2).

Step-loop technique: Technique in the *dynpro flow logic* for processing screen elements arranged in a table-type manner on the *screen* of a dynpro. The step loop technique is used to process *table controls* and their predecessors, the *step loops*.

String: *Elementary data object* of variable length, either *byte string* or *text string*.

String literal: *Literal* that is defined with characters contained in backquotes (`) (see Section 6.1.3). The length is minimum 0 characters, maximum 255 characters. The *data type* of a string literal is `string`.

Structure: Either a *structured type* in the *ABAP Dictionary* or a name for a structured *data object* in an *ABAP program*. You can access whole structures or merely by component. Structures that contain only *character-type flat components* can also be treated as *elementary data objects* in ABAP.

Structure component selector: Character -. A *component* `comp` of a *structure* `struc` can be addressed using `struc-comp`.

Structured type: *Data type* of a *structure*. Contains data types other than *components* (see Section 6.3.4).

Subclass: *Class* that was derived by means of inheritance from a *superclass* (see Section 7.2.1).

Subquery: `SELECT` statement that can be used within the `WHERE` condition of *Open SQL* statements for a subquery.

Subroutine: *Procedure* that can be defined in every *ABAP program* (except *class* and *interface pools*), but only outside of classes. Can be called from any program. Begins with `FORM` and ends with `ENDFORM` (see Section 4.2.3).

Subroutine pool: *ABAP program* that usually contains *subroutines* that are called from other ABAP programs. Does not support its own dynpros.

Subscreen: *Screen* of a *subscreen dynpro* (see Section 25.2.6).

Subscreen area: Area within a *screen* in which other screens can be represented as *subscreens* (see Section 25.2.6).

Subscreen dynpro: *Dynpro* whose *screen* can be displayed as a *subscreen* in a *subscreen area*.

Substructure: *Component* of a *structure* that is structured itself.

Superclass: *Class* from which *subclasses* are derived through *inheritance*.

Surrogate area: Portion of the characters that can be displayed in *Unicode* (U+1001 to U+10FFFF) which includes, for example, musical notes or more specific Asian characters. Addressed directly in *UTF-8* and *UTF-32*, and in *UTF-16* through combinations of specific low and high surrogate characters.

Symbol: Graphic element in *lists* (see Section 27.2.1).

Synchronous Remote Function Call: *Remote Function Call* with which the remotely called function is waited for at the end of processing (see Section 39.2.1).

Synchronous update: Execution of *update function modules* of high priority, when the calling program waits for the update to finish. The synchronous update is started by `COMMIT WORK` with the addition AND WAIT (see Section 33.3.1).

Syntax check: Static check of the *ABAP source code* to check if the syntax is correct. The syntax check is called in the *ABAP Editor* via **Program • Check • Syntax**, or via the statement SYNTAX-CHECK (see Section 38.4).

Syntax error: Violation of the ABAP syntax rules. Syntax errors are displayed after the *syntax check* by the *ABAP Editor*. A program that has syntax errors cannot be executed.

System class: *Class* of the *class library*, in which language-related functionality is implemented. As a rule, the name begins with CL_ABAP_ or CL_SYSTEM_ (see Section B.1).

System code page: *Code page* that is released for usage on an *application server*. In *Unicode systems*, the system code page is always *UTF-16* with platform-dependent *byte sequence*. In non-Unicode systems, the system code pages are defined in the database table TCPDB. In Non-Unicode-*Single-code-page systems* there is only one system code page. In *MDMP systems* there are several system code pages. The code page of the *text environment* of an internal session is always a system code page. The system code page of the current text environment is the active system codepage of an internal session.

System field: A predefined *data object* that can be filled contextual by the *ABAP runtime environment* and can be analyzed in the program (see Table 5.8).

System log: Central buffer storage for recording system errors on an *applica-*

tion server. You can call the system log via the *transaction code* SM21.

System toolbar: Part of a *window*. Contains predefined and *icon*-represented *push buttons* to operate the program, as well as an *input field* for the direct input of *function codes*. Part of the *GUI status* set with SET PF STATUS. Created with the *Menu Painter* tool. Named *standard toolbar* in the *ABAP Workbench*.

Table body: Description of actual *internal table* for internal tables with *heading line*. The table body is addressed by attaching [] to the table name (or a *field symbol* or a dereferenced *data reference variable*). Internal tables and table bodies are identical for internal tables without header line.

Table category: Part of the *data type* of an *internal table*. Specifies the type of storage and access. Table categories include *standard tables*, *sorted tables*, and *hashed tables* (see Section 6.3.5).

Table cluster: *Database table* in the *database* that contains the data of several *cluster tables*.

Table control: *Screen element* for displaying and processing tabular data with a special *user interface* (see Section 25.2.5 and 25.3.10.1).

Table index: An internal line number in *index tables* (*standard tables* and *sorted tables*). Each table line in an index table has a unique line number, which is managed by the *ABAP runtime environment* in a logical index. The line numbers start at 1 and run consecutively and without gaps, up to the current number of lines in the table.

Table key: Columns of an *internal table* or of a *database table* whose content identifies table rows.

Table parameter: Obsolete *formal parameter* of *function modules* or *subroutines* that is typed as an internal *standard table* with header line (see Section 4.2.3).

Table pool: *Database table* in the *database* that contains the data of several *pool tables*.

Table type: *Data type* of an *internal table*. Defines *row type*, *table category*, and *table key* of an internal table. The table can be *generic* regarding the key (see Section 6.3.5).

Table work area: Structured *interface work area* that is declared using the statements TABLES or NODES with reference to an identically-named structure or *database table* of the *ABAP Dictionary* (see Section 6.9).

Tabstrip: Short form for *tabstrip control*.

Tabstrip area: Area of a *screen* on which *tabstrips* can be displayed.

Tabstrip control: *Screen element* that consist of several *tab pages* and is displayed as a tab (see Section 25.2.6 and 25.3.10.2).

Tabstrip page: Page within a *tabstrip*. Each tabstrip page has a *tab title*.

Tab title: A single-line element located at the top of a *tabstrip page* that is linked to a *function code* and selects tabstrip pages when you click on it once.

Termination message: *Message* of *message type* A. Termination messages are displayed in a *dialog box* and then terminate the running program (see Section 28.1.2).

Test: Combination of tests of one or several *ABAP programs* in *ABAP Unit* for which a *test run* can be executed.

Test class: Specific local *class* of a program, in which tests for *ABAP Unit* are implemented in the form of *test methods*. A test class groups together related tests that use the same *fixture*. Test classes are defined using the addition FOR TESTING of the statement CLASS. Test classes can only be used as part of *test runs* and are not generated as standard in productive systems.

Test method: Special *instance method* of a *test class* in which a test is implemented. Test methods are defined using the addition FOR TESTING of the statement METHODS, and called during a *test run* of the *ABAP Unit* tool.

Test run: Execution of a *test task* in *ABAP Unit*. Test runs for test tasks of an individual program can be started directly in the corresponding editor by choosing **Program** or **Function Module • Test • Module Test** or **Class • Module Test**. More detailed test runs are executed using the *Code Inspector*. After a test run the result is displayed on the user interface of ABAP Unit.

Text element: Component of an *ABAP program*. Contains texts that can be accessed in the ABAP program. Text elements are *list headers* (*standard page header*), *selection texts*, and *text symbols*. The text elements are created in multilingual *text pools* of the program and can be used when loading a text pool in the program. Text element maintenance is called using the *transaction code* SE32.

Text environment: The text environment is part of the *runtime environment* of an *ABAP program* and is made up of a language, a *locale* and a *system code page* (see Section 35.1.2). All programs in an *internal session* have a common text environment. As a default, the text environment of an internal session is determined by the *logon language* and can be set by the statement SET LOCALE (see Section 35.3). The language of the current text environment is contained in the *system field* sy-langu.

Text field: In ABAP, *data object* of *data type* c. In *dynpros*, *screen element* that serves the sole purpose of displaying text and on which no *user actions* are possible. A text field of a dynpro is not connected with a *dynpro field*.

Text-field literal: *Literal* that is defined using characters enclosed in single inverted comma (') and that can be linked with a *text symbol* (see Section 6.1.3). The length is a minimum of one character and a maximum of 255 characters. The *data type* is c in the length of the specified characters.

Text language: Identification of a component of the type LANG of a *structure* defined in the *ABAP Dictionary* or a *database table* (as of Release 6.20). When a new structure is created the first component of the structure LANG is identified as the text language, by default. Only one component of this type can be identified as the text language, if there are several of these components. The text language is used when the structure is transferred between *MDMP systems* and *Unicode*

systems for the conversion of the character-like components.

Text-like data type: *Data type* whose *data objects* contain texts. The corresponding *predefined data types* are c and string. The corresponding *generic data type* is csequence.

Text pool: Component of an *ABAP program*, that contains the *text elements* of the program. For a program, multiple text pools in several languages can be defined. When you load a program into an *internal session*, the text elements of the text pool of the *logon language* are read in by default. If this text pool does not exist, the text pool is used which is specified in the *profile parameter* zcsa/second_language (since Release 6.20). If none of these text pools exists, then a blank text pool without text elements is loaded. During program execution, you can load the text pool of a different language with the statement SET LANGUAGE (see Section 35.2).

Text string: *Data object* of the *data type* string.

Text symbol: *Named data object* of an *ABAP program*. It is maintained as part of the *text elements* of the program and addressed in the program using the name text-###, whereat ### is the three-character ID of the text symbol. A text symbol has the *data type* c and the length defined by *mlen* in the text elements. If the text symbol is not in the currently loaded *text pool*, text-### is handled like an initial one-character text field. A text symbol can also be linked with *text field literals* by using the syntax 'Literal'(###) and thus replaces them in the program if it exists in the currently loaded text pool (see Section 2.2.5).

Time field: *Data object* of type t that contains a time specification in the HHMMSS format. At calculations the content of the time field is converted into the number of seconds since 00:00:00. There are time stamps available for combined date/time specifications of higher accuracy.

Time stamp: Date and time information in a *data object* of the *data type* p without *fractional portions* (short form) or of the length 11 with seven fractional portions (long form). The *decimal places* before the decimal point display the date and time in the form YYYYMMDDHHMMSS. In the long form, the split seconds are also displayed after the decimal point. See section 36.1.2

Title bar: Component of the *GUI* that contains the *GUI title* of a *window*. The title bar is set by a SET TITLEBAR statement (see Section 25.3.4).

Tool bar: Name used for *system tool* bar in the *ABAP Workbench*.

Top include: *Include program* used for the global data declarations of an *ABAP program*. The top include should not be used to implement *processing blocks*. As of Release 6.10, this is checked by the *extended program check*.

Transaction: Execution of an *ABAP program* using a *transaction code*. There are *dialog*, *report*, *parameter*, *variant*, and (as of Release 6.10) OO *transactions*. A transaction is started by entering the transaction code in the input field on the toolbar or by means of CALL TRANSACTION or LEAVE TO TRANSACTION statements.

Transactional Remote Function Call: Remote Function Call in which the function called remotely is flagged for execution and started by a COMMIT WORK statement (see Section 39.2.3).

Transaction code: Twenty-character name connected with a dynpro, another transaction code, or (as of Release 6.10) a *method* of an *ABAP program* that is used to execute programs. Transaction codes linked with dynpros are possible for *executable programs*, *module pools*, and *function groups*. *Parameter transactions* and *variant transactions* are linked with other transaction codes. Transaction codes that are linked with methods are allowed for all *program types* except *include programs*. Maintenance and administration via transaction code SE93.

Transaction variant: You can use transaction variants to input fields on several *dynpros* in a *transaction*, to change the attributes of *screen elements*, and to hide entire *screens*. Maintenance and administration using the *transaction code* SHD0.

Transparent table: *Database table* defined in the *ABAP Dictionary* that has one instance in the *database* with the same name and the same columns as the definition in the ABAP Dictionary. The data in transparent tables can be processed from outside the *SAP systems* via the programming interface of the database.

Treatable exception: *Exception* that can be treated in the program and that does not lead to a *runtime error* when treated. As of Release 6.10, all treatable exceptions are implemented by means of *exception objects* and can be treated using TRY-CATCH-ENDTRY statements. Before Release 6.10, selected runtime errors were catchable with CATCH-ENDCATCH. See Chapter 15

tRFC: → *Transactional Remote Function Call*

Trusted system: *SAP system* that is classified as a trusted caller of *Remote Function Calls* in a *Trusting System*. The trusted system provides the *RFC client*. Classification takes place via *transaction* SMT1. Trusted systems log on to the trusting system without transferring a password. User-specific logon data is checked in the trusting system.

Trusting system: *SAP system* that trusts a *trusted system* in calls via *Remote Function Call*. The trusting system provides the *RFC server*. The trusting systems can be displayed in a trusted system using *transaction code* SMT2.

Type: Abstract description of an *object*. Either a *data type* for a *data object* or *object type* for an object in *ABAP objects*. The corresponding *generic data type* is any.

Type assignment: Definition of a generic or complete *typing* for *formal parameters* or *field symbols*. Specifies in which operand positions a formal parameter or field symbol can be used and is used for checking the *data type* of an assigned *data object* (see Chapter 8).

Type class: System class of the *Run Time Type Services*. The *static methods* of the type classes generate *type objects* from available *types* or construct new types.

Type conversion: Converts the contents of a *data object* during the *assignment* to a data object with a different

data type according to *conversion rules* (see Appendix A).

Type group: *ABAP program* that. Contains the definitions of globally visual *data types* and *constants* and which is loaded by using them. Does not support any *dynpros* of its own.

Type name: Name of a *type*. In a program, only the *relative type name* is known and statically usable. The *absolute type name* can only be used in dynamic statement forms.

Type object: *Instance* of a *type class*. Type objects describe or represent a *type*. Type objects are created with the *static methods* of the *type classes*. The type class and the possible attributes of type objects determine the technical properties of the type. *References* to type objects can be used, for example, after the HANDLE addition to the statements CREATE DATA and ASSIGN.

UCS: Abbreviation for *Universal Character Set*. 4-byte *character set*, standardized according in ISO-10646, which contains all other character sets. The UCS character set is currently identical to the *Unicode* character set, in other words it contains no additional characters not contained in Unicode.

Unicode: Language-independent *character set* for international data processing (*www.unicode.org*). Subset of the UCS character set according to ISO-10646. 1114111 characters numbered hexadecimally by U+0000 to U+10FFFF can be displayed in Unicode. The Unicode character set is normally accessed using a *UTF-character representation*.

Unicode character representation: *Character representation* defined for

Unicode. SAP supports the representations *UTF-8*, *UTF-16*, and *UTF-32*, whereat the *byte order* can be platform-dependent.

Unicode check: *Syntax check* for *ABAP programs* that are to be executable in a *Unicode system*. The Unicode check was tightened as of Release 6.10. It is activated in the *program attributes*.

Unicode fragment view: Splits *structures* into *alignment gaps*, *byte-* and *character-like* areas, *numeric data objects*, *strings*, *reference variables*, and *internal tables* (see Section Appendix 31).

Unicode program: A Unicode program is an *ABAP program* in which the *Unicode checks* are run effectively and in which certain statements involve different semantics from those that apply in non-Unicode programs. A program of this kind usually returns the same results in a *Unicode system* as in a non-Unicode system.

Unicode system: *Single-code-page system* in which characters are encoded in *Unicode character representation*. The *system code page* for a Unicode system is currently *UTF-16* with a platform-dependent *byte order*. All ABAP programs in a Unicode system must be *Unicode programs*.

Unit key: Component of a structure or database table of the type UNIT, defined in the ABAP dictionary. A unit key can be linked to a quantity field of a structure or database table. The Unit key can contain a unit abbreviation from the table T006 and determines the unit for the unit field.

Up cast: Also called *Widening Cast*. Assignment between reference variables in which the static type of the target variable is more general than or the same as the static type of the source variable (see Section A.5.2). Compare *down cast*.

Update function module: *Function module* for which the property **update module** is selected in the *Function Builder*. It is the basis of the *update*. Generally, an update function module contains changing database accesses and, with the statement CALL FUNCTION ... IN UPDATE TASK, can be registered to later execute the statement COMMIT WORK. When an update function module is created it is assigned either a high or low priority level (see Section 33.3).

Update module: → *Update function module*

User action: Action performed by a user on a *control element* of the *user interface*. Leads to the *dynpro event PAI*, if the selected control element is linked to a *function code*.

User interface: All the *control elements* in an *ABAP program*. Consists of the graphical interface (*GUI*) in a *window* and the *function keys* and other keys of an input device (keyboard or hardware components that simulate keyboards, such as bar-code readers).

User master record: A user master record must exist before a user can *log on* to an *SAP system*. The record determines which actions a user is allowed to execute and which *authorizations* they possess. Furthermore default settings, such as the way in which *decimal separators* are displayed in *lists*, are recorded in the user master record. User master records are maintained in user maintenance (*transaction code* SU01).

User name: Name of a user that is required for logon to *SAP systems*. Together with the *password*, the user name allows authorized use of SAP systems.

User session: Status between the *logon* and logoff of a user in an *SAP system*. The user can work with the SAP system during the user session.

UTC: Abbreviation for Universal Time Coordination. Basis for calculating worldwide time specifications. The UTC reference time is based on Greenwich Mean Time (GMT) but is not a time zone. It has no daylight- saving time and takes into account the time variance caused by the rotation of the earth. This variance may not exceed Greenwich Mean Time by more than an average of 0.9 seconds per year. In ABAP, UTC time specifications occur, when dealing with time stamps.

UTF: Abbreviation for Universal Transformation Format. Different representations of the *Unicode character set*. All UTF character representations uniquely refer to the Unicode-defined characters and can be transformed in each other. The representations differ only in the type of addressing. See *UTF-8*, *UTF-16*, and *UTF-32*.

UTF-8: 8-bit *Unicode character representation*. *ASCII* characters are represented by one byte. Other European characters are represented in 2 bytes. Most Asian characters are represented in 3 bytes. The characters in the *surrogate area* are addressed directly using 4 bytes.

UTF-16: 16-bit *Unicode character representation*. In this representation, all characters are displayed using 2 bytes. The characters in the *surrogate area* are addressed by combinations of special low and high surrogate characters.

UTF-32: 32-bit *Unicode character representation*. In this representation, all characters are addressed using 4 bytes.

Value range: **Amount of** allowed values for a *data object*. The values allowed for a data object are determined by its *data type* (see Table 5.2).

Variable: *Named data object* whose value can be changed during the runtime of an *ABAP program* (see Section 6.4).

Variant: Set of input values for *selection screens*. Can be used when accessing selection screens to enter preallocate values in the *input fields*. You can create variants on a selection screen via **Goto • Variants** and transfer them, for example with a SUBMIT statement (see Section 10.2.2).

Variant transaction: Special *transaction code* used to link a *dialog transaction* with a *transaction variant*. When a variant transaction is accessed, the dialog transaction is called and executed with the transaction variant.

View: Grouping of columns in one or more *database tables* according to application-specific criteria. In the *SAP system,* views are defined in the *ABAP Dictionary* and can be referenced as data types like *flat structures*. Views can be used like database tables in reading *Open SQL* statements (see Section 29.2).

Visibility section: The *declaration section* of a *class* can be subdivided into up to three visibility sections. These areas are *public*, *protected*, or *private* (see Section 7.2.1). They define the visibility of the *components* of the class and thus, the *interfaces* of the class for its users.

Warning: *Message* of the *message type* W. Warnings during *PAI* processing of *dynpros* make screen fields ready for input again (see Section 28.1.2).

Weak reference: Reference to an *object* that does not retain the object when the *Garbage Collector* is executed, unlike *object references* in *reference variables*. Weak references are represented by objects of the *class* CL_ABAP_WEAK_REFERENCE in *ABAP Objects* (see Section B.1.12).

Web Application Builder: Tool in the *ABAP Workbench* for creating *Business Server Pages*. Can be accessed by means of the menu path *Create Web Objects BSP Application* in the *Object Navigator*.

Web Application Server : → *SAP Web Application Server*

Web AS: → *SAP Web Application Server*

Web dynpro: Technology used to create platform-independent web-based interfaces. Available since Release 6.30 for *SAP Web Application Server Java,* and available SAP-internally since Release 6.40 for the SAP Web Application Server ABAP.

Widening cast: → *Up cast*

Wildcard character: Character that substitutes other content. In character string processing, " *" usually stands for any *character string* and " +" for any individual character (see Section 13.2.2). In WHERE-conditions of *Open SQL* with the *operator* LIKE "%" stands for any character strings and "+" for individual characters (see Section 29.2.4). The special functions of wildcard characters can be canceled using escape symbols.

Window: An area on a screen delimited by a frame. In the *SAP GUI*, a window comprises a *title bar, menu bar, tool bar, application toolbar, screen, status bar*, and possible *scroll bars*.

Work Area: Description for a *data object* that is particularly useful when working with *internal tables* or *database tables* as a source for changing operations or a target for reading operations.

Work process: Component of an *application server*. Work processes execute written applications in ABAP. There are various types of work processes for different applications: Dialog, enqueue, background, spool, and update work processes. Each work process is registered for the complete runtime of the *SAP system* as a user in the *database system*. In the *dialog processing*, a work process is assigned to the *ABAP program* for the duration of a *dialog step*.

XML: XML (Extensible Markup Language, *http://www.w3.org/XML*) is a generic model for the structuring of data. XML has a generic syntax (markup) to display elements of the model in a text format. The display in text format enables the display of structured data without using the program that created this data. ABAP data can be transformed to XML and back using *XSL transformations* and *simple transformations*.

XSLT: XSLT (Extensible Stylesheet Language Transformation, *www.w3.org/TR/xslt*) enables the conversion of XML formats into any other *XML* formats. The *ABAP runtime environment* contains a *XSLT processor* for executing *XSL transformations*.

XSLT program: → *XSL transformation*

XSLT processor: System program to execute *XSL transformations*.

XSL transformation: Program written in the XSLT in the *repository* (XSLT program) for the transformation of XML documents. The call of a XSL transformation is made with the CALL TRANSFORMATION statement. With implicit *serialization* and *de-serialization*, the direct conversion of ABAP data into XML formats and vice versa is possible (see Chapter 40).

F   Notes on the CD-ROMs

The three CD ROMs contain a test version of SAP Web Application Server 6.20. The Web Application Server is the successor to the SAP Basis system and can be used as an HTTP(S) server.

System Requirements

▶ Windows 2000, Service Pack 2 or higher;
  Windows XP (Home or Professional)

▶ Internet Explorer 5.01 or higher

▶ Min. 192 MB RAM

▶ Min. 512 MB paging file

▶ Min. 3.2 GB hard disk space

Installation

You will find instructions for installing, using, and managing the SAP Web Application Server on the first CD (kernel). Follow the instructions in the file Web_AS_demo.htm which opens when you insert the CD. A tutorial for creating Business Server Pages (BSP) is also available.

Additional Information and Support

SAP offers the test version of the Web Application Server free to the readers of this book. The CDs were carefully produced and tested by employees of SAP. Neither SAP AG nor Galileo Press GmbH can be held responsible for any damage resulting from an incorrect installation of the software.

Neither SAP nor the publishing house can provide further support. We ask for your understanding in this respect.

Index

Leverage the value of your business with SAP's new infrastructure

Acquire unparalleled insights from four exclusive sample case studies

312 pp., 2005, US$ 69.95
ISBN 1-59229-041-8

SAP NetWeaver Roadmap

S. Karch, L. Heilig, C. Bernhardt, A. Hardt, F. Heidfeld, R. Pfennig

SAP NetWeaver Roadmap

This book helps you understand each of SAP NetWeaver's components and illustrates, using practical examples, how SAP NetWeaver, and its levels of integration, can be leveraged by a wide range of organizations.
Readers benefit from in-depth analysis featuring four actual case studies from various industries, which describe in detail how integration with SAP Net-Weaver can contribute to the optimization of a variety of essential business processes and how the implementation works. Finally, detailed coverage of SAP NetWeaver technology gives you the complete picture in terms of architecture and functionality of each component.

>> www.sap-press.de/955

Gain in-depth knowledge on SAP's new UI technology

356 pp., 2005, US$ 59.95
ISBN 1-59229-038-8

Inside Web Dynpro for Java

Chris Whealy

Inside Web Dynpro for Java

A guide to the principles of programming in SAP's Web Dynpro

This book teaches readers how to leverage the full power of Web Dynpro - taking it well beyond the standard "drag and drop" functionality. You'll start with basics like MVC Design Pattern, the architecture, event handling and the phase model. Then, learn how to create your own Web Dynpro applications, with volumes of practical insights on the dos and don'ts of Web Dynpro Programming. The book is complemented by a class and interface reference, which further assists readers in modifying existing objects, designing custom controllers, etc.

>> www.sap-press.de/937

Collaborative Processes,
Interfaces, Messages, Proxies,
and Mappings

Runtime, configuration,
cross-component processes,
and Business Process
Management (BPM)

270 pp., 2005, US$ 69.95
ISBN 1-59229-037-X

SAP Exchange Infrastructure

www.sap-press.com

J. Stumpe, J. Orb

SAP Exchange Infrastructure

If you know what SAP Exchange Infrastructure (SAP
XI) is, and you have seen the latest documentation,
then now you will want to read this book. Exclusive
insights help you go beyond the basics, and provide
you with in-depth information on the SAP XI architecture, which in turn helps you quickly understand
the finer points of mappings, proxies, and interfaces.
You'll also benefit from practical guidance on the
design and configuration of business processes.
Additionally, in a significant section devoted to step-
by-step examples, you'll discover the nuances of
various application scenarios and how to tackle their
specific configurations.

>> www.sap-press.de/934

Gain first insights into the Composite Application Framework

300 pp., with CD, approx. US$ 69.95
ISBN 1-59229-048-5, aug 2005

SAP xApps and the Composite Application Framework

www.sap-press.com

J. Weilbach, M. Herger

SAP xApps and the Composite Application Framework

This book provides you with a detailed introduction to all of the SAP components that are relevant to xApps, especially the integrated SAP NetWeaver tools (Composite Application Framework – CAF) for creating and customizing your own xApps. This unparalleled reference contains exclusive information, practical examples, and a wealth of screen shots from the CAF, taken from actual pilot projects. In addition, you'll uncover the ins and outs of SAP partner programs for developing and certifying your own xApps, and lots more.

>> www.sap-press.de/1017

**Web AS and Java:
The guaranteed future
for your Web business**

520 pp., with DVD, approx. US$ 69.95
ISBN 1-59229-020-5, june 2005

Java Programming with
the SAP Web Application Server

www.sap-press.com

K. Kessler, P. Tillert, P. Dobrikov

Java Programming with the SAP
Web Application Server

The 6.30 version of the Web Application Server
represents the conclusion of Java Engine implementation by SAP.

This book covers all the areas in which Java can be
applied on the WebAS in future, starting from the
architecture of the Web AS and the installation of
IDE. You get in-depth information on database and
R/3-access and on surface-design using the new SAP
technology Web Dynpro, plus development of Web
services and basic information regarding Java
messaging in SAP systems.

This book is aimed at Java-developers who want to
branch out into the SAP-world and equally at ABAP
programmers, who want to know in which direction
Web AS is going in future.

Interested in reading more?

Please visit our Web site for all
new book releases from SAP PRESS.

www.sap-press.com